Changing Men

and Masculinities in

Latin America

▪ ▪ ▪

Changing Men

and Masculinities in

Latin America

....

Edited by Matthew C. Gutmann

DUKE UNIVERSITY PRESS

DURHAM AND LONDON 2003

2nd printing, 2004

© 2003 Duke University Press   All rights reserved
Printed in the United States of America on acid-free paper ∞
Designed by Rebecca M. Giménez   Typeset in Scala by Keystone
Typesetting   Library of Congress Cataloging-in-Publication Data
appear on the last printed page of this book. Acknowledgments
for the use of copyrighted material appear on page 417 which
constitutes an extension of the copyright page.

FOR OUR TEACHERS AND STUDENTS

■ ■ ■ ■

CONTENTS

■ ■ ■ ■

Acknowledgments   ix

MATTHEW C. GUTMANN, Introduction: Discarding
    Manly Dichotomies in Latin America   1

MARA VIVEROS VIGOYA, Contemporary Latin
    American Perspectives on Masculinity   27

URBAN MEN AND MASCULINITIES

CLAUDIA FONSECA, Philanderers, Cuckolds,
    and Wily Women: Reexamining Gender Relations
    in a Brazilian Working-Class Neighborhood   61

AGUSTÍN ESCOBAR LATAPÍ, Men and Their
    Histories: Restructuring, Gender Inequality, and
    Life Transitions in Urban Mexico   84

FRANCISCO FERRÁNDIZ, Malandros, María Lionza,
    and Masculinity in a Venezuelan Shantytown   115

NORMA FULLER, The Social Constitution of Gender
    Identity among Peruvian Males   134

STANLEY BRANDES, Drink, Abstinence, and
    Male Identity in Mexico City   153

REPRESENTATIONS AND PRACTICES

FLORENCIA E. MALLON, *Barbudos,* Warriors, and
Rotos: The MIR, Masculinity, and Power in the
Chilean Agrarian Reform, 1965–74   179

DANIEL BALDERSTON, Sexuality and Revolution:
On the Footnotes to *El beso de la mujer araña*   216

PETER M. BEATTIE, Measures of Manhood: Honor,
Enlisted Army Service, and Slavery's Decline in
Brazil, 1850–90   233

MIGUEL DÍAZ BARRIGA, *Vergüenza* and Changing
Chicano/a Narratives   256

X. ANDRADE, Pancho Jaime and the Political Uses
of Masculinity in Ecuador   281

SEXUALITY AND PATERNITY

RICHARD PARKER, Changing Sexualities:
Masculinity and Male Homosexuality in Brazil   307

JOSÉ OLAVARRÍA, Men at Home? Child Rearing and
Housekeeping among Chilean Working-Class Fathers   333

HÉCTOR CARRILLO, Neither *Machos* nor *Maricones:*
Masculinity and Emerging Male Homosexual
Identities in Mexico   351

DONNA J. GUY, Rape and the Politics of Masculine
Silence in Argentina   370

Contributors   393

Index   399

ACKNOWLEDGMENTS

■ ■ ■

The original impulse for this volume emerged from a desire to share with English-speaking readers recent scholarship by specialists in the field of men and masculinities in Latin America who themselves are from and reside in Latin America. I am delighted to be able to include in this collection essays by some of the foremost chroniclers and analysts of men and masculinities in Argentina, Brazil, Chile, Colombia, Ecuador, Mexico, Peru, Venezuela, the United States, and Spain. I am very grateful to the authors of the chapters published here for accepting the invitation to participate in this effort and, even more, for their unfailing graciousness and couvade-like generosity in bringing our project to completion.

This collection of essays is quite consciously an attempt to extend feminist theory and gender studies in Latin America in new directions, which is appropriate given our great debt to those pioneers in women's and feminist studies who, far more than was the case in the United States or England, for example, provided the impetus and personnel that enabled scholarship on men and masculinities in Latin America to emerge in the first place.

With great good fortune we are able to build here on several recent collections devoted to studying men and masculinities in Latin America that have only appeared in Portuguese or Spanish, and I therefore wish to acknowledge the enduring influence of compilations by scholars such as

Ondina Fachel Leal (*Corpo y significado: Ensaios de antropologia social* [Porto Alegre: Editora da Universidade, 1995]); Mara Viveros and Gloria Garay (*Cuerpo, diferencias y desigualdades* [Bogotá: Universidad Nacional de Colombia, 1997]); Teresa Valdés and José Olavarría (*Masculinidad/es: Poder y crisis* [Santiago: ISIS Internacional/FLACSO, 1997], and *Masculinidades y equidad de género en América Latina* [Santiago: FLACSO/UNFPA, 1998]); Susana Lerner (*Varones, sexualidad y reproducción: Diversas perspectivas teórico-metodológicas y hallazgos de investigación* [Mexico City: El Colegio de México, 1998]); Richard Parker and Veriano Terto Jr. (*Entre Homens: Homossexualidade e AIDS no Brasil* [ABIA, 1998]); Norma Fuller (*Paternidades en América Latina* [Lima: Pontificia Universidad Católica del Perú, 2000]); and Mara Viveros, Norma Fuller, and José Olavarría (*Hombres e identidades de género: Investigaciones desde América Latina* [Bogotá: Universidad Nacional de Colombia, 2001]).

Earlier versions of several papers in this volume were presented at a conference on "Male Friendship and Homosociality in Latin America" at Brown University in April 2001. I am therefore most grateful to the Provost's Office and the Watson Center for International Affairs at Brown and to the Hewlett Foundation for financial sponsorship of that conference.

For conspiratorial inspiration my appreciation goes to Red Les Hechiceres, good witches and colleagues who consistently seek to expand the ranks of researchers examining all forms of gender inequality in Latin America and to carefully develop theoretical frameworks grounded in the actual joys and hardships of men and women in the Americas and not simply to repeat trendy aphorisms. My thanks in particular to Mara Viveros: I still haven't learned the words to that song, and I sing it just the same.

I am grateful to several people who reviewed individual essays that appear in this collection, including Lawrence Cohen, Bob Connell, Miguel Díaz Barriga, Norma Fuller, Jonathan Inda, Nelson Minello, José Olavarría, Ruben Oliven, Linda-Anne Rebhun, and Patricia Zavella, and to the anonymous reviewers for Duke University Press for their many important contributions to the final version of this collection. Thanks to María Elena García for assistance in translating one essay and editorial work on several others; to Paul White for editorial help; and to Kathy Grimaldi, Matilde Andrade, and Shirley Gordon in the Department of Anthropology at Brown

University for secretarial support. Valerie Millholland, Miriam Angress, Rebecca Johns-Danes, Joe Abbott, and everyone else at Duke have been enthusiastic and careful in their stewardship of this project; it has been a pleasure to work with them on this book.

To Maya, Liliana, and Michelle—for all their help, in all their ways.

This book is dedicated to our collective teachers and students. Despite our diverse cultural and disciplinary backgrounds, methods of research, and styles of writing, the authors of the chapters in this book have all experienced the pure pleasure of learning from those special women and men whom we have gratefully come to name as our teachers, those who have approached the craft of educating others in the broadest sense as a calling and a passion. Similarly, perhaps, we all share the hope that at least for some of our students we will come to be counted among their memorable teachers.

Matthew C. Gutmann

Oaxaca de Juárez, May 2002

Changing Men

and Masculinities in

Latin America

■ ■ ■

MATTHEW C. GUTMANN

Introduction: Discarding Manly

Dichotomies in Latin America

■ ■ ■

Among the most extraordinary cultural migrations is female identity. Without a doubt
masculinity is modified: to be under the orders of women upsets psychic hierarchies, to not
share in domestic chores is to run the risk of divorce, and to accept household democracy is
no longer so arduous . . . but the great change occurs in the space of historic subjugation.
—*Carlos Monsiváis,* AIRES DE FAMILIA

We need studies that concentrate on men and masculinities, on men as
engendered and engendering beings in Latin America. We may not always
need them, but we do in the early twenty-first century. For the authors of
chapters in this volume a focus on men and masculinities represents a key
element in the broader study of gender relations, identities, and inequalities throughout the Western Hemisphere. Thus the impetus for this book
on men and masculinities in Latin America derives from a recognition
that we know too little about men-*as-men* in this part of the world, a desire
to extend our research on gender to include men as well as women, and a
commitment to ground our exploration of men and masculinities in the
Americas within an overall framework of gender/sexuality analysis. Yet
Changing Men and Masculinities in Latin America is not intended to provide

a counterpart, complementary or otherwise, to studies of women in the region. Still less is it part of a backlash reaction to feminism and scholarship that has only begun to uncover myriad secret histories of women in Latin America. Building on diverse feminist currents, the chapters in this book take as axiomatic the power imbalances rooted in relations of gender/sexuality in the region. Regardless of how diverse they may be in Latin America, no adequate account of the ideas and practices, the dreams and fears associated with men and masculinities there is possible without reference to these inequalities.

In editing this book I have tried to gather chapters that reflect the diversity of disciplinary approaches to the study of men and masculinities in Latin America, research that represents the work of leading scholars of the field who write and teach about this subject in Latin America, as well as in the United States. In this introduction I provide an overview of some of the central themes raised in the chapters to follow. I also try to anticipate readers' questions—for instance, about how far we can generalize about regions and genders—and in the process I hope to provoke further reflection and discussion about certain theoretical assumptions that underwrite many of the contemporary studies of men and masculinities in Latin America. I especially would like to push the envelope a bit with respect to three concerns: (1) the relationship between local and global changes in gender/sexuality in Latin America; (2) the question of whether there is anything typical and/or sui generis about gender and sexuality among men in Latin America; and (3) the relative benefits and problems with continuing to study men (or women) as opposed to always and necessarily studying gender/sexuality overall in Latin America or any other part of the world.

How to Study Men and Masculinities in Latin America

Scholars of men and masculinities in Latin America describe and utilize the term *masculinity* and the related concepts of male identity, manhood, manliness, and men's roles in at least four distinct ways. In fact, most scholars writing on this subject use more than one of the four frameworks, which indicates how fluid these concepts are and occasionally signals a lack of theoretical precision in approaching this issue.

The first concept of *masculinity* argues that it is anything that men think, say, and do. If men are involved, then so too must be masculinity. The second concept holds that masculinity is what men think, say, and do to distinguish themselves as men. Accordingly men may achieve (or strive to achieve) masculinity at some times more than others. Third, masculinity is seen by some as a quality that certain men have more than other men, either because they were born that way or because of some personal kind of achievement. Finally, other scholars of men and masculinities in Latin America have sought to emphasize the overriding significance of women to the negotiation of masculinities for most if not all men at most if not all times in their lives.

To a certain extent in recent scholarship these four ways of describing men and masculinities in Latin America represent analogous approaches. They also correspond to specific historical and cultural conditions in Latin America, for instance, in relation to the broad influence, beginning in the 1970s, of feminism and feminist movements within academia and society more generally. As such these four approaches are indicative of social histories in the region and also of personal ones, which is why they may also illustrate particular stages in individuals' subjective histories.

In both social and personal histories, what it means to be a man in Latin America can often best be appreciated in relationship to hegemonic masculinities in the region. The dominant male ideological expressions of these hegemonic masculinities—for instance, homophobia, machismo, and misogyny—are not simply individual expressions of interpersonal relations in families and households but also pertain to the very foundations of gender inequalities within these societies and internationally.[1] Informed by theoretical work on manhood, virility, and their conceptual and practical opposites, several chapters in *Changing Men and Masculinities in Latin America* use the phrase *hegemonic masculinity* to provide greater depth to the model and new manners in which it may be utilized in specific cultural contexts in the region. In particular in this volume we try to capture the complex interplay between normative and practical manifestations of masculinity in these social settings and to demonstrate how they have been accepted sometimes and challenged at other times by women and men throughout the hemisphere. Although norms certainly provide an omnipresent environment within which men and women negotiate various forms of masculinity, we err when we neglect to carefully distinguish among cultural customs, traditions, and truisms on one hand and the actual ideas and lived experiences of men and women that pertain to men and masculinities in Latin America.

Our grasp of changing male identities and practices in Latin America may be tempered by how we understand the relation of hegemonic masculinity to women in general and to other forms of masculinity that are marginal and subordinate. Among the most obvious and studied of these latter categories are those relating to men who have sex with other men, working-class men, and men who are subject to racism of one kind or another. Yet despite the fact that the organization and distribution of men and masculinities occurs in distinct ways throughout the region and is constrained by preexisting gender relations, these restrictions are historically contingent and constantly disputed by an array of social actors. The notion of changing men and masculinities can thus be employed both as an appraisal of a process underway and as a call to action (see Chant and Gutmann 2000).

With respect to the study of homophobia in Latin America, for instance, one thing is certain: it is not just for queers anymore! Uncovering, understanding, and contesting homophobia should no longer be regarded as the responsibility of gays alone. No longer should homophobia be dismissed by some as applying only to the ideas and actions of heterosexuals against homosexuals; it must instead be understood in a broader sense as incorporating feelings of homosocial discomfort and engendered ideologies of domination and subordination.[2] It is not surprising that homophobia receives more systematic attention in studies of subordinate masculine practices (for example, homosexual, transvestite, cross-dressing, gay, drag-queen men) than in studies of heterosexual men in Latin America.[3] Surely, however, there is a need for scholars whose research is more concerned with self-identified heterosexual men to also adequately address matters such as homosocial desires, fears, experiences, and prejudices in relation to topics such as male friendships and social spaces. Mara Viveros (2002) reports, for instance, that in Quibdó, Colombia, male youth routinely use the epithet *maricas* (queers) when referring to other youth who have demonstrated a lack of *lealtad* (loyalty). Viveros concludes, "To betray the group constitutes the worst crime and a youth who was accused of being a traitor

4 ▪ ▪ ▪ Matthew C. Gutmann

was labeled a 'marica,' not for his sexual practices but because of his disloyalty" (208). In this volume Peter Beattie's chapter addresses a similar point regarding the role played by homophobia in a formally heterosexual context of soldiers in late-nineteenth-century Brazil, given expression in attempts to reform "inverts" and suppress same-sex desires.

Further, although homophobia has often been approached in Latin American studies as necessarily involving men engaged in same-sex sex, many classic ethnographies and histories of the region (e.g., Freyre 1956 [1933]; Lewis 1961) have described tacitly, and less often explicitly, clear patterns of homosociality, the social bonds between men, that are found in a variety of social spaces. These ethnographies have extremely diverse implications. Homosociality exists in relation to women, who are by definition supposedly excluded from sharing these relationships, and it is relevant in relationships among men, including homophobia and same-sex sexual desires and practices. Homosociality and homophobia are thus, of necessity, central to the study of all scholars of men and masculinities in Latin America and elsewhere.

In the 1980s and 1990s, studies of men-as-men in Latin America developed in the wake of earlier feminist research by women and as an extension of these other studies. More than was true in the United States, studies of men-as-men in Latin America were usually framed by feminist theories of gender oppression, regardless of whether the primary focus was on heterosexual men or men who have sex with other men. That is, from the beginning in studying men as engendered and engendering beings, in Latin America there has been a more unambiguous adoption of critical feminist lenses for understanding men-as-men within general paradigms delineating power and inequality. The parallel "me-tooism" that developed in certain wings of men's studies in North America and Europe has been far less influential in Latin America, although, to be sure, a translation into Spanish of Robert Bly's mythopoetic manifesto on Iron John, *Hombres de Hierro: Los ritos de iniciación masculina del Nuevo Hombre,* was quickly brought into print in 1992. Scholarship in Latin America on men and masculinities has been marked by feminist theoretical frameworks; indeed, many women who have long been active in research and activism around women's oppression have been leaders in the emerging study of men and masculinities in the region.

The contributors to the present volume are among those for whom the study of unjust regimes of coercion and control is a principal rationale for studying men and masculinities in Latin America. The influence of Marxist and Foucauldian theories of power and change are evident throughout the chapters. The authors of this collection are also cognizant of the fact that there have always been distinct objectives in studies of men and masculinities. Among the methods employed in the chapters of this book to underscore these tensions as they relate to questions of difference and inequity are two worth mentioning here. One is the need to include women in studies of men and masculinities. This entails examination of the relationship of women to men and masculinity, illustrating how women may be practically incorporated into research focused on men, and learning from more nuanced treatments of women to critique monochrome debates on essentialized male natures and constructions of masculinity. Another method used to highlight the centrality of gender power imbalances in these chapters involves the description and explanation of hierarchies among men themselves that are associated with more hegemonic and more marginalized men and masculinities.

As Mara Viveros shows in her survey in this volume of contemporary perspectives on masculinity in Latin America, "In Latin American societies—multicultural with a broad array of social classes—it has become necessary to think about the various ways in which masculine identities are constructed in various social sectors, ethnic groups, and sociocultural contexts." In her own research Viveros has demonstrated what she calls "the overlap between gender and ethnic-racial identities," such that the masculinities of one ethnic-racial group emerge in contrast to other ethnic-racial masculinities, as men use aspects of their corporeality in constructing their ethnic-racial identities as much as their gender identities. Discussing ethnic-racial and class divisions, Norma Fuller shows in her chapter how working-class men in Peru may recognize the existence of racial hierarchies but cleverly invert them by claiming the virile attributes for themselves and feminizing the men of the dominant class. In this way men from the popular sectors, and those with Indian or black ethnic or racial features, can claim to be more masculine than *mestizo* (mixed-race) men (see also Fuller 1997). In Miguel Díaz Barriga's contribution, as well, the concordance of class, race, and region is developed in order to understand questions of somatization of social inequalities and to chart actual trans-formations as they transpire.[4]

In the chapters by Richard Parker and Héctor Carrillo the "overlap" between gender and sexual identities and practices is demonstrated in relation to AIDS in Brazil and Mexico. In each case the authors emphasize the changing and emerging character of gay communities in these coun-tries and the role that public health prevention and treatment efforts have played in tandem with such sociocultural developments.

Using a number of theoretical frameworks in which an emphasis is placed on male-male or male-female relations, or combinations of these, the study of men and masculinities in Latin America has emerged in the last two decades as a component part of feminist gender studies in gen-eral. Sensitive to broader institutional and cultural patterns of power in-equities, this scholarship initially emerged from social movements aimed at resolving problems most affecting women and the male gay commu-nities and has resulted in a far richer understanding of what it means to be a man today and historically in Latin America.

Inversions, Conversions, and Perversions

Try as we might to describe and champion a vast diversity of masculini-ties and femininities in Latin America, there is no mistaking the fact that talk of dichotomous dualities, for instance that positing male and female worlds, recurs with what may be for some a frustrating regularity. Nor is the blessed distinction between sex and gender, that is, between bodies and culture, still found to be nearly as useful as many scholars in gender studies once presumed and hoped. As is evident in the papers by Daniel Balderston, Claudia Fonseca, and X. Andrade, for example, the separa-tion of bodies and minds, of biologically essentialized sexualities and cul-turally restricted genders, is most problematic. Given that gender itself is grounded in physical sexuality and the manner in which the latter is understood, contested, organized, and practiced by societies, many schol-ars today are loathe to treat either category in conceptual isolation from the other.

In the field of biology, too, former hallowed notions of sex and sexuality are increasingly challenged not so much by new findings as by new approaches to understanding what we know. In a recent landmark study of gender politics and the construction of sexuality Anne Fausto-Sterling (2000) provides evidence of the existence of at least five biological sexes (hermaphrodites, male pseudohermaphrodites, female pseudohermaphrodites, females, and males). Thus even male-female dimorphism, which has been used to explain behavior like the mating practices of various species—with greater dimorphism among gorillas, for instance, supposedly correlating to lower rates of "monogamy"—must be called into question for many of its essential theoretical biases. Still, despite the work of some scholars to break with binary thinking, such models die slowly, and male/female divisions are still the foundation for much gender research in Latin America. A parallel model is found in some studies whose subject is same-sex sex among men, where rigid active/passive contrasts aimed at explaining why active, penetrating men are not necessarily considered homosexual or gay by themselves or by others in society more broadly. As Parker shows in his chapter in this volume and elsewhere (e.g., 1999), although retaining useful elements, the active/passive taxonomy can miss as much as it captures with respect to changing norms and actual sexual practices (see also Lancaster 1998; Núñez 2001).

A term employed popularly in Mexico and among Mexicans in the United States may help to demonstrate in another way the perils of dichotomous modeling of gender/sexuality in Latin America. Among Mexicans of various persuasions in different locations the term *mayate* is used to mean quite different things. Among self-identified heterosexual men in Mexico City, for example, *mayate* generally refers exclusively to *homosexuals,* although what *homosexual* means to different people varies considerably (see Carrillo, this volume; Núñez 1994). Among Mexicanos in the United States, and among some Mexicanos in Mexico who have lived in the United States, the word *mayate* is used most often to refer in a disparaging way not to homosexuals but rather to African Americans. Only one of my acquaintances in Mexico, a cab driver in the Federal District who had earlier lived many years in Chicago, used *mayate* to refer to both homosexuals and blacks. Yet even for him *mayate* mainly was utilized to refer to African Americans, whereas the word he most commonly employed to vilify a homosexual was *maricón.*

Etymologically the term *mayate* originally meant simply a dung beetle.

Perhaps it has come to refer to those perceived as racial and sexual outcasts in part because of their assumed political and sexual passivity. The use of the term *bagaxa* in Brazil seems to have similar racial-sexual semantic overlap (see Beattie, this volume).[5] In analyzing the term *mayate* we can see some of the inherent problems in dichotomous modeling of men and masculinities in Latin America—Mexicans/African Americans, hetero-sexuales/maricas. In the case of each definition of *mayate* there is a tacit judgment regarding the active and passive political and sexual roles played by each of these groups, yet the very polyvalence of the expression puts the lie to neatly bounded categories of analysis.

With both so-called political passivity and sexual passivity there is evidently more at play than is perhaps immediately apparent; both forms of assumed passivity represent territories that remain to be more fully charted. Clearly one obstacle that must be overcome in studying sexual passivity in Latin America is the notion that passivity is the mirror opposite of activity. Part of this conflation results from confusion over power and control in sexual politics and choice. In her study of transvestites, queens, and machos in Mexico City Annick Prieur (1998, 129) makes a similar point when she insists that, although her informants are victims of symbolic (and not-so-symbolic) violence, they are also in just as real a sense actors who *choose* certain elements of their lives; they are not simply the passive subjects of history. In an entirely different way Elizabeth Brusco (1995) shows in her study of evangelism and machismo in Colombia how the attempts by women to convert their (often lapsed) Catholic husbands to Protestantism has as one aim the cultural pacification of men. These women expect the men to stop drinking and womanizing after religious conversion, in this manner actively promoting certain forms of gender equity through the channeling of men into more passive pursuits.

The pull to dichotomize persists despite continuous efforts of scholars to nuance, qualify, and hedge on men and masculinity in Latin America. One countervailing compulsion stems from the fact that among men and women throughout the hemisphere a consistent point of reference for determining what a man is when compared to a woman (or to some other men, for that matter) is the body. Whether this involves rudimentary matters of strength and sexual dimorphism or age and the achievement of manhood with puberty, the body is often the arbiter of last resort and bodily political economies—the inscription of societally based inequalities on bodies—often provide the currency in which identities and interests are exchanged. How men and women in the region engage in verbal play with these corporal reference points, how they perform with more or less skill the gestures associated with masculinities and femininities, and how they defy concepts and practices prevalent in the worlds into which they were born are the subjects of Fonseca's chapter on the discourse and substance of philandering in Porto Alegre, Brazil, and Andrade's chapter on political pornography in Guayaquil, Ecuador.[6]

As both Fonseca and Andrade reveal, although determining the significance of issues like sexual license and vulgarity is not simply a matter of recording accepted cultural standards, we must not overlook the influence of dichotomized cultural values and customary practices. In addition to the examples they present I would offer another: the distinct way that virginity and sex are approached in many if by no means all cultural contexts in Latin America. Although dichotomous male/female definitions of virginity and sex are indisputably familiar in other parts of the world, we might well benefit by continuing to ask if there are not certain common if never axiomatic differences that are still experienced by men and women *as* men and women in the region. More specifically, and without tumbling into the circumlocutions of Bill Clinton on the subject, if a woman loses her virginity in Latin America, or simply "has sex," for instance, her orgasm is not necessarily implied in the act. In contrast, if a virginal man penetrates the same woman's vagina and does not ejaculate, has he lost his virginity and had sex? For most of Latin America orgasm and ejaculation are implicitly required for a man to lose his virginity and have sex, whereas orgasm is not necessary for women in the region to lose their virginity or have sex. What the implications of such conceptual distinctions grounded in gender difference for men and masculinities in Latin America may be does vary from one context to another. Depending on factors such as historical period, country, and class, a woman in Latin America who loses her virginity before marriage, for example, may face severe punishment or no social opprobrium whatsoever. Donna Guy's chapter on rape in late-nineteenth- and early-twentieth-century Argentina explains how courts determined what constituted sexual crimes and how they meted out punishments for the same or silently disregarded rape. Both Guy and Beattie also mention *defloramento/defloramiento* (deflowering), that quaint legal expression signifying a profound change in women's sexual status. In Brazil during the late nineteenth century young women between the ages of sixteen and twenty-one who had sex with men, for instance, were legally considered to have been seduced with false marriage promises or pledges the man did not keep. They had been deprived of their virginity and thus were judged to have been deflowered. If a man had sex with a girl who was under sixteen years of age, he was considered guilty of statutory rape. (Again, this phenomenon was hardly unique to Latin America; rather, the argument here is simply that such legal and cultural restrictions have formed an integral part of the history of men and masculinities in the region.)

Perhaps bodily referents are not so simple today, but at the same time differences that might seem patently cultural in origin—such as those pertaining to virginity and what constitutes a sexual act—can shed light in places some would prefer to keep under the covers. This is true despite the transparently artificial nature of dichotomous taxonomies employed to highlight gender/sexuality disparities. The imagined perversions of passive partnership in sexual acts between men are simultaneously subject to metaphorical and practical conversion, including by the men themselves who are so engaged.

All in all the finest studies of men and masculinities in Latin America stick closely to observed events, emotions, and practices and provide new documentation and insights into long-standing issues related to active and passive, homophobia and homosociality, and the relation of femininity to masculine identities. When studies dip into overgeneralized claims based on little more than speculation, hearsay, and wishful thinking, they tend to reinvent hackneyed truisms. Hence, regardless of the importance of exploring alleged Latin American sexual shibboleths and making clear the influence these have on the ideas and behavior of men and women in the region, the greatest necessity is to ground one's inherently limited empirical findings in a thorough understanding of specific cultural histories and conditions. The point in comparing these actual case histories to putative norms is not simply to measure them against one another but, even more, to better understand the mutually conditional relationship in Latin America between gender/sexuality bylaws and the contradictory ways actual men and women there conduct themselves in life.

Is There a Typical Latin American Gender/Sexuality?

In September 1998 I organized a session at the Latin American Studies Association meeting in Chicago with the tongue-in-cheek title "Is There a Latin American Sexuality?" Fortunately the invited panelists—including Donna Guy, Richard Parker, Rafael Ramírez, Lynn Stephen, Teresa Valdés, and Mara Viveros—understood the question more as a collegial goad and less as a rhetorical query whose implicit intent was to reaffirm an already established fact. At that panel there was ample evidence of the reluctance on the part of many scholars of gender and sexuality in Latin America, myself included, to generalize beyond narrowly defined populations. Indeed, many of us have devoted considerable time and energy to describing the diversity of manhoods and womanhoods in the hemisphere and to reining in some of the more outrageous (and racist) generalizations about men and women in Latin America. The point was not then and is not now to blithely essentialize or exoticize gender and sexuality for the region. We were attempting to better understand what might be common in various parts of the hemisphere and even more why so many people, specialists and lay observers alike, continued to affirm generalizations about "Latin American men" and "Latin American women."

Aside from finding pan-Latin frameworks altogether inaccurate, panelists volunteered examples of why sexualities in Latin America had to be placed squarely into a context of global processes of change. Several speakers offered lucid testimony showing global transformations underway in the late twentieth century that carried profound implications for sexualities in the Latin Americas. Economically, these changes were evident in tracing the impact of neoliberal programs on reproductive health programs, the growing numbers of women working outside the home for money, and the expansion of international sex markets. Politically, men and masculinities in Latin America have been impacted in dramatic ways by feminist projects in the region and globally, by urban movements for social services in which women have often played a significant role and in which men have been challenged by women's independence and initia-

Young man in Oaxaca, Mexico, herding goats. Photograph by Matthew C. Gutmann.

tive, by general trends toward democratization that have raised new issues of cultural citizenship including with respect to gender divisions of labor, and by AIDS activism in many countries of the region. Demographically, mass access to modern forms of contraception, and the consequent fall in birthrates, has tested gender/sexuality identities, behavior, and roles in intimate and associational ways, and the fact that girls' attendance rates at school have risen more quickly than boys' has had obvious implications in numerous ways, including the training and qualifications of women and men for various sectors of employment. The shift from more uniformly differentiated divisions of household labor in the countryside to situations that have given rise to greater fluidity in gender employment patterns as a result of modernization and urbanization has accordingly had dramatic consequences for men and women as they have become more thoroughly incorporated into wage labor relations.

With respect to employment, financially supporting one's family and work in general are without a doubt central defining features of masculinity for many men and women in various parts of the Americas. As shown by Fuller in her chapter, for a variety of reasons "the public sphere sustains and legitimizes masculine predominance. It is the locus of achievement and should be regulated by honesty, efficiency, and contributing to the common good." She goes on to report, "Within this sphere work is represented as the key dimension of adult, masculine identity." Similarly, José Olavarría writes in his chapter, "In Chile, as elsewhere, the workplace and the home were separated—particularly in urban areas—only as a result of the industrial revolution, which detached the site of production from where people lived." Among the implications of these developments, he notes, was "a nuclear family in which the father/patriarch played the role of head of the household and provider and in which the mother took charge of domestic matters and child rearing in the home" (see also Olavarría and Parrini 2000).

In her pioneering history of men and masculinity in the Chilean Movement of the Revolutionary Left (MIR) in the decade beginning 1965 running through the coup in 1973 and the years of repression that followed, in a very different way, Florencia Mallon here also explores transformations in men's conventional role as *paterfamilias*. Documenting the ways that the MIR leadership was able to effect a "gendered transgression" by challenging "the ideal of masculinity deployed by the more traditional organized left, one that emphasized disciplined work habits and responsible family behavior," which she contrasts to the seductive heroics embodied by "the image, the experience, the incorruptibility of Che," Mallon argues that "the promises of revolutionary [masculine] salvation that built on the figures of the *barbudo* and the warrior-victim were, in the end, empty."

In Mexico the narratives Agustín Escobar collected in Guadalajara revealed "the importance of the conditions in which men grew up: where they had lived, the poverty that forced them to find work at a young age, and the ways in which their parents negotiated whether their son would work or stay in school." In my own research in Mexico and with Mexican migrants living in the United States I have often heard talk of a particular intermediate category of fathers, between those who are present and active in the parenting of their children and those who desert their families and are never heard from again. These intermediate-status fathers are known popularly as *padres de cheque*, check fathers, because they are men whose paternity is established and validated primarily through their periodic remittances to households in which they have long since ceased to reside.

In discussing fatherhood in this collection, in addition to the contribution by Olavarría, the chapters by Stanley Brandes, and Francisco Ferrándiz disclose one of the more irksome clichés regarding men and masculinities in Latin America: the supposedly uniform significance and value for men in this region of having children to prove one's virility through the procreation of many offspring, particularly male progeny. Undoubtedly for the foreseeable future, debates about procreation and related issues such as abortion will continue for some time in Latin America, the Catholic Church doctrine will maintain its hegemonic control over legislation in most countries of the hemisphere, and pronatal voices will remain well publicized in the media.[7] At the same time, for many if not all men in Latin America in the early twenty-first century, being a father entails far more than providing the seed for propagation of heirs. Whether narrowly conceived as a matter of financial responsibility, or understood in a more full-bodied sense to involve the active participation of men throughout the lives of their children in as many aspects of their lives as possible, with these and other similar studies we have ample proof of the centrality of fatherhood broadly conceived in the lives of large numbers of men if by no means all men in distinct regions of Latin America.

The stereotype that for all men in Latin America fatherhood is tantamount to insemination and producing (especially male) progeny is prevalent not only outside the region but also within it. In fact, this formula is sometimes deployed by men and women in Latin America as a way to poke fun at men regarded as hopelessly antiquated in their thinking and behavior. But if fertility rates in countries throughout Latin America have fallen sharply in the last several decades, this by no means indicates that men are having sexual intercourse with women less than they used to or that fathering children has become less important for men. Instead, I would argue, sex has become less tied to procreation and more to sexuality. This is related as well to Parker's conclusion in his chapter that among male homosexuals in Brazil the economy of sexuality has come to be organized more around the symbolic value of sexual desires or sexual identities than of sexual roles. In a sense the changing standards associated with both fatherhood and same-sex sex among men in Latin America are aspects of the same process of emerging sexualities that give priority to desire over more traditional mores emphasizing function and performance.

Balderston's examination here of footnotes that reveal many of the theoretical sources utilized by Manuel Puig in writing his famous novel *The Kiss of the Spider Woman* lend further credence to the importance of documenting the influence on gender and sexual politics in Latin America of ideas originating in Europe and the United States. With respect to terminology and more fundamentally to exploring issues such as same-sex sex, tracking the labyrinthine course of same-sex desire and practices in Latin America requires a familiarity with global factors and postulates (see also Wright 2000). The cross-pollination of theories of homosexuality, for example, has always reflected not only the prevailing assumptions in the metropoles but also the prevailing assumptions there about the rest of the world. In the case of Latin America, definitions of Latino/aness in general and Latino/a gender/sexuality in particular—and reputed correlates like machismo—these assumptions reveal cosmopolitan prejudice as much as insight. On a practical level, in countries like the United States the contradictoriness of ideas about homophobia in Latin America is given expression when experts on men and masculinity in the region are asked to testify for men seeking political asylum on the basis of discrimination and intolerance against homosexuals in other Spanish-speaking countries of the hemisphere. This has happened repeatedly to several authors in this collection. To deny homophobia in these countries would be absurd, yet to exploit racist stereotypes about Latino machismo is for many scholars equally indefensible.

Despite our efforts to accentuate historical particularism *and* global contextualism at the LASA panel in 1998 I was struck by the creeping suspicion—and I do not think I was alone in this feeling—that despite differences of class, ethnic group, region, and generation, it was not just in the popular imagination that Latin America was seen as constituting in some palpable sense a coherent area of historical and cultural commonalties with respect to certain aspects of gender and sexuality. That is, despite the real and unanimous acknowledgment of the profound impact of globalization on sexualities throughout Latin America, there was simultaneously the deep-seated sense that these global influences were still filtered through particular, local, Latin American contexts. For this reason, in order to understand men and masculinities in the region, we were compelled to seek more than simply the Latin versions of global trends and transformations.

One widely discussed example of this would again be the active/passive

In a jumble of global and local imagery, the macho histrionics of Jim Morrison (whose face is on this T-shirt) and his rock band, The Doors, remain popular in Mexico City. Photograph Matthew C. Gutmann.

dichotomy that, albeit in a more nuanced manner, continues to serve the conceptual purposes of historians, anthropologists, and others studying men who insert themselves into other men and those who are entered in Latin America. Yet given the profound influence of models of sexuality from Europe and the United States in particular (for example, the widespread adoption in the social sciences, media, and popular vernacular of the term *gay*), and the shift in many parts of Latin America from traditionally popular notions of active/passive role playing to the invention of gay and homosexual identities and practices, what if anything today is particular to Latin America, for instance, same-sex sexuality? One possible answer lies in the analysis closely linked to a revised active/passive framework that posits Latin American regimes of sexuality that are more supple than their U.S. counterparts in accounting for greater ambiguity than straight/gay labels allow, as when practice (and agency) more than identity (and essence) emerges as the crucial distinction delineating frequently alternating (more) dominant and (more) submissive participation in sexual encounters among men and between men and women (see Lancaster 1998).

Another example of a theme common in discussions of sexuality in Latin America is the bellwether term *machismo*; although fewer scholars today argue that all Latin American men exhibit an obvious and identical machismo, or that machismo in the sense of sexism is unique to Latin America, both popular and much scholarly literature maintain a tacit view that machismo is ubiquitous if not universal in the region. And without doubt machismo is a most common equivalent for sexism throughout the world today, although as I have tried to show elsewhere, it is a term with a remarkably short word history and one whose etymology derives as much from international political and social currents as from cultural artifacts peculiar to Latin America (see Gutmann 1996).

In a further effort to resist the trend toward increasingly particularist studies we might ask, too, about the extent to which we can justifiably generalize regarding the impact of far-reaching events and movements (such as revolution, world war, feminism, neoliberalism) on men and masculinities in Latin America, both historically and in contemporary societies. Part of this inquiry into the larger issues that form the basis for changing men and masculinities in Latin America must be devoted to tracing the influence of ideas and practices in countries like the United States about countries in the rest of the hemisphere. Although commonplaces about such matters are epidemic, we still do not know enough about the role of the United States today and historically in helping to define and circumscribe "Latin" manliness and its opposites.

The Politics of Masculinity

One question alluded to at the beginning of this introduction remains to be resolved: Why even have a volume on men and masculinities instead of one on men and women and gender in general? Is it time to put an end to women-centered and men-centered studies and get on with the business of gender-in-general studies? Obviously I believe not, and I think the papers in the volume provide numerous reasons why not. The short answer to why men-as-men studies are useful today relates to a rather distinguishing feature of studying men and masculinities in Latin America and elsewhere around the globe: without exception, on the grand level of societies, and in far more varied ways at the interdependent level of families, households, and neighborhoods, men are in positions of power and control. At least in the contemporary world the politics of masculinity requires studies that focus on men-as-men.

Although there are real, ongoing problems of binary frameworks, this does not obviate the need to focus, at least some of the time, on men or women. Nonetheless, inherent in the fourth conceptual framework for understanding masculinities in Latin America—the importance of women to the construction, performances, and practices associated with men and manhood in the region—is the recognition that most men in most parts of Latin America most of the time live with and around women. Notions of separate women's worlds and men's worlds, then, are emphatically no more than idealized representations of lives as they are lived and experienced by some and by no means all men and women. If a central aim of the study of men-as-men in Latin America is to critique gender and sexual inequality, a focus on men and masculinities will not make us complicit in reinforcing such archetypal polarities. Political changes must occur before our framework transforms so thoroughly that the study of gender/sexuality becomes harmful if mainly focused on either men or women. Until men are routinely understood as engendered and engendering beings, the sway of women over men will be held suspect. Studies of men's influence on and control over women and research on the relationships between mothers and male children are still far more common than those examining the impact of adult women on adult men.[8] In addition, until men are routinely understood as engendered and engendering beings in scholarly venues, the control of some men by other men will be a topic assigned (and often consigned) to gay studies and queer theory alone.

In his ethnographic portrait of an Alcoholics Anonymous group he calls Moral Support in Mexico City, Brandes demonstrates well in his chapter the value of examining spaces of self-reflection and protection of men by men, as well as the obvious relevance for men in this group of men and masculinity in contrast to women and femininity. As he writes, "Among working class Mexican men, like those in Moral Support, sobriety and the abdication of arbitrary power over spouses might well be considered effeminate. Whatever they feel inside, it is rare for men to express guilt openly over mistreatment of women. In Alcoholics Anonymous, by contrast, men can abstain from drink and ask women in public for forgiveness without necessarily casting their masculinity in doubt."

The unsteady transition in many university programs in Latin America from women's studies to gender studies (or to gender and women's studies) reflects an attempt to identify men as engendered and engendering beings, to incorporate men and the study of men and masculinities into university research and syllabi, and to recognize that gender entails more than simply adding women and men together, as if women + men = gender. In Mexico efforts to break with such an equation have been especially evident in recent studies on topics as diverse as the relationship among rock 'n roll, nationalism, and the "death of masculinity" as it once was (see Zolov 1999), to analyses of the differential participation and impact of men and women in migratory streams toward El Norte (see Barrera Bassols and Oehmichen Bazán 2000), to recent work on male fertility, men's reproductive health, and masculinity as a "risk factor" in health problems generally (see de Keijzer 1998; Figueroa 1998; Lerner 1998). Nonetheless, we have some distance still to travel: in the *Diccionario del español usual en México* (Colegio de México, 1996, 459) the fifth definition of *género* is "*Estudios de género:* Aquéllos dedicados a investigar el lugar que corresponde a las mujeres en la sociedad (Gender studies: Those dedicated to researching the place of women in society)."

With respect to announcements of the death of antiquated masculinity, one need not adopt the view that a New Man has surfaced from the Argentine pampas to the shallows of the Rio Grande or claim that challenges to men and masculinity are novel phenomena of our contemporary age in order to recognize that men and women throughout Latin America have been grappling with what seem to many to be new ideas and relationships related to their masculine identities. Men who seek to distance themselves from certain confining roles and identities are the subjects of Ferrándiz's essay on a shantytown of Caracas, Venezuela, where many men "are raised and expected to conform to tough models of masculinity." In his chapter he talks of "wounded masculinity" and of "masculinity tracks" that often bring the violence of street life into contradiction with the cultural prescription that men must provide financially for their families.

Curiously perhaps, one conclusion from several essays in this volume seems to be a reversal of an old feminist paradigm that associated men more with culture and women with nature. Whereas other commentators have gone so far as to argue that, in popularly conceived versions of dichotomous men and women, girls develop into women rather naturally whereas boys must be turned into men through human intervention, our authors find evidence of other experiences in which men are broadly associated with rather instinctual behavior and in which, ultimately at least, women are able and expected to control situations. The extent to which men are "domesticable" is also part of popular discourse regarding male sex drives.

Central to the studies in *Changing Men and Masculinities* is the emphasis on change, changing the politics of men and masculinities. Without seeking an eviscerated version of transformed manhood—still less, anything promoted as New Men and Masculinity—these essays develop the theme of change by squarely addressing questions of basic social inequalities between men and women, as well as among men of different ethnic-racial groups, men of different sexual orientations, and men of different classes. These are the politics of masculinity.

Other Goals of the Volume

This project began as five anthropological papers that were published in 2001 in the U.S. journal *Men and Masculinities*. Those five essays are presented here in the chapters by Andrade, Díaz-Barriga, Fonseca, Fuller, and Viveros Vigoya, in some cases as revised versions. I also invited several other scholars to contribute chapters. The result is an interdisciplinary panorama of contemporary research by sociologists, historians, literary critics, public health researchers, and activists on men and masculinities in Latin America, benchmark studies by some of the leading scholars working in this field who live, research, and teach in Latin America.

In the 1990s several North Americans wrote outstanding ethnographies and histories in English of men and masculinities in Latin America (see, e.g., Carrier 1995; Lancaster 1992; Limón 1994; Parker 1999; Stern 1995). During the same period there was a "boom" in research on this subject written in Spanish and Portuguese by sociologists, anthropologists, historians, literary critics, public health workers, and others in Latin America (see Viveros Vigoya's essay here). But very few of these Spanish and Portuguese studies were translated into English (for an exception see Ramírez 1999), and for this reason many English-only scholars have not had access to the investigations and conclusions of their Latin American colleagues. To be sure, more than a matter of translation is involved. With this volume we seek to redress not only linguistic obstacles to collegial exchanges but also to help facilitate the ongoing process of learning from different conceptual frameworks, methodological styles, and research questions of those engaged in studying men and masculinities in Latin America. Thus, together with studies by people resident in the United States, we are able to offer here to English readers current work by others engaged in studying men and masculinities who have pioneered the field in Latin America.

Another goal of this collection is to take advantage of the widespread interest in men and masculinities across diverse academic disciplines and areal concerns. This volume provides examples of significant research in the region on topics as varied as fatherhood, sexuality, machismo, health, housework, and sports; the impact on men of women's participation in social movements; the extent to which we may generalize for the region as a whole about men and masculinities; and the intersections of class, race, and ethnicity with masculinity in the region. With chapters on Argentina, Brazil, Chile, Colombia, Ecuador, Mexico, Peru, Venezuela, and the United States this volume provides ample coverage of the region so that differences and similarities for the Latin Americas may be highlighted. And, as should be obvious by the inclusion of Díaz Barriga's essay on Chicana and Chicano narratives, Latino/as in the United States are definitely part of what constitutes Latin America.[9]

In addition to geographical and disciplinary breadth, methodological diversity will also be quickly apparent to the reader. I have purposely placed chapters based on historical and ethnographic anecdotes side by side with others utilizing self-report epidemiology, next to others that utilize statistical findings, and alongside still others highlighting literary criticism. The wealth of approaches in research on men and masculinities in Latin America requires nothing less.

Words such as *competition, pride, responsibility,* and *sacrifice* are casually and sometimes exclusively associated with men in Latin America. Yet it takes no great effort to show how these terms may also be usefully applied to women as well. This observation in no way negates the importance of discourse, definitions, and customs, but it does point to the vital distinction between norms and practices and the perils of dichotomous modeling and the attendant need to discredit hackneyed gender dichotomies and dimorphisms in Latin America. Recognition that stereotypically feminine qualities such as self-control, devotion to others, and composure are in specific contexts valued attributes of men, too, by no means denies gender divisions or, still less, gender inequalities. It does point to a confluence of similar qualities in particular circumstances in men and women and by providing a counterpoint to conventional gender differentiation shows that such dichotomies are more fragile than analysis of norms alone can reveal. Borrowing from Mallon here, by planting our feet firmly on the ground we can see that it is high time to discard romantic concepts of dichotomous men and masculinities in Latin America.

Notes

1. Australian sociologist R. W. Connell was among the first scholars to apply this Gramscian term to the study of men and masculinities. In *Gender and Power,* e.g., Connell (1987, 186) defines hegemonic masculinity as constructed in relation to women and to subordinated masculinities, as closely connected to the institution of marriage, and as decidedly heterosexual.

2. On this point see, e.g., Kimmel 1994.

3. See Carrier 1995; Green 1999; Higgins and Coen 2000; Kulick 1998; Prieur 1998.

4. For a fine recent study of masculinity among an indigenous population in Guatemala see Santiago Bastos (1999).

5. See Gutmann (2002, 105). Higgins and Coen (2000, 114) write that *mayate* "often means an active gay male or one who penetrates. It can also refer to a very masculine male who is involved in some kind of street hustle, including sex, crime, and sometimes violence." See also Prieur (1998) for the more nuanced connotations of the term *mayate*

as employed by some male prostitutes and transvestites in the Nezahualcóyotl area east of Mexico City. *Mayate* among these men refers not to all men who have sex with other men, and still less to African Americans, but only to "a man who looks like a man and has sex with men who are regarded as *homosexuales,* and usually also with women" (Prieur 1998, 26).

6. For recent scholarship in Latin America on the body see also Leal 1995.

7. At the dawn of the twenty-first century many men were at least complicit in their government's refusal to legalize abortion in any but a handful of countries in Latin America, thus contributing to the control of women's reproductive options by men. On this issue, and so many others, the relationship of the Catholic Church to masculinity in Latin America remains to be uncovered.

8. For recent attempts to cope with this concern see Fonseca, this volume; Gutmann 1997; and Valdés, Benavente, and Cysling 1999.

9. For other studies of masculinity and Latinos in the United States see Limón 1994; Mirandé 1997.

References

Barrera Bassols, Dalia, and Cristina Oehmichen Bazán, eds. 2000. *Migración y relaciones de género en México.* Mexico City: GIMTRAP / UNAM.

Bastos, Santiago. 1999. "Concepciones del hogar y ejercicio del poder: El caso de los mayas de ciudad de Guatemala." In *Divergencias del modelo tradicional: Hogares de jefatura femenina en América Latina,* ed. Mercedes González de la Rocha, 37–75. Mexico City: CIESAS / Plaza y Valdés.

Bly, Robert. 1992. *Hombres de hierro: Los ritos de iniciación masculina del Nuevo Hombre.* Mexico City: Planeta.

Brusco, Elizabeth E. 1995. *The Reformation of Machismo: Evangelical Conversion and Gender in Colombia.* Austin: University of Texas Press.

Carrier, Joseph. 1995. *De los Otros: Intimacy and Homosexuality among Mexican Men.* New York: Columbia University Press.

Chant, Sylvia, and Matthew C. Gutmann. 2000. *Mainstreaming Men into Gender and Development: Debates, Reflections, and Experiences.* Oxford: Oxfam.

Connell, R. W. 1987. *Gender and Power: Society, the Person, and Sexual Politics.* Stanford, Calif.: Stanford University Press.

de Keijzer, Benno. 1998. "El varón como factor de riesgo." In *Familias y relaciones de género en transformación: Cambios transcendentales en América Latina,* ed. Beatriz Schmukler. Mexico City: EDAMEX.

Fausto-Sterling, Anne. 2000. *Sexing the Body: Gender Politics and the Construction of Sexuality.* New York: Basic Books.

Figueroa, Juan Guillermo. 1998. "Algunos elementos para interpretar la presencia de los varones en los procesos de salud reproductiva." *Revista de Cadernos de Saúde Pública* 14, supp. 1:87–96.

Freyre, Gilberto. 1956 [1933]. *The Masters and the Slaves: A Study in the Development of Brazilian Civilization*, trans. Samuel Putnam. New York: Knopf.

Fuller, Norma. 1997. *Identidades masculinas: Varones de clase media en el Perú*. Lima, Peru: Pontificia Universidad Católica del Perú.

Green, James. 1999. *Beyond Carnival: Male Homosexuality in Twentieth-Century Brazil*. Chicago, Ill.: University of Chicago Press.

Gutmann, Matthew C. 1996. *The Meanings of Macho: Being a Man in Mexico City*. Berkeley: University of California Press.

——. 1997. "The Ethnographic (G)Ambit: Women and the Negotiation of Masculinity in Mexico City." *American Ethnologist* 24, no. 4:833–55.

——. 2002. *The Romance of Democracy: Compliant Defiance in Contemporary Mexico*. Berkeley: University of California Press.

Higgins, Michael, and Tanya Coen. 2000. *Streets, Bedrooms, and Patios: The Ordinariness of Diversity in Urban Oaxaca: Ethnographic Portraits of the Urban Poor, Transvestites, Discapacitados, and Other Popular Cultures*. Austin: University of Texas Press.

Kimmel, Michael S. 1994. "Masculinity as Homophobia: Fear, Shame, and Silence in the Construction of Gender Identity." In *Theorizing Masculinities*, ed. Harry Brod and Michael Kaufman, 119–41. Thousand Oaks, Calif.: Sage.

Kulick, Don. 1998. *Travesti: Sex, Gender, and Culture among Brazilian Transgendered Prostitutes*. Chicago, Ill.: University of Chicago Press.

Lancaster, Roger. 1992. *Life Is Hard: Machismo, Danger, and the Intimacy of Power in Nicaragua*. Berkeley: University of California Press.

——. 1998. "Sexual Positions: Caveats and Second Thoughts on 'Categories.'" *Americas* 54, no. 1:1–16.

Leal, Ondina Fachel, ed. 1995. *Corpo e significado: Ensaios de antropologia social*. Porto Alegre: Editora da Universidade.

Lerner, Susana, ed. 1998. *Varones, sexualidad y reproducción*. Mexico City: El Colegio de México.

Lewis, Oscar. 1961. *The Children of Sánchez: Autobiography of a Mexican Family*. New York: Vintage.

Limón, José. 1994. *Dancing with the Devil: Society and Culture Poetics in Mexican-American South Texas*. Madison: University of Wisconsin Press.

Mirandé, Alfredo. 1997. *Hombres y Machos: Masculinity and Latino Culture*. Boulder, Colo.: Westview.

Monsiváis, Carlos. 2000. *Aires de familia: Cultura y sociedad en América Latina*. Barcelona: Editorial Anagrama.

Núñez Noriega, Guillermo. 1994. *Sexo entre varones: Poder y resistencia en el campo sexual*. Mexico City: UNAM/Porrúa/El Colegio de Sonora.

———. 2001. "Reconociendo los placeres, desconstruyendo las identidades: Antropología, patriarcado y homoerotismos en México." *Desacatos* 6:15–34.

Olavarría, José, and Rodrigo Parrini, eds. 2000. *Masculinidad/es: Identidad, sexualidad y familia*. Santiago: FLACSO.

Parker, Richard. 1999. *Beneath the Equator: Cultures of Desire, Male Homosexuality, and Emerging Gay Communities in Brazil*. New York: Routledge.

Prieur, Annick. 1998. *Mema's House, Mexico City: On Transvestites, Queens, and Machos*. Chicago, Ill.: University of Chicago Press.

Ramírez, Rafael. 1999. *What It Means to Be a Man: Reflections on Puerto Rican Masculinity*, trans. R. E. Casper. New Brunswick, N.J.: Rutgers University Press.

Stern, Steve J. 1995. *The Secret History of Gender: Women, Men, and Power in Late Colonial Mexico*. Chapel Hill: University of North Carolina Press.

Valdés, Teresa, M. Cristina Benavente, and Jacqueline Cysling. 1999. *El poder en la pareja, la sexualidad y la reproducción: Mujeres de Santiago*. Santiago: FLACSO.

Viveros, Mara. 2002. *De quebradores y cumplidores: Sobre hombres, masculinidades y relaciones de género en Colombia*. Bogotá: Universidad National de Colombia.

Wright, Timothy. 2000. "Gay Organizations, NGOs, and the Globalization of Sexual Identity—A Bolivian Case." *Journal of Latin American Anthropology* 5, no. 2:89–111.

Zolov, Eric. 1999. *Refried Elvis: The Rise of the Mexican Counterculture*. Berkeley: University of California Press.

MARA VIVEROS VIGOYA

Contemporary Latin American
Perspectives on Masculinity

■ ■ ■

Only in the late 1980s did research begin in Latin America that described men as having gender and producing gender. Until then men were identified with humans in general, and male privilege made the problem of men as such invisible. The work of Latin American feminists led to many studies of women but ignored the male perspective because despite the fact that gender studies in Latin America have long asserted the need to emphasize the relational aspect of the concept of gender, most of these studies centered their attention on women alone.

The emergence of the theme of masculinity as a topic of research occurred concurrently with the growth of men's groups interested in transforming their practical gender relations because they considered these a source of oppression and dissatisfaction not only for women but also for themselves. Thus, in recent years numerous books and articles on men and masculinity have been published in many Latin American and Caribbean countries, and there has been a proliferation of workshops devoted to "personal growth" in which these topics have been subject to reflection and discussion. At the same time, at an institutional level both nongovernmental organizations and gender studies programs in some universities have incorporated masculinity into their policies, activities, and academic programs.[1]

The growing presence of men and masculinity in gender studies and workshops reflects the powerful shifts in gender relations in Latin America in the past thirty years. Economic, social, and cultural changes have characterized the period—noteworthy among them are women's insertion into the labor market and the impact this has had on daily life, sexual roles, and traditional dynamics in the family—and have made it all the more necessary to understand and transform the place of men in present gender relations, both between men and women and among men themselves. In a sense it is already commonplace to refer to the so-called crisis of masculinity in Latin America, an expression of the clash between attributes culturally assigned to men and subjective reactions on the part of men to important social, economic, and ideological changes that produce this gap and that are instigated and supported in various ways by women (Gutmann 1999; Valdés and Olavarría 1997; Viveros 1997). As such, the crisis of masculinity refers to challenges faced by men with respect to contemporary masculine identities and practices associated with men that are out of synch with those commonly regarded as "traditional" in some sense.

Beginning in the 1980s, studies on masculinity in Latin America revisited some of the themes common in English-speaking countries when the field of "men's studies" first began. I have in mind Kenneth Clatterbaugh's (1997) eight perspectives on understanding and explaining masculinity, Michael Kimmel's (1992) discussion of the two dominant orientations of men (confronting their role in women's oppression and seeking to recuperate positive values associated with masculinity), and Robert Connell's (1997) four definitions of masculinity, each more easily distinguished in theory than in practice.

Masculinity Enters Gender Scholarship

In what follows I examine how some studies published in Latin America in the late 1980s and 1990s approached the theme of the masculine. This selection is far from exhaustive, nor does it offer a full panorama of present debates on masculinity in Latin America. It reflects my own biases and interests and necessarily leaves much material uncovered. Nonetheless, in this review I attempt to offer useful information about contemporary debates on masculinity and to stimulate discussion and analysis on the process of constructing this theoretical body of work. I organize the review around several themes that have been important in Latin America in this period: the construction of male identity, fatherhood, practices and representations, homosociality, and men's reproductive health and sexuality.

Scholarship on men and masculinity in Latin America has been carried out principally in anthropology, sociology, and social psychology. The dominant theoretical orientations have been constructivist, grounded in the notion that the categories we use to perceive, evaluate, and think are socially constructed. These new research perspectives have allowed new qualitative methods of investigation that are used to take into account complex problems such as the relationship of power to gender relations (Parker 1995). Similarly, the importance of not only behavior but also discourse has been emphasized, showing how the hegemonic position of men is presented, defended, and justified (Ramírez 1995). Finally, it is necessary to reiterate that contemporary studies of masculinity occur within the context of profound transformations in Latin America generally, in complex societies that are largely urban, in the huge numbers of women incorporated into the labor market, and in stronger and weaker feminist movements that have questioned male privilege in public and private spheres. In Latin America the so-called crisis of masculinity has emerged from these social and economic changes as well as from the significant impact of women in diverse social movements.[2]

The Construction of Male Identity

As pioneering studies, largely exploratory in character, most research on masculinity has faced the challenge of recognizing and analyzing what it means to be a man and the consequences of being a man within a Latin American context. Indeed, one of the principal themes analyzed is the construction of masculine identity. Among the first Latin American studies seeking to answer these questions was Sócrates Nolasco's (1993) *O mito da masculinidade* (The myth of masculinity) and Rafael L. Ramírez's

(1993) *Dime capitán: Reflexiones sobre la masculinidad* (What it means to be a man: Reflections on Puerto Rican masculinity [English translation, 1999]).

Nolasco (1993) studied twenty-five middle-class men between twenty-five and thirty-five years of age, analyzing the oppressive forms in which Brazilian men are traditionally socialized—their relation to work, themselves, their partners, friends, and children—and thereby questioning the social parameters through which to define what a man is. Nolasco proposes that in various countries increasing numbers of men are seeking other paths, therapies, and communities that will allow them to discover another kind of subjectivity, one in which emotions are not classified according to a sexist referent and in which emotions are not regarded as something harmful and irrational. In Nolasco's analysis the principal tensions experienced by men derive from attempts to adapt themselves to social roles that in fact do not correspond to their abilities or their desires. Until now, according to Nolasco, in defining masculinity men's self-perceptions have been grounded in vague concepts of authority and tradition. One difficulty for them has been how to construct self-images that accord with different aspects of their identities and not simply with what is socially expected. In the same way, Norma Fuller discusses in this volume a related schism between norms and behavior among men in contemporary Peru. The stereotype of the macho excludes such subjective dynamics, making individuals believe that men are made from a series of absolutes: they never cry, they must be the best, they must always compete, they must be strong, they must not get affectively involved, and they must never retreat. This is the model that some men are attempting to overcome.

Ramírez (1999) explores the construction of masculinity in Puerto Rico from an interpretivist perspective. The study begins with a critique of how the term *machismo* has been used and continues with a description of diverse masculinities in distinct ethnographic contexts. Ramírez also insists that the dominant ideology of masculinity is reproduced among men in homosexual relations, and he concludes his study by suggesting the possibility of constructing a new masculine identity, one stripped of the power games and competition present in the traditional male role. Using secondary sources, Ramírez presents his interpretation of what it means to be a man in Puerto Rico, concluding that in Puerto Rico, "masculine identity is embodied in the genitals and is articulated with sexuality and power" (1999, 48) and that "encounters between men are based on power, competition, and possible conflict" (1999, 58).

Unlike Ramírez (1999), Nolasco (1993) attempts to distinguish his study from feminism, arguing that the organization of groups of men cannot be characterized as a political movement and that each of these movements has its own characteristics and dynamics. Nolasco also criticizes what he sees as the association made by early feminism between patriarchy and men and the representation of women as virtuous and men as fundamentally bad.

The Importance of Social Context

Some authors, such as Henao (1994, 1997), Gutmann (1993, 1996), Escobar (1998), and Valdés and Olavarría (1998), have approached the study of male identities by paying special attention to the impact on gender relations of the economic, political, social, and cultural contexts in which these relations are defined and redefined. In Colombia writers such as Hernán Henao have shown interest in the topic of male identity within the framework of national and international changes that have occurred in the last thirty years. In a study based on life histories of forty-five drug addicts Henao (1994) reflects on the search for male identity that is resolved through denial, fear, and the impossibility of responding to challenges facing men in today's world. He argues that for men who feel powerless, fearful, and incapable of coping in a world "in which subjects have disappeared," the language of psychoactive/psychotropic drug users provides a way to speak. In a later study Henao (1997) shows how changes in gender roles and values gained in strength following the 1960s as a result of feminist movements. To illustrate these changes, he refers to men in the contemporary world, comparing "men who must enter and live in the home" with those whose roles and values were previously determined outside the domestic context.

Gutmann (1993) points to the effects of the Mexican economic crisis of 1982 on traditional roles and values associated with men and women. On the basis of an ethnographic study of intergenerational differences in masculine identities in the *colonia popular* of Santo Domingo, situated in

31 ▪ ▪ ▪ Latin American Perspectives on Masculinity

one of the major areas of land invasion in Mexico City, Gutmann analyzes the impact of the crisis on daily life for the inhabitants of the *colonia*, in particular the important connections between women's involvement in paid work and the growing participation of men in housework, leading to an "erosion of machismo" (see also de Barbieri 1990). At the same time, he posits a critique of stereotypes regarding machismo among Mexican men, especially men from the poorer strata, seeing such stereotypes as incomplete and deceptive if understood as adequate representations of how men see themselves and how they are viewed by the women with whom they share their lives. One of the chief merits of Gutmann's work is the relationship established between individual processes of identity construction and the shifts experienced in Mexican society in the 1970s and 1980s, including economic transformations and crises, struggles for ethnic identities, and ecological catastrophes.

Agustín Escobar Latapí (1998) also looks at the impact of economic and social restructuring in Mexico on the lives of Mexican men, but in contrast to Gutmann (1993) he focuses not on the daily experiences of men but rather on the descriptions they gave of events and transitions that define the key points in their lives in relation to their families, schooling, migration, and work. On the basis of an analysis of the life histories of men in Monterrey, Guadalajara, and Mexico City, Escobar arrives at the following conclusions: in the first place mothers play a determining role in the rearing, schooling, and initial work experiences of their sons. Mothers later help in the domestic arrangements and care of grandchildren in the families their sons form and play a less significant role in decisions relating to their sons' activities in the public realm. Second, although there are clearly changing patterns with respect to male attitudes toward their wives working outside the home, it is not the case that gender relations are everywhere constructed through egalitarian negotiations. Nonetheless, Escobar reports men seeking new relationships with women and a softening of notions that men alone have responsibility for economic support of families and that the role of women is exclusively tied to the family. Throughout Escobar shows that these changes in male attitudes and behavior have been prompted by recent social and economic shifts underway in the country. In his contribution to the present book Agustín Escobar

Latapí significantly goes on to note a "softening" of male attitudes with respect to women's entry into the labor market in Mexico.

The work of Teresa Valdés and José Olavarría (1998) in Santiago, Chile, also indicates the importance of contextualizing the construction of male identities within the framework of overall changes in that society. Valdés and Olavarría maintain that it is impossible to talk of a unitary Chilean masculinity, and they underline the multifaceted character of gender identities despite the relative cultural homogeneity of the country as a whole, the continuing strength of certain hegemonic models of masculinity grounded in relationships of male domination in households and more broadly in society, and the powerful mark left by seventeen years of military dictatorship on male identities in Chile. Analysis of the life histories of men from the upper-middle and popular strata in three distinct stages in their life courses allowed the authors to affirm that the hegemonic model of masculinity is fairly generalized among men in Santiago, regardless of their social situation. This model is reproduced from one generation to another through various spheres of socialization, and it is reinforced daily in different spaces of homosociality, although as Olavarría notes in this volume, generational differences exist in urban Chile and are important in various spheres of social life, including housework and sexuality. Nevertheless, faith in the hegemonic model structures the lives of older men and men from the popular sectors more than those of younger men and those from middle sectors, who are generally more critical of the model and more often seek to distance themselves from it. But not even these latter men seriously question social mandates that derive from this model or entertain notions of living other ways as men, and their discontent has more to do with the impossibility of modifying family roles—within which they feel imprisoned—than with a full condemnation of the dominant paradigm.

Masculinities and Social Classes

In his work on men in Guatemala Santiago Bastos (1998) sets out to understand gender relations as they are manifested in internal dynamics of households in popular sectors. Offering an analysis that goes beyond simply positing male domination, Bastos compares the behavior and activities that occur in indigenous and nonindigenous households located in the same working-class neighborhoods of Guatemala City. He examines the manner, often implicit, in which economic responsibility and domestic authority operate. He proposes that we conceptualize the activities of heads of households as analytically discrete, in part normative and in part actual and practical. He also notes that various members of households enjoy the possibility of exercising power, and he describes the complex interrelation between responsibility and authority in heading a household. In another article on the same theme Bastos (1999) explains certain ambiguous behavior by men in popular sectors through the "double system" of masculinity. On one hand, the image of manhood is constructed with reference to men's capacity to fulfill their roles as economic providers, obtaining through such provision social recognition and the possibility of imposing their authority on women and children in the home. On the other hand, men must present an image of themselves free from social ties, in particular from those with women. These two sides of the adult male image, Bastos reasons, can spawn destructive and self-destructive behavior among these men.

With a similar analytic perspective Marie Dominique de Suremain and Oscar Fernando Acevedo (1999) show in their study on heads of households and fatherhood among popular sectors of the population of Medellín, Colombia, that concurrent with new social and parenting demands on fathers, the objective obstacles impeding a positive realization of this paternal role have multiplied. By *obstacles* they mean the social conditions prevalent among the popular sectors in Colombia—unemployment and/or unstable employment, and "displacements"[3]—and factors related to transformations in families in Medellín such as the increase in marital separations and women's adoption of new roles. That is, there is a tremendous gap between the model of an ideal father, which is increasingly common, and the actual possibilities of putting this model into practice, especially in the popular sectors. This disparity has negative consequences as much for men themselves as for the whole family group, increasing discord between genders and generations.

Norma Fuller (1993, 1996) is one of the few scholars who have dealt with the construction of masculinity in dominant social sectors in Latin

America (see also Kogan 1996). Fuller (1993) argues that in the middle class, Peruvian men have not experienced significant changes as much as women because the latter have entered spheres traditionally considered masculine and have in this way acquired new freedoms. Thus, if men have seen reason to question existing male models, it is because of the transformations undergone by women. In a later study Fuller (1997) analyzes representations of masculinity characteristic of middle-class Peruvian society. She concludes that masculinity is configured in three ways in that country: natural (manliness), domestic (father, husband), and outside (work, politics). Each figure is based on different, and sometimes opposite, moral codes. Every man must confront each of these contradictory demands throughout his life, giving play to each depending on his stage in the life course and the particularities of his personal life. Fuller (1997) similarly argues that although these representations have become more egalitarian, significant discord persists between the formal representations and the practical activities of this population.

Masculinities and Ethnic-Racial Identities

In Latin American societies—multicultural with a broad array of social classes—it has become necessary to think about the various ways in which masculine identities are constructed in various social sectors, ethnic groups, and sociocultural contexts. Authors such as Octavio Paz (1959), Milagros Palma (1990), and Sonia Montecino (1991, 1995) have argued that the exaggeration and arbitrariness of masculine domination held to be so prevalent in Iberian colonial societies are produced by the real and symbolic illegitimate births that mark these societies. For these authors the figure of the Malinche constitutes a founding myth embedded in the Latin American social order because what is masculine is constructed in problematic relation to what is feminine from the perspective of the child or the absent father.[4] Although, as Fuller (1996) argues, this perspective has the advantage of considering the historical specificity of Iberoamerican societies to explain the dynamic of gender relationships, it also ignores the modernization processes of which these societies are currently a part, as well as the particularities of each.

Other work on this subject includes research in Brazil by Ondina Fachel

Leal (1992a, 1992b) considering the connection between cultural identity and gender identity. Drawing on her work on *gaúcho* culture,[5] Leal (1992a, 1992b) notes that *gaúcho* identity is strongly linked to masculine identity and describes cultural expressions of the former, such as myths, enchantments and seduction magic, verbal duels, and representations of death. In "Suicidio, honra e masculinidade na cultura gaúcha" (Suicide, honor, and masculinity in gaúcho culture), Leal looks at the meaning of masculine suicide in Rio Grande do Sul, the region where *gaúcho* culture is concentrated in Brazil, where suicide is a common practice and death represents a challenge and an opportunity for men to prove their masculinity. When a *gaúcho* loses his strength and is no longer capable of taming nature, he simultaneously abandons his *gaúcho* identity and his masculinity. His defeat is perceived socially as a feminization and as a cultural death and is experienced by him as his own death.

Joel Streicker (1995) analyzes the links established among class, race, and gender in daily life in the coastal city of Cartagena, Colombia. In particular, Streicker examines the interactions between these three categories in the everyday discourse of the residents of one barrio in Cartagena, claiming that the interdependence of race, class, and gender is related to the naturalization of difference and provides a powerful way of neutralizing social and individual subjectivities. The notion of masculinity is constructed not only in opposition to femininity but also in contrast to the masculinity of black men and rich men: the first group is considered dangerous and associated with what is animal, whereas the second is perceived as more feminine because rich men are seen as more interested in themselves and more subject to restrictions imposed by their wives.

From this perspective Mara Viveros (1998, 1999) analyzes the representations of masculinity of a group of adult men from middle-class sectors of Quibdó, the capital of the Chocó region of Colombia, where the largest percentage of the Afro-Colombian population lives. The author contends that sexual performance and a capacity for seduction and conquest are traits linked to black and masculine identities. Rather than confirming the racist stereotype that black men are obsessed with sex, this finding illustrates the overlap between gender and ethnic-racial identities. If one takes into account that identity is a relational construct, it is evident that Chocoan male masculinities have emerged in contrast to nonblack masculinities because Chocoan men have in this manner utilized their corporeality in constructing their ethnic-racial identities as much as their gender identities.

In summary, these diverse works document changes in the behaviors of men in the last two decades in Latin America, a region often described as *macho*, a debatable term used to characterize prevailing gender relations marked by a powerful domination of women by men (see Fuller 1998; Gutmann 1998). Even if some studies point out that masculine identity is constructed around power and competition linked to traditional masculine roles and indicative of repressed emotional expression, in others the deep fissures produced in this model are demonstrated, driven many times by changes promoted by women. At the same time, the multiple meanings of masculinity are generally highlighted because of class differences and because of differences within classes relating to particularities of education, age, and moments in the life cycle.

Masculinity is not an essential or static quality but a historical manifestation, a social construction and cultural creation. One must avoid asserting the existence of a black, *gaúcho,* or working-class masculinity in Latin America. It is important to recognize multiple masculinities, but one must also understand the relationships that exist among them and note that gender identities and class or ethnic-racial identities are acquired simultaneously and generate social practices marked by these multiple identities (see García de León 1994).

Fatherhood: Practices and Representations

In many studies of masculinity fatherhood has emerged as the highest form of male responsibility. Fuller (1997) points out that the paternal figure is determinate in the construction of masculine identity in Peru, regardless of whether the father is present or absent. Fatherhood represents the attainment of adult status and constitutes the most important experience in men's lives. It inaugurates a public display of the complete, virile, and responsible man. For Fuller paternity has a natural, domestic, public, and transcendental dimension. It is natural because it is the ultimate proof of virility; it is domestic because it allows men to rehearse their public sides by linking sons to the values necessary to perform in the public sphere; and it is transcendental because it ensures the continuity of life and transforms man into the creator. Last, Fuller highlights the existing imbalance between the model of the devoted father, described as ideal, and the gendered division of labor that alienates men from domestic chores and child rearing.

In *O Mito da Masculinidade* Nolasco argues that paternity in Brazil represents the most conflictive dimension of masculine identity, which is most challenging to achieve in practice. Nolasco examines the father-son link with the aim of reaching a better understanding of what happens to men who, despite the fact that some of their own fathers were absent, attempt to create a sense of belonging and involve themselves with their own children more completely than did their own fathers. In young fathers this novel situation may spark feelings of fear, pleasure, and strangeness. Nolasco argues that the image of the contemporary father in Brazil is constructed around the notion of complicity, pleasure, and gratification more than around a divine and moral image. For Nolasco fatherhood is a way men insert themselves into society to fuse the processes of masculine identity construction with the authoritarian model that is performed by men.

Hernán Henao (1997) describes recent changes in the manners of being a father in Colombia. Drawing on a series of field studies in the Antioquia region of that country, Henao points out that the image of the traditional father has existed precisely because of the discourse promoted by mothers and priests. The traditional father has been "an unreachable being, one who disappears in everyday events" (cited in Viveros 2002, 80). Today, on the contrary, fathers are expected to interact more with family members and to enjoy their home environment, very different from the fathers of bygone times, when male roles and values were determined by men's lives outside the domestic sphere. As Henao suggests, these new demands on the father began taking shape in the 1960s, with the feminist movements at the time, and acquired a particular salience in the 1990s, when Colombian men began to become aware of the gender problematic.

Benno de Keijzer (1998) notes the existence of various types of fatherhood in Mexico. He describes fatherhood as a position and a function that changes historically and has notable variations from one culture to the next, for example, in distinct social classes and ethnic groups within each country. De Keijzer makes an important distinction between biological paternity and social paternity because in the absence of the biological father, other men (grandparents, uncles, older brothers, or nonrelated adults) may assume fatherly duties. Also, de Keijzer points out that in Mexico, despite the fact that being a father holds great cultural value, when men from diverse rural and urban backgrounds in Mexico are asked how they define their manly qualities, fathering responsibilities are not often mentioned. Instead, other qualities, such as being a boss, worker, or provider and being strong, risky, brave, or a womanizer, are more frequently associated with true masculinity.

De Keijzer (1998) elaborates a typology of fathers from his own research experience. He refers, for example, to the model of the absent or fugitive father, involving several scenarios: homes in which mothers provide the only or principal income, a growing phenomenon; single, adolescent men who flee because of an unexpected pregnancy; immigrant fathers who maintain intermittent contact with their children and intervene in child rearing as regulators more than as active participants; and divorced men. At the same time, in many regions of Mexico the traditional or patriarchal father still predominates. He provides for his family but feels incompetent in child care and domestic chores; he considers that expressing affection can diminish his authority and therefore generally seeks to maintain a distance with his children. If he does approach them, he does so only with male children, beginning from the time he can communicate with them verbally. For de Keijzer these men represent a risk factor and a strain on the whole family, especially when they impose themselves through domestic violence associated with alcoholism. Similar issues are explored by Stanley Brandes in his chapter here on an Alcoholics Anonymous group in Mexico City in the late 1990s.

Next de Keijzer (1998) discusses an emerging kind of father in Mexico who pretends to be egalitarian. In Mexican culture such fathers are sometimes the objects of jokes and ridicule aimed at discouraging any changes in gender relations. Finally, de Keijzer highlights how men incorporate into their paternal practices a combination of traits of the different types described and how they change as fathers at different moments in their lives—authoritarian fathers may become tender, loving grandfathers—and in their relationships with different children. In other words, fatherhood is understood as an ambivalent and contradictory sphere for many men.

In his ethnographic study on changing gender relations in Colonia Santo Domingo in Mexico City Gutmann (1996) explores themes associated with fatherhood, such as the precarious connection between masculine sexuality and reproductive imperatives, the importance of blood ties and their relation to abandonment and adoption, and popular concepts about family, adultery, and polygamy. For Gutmann diverse paternal practices existing in Mexico reveal the ambiguous character of masculinity there. In this context he critiques simplistic notions of masculinity, concepts that reduce it to stereotypical irresponsibility and violence. Similarly, he argues that no solitary model of Mexican masculinity exists against which men can compare themselves or be compared. The results of his research lead to an opposite conclusion: for many men, being a committed parent is a central characteristic of being a man. Even the economic responsibilities of fatherhood are realized in diverse ways, from arranging to share free time with children to passing on technical knowledge to children. Further, Gutmann shows how the ideas and practices related to fatherhood are elaborated differently in a range of social classes. Thus, in popular classes with lower educational achievement and few economic resources, it is not rare for men to care for small children, whereas in social sectors with more resources, maids and nannies assume the majority of child care. In conclusion he argues that ethnohistorical research must be conducted to tease out class, regional, and generational differences with respect to the practices of fatherhood.

Last, it is worth mentioning the topic of adolescent fatherhood, which has been largely ignored in examinations of fatherhood in Latin America. In a recent study on adolescent male fatherhood in Brazil Jorge Luiz Cardoso (1998) points to a "wall of silence" erected by institutions, researchers, and individuals affected in Brazil. Cardoso suggests, for instance, that even when an adolescent father tries to play an active role in rearing his son or daughter, social institutions may impede or deny him the right to take on this role. Cardoso argues that the silence that surrounds adolescent fatherhood implies a perverse relation between society and these youths. By socially invalidating adolescent fatherhood, society legitimizes father absence and prevents these teenagers from seeing themselves as fathers who should assume their fathering responsibilities. Cardoso's study concludes that by culturally attributing conception and

Men/Sex/Men. HIV/AIDS prevention postcard used
in interventions in gay commercial venues. Brazilian
Interdisciplinary AIDS Association (ABIA).

child rearing to women alone, the widespread perception in Brazilian
society that children belong exclusively to their mothers is perpetuated,
and adolescent fathers continue to be regarded merely as sons and not as
potential fathers. For this reason it is necessary to create a support network
for these fathers so they may assume their roles as historic subjects and as
social actors who can and must participate in the construction of their own
human destiny and of the society in which they live.

As shown in many of these studies fatherhood in Latin America is a
complex concept, a subject that sits at the crossroads of multiple social
science disciplines. From varied perspectives the studies provide evidence
of the changing concepts and conduct related to child care and child rear-

ing, family and gender roles, and the effects of these changes on representations and practices pertaining to fatherhood in the region. In particular, these studies illustrate the contradictions of contemporary fatherhood in Latin America, the impact of socioeconomic and political changes on intrafamilial relations, the progressive deinstitutionalization of fathers' roles—increasingly more independent of authority—and the growing importance of fatherhood for masculine life projects. Changing patterns of fatherhood are implicated in more general transformations in gender relations, in the meanings assigned to infancy, in the expression of intimacy, and in representations of masculinity.[6] Finally, as noted, many authors point to a great variability in the experience of fatherhood according to men's socioeconomic and ethnic-racial allegiances, their generations, their primary experiences, specific moments of the life cycles in which they find themselves, and the sexes and ages of their children.

The Realms of Masculine Homosociality

Another important dimension of masculinity is its expression in public spaces, including symbolic spaces of power in which women have traditionally not been present. As Marqués (1997, 28) points out, "in earlier Western patriarchal societies, most social life took place in exclusively male spaces, so that homosociality was an inevitable fact."

Denise Fagundes Jardim (1992) presents a suggestive reflection about the social construction of male identity among the working class in Porto Alegre, Brazil. In her description of the *butecos* (bars where working-class men gather) Jardim shows how men in Porto Alegre appropriate this social space to construct masculine territories. In these transitional spaces between the public work space and the private space of family life, conversations about politics, sports, or business are privileged, and when someone touches on a topic about private life, it is discussed from an impersonal and coded perspective, with little direct reference to the personal lives of those gathered. In the aesthetic of these spaces one observes how food, drinks, and sounds are given masculine meanings.

In another article about the same topic Jardim (1995) highlights the importance for men of being able to share moments with other men in which they can reflect on ideal masculine behavior. For Jardim the relationship established among these men in these bars is a performative experience expressed through controlling alcohol consumption, managing the physical space of the bar, and producing a positive public image of themselves and their work. In particular, they seek to present themselves as workers and providers for their families and to contrast this image with the negative figure of the Brazilian *malandro* (street-smart hustler). Jardim concludes that the *butecos* constitute privileged spaces for male socialization in which discourse about the meanings of being male is produced and reproduced.

In his article on sports in Brazil Edison Luis Gastaldo (1995) describes male relationships within a martial arts academy, Full Contact, and analyzes the practices and representations of the body by one group of participants. According to Gastaldo the men's discourse about the relation of their bodies to this sport is characterized by three traits in particular: the utilization of the body for sparring, the rejection of pain, and the acceptance of rules that control this martial art. Even if this article does not make explicit the relation between the social uses of the body and male identity, the description and discourse analysis of the practitioners of this sport suggest that the emphasis placed on overcoming pain and exhaustion by submitting to a strict regimen is part of constructing a masculine form of perceiving and molding the body.

Eduardo P. Archetti (1998) examines the inherent complexity of models of masculinity by analyzing classic tango texts, as well as the songs of football fans, thus incorporating two cultural spheres representative of both Argentine identity and masculinity. Archetti shows, for example, that the narrator of tango texts is generally a man (son) who passes his free time with friends in a café (his second home), desires romantic love from a woman, and idealizes maternal love, the only feeling considered enduring. In the lyrics of tango songs psychological and moral dilemmas are also presented regarding the men's unconventional desires for *milonguitas* (young unmarried women from the lower middle class) and respect for social and familial norms, incarnated in the mother. In the tango the central masculine figures are not only those of the romantic lover (a transgressive masculine image) and the cynical *bacán* (someone who is suave and generous) but also those of the *compadrito* (the elegant seducer of women and arrogant rival of other men) and of the *compadrito* in crisis—the man who, deceived by one woman, may still be redeemed by the love of another.

These explicit and implicit meanings of masculinity are also found in the songs of football fans. Unlike the tango, however, the world of football is exclusively masculine. Through these songs fans dramatize gender identities and establish the limits of positive and negative aspects for what is supposedly defined as masculine. By vehemently defending their masculine identities and disqualifying those of their adversaries, they affirm the criteria used to organize relationships among men: dominion, control, and power. (In the present volume X. Andrade's study of political pornography in Ecuador illustrates a similar manipulation of such masculine traits to quite different ends.) In summary, through the study of the ritual spheres of tango and football Archetti (1998) shows how masculinities are unstable because men do not limit themselves to the reproduction of a hegemonic, heterosexual, Argentine masculinity but rather construct and negotiate multiple masculinities in varied spheres and with different actors.

The work site is another space affected by gender relations, involving as it does differences and inequalities in jobs, income distribution, working conditions, and the classification of work as appropriate to male or female. This is illustrated in a study by Virginia Guzmán and Patricia Portocarrero (1992) through analysis of the life histories of male and female workers in Lima, Peru. In particular, Guzmán and Portocarrero examine the value assigned to women's and men's labor in factory work spaces and the ways in which gender and broader social identities are linked. The authors maintain that women's presence in factories is not entirely accepted and that the values most esteemed in this environment are those most associated with "virile" qualities such as strength, capacity for resistance, the possession of technical knowledge, and the exercise of power. They also point out that the factory is occupied materially and symbolically by men and that discourse in the union is also dominated by notions of dominant masculinity, clearly linked in turn to a conceptualization of public space and citizenship as male privileges. In other words, despite the fact that workplaces, historically masculine, have become mixed, women do not occupy the same position as do men in the organization of institutions, and the notion of work continues to be regarded in masculine terms (see also Pesce 1988).

Such studies highlight the importance that men ascribe to these spheres of masculine homosociality in Latin America, where the very competition among men allows them to validate their maleness. As David Leverenz argues, "ideologies of manhood have functioned in relation to the gaze of male peers and male authority" (cited in Kimmel 1994, 129). In a sense one could say that encounters between adult men in these spaces mitigate the forces that drive the masculinity of young gang members. Francisco Ferrándiz, in his chapter in this volume, also discusses attempts by gang members in Caracas to break with more youthful expressions of masculinity, as when the men try to shoulder more responsibilities as fathers and husbands. With modernity there emerges a feminine presence in spaces that have been regarded as proverbially masculine, such as cafés, bars, places of recreation and sport, workshops, and factories. Despite the fact that the concept of masculinity "may be competing, contradictory and mutually undermining" (Cornwall and Lindisfarne 1994, cited in Archetti 1998, 200), and despite the recent increase in encounters between men and women in time and space, however, often in Latin America there has been a tendency to reproduce relations grounded in hegemonic masculinity, that is, to ignore or subordinate women.

Men's Reproductive Health and Sexuality

In recent years men's role in reproduction has become an important focus of studies on masculinity in Latin America. Scholars began by questioning the exclusive emphasis on women in reproductive health research, seeking instead to examine men's influence on women's health and on reproductive decisions in general. Important studies, such as those of Juan Guillermo Figueroa (1998a, 1998b) in Mexico, Hernando Salcedo (1995) and Viveros and Gómez (1998) in Colombia, and Tolbert, Morris, and Romero (1994) in Latin America, have attempted to fill this void. Figueroa (1998a, 1998b), for example, seeks, first, to conceptualize the ways Latin American scholars, educators, and activists have interpreted reproductive health in the male sphere and, second, to analyze how men may be "located" within reproductive health processes. A particular theme discussed by Salcedo (1995) and Tolbert, Morris, and Romero (1994) is the way in which gender relations affect decisions made in relation to abortion. Viveros and Gómez (1998) discuss male sterilization in Colombia as a contraceptive decision taken in a specific social context that defines and limits men's contraceptive options, models of masculinity, and the meanings of fatherhood and sexuality.

To incorporate men more explicitly in reproductive health research, Figueroa (1998a) utilizes aspects of traditional demographic analysis linked to fertility in order to identify more comprehensive indicators of individual experiences involved in fertility and the reproductive process overall. Subsequently, Figueroa (1998b) argues that by ignoring existing power relations between men and women, the medicalization of fertility can tend to endorse existing and exclusive "gender specialization." Men are in effect treated as agents who can impede or facilitate the regulation of fertility but as ultimately incapable of regulating it. He concludes by proposing several analytical and methodological strategies to uncover the presence of men in the reproductive health sphere.

Tolbert, Morris, and Romero (1994) discuss the relationship between gender relations and decisions to have abortions by couples in Colombia, Peru, Mexico, and elsewhere. They note that couples whose relationships were characterized by a greater gender equality were more candid in their negotiations about abortion. In a similar way, based on seventy-two formal interviews with Colombian men who wrestled over abortion decisions, Salcedo (1995) analyzes the relationship between masculinity and abortion, including masculine representations of sexuality, reproductive life, and feelings of desire. In his study Salcedo evaluates men's first reproductive event as a male rite of passage, discusses men's tendency to separate reproductive desire and sexual desire, and examines the relation between men's desire for heirs and women's own affective lives. Salcedo concludes by calling on men to participate more in reproductive decisions and to seek alternative ways of thinking about fatherhood.

Still other studies on men's reproductive health and sexuality in Latin America, such as those of Luis Leñero (1992), Armando Gomensoro et al. (1995), and de Keijzer (1995), seek to link male identity construction with particular sexual and reproductive behaviors of men. In case studies of Mexican men in urban areas Leñero discovers men whose apparently respectful attitudes toward women actually hide a persistent "neomachismo." As Leñero points out, this neomachismo is manifest in real and spontaneous behavior that in fact seeks to perpetuate male privilege. Nor is the use of birth control by some men necessarily tantamount to assuming responsibility for family planning; indeed, it can indicate the opposite: fleeing marital and familial commitment and responsibility by adopting a defensive attitude toward women.

In their study of three hundred Uruguayan men Gomensoro et al. (1995) come to similar conclusions. Their findings show that men may change some opinions about family, couples, sexuality, and some of their social roles but that they often preserve a deeper set of "existential infrastructures." For this reason, according to the authors, relationships between couples and families are paradoxically more conflictive than ever before. In response to this crisis the authors propose a "new masculine condition."

De Keijzer (1995) links masculine socialization to certain forms of intrafamilial violence, abuse, and sexual punishment, to the limited use of birth control and participation during pregnancy, and to the principal causes of male mortality. Drawing on the triad of violence described by Michael Kaufman in *Beyond Patriarchy* (1987), de Keijzer (1995) conceives of "masculinity as a risk factor" in three arenas: men's relationships with women, their relationships with other men, and their relationships with themselves. In each arena de Keijzer explains how hegemonic masculinity has a notably harmful impact on men's health.

Each of these studies attempts to reveal men's involvement in a realm traditionally assigned to women—the reproduction of the species—and to study male behavior and attitudes in sexual and reproductive health in their own right and from male points of view in various cultural contexts in Latin America. Although it has generally been argued that masculine sexuality is characterized by its separation from reproduction, these studies show how, by questioning the relationship between masculine identity and values associated with sexuality, male participation in different reproductive events (for instance, birth control, abortion, fatherhood, and sterilization) has been made problematic. At the same time it is clear that a rift still exists between adoption of a modern discourse emphasizing male participation in reproductive decisions and the construction of new models of family life and gender relations on a more democratic and equal basis throughout the region.

In Latin America there is a tendency to associate masculinity with heterosexuality and to associate homosexuality with femininity and passivity. However, several studies (Cáceres 1995; García 1994; Serrano 1994) point to the fact that adoption of traits or behaviors identified as masculine or feminine, as indicating passive or active roles in sexual relations, is independent of sexual orientation. Thus, many scholars have attempted to show that homosexual or heterosexual behavior is not necessarily linked to a differentiated sense of sexual identity (Parker 1995).

Writing in Colombia, José Fernando Serrano (1994) argues that homosexuality is a constructed category that refers to certain aspects of human life, that it involves more than sexual components, and that it carries with it certain implications for how life may be lived and a way of understanding and experiencing the world. Drawing on interviews with homosexual men from urban, middle-class sectors in Colombia, Serrano determines that no unitary homosexuality exists but rather a diversity of situations— multiple homosexual genders in which feminine and masculine components interact, varying according to individual lives. In a similar fashion Héctor Carrillo demonstrates in this volume the inherent problems attached to neatly dichotomized notions of what constitutes homosexuality in Mexico. At the same time, through their practices, homosexual men in urban Colombia assign new meanings to categories and roles imposed by society. In this way they resolve the tension between the identity socially suggested to them and the identities they develop and re-create.

In his study of sexual workers in Colombia Carlos Iván García (1994) develops a sociolinguistic analysis showing the relationship between masculine prostitution and processes of social violence and discrimination. In particular, García analyzes the language use and sociocultural characteristics of a group of sexual workers in Bogotá to understand the distinctive factors that coalesce to help form their identities. He also demonstrates the variety of situations implied by the word *homosexual* and the diversity of actors and social sectors involved in male prostitution in Bogotá.

In his article on health and bisexuality in Lima in the 1990s, Carlos Cáceres (1995) proposes a taxonomy of the range of experiences of homosexual men in Lima. The "characters" described by Cáceres are neither

HIV/AIDS intervention outreach on the gay beach in Copacabana, Rio de Janeiro. Brazilian Interdisciplinary AIDS Association (ABIA). Photograph by Emmanuelle Barabas.

static nor clearly defined but rather in a process of appearance and disappearance. In this way, in working-class sectors for instance, one finds the "active" or *mostacero* bisexual man, who does not question his basic heterosexuality, the effeminate *marica* or *cabro,* who will not call himself a man, and the transvestite, who expresses himself through aggressively exaggerated feminine mannerisms. In middle-class sectors one finds the *entendido,* who participates in clandestine homosexual encounters, the "married bisexual," the "bisexual gay," and the "gay," who participate fully in local homosexual culture and assume a macho style. Based on these characterizations, Cáceres proposes programs for AIDS prevention and sexual health that take into account the heterogeneity of sexual meanings.

Richard Parker (1995) is also interested in problems of sexual and reproductive health in relation to the development of sexual communities in Brazil and elsewhere in Latin America. In a survey of the state of academic research about sexuality Parker argues that some studies about gay communities in various developed countries point to an important correlation established between social development and support networks for gay communities and the resulting reduction of risk in sexual behavior. According to Parker the absence of such structures in developing countries largely explains the limited behavioral changes in sexual matters in these regions, although as he argues in this volume, in the 1980s and 1990s we may indeed speak of "a range of transformations in the social construction of (homo)sexual identities, cultures, and communities" in Brazil. The spread of HIV/AIDS and the emergence of new homosexual communities, each with its own institutional structures and social representations, have called attention to specific social dynamics and economic and political processes found in sexual communities, particularly in developing countries, albeit within the context of an increasingly globalized system.

Based on the studies examined, we may conclude that the relationship between sexual behavior and gender identity in Latin America is a very complex one and that the way in which sexual identities are constructed in different cultural contexts depends to a large degree on the categories and classifications utilized in each culture to treat sexuality. The focus of these studies has evolved from concern with actual sexual behavior to explorations of the sociocultural conditions in which such behavior occurs and to the cultural norms that organize sexuality. From this point of view local cultural categories and the classification schemes structuring and defining sexual experience in different contexts have been increasingly emphasized, as it has become evident that categories such as homosexuality and heterosexuality do not reflect the diversity and complexity of the lived sexual experiences and that homosexual and heterosexual behavior has been disconnected from a distinct sense of gender identity.

Final Reflections

Although there have been many advances in recent studies of masculinity in Latin America, there remain several unexplored themes that merit reflection and that should be future topics of academic interest. Research on the relationship between Latin American men and power, both institutional and individual, is required. Also needed are studies that show that within the same culture exist hegemonic and subordinate forms of masculinity, with tensions between them displaying "an interplay of alliances and contradictions which allow even more nuanced studies and a better understanding of individual behavior" (Minello 1996, 15).

Also, as noted by Teresita de Barbieri (1996), we need to better understand how men in Latin America have been affected by women taking over traditionally male jobs and, conversely, how men are coping in traditionally female occupations, such as nursing. Similarly, we need more studies about the effects of economic and social restructuring on men's life projects and experiences. In the area of reproductive health, as Marta Lamas (1996) points out, not only is it necessary to include men in analyses of reproductive health processes, but the symbolic dimension of the male body must be incorporated as well. To study masculinity requires not only viewing it as cultural and historic construction, that is, as a gender question; we must also attend to subjectivity, to the body as a cultural and psychological fact, and to the implications of sexual difference.

We also must ask new questions about masculinity. In recent years a certain type of literature has begun to emerge in Latin America that reiterates Robert Bly's (1990) arguments in his book *Iron John,* a book on masculinity that sparked sustained interest in the North American media for its discussion of the profound nostalgia that some men feel about lacking a life with meaning and the repercussions suffered by some men who were raised in homes where fathers were absent or where mothers supposedly had too much power. Bly's ideas reverberate in the work of certain Latin American authors, and several male groups and movements have developed in countries in the region as some men search for alternatives to the transformation of masculinity. As part of this movement in Latin America, workshops are proposed exclusively for men to reacquaint them with father figures and assist them in exploring positive attributes of masculinity (see, e.g., Cardelle 1992; Kreimer 1992).

Although there are positive aspects to these goals, the ambition to reinforce male power also reveals troublesome authoritarian strains and in some cases masks a reactionary, antifeminist posture in Latin America (Parker 1997). Their accent on a split in male identity may carry a critical message for women, making women responsible for their own situation, thereby strengthening traditional hegemonic masculinity (García de León

1994). On the other hand, the conclusions and solutions proposed by these kinds of analyses are inherently individualist—they point only to personal situations and interpersonal transformations, avoiding the importance of institutional, social, economic, and political situations and transformations—and masculinity is decontextualized from the real experiences of male-female relationships (García de León 1994; Kimmel 1992). In her chapter here Florencia Mallon provides a critical, and paradoxical, illustration of such decontextualization among former members of the revolutionary MIR organization in Chile in the 1970s.

In the academic world many of the new studies about masculinity ignore women's points of view about men because such viewpoints are not considered relevant to understanding masculinity. However, as has been argued in recent studies in Latin America, it is important to remember that men and women interact permanently in everyday life, that they affect each other with their activities and identities, and that feminine identities provide a point of reference for male identities (Gutmann 1997, 1999). For this reason it is necessary to approach masculinity from a perspective that allows for the multiple interactions of men with various kinds of women and different kinds of men, in other words, for "the different genders produced in society at any particular moment" (de Barbieri 1996). We should insist that masculinity in Latin America not be understood outside of a larger gender structure, defined as an ordering of social practice, and that the gender experiences of men are determined not only by their sex but also by the place they occupy within class, ethnic-racial, and generational categories in the societies in which they live (Fuller 1997).

Finally, it is necessary to continually demonstrate that inequalities in gender relations persist and that changes in masculine representations often constitute nothing more than adaptations to contemporary social conditions. To emphasize only the changes experienced by men and not the social transformations occurring among women can hide the fact that although some of the demands made by feminists are being adopted by "official" discourse in Latin American societies, gender equality is not present in everyday practice, nor is the process of masculine identity transformation in Latin America a homogenous one without contradictions.

—Translated by Matthew C. Gutmann and María Elena García

Notes

1. On this development see the interesting and detailed compilation by Valdés and Olavarría (1997).

2. I agree with Robert Connell's (1995) criticism of the concept of masculinity because masculinity is not a system in its own right but rather a configuration of a gender practice. In this sense it would be more rigorous to say that there is a crisis in the gender order.

3. *Displacements* refers to the more than one million people in Colombia who in the 1990s were forced to abandon their homes, fleeing violence perpetrated by one or another military group in that country.

4. Malinche was the sixteenth-century translator-mistress of Hernán Cortés, Spanish conqueror of what is today Mexico. Considered by some a traitor to the indigenous peoples whom Cortés subjugated, she has also more recently become a symbol for many feminist scholars of feminine independence and ingenuity.

5. The *gaúcho* is defined by the author as a rural cattle worker who lives in the southern Latin American pampa.

6. In fact, fatherhood is intimately linked to processes of male identity construction. Paternal meanings and practices are defined by a particular way of being and feeling masculine, of adopting some roles and rejecting others, and of allowing oneself to experience deeply affective feelings.

References

Archetti, Eduardo P. 1998. "Multiple Masculinities: The Worlds of Tango and Football in Argentina." In *Sex and Sexuality in Latin America,* ed. Daniel Balderston and Donna J. Guy, 200–216. New York: New York University Press.

Bastos, Santiago. 1998. "Desbordando patrones: El comportamiento doméstico de los hombres." *La Ventana* 7:166–224.

——. 1999. "Más allá de la dominación masculina: Algunas propuestas para la comprensión de la dinámica de poder en los hogares populares." Paper presented at the seminar Hogar, Pobreza y Bienestar en México, Guadalajara.

Bly, Robert. 1990. *Iron John: A Book about Men.* Reading, Mass.: Addison-Wesley.

Cáceres, Carlos. 1995. "Bisexualidades masculinas en la Lima de los noventa: Consideraciones de salud sexual." In *El amor y sus especies,* ed. L. Kogan, 39–57. Lima: Pontificia Universidad Católica del Perú.

Cardelle, Franck. 1992. *El desafío de ser hombres hoy.* Bogotá: Universidad Javeriana.

Cardoso, Jorge Luiz. 1998. "Paternidade adolescente: Da investigaçao à intervençao." In *Homens e Masculinidades. Outras palavras,* ed. M. Arilha, S. Unbehaum, and B. Medrado, 185–215. São Paulo: Ecos/Editora 34.

Clatterbaugh, Kenneth. 1997. *Contemporary Perspectives on Masculinity: Men, Women, and Politics in Modern Society.* Boulder, Colo.: Westview.

Connell, R. W. 1995. *Masculinities.* Berkeley: University of California Press.

———. 1997. "La organización social de la masculinidad." In *Masculinidad/es poder y crisis,* ed. T. Valdés and J. Olavarría, 31–49. Santiago: ISIS Internacional/FLACSO.

de Barbieri, Teresita. 1990. "Sobre géneros, prácticas y valores: Notas acerca de posibles erosiones del machismo en México." In *Normas y prácticas: Morales y cívicas en la vida cotidiana,* ed. José Manuel Ramírez-Sáiz, 83–105. Mexico City: Porrúa/UNAM.

———. 1996. "Certezas y malos entendidos sobre la categoría género." In *Estudios básicos de derechos humanos.* Vol. 4, ed. Laura Guzmán Stein and Gilda Pacheco O., 49–83. San José, Costa Rica: Instituto Interamericano de Derechos Humanos/Comisión de la Unión Europea.

de Keijzer, Benno. 1995. "La masculinidad como factor de riesgo." Paper presented at the seminar on Fertility and the Male Life Cycle in the Era of Fertility Decline, International Union for the Scientific Study of Population, Zacatecas, Mexico.

———. 1998. "Paternidad y transición de género." In *Familias y relaciones de género en transformación: Cambios trascendentales en América Latina y el Caribe,* ed. Beatriz Schmukler. Mexico City: EDAMEX.

de Suremain, Marie Dominique, and Oscar Fernando Acevedo. 1999. "Feminización de la pobreza y retroceso de la paternidad en sectores populares de Medellín." *Cuadernos Familia Cultura y Sociedad* 3–4:123–33.

Escobar Latapí, Agustín. 1998. "Los hombres y sus historias: Reestructuración y masculinidad en México." *La Ventana* 8:122–73.

Figueroa, Juan Guillermo. 1998a. "Algunas propuestas analíticas para interpretar la presencia de los varones en los procesos de salud reproductiva." In *Masculinidades y equidad de género en América Latina,* ed. Teresa Valdés and José Olavarría, 175–98. Santiago: FLACSO/UNFPA.

———. 1998b. "Algunos elementos para interpretar la presencia de los varones en los procesos de salud reproductiva." *Cuadernos de Saúde Pública* 14:87–96.

Fuller, Norma. 1993. *Dilemas de la femineidad: Mujeres de clase media en el Perú.* Lima: Pontificia Universidad Católica del Perú.

———. 1996. "Los estudios sobre masculinidad en Perú." In *Detrás de la puerta: Hombres y mujeres en el Perú de hoy,* ed. Patricia Ruiz-Bravo, 39–57. Lima: Pontificia Universidad Católica del Perú.

———. 1997. *Identidades masculinas: Varones de clase media en el Perú.* Lima: Pontificia Universidad Católica del Perú.

———. 1998. "Reflexiones sobre el machismo en América Latina." In *Masculinidades y equidad de género en América Latina,* ed. Teresa Valdés and José Olavarría, 258–66. Santiago: FLACSO/UNFPA.

García, Carlos Iván. 1994. "Los pirobos del Terraza: Interacción y discriminación sociales en un grupo de trabajadores sexuales." Senior thesis, Universidad Nacional de Colombia.

García de León, María Antonia. 1994. *Elites discriminadas*. Barcelona: Anthropos.

Gastaldo, Edison Luis. 1995. "A forja do homem de ferro: A corporalidade nos esportes de combate." In *Corpo e Significado*, ed. Ondina Fachel Leal, 207–25. Rio Grande do Sul, Brazil: Universidade Federal do Rio Grande do Sul.

Gomensoro, Armando, Elvira Lutz, C. Güida, and D. Corsino. 1995. *La nueva condición del varón*. Montevideo: Editorial Fin de Siglo.

Gutmann, Matthew C. 1993. "Los hombres cambiantes, los machos impenitentes y las relaciones de género en México de los noventa." *Estudios Sociológicos* 11, no. 33:725–40.

——. 1996. *The Meanings of Macho: Being a Man in Mexico City*. Berkeley: University of California Press.

——. 1997. "Trafficking in Men: The Anthropology of Masculinity." *Annual Review of Anthropology* 26:385–409.

——. 1998. "El machismo." In *Masculinidades y Equidad de Género en América Latina*, ed. Teresa Valdés and José Olavarría, 238–57. Santiago: FLACSO/UNFPA.

——. 1999. "Las fronteras corporales de género: Las mujeres en la negociación de la masculinidad." In *Cuerpo, diferencias y desigualdades*, ed. Mara Viveros y Gloria Garay, 105–23. Bogotá: Universidad Nacional de Colombia.

Guzmán, Virginia, and Patricia Portocarrero. 1992. *Construyendo diferencias*. Lima: Flora Tristán Ediciones.

Henao, Hernán. 1994. "El hombre finisecular en busca de identidad: Reflexiones a partir del caso antioqueño." Paper presented at the symposium on Sexualidad y Construcción de Identidad de Género, VII Congreso de Antropología en Colombia. Medellín: Universidad de Antioquia.

——. 1997. "Un hombre en casa: La imagen del padre de hoy: Papeles y valores que destacan 400 encuestados en Medellín." *Nómadas* 6:115–24.

Jardim, Denise Fagundes. 1992. "Espaço social e autosegregaçao entre homens: Gostos, sonoridades e masculinidades." In *Cuadernos de Antropologia* 7:28–41.

——. 1995. "Performances, reproduçao e produçao dos corpos masculinos." In *Corpo e Significado*, ed. Ondina Fachel Leal, 93–207. Rio Grande do Sul, Brazil: Universidade Federal do Rio Grande do Sul.

Kaufman, Michael, ed. 1987. *Beyond Patriarchy: Essays by Men on Pleasure, Power, and Change*. New York: Oxford University Press.

Kimmel, Michael. 1992. "La producción teórica sobre la masculinidad: Nuevos aportes." In *Fin de Siglo: Género y cambio civilizatorio*, ed. Teresa Valdés and José Olavarría, 129–38. Santiago: ISIS/Ediciones de las Mujeres.

——. 1994. "Masculinity as Homophobia: Fear, Shame, and Silence in the Construction of Gender Identity." In *Theorizing Masculinities*, ed. Harry Brod and Michael Kaufman, 119–41. Thousand Oaks, Calif.: Sage.

Kogan, Liuba. 1996. "Estudios sobre relaciones de género en los sectores medios y altos de Lima." In *Detrás de la puerta: Hombres y mujeres en el Perú de hoy,* ed. Patricia Ruiz-Bravo, 27–39. Lima: Pontificia Universidad Católica del Perú.

Kreimer, Juan Carlos. 1992. *El varón sagrado.* Buenos Aires: Editorial Planeta.

Lamas, Marta. 1996. "Hombres antes que masculinidades: O por qué el género no basta para comprender la diferencia sexual." Paper presented at VI Coloquio de Estudios de Género, Mexico City.

Leal, Ondina Fachel. 1992a. "Suicidio, honra e masculinidade na cultura gaúcha." *Cuadernos de Antropología* 6:7–21.

———. 1992b. "O mito da Salamandra do Jarau: A constituiçao do sujeito masculino na cultura gaúcha." *Cuadernos de Antropologia* 7:6–14.

Leñero, Luis. 1992. "Los varones ante sí mismos." In *De carne y hueso: Estudios sociales sobre género y reproducción,* ed. María del Carmen Elú and Luis Leñero Otero, 75–95. Mexico City: Instituto Mexicano de Estudios Sociales.

Marqués, Josep-Vincent. 1997. "Varón y Pariarcado." In *Masculinidad/es poder y crisis,* ed. Teresa Valdés and José Olavarría, 17–31. Santiago: ISIS Internacional/FLACSO.

Minello, Nelson. 1996. "Reflexiones sobre masculinidad." *Salud Reproductiva y Sociedad* 5:13–17.

Montecino, Sonia. 1991. *Madres y huachos: Alegorías del mestizaje chileno.* Santiago: Editorial Cuarto Propio/CEDEM.

———. 1995. "Identidades de género en América Latina: Mestizajes, sacrificios y simultaneidades." In *Género e identidad: Ensayos sobre lo femenino y lo masculino,* ed. Luz Gabriela Arango, Magdalena León, and Mara Viveros, 265–81. Bogotá: Ediciones Uniandes/Tercer Mundo.

Nolasco, Sócrates. 1993. *O mito da masculinidade.* Rio de Janeiro: Editorial Rocco.

Palma, Milagros. 1990. "Malinche: El malinchismo o el lado femenino de la sociedad mestiza." In *Simbólica de la feminidad,* ed. Milagros Palma, 13–39. Quito: Ediciones Abya-Yala.

Parker, Ian. 1997. "Hombre, mito y subjetividad psicoanalítica." *Archipiélago* 30:79–85.

Parker, Richard. 1995. "Estado de la investigación en sexualidad: Avances y desafíos sociales." Paper presented at I Seminario Taller Sudamericano en Investigación Sociocultural en Sexualidad, Santiago.

Paz, Octavio. 1959. *El laberinto de la soledad.* Mexico City: Fondo de Cultura Económica.

Pesce, Adele. 1988. "Los conflictos de sexo en el trabajo: Reflexiones a partir de una investigación empírica en Italia." *Sociología del Trabajo* 3:35–57.

Ramírez, Rafael. 1993. *Dime capitán: Reflexiones sobre la masculinidad.* Rio Piedras, Puerto Rico: Ediciones Huracán.

———. 1995. "Ideologías masculinas: Sexualidade e poder." In *A desconstruçao do masculino,* ed. Sócrates Nolasco, 75–83. Rio de Janeiro: Editorial Rocco.

———. 1999. *What It Means to Be a Man: Reflections on Puerto Rican Masculinity.* New Brunswick, N.J.: Rutgers University Press.

Salcedo, Hernando. 1995. *El aborto en Colombia: Exploración local de la experiencia masculina.* Bogotá: Universidad Externado de Colombia.

Serrano, José Fernando. 1994. "Diversidad cultural y homosexualidades." Paper presented at Simposio Sexualidad y Construcción de Identidad de Género, VII Congreso de Antropología, Medellín.

Streicker, Joel. 1995. "Race, Class, and Gender in Cartagena, Colombia." *American Ethnologist* 22, no. 1:54–74.

Tolbert, Kathrin, Karen Morris, and Mariana Romero. 1994. "Los hombres y el proceso de decisión respecto al aborto: Hacia un modelo de relaciones de género y el aborto." Paper presented at Encuentro de Investigadores sobre aborto inducido en América Latina y el Caribe. Bogotá.

Valdés, Teresa, and José Olavarría, eds. 1997. *Masculinidad/es poder y crisis.* Santiago: ISIS Internacional/FLACSO.

———. 1998. "Ser hombre en Santiago de Chile: A pesar de todo, un mismo modelo." In *Masculinidades y equidad de género en América Latina,* ed. Teresa Valdés and José Olavarría, 12–36. Santiago: FLACSO/UNFPA.

Viveros, Mara. 1997. "Los estudios sobre lo masculino en América Latina: Una producción teórica emergente." *Nómadas* 6:55–67.

———. 1998. "Dionisios negros: Sexualidad, corporalidad y orden racial en Colombia." Paper presented at the Latin American Studies Association congress, Chicago.

———. 1999. "Orden corporal y esterilización masculina." In *Cuerpo, diferencias y desigualdades,* ed. Mara Viveros and Gloria Garay, 164–84. Bogotá: Universidad Nacional de Colombia.

———. 2002. *De quebradores y cumplidores: Sobre hombres, masculinidades y relaciones de género en Colombia.* Bogotá: Universidad National de Colombia.

Viveros, Mara, and Fredy Gómez. 1998. "La elección de la esterilización masculina: Alianzas, arbitrajes y desencuentros conyugales." In *Mujeres, hombres y cambio social en Bogotá,* ed. Luz Gabriela Arango, 85–133. Bogotá: Universidad Nacional de Colombia.

Urban Men

and Masculinities

. . . .

CLAUDIA FONSECA

Philanderers, Cuckolds, and Wily
Women: Reexamining Gender
Relations in a Brazilian Working-
Class Neighborhood

■ ■ ■

During my 1986–90 field research in Vila São João, a working-class neighborhood about seven kilometers from downtown Porto Alegre (Rio Grande do Sul, Brazil), I was taken aback by the frequent references to *guampudos*, the local term for cuckold.[1] I had not solicited these commentaries. They had not shown up in the life histories I had collected during the initial phase of my fieldwork, nor were they present in the answers to a questionnaire I had applied on family organization. But on rereading my field notes I stumbled across references to *guampudos* on nearly every page. They popped up in daily banter between neighbors, in risqué jokes, and in succulent gossip.

The middle-aged matrons of Vila São João were experts on the subject: "Ah, Leco [a neighbor] didn't say hello this morning? It's because he didn't see you—his *guampas* [horns] got in the way!" Frequently, mothers and sisters would volunteer such information while describing the men in their family. A sister, while showing me her photo album, would quip,

"You see the girl in the photo here? That's the woman who put *guampas* on my brother." Or a mother would sniff, "My son, poor thing, began to drink because of his *dor das guampas* [literally, pain in the horns]." The men, too, join in the gossip. Although they generally avoid direct accusations, they allude frequently to *Ricardão,* that is, any man who goes out with a married woman. "In this neighborhood," someone observes, "there's more than one *Ricardão* jumping the fence when the husband is gone." Another man sniggers in agreement: "Nowadays, *guampas* come with hinges so they can be raised and lowered faster." The term is even used to classify a specific kind of sentimental music, somewhat akin to country and western: "Listen to those words," a man might prompt. "That's music for *dor das guampas.*"

The older women insinuate that in the good old days things were different. Mary is only thirty-five years old, but she insists that she is "old-fashioned" because, although she is fully aware that her husband sees other women, she could never consider the possibility of cheating on him. There is some indication, however, that the sexual liberty of married women has long been a popular topic of discussion among women as well as men. The barber on the corner describes the nightclub where he used to hang out in his youth, forty years ago, as a place for encounters. "The girls could find a husband and the married women could find something to keep them busy while their husbands were out working."

At the highest point in the neighborhood stands a white cement cross, in honor of the hill's informal name, *Morro da Cruz* (the Hill of the Cross). The first time I asked a pack of children the name of the area, however, I received a curious answer: "This here is called *Morro das Guampas.*" After a good number of snickers, one lad politely added, "It's because the first cross they put up was made of crooked wood. It looked more like a pair of horns than a cross."

In the Vila São João relatively few subjects escape the irreverent humor typical of daily interactions. However, certain themes are more popular than others. Male-female relations are a particular favorite, running through the stylized jokes built around anonymous subjects, the boisterous gossip about well-known relatives and neighbors, and the chiding jibes flung as half-serious accusations directly at one's partner.[2]

The constant joking about cuckolds was a surprise to me. In more than ten years of daily contact with Brazilian university professors I could recall but one instance involving such ribald humor: when a colleague, known for a certain rustic coarseness, teased another about the possible results of his wife's frequent trips. I had reason to believe that in the working-class neighborhood, where "traditional morality" supposedly weighed heavily on male-female relations, sexual decorum would be still more important. Anthropological literature on working-class populations in other Brazilian cities indicated that, following the general honor-shame model typical of the Mediterranean area, a woman granted her husband exclusive rights to her sexual favors in return for his material support, and, in the bargain, they both gained enhanced status as married members of a respectable family (Duarte 1987; Machado 1985; Sarti 1995). The difference between the behavior predicted and the behavior I encountered typifies the sort of anthropological puzzle that inspires closer investigation.

In this essay, therefore, I propose to probe the meaning of ribald jokes by locating them within the complex system of gender relations in the Vila São João. This line of investigation leads to the question of masculinity, but rather than centering on "masculine identity" (a major preoccupation in recent research), I propose to examine how men and women, moving through their usual social networks, use and are affected by culturally accepted definitions of maleness. Although these definitions include various virtues, from courage and loyalty to hard work and honesty, I have elected to investigate the attitudes linked directly to the conjugal relationship. Through the analysis of jokes and gossip about philandering men, gold-digging women, and, in particular, husbands of unfaithful wives, my aim is to better understand the power relations implied in images of sexual transgression.

In previous considerations of gender relations I have attempted to dethrone the conjugal relationship, the habitual center of academic debate on gender relations, in order to bring out the importance of other sorts of male-female bonds, be they between generations (mother-son, father-daughter ties) or between siblings (Fonseca 1991; see also Sacks 1979). When we shift the analytical focus away from the husband-wife relationship, the "war between the sexes" becomes an awkward metaphor, and the lines of demarcation between enemy camps begin to blur. In this essay, although marital relations have become the central issue, I continue to be interested in how members of the extended kin group view spouses within the group. In this way, rather than approach the conjugal relationship straight on (that is, with people talking about their own marital situations), I attack it, so to speak, from its soft underbelly. In the side comments made by informants about *other people's* marriages, the idea of marital transgression—in particular, transgressions involving adulterous wives and cuckolded husbands—comes to the fore.

A Question of Honor?

Like others who have studied Brazilian working-class families (Duarte 1987; Machado 1985; Sarti 1995; Woortmann 1987), at the outset of my research I viewed "masculine honor" and "feminine modesty" as notions that might help reveal important aspects of the local residents' gender relations.[3] As the ethnographic investigation advanced, however, the classical discussion on honor came to appear increasingly inadequate to capture the flavor and, more to the point, the fragility of male status in Porto Alegre. In this context the reexamination of gender relations called into question the necessary link between masculine honor and extreme forms of male dominance.

In recent years a number of ethnographies in various Portuguese (Almeida 1995), Greek (Herzfeld 1985), and Latin American (Gutmann 1996) settings have been published that mitigate the Anglocentric stereotypes of *machismo* that plagued many of the early studies on southern European men. One might add that even the classical studies did not entirely overlook the fear men had of their women's unruly conduct. Pitt-Rivers (1977), writing on the Andalusian town of Grazalema, aptly pointed out that the object of public shaming rituals such as the *vito* (or *charivari*) was generally the betrayed husband, not his unfaithful wife. Analyzing the situation, he concluded, "Women hold in their hand the power not merely to put pressure on their menfolk, but actually to 'ruin' them" (64). Gilmore (1987), in a subchapter of his study on Andalusian masculinity entitled "The Power of Women, the Weakness of Men," evokes a similar male dread of unbridled female sexuality.

Nonetheless, in this literature there appears to be a consensus that, despite episodic threats of individual female rebellion, the male-oriented norms prevail in most everyday situations. Gilmore (1987), in the most explicit example of this perspective, blends psychological with ethnographic insights to conclude that *machismo* is a sort of "compensatory mechanism [and that the] penis is the man's ticket to a sense of superiority. Andalusian males redeem their manhood by monopolizing the means of sexual reproduction" (Gilmore 1987, 150). Speaking then of women's inevitable "victimization," the author leaves us with the impression that the community's female members have little choice but to go along with the dictates of the masculine ego.

Noting that these ethnographic studies on masculinity were all written by male researchers, one might wonder if, somewhere along the line, there has not been a tendency to take some of the native's virile blustering too literally. This might result from the researcher's understandable empathy for the male point of view or from the informant's inclination, finding himself in conversation with another man, to exaggerate agonistic displays of maleness. Such skewing of information toward one focus or another is an inherent process of any methodological approach and therefore is not in itself a problem. Nonetheless, in this case circumstances coincide to create a gap: women, one might say, are pretty much left out of the picture. In his review article on masculinity Gutmann (1997) laments this absence, reminding us that "masculinities develop and transform and have little meaning except in relation to women and female identities and practices" and recommending that ethnographic investigations on men and masculinity include more research on "women's ideas about and experiences with men" (400).[4] Harking back to Gutmann's recommendation, I do not focus particularly on male speeches and opinions (although, certainly, these are plentiful in the public banter I recorded in my field diary) but rather on the uses that women make of male-related imagery. This perspective, as will be seen, gives us a slightly less-reverent view of male domination.

People in the Vila São João, when directly questioned about sexual morality, will no doubt reply that girls should be virgins until their wedding days, that married women should be chaste, and that men should dedicate themselves to supporting their wives and children. Normative speech may well paint an image of well-respected mutual obligations between husbands and wives. The all-pervasive humor, however, suggests another version of gender relations, one in which the reciprocity implicit in the conjugal pact, far from spelling out tranquility, seems to open the way for suspicion and one-upmanship as men and women endlessly vie to get the upper hand.

Men as Sexmongers

Men, whether married or single, are often kidded about being sexmongers. One hears laughing innuendoes about their sexual antics, both conquests and rebuffs, both extraordinary prowess and possible impotency. Even comments on treatment for venereal disease afford an opportunity to point out a man's "natural" inclinations. It is taken for granted by most denizens of Vila São João that, in their relationship with women, men just naturally aim for sex, at the least possible cost.

There are various stories about men who, in one way or another, manage to win a woman's sexual favors without giving much in return. In one illustrative case women gossiped about their recently separated neighbor, whose husband had just come through for a weekend visit: "He arrived with $3,000 *reas* [roughly U.S.$60 at the time] in his pocket, got everything he was after [an obvious reference to sexual favors] and before Vania [the wife] knew what was going on, he had left without spending a red cent." The best examples of male wiliness, however, appear in stories about young virgins.

Virginity, variously described as a jewel or crystal, is normally a serious subject. This "poor girl's dowry" is considered a precious coin, especially useful for achieving a "good marriage," that is, one in which the man will be a good provider. However, the normal system of marriage accentuates the vulnerability of this treasure. Approximately half the couples I had contact with (in general, those who were a bit older) were legally married. In local parlance no one makes a distinction between the couples who have a marriage certificate and those who are merely living together. They are all termed *casados*. To "get married" is often coterminous with a couple publicly setting up house together. When a girl's parents are opposed to her choice of husband, she may resort to *fuga* (elopement), running away for a day or two with her lover and confronting her parents with the (literally) consummated fact shortly afterward. According to traditional perspective the girl surrenders to her suitor in return for his promise to "hitch up" with her *(se amarrar)*. In the Vila São João it is quite common, however, for the seducer to try to get out of his commitment by claiming that the girl had other lovers before him. Such cases inevitably inspire a sort of community trial by gossip: Was he the girl's first lover or not? Was she really a virgin? Milene's son, for example, was being legally pressured to marry a thirteen-year-old girl who had lived with him for about six months at his parents' home. Milene defended her son, saying, "The girl didn't get pregnant. In any case, she'd lost her virginity long before coming to our house." She then elaborated with stories about her own brothers: "Jane [the wife of one brother] was only 15-years-old when she got pregnant. Her mother made a big to-do, but it was OK, my brother admitted it was him. With Caco [her other brother], things were quite different. The girl's parents had to threaten him with jail. That's why he ended up with her. Now, my oldest brother—you know, he still has a record at the police station because of a girl he got in trouble [*incomodou*]."

Such gossip is not intended to describe things as they should be but rather as they are. It is "obvious" that a man will try to have sexual relations without assuming conjugal obligations. Rather than see this as proof of one-sided male abuse, however, one should remember that women do not always correspond to the image of shrinking violets. On the contrary, in many stories they appear to have as many other things on their minds as the men do.

Women, in fact, are teased about their utilitarian approach to the opposite sex. Although young girls (those considered virgins [*meninas moças*]) are generally spared this teasing, an unaccompanied woman over a certain age may expect suggestions that she had best *arrumar um coroa* (roughly, hook an elderly sugar daddy) to take care of her and her children's basic needs.[5] Public banter points to this practical aspect of the conjugal relationship far more often than to romantic involvement. As one of numerous examples, I cite the case of Betty, a divorced woman, who was complaining to her neighbors that because she had no way of supporting her children, she might have to send them to live with her ex-husband and his wife. A neighbor retorted (with her own husband's laughing approval), "Get yourself together, woman! All you need do is find some rich *coroa*." Betty responded, in tones of mock tragedy, "I didn't manage to do it when I was 15, how do you expect me to do it now that I'm thirty?"[6]

The irony of the suggestion that a woman should try to hook a sugar daddy is that few men in the *vila*[7] would fit this bill. Most of them are unskilled laborers: Nei, a young father of five, loads trucks for a living; Giba, twenty-seven, works as a night janitor in the local supermarket; Touro sells lamps door-to-door in the nearby upper-class neighborhoods; Zeca sweeps up sawdust in a friend's workshop; Lirio helps his brother sell vegetables at the farmer's market; Cuia did good business for a while fixing up and reselling motorcycles, but after a police crackdown on unlicensed vehicles, he was forced to look for work at a nearby construction site. With such jobs few men go very far in terms of prestige or buying power.

Coincidentally, the most highly qualified and prestigious jobs (for example, police work or driving a bus) are associated with sexual conquest. People say that when a man is in such a line of work, "There's nothing he can do about it. The women are all over him." However, even policemen and bus drivers feel their masculinity threatened by their inferior class situation. I remember, for example, how a recently separated bus driver became very angry when he learned that his ex-wife was looking for a "better marriage": "What does she want," he asked, "a doctor or a lawyer maybe?" He could not understand that his wife was not referring to money or status but to the sort of helpmate who would treat her more kindly.

The inferior status and limited economic opportunities of unskilled manual laborers exacerbate the fear of female betrayal. After all, if a man fails to uphold his end of the implied marital bargain, why should his wife uphold hers? If he fails to provide a comfortable existence for his wife and children, why should the woman feel obliged to be faithful?

Cuckolds and Their Wily Wives

Malandragem (roguishness) has often been associated in the anthropological literature on Brazil with the male spectrum of activities (DaMatta 1979; Oliven 1987). Women are not generally included in the category of *malandros*. When researchers describe a group's representations of the universe of feminine activities, they tend to emphasize normative images: the *santa* (the good mother and faithful wife) or the *piranha* (the promiscuous woman). In my work on the Vila São João, on the other hand, these

Threesome. HIV/AIDS prevention folder for sexually active bisexual men. Brazilian Interdisciplinary AIDS Association (ABIA).

exaggerated figures appear less relevant in day-to-day exchanges than images of the *malandra* (wily woman). Particularly in jokes and gossip, one sees insinuations that even if a woman gets the masculine support she is after, she may not fulfill her end of the bargain. She may not grant the monopoly of her sexual favors to the man who supports her, thus inflicting on him the humiliating status of *corno manso* (tame or willing cuckold).

The abundant anecdotes about such women are not always told in accusatory tones. A respectable lady, married to the same man for over three decades, speaks in frank admiration of her goddaughter: "She's a *malandra*. She hooked up with some senile old man. He gives her everything—a television, games for the children—and she has others [lovers]. Good for her!"

In another episode a woman rubs together thumb and forefinger (a gesture signifying money) to tell me how *esperta* (clever) the neighbor's daughter was: "Her first man—the one who bothered her—had lots of money. Now he sends her an allowance every month, to support her and the kid. He even bought a house for her to live in." Still another woman admires her brother's choice of lover: "His girl friend was the maid for a rich old couple. When the fellow's wife died, she stayed on with the old man. Now she does what she wants with his money. She bought a motorcycle for my brother. They're just waiting for the fellow to kick off so they can get married."

Despite being described in certain situations with good-humored directness, women's sexual adventures are not condoned as men's are. It is significant that no woman would brag publicly about her own sexual exploits. The admiration she expresses for her "clever" neighbor or sister-in-law may be laden with irony, conveying a more disparaging view of the girl's loose ways. Moments of complicity, when one woman confesses her sexual adventures to another, are also charged with ambivalence. Sinara, for example, on hearing the confession of her daughter's marital infidelities, appeared genuinely concerned. She advised her daughter to be more *malandra,* lest her indiscretions jeopardize a long-standing marriage with "the father of her children," who was, coincidentally, a good provider.

Finally, people make a clear distinction between cheating on a *coroa* (an older man, often married to another woman, who, in local logic, "asked for" what was coming) and cheating on a husband, that is, a neighbor and friend. In cases of the latter sort gossip carries a tone of frank disapproval. Milene speaks with a mixture of scorn and pity of the elderly couple living beside her: "He was a cuckold and didn't even care. I remember that when we were little, we used to tease his son a whole lot. We would say, 'Your Ma is there in bed with a big thug.' He would cry and cry . . . but his father never did anything."

From the various bits of gossip I registered, I have the impression that this case is not atypical; in other words, most cases of female transgression seem to occur without serious repercussions. Among the dozens of narratives I collected on unfaithful women, I registered only one case of separation justified by the wife's adultery and one case of violence by a husband against his wife's lover.

Considering the enormous publicity given to crimes of passion in the national and local papers, the absence of such material in my field notes is surprising. In the neighborhood I worked in it appeared that the betrayed husband has, in fact, few and unappealing options. If he denounces his wife's wrongdoings, he exposes himself to public ridicule, which only an act of dramatic violence could erase. I deduce from the lack of violence in the stories about unfaithful wives that either the all-pervasive gossip is simply untrue or that most men find the "virile" solution distinctly distasteful. Their basic option is to maintain silence—a silence that, nonetheless, invites others to manipulate the fear of exposure.

Women Use the Threat of Cuckoldry against Other Women

Even if the stories were no more than malicious gossip, and even if they had very little to do with the real behavior of women, one would still have to admit that people *believe* that female adultery is common and, in most cases, goes unpunished. The fear of "bearing horns" thus haunts a great many men—a fear that, in able hands, becomes a weapon for powerful manipulation. The question is by whom and against whom? Rather than see the gossip about loose women as a symptom of male domination, one should ask how and why this gossip is activated by certain individuals against others.

As pointed out in the beginning of this article, everyone makes jokes about adultery, but, in general, only women name names. Women, it might be added, do not talk about just anyone but rather about other women with whom they entertain a specific relation—that of competitor for a certain man's attentions. Occasionally, for example, I would hear a new wife accuse her husband's previous spouse of having had lovers. By doing this, she not only highlights her own virtues, but she also indirectly allays suspicions that she might be responsible for the breakup of her husband's previous marriage.

There is still another category of women who seem to make an art of gossiping about their rivals' misbehavior: mothers and sisters, in my experience, delight in casting suspicion on their female in-laws. Let us remember the comments quoted at the beginning of this article: "You see the girl in this photo here? That's the woman who put *guampas* on my brother," and "My son, poor thing, began to drink because of his *dor das guampas*." It is no coincidence that these speakers were women defending their male relatives against less-than-honorable wives and girlfriends.

Ironically, it is these same women—mothers and sisters—who will make jokes to emphasize the sexual virility of their male relatives. According to a certain widow, "My son was so handsome that, at his funeral, besides his wife, there were five other women crying over the coffin." An adult daughter comments on the escapades of her father, who is going through a rough period with his present wife: "It would appear that he's next door all the time, consoling the widow who just lost her husband. Consoling! You can imagine how!" A sister describes her brother's behavior with an ironic laugh: "He went with me to the bingo parlor but, before I knew it, he had disappeared. When I went to look for him, there he was in a corner kissing and hugging a young black girl." To sum up her story about her son's chronic adultery, a certain mother explains to me: "You have to understand, he's a bus driver. The girls are always all over him. He can't refuse. If he didn't take advantage of the situation, they'd say he was a homosexual *(puto)*." On relating her son's various sexual feats, another woman breaks into laughter (despite her initial efforts to maintain a dispassionate tone): "What a shameless creature! He just won't stop, but it's no use. Some men are like that. Last year, when he was in the hospital, I went to visit him and I ran into his wife blubbering at the door. 'What is it?' I asked . . . and then I looked and saw: there were two other women—his little girlfriends—who'd got there before her."

To avoid classifying this apparent contradiction between the exaltation of male relatives' philandering and the accusations against their supposedly unfaithful wives in terms of the long-criticized "double standard" (Pitt-Rivers 1977), one should remember that the women who denounce the shameless behavior of their sisters-in-law and daughters-in-law may well brag about the cleverness of their goddaughters and neighbors for the same sort of adventures. In other words, the difference between "shamelessness" and "cleverness" may not depend as much on what actually occurred as on the relationship between the person who is describing the act and the person who committed it. But why, one might ask, would women be interested in besmirching the image of their female in-laws?

In a previous study on a poverty-stricken squatter settlement, I examined in detail the importance of blood ties and the way these ties rival the conjugal bond (Fonseca 1991). Just as in many other lower-income groups (see Stack 1974), blood relations form the nexus of an extended kin network, guaranteeing the continuity of social ties despite conjugal ruptures and remarriages. In the Vila São João, although slightly more prosperous and with a higher rate of conjugal stability than in the *vila* of my previous study, a great many men still maintain daily contact with their parents or siblings. Wives thus find themselves competing with in-laws for their men's time, money, and services rendered.

Female relatives, like wives, make themselves useful by furnishing their men with minor domestic comforts. Whether separated or still married, a man knows he can usually find a meal or a bed in his mother's home and, often, in his sister's home. Fathering children is definitely a point of masculine pride, but neither marriage nor coresidence with his children's mother is necessary for him to acquire paternal status. Instead of his wife, a man's mother or sister may raise his children (see Fonseca 1995). In fact, with the exception of begetting his children, the only other feminine role a mother or sister cannot properly perform is that of sexual partner. Is it, then, a mere coincidence that often it is these female relatives who point out brothers' and sons' vulnerability to "unfaithful" wives and that it is a man's mother and sister who generate gossip and jokes about cuckolds to undercut his wife's principal political advantage? Their banter is a constant reminder that the wife's specific talent of enhancing her husband's prestige and giving birth to his children is accompanied by the constant threat of infidelity. It contributes to the idea that, considering the manifest fragility of the conjugal tie, survival and reproduction should be organized around more secure relations, that is, the ones defined by blood.

The Target of Social Stigma

The way mothers and sisters use images of male cuckolds to cast aspersions on the virtue of their female in-laws would not necessarily be incompatible with modes of male domination. One may imagine that to avoid ridicule, men would insist more than ever on their wives' subordination. Certainly, the masculine fear of horns explains a husband's occasional attempt to confine his wife to the house, forbidding her to hold a job outside the home. It also explains in part the zeal with which some men execute their protective role, staying close to home. There are, nonetheless, a number of other signs indicating that the fear of cuckoldry is a double-edged sword, swinging just as easily against men as against their wives.

In the first place I would argue that there are no firm sanctions against a woman's sexual transgressions. I have already mentioned that men rarely impose publicly perceptible sanctions on their allegedly adulterous wives. But other members of the community might be charged with this responsibility. For example, according to the ethnographic literature on Mediterranean honor, a woman's blood relatives are often the major guardians of her sexual behavior. The shameful behavior of a mother or sister could mar a man's reputation as much as his own wife's (see, e.g., Bourdieu 1972; Kressel 1981; Pitt-Rivers 1954, 1977). An extreme example would be Corsica, where the term *cuckold* is applied not only to the brother, father, or husband of a dishonored woman but also to any man who lacked the courage to avenge other offenses (such as murder) committed against the clan (Knudsen 1988). The Vila São João is a different story.

Similar to the pattern in most Western countries, I find among verbal offenses employed in the *vila* references to the morality of a man's female relatives: expressions such as "son of a bitch" or "I 'ate' your sister."[8] However, I never saw signs of anyone taking these insults literally. Men may make it a point of honor that their sisters and daughters be respected. If, for example, a reputed virgin's first lover refuses to marry her, he may well be confronted with serious threats from her male relatives. On the other hand, punitive measures are hardly ever brought against the girl.

Barring masculine retaliation, one should not ignore the possibility of community sanctions—ostracism, for example—against unchaste women. But there, again, my material fails to yield supporting evidence. Despite the presence in the *vila* of numerous single mothers, as well as many women on a third or fourth "husband," only two or three of them—all particularly poor—were regularly criticized by their neighbors. The implication was that these women were stupid rather than immoral. They had not managed to "hook" a stable partner and so, along with their children, were condemned to lives of hardship.

At one point I was convinced I had found evidence of belief in divine sanctions against adulterous wives. The death of Dona Lucia, struck down by a heart attack at age forty-eight, was interpreted by Gina, one of my key informants, as a punishment from God because the deceased woman had supposedly been unfaithful to her husband with a string of different lovers. ("I heard this," claimed Gina, "from Dona Lucia's own niece.") However, close evaluation of my field notes helped me to contextualize this incident. I met Dona Lucia several years before she died. At the time, I had a series of conversations with her neighbors and adult daughters who, when they spoke of her, inevitably brought up her husband's shameless behavior: "He kept another woman for years, abandoned his family, sold the house, and gave everything he had to his new lover." Sometime later the "abandoned" woman, Dona Lucia, got together with a new helpmate, a "widowed gentleman" who lived with his mother a couple of blocks up the street: a "good husband," owner of various city lots, and an abstemious teetotaler. In other words, for years this woman's escapades, if they were indeed real, seem to have evoked little if any indignation among the people around her.

Gina's particular interpretation of Dona Lucia's untimely death could possibly be attributed to her evangelical upbringing. It is, nonetheless, evidence of the existence in the *vila* of a more normative discourse on female morality, one close to that seen by other researchers as a sort of hegemonic ideal (Almeida 1995). As I see it, however, the question is not whether this sort of normative discourse exists but rather *how much weight it carries*. In the case of Dona Lucia it does not seem to have seriously affected her lifestyle.

In my notes women targeted by gossip as possible adulteresses suffered no particular discrimination by their neighbors. They received visits, took part in *rodas de chimarrão*,[9] and shared childcare responsibilities just as any other woman in the neighborhood. With the exception of Gina's condemnation of Dona Lucia, I never heard a woman accused of adultery except to sneer at her poor or naïve cuckolded husband. On the other hand, several men were pointed out to me as cuckolds by people who offered no particular comment or information on their guilty wives.

It appears that in the *vila* the socially accepted sanctions against female adultery are not sufficiently ominous to ward off occasional offenders. One might add that men seem to suffer as much, if not more, stigma than their unfaithful wives. In fact, there appears to be a basic asymmetry in the social stigma attached to the breach of the conjugal pact. The girl, seduced and abandoned, especially if she has gotten pregnant and had a child, may find it hard to muster a living. In general, however, she will suffer no stigma for having been abandoned. On the contrary, people tend to take pity on her. She will spin laments about how her husband spent all his money on other women, leaving his children to go hungry. She will tell long stories about how much she has suffered, thus garnering a reputation as a courageous fighter who, despite all odds, has been able to keep her family together and raise her children. An ex-husband, on the other hand, will usually not dare to complain publicly about his wife's treatment of him. Even if his wife breaches the marital contract, taking lovers or bearing children out of wedlock, he must suffer in silence because any reaction on his part would cause him to publicly assume the humiliating status of cuckold. In short, to call a man a cuckold appears to be a more frequent and searing accusation than to call a woman shameless.

Nothing illustrates this masculine vulnerability better than a scene I witnessed one day while chatting with Dona Rosa, a plump sixty-year-old matron, at her front gate. She was going on, misty-eyed, about all the hardships she had been through, giving considerable emphasis to her drunk and philandering husband's perfidy. Suddenly, changing her focus to a figure behind me, a passerby on the other side of the street, she cackled, "Hello there, you old cuckold, did your wife let you out to graze?" Waiting only for an affable wave from the elderly gentleman in question, she resumed the refrain of her story in the same tragic tone as before. Were I to heed only her narrative, the one spun specifically for my ears, I might reinforce the hypothesis of woman's eternal victimization. But after reflecting on Dona Rosa's humorous assault on her old friend, I was forced to concede that things just are not that simple.

This story gains still more significance when one considers that Rosa was kidding the same man commented on by Milene: the one who in his youth "was a cuckold and didn't even care." No doubt it could be dangerous to openly taunt a younger man in this way. But, now an old man, this fellow had little choice but to play along with the joke, accepting the part of clown and publicly exhibiting the Achilles heel of the masculine ego common to all men in the *vila*.

How Women Use the Threat of Cuckoldry against Men

Humor in the Vila São João, "like humor in any society, uses things which are ambiguous or taboo and plays with this in different ways"

(Seeger 1980, 69). In his work among the Suya Indians, Anthony Seeger, like many researchers, sees humor as a sort of escape valve that permits people to let off steam about society's repressive norms rather than change them. It would be imprudent, however, to presume that jokes serve this function in every situation. For example, Natalie Davis (1975), in her essay on early modern France, "Women on Top," suggests that the boisterous humor surrounding images of "unruly women," from carnival costumes and *charivaris* to plays and picture postcards, undermined as much as it reinforced conventional patterns of authority: "I want to argue that the image of the disorderly woman did not always function to keep women in their place. On the contrary, it was a multivalent image that could operate . . . to widen behavioral options for women within and even outside marriage" (131).

Following this logic, I suggest that humor holds an important part in the transmission of values from one generation to another. To illustrate this hypothesis, I cite an anecdote from my field notes. Dona Alcina vigorously bemoaned the "shamelessness" of her ex-daughter-in-law, who "took up with somebody else": "When she and my son separated, she got everything. The sound box, the color television, the set of crystal, everything!"

There is no doubt that the emphatic tone of her discourse resulted in part from the presence of three nieces *(meninas moças)* for whom she was caring at the time. Certainly, she would not want her charges to copy the example of her unfaithful daughter-in-law. However, one might ask which message the youngsters were picking up: the shameful aspect of the daughter-in-law's behavior or its lucrative rewards? After all, the woman was able to exert her liberty and still get away with "everything."

The inspirational character of this irreverent humor comes out even more strongly in the following apocryphal story told by a woman to her female cronies:

A recently married woman was strolling through the countryside with her new husband when she saw two lovebirds grooming one another. "Isn't that beautiful," she said to her new spouse, "the way they court one another with such tender care? . . ." A few minutes later, they encountered a bull coupled with a cow. "That's the way I like it," said the husband. "Bam, slam, and you're finished." The wife's response: "Yes, I see. However, please take note: Birds do not grow horns."

This is an explicit example of how women may turn conservative morality dictating female fidelity to their own advantage.

. . . .

Why, one might ask, do women in this Porto Alegre *bairro* appear less resigned and men less dominant than those described in many other ethnographies of Brazil's urban poor? To answer this question, one could endorse the hypothesis that in Rio Grande do Sul particular historical conditions created a regional cultural complex quite different from the Mediterranean complex dominant in the rest of Brazil. Supporting evidence would point to a tradition of border wars (which often left women running the homesteads), a cattle economy of freedom-loving cowboys (whose nomadic ways took precedence over the imperatives of family honor),[10] and a heavy contingent of northern European immigrants with a non-Mediterranean pattern of gender relations. Critics of this approach would protest, however, that wars and female-headed families were common throughout colonial Brazil and that Rio Grande do Sul (especially the lower echelons of society) has never been so European as the state propagandists would have us believe.

Another, and considerably more tempting, approach to the analysis of the ethnographic data presented in this essay would highlight cultural transformation. Many observers would name the 1980s *reabertura democrática*, during which time Brazil emerged from a twenty-year military dictatorship, as a turning point in the history of social mores in Brazil. Starting in this period, the 1978 legalization of divorce, the repeated negative publicity given by national media to "crimes of honor,"[11] an increasingly active women's movement, and a growing presence of the State in family affairs were influences that left their mark on people's attitudes. In Rio Grande do Sul, a left-leaning political tradition that brought the National Worker's Party (PT) to power in the late 1980s might have produced a particularly progressive version of more general national trends. Following this line of analysis, one can better understand the freewheeling humor described in this paper as an indication of behavior and attitudes that only a few decades before would have been regarded as unspeakable transgressions.

Indeed, anthropologists working on gender relations in different Latin American settings, from northern Brazil to Mexico, have reported how members of today's younger generation adopt attitudes not so different from those embraced by their North American counterparts (see Gutmann 1996; Rebhun 1999). Such observations would be valid for many young couples I knew in the Vila São João as well. Much of this literature, however, has tended to rank these new attitudes in value-laden terms (*transformative* vs. *archaic* consciousness, for example). Such an approach keeps us from exploring the subtleties embedded in the so-called traditional modes of behavior—those that differ substantially from the researcher's (and some feminists') idea of politically correct gender relations.[12]

No doubt, geopolitical specificities and cultural change have much to do with what I observed in the *vila*. Nevertheless, it is possible that the conclusions I draw from my ethnographic research are also related to the particular epistemological slant I adopted to analyze this scenario. In particular, tacitly guided by the notion of "variant masculinities," I have questioned pejorative stereotypes of "traditional" (or in this case "Latin") gender relations, suggesting that hegemonic narratives of male dominance do not always reflect the reality of everyday behavior.[13] Working with jokes, kidding, gossip, and other "spontaneous" discourses emanating from the inhabitants of this urban *bairro*, I have attempted to zoom in on these everyday practices. Humor should not be seen as the sole key to understanding male-female relations in this Brazilian setting. Certainly, the stereotypic images behind ribald jokes do not take into account much of the simple, ordinary affection and companionship between men and their wives. They do, however, have the advantage of being different from the stereotypes that underwrite normative discourse and, consequently, help to counteract the juridical bias that casts people's experiences in terms of univocal laws. In this ethnographic study of gender relations in the Vila São João I have thus used spontaneous speech events—jokes and gossip—as an opening onto variant discourses that might be overlooked by research methods centered on hegemonic norms. In the process I hope to contribute to the growing trend toward more nuanced and contextually specific analyses of masculinity in Latin America.

Notes

1. Throughout Brazil, as in much of southern Europe, the husband of an adulterous wife is depicted as having horns, which in Portuguese may be rendered as *guampas, cornos,* or *chifres.* Thus, the cuckold is referred to, depending on the region, as *guampudo, chifrudo,* or *cornudo.*

2. See Leal (1987) and Motta (1998) for more on the playful manner in which men and women from working-class populations in Porto Alegre deal with the subject of sex.

3. Researchers working in other parts of Latin America have developed alternative theoretical frameworks centering on machismo/*marianismo* in Mexico (Stevens 1998) and respect/reputation in the Caribbean region (Giraud 1999). In central and southern Brazil, where neither Spanish American Catholicism nor the closed nature of island contexts pertains, researchers have traditionally preferred the analytical perspective provided by the literature about Mediterranean honor.

4. Recently women researchers have made inroads into the study of masculinity, touching on dimensions of male identity, such as sexuality and emotional fragility, that may be more easily probed by female interviewers (Boff 1998; Buffon 1992; Jardim 1995; Leal 1989; Lecznieski 1995; Victora 1992). In the area of gay studies we have yet another important approach to Brazilian masculinity (see Fry 1982; Mott 1987; Parker 1991; Perlongher 1987; and Silva 1993).

5. See Goldstein (1999) for the racial overtones of this "*coroa* complex."

6. Men also may be accused of being fortune hunters, trying to "hit the jackpot" *(fazer o golpe do baú)* by marrying a well-off and generally older woman for her money. But in the case of women such tactics appear to be tolerated and, at times, even encouraged, whereas in the case of men they are commented on with snickers bordering on ridicule.

7. *Vila,* a synonym of *bairro,* is the term used in southern Brazil to designate an urban neighborhood.

8. "To eat" *(comer)* is a slang form of referring to the active partner's role in a sexual relationship.

9. *Chimarrão* (or *erva mate*) is a hot tea served in a single gourd normally passed among the different participants in a group.

10. See Leal (1989) for a development of this hypothesis.

11. For example, during 1979 newspapers gave considerable coverage to the "Doxa Street" trial, in which a middle-class lawyer, following a principle inherited from the centuries-old Philippine Codes, sought to justify the murder of his supposedly adulterous wife as being in legitimate defense of his honor (see Corrêa 1981; Grossi 1993).

12. Recent studies that explore this terrain include Gregori (1992); Grossi (1998); Leal (1989); and Muniz (1996).

80 ▪ ▪ ▪ Claudia Fonseca

13. The term *variant masculinities* has been inspired by the work of Lindisfarne (1994) and Connell (1987).

References

Almeida, Miguel Vale de. 1995. *Senhores de Si: Uma interpretação antropológica da masculinidade.* Lisbon, Portugal: Fim de Século.

Boff, Adriane. 1998. *O namoro está no ar . . . na onda do outro.* Santa Cruz, Brazil: EDUNISC.

Bourdieu, Pierre. 1972. *Le sens de L'honneur: Esquisse d'une théorie de la pratique précédé de trois études d'ethnologie kabyle.* Geneva, Switzerland: Librairie Droz.

Buffon, R. 1992. "Encontrando o homem sensível? Reconstuções da imagem masculina em um grupo de camadas médias intelectualizadas." Master's thesis, Department of Anthropology, Universidade Federal de Santa Catarina, Brazil.

Connell, R. W. 1987. *Gender and Power: Society, the Person, and Sexual Politics.* Cambridge, Mass.: Polity Press.

Corrêa, Mariza. 1981. *Os crimes da Paixão.* São Paulo, Brazil: Brasiliense.

DaMatta, Roberto. 1979. *Carnavais, malandros e heróis: Para uma sociologia do dilema brasileiro.* Rio de Janeiro, Brazil: Zahar.

Davis, Natalie. 1975. *Society and Culture in Early Modern France.* Stanford, Calif.: Stanford University Press.

Duarte, L. F. D. 1987. "Pouca vergonha, muita vergonha: Sexo e moralidade entre as classes trabalhadoras urbanas." In *Cultura e identidade operaria: Aspectos da cultura da classe trabalhadora,* ed. J. S. L. Lopes, 203–26. São Paulo, Brazil: UFRJ/Marco Zero.

Fonseca, Claudia. 1991. "Spouses, Siblings, and Sex-Linked Bonding: A Look at Kinship Organization in a Brazilian Slum." In *Family, Household, and Gender Relations in Latin America,* ed. E. Jelin, 133–60. London: Kegan Paul.

———. 1995. *Caminhos da adoção.* São Paulo, Brazil: Cortez.

Fry, Peter. 1982. *Para ingles ver.* Rio de Janeiro, Brazil: Zahar Editores.

Gilmore, David. 1987. *Aggression and Community: Paradoxes of Andalusian Culture.* New Haven, Conn.: Yale University Press.

Giraud, Michel. 1999. "Une construction coloniale de la sexualité." *Actes de la recherche en sciences sociales* 128:46–55.

Goldstein, Donna. 1999. " 'Interracial' Sex and Racial Democracy in Brazil: Twin Concepts?" *American Anthropologist* 101, no. 3:563–78.

Gregori, Maria Filomena. 1992. *Cenas e queixas: Um estudo sobre mulheres, relações violentas e prática feminista.* Rio de Janeiro, Brazil: Paz e Terra.

Grossi, Miriam. 1993. "De Angela Diniz a Daniela Perez: A trajetória daimpunidade." *Revista de estudos feministas* 1, no. 1:166–68.

———. 1998. "Rimando amor e dor: Reflexões sobre a violência no vínculo afetivo-conjugal." In *Masculino, feminino, plural: Gênero na interdisciplinaridade*, ed. Joana Pedro and Miriam Grossi, 293–314. Floianópolis, Brazil: Ed. Mulheres.

Gutmann, Matthew. 1996. *The Meanings of Macho: Being a Man in Mexico City*. Berkeley: University of California Press.

———. 1997. "Trafficking in Men: The Anthropology of Masculinity." *Annual Review of Anthropology* 26:439–86.

Herzfeld, Michael. 1985. *The Poetics of Manhood: Contest and Identity in a Cretan Mountain Village*. Princeton, N.J.: Princeton University Press.

Jardim, Denise Fagundes. 1995. "Performances, reprodução e produção dos corpos masculinos." In *Corpo e significado: Ensaios de antropologia social*, ed. Orlandina Fachel Leal, 193–206. Porto Alegre, Brazil: Editora da UFRGS.

Knudsen, Anne. 1988. "Men Killed for Women's Songs." *Culture and History* 3:79–97.

Kressel, G. M. 1981. "Sororicide/Filiacide: Homicide for Family Honour." *Current Anthropology* 22, no. 2:141–58.

Leal, Ondina Fachel. 1987. *A leitura social da novela das oito*. Petrópolis, Brazil: Editora Vozes.

———. 1989. *Gaúchos: Male Culture and Identity in the Pampas*. Ph.D. diss., Department of Anthropology, University of California, Berkeley.

Lecznieski, Lisiane. 1995. "Corpo, virilidade e gosto pelo desafio: Marcas de masculinidade entre os guris de rua." *Horizontes Antropológicos* 1:95–112.

Lindisfarne, Nancy. 1994. "Variant Masculinities and Variant Virginities: Rethinking 'Honor and Shame.' " In *Dislocating Masculinity: Comparative Ethnographies*, ed. Andrea Cornwall and Nancy Lindisfarne, 82–96. London: Routledge.

Machado, Lia. 1985. *Família, honra e individualismo*. Série de antropologia social no. 47. Brasília, Brazil: Universidade de Brasília.

Mott, Luiz. 1987. *Dez viados em questão*. Salvador, Brazil: Edições Espaço Bleff.

Motta, Flávia de Mattos. 1998. *Velha é a vovozinha: Identidade feminina na velhice*. Santa Cruz do Sul, Brazil: Edunisc.

Muniz, Jacqueline. 1996. " 'Os direitos dos outros e outros direitos': Um estudo sobre a negociação de conflitos nas DEAMs/RJ." In *Violência e política no Rio de Janeiro*, ed. Luiz Eduardo Soares, 125–64. Rio de Janeiro, Brazil: Relume Dumará.

Oliven, Ruben. 1987. "A mulher faz (e desfaz) o homem." *Ciência Hoje* 7, no. 37:54–62.

Parker, Richard. 1991. *Bodies, Pleasures, and Passion: Sexual Culture in Contemporary Brazil*. Boston: Beacon.

Perlongher, Néstor. 1987. *O negócio do michê: Prostituição viril em São Paulo, Brazil*. São Paulo: Brasiliense.

Pitt-Rivers, Julian. 1954. *The People of the Sierra*. London: Weidenfeld and Nicolson.

———. 1977. *The Fate of Sachem or the Politics of Sex: Essays in the Anthropology of the Mediterranean*. Cambridge, U.K.: Cambridge University Press.

Rebhun, Linda-Anne. 1999. *The Heart Is Unknown Country: Love in the Changing Economy of Northeast Brazil.* Stanford, Calif.: Stanford University Press.

Sacks, Karen. 1979. *Sisters and Wives: The Past and Future of Sexual Equality.* Westport, Conn.: Greenwood.

Sarti, Cynthia. 1995. "Morality and Transgression among Brazilian Poor Families: Exploring the Ambiguities." In *The Brazilian Puzzle: Culture on the Borderlands of the Western World,* ed. David Hess and Roberto DaMatta, 114–33. New York: Columbia University Press.

Seeger, Anthony. 1980. *Os índios e nós: Estudos sobre sociedades tribais brasileiras.* Rio de Janeiro, Brazil: Campus.

Silva, Hélio R. S. 1993. *Travesti: A invençao do feminino.* Rio de Janeiro, Brazil: Relume Dumará.

Stack, Carol. 1974. *All Our Kin.* New York: Harper.

Stevens, Evelyn. 1998. "Machismo and Marianismo." In *Crossing Currents: Continuity and Change in Latin America,* ed. Michael Whiteford and Scott Whiteford, 125–32. Upper Saddle River, N.J.: Prentice-Hall.

Victora, Ceres. 1992. "As relações de gênero na Vila Divina Providência ou o que elas esperam deles." In *Cadernos de antropologia (Cultura e identidade masculina)* 7:15–28.

Woortmann, Klaas. 1987. *A família das mulheres.* Rio de Janeiro, Brazil: Tempo Brasileiro em co-edição com o Conselho de Desenvolvimento Científico e Tecnológico.

AGUSTÍN ESCOBAR LATAPÍ

Men and Their Histories:

Restructuring, Gender

Inequality, and Life Transitions

in Urban Mexico

▪ ▪ ▪ ▪

This essay explores the changing experiences and power relations of men in Mexico's three largest cities—Mexico City, Guadalajara, and Monterrey— in terms of the actors themselves and with respect to the factors shaping key transitions in their lives. This essay also attempts to implement an "empathic" approach to men's lives. Forty life histories form the core of this qualitative, process-oriented, and case-study counterpart to a large survey conducted on occupations, social mobility, and household organization that was carried out in these and other Mexican cities.[1]

Throughout Latin America the gender structure of the labor force has shifted appreciably during the past twenty years. In Mexico, as elsewhere, the main change consists in the rapid increase in the rate of women's participation in the labor force (García and Oliveira 1994; González de la Rocha and Escobar 1986). Although this change has been most clearly noted among working-class women, it is a societal change in the sense that women in all social classes participate more intensely in employment and remain working throughout their childbearing years. Together with this change some analysts have found a narrowing of gender income differentials within occupational categories (Parker 1996) and in occupational achievement (Escobar and Cortés 2000).

This change may have a discernible effect on gender power differentials within the household, but this is a matter of some debate. Although some analysts contend this is clearly the case (Safa 1995), others provide less-straightforward answers and conclude that, although among *mestizo*[2] families women's work and income can in fact undermine men's power and authority, among indigenous families the collective nature of the creation and provision of incomes hinders any such power shift (Bastos 1999). In terms of the power and authority of Mexican men within the household, Gutmann (2000) has noted two things. First, there already was more variation in men's roles and men's power than previously thought. Second, the current trend is toward greater variation, including greater male participation in household work and household affairs, and a growing recognition of the importance of women's work.

This text explores the nature and extent of this change in men's power and authority from a different perspective, namely that of *life transitions,* with an implied shift in emphasis from the construction of daily life to the construction, change, or destruction of life perspectives. The fundamental assumption is that if there has been a power shift, women will figure more prominently as *actors,* making, or participating in, decisions that affect men's lives. The object of the narrative section in this essay is to discern precisely who the actors in these changes have been and whether women's agency is more clearly discernible among younger, as opposed to older, men. Age is therefore the primary division in the case studies. The other fundamental dimension is social class because class marks a clear contrast in property, opportunity, and the ability to plan one's life. The case studies for this essay were collected from men in widely different social classes, from the propertied bourgeoisie to unskilled workers and informal street vendors.

The men whose histories I recount in this chapter were eager to tell their stories as part of their efforts to understand themselves and to make themselves understood by others. Accounting for their lives seemed vital to them. And, as I learned to listen and provide a context within which they could express themselves—in the interviews, I rarely needed to provide them with more than a few historical markers—I realized both that they were asking to be appreciated for the men they had become and that their experiences of masculinity were diverse—and diversifying (Gutmann 2000). Work, family, and marriage were approached and understood in many more ways than I expected. Whereas for some men being a man seemed an obvious part of their identity, for others masculinity appeared far more ambiguous. Whereas for some work was the axis around which they could order and make sense of their lives and lay the foundations of their identities, for others this domain was merely one part of their lives and in no way defined their overall identities or sense of purpose. These men and their histories illustrate well the search for contemporary identities at a time when men's power and identity are no longer taken for granted and when previously dominant forms of discourse have crumbled.

Nonetheless, these histories should not be approached naively. In gender studies of the last quarter-century women have had to discard language justifying male domination as part of the process of sorting out their lives. As they did this, the stories men told about themselves became seriously suspect. Veiled justifications for domination were thus a matter of concern in the interviews, as men described transitions in their lives, the reasons for these changes, and the other people who shared in these events and in subsequent analysis of the men's discourse.

There were, roughly, two kinds of history telling. The first conformed to what I expected as a researcher in a fairly traditional, male-dominant society. This discourse, albeit with variations, assumed women's supportive role as either obvious or the most convenient and rational arrangement for men and society in general. In this kind of history, with respect to their sons, women played a key role as mothers when their sons were children and later faded into the background as the boys became men, entered the world of work, and married. Where women were forced to stay out of the labor market after marriage or their economic role was ignored, this kind of discourse had changed little. This discourse was more common in Monterrey and Guadalajara than in Mexico City.

The other kind of personal history was most prevalent in the capital city, especially among younger men there. Although women similarly represented a dominant influence during their sons' childhoods, in Mexico City they continued to play an important role later in men's lives more than was the case in Monterrey and Guadalajara. Men here also talked of marriage partners in more variable and negotiable terms. This is not to say that the gender divisions of labor in the household and the marriage were truly equal, simply that women's interests and opinions and men's participation in domestic affairs were more important in Mexico City than in the other two cities. With a discourse distinguished by its explicitness and range, men also expressed a willingness to establish a certain "contract" in their marital relationships that often did not conform to previous dominant patterns.

Male Agency, Social Contracts, and Sexual Contracts

Men in this study were asked to discuss (1) the major influences on turning points and decisions in their lives; (2) which people had played the biggest roles in their lives; and (3) how they had made important decisions in their lives.[3]

My own assessment is that most men were aware of the primary causes, reasons, and persons influencing the most significant changes in their lives. Further, the setting provided by myself and the firms for the interviews allowed them to express themselves honestly, with the possible exception of the formal manufacturing workers in Monterrey, who claimed a high degree of satisfaction with their jobs and with the labor policies of their employers.[4] Interviewees with experience in psychotherapy and psychoanalysis were far more articulate but more difficult to "center" along the themes I suggested. They believed intimate family relationships had been more important than social factors, and in general their assessments of their mothers' roles vis-à-vis their fathers, themselves, and their siblings were less positive. These men tended to assign less responsibility to their fathers for their later personal problems, whereas men who had not undergone therapy were more prone to describe their mothers as having sacrificed themselves for their families.

In general I noted changes in the relative power of men and women as expressed in the lives of men of different ages. Whereas older men identified maleness with their own fathers, male peer groups, male working groups, and the absolute preservation of male domination, younger men often referred to the greater role played by women in some or all these features of life, and, in explaining the differences between their actions and those of older generations, they attributed a greater role to women's agency in their own lives.

The narratives I collected revealed the importance of the conditions in which men grew up: where they had lived, the poverty that forced them to find work at a young age, and the ways in which their parents negotiated whether their son would work or stay in school. Other factors impinged on the men's childhood: fathers who left mothers, mothers who died, the re-marriages of parents, and the need to leave one's natal village and seek relatives and a new life in Mexico City or Monterrey. A second issue the men noted was how and when they began working and the conflicts that often occurred in one's family over continuing in school or starting to work. A third set of related events concerned the time when men left their home, normally after getting married or just moving in with a woman, and the strains that developed in the new home over contributions to the household budget. Finally, undoubtedly interactions between men's parents and in-laws and couples were especially important for the younger generation and a key to understanding subsequent employment trajectories.

Gender and Employment Inequality

Arguing that economic transformation has led to changes in gender power relations begs one question, namely, whether economic transformation has in fact led to changes in gendered participation in the economy. In Mexico restructuring has entailed a sharp increase in women's participation in employment. What has not been established, however, is the extent to which this growing participation has remedied gender inequality in employment.

There are two issues regarding gender inequality in employment: wage inequality and opportunity inequality. Few studies show the extent of wage inequality and whether it is growing or not. Roberts and Escobar (1997) showed that although most incomes from work rose from 1987 to 1994, increases were greater for men than for women. On average the male/female gap in equivalent deciles in the income distribution was roughly 30 percent. Also, they showed that the highest decile of the male income distribution rose considerably faster than the top decile of women's income distribution. Other recent research, however (Parker 1996), relying on median incomes in the main occupational categories, controlled for education and showed that gender income inequality per occupation and schooling levels was typically less than 15 percent. If both analyses are correct, this would indicate that most income inequality is rooted in gender segregation, that is to say, in women's inability to reach the higher-paying occupations to the same extent as men, not in pay discrimination within occupational positions.

Other research (Escobar 1999; Escobar and Cortés 2000), using retrospective social mobility analysis, has concluded that gender inequalities in labor-market achievement diminished substantially after 1982. This fall was owing to a number of other changes. For one thing, the sons of professionals, employers, and upper management are less able to inherit their parents' position today than they were twenty or thirty years ago, whereas women from the same social class have on the contrary improved their chances of maintaining a privileged class status. The combination of less achievement by men and more by women has brought about a near equality in achievement opportunities for men and women in the privileged classes. Among other classes the gap has also narrowed, although to a far lesser degree. The classes in which children showed the least changes in the direction of gender equality in occupation achievements were the most involved with informal employment.

All these developments in the employment market have meant that (1) men will be increasingly working with more women, and (2) some of these women will hold positions equal to or higher than those of men, thus, except in informal occupations, reversing traditional male authority at work.

These findings in turn suggest there will be three kinds of husband-wife relationships: first, men married to women in professional and non-manual occupations will feel the pressure to change both because of increased work and increased achievement equality. Second, men married to other working women will experience the need for change based primarily on the intensified work (and earnings) of their spouses, although parity in income levels has usually not been achieved. Finally, because women's participation rates have risen but have not equaled those of men, other men are still married to nonworking women, and pressures for change will be visible only from nonoccupational sources (a generalized ideology of equality, for example) and from kin, religious, and peer groups.

In the following sections I will summarize the major transitions in men's lives, and attempt to relate them to the changes and diverse patterns detailed above.

Catastrophes and Constructions: Salient Aspects of Men's Histories

"Life transitions" may occur at different times. The first major life transition found in these case studies, however, has to do with the loss of one or both parents or a drastic separation from the boys' families at an early age. This transition, which is experienced as a catastrophe thrust on their lives, given that they rarely play an active role in it, has a clear class dimension. But some change is also evident between the two cohorts, with the younger generation suffering fewer catastrophes of this sort, in spite of the economic worsening implied by the various Mexican crises of the 1980s and 1990s. Among the older cohort in this study many men reported they had lost a parent when they were still a child. This happened particularly often to the sons of peasants, the self-employed, and construction workers. Alcohol addiction seems to have been a frequent reason for a parent's early death, although in some cases the men may not have ever realized this was the true cause. In Monterrey a parent's death at an early age seems to have happened less frequently, perhaps because of the fact that, in spite of the risks of industrial work, men in Monterrey were relatively more healthy forty years ago than men in other Mexican cities. One man had been left an orphan in his youth. Shortly after his father's death the firm hired him when he was still a teenager. The young man quit school, and the difference in the income he earned compared to what his father had earned was minimal; thus the family was able to stay together.

In the case of another informally self-employed man from Monterrey, following his mother's death when he was still a child, his father soon found another woman. The boy's stepmother only fed him when his father was present, so he ran away from home at age nine and began a series of informal jobs: cleaning buses, assisting a baker, street selling. He found various kinds of sleeping and household arrangements with his employers, in the company of other runaway boys, and as an adoptive child in families who gave him food and shelter in return for some of his earnings. After eighteen months his father and stepmother found him and forced him to return home. Still he did not quit work and in fact contributed substantially to his household, even enjoying a little autonomy and recognition. He was never happy there, however, one reason he married quite early: "I wanted a woman to look after me."

The strategies employed after the death of a parent are crucial at this stage. In another case in Guadalajara, after the husband of one woman died, she sent her sons to work and at the same time conferred on them the new status of "family heads." As the workers in the family the young men were allowed to participate in decisions about allocation of money and the activities of their younger siblings. This family stayed together until the eldest brother renounced his responsibilities and fled to the United States, whereupon he cut off all ties to them. Two younger brothers then took his place. All the children in this family attended more school than their parents had, a few of them even graduating from college. Another case illustrates how families may be more crucial for survival than households. When her husband died, a mother found another husband who, nevertheless, refused to be burdened with the woman's boys, aged six and eight. In a rare instance of abandonment by the mother, the two children were then left with their grandparents, who became, in the words of one of them, their "true parents."

Parental deaths were less common among the younger cohort of the study, but there were several instances of family breakups, caused mainly by the father's leaving, which is why several men reported that they had been brought up in families headed by single mothers. Most of these men depicted their mothers as having been courageous and able to face and solve problems. Making new economic arrangements was especially crucial. When one boy's father left, the owner of the middle-class building where his family were tenants offered his mother the janitor's apartment free of rent provided that they cleaned and cared for the whole building. In his interview he remarked that this arrangement allowed the children to continue studying; they all completed high school, and one obtained a college degree.

At this early stage in their lives some boys lost their security when one of their parents died. When their father died, the mother became the crucial actor. Usually, she rearranged the household division of labor to assure the creation of new income earners, in some cases distributing power and authority to the new workers. These rearrangements show mixed success: in one case the new "breadwinner" fled soon after, whereas in another she managed to devise a collective income-generating arrangement and, at the same time, made it possible for her children to continue their education. When the mother (or the stepmother) refused to protect the child, he was forced to leave, either in search of food and lodging or because he was forcibly placed under another family's care.

Migration and Urbanization

In the rapid urbanization of Mexico between 1950 and 1970, whole families with young children resettled in Guadalajara, Monterrey, and Mexico City. From the vantage point of the year 2000, modernization-cum-urbanization is often seen as the "golden age of Mexican development." Although this may be true (workers and peasants acquired more assets and better jobs and education than at any other time), older men's histories show that the transition from rural to urban settings and jobs was often traumatic and in some cases divided families and produced significant breaks. There are also regional variations in this transition. Typically, men's work trajectories were unstable. But whereas immigrants to Guadalajara showed some degree of occupational diversity before arriving in the city—many worked in small stores, on commercial poultry farms, and at other semiurban, cash economy activities—those entering manufacturing jobs in Monterrey almost invariably had a background as impoverished agricultural laborers. A smaller number of young men were sent by parents who owned shops or businesses in the wealthier towns in the north, such as Tampico and Reynosa, to study at a local university. Later these people often found managerial jobs in the Grupo Monterrey, a powerful industrial group in that city.

Sons often worked in the same firms as their fathers. Companies were growing and minimum-age hiring laws were not enforced in the Mexican construction industry. But it was not always the fathers who found jobs for their sons. More resourceful, better educated, and attracted by the new

Man watching soccer match in Mexico City with his son. Photograph by Matthew C. Gutmann.

world of modern industry, sons often found formal jobs first and then told their fathers of entry-level openings.

The impact of urbanization and modernization in Mexico City was evident in several ways. In some cases immigrants' fathers were peasants or craftsmen who became masons, mechanics, carpenters, or jewelers. Sometimes migration was associated with family breakups, and boys and their mothers found temporary shelter with relatives, later moving out as they found jobs. There was also "passive" migration as a result of urban expansion, which opened up different options: it became possible to shuttle to and from the city every day, while the household remained a primarily agricultural production unit. In these cases there was considerable pressure on the household labor pool. Wages were welcome, but fathers often refused to free their children from rural production duties.[5] In some cases peasant mothers played a crucial role in shaping their children's lives, for instance, by limiting the amount of work a boy devoted to the land and by helping to convince their husbands to let sons attend high school. Families in Mexico thus employed diverse strategies with respect to schooling their children (González de la Rocha 1994). In the histories I collected interventions by mothers served to allow older children to work in the urban economy, in this way providing an income base for younger children to continue their schooling. In one case the eldest boy replaced his father farming the family land, his two older sisters secured wage jobs, and four younger children stayed in school much longer (although only one obtained a nonmanual job).

The fate of children in these cases had more to do with household strategy and sibling order than with gender. The eldest boy was "sacrificed" as he, to some extent following a traditional peasant pattern in highland Mexico, kept control of the land but did not marry and was responsible for his parents in their old age. Arrangements like these could lead to significant tears in the family, most of which were later repaired. Years after such breakups, fathers might reappear to provide credit, free land for their houses, contacts, or to act as business partners. The younger cohort in this study produced fewer immigrants, and among those who had migrated a larger proportion had urban work experience before arriving in the city.[6]

When young men in their early twenties managed to secure good jobs or to start small, successful businesses, their families could become a burden. Some showed a sense of loyalty and responsibility, whereas others broke away, often in dramatic ways. In 1970 a young worker in Monterrey decided to leave the carpet-installation business he worked for and start an independent one. He became very successful, adding a home decoration line to the carpet business, but his family placed increasing demands on his income, in his view impeding further development. He moved to another quarter of the city, hidden from his relatives and, thanks to his whiteness and his ability to incorporate middle-class manners and lifestyle, was "born again socially," although his girlfriends at the time were genuinely intrigued by his apparent lack of family and background. This breakup was never repaired, and at the time of his interview the man still did not have contact with his family.

Another worker, arriving in Mexico City with his mother from a poor peasant household, secured a low-paying job as a laborer for a public works construction company. This was heavy, dangerous outdoor work, and the pay was barely enough for him and his mother to survive. Yet as soon as he seemed stable and news reached his younger brothers in the village, they came to join him and their mother. The man was forced to stop his search for better work and instead show himself to be a reliable, deferential worker who deserved the chance to bring his brothers into the company. What was more, before he succeeded in placing them, he had to work extra time to provide more income for all the members of his household.

As young men entered the workforce and various metropolitan economies, there was a clear shift in agency from their mothers (and to a lesser extent their fathers) to themselves and their ability to mobilize their social resources. In some cases, however, men mobilized these resources for others—their mothers, brothers, and sisters mostly but also other relatives. As these young men became economically independent, the household balance of giving and receiving shifted drastically, which led some of them to break their family ties for good. However, although most household histories as told by women emphasize the moments in which men (older children or spouses) abandoned their families, in some of these histories men have insisted on the effort implied in staying within the family fold. Although there are very significant histories of breaking away and "disappearing," men, somewhat understandably, prefer to emphasize how they have continued to fulfill their duties in spite of growing burdens as now capable, breadwinning members of their families. There is no guilt in separation, at least at this stage in men's lives. Yet among the younger generation, breaking away in youth is less attractive. Part-time jobs pay less, and firms are less interested in financing their training and education, making them dependent on their parents' help for longer periods. In this sense urban Mexico seems to have passed from a combination of state-sponsored public and "private" sponsorship of training and education centered in the company (most clearly visible in Monterrey) to a "private" sponsorship of education dependent on families, whether parents or older siblings. In most cases intergenerational ties either remain or are later rebuilt, as the following sections show.

Personal Advancement and the Marriage Contract

These men's histories provide considerable detail about what they considered their struggles for advancement. Some of them had had remarkable careers. In a few cases in Monterrey this may have been related to the fact that the interviewees were selected by the corporate director of industrial relations and by chiefs of personnel in the plants, but cases of substantial social mobility were evident throughout the study, illustrating the extent and significance of Mexico's urbanization and modernization. I found the son of a very poor sharecropper who became the industrial relations manager in one of Mexico's largest rolled-steel production plants, the orphaned son of peasants who held a postgraduate degree and led a district tribunal in Guadalajara, and other less-impressive but still significant examples of social mobility. The case of the carpet layer who became a literature professor in the United States is also relevant, although it reveals more a transnational opportunity structure. These are the histories that explain certain kinds of the cross-class mobility noted in the previous section. Although the stories collected here do not allow an assessment of the extent of mobility after the crisis of 1994–95, they do show that occupational mobility was increasingly predicated on educational mobility. Most cases, of course, showed less striking change. The children of peasants, laborers, and workers generally became workers, low-level nonmanual workers, and skilled operators or craftsmen.

There was a systematic difference between younger and older men in terms of how these Mexican men described their marriages. Older men talked little about the specifics of their marriages, yet their point of reference seemed to be a hegemonic marriage contract from the past: male breadwinner, mother-housewife who is rather domestically confined, and joint responsibility vis-à-vis the children. Although this reference point remained unarticulated during the interviews, deviations and violations were detailed, justified, explained, or revealed, sometimes with admissions of guilty feelings harbored by the men. With very few exceptions older men did not speak of their wives as having failed. They regarded themselves as the source of most marital problems, with overwork, work-related pressures and lifestyles, and alcohol abuse as justifications for their not having fulfilled expectations.

Younger men described discussions, disagreements, and breakups or changes in this arrangement as time went by, whether with one or a series of partners. To most of them the marriage contract was simultaneously explicit and variable: it was an agreement that needed to be modified and explored. It was not fixed. The terms and conditions of gender relations in marriage were different from those of their parents and tended to evolve into much clearer arrangements as time went by. Explicit contracts allowed men to express their own expectations in the "partnership" and to be taken "as they were," not to be measured against an unspoken ideal. This also seemed to free them from guilt. Whereas the first generation had only themselves to blame, given that women had no responsibilities outside of the home, and no older men spoke of the shortcomings of housewives and mothers, the second generation pointed to problems "caused" by their wives or their wives' ambitions, achievements, and, sometimes, selfishness.

When men talked about this subject, however, I had the feeling that their particular life stage substantially influenced what they said. With respect to their marital arrangements, life histories got confused with social histories. Around half the men, both young and old, however, spontaneously referred to having a "moral agreement" with their wives. I had not heard the phrase since conducting fieldwork in Guadalajara in 1982, and its relevance in all three cities in the 1990s, and its persistence as a concept, was a significant finding of our study. Men's use of the phrase "moral agreement" in this way implied not simply a formal contract but also an arrangement subject to negotiation and to a unique standard of application for each couple.

What men described, however, was far from a "sexual contract." Although sex was unquestionably a central part of the agreement,[7] most discussions and negotiations concerned money and decisions about housing strategies, children's education and perspectives, the use of money, and the rights and obligations of each partner regarding leisure. This, however, entailed communication. All men in Monterrey, and most young men elsewhere, claimed emphatically that they had better communication in their marriages than had been true for their parents. The more articulate explained that marriages break up primarily because partners do not know what to expect from each other: "I will not promise you what I can't give you, but I will give you what I can, and you must tell me what you want and what you can give me," as an industrial relations manager in Monterrey put it.

In some cases history played an undeniable role, reflecting the ideological sea changes, economic crises, and long-term income reductions accompanied by growing employment instability in Mexican cities in recent years. Three examples illustrate certain of these influences. The first man was a mechanic who owned a truck parts shop and two minibus jitneys. His girlfriend lived with her mother and an uncle. The uncle raped her. She was afraid and in shock. The boyfriend, who was then studying mechanical engineering, found her shelter at a Sacred Heart convent. She lived there for more than one year and in that time was taught liberation theology. Later they decided to live together although not to get married, and because she was at a disadvantage as a woman, she would study first, while he worked to support them both. Then their roles would be reversed. They would also delay having children. This story shows both ideological change and the creation of a substantively different marriage contract.

After long absences resulting from drinking, unfaithfulness, and economic irresponsibility, two older men, one in Guadalajara and the other in Mexico City, were "born again" within their marriages and families. Alcoholics Anonymous and religious conversion to a "Christian" faith were key in this change.[8] They wanted to re-create a traditional marriage. In one case it seemed to work. In the other the man was unhappy because his wife, after having handled life on her own for many years, did not initially welcome him back, although eventually he did rejoin her.

As a consequence of women's paid work, more than half the men in the younger group met their current spouses at work. The second most frequent place where partners met was high school or university. (Men in the older group rarely had met their spouses in these places.) The most common sites for couples to meet were the corporate headquarters,[9] and the administrative offices of production plants, where women worked as secretaries or administrative assistants. Monterrey was a relative exception because even younger men and women there worked in rather sex-segregated environments. Most men interviewed in Monterrey met their spouses at church, in a neighborhood social club, or in a youth group.

Static and Evolving Marriage Contracts

Once they entered the labor market, men privileged school, work, and work-related social groups to explain their accomplishments, promotions, and the establishment of businesses. Some referred to joint family strategies in two-career households. But analysis shows there were several marriage patterns and that these interacted with men's careers. There were almost no exceptions, however, to initial marriage to social equals. In sum, with respect to marriage and career, one lesson and two general patterns emerged from this study.

The lesson was that there were many kinds of marriage, with variation on how explicit marital agreements were and the precise relationships they entailed, particularly among younger couples. As time passed, there was a tendency toward greater explicitness and greater variation. The first general pattern was that "marriage horizontality" went beyond the generalities of social class at the time of marriage. The sons of workers and peasants married the daughters of workers and peasants, thus bringing together similar pasts as well as similar current situations. The other general pattern was that social mobility created severe marital strains. These strains led to either a rearrangement of the marriage contract or dissolution of the marriage. In the new context, in which women's work and, in some cases, women's careers were not usually relinquished, the couple needed to reestablish the terms of their relationship as the situation of each evolved. This development could also have resulted from the instability of men's careers in the context of employment instability that has become the norm since the early 1980s. Although in this latter case most women still supported their husbands' careers and provided solidarity, safety, and often an income during their periods of unemployment, devotion was less common than before.

One case brings together both the lesson and the general patterns. The mechanics instructor mentioned earlier who taught at a construction industry training center, and who owned a truck parts shop and two "minibuses," quit his studies to earn more and allow his spouse to finish her studies first. His opportunity to study would come later. His wife studied general nursing, then specialized nursing, and subsequently joined a social circle of physicians and health professionals. She started to look down on him, and he felt he did not fit among her friends because of his grease-stained clothes, beer belly acquired after he quit sports to work longer shifts,[10] and his foul-mouthed mechanic friends. Everything about him, he said, contrasted with the whiteness, discipline, and professional order of the medical profession. They broke up before he had a chance to return to the university. This marriage had been, in his words, based on gender equality and the teachings of liberation theology. In contrast, his second wife was far less a dominant figure in their marriage, and she had no pretensions. Still, he knew she was crucial to the management of his other businesses while he taught most of the day.

A second case in point concerns the bank manager mentioned above. The man lost support from his family when he got a girl pregnant in his small, rural town in Guerrero. They said the girl was a *mal partido*, a socially unattractive spouse. He had to leave the town and live with his common-law wife until their baby girl died and the woman returned (possibly at his initiative) to her parents' home. He stayed single for several years, wounded by his initial experience with marriage. He began a slowly rising career in a bank and started living with an office employee who worked for the Federal Highway Police. He decided she was not good for him and stopped seeing her. The woman he was married to at the time of the interview was a coworker at the bank, where they met; they had two children, and he claimed to be satisfied.

One major question in the project concerned the rearrangement of domestic life and work as women's employment in general grows. There were diverse patterns. In the cases just mentioned one wife managed the husband's two independent businesses, whereas the second was still a bank employee, working the same long hours as her husband. The economic benefits were different but significant in each case. In the first example above, income from the two independent businesses was greater than that from the man's "official" teaching job. In the second the wife's income was lower than her husband's but still significant.

In Monterrey we noted another distinct pattern. The wives of workers, employees, and managers in the Grupo Alfa stayed at home but were far from idle, nor was their work limited to housework—employees and managers generally hired domestic employees. Most of the women had performed waged or salaried jobs while single, which was often how they met their future husbands. Most had either an income-earning activity or socially relevant commitments: running a small eiderdown workshop, teaching aerobics, owning a beauty parlor or a shop, or performing volunteer work for organizations such as the Downs Association or the Christian Family Movement.[11] There was unanimous agreement among the men interviewed concerning the paramount importance of their wives' domestic role and the fact that the men did not want them to work "for other men." Some men recognized that this caused strains in their relationships, but they insisted on this arrangement and their wives complied. Although younger women had not quit their jobs at marriage, they did when the first child was born, an event delayed by either natural or artificial means. Still, their careers were never seen to be as important as the careers of their husbands.

Apart from these straightforward cases there was a general tendency for a more unmentioned form of cooperation from the wives in the younger generation, even those who had full-time positions. Many men mentioned there had been times when, in order to get promoted or earn more, they had to study at night, work extra hours, and hold two jobs. During these periods the tacit condition was total cooperation from their wives and children or, in one case, remaining single and living at the parental house until the man's early thirties. Although these men, in Guadalajara and Mexico City, said they shared domestic work, the fact is that, when they had to make a strong push ahead, their wives did the extra household chores, often without quitting their own jobs. After those critical periods men reentered the world of domestic responsibility. But, with the exception of the mechanic mentioned in the last section, none subordinated his career to his wife's. Wives' participation in this effort included mutual agreement about what the family would do with the added income. The usual understanding was that it would be used for clearly defined projects, like building a house or an extension or paying for private schools. At times women were the key players in making these decisions.

Intergenerational assistance

It is usually assumed that women's new role as cobreadwinners above all forces a shift in the relationship with their spouses and that it is the male spouses who have to adapt, accept a new household division of labor, and take on new responsibilities. Although this is often the case, we found that women's careers depend as much on intergenerational cooperation and assistance as on men's shifting roles in the household. This intergenerational assistance has been made possible by several interconnected forces. First, the older generation (those in their sixties) are living longer than their own parents did, and they remain healthy longer. Second, that generation accumulated assets during Mexico's period of rapid development that their offspring cannot yet match because of falling real incomes for Mexico's lower-middle and working classes. Third, they were the first in the demographic transition, which meant they had fewer children and can therefore care for a larger portion of their grandchildren than their own parents could. Fourth, and last, Mexico's rapid urbanization is mostly over, which means that in Mexico's largest cities couples in their thirties and forties are more likely to live in the same city as their parents than was the case for the previous generation. Intergenerational assistance is of such relevance that the younger couple's place of residence is often defined by its proximity to the wife's mother (or parents). Intergenerational assistance can accurately be portrayed as a transfer of monetary and other resources from the generation that benefited from Mexico's urbanization and modernization to that of their own children, often beset by economic woes and by a situation in which two jobs are necessary to merely get by (or as a subsidy from the older household to the firms paying less and the state, which fails to provide childcare and other services). But it is also a mechanism that can provide for the care and inclusion of the elderly in the lives of the younger generation. Regardless of the generation providing or receiving assistance, however, men usually provide money, whereas their sisters and wives provide care and company, whether as baby-sitters or as caregivers for the old and infirm. Intergenerational cooperation, therefore, has to a certain extent shielded men from some of the household rearrangements they would otherwise have had to accept.

A surprising finding of our study revealed that, when a woman worked outside the home, it was usually not her husband but her parents, or even grandparents, who assumed some responsibility for the woman's previous household duties. This was true especially in the case of younger women. Older couples had often formed in times of rapidly changing, high-mobility urbanization and modernization; they often lived away from their parents, who in any case had little to offer their many children. Their parents were peasants, sharecroppers, or newly arrived urban workers toiling at the bottom of the labor market. They had aged quickly and died young.

Younger men in our interviews in Guadalajara, Mexico City, and Monterrey often delayed marriage, thus lengthening economic dependency on their parents. They also relied on their parents in rough times. And many young couples, especially two-career couples, depended on economically stable, healthy grandmothers and grandfathers to act as nannies and cooks, to provide shelter when needed, and to furnish loans and advice on business and job contacts. Real estate was particularly important in this respect. Many interviewees' parents, even working-class or peasant-origin parents, owned or bought land or a house that later became very valuable; they enjoyed all or most urban services, even if they were initially part of a shantytown.

The much higher level of education achieved by the younger generation was also directly related to the stability and urban settlement of their parents. Delayed marriage stemmed from both longer schooling and the younger generation's inability to become economically independent early in their adulthood. In Monterrey, especially, it was key for the younger group to be able to count on their parent's help for a longer time. The sharecropper's son who is now chief of industrial relations in Monterrey married at thirty-seven. He lived with his parents in a well-built house in one of the *colonias obreras* (worker districts) in Monterrey. Although he contributed financially to the household, had he married earlier, his commitment to the family would have been much greater, and he would have faced enormous obstacles studying and working simultaneously and traveling to distant plants for more than fifteen years. The longer lives and greater asset accumulation by parents of the younger group of men allowed the latter to suffer a smaller decline in quality of living than suggested by lower current wages, growing employment instability, and less company support for further schooling at employers' expense. They benefited from domestic work done by mothers or mothers-in-law and by their willingness and ability to mind grandchildren. Ironically, a generation of women was relegated to the home but performed significant feats in terms of constructing an urban asset base that was still providing significant support to their adult, married children.

Two-career families were especially dependent on these networks. In the case of the bank manager, his wife's mother had provided valuable help, picking up the children after school and looking after them at night, when the manager and his wife attended special training courses and seminars that helped gain them promotions.[12] The Guadalajara judge also was part of a two-career couple, and again his parents-in-law were extremely helpful.

Nonetheless, the long lives of the younger generation's parents had another side. Many younger men talked of elderly, frail, widowed mothers or fathers who depended on their children for help and money. In Monterrey, because of the select nature of the interviewees and their level of asset accumulation, these poor parents were rare. But they were common in the other two cities, where stable employment was less common and pension payments were ridiculously low, after the inflationary period running from 1982 to the early 1990s. Pensions were rarely mentioned as significant; on the contrary, men talked of arrangements in which they provided money while their sisters or their wives looked after their mothers. Usually an elderly mother lived with a married daughter. Although men reported providing money, two emphatically said they tried not to give them a set monthly amount so that their brothers and sisters would not think they would take that responsibility alone.

In sum, the elderly generation was a significant presence among the younger group of men. Usually parents helped their adult sons in myriad ways. Although the remarkable social mobility of the older group was a product of their own efforts, of government and company training programs, and of the expansion of modern employment, the upward mobility of younger men was less common and far more closely pinned to parental help. In the 1990s firms demanded prior job skills, and further schooling was made more difficult by the growing intensity of work and increasing restrictions on absences related to further training. A few men resorted in the past to informal work because it provided flexible hours, but income from these activities was in decline. There was a clear historical change that passed the cost of schooling and training on to families, which in the future will probably lead to more inequality in the opportunity structures. In a related finding middle-class families are investing equally in the education of their sons and daughters, aided by an early transition in fertility levels, whereas informal and working-class families are still giving preference to their sons.

Even in families not conforming to the two-career pattern, women's paid work was increasing. This illustrated the diversity in the employment opportunities of men and women, the growing possibilities for women as compared to the previous generation, and the significant gender barriers still prevailing in many cases. In a Mexico City branch of the largest national bank, a man we interviewed met and married another employee. She rose far more rapidly in the bank hierarchy than he did. Yet when she got pregnant for the second time, she was fired, which, he reported, was company policy. He became so actively involved in the defense of his wife's case at the labor hearing that he was threatened with being fired and ostracized. Because they could not afford to lose both jobs, he acquiesced and stopped collaborating in her case. Almost two years after the event his wife still had not returned to work. The lesson seemed clear: although in many instances women were rising faster than men, there were still significant gender barriers.

Overall, however, there are structural reasons for lower rates of upward mobility today. Calamities are most common among the poorest, lowest-skilled workers. An older worker at a construction firm in Mexico City had two daughters. They had to quit university studies when their older brother, who was already at work and the main breadwinner, was killed by a bus. Another son of a worker was killed in a car accident in which a drunken friend was driving. The eldest son of another worker was mentally retarded because the doctors at the clinic where his wife was giving birth were too interested in a boxing match on TV and were careless. Informal microbusinesses were also especially vulnerable. Partners fled with profits or merchandise, buyers disappeared without paying, and some incurred financial debts for years. Many working-class men and women never received their degrees because they could not find two or three months to write their theses or because they could not afford the degree-granting procedure in a public university. Their subsequent occupational performance reflected these failures.

Other men were evidently quite satisfied with an uneventful working life. There were technicians, low-level bank employees, mechanics, and manufacturing workers who said they were happy because they had bought or built a house or because other people at work respected their skills. Men were eager to talk about the ways they had solved a technical problem, and this satisfaction was hardly diminished by the cool reception their achievements elicited from superiors. Many men in all three cities remarked on significant nonwork satisfactions, notably the fact that they thought they had much better communication and a much better relationship with their wives than their fathers had had with their mothers.

A midlevel manager at Grupo Alfa had only recently, at forty-five years old, reached his father's position in the company, despite the fact that, unlike his father, he had a university degree. He was happy and proud that he survived the group's crisis from 1981 to 1985, when he joined his wife's home-based microbusiness, which became the sole basis for family survival. He also told of his satisfaction with his new job and the volunteer work he performed with his wife. Perception of achievement varied enormously. The general director of a large bank interviewed in Mexico City carefully avoided showing pride in his position. He credited his university teachers and his mentors at the bank, but he also admitted he deserved the position and, reluctantly, talked of his large assets. But he was far more concerned with his life as a series of major events that he was slowly discovering with the help of psychoanalysis. He traced his roots to Italian nobility, and his father was among Mexico City's most respected physicians in the 1930s and 1940s. Thus he may have taken for granted a certain standard of wealth, prestige, and power that would be alien to most Mexicans. His challenge in life lay instead in this inner struggle for self-discovery.

This story contrasts with that of a young technician in Monterrey who spent a week alone on a mountain repairing a microwave radio relay station and did so with no help, little training, and inadequate tools. It also contrasts with the story related by a manufacturing worker who told me how he built his house with his own hands over a period of several years and that it was finally a "good, solid house." Many men who did not experience significant upward mobility stressed their ability to spend time and communicate with their families, to overcome significant technical challenges that went unrecognized, and to reconcile their present with their past.

Perceptions of Competition with Women

As was true generally in Mexico, in Jalisco's textile mills of the 1920s and 1930s the labor force consisted almost exclusively of women. Indeed, women founded the first textile workers' union, and the legendary María Díaz became a cult figure for workers nationally (Gabayet 1988a). As wages rose during the 1940s and 1950s, however, men took over the union, and systematic cliquing and party politicking excluded women from work under the rationale that women did not need the jobs because men could earn the money and women would be far more comfortable (and appropriately secluded) at home. During the 1980s and 1990s, however, women flooded back into the labor market, and, although gender segregation at work persists, it is much weakened. It is therefore important to explore men's gender attitudes and decisions at work and to explore whether this renewed female presence has been met by organized resistance or even, possibly, whether women are using the same cliquing and politicking men used before, therefore becoming limiting agents in men's working lives.

Women's growing participation in paid employment and declining levels of gender achievement inequality suggest that men faced situations in which they competed against women. In these histories, however, there were few accounts of this happening, or at least of men's awareness of such competition. A Monterrey manufacturing worker decided not to take a promotion in a new plant because the firm was going to hire women workers; a shoe stitcher in Guadalajara left his job because there were only women around him, and he liked male-based environments and weekend drinking among coworkers. Bank employees in various instances described discriminatory practices against women but showed no antagonism toward their companies. According to one man, in the 1970s banks only hired beautiful, single women as cashiers; never taken into account for promotions, the women were pressed to quit after marriage. After Mexican banks were nationalized in 1982, there was more gender equality, and many married women entered the bank or stayed in it.[13] In the 1990s, this employee said, women could stay in the bank if they worked just as much as men and never asked for gender-specific concessions. They were fired as soon as they became pregnant or had to be absent because of an illness in the family. With restructuring, this bank's payroll in Guadalajara had shrunk 30 percent in the previous five years, yet men did not report more male or female layoffs. With two exceptions women's entry into various levels of the employment structure was not perceived as a threat, although more men were working with women and under their supervision.

Men in Monterrey consistently reported that their number-one priority in the coming years was to help secure a better future for their families; many spontaneously spoke of specific goals like helping their children with schoolwork and joint participation in after-school activities, particularly intense in that city, where almost all the interviewees belonged to social and sports clubs and a few to voluntary organizations. Among the younger men, however, securing a better job and somehow owning a house were the main objectives.[14]

Unlike the situation in the 1940s and 1950s, women's entry into paid employment in the recent period of restructuring has been based on a weakening, rather than a strengthening, of labor organizations. Men and male unions have therefore not resisted this movement, which has been characterized to a great extent by family, rather than gender or labor, solidarity. This development has also been made easier by the fact that, unlike what happened in the 1940s and 1950s, the occupations expanding most rapidly during the 1980s were mostly informal and therefore undesirable to men in stable jobs. But this expansion certainly, by 2000, had penetrated occupations and jobs that until recently had been considered masculine. The change in terms of the construction of men's lives has more to do with the microstructures of authority and power at work. Women can be men's equals or superiors, and this is a sea change that also subjects men's advancement to some women's decisions. But men have so far been more successful at cornering upper-level occupations in the private sector. Women in Monterrey rarely decide men's futures, whereas in the public sector (in Mexico City, for example) it is not rare. With some exceptions, such as those cited above, the expansion and entry of women into male occupational niches has been a surprisingly silent phenomenon. It remains to be seen, however, whether the women leaders of in-bond plant unions, which employed women almost exclusively until 1980 but now employ growing numbers of men, will succeed in retaining their positions or whether they will be driven out of them by men, as their counterparts were in the 1930s.

Final Remarks

Gender relationships in urban Mexico are changing. These changes allow for much greater variation in gender roles today than before, and, although leading to greater equality, significant forms of inequality are retained. As to the significance of these transformations, first, change is responsible for a "surfacing" of gender roles and gender discourse. For older generations the normative divisions of labor in the family and at work required neither justifications nor explanations. There was also little elaboration on the dominant gender order. Older men in this study believed there was not much to explain, that their particular relationships and their attitudes toward women and their partners required no justification. This "old" form of dominant discourse was therefore largely blanketed by silence because men adhered to a fixed form of marriage contract.

It was therefore significant that younger men more often carefully described and explained why they opted for particular arrangements. The "old" forms of gender relationships were updated by means of a new discourse describing women as intelligent, enterprising persons supporting the advancement of the other members of their families, as socially responsible persons engaged in voluntary work, or as, finally, successful microentrepreneurs in household-based, "gender correct" economic activities.[15] Although this was a validating discourse, it was still a change from that of the older group, for whom there was no need to elaborate on women's more subordinate, supportive, and secluded role. Among other younger men, of course, the change was even more evident, as they had decided with their spouses to do things differently than their parents had, and the change from the previous generation was a significant part of their very descriptions of their own histories.

This means that as the old hegemonic forms of discourse and gender relationships have crumbled, numerous others have arisen, and these "new" discourses became more elaborate and visible. Naturally, there has been a price for men. With fewer guarantees that they will have their way with women, there was growing uncertainty. But there were some important gains for men in this change. Older men felt the burden of responsibility, and many showed significant guilt at not being "up to snuff."

Alcoholism, economic irresponsibility, and adultery were all their fault. Their wives could not be held responsible for men's acts because men had, or thought they had, all the power at home. Women were seen as selfless, whereas men often confessed to being selfish and later repentant for the consequences of their acts—their wives, for example, had to take very menial jobs laundering clothes or as servants when men did not provide for the households; children became ill or died for reasons men believed were connected to their irresponsibility.

Younger men in contrast felt more free to criticize their wives. They pointed to instances of their wives' irresponsibility and selfishness and to ways in which, according to them, their wives had gained an unfair advantage at home or, less frequently, at work. Responsibility, recognition, and guilt were therefore shared. But histories centered less on women's shortcomings. What was remarkable was how younger men referred spontaneously to discussions with their wives and how they felt they had jointly decided important issues. This was true even for couples adhering to the "updated" version of the old marital division of labor.

Ironically, then, the dominant, generally understood discourse shaping the gender roles of older men was either vague or private, whereas change to a more variable form of gender relations at home and work, which is negotiated by partners and therefore apparently more private, is in fact more open and public.

Nonetheless, the substance of change should not be overestimated. New forms of discourse still conceal many inequalities. In this study, I did not delve into housework. A number of Mexican gender studies have already established a growing involvement of men in domestic chores (García and Oliveira 1994). But the relationship of the domestic order to men's and women's careers was detailed in these histories, and they showed that, although some men have actively committed themselves to their wives' careers, in most cases the "moral agreement" entails privileges for men. Also, although we did find that many younger women enjoyed much more freedom related to their involvement in the world of work, the cost of this change is only partly borne by their spouses; young women's mothers proved to be extremely valuable to them. Grandparents, in many ways, are paying a significant portion of the costs that restructuring has entailed. And, although this can clearly be observed in the case of healthy, economically stable grandparents via their assistance to younger couples, it is even more true of the elderly, sick, and poor parents receiving only occasional help from their children (children who, sometimes, have "moved in" to help them, thus enjoying some of the benefits of the assets of these elderly parents) (Varley and Blasco 1999).

Perhaps the most significant nonfinding is related to perceived competition from women at work. According to the survey, women have successfully entered previously male occupational strata in large numbers. Their presence is often recognized, but I found no sense of male solidarity or male cliquing against women, and competition was expressed in very few cases. Some of this lack of expression may be related to labor-market segregation and to the persistence of gendered niches in the employment structure. But this survey and other studies have shown that women are entering male employment niches. There are two nonexclusive labor-market explanations for this lack of resentment on the part of men. First, substantial labor-market reorganization has meant the employment of women in a context of high mobility masking this process. That is to say, women have rarely entered en masse to take men's jobs. Rather, as old departments close, and new ones are set up, the labor force changes. Second, falling incomes and growing worker disorganization have meant that men cannot prevent women's entry into work. These women are only doing what their wives and sisters are doing, and men have no solid worker organizations to avert the process in any case. Today, declining real incomes, disorganized workers, and the need for more employment in one's own family seem to have softened male attitudes.

It is possible, of course, that I may not have pushed interviewees hard enough. But I intended, whenever possible, to listen to their histories.

Notes

1. This essay reports some of the findings of the project "Age, Gender, Family, and Work in Urban Mexico," financed jointly by the Ford Foundation and Mexico's Science Council (CONACYT). The three cities were Mexico City, with a population of roughly thirteen million at the time of the survey; Guadalajara, Mexico's second-largest city, with a population of 3.5 to 4 million; and Monterrey, Mexico's third-largest city and its most manufacturing-intensive, comprising just under three million inhabitants. The survey

included 11,200 households and 24,000 persons 18 years old and older, including 16,000 providing a full labor mobility history. Partial results have been published in Escobar 1999. The men interviewed for this paper were selected independently from the survey. A book on labor, social mobility, and household arrangements is currently under revision for publication.

2. *Mestizo* is a term used in Mexico to refer to "mixed race" people, that is, the vast majority of the population who do not identify themselves ethnically as either members of an indigenous group or those referred to generally as "Spanish."

3. If these topics did not arise otherwise in the interview, the men were asked to talk explicitly about (1) the occupations and social status of their parents, and family life in their youth; (2) the same for their spouse's family; and (3) their own and their families' future, and what was necessary for them to achieve goals they had.

4. I am convinced these Monterrey companies were among the best private firms in this regard in Mexico, but still I believe I was given guarded responses. In one firm I realized after the interviews that the industrial psychologist had in fact eavesdropped from an adjacent office. This unfortunate incident may prove the Monterrey workers right in their assessment of the lack of absolute confidentiality that I had promised them.

5. This resistance by the fathers was related to the fact that they controlled all income from the land, to the novelty of urban occupations, and also to the fact that families holding communal *ejido* land could lose it if they failed to work it. Those who kept the land were wise. Rising land values in the metropolitan area and the illegal sale of part of their *ejido* plots to working-class residents of Mexico City later provided them with needed capital.

6. On the urbanization of Mexico see Roberts and Escobar (1997).

7. Thus, an informal street vendor in Monterrey wounded his father-in-law in a machete fight because the latter found him with a prostitute. The son-in-law explained that he was justified in seeking prostitutes because his wife had refused him sex after the birth of their first child.

8. In Mexico "Christians" is the name usually given to Protestants, as opposed to Catholics.

9. Some young women working at corporate offices were the daughters of high-placed executives, had a university degree, spoke three languages, and had significant responsibilities. Nonetheless, they all stopped working after they married.

10. Before this, he had been part of a soccer team, training and playing several times a week.

11. Most of these activities are unlikely to be reported in employment surveys as jobs.

12. Mexican banks have always required extremely long working hours.

13. In the women's case studies I collected, two bank employees reported their desire to remain in the bank after marriage because of excellent health care packages for the whole family and low-interest mortgages offered employees. These perks, however, had become less common.

14. In Monterrey no younger manual workers owned a house, perhaps the flip side of parents living longer and the impact of their lower incomes.

15. In one case (the forty-five-year-old Monterrey executive) this microenterprise was the family's only source of income when the husband was dismissed from his job in 1981.

References

Bastos Amigo, Santiago. 1999. "Concepciones del hogar y ejercicio del poder: El caso de los mayas en la ciudad de Guatemala." In *Divergencias del modelo tradicional: Hogares de jefatura femenina en América Latina*, ed. Mercedes González de la Rocha, 37–75. Mexico City: CIESAS/Plaza y Valdés.

Escobar, Agustín, and Fernando Cortés. 2000. "Nuevos patrones de acumulación: ¿Nuevos modelos de movilidad social?" Paper presented at Economic Commission for Latin America and the Caribbean, Santiago de Chile.

Escobar Latapí, Agustín. 1999. "Los hombres y sus historias: Masculinidad y reestructuración en México." In *Género e Trabalho na Sociología Latinoamericana*, ed. Alice Rangel de Paiva Abreu and Laís Abramo, 197–226. São Paulo: ALAST.

Gabayet, Luisa. 1988a. "Antes éramos mayoría . . . las mujeres en la industria textil en Guadalajara." In *Mujeres y sociedad: Salario, hogar y acción social en el occidente de México*, ed. Luisa Gabayet et al., 91–107. Guadalajara: El Colegio de Jalisco/CIESAS.

García, Brígida, and Orlandina de Oliveira. 1994. *Trabajo y vida familiar en México*. Mexico City: El Colegio de México.

González de la Rocha, Mercedes. 1994. *The Resources of Poverty: Women and Survival in a Mexican City*. Oxford: Blackwell.

González de la Rocha, Mercedes, and Agustín Escobar. 1986. "Crisis y adaptación: Hogares de Guadalajara." Paper delivered at the III Encuentro de investigación demográfica en México (SOMEDE), El Colegio de México.

Gutmann, Matthew C. 2000. *Ser hombre de verdad en la ciudad de México: Ni macho ni mandilón*. Mexico City: El Colegio de México.

Parker, Susan. 1996. "Niveles salariales de hombres y mujeres: Diferencias por ocupación en las áreas urbanas de México." In *México diverso y desigual*. Vol. 4, ed. Beatriz Figueroa Campos, 373–90. Mexico City: El Colegio de México/SOMEDE.

Roberts, Bryan, and Agustín Escobar. 1997. "Mexican Social and Economic Policy and Emigration." In *At the Crossroads: Mexican Migration and U.S. Policy*, ed. Frank Bean et al., 47–78. Lanham, Md.: Rowman and Littlefield.

Safa, Helen I. 1995. *The Myth of the Male Breadwinner: Women and Industrialization in the Caribbean.* Boulder, Colo.: Westview.

Varley, Ann, and Maribel Blasco. 1999. "Family Diversity and Housing for Older People in Mexico." Paper delivered at Migration, Immigration, and Transnational Families, a research and policy workshop organized by University of Texas at Austin and Universidad Iberoamericana. Universidad Iberoamericana, Tijuana, Mar. 26–27.

FRANCISCO FERRÁNDIZ

Malandros, María Lionza,

and Masculinity in a

Venezuelan Shantytown

∎ ∎ ∎

Para Omar y su estela de risas

Mug Shot

Profile of E. H.: twenty-seven years old.[1] Medium height. Slim. Dark skinned, mestizo. Bright black eyes. Visible elbow scar. Swinging body language. *Calé*–popular speech. Worn-out T-shirt. Sport shorts. Baseball cap. Barrio-shantytown dweller. Street rambler. Formally unemployed. No bank account. No registered property. Uneducated. Undernourished. Short-term jailbird. Spiritist.

Click.

If we were to regard E. H.'s public persona from the point of view of Venezuela's prevalent official discourses and practices of exclusion, he would no doubt belong to the brand of dangerous *barrio* (shantytown) youngsters and grown-up men lumped under the label of *malandros* (street-smart thugs). As an ordinary inhabitant of the shantytowns of Caracas, E. H. personifies in his very flesh and personal style the *suspicious appearance* named by Julio de Freitas (1995, 3–4) as typical of the streets of Venezuela's capital city. E. H. is an ordinary *tierrúo* (mud dweller)—a derogatory term for one who lives in the barrio—who, once out of his immediate urban territory, his shantytown, frequently notices that others cross the street to avoid him, that merchants lock their shops when they spot him, that police officers comment on how he does not fit in and that they may reach for their guns or harass him, that taxi drivers speed away after refusing him a ride.[2]

Given such a hegemonic, essentialized, and internalized view of men living in the shantytowns, E. H. is in all likelihood just a hopeless and genuine delinquent. Yet there is more. Men from the popular urban sectors in Venezuela often are depicted as savages, barbarians, and parasites, people who are predisposed to random violence owing to little more than their "lack of character."[3] In a context in which social stigma is assigned randomly to a whole population according to crude considerations of class and gender, being a malandro thus becomes the preeminent form of masculinity available to male inhabitants of the shantytowns. The social, psychological, and cultural mug shot of a stereotypical thug of the shantytowns communicates a disturbing image of a tough guy, drug addict, heavy drinker, lawbreaker, sexual predator, irresponsible father, merengue and popular salsa fan, a man bent on easy and fast money, a treacherous gambler, mostly uneducated and coarse, one deeply immersed in the culture of weapons, unreliable, criminal, vengeful, fearless of an early death, a ruthless assassin, someone who would kill for just a pair of shoes, and, ultimately, a man who is thoroughly incorrigible.

The widespread influence in the social imaginary of this hegemonic prototype of the malandro and popular lawbreaking man no doubt acts to obscure the structural causes of poverty, unemployment, and "informal" employment in the Venezuelan popular urban territories. Simultaneously, this same process, which in Venezuela produces delinquent and disposable bodies—particularly male bodies—also turns most youngsters and men in the shantytowns, regardless of their particular biographies or life projects, into potential targets of systematic discrimination, arrest, torture, and violent death by the state and its agents.[4] E. H., like most of his peers and other barrio men, lives his life trapped in a forced gender identity that mostly breeds stigma, suspicion, and abuse.

Of course life in the shantytowns of Caracas, Venezuela, is complex. Conditions are ripe for the emergence of pockets of violence. Residents have to endure the neighborhood professional criminals, the murderous practices of petty and grand delinquents, and many other forms of structural violence, not the least of which is wholesale police repression. Many men in Caracas are raised and expected to conform to tough models of masculinity. Yet the presence of criminality in the shantytowns and the dominant cliché of masculinity as a realm of impenitent delinquency does not, as certain public discourses would have it, transform all men into undesirable and menacing offenders, beyond redemption, worthy only of extermination.

In many ways shantytown dwellers have absorbed these hegemonic stereotypes about men and masculinity that circulate in the media, political policy reports, and other official sources of public opinion. "This barrio is still clean, believe me," Hermes told me one day in the heart of one of the more infamous popular neighborhoods in Caracas, Los Mangos de La Vega, a place other friends advised me not to go near even in daylight. "You can come here anytime, if you're careful, of course. But never ever go to any of the shantytowns of El Valle. All you'll find there are *puros malandros*. Dangerous men. There they'll kill you for nothing." Most barrio residents are quick to point out that the stereotype about their own neighborhood does not accord with their own experiences, whereas they are quite sure that *malandrismo* is the dominant male way of life in other areas of the city with which they have less familiarity. Therefore they are as eager to express their negative opinions about other poor neighborhoods as the inhabitants of middle- and upper-class areas are quick to denigrate all popular barrios.

This essay is concerned with the interface of youth, gender, stigma, and everyday violence in urban Venezuela, resulting in the production of what I call a *wounded masculinity*. Drawing on the life history of E. H., we trace the parameters of structural and discursive violence to establish the stigmatized and coercive framework in which E. H. has deciphered his life and constructed his gender identity. Given the generalized nature of outcast, delinquent, and highly restricted masculinity in Caracas's shantytowns, E. H.'s life may seem unexceptional. In fact, at first glance E. H. seems to have done no more than travel through life on his way to becoming a reckless criminal. Yet his biography is multifaceted and full of texture, and understanding how he has employed diverse survival strategies calls for a nuanced understanding of what it means to be a man in Venezuela's urban peripheries. Moving from street child to shoe-shine boy, abandoned car dweller, drug addict, gambler, petty thief, informal worker, occasional prisoner, enthusiastic looter during the *caracazo*,[5] husband and father, anthropologist's informant, and spiritist healer, E. H. has journeyed across the perimeters and territories of social and gender stigma. His categorically ambiguous experience of being a man in the informal sector of this once rich oil country is not uncommon.[6] Many men in the shantytowns are trapped by highly gendered identity and behavioral expectations that, as in E. H.'s case, collide with their life projects.

A Picture in Motion

It was no easy task to get E. H. to talk about his life. The life he had lived was, in his opinion, too average, not worth any attention. Yet this history, perhaps because of its "antibiographical" status,[7] may be important to the understanding of how Venezuela's modernity and its associated ideologies are experienced at an everyday level in Venezuelan shantytowns. Although his style of life does not exhaust all possible forms of male experience in the shantytowns, it is representative of the lives of many men who unravel their lives in contexts of low intensity urban violence. Thus I come to the central question guiding this study of one man's ordinary life in a Caracas shantytown: How has E. H. experienced, endured, and eventually resisted forms of masculinity imposed on him by the very act of beginning life in a poor family in the urban popular territories?

E. H. was born in a shantytown on the southern edge of Caracas to a woman E. H. himself calls "a cabaret lady" and a man with whom E. H. has had little contact in his life. Unhappy and harassed at home, he also resisted going to school, although he remembers that to hide his truancy he would give his mother fake drawings and other kinds of invented homework. E. H. spent most of his time roaming the streets of his shantytown for money, play, and excitement:

I'd take off with my notebooks and stuff but I would never make it to school. And when I got home I had my pockets full and would bring every thing I could think of to my mom. Food and everything, you know. And I still had some money left. But when my mother got home, always drunk, she would start tormenting me. She would send me to the shower and then hit me with her belt, after my back was wet. I guess her bad temper ended up driving all of us mad.

As his mother, Rosa, suggested to me, her rude behavior toward her children—five boys from different fathers—stemmed mainly from her desire to toughen them so they would be ready for the kind of life she said she expected for them.[8] When E. H. was eight years old, weary of his mother's beatings, he ran away from home and started a life in the streets, which he found to be a distinctively male space of socialization.[9] In dire straits and unsupported by his family, E. H. was quickly forced to master the circuits of the informal economy, the *rebusque,* in his barrio. He survived by shining shoes and cleaning windshields, tasks he had occasionally performed before he left home. He still remembers the sense of empowerment he achieved by earning his own money and fully enjoying his freedom in the streets—no timetables, no formal education, no family obligations.

During this time E. H. slept, along with other kids, in abandoned cars on the outskirts of his barrio. With the promise of daily food and clean clothes, his mother would come by once in a while to try to convince him, "in quite a loving way," to return home. And on more than one occasion he did go home for a while. But before long he would confront the old patterns that had driven him away before, and, inevitably, he returned to the streets. There E. H. was regularly exposed to the most extreme and routinized forms of street violence. When he was barely ten, one of his older brothers was killed in a gang fight. Only six months later, a second brother died in similar circumstances.

E. H. told me of another incident that took place a little later, one that remained a crucial reference point in his memories of childhood. Now the oldest son alive, this incident pushed his emergent masculinity to the fore and led him for the first time into a potentially serious skirmish with the police and judicial system. After finding his mother severely beaten and bleeding in the street one day, E. H. felt compelled and felt pressure from others to kill his mother's assailant in order to restore the honor of the family. This was true despite the fact that E. H. was a runaway and at the time had a tormented and distant relationship with his mother. When he was already in the chase, a female relative talked him out of seeking revenge by convincing E. H. that if he were caught he would destroy his own life for that of a worthless man. When E. H. told me about this incident a few years later, it seemed that he had never been truly comfortable with the status he had been obliged to assume as the main protector of his family's reputation. In what many people, including his mother, considered a lack of manliness, E. H. decided against retaliation, and he returned to the streets to live his own life. "[But] it was not cowardice on my part not to kill that sucker," he told me. "Simply that I had a really pure heart. I still see the guy who did it around, and sooner or later I'll get him with a few needles."[10]

At this point, however, E. H. was still a child in many respects. First, he had run away from home; then he had failed as his family's defender when he showed himself incapable or uninterested in hunting down the man who had assaulted his mother. In his quite conventional fall from grace E. H. became ensnarled in street life. He became a drug addict, a petty trafficker of marijuana, amphetamines, and *aguardiente* (liquor). He became increasingly involved with gangs of street children and even of older men.

> I started to consume drugs, to brag, and to play games of chance with malandros, but *true* malandros, let me tell you. I was the only *pelao*-kid hanging out with them. Even though I was a kid, I could easily drink three bottles of *caña clara*—rum liquor and still be able to stand up. I tried to be nice to everybody, and nobody harassed me. Whenever we took pills with liquor we'd go crazy. We became fearless. We felt we could fight three guys, or five guys, if we wanted, I mean fist fights, you know. Once they got me and hit me really hard; I was left unconscious down there at the edge of the barrio, and nobody cared. I don't remember how long I lay there. Next day my whole body hurt, but I took a few pills and the pain disappeared. I was fine. You feel like superman.

Fuel Embodied

E. H. remembers this time of initiation into male routines and excesses in a confused way. He seems always to have been intoxicated, moving from abandoned car to abandoned car, learning to be a *real* man among *real* malandros. Yet in their toughness and apparent invincibility he and his peers were strikingly vulnerable even when high on drugs. At his mother's house he told me a story that revealed the traumatized space in which many barrio neighbors led their everyday lives. The low price of gasoline, subsidized by the Venezuelan state, turned this product into a preferred narcotic for the generation who shared the streets with E. H. in the late 1970s and the 1980s. At times the hallucinations induced by gasoline, the perverse fuel of Venezuela's modernity, were crude visualizations of the structural exclusion to which these youth were subject and illustrations of the local, wounded space of their everyday experiences.[11] E. H. conveyed such images of terror to me one afternoon in his shanty, with a vision that was still vivid in his memory:

> When I was in the streets, I used to consume gasoline a lot. We would get a bottle of gasoline and inhale in it. See, this stuff makes you see planes, like planes falling down on you, and you get terrified and run like crazy. Or, then, like a train at full speed trying to run you over. Can you imagine? A train running all over the place in this *cerro* [hillside]? It doesn't make any sense. And suddenly you can see a whole army chasing you down, and then you start running all over the hill like crazy, looking for a safe spot. Where? People thought we were nuts; they just couldn't understand. But it was so real to us. And after you came out of your burrow, so to speak, you were still asking your *panas*-buddies in terror, "Are the police still here? Are the authorities still after us?" "What authorities?" they'd say. "There's nothing here."

They had reason to fear. Since they began to toddle, these youths had been officially marked as incurable delinquents, as children without a childhood and later as youth without a future. Young or mature, respectable workers, students, or evildoers, shantytown men are indiscriminately treated as malandros by the various police agencies and the military. "There is some kind of death penalty for barrio men," E. H. and his spiritist friend Maimai told me on one occasion. "The order from the government is 'Shoot the malandros, *plomo al hampa*, lead for the scum.'"[12] That could mean death for them or any of their peers and neighbors.

As is frequently the case in poor areas of Caracas, at times during my fieldwork I could not enter E. H.'s shantytown because it was occupied by police carrying out "cleansing operations." During these interventions, as my informants (most of them spiritists) declared, no one was safe from indiscriminate harassment, and shootouts were all too common.[13] Whether in the narrow streets and alleys or hidden in fragile shanties, no one could escape the crossfire.

To be sure, police harassment and military hair triggers are not the only forms of daily danger in the shantytowns. Life in the heart or on the periphery of delinquency always involves long-lasting *culebras*. *Culebra* literally means "snake," and in Caracas it refers to an enduring feud. It can apply to a dispute between people, neighborhoods, or situations—or a combination of them—that may eventually erupt into violence. Being able to negotiate these culebras successfully, to impose fear or respect into your culebras, is highly valued as a sign of manliness in the streets. After seven years wandering around, E. H. was profoundly immersed in this world of toughness, aggression, and payback. Within this logic of masculinity he proudly carried a "medal" in his right elbow, a scar from a gunshot wound he received in an attack that stemmed from the deaths of his brothers. Yet at that point in his life he felt trapped: "When I reached fifteen, I started to wonder about my life and my expectations, and I decided that I wanted something else. I could see some younger kids and I thought, 'These guys will be something in life, and I will still be in this mess.' The life I was living, you know, was a 'bad life.' It was not appropriate for me. I wanted out."

A few years later, on July 5, 1985—a date he emphasized a few times during our conversations—he decided to leave the streets. Because life choices for barrio men are limited, particularly when these men are branded with the stigma of the malandro, the only way to break completely with his former life was for E. H. to join the army. He was eighteen. The army offered him a respite from the pressures of the streets and a fresh environment from which to reconsider his life. According to his narrative he used military discipline against his addictions and managed to quit alcohol and drugs, at least partially. He did not stop consuming drugs and alcohol entirely, but these substances stopped being central to his identity and his relationships with other men. He thinks of his stay in the military as a turning point in his life, and he showed me his military I.D. with pride to demonstrate, I think, one of the few pieces of evidence besides his police record that he has of his legal existence.

E. H. returned to Caracas, determined to start anew, but found himself haunted by unresolved issues that he just could not ignore. He soon realized that there were old paths that he had to go round, risky gatherings to avoid, certain police officers to evade. His old culebras, even if subdued, were still alive. And new and disturbing ones appeared. His younger brother was killed by a gang when he was still a teenager. Later his brother's killers, led by the well-known gangster Canelón, showed no compunction in roughing up those who attended the funeral. In what he considered one of his most visible acts of public courage, E. H. confronted them but was outnumbered. Still, he was one of the few who managed to hold on to his wallet. With the death of his third brother E. H. was quickly transformed, one more time despite his best intentions, into a main participant in a new blood feud. Again expectations were raised in the shantytown as to how he should react to this new murder.

E. H. was furious with the head of the gang that had enlisted his brother to fight Canelón's gang. According to E. H. this malandro was recruiting and arming youths like his deceased brother to fight on the front lines against other gangs for control of the barrio's territories. He thought this was immoral and cowardly even according to the codes of street violence. Yet E. H. decided to start with Canelón. He went to the top of the hill with a gun to avenge his brother. Once he arrived he was promptly surrounded by members of the gang who told him that the blame was not theirs. Rather, E. H. should confront the leader of his brother's own gang, the one who put him at risk. Then, looking downhill, one of the rival gang members gave E. H. the gun that had been used to kill his brother and urged him to retaliate against the appropriate person. E. H. knew that his life had been spared so he could carry out this dirty job for Canelón and his gang. He never used the gun, though, and instead gave it to a friend. Again, he refused to take part in violence. Presumably, in the eyes of his culebras, he gave up a good share of masculinity along with that symbolically and emotionally charged gun.

Adding to his renewed tribulations in the streets, employment opportunities in the formal sector were slim. E. H. applied a series of more or less legal strategies for survival in the informal sector. In times of dire need he resorted to picking pockets. A petty theft in the popular market where E. H. often spent time in search of low-paying and temporary jobs resulted in his main brush with the judicial and penal system. After he was arrested, he spent two terrifying weeks in jail; he was released quickly only because of the insignificance of his offense. According to E. H., a compassionate lawyer or secretary tore up the record of his crime, *"ras, ras, ras, ras,"* and let him go.

> I don't recommend prison to anybody. In jail, I had to sleep very close to the bathroom door, and everybody had to step on me to get in, to jump "over my dead body," you could say. As people were released, I managed to move my sleeping place away from the bathroom, little by little. I remember I had my life threatened by one guy who was trying to control the cell. He bragged that he was there for theft, rape, homicide, and demanded that everybody had to obey his orders. He accused me of having turned him in. "You are wrong, you are wrong," I would tell him. He was testing me, ready to stab me to death if I flunked. These guys are really satanic, let me tell you. They do not stab you once in the heart, you know. They sew your whole body up. They leave you like a colander and nobody cares. Fortunately I managed to get out of that hell after a couple of weeks. I had to beg and scream out my innocence to the official who was there, but I was released with no charges.

Because of the cruelty of Venezuela's penal system, and the sluggishness and corruption of its justice system, E. H. was truly blessed to come out relatively unscathed. Indeed, aside from the constant tragedy that was his family, E. H. was somewhat lucky; he could even contemplate being able to emerge from his years in the streets alive and without any serious blood debts. His police record was short and his experience with institutionalization minimal, albeit traumatic. Nonetheless, until the day he dies E. H. will be a malandro. This has been his fate from the day he was born. With few chances of securing steady employment or being considered an integral part of Venezuela's future, no matter how much he struggles, E. H. will never shake off his murky past in the streets or his suspicious appearance—attached as they are to his skin and his cultural style—or his culebras. He had always been uneasy with the expectations of others, and after his short jail term and his experience with Canelón and his gangland associates, E. H. definitely wanted out, somehow. . . .

Although he never told me exactly how he turned his life around, the fact was that by the time I met him, E. H. had reconciled with his mother—"There is only one mother"—and eventually married a young woman from his shantytown, with whom he had two children. In the meantime he had also become a spiritist. These changes in his life entailed a reconsideration of the terms and activities by which he constructed his masculinity.

Shaking Uncontrollably

I met E. H. in January 1994, deep in the forest on the mountain of Sorte, the main pilgrimage site of the Venezuelan spirit possession cult of María Lionza, during an early fieldwork stay with a spiritist group based in E. H.'s shantytown.[14] He had joined the group a year earlier, when he discovered in spiritism a fresh environment in which to establish networks of solidarity, make a living, and refashion his local identity. During our sojourn in 1994 we spent four days on the mountain, while the spiritist party performed healing rituals and initiation rites. A ceremony performed to develop E. H.'s mediumship ended in failure when he did not "receive" any full spirit, only mild trembling.

During the nightlong ceremonies E. H. asked the spirits to disclose the whereabouts of Canelón. After a member of his gang killed E. H.'s little brother, he had twice tried to murder E. H. Now Canelón had disappeared from the shantytown, and E. H. wanted to know if he was about to return or if he might even be dead. Eventually a popular malandro spirit, Ismael, arrived in the body of a medium.[15] The spirit told E. H. that Canelón was out of the picture for good and therefore that E. H. did not have to leave the shantytown. E. H. could disengage from at least this culebra and would be left alone.

After our initial contact in Sorte I began to visit some of the members of this small spiritist group regularly in Caracas. In addition to its religious routines the group also functioned as an economic unit, at least for its three core members. In the wee hours of the morning, Maimai, Roberto, and E. H. would often go to a nearby wholesale market to buy a few products such as fruits and vegetables. Maimai had bought an old and shabby van with the money he won in a lottery, on a number recommended by one of their main spirit protectors, the Viking Robinson. Most of the petty economic activities of the group revolved around this vehicle. After securing various inexpensive products, they would drive to the foot of the shantytown, place them in the open door of the van and await potential buyers. With the fruits and vegetables they also offered spiritist services such as counseling, diagnosis, spiritual checkups, and "*tabaco smoking*" (divination with cigars).

During the day Maimai stayed with the van, their base of operations, while the rest of the group looked for alternative ways to earn some money. E. H. usually went back to the market to work as *carretillero* (loader and gofer), but competition was high, local mafias were very active, and sometimes E. H. would come back with empty pockets. Occasionally he worked as a bricklayer, but that was as a last resort. When his tools were stolen one day, that ceased to be even a possibility.

By the end of the day, when sales had declined, Maimai split the sparse revenue among all those (other than me) who had joined in the group's activities that day. The money was divided into uneven shares, depending on the nature of each member's work contribution and the total time each had spent under the sun. On particularly bad days a system of reciprocal loans went into effect, as E. H. or Roberto shared the money they had earned in their separate activities. When everyone was satisfied that the money had been "evened out" for the day, they bought food for their families—the mandatory *harina de pan* (maize flour) to cook *arepas* and, if they were lucky, something extra, such as chicken, canned sardines, or raw liver, depending on the earnings of the day.

In this new role of family provider, during this time E. H. was also building atop his mother's concrete shanty a wooden shack—*rancho de tablas*—for his family. He roamed the dumps surrounding the wholesale market, also a very competitive environment, looking for scraps in the garbage. The most valued were wooden planks and zinc sheets. Sometimes he walked by content with some newfound treasure on his head, ready to climb to the top of the hill. Other times he returned frustrated with only dirty fingers. Not well secured to his mother's shanty, E. H.'s shack was always on the verge of collapse from heavy rain and wind. Yet sprucing up that precarious home, the only shelter E. H. was able to provide for his nuclear family, became a major life project for him.

No matter how well they had done in selling and building, their day was far from over when they closed their stall. In the late afternoon the group usually drove to a neighboring outdoor spiritist shrine to look for potential clients and to develop their own mediumship. It was during these afternoon ceremonies, and during the occasional ceremony in their shanties, that I could follow E. H.'s *materia* (medium activities). As an apprentice at the time, E. H. was looking for affinities in the pantheon of spirits in order to start formal negotiations with certain spirits who might possess his body. From the great array of spirits in the cult, each medium selects those with whom, for one reason or another, he or she may feel a special connection. That means that each spiritist cultivates a different pool of spirits to work with. The patient development of these affinities is crucial to the future spiritist persona of the medium, as well as to his/her public identity as a healer. Quite often, in fact, the name of a particular spirit becomes associated with that of the medium.

It has become commonplace to identify and celebrate the flexibility of gender identities. As such, they are necessarily unfinished, precarious, multiple. As we will see below, mediumship is a prolific ground for gendered ebb and flows, mostly in the form of what Roger Lancaster calls *carnal transactions* (1997, 564–66). In fact, E. H.'s development as a medium provided him with an effective means for building a more fluid gender identity, according to other models of masculinity beyond the malandro type. Yet, beyond the identity flux, E. H.'s case also refers to another relevant fact: the profound discomfort that individuals or groups of people might feel toward expected social and gender roles and behavior. This is particularly true with respect to identities and lifestyles as harsh and troubling as that of the malandro, which, as I suggested at the beginning of the paper, can also be regarded as one form of wounded masculinity, enforcing a strong and tragic pressure on males in the shantytowns.

Like some of his spiritist companions, I was surprised initially by E. H.'s steadfast refusal to be possessed by malandro spirits, who embody most traits of the stereotypical delinquent and constantly refer to scenarios of street violence. They thus represent the kind of masculinity from which he was trying to escape at that point in his life. We all thought that this was to be E. H.'s "natural" entry into spiritism. But E. H. said "no."[16] His attempts to build a home, be a responsible father, and maintain a monogamous marriage already represented a rupture from what was expected of the stereotypical malandro. Now, publicly rejecting any "overture" toward the malandro spirits was yet another way of showing his anxiety about what was expected of him in life. He felt as if he were in a cage.

Instead, E. H. showed an interest in simultaneously approaching three nonmalandro male spirits: the Indian *cacique* Tacataca, the African Changó, and Raúl Sánchez Valero, an old healer from the Andes. The spirits in the pantheon always hold many popular memories that are mapped in sophisticated ways onto the bodies of the mediums during trance. These corporeal memories are unquestionably gendered. Speaking in overall terms, the Indian male warriors such as Tacataca exhibit—and transfer to their mediums—local senses of courage, dignity, loyalty, and resistance. As victims of the colonial regime, they stand for an injured, sober, yet heroic masculinity. The Africans, including many members of the Cuban santería like Changó, loosely convey experiences of suffering from the time of slavery in Venezuela. They are the tortured, stigmatized, forgotten, and Maroon fighters against colonial power. And *chamarreros* such as Sánchez Valero stereotypically elicit nostalgic local memories of rural Venezuela. As male spirits they usually come across in possession as womanish, obscene, overly sexist, heavy drinking, humorous, grouchy, wise, tender, reliable.

Identification by mediums with the entities possessing them goes beyond nominal attributions. During trance materias feel them deep within their bodies—their smell, their taste, their weight, their caprices. Even outside ritual settings, in their everyday life, they perceive their spirits inside their skins. They constantly talk to them and smoke cigars to get answers. They sense their evanescent presence in breezes, temperatures, and noises. Spirits also infiltrate their gestures, tastes, and moods. In fact, many male mediums refuse to be possessed by female spirits because they believe that these spirits would feminize—and thus publicly ridicule—them. Mediums acquire in this way a new corporeality in their constant rubbing against the spirits, and this kind of identification, which crosses all sensorial paths, entails a whole universe of deeply gendered intimacy unknown to the uninitiated.

Further, the different types of entities and their possible combinations are not stable in the bodies of their mediums. They remain in constant tension and adjust over time. As if they were pieces of a kaleidoscope, these embodied images activate or deactivate according to circumstance and to the evolving preferences of the mediums. It seems clear that the three categories of spirits initially selected by E. H. to develop his mediumship offered him three distinctive corporeal "masculinity tracks"—as well as their multiple entanglements—to refashion his gender identity away from its hegemonic inscription as a malandro.

When I met E. H., however, the presence of the spirits in his body was embryonic. Still a beginner, he was just learning the ropes of trance, slowly discerning the different facets of this new form of closeness. In his shack E. H. had built an altar, which he tended daily. He prayed to his select spirits, lit candles for them, smoked tobacco, carried images of them in his pockets, and thought about them often. In the afternoons or on weekends he would gather with his spiritist companions and organize a ceremony. They created imaginative *velaciones* (sacred spaces) from spiritist symbols in order to lie down and invoke the spiritual forces. They carefully tended each other's rituals. They gave their entire bodies over to spiritual possession. But each attempt by E. H. to enter a trance, no matter the spirit invoked, resulted in uncontrollable shaking until he was absolutely drained of energy.

Presumably, if E. H. continued his spiritist development properly he eventually would become a good medium, able to enter sophisticated and more serene trances with his preferred spirits. But E. H.'s uncontrollable shaking is the essential image I recall from our relationship—E. H. shaking in his shanty in front of his spiritist altar; E. H. shaking in outdoor shrines, his arms extended ahead parallel to one another, his eyes rolled back. Convulsions are common in such early phases of spiritual development, when the medium is learning to embody certain previously unknown presences and when spirits—in this case Tacataca, Changó, and Raúl Sánchez Valero—fight among themselves for preeminence in the flesh. Yet in E. H.'s case they were clearly connected to the discomfort he had felt all his life about who he was and what was expected of him. E. H.'s shaking was a signal of transition, paralleling his most recent efforts to get off the streets and its routines. He was shaking against a cruel stereotype imposed on him, against a wounded masculinity, against powerlessness, against the killings and the mourning, against the lack of a future. He was shaking for a more nuanced sense of gender and identity, for a new persona, for a fresh horizon in his life.

Notes

1. This was in 1993–94. I met E. H. when I was doing fieldwork in Venezuela.

2. Fieldwork (1993–94) on the cult of María Lionza was supported by an MEC/ Fulbright doctoral grant and by R. L. Lowie and R. H. Olson travel grants (UC Berkeley). My thanks as well for a Rockefeller Fellowship, administered through the Institute of Violence and Survival at the Virginia Foundation for the Humanities and Public Policy (VFH) during fall of 1996. An earlier version of E. H.'s life story was published in Ferrándiz 1999a.

3. See Coronil and Skurski (1991, 322–34); and España (1993, 160–61). In fact, these designations are generally extended to all barrio dwellers.

4. Police operations on shantytown men—delinquents—are one crucial way in which these stigmatizing stereotypes are acted on in deeply traumatic ways. For an expanded discussion of these operatives, including kidnapping, torture, and indiscriminate arrests or deadly shootings, see PROVEA (1992) or any of their annual reports. For a study of the *criminogenic* quality of these state interventions (i.e., the production of penal antecedents for many men) see Tosca Hernández (1989, 2000). For testimonies and analysis of repressive practices on street children, especially boys, see Pedrazzini and Sánchez (1992); Duque and Muñoz (1995); and Márquez (1999).

5. *El caracazo* refers to a widespread (and violently repressed) popular rebellion against austerity measures that took place in Venezuela in 1989. For an analysis of the social wounds left behind by *el caracazo* see Coronil (1997) and Tulio Hernández (2000).

6. In this sense the task of deconstructing the gendered dimensions of the *malandro* parallels Gutmann's (1996) revealing critique of Mexican stereotypes of *machismo*.

7. Ignasi Terradas shows us how fruitful it can be to preserve from oblivion those antibiographies or lives "which reveal the silence, the emptiness, the chaos that a certain civilization has cast over a certain person, making him/her conventionally insignificant" (1992, 13).

8. Rosa herself had been severely beaten by her mother and quite a few men during her life.

9. Although there are obviously girls and young women on the street everywhere in the world, often engaged in prostitution, as many commentators have written, most of those living in the streets are boys. Further, while these factors vary cross-culturally, girls tend to be more constrained than boys by domestic tasks and compromises, not the least of which is raising their siblings. For Latin American perspectives see Scheper-Hughes and Hoffman (1994, 18–19); and Márquez (1999).

10. Here E. H., who was a spiritist when I met him, is referring to the possibility of settling this old account through magic.

11. It has become commonplace among critics of Venezuelan oil modernity to resort to metaphors such as "malediction," "bulimia," "wreckage," "perversion," and "devil's excrement" to characterize the impact of the oil economy on the economic, social, cultural, and political fabric of the country. See, e.g., Izard (1986); Briceño León (1990); Watts (1992); and Coronil (1997).

12. This is known in Venezuela as the *doctrina Betancourt,* "shoot first, then ask." See PROVEA (1992, 28). It is common to hear testimonies in the shantytowns and read reports in the press about men and children who are considered *sane* by their neighbors before they are killed by police, who are then, *postmortem,* officially declared to have been dangerous delinquents.

13. PROVEA (1992, 17) has denounced human rights abuses and violations committed during these police operations and stated that, contrary to government assertions, they should not be blamed on the "excesses of isolated officers acting on their own." In their own words, "what we have is a systematic pattern of repression which is painstakingly elaborated, learned, and conducted by the police corps, aimed at creating a disorienting social environment among the population which prevents the articulation of any organizational movement of resistance against the implementation of a certain [liberal] economic program with well known results."

14. For classic and more recent analysis of this widespread form of spirit possession in Venezuela see Barreto (1990, 1994); Clarac de Briceño (1992); Ferrándiz (1992, 1995, 1996, 1997, 1999b); García Gavidia (1987); Martín (1983); Pollak-Eltz (1972); and Taussig (1997).

15. For an analysis of the impact of malandro spirits in the cult of María Lionza in the early 1990s see Ferrándiz (1996, 1999c).

16. It is important to point out that among spiritists E. H.'s rejection of the malandro spirits can be considered as "normal" as not. During my fieldwork in Venezuela I found that many youngsters were fascinated by these new spirits and found in them a suitable embodied space to refashion their gender and social identities in nonhegemonic ways. In fact, the malandro spirits project all the ambiguities that shantytown dwellers have regarding street delinquency. See Ferrándiz (1999c).

References

Barreto, Daisy. 1987. *María Lionza: Mito e historia.* Caracas: Escuela de Antropología/Universidad Central de Venezuela. Unpublished manuscript.

———. 1990. "Perspectiva histórica del mito a María Lionza." *Boletín Americanista* 39–40:9–26.

———. 1994. "Plasticité et résistance: Le mythe et le culte de María Lionza au Venezuela." *Gradhiva: Revue d'histoire et d'archives de l'antropologia* 15:81–88.

Briceño León, Roberto. 1990. *Los efectos perversos del petróleo.* Caracas: Fondo Editorial Acta Científica Venezolana.

Clarac de Briceño, Jacqueline. 1992. *La enfermedad como lenguaje en Venezuela.* Mérida: Talleres Gráficos Universitarios.

Coronil, Fernando. 1997. *The Magical State: Nature, Money, and Modernity in Venezuela.* Chicago: University of Chicago Press.

Coronil, Fernando, and Julia Skurski. 1991. "Dismembering and Remembering the Nation: The Semantics of Political Violence in Venezuela." *Comparative Studies in Society and History* 33:288–337.

De Freitas, Julio. 1995. "Bárbaros, armados y peligrosos: La eficacia del discurso sobre la violencia popular urbana." In *Historias de identidad urbana: Composición y recomposición de identidades en los territorios populares urbanos,* ed. Emanuele Amodio and Teresa Ontiveros, 147–60. Caracas: Fondo Editorial Tropykos.

Duque, José Roberto, and Boris Muñoz. 1995. *La ley de la calle: Testimonios de jovenes protagonistas de la violencia en Caracas.* Caracas: FUNDARTE.

España, Luis Pedro. 1993. "La naturaleza de la violencia social." *SIC* 554:160–62.

Ferrándiz, Francisco. 1992. "Dimensions of Nationalism in a Venezuelan Possession Cult." *Kroeber Anthropological Society Papers* 75–76:28–47.

———. 1995. "Itinerarios de un médium: Espiritismo y vida cotidiana en la Venezuela contemporánea." *Antropología* 10:133–66.

———. 1996. "Malandros, africanos y vikingos: Violencia cotidiana y espiritismo en la urbe venezolana." In *Antropología de América Latina,* ed. Carlos Caravantes, 125–37. Zaragoza: Actas del VII Congreso Nacional de Antropología Social.

———. 1997. "A Trace of Fingerprints: Displacements and Textures in the Use of Ethnographic Video in Venezuelan Spiritism." *Visual Anthropology Review* 13, no. 2:19–38.

———. 1999a. "Brevísima historia de E. H.: Espacios de trauma, estigma y peligro en las vidas de los niños y jovenes de los *barrios* venezolanos." *Antropología de las edades,* ed. Carles Feixa, 181–90. Santiago de Compostela: FAAEE/AGA.

———. 1999b. "El culto de María Lionza en Venezuela: Tiempos, espacios, cuerpos." *Alteridades* 9, no. 18:39–55.

———. 1999c. "Juventud, estigma y violencia: El caso de los 'espíritus malandros' en Venezuela." *Joven(es)* 8:186–212.

García Gavidia, Nelly. 1987. *Posesión y ambivalencia en el culto a María Lionza: Notas para una tipología de los cultos de posesión existentes en América del sur.* Maracaibo: Universidad del Zulia.

Gutmann, Matthew C. 1996. *The Meanings of Macho: Being a Man in Mexico City.* Berkeley: University of California Press.

Hernández, Tosca. 1989. "Los problemas de la legitimación: La legitimación de los problemas sociales." In *Legitimidad y sociedad,* ed. L. Gabaldón et al., 113–78. Universidad de los Andes: Alfadil/Trópicos.

———. 2000. "El desafío de la violencia en el actual sistema político venezolano." Unpublished manuscript.

Hernández, Tulio. 2000. *Celebración de estar vivos.* Caracas: Biblioteca de Autores y Temas Tachirenses.

Izard, Miguel. 1986. *Tierra Firme: Historia de Venezuela y Colombia.* Madrid: Alianza America.

Lancaster, Roger. 1997. "Guto's Performance: Notes on the Transvestism of Everyday Life." In *The Gender/Sexuality Reader,* ed. R. Lancaster and M. Di Leonardo, 559–74. London: Routledge.

Márquez, Patricia. 1999. *The Street Is My Home: Youth and Violence in Caracas.* Stanford, Calif.: Stanford University Press.

Martín, Gustavo. 1983. *Magia y religión en la Venezuela contempránea.* Caracas: Ediciones de la Biblioteca de la Universidad Central de Venezuela.

Pedrazzini, Ives, and Magaly Sánchez. 1992. *Malandros, bandas, y niños de la calle: Cultura de urgencia en la metrópoli latinoamericana.* Caracas: Vadell Hermanos Editores.

Pollak-Eltz, Angelina. 1972. *María Lionza: Mito y culto venezolano.* Caracas: Universidad Católica Andrés Bello.

PROVEA. 1992. *Situación de los Derechos Humanos en Venezuela: Informe Anual (Octubre 1991-Septiembre 1992).* Caracas: Programa Venezolano de Educación–Acción en Derechos Humanos.

Scheper-Hughes, Nancy, and Daniel Hoffman. 1994. "Kids Out of Place." *NACLA: Report on the Americas* 27, no. 6:16–23.

Taussig, Michael. 1997. *The Magic of the State.* New York: Routledge.

Terradas, Ignasi. 1992. *Eliza Kendal: Reflexiones sobre una antibiografía.* Bellaterra: Servei de Publicacions de la Universitat Autónoma de Barcelona.

Watts, Michael. 1992. "Oil as Money: The Devil's Excrement and the Spectacle of Black Gold." In *Money, Power, and Space,* ed. S. Corbridge, R. Martin, and N. Thrift, 406–45. Cambridge: Blackwell.

NORMA FULLER

The Social Constitution

of Gender Identity

among Peruvian Males

∎ ∎ ∎ ∎

In this essay I use a contemporary feminist theoretical approach to ana-lyze representations of masculinity characteristic of the urban culture of the middle-class and popular sectors in Peru. Two additional issues are also examined: how discourses regarding masculinity intersect with re-gional, class, and generational identities and how gender identity is linked to macrosocial processes. The data analyzed were obtained carrying out in-depth interviews with a sample of 120 men. This sample was pro-portionally divided by class origin (middle-class or popular sectors) and age (younger and older adults). All interviewees were born in an urban environment or migrated to one of the three cities studied before they were five years old. An urban sample was chosen because in recent de-cades Peruvian cities have undergone drastic changes in the size of fam-ilies, levels of education, and feminine participation in the public sphere. Their populations have also been in contact with ideas from the outside world through tourism, migration, and the media, which provide infor-mation about the discourses of the women's liberation movements, the alternative sexualities that have contributed to the redefinition of gender relations elsewhere, and new representations of the characteristics of each gender.

Each of the three cities chosen has a clearly defined regional culture. Lima, the capital of Peru, had a population of more than six million people in 1990. It is the brain center of the nation, it is well integrated into the international world, and it constitutes the most modern part of the country. About 30 percent of the population of Peru lives in Lima, and most of the country's industrial production, commerce, and services are located there.

Cuzco, in the Andes mountains, had nearly 270,000 inhabitants in 1990. It was the capital of the pre-Hispanic Inca Empire (roughly A.D. 1200–1500) and today is one of the most important centers of *mestizo* (racially mixed) and Andean culture in the nation. Its economy is based on agricultural production, mining, and tourism (it is a national and international tourist attraction). The city is a combination of a local identity that imagines itself to be the heir of a pre-Hispanic tradition and the profound influence of Western discourses and fashions.

Iquitos, similar in size to Cuzco, is a river port in the heart of the Amazon basin region leading on to Brazil and the Atlantic Ocean. It is a frontier town whose principal revenue comes from logging, oil drilling, and its role as an administrative, commercial, and military center serving the whole northeastern Peruvian Amazon region. Various waves of migrants have come from other urban centers to Iquitos to exploit natural resources. Much of the identity of its residents revolves around two issues: quick riches from natural resource booms and opening up new territorial frontiers, and the defense of Peruvian national boundaries. Most of the popular sectors of the city comprise indigenous people who have adopted urban habits even as they maintain their ties with their native communities. The middle class is composed of descendants of the various migrations. Contact between the two traditions has resulted in a system of interethnic relations that is profoundly hierarchical. Moreover, discourses on masculinity in Iquitos and Cuzco in large measure reproduce the scale of hierarchies that position the capital, Lima, in a hegemonic position over Andean and Amazonian cities.[1] The latter, for their part, identify themselves with regional cultures and construct their identities in contrast to the existing order.

For the purposes of this study I defined the middle class as those people dedicated to small or medium-sized commerce and industry, middle- and upper-level white-collar workers, and professionals. To establish a clear difference between the middle-class and popular sectors, I chose the middle-class sample from people who had pursued or were pursuing higher education and whose parents belonged to the middle class. The Peruvian middle class is particularly important because it occupies a leadership position in the intellectual, political, and economic life of the country. I defined popular sectors as those sectors of the population whose members did not have higher educations or hold lower-level white-collar jobs, were workers, or were small vendors. Popular sectors represent 80 percent of the population of Peru.

The age groups were made up of men from twenty-three to thirty and forty-five to fifty-five years of age. The reason for dividing the sample into two cohorts was to bring out differences stemming from the different stages in the life course in which the men interviewed found themselves, as well as to be able to compare an older generation of men—who were socialized in traditional patterns of gender relations and who have more often played the role of witnesses than participants in recent changes in discourses and gender relations—with a younger generation of men, who inherited these changes and have come of age through them.

The Constitution of Masculinity

My first point is that gender identity is constituted within a multiplicity of differences of age, class, ethnicity, and other factors. A man's experience of gender is not only determined by his sex but also by the place he occupies within racial, ethnic, class, regional, institutional, and other categories in the society in which he lives. Therefore, we cannot speak of one masculinity but must recognize the existence of multiple masculinities defined contextually. Finally, gender identity should be put into a broader context. It is the expression of a sociopolitical order based on the control of strategic means of production and reproduction, including kinship structure, economic and political systems, and the symbolic power that defines the patriarchal order as "the real world" (Bourdieu 1999; Irigaray 1974).

As for Peruvian culture, the men studied all share the same general definition of masculinity, although the existing differences in regional cultures, class, social status, or stage in the life course lead to differing emphases on particular qualities or themes. The representations of masculinity of the interviewees appear in three different configurations that are not necessarily consistent with one another: the natural, the domestic, and the "outside" (public, street). The natural aspect of masculinity refers to men's sexual organs and physical strength. These characteristics are, according to them, the nucleus of masculinity because they are based on features that are defined as innate and unchangeable.

On the basis of these characteristics every boy is expected to develop daring and prove that he is sexually active. This task is accomplished by the primary socialization that takes place in the home, at school, and within the peer group. This process converts the natural facts of sexual and reproductive difference into courage and active sexuality (the qualities that make up virility). Virility is defined as that aspect of masculinity that cannot be tamed. Should virility be totally controlled, the man would run the risk of being emasculated and converted into being feminine. Femininity acts as a threat of contamination that is exorcised through the constant repudiation of all expressions of it in boys (Butler 1993). In this way the boundaries of masculinity are constituted, and an identity is produced that is opposed to that of women in the family (sisters, mother).

Outside space consists of the public and the street. The street is associated with virility and is a dimension of the outside world that is disorderly and opposed to the domestic realm. It is the arena of competition, rivalry, and seduction. From an early age the peer group transmits a masculine culture of the street that is opposed to domesticity and centered on the development of strength and virility. Peer groups transmit to boys one of the most important messages of masculine culture: to be a man signifies breaking some of the rules of the domestic world. The school occupies an intermediate space because it situates the boy in a condition of dependency (similar to his status in the family) and transmits public knowledge (indispensable for insertion in the world of work and politics), but to the extent that it brings together boys of the same age it constitutes a privileged space for the reproduction of peer culture.

As boys mature, they are expected to gradually leave behind the ideals of virility and enter adulthood. They stop being youngsters in order to become real men and enter the period of *hombría* (manliness). To Peruvian men, although virility is represented as natural and the core of masculinity, *hombría* is represented as a cultural product. It is something that every man must attain and requires responsibility, achievement in the outside space, and the recognition of one's spouse and peer group. The qualities associated with manliness belong to the spheres of both domesticity (family, marriage, fatherhood) and public life (work, politics). The domestic sphere corresponds to the realm of family and marriage and constitutes the nucleus of the affective. For Peruvian men to attain *hombría* and be worthy of respect, they must become husbands and fathers. It is in the family setting where men actually exercise authority, and in the end it is because they have to maintain a family that they strive to succeed in life. Nevertheless, domestic space is a contested arena.

Despite the fact that the public sphere is more visible and prestigious, in the home women occupy a structural position relatively equal to men because, from a domestic point of view, the home is defined as feminine, and everyday life is primarily under women's (mothers' and wives') rule. Although men hold the ultimate authority, especially with respect to matters related to the outside world, the house itself (especially the kitchen) is defined as feminine; therefore, when a man is inside its walls, he runs the risk of being feminized simply by his presence.

The public sphere sustains and legitimizes masculine predominance. It is the locus of achievement and should be regulated by honesty, efficiency, and contribution to the common good. Within this sphere work is represented as the key dimension of adult, masculine identity. To enter the world of work signifies the acquisition of the status of adulthood; it is a prerequisite for establishing a family and the principal source of social recognition. An adult man who fails to obtain a job that the peer group considers adequate and prestigious will lose the significance of any other form of personal achievement and become a *pobre diablo* (poor devil), someone lacking social recognition.

The Masculine Body

For the men interviewed in this study the body is composed of matter and appearance. The matter of the masculine body is also composed of two elements: sex (the sexual organs, represented by the penis) and strength (muscles, capacity). Appearance is made up of the face and adornments. The face is associated with the expression of inner qualities. Body appearance is what other people see and must be presentable and properly adorned to communicate the man's social worth. As Lucho, a forty-year-old working-class man from Lima, explains, "The first thing people look at is your face, your expression. Apart from that you have to be well dressed, presentable." The term *presentable* alludes to "who I am" in social terms, the acknowledgment that one expects from another to confirm one's own sense of masculinity or worth. In sum, there are two bodily dimensions: matter, whose seat is sex and strength, and appearance, which sends out signals through the face and external bodily adornments:

Matter (sexual organs, strength)
***
Appearance (face, adornment)

Strength, in turn, divides into qualities associated with virility and manliness. In terms of virility, strength relates to the attractiveness that emanates from hard, muscular bodies. Virility is centered in the sexual organs but is realized in the capacity to attract women because, according to the men interviewed, what arouses female desire is a muscular body that expresses strength. That is why men condition their bodies through sport and physical exercise, which stimulates, builds up, and expresses those aspects that make the male body attractive.

Strength is also transformed into manliness (capacity to work, respectability). Strength is the source of vigor (vigor = capacity to work [*vitalidad*]) and of courage (courage = self-confidence [*valentía*]), which enable a man to protect his family and command respect from other men. According to Rolando, a fifty-one-year-old working-class man, "Without physical strength, a man is nothing. When a man is physically strong he is respected in society. Nobody messes with him or tries to take advantage of him." That is because men provide (through their work) and protect and therefore occupy a senior position in the family.

Furthermore, strength, the quality that is the source of masculinity, dramatizes one of the great themes of the male identity: to be or not to be, to achieve or not to achieve. Although supposedly anchored in matter, strength must be achieved, improved, and communicated. Strength is not a quality that one is born with; it is acquired and accumulated. Thus, for Dante, a forty-two-year-old middle-class man from Cuzco, men exercise their bodies in order to build up muscles. As he relates, "For a time I lifted weights because I wanted to build up my pectoral muscles and arms. I was always measuring myself to see if I was getting bigger and things like that. I jog regularly and play soccer whenever I get the chance; or go swimming. I always look after my body to keep my stomach from growing. The main thing is to keep fit for when you go on long walks and things like that." Therefore, for Peruvian men, apparently the most natural trait, which is at the heart of male superiority, is also the most artificial and most closely associated with social qualities.

The emphasis on different bodily qualities varies according to stage of life. Young men talking about bodies focus on themes typical to their stage in life: courtship, competing with other men, and preparing themselves to embark on their working lives. The body sends out signals that show that a young man is attractive and capable of struggle and work.[2] Accordingly, young men are supposed to strive to acquire strength and vigor. For mature men strength has less to do with being attractive and more with capacity for work and vigor. According to Rolando, a fifty-one-year-old working-class man from Iquitos, "The important thing is to be strong. I feel relaxed because I'm completely healthy, which means I'm strong and I can work. My arms are strong. That is why the most important parts of the body are the arms and legs." On the other hand, different social classes attach varying importance to different attributes. Thus, middle-class men attach less priority to vigor, ascribe greater importance to intellectual and expressive capacities, and invest heavily in their appearance.

Beauty in the strictly corporal sense covers two aspects: the aesthetically beautiful and the attractive. Aesthetic beauty is associated with delicacy, softness, and fine features. This is a feminine trait because it rests on the opposition between delicacy/softness and strength/robustness/hardness. Women possess beauty (soft/delicate), whereas men are handsome (attractive/strong). Male beauty is called attractiveness and is directly associated with the strength expressed in a hard, muscular body, in firm thighs and buttocks. According to Homero, a twenty-seven-year-old working-class man from Lima, "For a man to be attractive, he must be over 5'7", have a good-size chest, good arms, good abdominal muscles, good legs, and a good butt. Because the girls say, 'Look at his butt!' or 'Look at those legs!' "

Seen from another perspective, beauty is associated with typical Caucasian looks and conforms to the guidebook of racial and class features on which the differences between the social orders in Peruvian society are built. Thus, for most of the men of the popular sector interviewed, a handsome man has white skin, blond hair, and blue eyes. However, this kind of beauty is founded on the attractiveness that emanates not from the body but from the face. In other words, it has to do with the harmony and softness of traits that are associated with femininity. As Ruso, a twenty-three-year-old working-class man from Lima, said, "A handsome man is [a] man who is attractive, who takes care of his appearance, who looks after his body. He'd be a man who is handsome and has bearing. But a man cannot be good looking. That's absurd. Only gringos [Caucasian men] are good looking."

By attributing this quality to light-skinned men, working-class men recognize the existence of racial hierarchies but invert them by claiming the virile attributes for themselves and feminizing the men of the dominant race. The men from the popular sectors, and those with Indian or black ethnic or racial features, can claim to be more masculine than the men of the dominant racial or ethnic groups. Their attractiveness lies in their bodies, in the very essence of their masculinity, whereas the attractiveness of men of other races resides in their beauty, a quality symbolically associated with femininity. Oscar, a forty-two-year-old working-class man from Lima, put it this way: "A woman would say that a good-looking man is tall, white, with light colored eyes, and blond because here [in Peru] we are racist."

Therefore, the body is where race and ethnic relations in Peruvian society play out against each other. The body not only reproduces but also revises and questions the hierarchical order of races. Through attribution of aesthetic superiority to the dominant race, racism is registered and internalized, whereas the subordinate position of Peruvian men is symbolically reversed by attributing subordination to femininity or to the foreigner. Just as the body could be considered a metaphor for the social world (Douglas 1973), the masculine body is a symbolic space where race and ethnic relations in Peruvian society are expressed, dramatized, and questioned.

The Public Sphere: Work and Politics

As men leave school and enter the labor market or follow college studies, they are expected to learn to be responsible, assume positions in the public sphere, and leave behind the juvenile world. Solid mutual help networks are also established during this period. They are based not solely on complicity and the solidarity of the peer group but also on issues in the public sphere. These masculine networks of solidarity are one of the means that, in the future, will sustain and guarantee the monopoly of adult men in the public sphere.

A high proportion of the forty-to-fifty-five age group identifies politics as a masculine activity and has participated in political groups or parties, neighborhood organizations, or work-related associations. According to those interviewed, participation widens their horizons and makes them feel part of a larger community than the family or the peer group; it makes them public men. For a significant proportion of middle-class men from Cuzco and Iquitos, participation in the development of local alternatives that will diminish the predominance of the capital city, Lima, over their regions is part of their life plans and of their regional and national identities. The participation of men from popular sectors in public life is centered on work-related and neighborhood organizations. Thus, levels of political participation reproduce regional and class hierarchies at the same time that they question them.

Nevertheless, politics, ideally the most noble of public activities, is also the most contradictory. Some of those interviewed see politics as corrupt and arbitrary; another group of men thinks that investing time and effort in public activities implies neglecting their work and thus their family obligations. In other words, individual interests and the moral indeterminateness of the public sphere tends to keep some men away from it. For such interviewees politics is something they engaged in during their juvenile period but gave up when they entered the world of work and family. Among the young adults interviewed in all three cities, the levels of political participation (in parties and unions) were considerably lower, reflecting the crisis in

Peruvian organizations of this type during the last decade and the decline in utopian views that sustained political discourses before the 1980s.

According to the men interviewed in this study, work is the key dimension of masculine identity. Entering the world of work signifies achieving the status of an adult, constitutes a prerequisite for establishing a family, and is the principal source of social recognition. For Peruvian men, to work means to have dignity, to be capable, and to be responsible: the three qualities characterizing manhood. To have dignity implies transcending the animal condition and becoming a human being. To be capable is to have the ability to transform nature and oneself and, above all, to obtain a place in outside (masculine) spaces. To be responsible means being able to maintain oneself and, especially, one's family. The latter is the ultimate justification for work and the foundation of masculine predominance over women and children. Men hold the authority within the family because they are supposed to maintain and provide for all its members. Therefore, work is the main foundation of masculine identity, in its version of manliness, because it transforms the male into a man, as opposed to an animal, guarantees him a place in masculine space, and allows him to become responsible and the head of a family. By extension, those who do not find a way to enter the world of work join those representing alternative, marginal versions of masculinity, such as criminals or those who are lazy. These last will be considered masculine insofar as they possess those manly qualities that constitute the core of masculinity, but they will never be respectable and in this sense will never be viewed as "true men."

Work is also represented as a masculine space par excellence because it is where a man meets his peers. As the areas for masculine socialization decline in adulthood, the place of employment progressively becomes the only homosocial context. It is an environment that establishes a counterpoint with the home, the feminine space in which men do not entirely belong and in which they are in a subordinate position to the wife or the mother. According to El Zambo, a fifty-three-year-old *albañil* (construction laborer) from Lima, "For me it means a lot of things. You work to bring something home and it takes your mind off things. At work, you go there, you clean up, you laugh, you tell jokes. Because in every home there are problems, but at work you have another kind of happiness, it's a second home."

Representations of work go through modifications during the life cycle. During youth, to work means attaining personal autonomy from the family of origin and is the key to entering the masculine world. To have a job allows a man to obtain the main symbol of manhood: the ability to provide. In addition, to have an income enables a young man to participate in the exchange of mutual invitations, in gatherings during which alcoholic beverages are consumed, and in other activities that allow him to obtain a place in men's networks. According to Sabio, a forty-year-old tourist guide from Cuzco,

> The first money earned is a landmark in the life of a young man. It was a great satisfaction because, well, I could look after myself. I could have my first money and could invite people with my own bucks. I felt that I was independent of my family. Suddenly it even gives you a certain authority. You know, you earn your money and then you are somebody. You can treat people, share, give, and to a certain degree, you can even influence certain situations.

Young people from popular sectors associate entering the labor market with adventure and new experiences that reaffirm their masculinity. Furthermore, earning money allows them to court women and to brag to their peers about their sexual or romantic exploits. For their part, middle-class young people delay their entry into the labor market because, as a rule, they attend university or a specialized academy. In this way they extend their youth. In contrast, young people from popular sectors obtain adult status earlier in life. I hypothesize that because they start to earn money earlier and thus become potential providers, their courting relationships more quickly lead to living together or getting married. This difference accentuates the gap between social classes because, whereas middle-class young people can invest in studies and in developing their networks of male friends, young men from popular sectors have to spend most of their resources providing for their families, thus jeopardizing their chances of obtaining better jobs in the future. This is more pronounced in Iquitos and Cuzco than in Lima, where there is a higher standard of living and more opportunities to go to college.

Just as there have been recent changes in the domestic sphere in Peru, the public sphere is also being redefined to accommodate women. Middle-class women are now getting college educations and entering the labor market, and popular-sector women have become important social actors. The interviews show a corresponding dramatic change in gender representations. All of the men interviewed agreed that women have as much of a right to work as men and thought that both men and women should contribute to household income. They are also conscious of job-related discrimination against women and consider it a leftover form of machismo.

Nevertheless, there are indications that not everything has changed. Men from popular sectors generally have jobs that require physical strength and geographical mobility. Both of these are identified with masculinity. In general, the greatest division of labor by gender can be found in jobs held by people from popular sectors. Middle-class men, on the other hand, identify masculinity with the capacity to command and with authority, characteristics that, according to them, are necessary for management positions. At the same time, the realms in which masculine solidarity networks are constructed that guarantee access to networks of influence, alliances, and support are reproduced through a masculine culture of sports, alcohol consumption, visits to whorehouses, or stories about sexual conquests. These mechanisms assure a monopoly of, or at least, differential access by, men to the public sphere and are a key part of the system of power in which masculinity is forged. Finally, as various researchers have already pointed out (Fuller 1997; Valdés and Olavarría 1998), current changes in gender relations have questioned the legitimacy of masculine dominance, but these have not necessarily involved as dramatic a challenge to men as they have for women with respect to the foundations of masculinity grounded in the identification of maleness with economic responsibility and authority over women and the family.

The Domestic Sphere: Matrimony and Fatherhood

According to the men interviewed, matrimony inaugurates adult life because when a man gets married, he breaks his dependency on his family of origin and acquires the symbols of manliness in its domestic version: control over the sexual favors of a woman and authority. His authority is based on his capacity to provide his family with the resources that are defined as masculine: material goods and social prestige. The woman offers sexual favors and domestic service. This relationship is defined as complementary and balanced because together the man and the woman make possible the family enterprise.

At the same time, according to the samples in all three cities, courtship and marriage relations are the place where gender, race, and class hierarchies are played out. The theme of interethnic relations occupies a central place for Peruvian middle-class men, for whom the affirmation of virility is associated with the sexual use of women from subordinate ethnic groups or classes, whereas matrimonial alliances are regulated by strict ethnic and class endogamy. The politics of sexual use of women from subordinate classes or groups tends to be less prevalent among middle-class young adults from Lima because of changes in erotic sensibility and the fact that the acceleration of the process of liberalization of sexual customs has increased the possibility of having sexual relations with young women in the same social group. In general, it is clear that gender politics is key for both the reproduction of social hierarchies and for their modification.

In urban Peru the marriage ceremony—which is always celebrated in the middle class and only sometimes in the popular sectors—marks the public celebration of the couple's rite of passage into adulthood, as well as the consolidation of affinal ties between the families of the couples who, by presiding over the ceremony, publicly accept the birth of these new relations and the public constitution of a new reproductive and productive alliance. For young Peruvian men the ceremony dramatizes not only a new identity as husband and head of household but also an abrupt break with adolescence. Young men must say good-bye to their friends, to bachelorhood, and to a time when they could freely roam about unattached. Their relationships with the street and with peers are redefined, and henceforth domestic life will take priority, as was made clear in this study when men related the changing character of their lives throughout adulthood.

In contrast to the middle-class sectors, where marriage marks men's entry into adult life and consecrates the masculinity of the initiates, among the popular sectors, especially in Cuzco and Iquitos, the process is slower and more gradual, as one of the two separates from her or his family and moves in with the family of the other. Only after an extended period does the couple establish a neolocal residence of its own.

Control over the sexuality of the spouse and authority over her and over the whole family is a key component of masculine identity in the men studied. In Peruvian culture, for men as well as for women, a man whose wife does not recognize his ultimate authority over her and over the family symbolically loses his masculinity and is said to be effeminate and tied to his wife's apron strings. In addition, recognition by the wife is never unconditional: it must be exchanged for respect. This makes the domestic sphere a domain where the basis of masculine identity can be most affirmed or most questioned.

From the domestic point of view Peruvian men define themselves as the providers and persons responsible for their families. As most of the interviewees stated, their principal goal in life was the progress of their families. Nevertheless, in their narratives it was evident that domestic values collided with masculine values because the men conceived masculine sexuality as a natural tendency that could not be totally controlled within marriage; if it were, it would run the risk of being feminized and thus emasculated. El Zambo commented in an interview: "As a man you have the right to be with a woman or to go drinking with friends, because if you don't, then people will laugh at you and say, 'This guy's no man,' or 'You're bossed around by your woman.' And my woman has never bossed me around."

On the other hand, men usually obtain the resources that they offer to their families in the public sphere, and to do so, they must invest time and resources to maintain their masculine solidarity networks. But hanging out with friends or taking care of business implies utilizing resources that, from a domestic perspective, might otherwise go to the family. As Manuel recounts, "Sometimes I decide to travel without asking my wife. When I get back I tell her, 'You know what? I had to go to such-and-such a place for work.' That usually gets her mad because she thinks I've gone off with another woman and that I have another home." These conflicts show that there is a constant and unrelieved tension between the virile and public aspects of masculinity and its domestic version. It is a credible hypothesis that in those families in which the wife can contribute public resources, this dichotomy is less sharp.

Fatherhood

According to the narratives of the men interviewed, paternity consecrates adult *hombría*. Every part of their lives is reinterpreted in light of this experience (Fuller 2000). When men stop being sons and become fathers, the "preferential tie" to friends is decisively cut, and the marriage is redefined and consolidated. In the end men's activities in the public sphere—work and politics—take on new meanings: fathers work and accumulate goods and prestige to provide and care for their families. At the same time, men acquire public identities on becoming the representatives of their families. This transformation represents a new stage in the life course, the point of perfect manhood when the men are no longer immature youths but rather men in the full sense of the word.

Despite the fact that the men interviewed unanimously described fathering as something they profoundly sought and as part of their life projects, this choice was not simply a matter of free will. In urban Peruvian culture those who are not parents never achieve the full status of adults. For this reason many describe how they have faced (and suffered) pressure from peers and family members to have children. Chochera, a forty-four-year-old worker from Lima stated,

> Children, whether boys or girls, make a man more of a man. Because you feel more . . . more mature, more of a man, like something in the eyes of others. For example, I have a close friend who lives here. He's been married for many years and he has no children. And there are those who will tell him, "Listen, man, you don't have any kids. You can't anymore. So it's like you're not here, you're not part of the world, you don't do anything, and there's no meaning to you." And others will say, "Yeah, I belong here. I have a son. I have a daughter."

Thus in urban Peruvian culture a man who is not a father cannot be a bona fide man because his virility and his capacity to contribute to the social order—two fundamental axes of masculinity—are in question.

In other words, for all the men interviewed, the manner in which the capacity to have children is translated into fatherhood in its public and domestic dimensions is responsibility. To be a father is not to procreate but rather to socially assume the bond with a son or a daughter and to dedicate oneself to forging this tie, that is, to give it material, social, and moral substance. To become a man, virility must be accompanied by responsibility.

The father figure is defined as the one who determines the destiny of his children. Fathers who are present and provide for their families guarantee future success for their children, whereas those who abandon their families condemn their children to poverty. Thus, the father is a contradictory figure because his presence is defined as crucial, but the possibility of his absence is always latent. The latter experience marks the personal history of a good number of the men interviewed. The motives of these fathers for abandoning families were infidelity, extreme domestic violence, and moving to get a job. Thus, even though the father represents public values and provides strategically important material and symbolic goods for the family, the nature of his sexuality, the possibility of abuse of power implicit in his position as an authority figure within the family, and his integration into the public sphere are opposed to his paternal role. This opposition is more evident among popular sectors because there are fewer family controls over the behavior of men, legal controls are less enforceable, and levels of poverty and labor instability can negatively affect the geographic stability of men and their capacity to support the family with resources from the public sphere. Popular-sector men from Iquitos, who had the highest level of fatherless households in the sample, also displayed the greatest contradiction between a high value attached to paternity and an intense hostility toward their own fathers.

Contradictory Identities

The opposition between the domestic sphere and masculine sphere (street, public) is expressed in the coexistence of three parallel discourses: the domestic discourse, which emphasizes reciprocal complementarity and solidarity in the conjugal enterprise; the discourse of virility, which emphasizes masculine predominance, solidarity among men, and inter-gender hostility; and the public discourse, which identifies manhood with the monopoly of the public sphere. This counterpoint between discourses that are often opposed to each other is one of the most important themes of masculine identity in the samples studied. Each age group emphasized different aspects of the global masculine culture. Young adults stressed solidarity and competition among men, the importance of being accepted in masculine spaces, and affirmation of their own virility. Adult men stressed their marriage duties and marriage conflicts, paternity, and recognition they had obtained in the public sphere (work, politics).

According to the men interviewed in this study, work is the key dimension of masculine identity. Work is also represented as a supremely masculine space because through work men accumulate the social and productive capital that represents their primary contributions to their families, thus allowing them to gain recognition from their peers and guarantee their gender dominance.

However, work is also the sphere of gender relations that has undergone the most dramatic changes during the last decades. All the men in the groups studied have been influenced by new discourses that question male predominance and show themselves to be relatively open to the idea of equality of the genders, especially when it comes to education and jobs, both of which seem to be well on their way to degendering in Peru.[3] Nevertheless, representations of masculinity in all the populations studied are based on presuppositions that imply the authority of men over women, the identification of men with the public sphere, and the repudiation of femininity. In sum, two tendencies coexist: one leading toward the growing degendering of public space and the other based in representations of virility, intragender solidarity, and masculine predominance.

According to the men interviewed, matrimony inaugurates adult life. From the domestic point of view the man defines himself as the person mainly responsible for the family. Nevertheless, domestic values collide with masculine values. This implies that there is a constant and unresolved tension between the virile, public aspects of masculinity and its domestic version.

The middle-class men and young adults demonstrated evidence of having been influenced in the direction of greater equality by changing conceptions of women's rights and courtship behavior. At the same time, in Peruvian society courtship and marriage relations are where gender, race, and class hierarchies are played out because the affirmation of virility is associated with the sexual use of women from subordinate ethnic groups or classes, whereas matrimonial alliances among middle-class sectors are regulated by strict ethnic and class endogamy.

In the three cities paternity consecrates adult *hombría,* and all the men interviewed share a highly idealized notion of fatherhood. Nonetheless, the father figure is frequently the object of general criticism because fathers' activities set in motion many of the contradictions personified by masculinity and the gender system overall in Peru.

Most generational differences stem from the fact that youth and adults occupy different stages of the life cycle and, thus, emphasize different aspects of the masculine global culture. Youth tend to privilege camaraderie and competition among men, the importance of locating oneself in masculine spaces, and affirming one's virility. In contrast, adult men focus their stories on marital responsibilities and conflicts, fatherhood, and earning public recognition in areas like work and politics.

However, young men show some differences in erotic sensibility and their views concerning the rights of women. An important proportion of youth reject the separation between sex and affection that is characteristic of masculine sexual practices. In a similar fashion young men frequently think that it is no longer possible to impose on women controls that were considered normal in previous generations. Furthermore, the great majority of them agree that men and women have the same political and labor rights and that it would be wrong to believe otherwise. These changes may be related to the fact that they have been more exposed than adult men to discourses regarding the rights of women.

Nonetheless, such critical attitudes exist simultaneously with definitions of masculinity that are identified with domination in the public sphere, authority in the family, and control of female sexuality. To reject these principles would require calling into question the foundations of their gender identity. Thus young men are confronted with challenges whose outcomes are difficult to forecast because the changes occurring in the position of women affect all facets of their lives but come into conflict with the corporal and emotional underpinnings of their manhood.

Notes

1. Peruvian society inherited a social order imposed during the three centuries of Spanish domination. The colonial society was conceived as a product of conquerors (Spanish) and conquered (Indians). Outside the Spanish and Indian republics, without a precise place in the dual order, were the *mestizos* and the slave populations of African origin. After the wars for independence the juridical and political system supporting the colonial classificatory system disappeared, but the ethnic and racial boundaries continued to influence social relationships and were reinforced by Western cultural and economic domination. Each city reproduces these hierarchies at the local level, but on a national scale Lima is also considered more Westernized, whereas Cuzco is associated with Quechua-speaking (Inca) populations and Iquitos with native peoples of the Amazon region.

2. Twenty-three (of sixty) young men underscored the importance of having an athletic body. Of these, seventeen were from the working class and five from the middle class. Only ten (of sixty) adult men stressed this quality.

3. *Degendering* is defined by Gutmann (1996) as a "decentering of the perceived wisdom that associates practices especially with men or women" (190).

References

Bourdieu, Pierre. 1999. *La domination masculine*. Paris: Seuil.

Butler, Judith. 1993. *Bodies That Matter: On the Discursive Limits of Sex*. New York: Routledge.

Douglas, Mary. 1973. *Poder y peligro: Un análisis de los conceptos de contaminación y tabu*. Mexico City: Siglo XXI.

Fuller, Norma. 1997. *Identidades masculinas: Varones de clase media en el Perú*. Lima, Peru: Pontificia Universidad Católica del Perú.

———. 2000. "Significados y prácticas de paternidad entre varones urbanos del Perú." In *Paternidades en América Latina*, ed. Norma Fuller, 35–89. Lima, Peru: Pontificia Universidad Católica del Perú.

Gutmann, Matthew C. 1996. *The Meanings of Macho: Being a Man in Mexico City*. Berkeley: University of California Press.

Irigaray, Luce. 1974. *Speculum, d'autre femme*. Paris: Les Editions de Minuit.

Valdés, Teresa, and José Olavarría. 1998. "Ser hombre en Santiago de Chile: A pesar de todo, un mismo modelo." In *Masculinidades y equidad de género en América Latina*, ed. Teresa Valdés and José Olavarría, 12–35. Santiago, Chile: FLACSO.

STANLEY BRANDES

Drink, Abstinence, and

Male Identity in Mexico City

■ ■ ■

This essay, concerning an Alcoholics Anonymous group in a poor district of Mexico City, analyzes a social setting in which members are forced to reflect on the multiple meanings of masculinity. The group, which I call Moral Support, is made up entirely of working-class men who migrated to the city a generation ago in an attempt to improve their economic circumstances. Each of the men suffered serious emotional and physical trauma as a consequence of excessive drink. After years of vain attempts to control their habit they found relief through membership in Alcoholics Anonymous.

For these men, as for many others in Mexico, abstinence from drink presents acute problems. Throughout large segments of Mexican society, alcoholic drink is an inherent part of the male role. When men abandon drink radically, as membership in Alcoholics Anonymous requires, they are forced to question their own gender identity. For this reason, in Moral Support, as in other A.A. groups of its kind, much of the therapeutic work involves testing and manifesting one's manhood. Through personal stories delivered at group meetings, the men both critique and affirm traditional definitions of masculinity. The thrice-weekly meetings allow for, and even demand, the individual and collective assessment and assertion of male identity.

Consider, first, some of the ways alcohol defines the male role in Mexico. Christine Eber, a specialist on gender and alcohol, finds evidence that from ancient times through the colonial period men were given "more leeway to drink" than women (1995, 23). This pattern has persisted to the present day. Drink is virtually a prescribed feature of religious ritual and ritualized encounters of all kinds in which men frequently participate. The most obvious examples come from the religious realm. Throughout Mexico male drinking is and long has been essential to the ritual process (e.g., Brandes 1988, 174–78; Madsen and Madsen 1979; Taylor 1979, 61; Warren 1985, 92). In fact, this relationship extends beyond Mexico to much of Latin America (e.g., Doughty 1979, 73–74; Heath 1985; Leacock 1979; Nash 1985, 208). At Mass it is the priest—without exception a man—who takes communion by drinking wine. During rites of passage, particularly baptisms and weddings, it is principally the male celebrants who publicly exchange bottles of liquor and consume them as a formal part of the ritual process. Ingham (1986, 151) states that in the central Mexican town of Tlayacapan, located less than two hours from Mexico City, "drinking is a typically male behavior. Women may drink a little at fiestas, but rarely to intoxication, and what sipping they do usually takes place apart from the men in their lives. Men, by contrast, may drink heavily at fiestas, during Carnival, on weekends, or just about any time, for that matter." At the fiesta of the Tastoanes in Zapopan, on the outskirts of Guadalajara, male clown figures who are able to perform their role to the spectators' satisfaction are "rewarded with a jug of *huariche*, which is a local term for hard liquor, usually mescal or tequila" (Nájera-Ramírez 1997, 19). The traditional ceremonial role of male folk healers and public officials in Mitla, in the state of Oaxaca, "lends itself to continuous drinking" (Parsons 1936, 187).

Male drink routinely occurs during life-cycle rituals and community fiestas. In rural Mexico hired musicians, who are almost always male, receive food and alcoholic drink in return for playing at family and community celebrations (e.g., Foster 1983, 138; Nutini 1984, 152). During All Saints and All Souls Days (November 1–2) family members place items favored by the deceased on gravesites and home altars. Liquor often figures among these offerings in altars dedicated to deceased male relatives.

This is never the case with females. Even if it is known that a deceased mother or sister had favored a particular alcoholic beverage, the family would try to hide rather than announce that preference. Public display could only bring shame on the deceased and her relatives. During community fiestas male cargo holders, or *mayordomos* (religious and/or civil officeholders, who assume these posts on a rotating basis), are expected to distribute and imbibe large quantities of alcohol. A particularly rich anthropological literature describes the duties of cargo holders in the Indian villages of highland Chiapas, where alcohol occupies a central ritual role (e.g., Bricker 1973; Cancian 1965; Nash 1985; Vogt 1993). In Chiapas, too, legal disputes are often settled through the presentation of bottles of liquor by the offender to the victim. With the exception of litigation between long-married spouses, it is always men who give and receive alcoholic beverages in these transactions (Collier 1973, 24–27, 100–103).

Mexican men demonstrate friendship through drink. Lomnitz (1977, 175–80) and Gutmann (1996, 177) both show that alcoholic consumption is intrinsic to male friendship in Mexico City. Throughout Mexico, when boys are young and prohibited from imbibing alcohol, they often play at being drinking buddies. Girls never play at this game. As teenagers or newlyweds forming friendships, men sometimes say to one another, "We'll have to get drunk together some day!" It would be highly unusual for a woman to make such a statement. Gutmann (1996, 173) observes in Mexico City that "Every day, and even more so on holidays, men are found sipping *las copas*—alcoholic beverages—in the streets." He adds a cautionary note, however: "What of those men who were at home and sober throughout that day? Were those men, at least implicitly, less manly than those who were drunk in the streets?" (174). The answer is, of course, "No." But drinking in the streets is a normal, predictable occurrence for men, whereas for women it is likely to be scandalous.

Given the centrality of alcohol in the life of the Mexican male, it is no wonder that problem drinking is the leading cause of death among males in the so-called productive years of life (35–65). Mortality from alcohol results directly through cirrhosis or indirectly through accidents and homicide (Menéndez 1990, 9). Moreover, data show that poor men—particularly rural migrants to the city who work in construction and other manual jobs—suffer the most from alcohol excesses (Menéndez and Di

Pardo 1996, 173). However, these problems are not unique to the city. In the state of Morelos, Romanucci-Ross found a strong correlation linking masculinity, violence, and drink: "That men are more involved in violence and killing reflects not only the divergent codes of behavior . . . but also the exclusive right of men to non-ceremonial drinking and drunkenness (women drink moderately and only at fiestas). The tie-in between aggressive violent behavior and alcoholism is nearly complete, in my opinion— that is, the aggressor is almost always either a heavy drinker or an alcoholic and is in most cases intoxicated when the aggression is committed" (Romanucci-Ross 1973, 136).

In Mexico, as in most parts of the world, drink and drunkenness are certainly not exclusive to men. Nor does a man necessarily lose his male identity if he abstains from alcoholic drink (Gutmann 1996, 173–95). However, manhood and drinking are closely enough linked in ideology and observable behavior that men—at least, most men in the Mexican laboring classes—come to associate imbibing and inebriation with male identity. In Mexico it is easy for a man to question his gender identity should he decide to give up alcohol once and for all. An analysis of Moral Support meetings shows how one group of working-class men tries to manage this problem.

Officially, no Alcoholics Anonymous group can or should claim social exclusivity based on gender or any other aspect of social identity. Alcoholics Anonymous meetings always begin with the proclamation, "Alcoholics Anonymous is a group of men *and women* [emphasis mine] who share their mutual experience, strength, and hope to resolve their common problem and help others to recuperate from alcoholism. The only requirement to be a member of A.A. is the desire to stop drinking." Nonetheless, in Mexico members overwhelmingly are men. In 1991 a study team reported that men constitute 91 percent of the A.A. members in Mexico City (Rosovsky, Casanova, and Pérez 1991, 138). "In the rest of the country," states the senior author, "this proportion is even bigger" (1991, 1). The 1991 survey demonstrates that the number of women in A.A. has increased slightly over time; but, as the study team laments, "there still persist discriminatory attitudes of machismo and paternalism towards women, which makes women's participation difficult" (142). In a recent overview of women's drinking patterns Margarita Vega proposes that Mex-

Man in Mexico City gesturing. "Do you want a drink?"
Photograph by Matthew C. Gutmann.

ican women need a therapeutic outlet other than Alcoholics Anonymous: "A woman who has developed alcoholism is more alone, so that she requires more social support. Psychologically it has been found that women who arrive at A.A. bring with them different emotional problems: they feel more guilt than do men, their self-esteem is more affected, and these necessities need to be taken into account" (Vega 2000, 4A). Moreover, it should be noted that the demographic profile within Mexico of members in A.A. is not radically different from that of other countries with respect to gender. Mäkelä et al. (1996, 171) state, for example, that "men in all countries have constituted and still constitute the majority of members."

When working-class men join an Alcoholics Anonymous group in Mexico City, they in essence substitute one group of male friends for another. Lomnitz (1977, 175–80) found that in Mexico City during the 1970s, male construction workers developed exclusively male friendships.

They called their friends *cuates* (twins). Lomnitz found that above all "the act of getting drunk" (176) brings about this bond because "getting drunk together represents a high degree of trust" (177). As one of Lomnitz's informants put it, "When you are sober you cannot say the kinds of things you can say when drunk; these are your truths" (176). Another man told her, "I do not drink so I don't have any friends" (177). (In August 2000 a man from Matehuala in the state of San Luis Potosí told me exactly the same thing.)

Now, a generation later than Lomnitz's study, the men of Moral Support use the same terminology as did Lomnitz's informants. Repeatedly, in personal stories, recorded life histories, and daily conversation, group members refer to former male friends from their days as active alcoholics as *cuates*. They distinguish *cuates* from their new male companions, those from Alcoholics Anonymous in general and Moral Support in particular, who are known as *compañeros*. *Cuates* emerge in life history narratives as evil creatures, luring their so-called friends into cantinas and seducing them to have yet another drink. *Compañeros,* on the other hand, represent recovery from the insalubrious effects of alcohol.

Given that Alcoholics Anonymous proclaims alcoholism to be a mortal illness, the men of Moral Support think of their former *cuates* as nothing short of harbingers of death. David speaks bitterly of the treatment he received from former drinking companions when he tried to distance himself from them: "I had to withstand humiliation from my buddies because then they'd see me and [say] 'Hey, come over here and have a drink.' " His response (a common one) was to refuse on the grounds that "I'm on medication." But the friends would taunt him by accusing him of being cowardly: "It's that they'll hit you. . . . [They say] you're afraid . . . [that] your wife will scold you . . . [or] you've become an *hermano*," that is, a "brother," or Protestant fanatic:

> They think that because I stopped drinking that I'm a Protestant or I'm an Evangelist, etc. You know? So that's what I had to suffer, because it's unbearable. They're unbearable things, that they're just poking and poking you with the intention of making you fall back down, fall back into drinking again. . . . Because they told me over and over, "No, it's that those at home will punch you" or "they'll scold you" or "you're

a . . ." or "You've become an *hermano*" or "repentant drunk," you know, things like that. Because, those people didn't get it, they didn't understand. And by then I more or less could envisage that what I was saving was my skin, it was my life itself. That's what I was saving, without worrying about theirs, because they wanted to live like that. But I didn't want to live like that anymore. I wanted to release myself from the hell into which I had sunk, that mud hole that was alcoholism, that quicksand from which so many times you desperately want to escape and can't.

After more than a decade of sobriety David still has to negotiate invitations to join former buddies in a drink. But, as he says, "It's stupid, for example, that I as [a member of] Alcoholics Anonymous, instead of seeking out beneficial friendships, should enter a cantina. Because, thank God, I don't even step foot in a cantina anymore. . . . That's not my scene."

Renaldo, at age sixty-four and with seventeen years of sobriety, recalls that he started drinking when he was sixteen. At first he would drink alone, frequenting cantinas located in the closest large town to where he lived. All this occurred in his native state of Querétaro, immediately after the government opened the first highway leading from the small *ranchería* of Comalones to the nearby capital city:

Querétaro was far from where I lived, far from Comalones. More or less, hmmm, walking it was more or less two hours from there. And, well, when they opened the highway—because there weren't any highways before—we didn't know anything about busses at that time, we didn't know what a car was, we didn't know what a radio was, nothing, nothing. All of that was, hmmm, as they say, dead; it didn't exist. It was only later that we started to see all of that, when they opened the road. . . . And that was when I started to go to the cantina.

The little *ranchería* of Comalones, as it turns out, had cantinas of its own. But Renaldo would walk the two hours to Querétaro to avoid being detected. "I didn't like to drink there [in Comalones] because I was ashamed. I was ashamed that they would see me drinking and so, in order for them not to see me, well, I went all the way to town. I'd come back late at night." At age sixteen, states Renaldo,

I started to go, but they didn't let me in, they threw me out. They didn't let minors enter the cantina and I asked permission to enter. I told them I was going to take a piss, right? But then, while I was there, I'd have to have a tequila. Right? In my hometown, they drank tequila a lot. And, well, that was where I started. Afterwards, when I grew up, they let me in. Once I was eighteen years old they let me enter the cantinas and . . . that was where I started to get caught up in alcoholism. . . . And, well, I started to like it. . . . Actually, when I started to drink, I didn't have friends. I was alone, right? Afterwards, I needed company to drink. Afterwards, I got together with friends to drink and drink and, well, *echar relajo,* as they say . . . that is, to be laughing there in the cantina, to be, hmmm, playing, playing pool.

Renaldo, like others in Moral Support, draws a picture of drinking as a social act. Once he had come of age, his solitary drinking ended, and he began to binge on drink with friends. As a migrant to Mexico City, already married, Renaldo began to drink even more heavily. "That was when I started to drink, hmmm, with fervor—you know? Because here is where I got together with people who were alcoholics and, well, I ended up being that way afterwards. They were *alcoholizados* [literally, alcoholized, i.e., hooked on alcohol], good at drinking and, well, I started to hang around with them."

David and Renaldo are typical of the men in Moral Support. Friendship—specifically male friendship—was the foundation of their drinking careers, just as friendship is what helped them to escape. When David first attended an A.A. meeting, he fought against the program:

I thought that there [at the group meeting] they were going to give me an injection, you know, to tell me that this is how you go about stopping to drink until you definitively stop. But, no, it was completely the opposite. They told me that if you want to quit drinking, come and listen, join with us, join up with the triumphant ones. I didn't understand anything, I didn't understand a thing, because . . . because I was blocked by my alcoholism—mentally blocked, physically destroyed, morally undone . . . and, economically, don't even mention it! . . . So I started going [to meetings] with this friend and little by little it started to affect me. Of course, I had to discipline myself, I had to make an effort, I had to make the sacrifice not to hang out with the people I used to hang out with, because the people who I used to drink with . . . of course, I had to separate myself from them for a reasonable time, you know.

Now an established member of Alcoholics Anonymous, David looks back to his initial encounters in A.A. He recalls the enduring validity of his *compañeros'* words: "Here [in A.A.] we're going to help you; here we're going to give you the weapons to defend yourself out there."

Scholars have pointed out that Alcoholics Anonymous meetings can become as addictive to the recovering alcoholic as was alcohol itself. One compulsion is replaced by another; the person who successfully abstains possesses a "gift for substituting people for alcohol" (Lomnitz 1977, 259). The men of Moral Support tell of experiences that confirm this analysis but only partially. The Alcoholics Anonymous group in fact becomes a substitute not so much for alcohol as for the former drinking buddies. One group of men replaces another. To carry out the Alcoholics Anonymous program properly requires a great deal of time away from home. Moral Support meetings occupy three evenings a week. Several of the men attend two groups, which meet on alternate days, which means that these men are out virtually every night of the week. Whether drinking or sober, the men of Moral Support like to establish connections with other men, who relate to alcohol in the same way they do. The quality of life at home for these men might well improve under the influence of the A.A. program. However, the actual number of hours they spend with the family is probably not much greater than it was prior to group membership.

There is no doubt, however, that the men of Moral Support perceive Alcoholics Anonymous as the salvation of the family. David, whose own family was torn asunder by his drinking problems, expresses the A.A. ideal:

I told you about *compañeros* who have arrived [at A.A.] almost destroyed, who almost don't have their lives anymore. And now, thanks to A.A., which exists not just in our country but throughout the world, we have that great hope to save ourselves from the claws of alcoholism, to be good citizens, to be good spouses, to be good children, to be good workers. So this is what you win from being a member of Alcoholics Anonymous. They move you from one place to a more positive place. . . . Above all, as I told you a while ago, the family [of an A.A. member] lives in tranquility, now that the wife is no longer wondering what time her drunkard will arrive home, in what state he's going to return—if he isn't going to come home beaten up and batter his own wife and kids. Or if he'll bring home money for the household expenses. Because . . . a drunk can't fulfill his responsibilities.

To fulfill responsibilities is one of the great precepts of Alcoholics Anonymous. And one's duty to family members is paramount. Of course, says David, men sometimes lure their wives into drink. "That is a grave error," he proclaims, "because afterwards it's not going to be one alcoholic, one drunk, but two. And if these two are heads of a family, it will be hell for the kids, a life of trauma, of sadness, of tears."

David's marriage, like that of so many alcoholics, was destroyed by his drinking. When drunk, he mistreated his wife badly. After joining A.A. he tried to win her back, but she was already lost to him. During most of my two-year field stint, the couple shared a house and kitchen, arranging their schedules to assure minimal contact. If they encountered one another within the confines of their tiny home, they did not even speak. Eduardo had a similarly sad experience with a common-law wife. She left him because of his alcoholic episodes, despite the fact that she had just become pregnant. Eduardo says:

So we broke up. She left my house, she left her poor home. I am from the state of Zacatecas; my *pueblo* is Jaramillo. So, well, with that woman I had a girlfriend. And . . . in reality, you know, it makes me so sad to remember that. Because all I did was ruin the life of that poor woman, of my wife. In reality, my intentions were good. But alcohol destroyed me completely. . . . Afterwards, she broke up with me, you know, she had to work for a while. I didn't give her alimony, because they didn't force me to and I didn't want to, me being the asshole [*culero*] that I am. I was angry because she had left my house, you know, and she only came looking for me after she had the child. So then afterwards she met another man and I think they live around here in Mexico City, I don't know where. The problem is that, from what I learned, what they told me, right?, that guy treated her really badly. Because then she became alcoholic, too, and she drank and she drank. They fought a lot. He beat her.

Eduardo describes himself as neglectful and irresponsible, attitudes born of his drinking career. His story is filled with images of violence. He harbors lingering feelings of hostility and self-recrimination. By official A.A. standards these feelings are sure indications that his drinking problem is only partly resolved, despite periods of sobriety.

The men of Moral Support are supremely conscious that alcohol abuse once exacted a terrible emotional and physical toll on the women closest to their hearts—above all, mothers and spouses, who suffered in ways very similar to Kaja Finkler's "women in pain" (Finkler 1994). The men of Moral Support differ from many other Mexican men in that they are openly repentant. Participation in Alcoholics Anonymous provides an outlet for their remorse, a space in which the expression of regret is interpreted as strength rather than weakness.

In the mid-1990s Eduardo experienced a terrible loss when his sister and mother died within six months of one another. Just afterward, Eduardo was able to tell me,

> Recently, in my last drinking bout, [I lost] my mom, right? My sister and my mom. . . . Well, I have felt bad, because once you lose the moral support of a mother—right?—of a sister, well, you feel bad. Especially with how much I made my mother suffer, you know, with my drinking habit. . . . Oh, I felt so bad. I would have celebrated eleven years in A.A. and, well, I relapsed again. And who bore the burden? My children, my woman, my mom, my *mamá*, because she was the one who took care of me, too—so much! On the eighth of November my mom dies. . . . Physically I didn't hurt my mother. But, morally, it was another story. Morally, I was always drunk. And she wondering if I had eaten or not, if I was drinking or not, where I was sleeping, what I was doing. All of that drained her, robbed her of sleep, robbed her of well being. And that's why they say that an alcoholic is a thief. By nature a thief. Because he robs tranquility, he robs his family of their sleep.

When Eduardo spoke to the group of his remorse, his voice cracked and he burst into tears, an indication, in the context of A.A., of sincerity, courage, and strength.

Among working-class Mexican men, like those in Moral Support, sobriety and the abdication of arbitrary power over spouses might well be considered effeminate. Whatever they feel inside, it is rare for men to express guilt openly over mistreatment of women. In Alcoholics Anonymous, by contrast, men can abstain from drink and ask women in public for forgiveness without necessarily casting their masculinity in doubt. In A.A. men come to realize, in David's words, that "if the head of [a] household is drunk, there is unhappiness, there is suffering, there are tears, there is illness, there is misery. All that is what alcoholism produces. Alcoholism destroys homes."

One of the main tasks of Alcoholics Anonymous is to help recovering alcoholics overcome internal conflicts and come to terms with their past. Some men, however, use the podium to assert their continued dominance over women. Raúl provides one such case. Raúl, a shoe repairman, is a stocky man about forty-five years old. He is neatly groomed but driven by an aggressive, combative impulse unlike anyone else's in the group. During my months with Moral Support Raúl faded in and out of meetings. On one occasion, after a lengthy absence, he was called to the podium and spent most of his personal history condemning his wife. The two of them had had a bad argument, he said, so he abandoned her and his children for eight months. That experience taught her a lesson, he said. She had to go begging from her brothers and sisters for beans and tortillas. He had warned her, "Your brothers and sisters are not going to support you, because they have their own children to take care of." He seemed pleased to report that his prediction proved right. They did not provide for their abandoned sister. At this point Raúl displayed the cruel, almost sadistic, side of his personality. Instead of eating "nice cuts of beef" on Sundays, he said, the children ate *"puros chilaquiles"* (only *chilaquiles*), a poor man's dish, made of leftover, dried-out tortillas. Rather than putting on new clothes at the beginning of the school year, the children wore hand-me-downs from their cousins, secondhand clothes and shoes. That taught her a lesson, Raúl repeated. He seemed as unconcerned about his children's welfare as about the well-being of his wife. To end his tale, Raúl reported that he and his wife have reunited. He had taught her a thing or two. (They have since separated, this time, it seems, permanently.)

Raúl, as I have said, is an exception. Others in Moral Support speak with deep remorse about the injuries caused to parents, wives, and children. Through involvement in A.A. they hope to redefine family relationships so

Teenage Alcoholics Anonymous poster in Mexico
City. "Do you suffer from a drinking problem? There
is a solution!!!!" Photograph by Matthew C. Gutmann.

as to maximize equality and mutual respect between spouses. This endeavor involves a redefinition of what it means to be a man. The men of Moral Support know that, as recovering alcoholics, they must abdicate as authoritarian rulers at home. They should share in household tasks and take responsibility for their children. To signal this new relationship, the men shun the common Mexican label *esposa* to refer to the wife. Instead, they refer pointedly to their wives as *compañeras*. This designation, they believe, automatically elevates their wives to a position of equality.

In fact, by using the term *compañera* the men symbolically conflate all categories of female partners. The term *compañera* refers without distinction to women who are legally married and to those who live in *uniones libres* (common-law unions). Long-term romantic companions are also potentially *compañeras*. Formal church marriage is normally more prestigious than a common-law marriage and results in a man acquiring a wife, or *esposa*. Hence, to substitute the term *compañera* for *esposa* is symbolically to eradicate a two-tier system, elevating those men who are formally married by a priest above those who are not. The term *compañera* helps to produce the common denominator that the men believe to be ideal.

The term *compañera* also equates the female partner with the male *compañero* in A.A. Symbolically, this usage elevates a man's significant other to a status beyond that of sexual partner, wife, and mother. It transforms her symbolically into a kind of friend, placing her on an equal footing with the men in the group. Likewise, to equate one's *compañeros* in Moral Support with the *compañera* at home is to convert the men into quasi kin. Symbolically, they become a kind of family. In the space of six months Eduardo suffered the death of two close female relatives: "my sister died the 26th of June, my mother the 8th of November," he says. "I was left alone and today I only have my *compañeros* from A.A. who are all of you—my friends, my true friends." The men of Moral Support regularly equate friendship with family. As reflected in the use of the terms *compañero* and *compañera*, friends become like family, family like friends.

At the conclusion of my fourth group meeting, when I announced to the group my desire to carry out the present research, David offered words of encouragement. "You are welcome into the group," he assured me. "You have a family here, because we are like a family." The men of Moral Support do more than substitute one group of males for another when they join A.A. For at least some of the men the group is a surrogate family.

Recovering alcoholics like the men of Moral Support cannot bolster their male identity by sharing drinks. In an abrupt reversal of norms, which George Vaillant interprets in psychoanalytic terms as a reaction formation (Vaillant 1995, 243), these men have come to consider drinking and getting drunk as the antithesis of manliness. That which they previously loved and cherished is now hated and rejected. Vaillant considers this emotional turnaround "essential for abstinence" (243). When it fails to occur, there exists a high risk of relapse.

Although the men of Moral Support can no longer express their masculinity through drink, alternatives are open to them. One is to assert a redefinition of masculinity that excludes alcoholic consumption. David requires constant reassurance. Each time he delivers a personal story, he states that Alcoholics Anonymous breeds *"hombres de verdad, hombres enteros, hombres íntegros"* (real men, whole men, complete men). He and several other men in the group use the podium to declare, *"Soy manso, pero no soy menso"*—that is, "I am tolerant and understanding but not cowardly." Arturo, whose small frame seems at odds with his strong will and fearless assertiveness, explained this formulaic expression to me. You have to be tolerant, he said, but you can't let people step on you. When people try to take advantage of you, you have to know how to *sacar las uñas* (show your claws). Arturo claims to suffer from *neurosis*, his term for uncontrollable anger. On several occasions, in disputes over policy issues, he stomped out of the meeting room angrily. Arturo is definitely not *menso* (cowardly), although his impetuousness tends to undermine his political effectiveness within the group.

I sat with David one morning on a threadbare sofa in the tiny parlor of the house he shares with his estranged wife. He mentioned that before entering A.A. he used to be a *machista* (sexist). I asked him to explain.

> Look, being a *macho* in our country . . . well, you hear much said about Mexican *machismo*, the *macho*. The *macho* is a person with no interest in feelings; he's the kind of person who is interested in nothing but what he does and he says. And, really, that can't be. . . . He likes to give orders rather than to do something himself, far from providing an example by putting his own words into practice. . . . And, before arriving at A.A., I was that person. I only liked to give orders, to say, "How come you haven't swept? Why haven't you dusted? Why haven't you made the bed?" Or, "Bring me this" or "Take this for me" or "do this thing for me." And, really, that's wrong.

David clearly has a capacity to empathize with women's heavy lot. Empathy was an emotion that he lacked before entering Alcoholics Anonymous.

David believes that since entering A.A. he has changed his ideas and habits. Living alone, separated from his wife, has forced him to learn to take care of himself:

> As I told you, it's not easy to live alone; it isn't agreeable to live alone. Take me, for example. I'm alone. At this moment, having your com-

pany serves me well, but, apart from this, I am happy. I feel happy because, as I mentioned to you, I go about my chores here, sweeping, watering the plants, dusting, washing clothes. Before I never did these things; it was because of my *machismo* that I didn't do them. I thought that chores were only for women and this is a serious error. . . . To think that chores are only for women to do is a grave mistake.

Being a man, to David, has little to do with abstaining from traditionally feminine activities like housework. Male identity seems to derive from competence at taking care of oneself. This opinion represents a radical departure from his former point of view.

Personal stories, which tend to ramble from topic to topic, regularly touch on the theme of household work. The redefinition of wives and live-in partners as *compañeras* implies a new sexual division of labor. Hence, the men claim that they collaborate at chores in a way that they never did before joining A.A. It is clear that a few of the men are happily married, a significant improvement over the family strife of their drinking years. Genaro, by far the most affluent of the group, takes his wife and children on a long road trip every Sunday. Renaldo participates with his wife in church activities. Emilio, whose wife and children share a single house with his brother's family, lives in apparent harmony with them all.

However, most married men in the group continue to suffer family problems. It is clear that the group meeting provides them a forum for airing their difficulties. Amador is one such person. Amador is in his late fifties and runs a small fruit-and-vegetable stand in the immediate vicinity of Moral Support. On the podium one evening Amador told his story. He drank steadily for over thirty years, from childhood. Life has been for him no more than "*un suspiro*" (a sigh). It has slipped away rapidly, he says. It has been "*triste*" (sad). The worst is that his children have turned out to be ingrates. Amador wonders whether his suffering has had any positive consequence at all. Neither his wife nor children show appreciation for what he has tried to do for them, he claims.

Jacinto also vents marital problems while on the podium. When he was an active alcoholic, he says, he and his wife would walk down the street and she would comment, "Doesn't that couple look nice? Don't they look like they really love one another and enjoy being together?" And he would say,

"That's the way they are. You and I are different." Now that Jacinto is in recovery, he claims that it is his wife, not he, who is difficult to be around. They do not get along. And as they stroll together, he is the one who now yearns inwardly to feel as happy as the couples they pass on the street. But he keeps this wish a secret, revealing it only to the group, never to his wife. Jacinto worries about compulsive masturbation and confesses his concerns to the group every time he delivers a personal story. However, he never explicitly connects sexual habits to marital infelicity. Rather than being symptomatic of marital unhappiness, it is a problem in and of itself, to be conquered and eliminated.

On the podium Renaldo tends to repeat himself and speak in generalities. Occasionally, however, he departs from this defensive strategy to deliver moving, detailed accounts of his alcoholic past. Once, as his personal story was drawing to a close, he departed from his well-worn tales, and his voice suddenly became dark. He told of returning home one day to find his wife with another man. The intruding lover escaped with Renaldo in pursuit. As he ran, Renaldo hurled stones at him with the intent to kill. But the man jumped over the adobe wall surrounding Renaldo's property and got away. At this point in the story the clock on the meeting-room wall sounded, indicating that Renaldo would have to yield the podium to another speaker. In a completely uncharacteristic move Renaldo exceeded his fifteen minutes and continued to talk. The incident was obviously traumatic, and Renaldo was drawing cathartic release from telling about it. After repeating the story several times, he ended with the rhetorical question, "When would I ever tell this story in the cantina?" The implied response was, "Never." Only to his *compañeros* in A.A. could such confessions like this be made. Renaldo on other occasions confessed how he would come home drunk from the *pulquerías* where he used to hang out. His wife would get so angry that she would beat him. When he first started attending A.A. meetings, he says, he used to think, "How can I admit that my wife would beat me?" But he now claims that speaking openly about these events has helped him to stay sober.

The personal stories that concern family problems imply an acceptance of traditional gender roles and values. Women should be faithful; they should not beat their husbands. Husband and wife should be happy together and enjoy a mutually satisfying sex life. In Renaldo's case, being cuckolded was a deeply shameful, emasculating experience. To tell this story to the group involved enormous courage, for the incident was a grave assault on his masculinity. On the other hand, he was sure to include in his narration his reaction on finding his wife with a lover: he thrashed out violently in an attempt to kill, which is exactly what traditional male norms would dictate. As for Jacinto, it is obviously hard for him to confess his marital unhappiness. However, his repeated, even casual, public confession of compulsive masturbation at least communicates to the group that he is sexually active, again important for any self-respecting male.

Masturbation emerges in other men's personal stories as well. Eduardo claims to worry about excessive masturbation. He says that he was "very young" when he started to masturbate, eleven years old. Although now, in his mid-thirties, he considers himself much too old to be masturbating, he nonetheless masturbates compulsively several times a day. Unlike Jacinto, Eduardo seems boastful, rather than distressed, when he talks about masturbation. Although Eduardo claims that masturbation makes him anxious, his jubilant tone of voice belies this assertion. Eduardo's confession implicitly serves as an announcement of his lively libido. Unmarried and romantically unattached, Eduardo consciously or unconsciously uses the personal story to communicate that he does not settle for complete sexual deprivation. Pursuit of pleasure is a necessary quality for any fully developed male.

Haydée Rosovsky (1991, 2) notes that sexual bragging is a normal feature of personal stories at Mexican A.A. meetings. Observations from Moral Support accord with her findings. David claims repeatedly in personal stories that, after more than a decade of sobriety, his alcoholism is well under control. He no longer needs A.A. to stay sober. Instead, he says, the group helps him control other negative impulses that linger despite his many attempts to overcome them. The strongest of these impulses, he says, are *envidia* (envy) and *lujuria* (lust). Without entering into explicit details David reveals in his public statement that he is a normally functioning Mexican male. Other *compañeros,* like Pedro, for example, do not hesitate to speak in public about their extramarital affairs. Pedro routinely brags about his uncontrolled sexuality. At the age of thirteen he had sex with a fifteen-year-old girl. Ever since then, he claims, he has thought about sex continuously.

Emilio is to all appearances happily married, yet his personal stories reveal long-term relationships with other women. As he puts it, this is the one problem that he has never been able to conquer. He has always been *mujeriego* (a womanizer), he confesses, with an air of combined pride and regret. Periodically, Emilio's personal stories concern the internal struggle he suffers at the end of the workday: should he visit *una vieja* (an "ol' lady") with whom he is carrying on an affair, or should he attend his A.A. meetings? Attendance at the meeting bears witness in and of itself to his moral strength, which operates as additional evidence of his masculinity. Emilio presents himself as a man battling to keep his libidinous drives within bounds. Sometimes his efforts succeed, sometimes not. In either case his masculinity is affirmed. Accounts like those of David and Emilio, told as public confessionals to a group of men, reproduce gender relations outside of the meeting context. In effect, they are sexual boasts. When narrated in personal stories, however, the boasts appear disguised as moral weakness. The open admission of that weakness is itself sufficient evidence of courage to demonstrate the manliness of the speakers. Moral Support speakers who use the podium to disclose uncontrolled sexual activity have nothing to lose. The confession inevitably reinforces their gender identity, despite their abstinence from drink.

Unmarried members of Moral Support confront a particularly grave form of sexual insecurity. Either they reside alone, which to most working-class Mexicans is a pitiful fate for any human being, or they live with married children and suffer the threat of being evicted by their own families. Their unhappiness and insecurity frequently emerge in personal stories. True, these men theoretically accept, even embrace, a redefinition of gender roles. They state that they strive for equality. They selflessly abdicate their traditional position as uncontested family power holders and demonstrate a willingness to carry out household tasks normally restricted to women. Yet no matter what new beliefs they might profess, these men have failed to fulfill an essential male role: to be the head of a household. They are not masters of their own home. This is probably why these are the men who use personal stories most explicitly to raise issues of gender identity.

For all but two or three of the men in Moral Support, living circumstances are anything but ideal. Those who reside alone or as dependents in the homes of relatives have a natural motive to leave the house: for human companionship, in the one instance, or escape from domestic unpleasantness, in the other. For the unhappily married men life outside the home is preferable to unhappiness within. The group provides all these men an escape into the public sphere. At the same time, for every one of the members of Moral Support attendance at meetings provides a culturally validated refuge away from family life, which is the principal feminine domain.

It is important to bear in mind that Moral Support consists only of men. This circumstance contributes to a perpetuation of certain patterns that they used to follow in the company of male drinking buddies. Open admissions of uncontrollable sexual activity and of the violent defense of one's honor are among the familiar themes carried over from pre-A.A. days. The repeated use of obscene language is another male speech pattern brought into the meeting room. One *compañero* starts almost every personal story with the confession, "*Sigo siendo culero*" (I'm still an asshole), a statement he would be unlikely to make in the company of women and children. The curse word *pinche,* which bears no particular lexical meaning but might be translated as the adjective "fucking," appears in almost every sentence of some personal stories. The common Mexicanism *chingar* (to fuck) emerges with similar frequency. And there are other speech patterns— including casual references to genitalia and erotic behavior—that, together with stories of sexual conquests and fantasies, impart a macho tone to Moral Support meetings. Even when the men confess personal weaknesses, the use of obscene language—especially language that draws attention to their own physical endowments—operates to counteract the message. On the podium one evening Emilio stated his constant nervousness at having to rise to the podium to speak. "*Me tiemblan los huevos*"—My balls quiver—he said. Pedro explained the fear he felt at giving up drink and joining Alcoholics Anonymous: "*Me costó un huevo, hasta los dos*" (It cost me a ball, even both). Only in exclusively male company may such statements be made. The assertions themselves highlight the unmistakable sexual identity of the speakers.

Paradoxically, too, the macho tone is reinforced through confessions of spontaneous homosexual desire under the influence of alcohol. Horacio, a stocky man in his mid-thirties, first arrived in the group about a month after I. Born and raised in Mexico City, he lived most of his adult life on the coast, where he married and had children. There he helped found an Alcoholics Anonymous group, which started out with five members. Horacio spoke movingly of his early suspicions that A.A. would fail to keep him sober. But he was proven wrong, he said. After this preamble, Horacio launched into an account of his "crazy" behavior as an active alcoholic. Whenever he got drunk, he would undress, stand nude in front of his *cuates,* spread his arms, and declare, "*¡Quiero hombre!*" (I want a man!). Iván, about the same age as Horacio, was convinced to join A.A. by his wife. She urged him over and over to find a "*grupo,*" but for a long time he resisted, claiming, "Look, I can go for two weeks without drinking, can't I?" The wife would reply, "But you always relapse." So he was convinced. Iván's main recollection is that the atmosphere in the *pulquerías* was "disagreeable." One detail in particular, he said, confused him. When men were urinating, they would grab one another's penises. On such occasions, he would think, "Hey, what's going on here?"

The men laugh nervously when listening to confessions of homosexual desire. Recorded life histories reveal many more such encounters than those that emerge during meetings, which provide a formal, public setting. One man even boasted in private to me that he has had sex with fourteen men, specifying at the same time that it was he who was always the partner to penetrate. He doubtless felt free to make this confession because, in the Latin American context, the active role in homosexual encounters is not necessarily stigmatizing (e.g., Carrier 1995, 15; Klapp 1964, 412; Lancaster 1992, 242; Paz 1961). Yet this man seems embittered because, after admitting to this experience on the podium, his anonymity was betrayed by a supposedly trustworthy *compañero.* It is uncertain whether the confessions of homosexual contact that emerge among men in Moral Support reflect widely shared experiences or whether they are even true. Nonetheless, by portraying homosexual wishes and encounters as part of their dark alcoholic past, the men seem to want to distance themselves from this kind of behavior in the present.

The relentless affirmation of heterosexuality is particularly noteworthy in the exclusively male context of Moral Support meetings. In this sort of close-knit, intimate setting, where men confess weaknesses, where they cry in front of one another and admit their faults, they strive to marshal whatever linguistic and behavioral mechanisms they can to demonstrate unquestioned masculine identity. As a result, a hypermasculine atmosphere prevails in the Moral Support meeting room.

The men of Moral Support manage to retain a sense of masculine identity while abrogating what used to be one of Mexico's rigid and longstanding gender codes: they remain steadfastly sober. To be sure, the members of Moral Support benefit in their search for identity from living in a highly fluid social context. Gutmann (1996, 9) captures the essence of the current social flux when he says that "there exists no stable set of determining and essential gender qualities that can adequately capture the situation for the region [Mexico and Latin America] as a whole; relentlessly emergent gender variations see to that."

It is perhaps easier to be a teetotaling male in Mexico City in the year 2000 than it was half a century ago. There are now over fifteen hundred formally registered Alcoholics Anonymous groups in Mexico City alone, and there are probably many more, like Moral Support, that resist formal affiliation with any central organization. In part A.A. owes its rapid expansion to the reshuffling of gender roles and ideals, which has proceeded rapidly during the past thirty years. Increasingly, the avoidance of alcohol is just another way of being a man. The men of Moral Support, and thousands of other men who constitute more than 90 percent of the A.A. membership in Mexico, need no longer feel like pariahs in their quest to remain sober. They can think of themselves as contributing to the social realignment occurring in their city and nation today.

Acknowledgments. I wish to thank Elizabeth Colson, Matthew Gutmann, Geoffrey Hunt, Roland Moore, and Linda-Anne Rebhun for comments leading to development of this paper. In addition, Suzanne Calpestri, Leticia Casanova, and Andrea Mitchell provided me superb bibliographical assistance. As Chester H. Kirk Fellow at Brown University during July 2000 I benefited from financial and intellectual support of the Center for Alcohol and Addiction Studies. The Center for Latin American Studies, Brown University, provided me generous hospitality during the month I was in residence. Place names and personal names in this chapter are disguised to protect informant and group anonymity.

References

Brandes, Stanley. 1988. *Power and Persuasion: Fiestas and Social Control in Rural Mexico.* Philadelphia: University of Pennsylvania Press.

Bricker, Victoria Reifler. 1973. *Ritual Humor in Highland Chiapas.* Austin: University of Texas Press.

Cancian, Frank. 1965. *Economics and Prestige in a Maya Community: The Religious Cargo System in Zinacantan.* Stanford, Calif.: Stanford University Press.

Carrier, Joseph. 1995. *De los Otros: Homosexuality among Mexican Men.* New York: Columbia University Press.

Collier, Jane Fishburne. 1973. *Law and Social Change in Zinacantan.* Stanford, Calif.: Stanford University Press.

Doughty, Paul L. 1979. "The Social Uses of Alcoholic Beverages in a Peruvian Community." In *Beliefs, Behaviors, and Alcoholic Beverages: A Cross-Cultural Survey,* ed. Mac Marshall, 64–81. Ann Arbor: University of Michigan Press.

Eber, Christine. 1995. *Women and Alcohol in a Highland Maya Town: Water of Hope, Water of Sorrow.* Austin: University of Texas Press.

Finkler, Kaja. 1994. *Women in Pain: Gender and Morbidity in Mexico.* Philadelphia: University of Pennsylvania Press.

Foster, Mary LeCron. 1983. "Tzintzuntzan Marriage: An Analysis of Concordant Structure." In *The Future of Structuralism,* ed. Jarich Oosten and Arie de Ruijter, 127–53. Gottingen: Herodot.

Gutmann, Matthew C. 1996. *The Meanings of Macho: Being a Man in Mexico City.* Berkeley: University of California Press.

Heath, Dwight. 1985. "Emerging Anthropological Theory and Models of Alcohol Use and Alcoholism." In *Theories on Alcoholism,* ed. C. Douglas Chaudron and D. Adrian Wilkinson, 353–410. Toronto: Addiction Research Foundation.

Ingham, John M. 1986. *Mary, Michael, and Lucifer: Folk Catholicism in Central Mexico.* Austin: University of Texas Press.

Klapp, O. 1980. "Mexican Social Types." *American Journal of Sociology* 69:409–15.

Lancaster, Roger N. 1992. *Life Is Hard: Machismo, Danger, and the Intimacy of Power in Nicaragua.* Berkeley: University of California Press.

Leacock, Seth. 1979. "Ceremonial Drinking in an Afro-Brazilian Cult." In *Beliefs, Behaviors, and Alcoholic Beverages: A Cross-Cultural Survey,* ed. Mac Marshall, 81–93. Ann Arbor: University of Michigan Press.

Lomnitz, Larissa Adler. 1977. *Networks and Marginality: Life in a Mexican Shantytown.* New York: Academic Press.

Madsen, William, and Claudia Madsen. 1979. "The Culture Structure of Mexican Drinking Behavior." In *Beliefs, Behaviors, and Alcoholic Beverages: A Cross-Cultural Survey,* ed. Mac Marshall, 38–54. Ann Arbor: University of Michigan Press.

Mäkelä, Klaus, et al. 1996. *Alcoholics Anonymous as a Mutual Help Movement: A Study in Eight Societies*. Madison: University of Wisconsin Press.

Menéndez, Eduardo. 1990. *Morir de alcohol: Saber y hegemonía médica*. Mexico City: Alianza.

Menéndez, Eduardo L., and Reneé B. Di Pardo. 1996. *De algunos alcoholismos y algunos saberes: Atención primaria y proceso de alcoholización*. Mexico City: Centro de Investigaciones y Estudios Superiores en Antropología Social.

Nájera-Ramírez, Olga. 1997. *La Fiesta de los Tastoanes: Critical Encounters in Festival Performance*. Albuquerque: University of New Mexico Press.

Nash, June. 1985. *In the Eyes of the Ancestors: Belief and Behavior in a Mayan Community*. Prospect Heights, Ill.: Waveland.

Nutini, Hugo. 1984. *Ritual Kinship: Ideological and Structural Integration of the Compadrazgo System in Rural Tlaxcala*. Vol. 2. Princeton, N.J.: Princeton University Press.

Parsons, Elsie Clews. 1936. *Mitla: Town of the Souls*. Chicago: University of Chicago Press.

Paz, Octavio. 1961. *The Labyrinth of Solitude: Life and Thought in Mexico*. New York: Grove.

Romanucci-Ross, Lola. 1973. *Conflict, Violence, and Morality in a Mexican Village*. Palo Alto, Calif.: National Press Books.

Rosovsky, Haydeé. 1991. "What Mexican Males Get in A.A." Unpublished manuscript.

Rosovsky, Haydeé, Leticia Casanova, and Cuauhtémoc Pérez. 1991. "Los características de los grupos y de los miembros de Alcohólicos Anónimos." *Anales del Instituto Mexicano de Psiquiatría*, 138–42.

Taylor, William B. 1979. *Drinking, Homicide, and Rebellion in Colonial Mexican Villages*. Stanford, Calif.: Stanford University Press.

Vaillant, George. 1995. *The Natural History of Alcoholism Revisited*. Cambridge, Mass.: Harvard University Press.

Vega, Margarita. 2000. "Alcohol, más dura contra la mujer." *Reforma* (Mexico City), Sep. 10.

Vogt, Evon Z. 1993. *Tortillas for the Gods: A Symbolic Analysis of Zinatanteco Rituals*. Norman: University of Oklahoma Press.

Warren, J. Benedict. 1985. *The Conquest of Michoacán: The Spanish Domination of the Tarascan Kingdom in Western Mexico, 1521–1530*. Norman: University of Oklahoma Press.

Representations
and Practices

■ ■ ■ ■

FLORENCIA E. MALLON

Barbudos, Warriors, and *Rotos*: The

MIR, Masculinity, and Power in

the Chilean Agrarian Reform, 1965–74

■ ■ ■

During the Chilean decade of agrarian reform (1964–73) the most radical agrarian mobilization evolved during the Popular Unity government of Salvador Allende (1970–73), marked by land occupations, street demonstrations, and "fence runnings." The Movement of the Revolutionary Left (MIR) was the main political party involved in this increasing effervescence, creating in September 1970 its rural arm, or front, called the Revolutionary Peasant Movement (MCR). Previously an urban student movement, the MIR would evolve during the 1970–73 period into the most consistently radical sponsor of agrarian unrest, changing its policy in the southern region so that it concentrated in large part on the countryside.[1]

Founded in Santiago, Chile, in August 1965, the MIR was from the very beginning, according to Hernán Vidal, a party dedicated to revolutionary agitation within the already existing and powerful Chilean left. To a country with a long tradition of leftist participation in parliamentary rule and electoral competition, the MIR set out to bring Cuban-inspired popular war. To a left with abundant, disciplined, and well-trained cadres, the MIR brought the frenetic activity and heroism of 1960s youthful rebellion and counterculture. The MIR's *Comisión Política* (Political Commission) was dominated by a group of tightly knit radical students at the University of Concepción, most of whom had grown up together in the small, upper-middle-class intelligentsia of the city. By the party's Third Congress in 1967 this charismatic and influential group, originally composed of Miguel and Edgardo Enríquez, Bautista Van Schowen, Andrés Pascal Allende, Nelson Gutiérrez, and Luciano Cruz, managed to get its supporters elected to a majority of the national offices on the National Committee and National Secretariat. Miguel Enríquez, then twenty-three years old, was elected the MIR's general secretary.[2]

The imagery of this young generation, which given the strong "agitprop" emphasis of the party's early years was an extremely important political tool, drew directly on the combination of the Cuban *barbudo*—the bearded and long-haired young romantic best symbolized by Ernesto "Che" Guevara—and the emerging "hippie" rebels who preached free love, danced to rock music, and stormed the barricades of the bourgeois state. The personal charisma of Miguel Enríquez was perhaps the most dramatic and relied substantially on the youth, good looks, and revolutionary moustache that so deeply resonated with the young idealists of the time. But Miguel also had an impressive talent for public oratory and personal drama, something he already demonstrated in 1964, when at the tender age of twenty he publicly stood up to a visiting Robert Kennedy at the University of Concepción.

Building at least in part on Miguel Enríquez's projection of a powerful individual persona, "as time went on," according to Hernán Vidal, not only Miguel but "his brother Edgardo and Bautista Van Schowen developed a political style that, during the MIR's great public ceremonies, drew on the romantic theatricality of light and shadow to present their best profiles, their good looks, virility, youth and daring, dressed in black, with abundant long hair, their firm and resolute attitude reflected in their level stares."[3] To this was added, in the last years of the 1960s, the romantic imagery of the party's first clandestine period, during which the national leadership participated directly in violent actions against targets representing the capitalist system, such as banks and large industries. Taken as a whole, this multifaceted image of the dedicated young *barbudo,* who risked everything in the name of revolutionary justice and emerged untouched and empowered on the other side, was heady stuff indeed. Although it built consciously and very effectively on the success of the Cuban Revolution, and on the ever more romanticized and rumor-filled legend surrounding Che Guevara, the MIR's construction of revolutionary masculinity also drew on elements of Chilean gender identities and sexual styles historically embedded in popular culture and politics.

One such persona or masculine style was the resistant and romantic working-class male. Referring to the mining regions of the Norte Chico, Jorge Pinto has identified this figure as the *lacho*, suggesting that they "were nothing more than transgressors of the matrimonial norm in the lower strata of society, popular lovers who were not willing to repress their feelings or 'the demands of the flesh.'" Elaborating in more detail for the south-central mining complex of El Teniente, Thomas Klubock has explored a similar image or figure whom he has called *el roto macanudo*. The nonwork cultural practices of the *roto macanudo*, Klubock has emphasized, were constructed in part as a rejection of company efforts to transform working-class men into responsible and monogamous husbands. By attaching Chilean slang words with positive meanings, such as *choro* (cool) or *macanudo* (great, or "far out") to the word *roto*, thereby transforming its customarily negative middle- or upper-class connotations of "hobo," "torn," "vulgar," and "uncouth," mineworkers appropriated the insult by turning it on its head. And they imbued the term with a new set of nested meanings that denoted style, good looks, and transgressive masculinity. In the countryside as well, Heidi Tinsman has argued, rural laborers and small producers appropriated the term *huaso*, often applied to them in a derogatory manner by landowners to mean "boorish," "stupid," or "country bumpkin," and imbued it with the trappings of resistant masculinity. "As many men explained in oral histories," Tinsman writes, "a *huaso* was so strong, independent and irreverent, that no man had a hold on him, not even the patrón."[4]

Although not consciously aware of it, therefore, the young *mirista* leadership deployed a transgressive masculinity that resonated broadly with the various forms of gendered rebelliousness—whether *lacho, roto macanudo,* or *huaso*—that had already taken shape in popular political culture. Probably a great deal clearer to them was the fact that such gendered transgression was a particularly effective challenge to the ideal of masculinity deployed by the more traditional organized left, one that emphasized disciplined work habits and responsible family behavior. Although debated and applied differently in the Communist and Socialist parties, the Chilean left in general had elaborated, across the twentieth century, a belief in the importance of proper and responsible family behavior and familial solidarity as a precondition to effective political action. The working-class family was considered the basic and most effective unit of class struggle, and both men and women were encouraged to carry out their prescribed roles within it.[5]

As Karin Rosemblatt has recently shown, this familial discourse was also strongly represented in the Chilean state apparatus, especially during the years of the popular front governments. Yet as was also the case with the imagery of the *roto,* working-class appropriations of family morality made something quite different out of the figure of the proper family man. By imbuing family responsibility with an egalitarian, even utopian, tinge, leftist activists claimed the high moral ground in their struggle with the upper classes. Especially in the Communist Party, Rosemblatt writes, "members could be called into the party's disciplinary control commissions and subjected to sanction for drinking, marital infidelities, or failing to support their families properly."[6] Leftist family morality was thus a double-edged sword. On one side, whether in the hands of government officials or leftist activists, it could be a weapon of social control. On the other side it could also become an ideal of working-class masculinity, honor, and dignity: the capacity, both moral and material, to support a wife and family.

In articulating 1960s rebellious *barbudo* imagery to a transgressive working-class masculinity, *mirista* leaders effectively countered both upper-class and leftist morality as forms of social control. In so doing, they promoted a heroic, resistant, and romantic subjectivity that was especially attractive to the younger generation of all classes. At the same time, however, this revolutionary narrative had two potentially large sociopolitical costs. One was the tendency to overlook the powerful attractiveness of family imagery, not only to the male workers and peasants who had never had the resources to actually support their families in an "honorable" way but also to the working-class and peasant women who yearned for economic security and familial stability and were not represented within the *mirista* romance. The other was the tendency to reproduce, within this extremely powerful articulation of a hegemonic revolutionary masculinity, the same kind of class, ethnic, and gender hierarchies that the organization was supposedly founded to erase. For after all, most of the rebellious, almost intuitively confrontational, young men attracted to this image could not be expected to meet the criteria of looks, style, and brash manliness of the *roto macanudo*. Those who did would perhaps not agree with the sense of moral purpose, personal risk, and extreme self-sacrifice symbolized by Che's bearded visage. And those attracted by the stubborn, eternally confrontational, and sacrificial *barbudo* might not be willing to hunker down to the centralized discipline of a small national directorate who supposedly did have it all.

In this chapter I trace some of the complexities of the MIR's constructions of masculinity through an in-depth look at the fortunes of a small group of local MIR activists in Cautín, the center of the MIR's experiment with radical agrarian reform. As we will see, the image of Che Guevara, as the ultimate *barbudo*, had extraordinary power over people's imaginations and morality, inspiring them to action. The central *mirista* leadership connected themselves effectively to Che's image and drew personal authority from it. At the same time, however, the discourses and images of transgressive masculinity woven into *mirista* practice were more complex and contradictory, causing rebellious resentment among some and self-aggrandizing behavior among others. Ironically, the most successful organizers and rabble-rousers, attracted to the MIR precisely because of their intensely confrontational style and demeanor, were also the ones the central leadership was unable to control. And at the local level people seemed most inspired by the images and practices of self-sacrifice and community solidarity that more closely resembled the sense of familial responsibility and utopia elaborated by the more traditional left.

Seeking Che among Working-Class Students: Temuco, 1967–71

When Che Guevara was killed in Bolivia in 1967, José Cárdenas was thirteen years old. At his grandparents' small store, or when his father sent him to Temuco's daily market to buy feed for the pigs and chickens they kept in their backyard, he had seen Mapuche peddlers arrive barefoot to sell their wares. He noticed how other classmates made fun of the Mapuche students at his school, so he made a point of personally befriending them. One of his teachers, María Marinao, herself of Mapuche origin, was a member of the Communist Party. Between his grandparents' preference for the leftist politics of the Popular Front, his teacher, and the things he saw going on around him, José had, "without having the script real clear yet in my head, but with that kind of emotional intelligence or intuition you have sometimes, I began to feel that people on the Left worried more about the poor, about the people as a whole."[7]

At his school he first joined the Communist Youth, but he also began to follow the heroics of a group of young, long-haired revolutionaries that included not only Che Guevara but also the daring young Chileans in the MIR. As part of a broader student movement, he watched as fearless and handsome MIR founders Miguel Henríquez and Luciano Cruz, with a certain Guevarist style, confronted the police and foiled their captors again and again. "When I got to the *liceo*," José remembered, "I was able to get in contact with people like this and I felt useful, I felt profoundly revolutionary. And in fact I dressed like a revolutionary, with a beret and a poncho, trying to be a bit more like the image of Che."

In such a context, when José read that the Bolivian Communist Party had not been committed to Che Guevara's efforts, and as a result was at least indirectly complicit with Che's death, he began to have second thoughts about his own involvement in the Communist Youth. In the Chilean Communist Party he began to see a complacency, a willingness to coexist with the system, that frightened him. And once again, it was the image, the experience, the incorruptibility of Che that served as his touchstone. As he began to focus on the contradiction between the CP's revolutionary promise and its accommodationist practice, "I made the very personal decision to leave the CP and get closer to the *compañeros* more committed to the revolutionary left."

At about the same time, when José was about fourteen, the Communist Youth had a meeting of its cadre at the school. Along with several other boys who were called forward to report, José made clear that "I couldn't keep working with them because I felt that the Party, and the youth working with them, were part of the system. I wanted to be honest about what I thought, because that's how I felt, and I felt it deeply. Several *compañeros* left with me at that point, about four or five, and we moved over to the Revolutionary Student Front (FER)."[8] In the FER, José remembered, he began to establish closer links with other young revolutionary students. This development coincided with an emerging crisis at home. José saw his father, a mechanic by trade, as basically interested in making money and rebelled against the older man's aggressive pressure to concentrate more on his studies. "He told me that I had to do what he said, because he was my father and was supporting me. Well, this actually motivated me to get more deeply into the FER and I slowly got more and more committed. And one day, when the old man started slapping me around, I left home."

José moved into a university student residence where he worked with other FER militants much older than he. "I admired these *compañeros*," he told me. "To me they seemed like small heroes, small gods. I think I held them up as mythical characters." Some of them advised José that he should return to his family, that it was not good to be living that way. But José felt good about the choice he had made; he felt equal to the others and that was a source of great satisfaction to him. His first assignment was to work with students in Pitrufquén, a few miles south of Temuco, where he spent about four or five months. Then, under the direction of some older students more directly connected to the MIR, he was sent to Villarrica, a city in the foothills of the Andes mountains to the southwest of Temuco. This was a more challenging assignment, farther away from home, and he prepared to move to Villarrica.

On his way out of town, when he stopped by to say good-bye to his mother, she began to cry. "I was the son who'd always given her the most problems," José explained. "That's why she loved me so much, and besides, I'd been sickly when I was little and that had brought us especially close." At the time, José could only focus on the all-consuming commitment he felt for his political work. There were no half-measures. He remembered a feeling of intense self-confidence, that everything would be easy. With that attitude he began to work in Villarrica with other members of the FER and the MIR's local committee. "We all lived together in the same house," José recalled, "sleeping bags on the floor, preparing food whenever one of us was able to bring something from home, or with donations that some of us got." For José this youthful adventure, almost like an extended camping trip, was also "a profound revolutionary cause" made even more intense by the shared experiences of many young rebels who, like him, were facing tensions or rejection at home.

In the early morning hours of May 5, 1972, José joined about twenty students, including members of the local MIR committee, in a *toma,* or illegal takeover, of a vacant house belonging to Leopoldo de Miguel. In a similar way to the *tomas* of landed estates that were proliferating in the countryside, this action was designed to dramatize the need for a dormitory to house the peasant and Mapuche students who came to Villarrica to study. The two domestic workers in charge of guarding the house were sympathetic to the students' cause, but the local judge refused to consider the students' demands—which in addition to the opening of a residence for Mapuche peasant students included the prompt payment of the domestic workers' back pay—and simply called in the police to throw them out. Sixteen occupants, including José and nine other minors, were imprisoned and charged with illegal usurpation and kidnapping. One of the leaders of the action was Manuel Barrientos.[9]

The illegitimate child of a Valdivia-based domestic worker and her boss, Manuel had been brought to a working-class neighborhood in Temuco by his aunt and uncle after the death of his mother. He had grown up somewhat wild, an intelligent misfit who got into trouble at school from a young age because he refused to respect authority. He chafed under his aunt and uncle's harsh discipline and their demand that he work as a peddler in the market while attending a commercial high school. Because he was extremely good at math, his uncle and aunt thought he should be an accountant or businessman; but he had a more abstract intelligence and, in addition to being fascinated by science fiction, wished to become a lawyer or a doctor.[10]

Manuel had been a physically small child who needed thick glasses from a young age. From early on he used his unusual intelligence to make his way in the adolescent world, writing extra-credit projects for his schoolmates and charging them in money or treats. By the time he was ten, he had already read *The Communist Manifesto* and Lenin's *State and Revolution,* both lent to him by the father of a classmate. He compensated for his lack of physical prowess by cultivating unusual skill with a knife: "From the time I was a little kid I enjoyed playing with a knife, so much so that it saved my life several times." And when he entered high school he responded to the teasing of the other boys by acting up to the point of getting suspended from school. "It was in tenth grade that I began to have problems," he recalled,

> because it was always the other guys who had the girls interested in them, and even when you're a little guy you've got that running around your head, especially if you're from a working-class neighborhood where the *machismo* is greater, and the other guys throw it up in your face if you don't have a girlfriend. And besides, it was very common in those days, I don't know what it's like today, but back then the young guys used to go out with older women. And so I'd see this going on, and it got me thinking, wanting to be like them and not like them, and this resulted in my doing things in school that weren't the best.

By the time Manuel was fifteen, he was working during the day and going to school at night, where he met Omar Garrido, a socialist teacher who served as a sort of role model. Originally from a working-class neighborhood, Garrido had studied medicine for two years until his money had run out and then finished a career in history and geography. Along with other older students from the nocturnal classes, some of whom were union activists, Manuel accompanied Garrido to drink a couple of beers after class. Often they would end up in the red-light district, drinking and dancing with the prostitutes, who would, according to Manuel, sit on the men's knees. These shared experiences helped bring the men closer to each other, Manuel remembered, as they would talk about their problems and the situation in the world. With Garrido he also shared the experience of being beaten when he got home late. Early one morning, when Manuel was trying to climb in through the window, his uncle leveled him with a blow to the face. But his friend got it worse, for "when he entered through the gate and opened the kitchen door, his father, that huge old guy, had grabbed the two by four they used to bolt the door, and hit my poor teacher across the shoulder, and for a month the poor man couldn't move his arm."

In 1968 a MIR organizer arrived from Concepción, according to Manuel, "a good speaker who could really drink and was really good with women, but his strongest loyalty was to the MIR." This led to the formation of the first secondary-school student group connected to the MIR through the local university organizations. Between 1968 and 1969, in addition to forming a "Che Guevara Nucleus" of the Socialist Youth in his neighborhood, Manuel worked with the local Maoist organization and, slowly, began to get closer to the MIR. His biggest ambition at that point was to follow other young MIR leaders into the countryside to work in the Mapuche communities near the city of Lautaro, slightly north of Temuco. When he brought up the subject with a member of the regional committee, however, he was rejected, even though, as he remembered, he was a year older than one of the young men who went. "My physical appearance, the glasses and everything, made me seem younger," Manuel recalled. "So they told me I was still a young kid and would do them no good."

After this rejection Manuel joined with other leftist students to form a group at his high school that, although not formally connected to the MIR, received literature and information from the MIR leadership in Concepción. The idea was to prove that they were not like the earlier leaders, the ones who had gone into the countryside but had also been heavy drinkers and partygoers and who, in Manuel's eyes, were not politically serious. They organized a regional conference for students from commercial high schools that drew representatives from across the south of the country, and they succeeded in getting people from their own group elected to most of the regional offices. This initiated what would become a longer term pattern for Manuel: using his superior intelligence and incredible capacity for hard organizational work to compensate for what, from his perspective, were the class- or gender-based slights he received from the MIR leadership.

By the middle of 1969 it was clear, even from Concepción, that Manuel's work at his high school was effective. The MIR began inviting him to meetings of the regional committee and offered him a position as leader of the secondary-school students. Manuel refused, not because he did not want to work with the students but because he was also interested in working with trade unions and shantytown dwellers. The MIR leadership accepted this new interest. Between 1969 and 1970, especially with the election of Allende, urban mobilizations intensified. Yet the MIR, as Manuel perceived it, seemed bent on developing its rural work above all else. "They were taking all the *compañeros* we had in the university, even from the schools, out to work in the countryside in the land recuperation movement," he remembered. Manuel opposed this one-sided strategy, not only because it kept taking away urban militants but also because he thought a strong movement in the city was necessary to support the rural mobilizations. For this reason, even though he was asked several times to go into the countryside, at this point he refused. "I was always a difficult son of a bitch, critical, and there were lots of things I didn't like about how the work was getting done." These tensions came to a head in mid-1971, when at a conference in Temuco Manuel and some of his *compañeros* presented a document critical of the MIR's lack of internal democracy.

The MIR's response was to send a surveillance team to keep track of Manuel's group. When they confronted the spies, a member of the regional committee was sent to talk to them:

We presented him with a document where we said that, even if the work in the countryside was correct, we also thought that if the goal was a rural guerrilla, it was necessary to work in a different way. Because the fence-runnings and estate takeovers implied that, at some point, the landowners or the military would begin a counteroffensive, and with those really good helicopters they could throw a couple of bombs, or with airplanes, and they'd make short shrift of all our pretty flags and banners. So it was important for our work to be a little less public and open. And again we raised the issue of the working class, and the fact that the workers needed to lead the process and all that, and it was then that they decided to sanction us.

Manuel and his friends were called before a group of regional and national leaders and accused of *desviaciones obreristas* (workerist deviations). Although several of his older *compañeros* were either expelled or marginalized from the party, it was decided that Manuel was too young to have played a leadership role. He was brought before the group of leaders at the very end, after they had decided to keep the workers and shantytown dwellers and throw out the older organizers. At this point Manuel's old rebellious streak came out in force. "I'd been waiting outside, next to the door, with my famous knife, seeing what happened to the others," he told me.

And I come up and see all those leaders there, about eight of them, and they tell me, so? What do you want me to say? I answered, you'll forgive me for saying so, and I don't mean it at a political level, but what you're doing is a wimpy dirty trick *(mariconada)*. We've done some work here, work that people recognize, and all you're doing is demonstrating that we're no different from the Communist Party. You're a bunch of bastards and shitheads, Stalinists, petty bourgeois.

When the meeting was over, Manuel was deemed capable of rehabilitation and was sent back to his commercial high school to "rest." He was also prohibited from going back to the trade unions or shantytowns where he had been working. But he was not willing to accept this prohibition, in part because of his own class pride and resentment. (He perceived the leaders who had sanctioned him as from more privileged backgrounds, people who had never known the hunger and privations of the poorer neighborhoods.) Already in the meeting he had refused to honor the prohibition, even suggesting that people at the grassroots would follow him out of the MIR if he were expelled, and shortly afterward he decided to test its limits directly.

When Manuel arrived at a Sunday meeting of the Che Guevara shantytown dwellers' association, he ran into the same MIR organizer who had accompanied them at the earlier sanctioning meeting, a man he remembered as belonging to a local landowner family. As Manuel got closer, the other man asked him where he was going.

To the shantytown, I understand there's a meeting, I told him, and people asked me to come. I'm a little late but I'm going in. No, he answered, the meeting's over. No matter, I said, I can still talk to people there. You're prohibited from coming in, he told me. That might be, I said, but I'm going in anyway. And the bastard takes out his pistol. Let me through, I told him, I'm not going to call you *compañero,* you son of a bitch, but shooting me would be ugly, to die at the hands of a comrade when I thought I'd always die at the hands of the enemy. But go ahead and shoot, if you're man enough.

One of the most persistent contradictions Manuel faced in the MIR was that the very same characteristics that made him a good leftist revolutionary—his rebellious attitude, grassroots tactics, and aversion to authority—did not stand him in good stead with the MIR's central committee. Indeed, in many ways Manuel Barrientos was a classic stumbling block for the MIR's brand of heroic revolutionary politics. Small and bespectacled, he did not fit the image of revolutionary masculinity so assiduously nurtured by the central leadership. Instead, he could be seen as a stereotype of the Communist Party apparatchik or mole, who could blend into the background and thus was especially effective behind the scenes. At the same time, however, his childhood experiences, and especially the abuse he had suffered from his aunt and uncle and his difficulties fitting into working-class adolescent male culture, had fostered in him an obstinate rebelliousness, a relentless capacity for confrontation that made it impossible for him to hunker down to party discipline. As he himself remembered, what had first attracted him to the MIR was his perception that they offered an alternative to the Stalinism he saw in the Chilean Communist Party. How ironic, then, that the very same party that promised heroic and uncompromising revolution, that held up the eternal rebel Che Guevara as their model, should then discipline his alleged deviations. Manuel's explanation for this contradiction went through a gendered class resentment: the leaders were members of the privileged classes, handsome and pampered, who had not known poverty or privation and used their status to drink and womanize rather than to pursue a principled revolution. And he channeled his frustrations by doing more of what he did best: marshaling his impressive intelligence into an almost frenetic form of grassroots organizing, combined with a heavy critique of the limitations of other people's political work.

After his confrontation at the Che Guevara shantytown, he was sent to work outside Temuco, in the Villarrica-Loncoche area, which included the mountain lumber region between Curarrehue and Panguipulli. There he found himself an ally, fellow organizer Julián Bastidas, sociology student from the University of Concepción, founding member of the MIR, and the nephew of the Bishop of Talca to boot. Julián defended him before the regional committee, emphasizing his good work, something that over and over seemed to protect Manuel from actually being expelled from the MIR. More or less at the same time, prompted by events at the *fundo* Chesque in Loncoche, where an armed group of landowners reinforced by police repelled an attempted invasion, killing Moisés Huentelaf, a Mapuche peasant leader and member of the MCR, the regional leadership had to reorganize the Loncoche-Villarrica local. The *miristas* who had supervised the Chesque action were forced to leave the area to avoid arrest, and in the subsequent shake-up about ten local organizers were expelled, as Manuel remembered it, because "in one way or another they took advantage of the responsibility they had to go out with girls" and did not carry their weight administratively. Bastidas was put in charge, Manuel recalled, because "he was a Christian Marxist, one of those for whom morality was fundamental."[11]

This reorganization gave Manuel a new lease on life, and he began planning the takeover of the empty house belonging to Leopoldo de Miguel, who he remembered was a pharmacist from Osorno living at the seaside resort of Viña del Mar who had already lost two landed estates to takeovers. Through a family member who worked in a factory the MIR had already helped take over, Manuel made contact with the domestic workers guarding the house. "I began to romance one of the girls there, so my presence would seem normal and nobody would find it strange to see me there all the time." As the planning proceeded, however, Manuel and Bastidas disagreed about Julián's participation in the action. "Julián wants to participate but I say no, because if we're caught they catch the head of the Local Committee and that brings us problems with the leadership and with all the work there is here." But Bastidas insisted, interestingly enough, by referring to Che Guevara: "And he brings out the whole story about how in the ambushes, and in all that stuff the leaders have always been there, and he begins talking about Che Guevara."

Manuel agreed, against his better judgment, to Julián's participation in the early morning action. Everything seemed to be going well when the local *gobernador* arrived, ostensibly to sign the agreement that would put in motion the expropriation of the house. But the local judge and police had other ideas, and they took advantage of the moment when all the invaders were talking with the representative of the central government to begin retaking the house. A fierce battle ensued, and, interestingly, Manuel's memory is that Julián's capture by invading police signified their defeat. "And suddenly I see Julián appear in the doorway there, this huge guy next to these tiny cops, and he tells me, there's no one left, he says, surrender.

No, I say, you can't be serious! And he tells me, it's an order, you bastard, surrender, he says, there's no one left you bastard. Well, if it's an order, I say. I throw one last kick at a cop who's standing there, and then I'm all peaceful."

Julián's role in the action helped crystallize the ambivalence Manuel felt for all members of the broader MIR leadership. On the one hand, he admired Julián because he was principled and moral and did not use his power to romance the girls or act irresponsible in other ways. Manuel also felt that Julián appreciated his talents and ability for hard work. Manuel even had a grudging admiration for Julián's personal connections in the region, the networks he had been able to form with those in power, which allowed them to get special treatment for the five days they were in the Pitrufquén jail on their way to Loncoche: "He'd developed a network and all that; the Fire Chief was his friend, the mayor, who knows, a whole bunch of people friends of Julián and so he got chicken, fruit, all kinds of things." Yet in the end Manuel could not shake the idea that Julián, this big tall guy, had surrendered to a couple of tiny policemen and had forced him to do the same.

Manuel Barrientos, Julián Bastidas, and José Cárdenas were all trans-ferred to the Loncoche jail, where they ended up sharing the prison with the peasants arrested in the Chesque action. Manuel and José both re-member that, with all those *miristas* together in one place, they were able to organize a variety of activities, including classes in political education and handicrafts. Among the books that circulated, recalled José, were Lenin's complete works, from which he read in particular the analysis of the 1905 Revolution and *State and Revolution*. Thanks to Julián, José remembered, he felt good about learning something while in jail.[12]

When he was released from jail a few months later, José returned to Temuco to live with his family. Although his parents had been extremely solicitous of him while he was in prison, his father traveling the dangerous mountain roads to visit him in Loncoche, living at home simply did not work out. José remembered that his father tried to become his friend, even to the point of buying him a suit and then suggesting, in a roundabout, embarrassed way, that they go out together to a bordello. But José had already decided, after talking it over with several of his *compañeros,* that when it came to sex, the revolutionary option was through a love relationship. Indeed, as one of them had put it, "he'd never fight in a guerrilla band, or go to the mountains, with a *compañero* who did not have the capacity to love, that in such a situation he needed *compañeros* who had known deeply what it meant to love, who were in love with life." So José pretended to be sick the night his father wanted to take him out and thus avoided having to confront the situation.[13]

His father's awkward attempts at male bonding were particularly repugnant to José because his interpretation of *barbudo* revolutionary morality had convinced him of the need to pursue a single love relationship. Different from both transgressive working-class masculinity and proper "family" behavior, the image of an ideal revolutionary companion was more commonly attractive to MIR national leaders and urban leftist intellectuals, although in reality most established leaders succumbed to the sexual temptations of notoriety and fell far short of this goal. At the grassroots, moreover, male activists more often added the behaviors and boastings of the *roto macanudo* to their obligations as family men. And all *miristas,* without regard for social class or ethnic background, were subject to the MIR's policy of compulsory heterosexuality, since known homosexuals were expelled from the party.[14]

It quickly became clear to José that the situation at home was not tenable. When Manuel "talked to us about our revolutionary commitment, and afterward said it would be good for us to join the local MIR committee on the coast," José jumped at the chance. By then it was the end of August/ beginning of September 1972, and the street demonstrations were heating up. There were railroad strikes, truckers' strikes, roadblocks, José recalled, and getting to Carahue "was a real adventure." Once he got there "it was a special day; there was a kind of euphoria, around the time that Allende visited."[15] After José was welcomed by the local committee, someone suggested he could spend some time at a local agrarian reform center affiliated with the MCR. This is how José ended up on the *asentamiento* Arnoldo Ríos.

Barbudos and Peasants: The Coastal Region, 1970–73

The product of the first *toma* of a landed estate organized by the MCR in December 1970, the *fundo* Rucalán near Carahue had also undergone a violent *retoma*, or reclaiming, by the landowner and his friends. "The starting point was 'Rucalán,'" claimed a November 1971 article in *El Rebelde* that then went on to list the seven armed confrontations that had occurred in Cautín during the UP government. In February of that same year, shortly after the creation of the *asentamiento* Arnoldo Ríos on the expropriated *fundo,* an open letter from the "Workers of 'Rucalán' to the General Public" had appeared in *Punto Final* with the headline "The Peasants Uncover the Intrigues of a *Momio* Landowner."[16] The Rucalán *toma* had been organized by a local land committee formed on the Mapuche community of Nicolás Ailío, located halfway between Carahue and the coastal port of Puerto Saavedra, that included as well non-Mapuche peasants and rural laborers from surrounding estates and from the fishing village of Nehuentúe. Represented by a banner that read across the middle "Asentamiento Arnoldo Ríos," decorated with a gun, and flanked by Che Guevara on the left and the logo of the MCR on the right, Rucalán was a most effective poster child for the MIR's general policy of armed mobilization of all the rural poor.[17]

The formal head of the *asentamiento* was Ricardo Mora, a landless day laborer from Nehuentúe who had married a Mapuche woman and been welcomed into her community of Pichingual. One of the three who received bullet wounds during the *retoma*, Mora had settled well into his public role of heroic peasant leader, stating in *Punto Final*, "If I die, I'll die defending all my *compañeros,* in our fight for bread, land, and socialism."[18] Yet at the same time, the intellectual and organizational power behind the scene was Heriberto Ailío, one of the founders of the local land committee in his community and a founding member of the MCR. In contrast to other MCR leaders such as Alejandro Manque or the Huentelaf brothers, Heriberto Ailío was not interested in public recognition. Although he did participate in other land invasions in his region, he mainly dedicated himself to making the *asentamiento* work and to producing enough to feed his family and the other relatives who had stayed behind in the community.

As an *asentamiento* created under Eduardo Frei's 1967 Agrarian Reform law, Arnoldo Ríos was a cooperative in which individual heads of households, in collaboration with state representatives sent by the agrarian reform agency (CORA), defined a production plan for the property. As Heriberto Ailío explained, the members of the cooperative, or *asentados,* worked the land in common, and part of what they produced went to pay back the loans and the agrarian debt. Although the majority of the property was farmed collectively, each household was also given about two hectares of private usufruct. In many cases, because the *asentados* were busy working on the communal enterprise, those two hectares were cultivated in a sharecropping agreement with a partner from one of the communities.

When the state intervened in the *fundo,* Heriberto Ailío recalled, poverty stopped knocking at people's doors. "Since we took nothing with us," he explained, "CORA gave us technical aid, fertilizers, herbicides, machinery, all those things. They gave us tractors to replace the oxen; cows, seeds, fertilizers; everything the *fundo* needed for the peasants to work it, CORA would give us."[19] Robustiano Ailío sharecropped his brother Heriberto's two hectares on Rucalán while also working the family lands in the community of Ailío. He also remembered the Popular Unity as a time of prosperity: "it was the first time we used fertilizer. The government at the time gave us broad technological support, [and] there was a lot of help in the countryside."[20]

But perhaps what most influenced the functioning of the *asentamiento* Arnoldo Ríos was the preexisting network of solidarity and exchange among the area's Mapuche communities. In addition to their agreements with sharecroppers from the communities, the *asentados* developed a system based on kinship that distributed food and other necessities from the *asentamiento* to the nearby communities. "We worked hard, [and] we saw tremendous improvements," Heriberto Ailío explained:

> In those days I was newly married. There was enough so my family could stock up, we never lacked for bread, for my house, for my family, and in addition back then we had an uncle living with us, and my mother and father who are since deceased. So I'd give to them, from what I made I'd give to them, and I could support two households.

[Q: Your parents also lived on Rucalán?]

No, they lived here [in Tranapuente].

[Q: So you'd bring things back here.]

Back here, exactly. CORA did a good job then, because they gave us the right to distribute some of what we planted to people. The entire community, all of it communal work, what we planted was tremendously productive. . . . We were able to keep the cooperative stocked, in fact we watched it grow, we were able to do things right in those years, no one was left owing money, we all came out well.[21]

The members of this successful cooperative were mainly those who had participated in the initial takeover, Mapuche and non-Mapuche peasants and rural laborers from several Mapuche communities and small towns located between Carahue and Puerto Saavedra. As Heriberto Ailío recalled, one of the principal motivations driving Arnoldo Ríos's success seemed to be kinship, particularly the ability economically to sustain a broad set of family ties. "We never lacked for bread," he told me; and he felt pride that, as a recently married man, he could support his family. Indeed, he contrasted this ability to the many frustrations his father had known as a day laborer on other people's properties, and he remembered the first day that he and his brother Robustiano had been able to buy enough flour with their wages so that they filled their stomachs with the freshly baked bread their mother made. At that point his father's eyes had filled with tears, and after dinner he had gone out to cut wood singing songs in the Mapuche language. The *asentamiento* was the first time that a sense of fulfillment could be generalized to all participating families, plus their kin in neighboring communities. There was a palpable sense of community solidarity and of male pride in being able to provide for their relatives.[22]

When José Cárdenas went to live on Rucalán, he felt this combination of prosperity and joy at a deep emotional level. It was like he had found a real home:

I remember, for example, the image of an old couple, two small old people, and the old guy was the loveliest old guy I'd ever seen; he was short and bald, with a bit of white hair, and he had such a special face. . . . He'd participated in the takeover; I don't remember his last name. I saw how close the two of them were; for me they were like the prototype of a real family. I'd always visit them to drink *mate* and eat potatoes and when the time came I helped them plant potatoes, throwing the seed down while riding horseback.[23]

This feeling of being at home deepened when José was invited to participate in a wedding celebration. He remembered that he was the only outsider who was invited and that he felt entirely included in the group. This sense of belonging nurtured in him a newfound generosity: "A few days before I'd received the money the Party sent me each month, I don't know how much it would be today, but I remember that I used it to buy the couple a pot. I'd never bought anything for anyone before, and I bought them a pot." Afterward he participated in the celebration, with a barbecue and wine, "and during the night someone passed me a guitar; now I don't play the guitar but for some reason, that night, it seemed like people thought I did. I don't know how long I sang and played, but everyone began dancing."[24]

For a youth hovering around his eighteenth birthday, who had never felt he belonged anywhere, this kind of solidarity was a heady experience. It deepened further with the family of Heriberto and Robustiano Ailío, the two brothers from the community of Nicolás Ailío in whose houses José lived. In addition to Heriberto's role as a leader of the MCR, he and his brother were the grandsons of the community's original *cacique* and thus had a certain traditionally based authority as leaders. Since Robustiano was also keeping track of the family household back in the community, José spent time in both houses, one in the community of Ailío and one on the Rucalán section of the agrarian reform cooperative. In both places he felt very much at home: "I have this very deep image and memory of having lived in their house. I was telling you the other day that I'd suddenly feel even the sheets on the beds, sewn from flour sacks, the cleanliness and texture of the cloth that I don't feel anymore today because now sheets are industrially made. All these kinds of things, they made me feel such a family-like spirit."[25]

In this context Heriberto Ailío was, for José, a father figure. "Something that really impressed me about Heriberto," he recalled,

was his fatherly capacity. You know, I never felt unprotected when Heriberto was near. He was a short, minute type of guy; you know how he is, but he gave me this feeling of protection. With his smile, for example, Heriberto would make me feel very protected. I think one of my big problems at that point in my life was having felt so unprotected in my own family; that whole issue I had, but Heriberto made me feel different. He made me feel happy, and at this very moment I'm feeling again the emotions and sensations I felt when I saw my friends, my *compañero* Heriberto, never a mean word, never a bad face, never a bad attitude.[26]

Even though José also remembered Robustiano Ailío as a protective figure, Robustiano was a kind of older brother, someone José could look up to. "I felt myself to be a revolutionary, a committed fighter who had left everything," José told me,

and I'd go out walking with him many times, in the early morning through the dense fog that came up from the river, to look at the fields. There was always a deeper meaning to the conversation, about why things were the way they were, and I always found something almost magical in what Robustiano would say. He was so much stronger; there was a special aura, something magical in his words and attitude. I'll always remember him with a gray baseball cap on his head, wearing a gray suit jacket.[27]

José himself made the connection that he played the role of the son, not only with the Ailío family but even earlier in the MIR's local committee in Villarrica, where, as the youngest of the bunch, he had actually been nicknamed "son." There was a sense of nostalgia when we talked, more than twenty years later, of his having lost something precious and meaningful. "Sundays have always been tedious, terrible days for me," he reflected, "but in Rucalán and Ailío I remember Sundays as happy days, when I'd play soccer with the other young people, or take walks with Reuche [Robustiano] looking for wild strawberries, and he'd talk to me about plants and things."[28]

He felt so much at home, José recalled, that he had to remind himself that he was there for political reasons. "Suddenly I'd remember that I had to do political work and so I'd begin talking with them and go out on horseback to Butalón which was behind Arnoldo Ríos. I'd visit the *com-*

pañeros and share their food." He would work in all the agricultural tasks; and, as he reflected on the experience more than twenty years later, he said, "It made me feel good; it made me feel important; it didn't matter whether anyone else knew what I was doing, but it made me feel important; maybe I had this idea of being the cool young guy; maybe it was kind of a colonial mentality; I don't know."[29]

Mario's self-criticism about his "being the cool young guy" with "a colonial mentality" was echoed in Manuel Barrientos's criticisms of some MIR activists' behavior in the same region. After getting out of jail in Loncoche Manuel had spent a couple of months in Temuco but was then sent to the coastal region, where a concentration of agrarian reform centers had emerged with ties to the MIR, to work in political education. After a couple of weeks in Carahue, Manuel remembered, he found out there was little actual cadre formation among the peasants living on the agrarian reform centers. So he went to the *fundo* Nehuentúe, known then as the Production Center Jorge Fernández, to see for himself.

> There I found Alejo, the *compañero* who was in charge, riding a beautiful white horse, wearing a white poncho with black markings on it, and he says hello to me still on top of the horse. They make me get up on another horse to look around the *fundo,* to get to know it, and they introduce me to people. Afterward we went back, and he says to Juan, another *compañero* who was standing there, take the horse, and the guy takes it, and unsaddles it, and all that. This seemed strange to me. I didn't say anything, but later with Anselmo, this guy I'd studied with in high school and who was working there, I said hey, buddy, what's this shit? First of all, this guy, I really don't know him, he's not among the ones who've been in the organization a while. And well, if he's in charge here, I guess that's the leadership's business, but does this kind of treatment go on all the time? Yes, he tells me. And you haven't complained? Well, yes, he said, but very gently.[30]

Things continued in the same vein the next day. Manuel got up early with Anselmo and went to help out at the dairy, around six in the morning, to see if anything needed to be lifted, moved, or stored. They were told no, and they drank some milk with the workers who were already there. There was nothing else for them to do until nine or ten in the morning, when the rest of the MIR *compañeros* got up and decided to have breakfast. Then there was the political meeting, after which lunch was served, then tea, and then dinner. The next day the routine was repeated, including, according to Manuel, having the horses ready and saddled. By that afternoon Manuel could stand it no longer:

> Listen, *compañero,* I told him, I want to clear up a couple of things, things I'm just not used to. First, I told him, you guys are actually using the landowner's house. The way you're treating people looks to me like the people from the organization have taken over the old boss's role. What I suggest, I said, is that first, you saddle and unsaddle your own little horse. Second, we get up early and have breakfast early, buddy. And finally, I said, it doesn't sit well with me to ask the people here to do things for us. We do them ourselves. Well, we got into a discussion, the guy kind of admitted it, and so then me and Anselmo set off for Imperial.
>
> The thing is, we also stopped in Ailío at another meeting, and well they didn't have a horse for the guy, but there was a similar kind of style. And in the evening, all the peasant *compañeros* were working, and the rest of us in the political meeting. So I said, excuse me, I don't know if anyone else wants to join me, but I'm going to go help the *compañeros.* If you want to continue the meeting, go ahead. So me, Anselmo, and two Mapuche *compañeros* from the local MIR committee all went off to help the workers, and we were there until two or three in the morning, working with them, and then returned to Imperial.[31]

The broader criticism contained in this narrative was, from Manuel's point of view, the lack of a serious political plan. As long as the leaders in the various centers did not take their work seriously, as long as some acted almost like university students on holiday, then the deeper, more critical work of consciousness raising and building party cadres would not prosper. From Manuel's perspective this kind of work needed to involve all local activists and peasant leaders in a democratic decision-making process. "What we were suggesting," he explained, "was the need to bring into the MIR *compañeros* who were workers, shantytown dwellers, peasants, Mapuches, who weren't only doing things as activists, but were also in the leadership. This was the only way. If you want a society for the majority, and fundamentally for the poor, you have to make sure they participate in decision making; otherwise it doesn't make any sense."[32]

Manuel's dissatisfactions with the MIR's work on the coast were very much in keeping with his earlier ambivalences and resentments and revolved around two main issues. The first was his familiar perception that MIR leaders tended to be from a privileged class background and to settle comfortably into this privilege in their political work. Thus Alejo, the leader on the ex-*fundo* Nehuentúe, rode around on a beautiful white horse, which was saddled for him by a local peasant, and cultivated a dashing look in a fancy white poncho. Thus the leaders got up late and did not work alongside the peasants in the production center. The second issue for Manuel was the ongoing authoritarianism and centralism that did not allow for the effective participation of lower-class activists. The two issues were clearly connected and went to the heart of the problems the MIR faced as a purportedly anti-Stalinist revolutionary organization, which nevertheless maintained a centralized and hierarchical party structure. Not surprisingly, therefore, when Manuel began pushing for an election of local leaders, the central committee decided to pull him out of the region, which they did at the beginning of 1973. When the coup came in September of that year, Manuel was back in Temuco.

José, too, went back to Temuco before the September 1973 coup; thus, neither he nor Manuel got to witness the end of the agrarian reform on the coast. For the Mapuche and non-Mapuche peasants who felt the brunt of the repression it was the end of a short-lived dream, and they were, in essence, left holding the bag. As Luis Ernesto Quijón, peasant organizer and survivor of two arrests and multiple tortures, put it in January 1997, the MIR organizers "didn't have to face up to the consequences. When [the repression] came they went off in one direction or the other, since they had the connections and the means, and they knew what to do. So who ended up paying for the broken china?"[33]

The "broken china" was a particularly apt metaphor for the violence, repression, and bodily injury caused by the September 1973 coup. But it could also be read to stand for the lack of responsibility and follow-through of the MIR leadership toward their grassroots. After fomenting a climate of confrontation, revolutionary violence, and a hegemonic masculinity of long-haired, daring youth, they simply pulled out. The peasants at the local level did not have the same option. Arrested, imprisoned, and tortured, they would have engraved on their bodies the consequences of this short-lived revolutionary romance. At a certain level this tragic, violent, and sacrificial denouement was a fitting end to the heroic and sacrificial narrative the MIR had been writing all along, a plot that began from the dramatic and selfless immolation of Che Guevara in Bolivia and was further layered and deepened by the listing of Chilean martyrs, such as Luciano Cruz and Arnoldo Ríos. Within this overall story Mapuche peasants ended up playing an especially crucial symbolic role as enduring warrior-victims.

Peasants, Warriors, and Perpetual Sacrifice:
Images of the Mapuche in the MCR

On October 23, 1971, Moisés Huentelaf was killed by landowner bullets during an attempted reclaiming of the *fundo* Chesque in Loncoche, which he and more than forty other peasant activists had taken over the day before. Along with his brother Félix and thirty-eight other peasant leaders from the southern region, Moisés Huentelaf had been present at the meeting on September 12, 1971, when the MCR was founded in Cautín. At a large demonstration in memory of Moisés Huentelaf held shortly after his death, Alejandro Manque, another founding member of the MCR from Loncoche, who had become a national leader for the organization, gave an inspiring speech in which he honored and commemorated his *compañero*. The only Mapuche sitting with the MIR central committee, Manque detailed the origins of the MCR in the mobilizations of Mapuche small proprietors and its expansion to encompass all the rural poor, and he called for a new agrarian reform law that would allow for the expropriation of all landed estates. He also emphasized the exemplary quality of Moisés Huentelaf as the epitome of unity and self-sacrifice: "The example of *compañero* Moisés Huentelaf shows us the combative way to struggle against injustice, misery, and hunger. It also shows us how to achieve revolutionary solidarity with others who are exploited in our land, because he already was an *asentado* (member of an agrarian reform cooperative) and had achieved, through struggle, access to land and work. But this wasn't enough for him. He continued fighting beside his *compañeros* who hadn't yet achieved land and bread."[34] Manque concluded by connecting

Huentelaf to the great hero icons of the MIR, emphasizing that they would continue fighting for land, bread, and socialism "along the trail already blazed for us by *comandante* Guevara, with the example of our comrade Luciano Cruz and now one more murdered by bourgeois bullets; no one will block our way, *compañero* Moisés, *hasta la victoria siempre* (onward always to victory)!"[35]

The combination of heroic sacrifice, combative struggle, and tragic victimization that united all three figures, brought even closer by their common demise—"murdered by bourgeois bullets"—helped construct an image of bravery that inspired, yet also distanced, the common man. Rather than dedicate himself to ensuring the security and prosperity of his family and community within his own agrarian reform center, Moisés Huentelaf had continued fighting for the rights of others. Indeed, all three men had shunned personal security, seeking instead to risk themselves in solidarity with others. To focus on the personal suffering such behavior might have caused was, in such a context, individualistic and counter-revolutionary: no suffering widows, hungry children, or mourning families were featured here. Quite the contrary, those left behind were also pictured as heroic, inspired by the sacrifice of their loved one to continue fighting. Yet there was also a difference between Luciano Cruz and Che Guevara, on the one hand, sons of the very same bourgeoisie charged with victimizing them, and the brave and sacrificial figure of the Mapuche peasant who had fallen victim to the violence of the landowning class that had victimized his ancestors for centuries.

Part of that difference was class exploitation and poverty, and the *mirista* press in 1972 featured prominently the images of long-suffering Mapuche peasants demanding their rights. In this context women and children were legitimate, indeed preferred, symbols of suffering, such as in the June 1972 march of three hundred women to Temuco to protest the imprisonment of "their sons, husbands, and brothers." Among the women demonstrating before the Court of Appeals were, according to *El Rebelde*, the wives of the Chesque peasants still in jail, the women from Lautaro who had been shot at while protesting poor medical attention for their family members who were rural workers, and the mothers of the students who had occupied the house in Villarrica. The common plight of these women, aptly represented by the photograph of Moisés Huentelaf's widow that graced an inset included with the same feature story, helped bond and symbolize the common plight of all the rural poor—"todos los pobres del campo"—that the MIR sought to represent.[36]

Yet as the originators of the struggle for the land, the Mapuche held a privileged position within the *mirista* imaginary. In one of the documents formulated at the founding meeting of the MCR, for example, entitled "The Peasant's Charter of Liberation," the most poetic section made direct reference to the Mapuche and to their ancestral suffering and usurpation: "Keep your *tralca* [Mapuche word for shotgun] behind the door and always well oiled so that you can defend yourself against your aggressive enemies, who are: the landowners, the bourgeoisie and the police who serve them, so that someday you can square accounts with all those who starved your parents and grandparents."[37]

Even clearer in this regard was the poem published in *Punto Final*, alongside the article about the events in Chesque, entitled "The Resurrection of Moisés Huentelaf." "You were born a slave, you died fighting, and you'll be reborn a *comandante* of the future republic that will crown the poor," the poem began, freely mixing revolutionary and mystical Christian metaphors. Immediately thereafter the author sought to establish the ancestral legitimacy of Huentelaf's image:

who would build you a monument now, huentelaf,
mapuche from the southernmost and oldest American forest,
your feet reeking of incessant war for the past four centuries,
guts howling, mouths covered by rocks,
stepping in the blood of your ancestors mixed in the mud of your hut
violated by the rain of four hundred years

In the next section of the poem the author connected the blood and suffering of the Mapuche people directly to Moisés Huentelaf's death, and through the symbolic hole left by the landowner's bullet, gave Huentelaf the ability to look back into his people's past and connect their deaths to present-day revenge:

who will build you the monument now, huentelaf,
that your own blood further reddened the old mud
through the hole opened in you by the boss's bullet

just like it's happened for four times one thousand two hundred
    moons.
Through that hole, moisés huentelaf, you count with your fingers
the ancient waves of your people's river of death,
and they all lie on their deathbeds sharpening the forgotten knives
in order to finally slice through the neverending thread of stories, one
    just like the other,
in which it's always the rich man who wins. Moisés huentelaf,
they've killed you so many times that you're more alive than ever
and it's too many deaths we carry with us and
it's time for our murderers to grieve.

Finally, in the last third of the poem the author plays with the imagery of
class and of Mapuche cultural identity, tying all the poor together, through
class and gender imagery, into a single message of freedom and liberation:

And how could they build you the monument, Indian,
if you were never seen at embassy cocktails, of you
there's barely an apocryphal trace in sociological treatises,
who will reconstruct your face now, huentelaf moisés,
if you gave no lectures or fashion shows nor
the inaugural addresses at symposiums on foreign investment.
You only plowed the earth with your teeth until that last furrow,
which you opened with your ribs, sowing precious testicles
so that history would have a definite sex, one
single species, male and female, called freedom.
You wanted to enter the summit meeting with your *trutruca*
leaning your music up against a pentagram made of fire, *roto*
    huentelaf.
Now that they killed you for the four hundredth time,
all those who, like you, moisés, are second class, we think
with our hands like we have across these long centuries that
only revolution will save you from the muddied waters.[38]

The especially poignant irony of this ancestral suffering, however—and
of the privileged status conferred on the perpetual warrior-victim who had
been killed four hundred times—was that it did not lead to a revolution

that saved the Mapuche from the "muddied waters." Instead, as the peasants arrested, tortured, and beaten on the ex-*fundo* Nehuentúe during the joint army and air force operation of August 1973 learned through personal experience, it led some directly back into the muddied waters, as leaders were tied to the legs of air force helicopters, flown around the area dangling free, and submerged in the waters of the Imperial River in an effort to force them to confess where the MIR had buried the weapons.[39]

"El MIR no se asila": No Safe Haven for Heroic Revolutionaries

Immediately after the September 1973 coup, the MIR leadership announced a policy of heroic revolutionary resistance. "El MIR no se asila" (the MIR does not seek asylum in the embassies) became one of the clandestine party's most important new slogans. This public image of continued and heroic resistance would culminate on October 5, 1974, when Miguel Enríquez met death head-on in a heroic gun battle at his safe house with two units of the *Dirección de Inteligencia Nacional* (DINA). But for most, the everyday experience of arrests and rumored tortures and disappearances generated a climate of fear and desperation, as the repressive forces used family members to blackmail activists still at large or the confessions of tortured prisoners to arrest or break the spirit of their comrades.[40]

When the air force helicopter had landed on the *asentamiento* Arnoldo Ríos on August 31, 1973, the soldiers had lined people up looking for Heriberto Ailío. No one said anything when the commander asked for him by name, even though he was standing right there. A fellow Mapuche activist had the presence of mind to tell Heriberto, in essence, to go look for himself. "It was a strategy he came up with to help me escape," Heriberto remembered. "So I left calmly, and walked calmly for quite a while until, suddenly, I felt the impulse, and began running." Heriberto Ailío hid out in the surrounding Mapuche communities, where he had many collaborators and friends, for a number of days. After the coup, however, he lost the contacts he had established to help him leave the region, and, knowing that the military was pressuring his family and others at the *asentamiento,* he decided to turn himself in.[41]

The military had identified him, Heriberto Ailío later learned, because

Hugo Ailío, a sixteen-year-old from his community who sold *El Rebelde*, had been found with copies of the newspaper and a picture of Che Guevara and tortured at the ex-*fundo* Nehuentúe. Hugo had been so afraid that, at first, he admitted a few things. Then he tried to stop, denying that he knew people; but at that point they began to pressure him harder, hitting him, applying electricity to his head, the soles of his feet, his mouth, lips, and nose. The moment came when he simply could not stand it any longer. "I just started quacking like a duck."[42]

The other person considered a traitor by many people from the coastal region was Gertrudis Quidel, a health promoter and leader who lived with Orlando Beltrán, head of the production center created on the ex-*fundo* Nehuentúe. After the August military operation she traveled to Santiago to meet with members of the Allende government and appeared on national television to denounce the tortures committed against her *compañeros*. She was arrested and tortured after the coup and forced publicly to recant her accusations. People from Ailío remembered that, later, even as she continued to visit Orlando Beltrán in jail, Gertrudis began dating a policeman. One day, the visitors for the Nehuentúe brought the news that Gertrudis had gone out one night with her boyfriend and had left the little son she had with Beltrán alone in the house. While she was out, the house caught fire, and the child—named Luciano Ernesto after the MIR's two martyred icons Luciano Cruz and Ernesto "Che" Guevara—died in the flames.[43]

Ironically, given how rebellious and difficult he had always been, it was Manuel Barrientos who wore the MIR's heroic postcoup straitjacket most comfortably. He did not do so by conforming to the public model of revolutionary sacrifice, however, but by remaining a compulsive behind-the-scenes organizer. Immediately following the coup, Manuel remembered, all contact was lost between the central committee and the regional organizations. After cutting his hair and changing clothes, he began sleeping in a different house every couple of nights. He stayed in touch with other activists, but it was hard to remain positive as comrades fled or were arrested. When a local charity organization with which Manuel worked was raided, it was decided he should leave Temuco.[44]

Manuel took the train north on September 22 and, until October 1974, stayed one step ahead of the police with the help of relatives. In Santiago he managed to reestablish contact with surviving *miristas* who were rebuilding a clandestine network based on regions of origin, but the siege was tightening around the MIR. Lumi Videla Moya, in charge of the network, was identified by MIR informant Marcia Merino and arrested in September 1974. Manuel decided to leave Santiago and began selling used clothes door-to-door in San Antonio, a working-class port south of Valparaíso. Visiting Santiago around the time of Miguel Enríquez's death, he saw people crying openly on the street as they read the news headlines. A contact at a Santiago movie house passed him a microfilm of the MIR's statement about Enríquez's death that was hidden in a pack of cigarettes. Unfortunately, his partner, a young *mirista* he had known in Villarrica, left it in their bag after reading it; this would cause Manuel problems after he was arrested a few days later.[45]

The civil police who arrested him in San Antonio initially did not know who he was. Even in Tejas Verdes, a notorious nearby concentration camp, he remained under the control of Military Intelligence rather than the DINA. This served as partial protection because of the intense and enduring competition between the DINA and other military intelligence services; but all that ended when the newspaper *La Tercera* broke the story that the "fourth man" of the MIR, "El Indio" Barrientos, had been captured and was being held in San Antonio. That very day he was blindfolded and transported to Santiago, to one of the DINA's torture centers at José Domingo Cañas. At his first interrogation, under the direction of the DINA's infamous MIR expert Osvaldo Romo Mena (*el guatón* Romo), and with collaborator Marcia Merino (*la flaca* Alejandra) present, Manuel was tied to the *parrilla,* a metal bed frame, and given electric shocks. But to his surprise this was the only time he was tortured with electricity. He remembers having admitted to working in the clandestine network under the direction of Lumi Videla, who was being held in the same facility, and they were brought face-to-face. Until his transport south to Temuco in the early days of 1975 Manuel remained "disappeared" in the bowels of the DINA torture network, between José Domingo Cañas and the concentration camps at Tres and Cuatro Alamos.[46]

During that time Manuel remembers the death of Lumi Videla, who was thrown over the wall of the Italian embassy, and the disappearance of several MIR comrades, including his Temuco *compañeros* Marcelo Salinas and Jacqueline Drouilly, who were married to each other. Although we discussed the question at some length, neither of us could quite figure out why he was not tortured or mistreated more, and the unspoken question between us was always why he had survived when so many of his comrades had not. At one point Manuel answered it by saying he'd always felt he was living on borrowed time. But on several occasions he also suggested that, in part, he survived because he did not fit the stereotype of the larger-than-life *mirista* hero.

"My looks did not inspire terror," Manuel concluded one day. "My appearance, and my way of talking, made them think I was worthless." What Manuel remembered most about his one electric torture session was that he took on a "Cantinflas-like" comic voice, and complained to his torturers that they couldn't tie his legs down so tight without hurting his varicose veins. Romo told him not to worry, that electricity was good for them because it improved the circulation; Manuel thanked him for the information. Everyone, Manuel recalled, was laughing by the end of his session. And this kind of self-effacing, clowning behavior became Manuel's defense and trademark, through which he revindicated his own humanity vis-à-vis his torturers while consciously exploiting the disbelief many felt when faced with a small, bespectacled man with varicose veins who allegedly was an important *mirista* activist. On his way out of Santiago toward Temuco in early 1975 he met up with a communist prisoner who had heard of "El Indio," a mythically strong *mirista* from the south: "He just looks at me and says hey, are you El Indio? Yes, I say. Hey, he answers, I don't know why, but the image I had was different, you crummy kid! I ran into him a couple of times in Paris later, and he always laughed about the image he'd created in his head, that of course didn't fit the reality of who I was."[47]

The dictatorship was still not finished with this atypical *mirista* mole. Only after several years' imprisonment and a military trial in Temuco was he finally released into exile in 1978. To the very end he organized the political prisoners and clowned before the authorities. Even in exile he remained a critic and a rebel, confronting founding MIR member Nelson Gutiérrez at the first meeting he attended in France. "His speech was very good," Manuel remembered, "very emotional. He ended up crying for our fallen *compañeros,* and talked about the thousands of resistance committees being formed in Chile." Although he did not want to accuse Gutiérrez of lying, Manuel raised his hand and explained that he had just left Chile a few weeks before and that "at least in Cautín, to speak of three resistance committees was already an exaggeration." It was time, Manuel concluded, "to plant our feet firmly on the ground."[48]

If we plant our feet firmly on the ground, we can see how Manuel's experience and subjectivity give the lie to the dramatic forms of romantic and revolutionary masculinity constructed by the MIR. If the MIR did not seek political asylum, many of the activists who survived did so by going into exile. If the ideal *mirista* went down fighting in a romantic shower of bullets, sacrificing his body and his life for a just cause, the surviving *mirista* had deflected his torturer's attention by complaining of varicose veins. And if we look beyond the central committee to the local activists, both Mapuche and non-Mapuche, we can also see that the promises of revolutionary salvation that built on the figures of the *barbudo* and the warrior-victim were, in the end, empty.

Yet the romance of Che Guevara, the kind of revolutionary whose refusal to believe in the impossible had garnered him both his improbable victories against Batista's troops and a lonely death in Bolivia, could still seduce; and, more than any other image, it crossed class, ethnic, and political lines. Mapuche peasants had mobilized for land under banners bearing Che's famous beret-clad head; ironically, the name "Che" meant "people" in the Mapuche language. Even infamous torturer *el guatón* Romo was seduced by the aura of the *barbudo* revolutionary when, nonplussed, he confronted Manuel, the *mirista* mole. Two decades later, having finally left the political party to which he had given the better part of his life, Manuel himself was still caught up in the frenetic and utopian organizing of his earlier years. If the hierarchy, authoritarianism, and lack of realism of a party built on revolutionary masculinity had finally expelled him, the image of Che continued to draw him back in. Indeed, when I visited Manuel in August 1997 and presented him with a copy of Paco Ignacio Taibo II's biography of Che, autographed by the author, he was visibly moved. José Cárdenas also held on to the image of Che. "Of course this was a profoundly romantic image I had," José admitted. But, he continued, "I can tell you that I'm not ashamed of having such a romantic idea of Che, even today, because it allows me to hold on to a sensibility, an ability I still have to feel awe, to be affected by the things happening around me, the things I live today on a daily basis."[49]

Notes

The research that forms the basis of this essay was carried out in Chile in 1996–97, on a UW-Madison sabbatical grant with additional support from the John Simon Guggenheim Foundation and an RISM Landes Fellowship from the Research Institute for the Study of Man. Follow-up visits were financed through a WARF Mid-Career Award (Aug. 1998 and 1999), University of Wisconsin-Madison, and the International Institute, UW Madison (1999). Eduardina, Heriberto, and Robustiano Ailío, Mario Castro, Gonzalo Leiva, Víctor Maturana, Enrique Pérez, Luis Ernesto Quijón, and Aldo Vidal were all key teachers about Cautín, the Pacific Coast, and the MIR. Magaly Ortiz transcribed the tapes of the oral interviews on which an important part of my analysis is based, for which I owe her a very special thank you.

1. Summaries of this movement and period are provided in Kyle Steenland, *Agrarian Reform under Allende: Peasant Revolt in the South* (Albuquerque: University of New Mexico Press, 1977); Florencia E. Mallon, "Land, Morality, and Exploitation: Discourses of Agrarian Reform in Cautín, 1938–1974," *Political Power and Social Theory* 14 (2000): 143–95; and Mallon, "The Mapuche Indigenous Community of Nicolás Ailío and the Chilean State, 1906–2000," ms. The Spanish term for "fence runnings" was *corridas de cerco*. This was a specifically Mapuche form of agrarian mobilization in which the fence of a large estate was moved back to its location on the neighboring Mapuche community's original land title.

2. Hernán Vidal, *"Presencia" del Movimiento de Izquierda Revolucionaria (MIR) (14 claves existenciales)* (Santiago: Mosquito Editores, 1999), 39–47.

3. Ibid., 48.

4. Jorge Pinto Rodríguez, "Ser hombre en el Norte Chico: El testimonio de un historiador," in *Diálogos sobre el género masculino en Chile,* ed. Sonia Montecino and María Elena Acuña (Santiago: Programa Interdisciplinario de Género, Universidad de Chile, 1996), 83–96; quotation on p. 84; Thomas Miller Klubock, *Contested Communities: Class, Gender, and Politics in Chile's El Teniente Copper Mine, 1904–1951* (Durham, N.C.: Duke University Press, 1998), 156–69; quotation on pp. 168–69; Heidi Elizabeth Tinsman, "Unequal Uplift: The Sexual Politics of Gender, Work, and Community in the Chilean Agrarian Reform, 1950–1973" (Ph.D. diss., Yale University, 1996), 114–15.

5. In *Partners in Conflict: The Politics of Gender, Sexuality, and Labor in the Chilean Agrarian Reform, 1950–1973* (Durham, N.C.: Duke University Press, 2002), Heidi Tinsman traces the way family politics and family metaphors permeated politics both from above and below, during the 1960s and early 1970s.

6. Karin Alejandra Rosemblatt, *Gendered Compromises: Political Cultures and the State in Chile, 1920–1950* (Chapel Hill: University of North Carolina Press, 2000), esp. chaps. 1, 2, 6, and 7; quotation on p. 216.

7. José Cárdenas, interview by author, Temuco, Apr. 15, 1997. I have changed the name of this individual for the purposes of this article, even though in principle he has always reiterated his permission for me to use his real name, because he has not seen this particular text in advance. Unattributed information and quotations in the paragraphs that follow come from the same interview.

8. The FER was the student front created by the MIR.

9. Archivo de la Intendencia de Cautín, Oficios Confidenciales y Reservados (1965–72), "Oficio del Intendente de Cautín, Gastón Lobos Barrientos, al Ministro del Interior, sobre la situación del Subdelegado de Villarrica con ocasión de la ocupación de un Inmueble en Aviador Acevedo 720, Villarrica," Temuco, May 29, 1972.

10. Manuel Barrientos, interview by author, Temuco, Jan. 14, 1997. As in the earlier case I have changed the name of this individual for the purposes of this particular article. Unattributed information and quotations in the paragraphs that follow come from the same interview.

11. Manuel Barrientos, interview by author, Temuco, Jan. 17, 1997. Unattributed information and quotations in the paragraphs that follow come from the same interview. On the events at the fundo Chesque see also "Lucha campesina: Un polvorín bajo tierra," *Punto Final,* no. 143, Nov. 9, 1971, 2–5.

12. Cárdenas, interview, Apr. 15, 1997; Barrientos, interview, Jan. 17, 1997.

13. Cárdenas, interview, Apr. 15, 1997.

14. Tinsman, *Unequal Uplift,* 198–201, makes clear that in rural unions during the UP, male comrades bonded through transgressive sexual conversation and raucous weekend entertainment following "leadership training sessions." The fact that homosexuals were expelled from the MIR was confirmed in interviews with surviving leaders broadcast in a TVN Special Report on Chilean television in 1994. Video copy in the ICTUS Archive, Santiago, courtesy of Steve J. Stern.

15. Cárdenas, interview, Apr. 15, 1997.

16. "El punto de partida fue 'Rucalán,' " in "Moisés Huentelaf murió luchando por la conquista de la tierra," *El Rebelde,* no. 8, Nov. 1971, 11. "Campesinos echan por tierra llas intrigas de un momio latifundista. Los Trabajadores de 'Rucalán' a la opinión pública," *Punto Final,* no. 124, Feb. 16, 1971, 26. The word *momio* is Chilean slang for ultraconservative and was used routinely by the left during the agrarian reform years especially. It denotes a mummified, rigidified state and is thus especially descriptive in the contexts in which it was used.

17. The organization of the land committee, the *toma,* and *retoma* is detailed in Mallon, "The Mapuche Community of Nicolás Ailío," ms., chap. 5. The banner from Rucalán appeared in photographs in *El Diario Austral,* Sep. 5, 28, 1973, 1 (in both cases). It is also interesting to note, in this context, that Arnoldo Ríos was a *mirista* student at the University of Concepción who died in a confrontation with students from the Communist Party. Steenland, *Agrarian Reform under Allende,* 91–92.

18. "El grito de la tierra," *Punto Final,* no. 124, Feb. 16, 1971, 25–28; quotation on 27–28.

19. Heriberto Ailío, interview by author, Community of Ailío-Tranapuente, Jan. 18, 1997.

20. Robustiano Ailío, interview by author, Community of Ailío-Tranapuente, Jan. 11, 1997.

21. Heriberto Ailío, interview, Jan. 18, 1997.

22. Ibid; and conversation with Heriberto Ailío, Community of Ailío-Huellanto Alto, June 21, 1997.

23. Cárdenas, interview, Apr. 15, 1997.

24. Ibid.

25. Ibid.

26. Ibid.

27. Ibid.

28. Ibid.

29. Ibid.

30. Barrientos, interview, Jan. 17, 1997.

31. Ibid. It is interesting that, when he is addressing the leader in Nehuentúe, Manuel uses the ultrafamiliar *tu* form of the verb that is common in Chilean slang— *ensillai* rather than *ensillas.* Also, when he refers to Ailío, he means the agrarian reform center where people from Ailío participated, that is, Arnoldo Ríos.

32. Ibid.

33. José Cárdenas, interview by author, Temuco, June 17, 1997; Luis Ernesto Quijón, interview by author, Community of Ailío-Tranapuente, Jan. 4, 1997.

34. Information on the events in Chesque is spread through various issues of MIR publications. See, e.g., "Lucha campesina: Un polvorín bajo tierra," *Punto Final,* no. 143, Nov. 9, 1971, 2–5; "En la senda de Moisés Huentelaf," *Punto Final,* no. 163, Aug. 1, 1972, 10–11; "Legalidad burguesa sigue impidiendo que la tierra sea de los campesinos," *El Rebelde,* no. 9, Dec. 1971, 10–11; "Moisés Huentelaf murió luchando por la conquista de la tierra," *El Rebelde,* no. 8, Nov. 1971, 11. Manque also gave a summary of the events in his speech, reproduced in "Huentelaf: 'Un muerto mas por las balas de los burgueses,' " *El Rebelde,* no. 8, Nov. 1971, 9–10; quotation on p. 10. The photograph of Manque and the central committee is also on p. 10 and is a good example of Hernán Vidal's point about revolutionary imagery, the use of black clothing, and the play of light and shadow.

35. *El Rebelde,* no. 8, Nov. 1971, 10.

36. "Patrones libres, campesinos presos, porque la ley es momia," *El Rebelde,* no. 33, June 6, 1972, 5–6, and inset, "Mujeres en la pelea" (7). For another use of the suffering wives and mothers in order to bond courageous and suffering men see "En Chesque se sigue luchando," *Punto Final,* no. 160, June 20, 1972, 26–27.

37. *El Diario Austral,* Dec. 31, 1970, 8: "Argumento del abogado defensor Miguel

Schweitzer a favor del recurso de amparo presentado a favor de Juan Bautista Landarretche y otros." The fact that this document was formulated at the founding meeting of the MCR is confirmed in "MCR: La revolución en el campo," *El Rebelde*, no. 28, May 2, 1972, 14.

38. Julio Huasi [most likely a pseudonym], "resurrección de moisés huentelaf," *Punto Final*, no. 143, Nov. 9, 1971, 3.

39. The main sources for the events of Aug. 29, 1973, are "El sur bajo régimen militar," *Punto Final*, no. 192, Sept. 11, 1973, 2–3; and an interview with Margarita Paillal [*sic*], a Mapuche peasant leader from Nehuentúe, that appeared in the last number of *Chile Hoy*, with her photograph on the cover, on the very day of the coup: *Chile Hoy* 2, no. 65, Sept. 7–13, 1973, 29, 32. I am grateful to Elizabeth Lira for the reference. Steenland, *Agrarian Reform under Allende*, 189–91, also provides a fairly extensive discussion of the incident. I deal in much greater detail with this military invasion in "The Mapuche Community of Nicolás Ailío," ms., chap. 5. It was one of several military expeditions in the month before the coup that were designed to check out the potential for resistance in areas known for their leftist militance.

40. For the campaign against the MIR see Ascanio Cavallo Castro, Manuel Salazar Salvo, and Oscar Sepúlveda Pachecho, *La historia oculta del régimen militar: Chile, 1973–1988* (Santiago: Editorial Antártida, 1988), 49, 51–60. DINA was the secret intelligence agency directly responsible to Pinochet and run by Manuel Contreras.

41. Heriberto Ailío, interview, Jan. 18, 1997. Heriberto Ailío is mentioned specifically in the story published by *El Diario Austral* on Sept. 3, 1973, as being one of the important organizers from the region still at large (1).

42. Hugo Ailío, interview by author, Concepción, Aug. 12, 1999.

43. Interviews with Manuel Barrientos, Apr. 14, 1997; Gloria Muñoz (name changed), Santiago, May 15, 1997; Heriberto Ailío, Temuco, Apr. 18, 1997, Huellanto Alto, Aug. 10, 1999; Robustiano and Eduardina Ailío, Tranapuente, Aug. 14, 1999; Patricia Valenzuela, Nehuentúe, Aug. 20, 1999. Although Robustiano, Eduardina, and Heriberto Ailío and Manuel Barrientos all remember the incident with the burning of Luciano Ernesto, Patricia Valenzuela, who lives in Nehuentúe, told me she did not remember it.

44. Manuel Barrientos, interviews by author, Apr. 14, 16, 1997.

45. Manuel Barrientos, interviews by author, Apr. 16, May 19, 1997.

46. Barrientos, interview, May 19, 1997.

47. Barrientos, interviews by author, May 19, 23, 1997; direct quotation from May 23 interview.

48. Barrientos, interview, Apr. 14, 1997.

49. Cárdenas, interview, Apr. 15, 1997.

DANIEL BALDERSTON

Sexuality and Revolution:

On the Footnotes to

El beso de la mujer araña

■ ■ ■

One of the most important reflections on Latin American masculinity, *El beso de la mujer araña* (The kiss of the spider woman), authored by Manuel Puig (1930–90), was published in Spain in 1976, the very year a brutal military dictatorship took over Puig's native Argentina. The novel, banned in Argentina until after the end of the military regime in 1983, consists of a series of conversations in a prison cell between an urban guerrilla, Valentín Arregui Paz, and a gay window dresser, Luis Alberto Molina. Much of the novel consists of a series of film narratives that Molina retells to Arregui; cinematic fantasy and identifications mediate the distance between the two men, who eventually make love (shortly before Molina's release). The following essay is based on a close study of a portion of the manuscripts to the novel and is limited specifically to eight footnotes, Puig's most extended reflection on theories of sexuality and on the relation between sexual liberation and political liberation movements. The larger issues at stake in the novel are, then, clearly reflected in the footnotes.

One of the most controversial aspects of Puig's novel is the series of didactic footnotes, eight in all, on theories of sexuality, especially on the origin and nature of homosexuality, and on the possibilities opened by sexual liberation movements. These notes establish a strange dialogue from below with the dialogue above, that of Luis Alberto Molina and Valentín Arregui, a dialogue that turns on the plural nature of masculinity.[1] Many readers, and most critics, have questioned the need for the series of footnotes (which some U.S. and European readers, in particular, have believed to be largely common knowledge), and there have been somewhat fruitless attempts to relate the precise matter of the notes to the events taking place on the upper parts of the same pages.[2] This essay, based on research into the sources of the footnotes and a careful examination of the manuscript versions of the material that became the notes, will take a somewhat different tack: to look at the series of notes as a brief treatise on the theory of sexuality and on the relationship between sexual liberation and broader social change. Given that Puig was famous for having eliminated the narrator from his fiction, the footnotes provide a unique point of access into his point of view.

The following essay is based in part on manuscript material that is being prepared for a critical edition in Colección Archivos in Paris by a team at the Universidad Nacional de La Plata consisting of José Amícola, Graciela Goldchluk, Roxana Páez, and Julia Romero.[3] The original manuscripts are in the possession of the Puig family in Buenos Aires; Goldchluk and Romero have tea and watch a movie every Wednesday evening with Puig's mother, choosing from the videotheque left by Puig, which consists of some thirty-five hundred films. This contemporary version of "Tea and Sympathy" has yielded access to a fascinating body of manuscript material, perhaps the most interesting such material to emerge in the field of Latin American literature since Ana María Barrenechea worked on the Cuaderno de Bitácora to Julio Cortázar's *Rayuela* (1963; Barrenechea edition of manuscript material 1983).

Because I will be dealing in some detail with the sources and versions of the eight footnotes, it would no doubt be helpful first to review their order and content. (I will not be dealing here with a ninth footnote, the one that completes the story of the supposed Nazi film, because it has little to do with the project of the notes on homosexuality and establishes a very different relation with the "text above," as Lucille Kerr calls it.) The first note (pages 66–68 of the first edition) appears in the middle of the third chapter, during the first half of Molina's retelling of the Nazi film involving Leni the chanteuse; it summarizes three theories of the physical origin of homosexuality (hormonal imbalance, intersexuality, hereditary factors) and the refutations of these theories by the British psychologist D. J. West. The second note (pages 102–3, near the beginning of chapter five, before Molina's interior monologue on the story of The Enchanted Cottage) is concerned with three "lay" theories of the psychic origin of homosexuality (theories of seduction, segregation, and perversion) and ends with an introduction to Freud's theories of its origin in infancy. The third (pages 133–35, in chapter six, the one in which Valentín tells the story of the film involving a race-car driver) continues the discussion of the theories of Freud and his orthodox followers (including his daughter Anna) on child psychology, the infantile libido, original bisexuality and the function of repression. The fourth (pages 141–43, in chapter seven, which opens with Molina's singing a bit of the bolero "La carta" and continues with Valentín's deciphering of a coding letter about "uncle Pedro") focuses on the orthodox Freudian theory that male homosexuality arises from an excessive identification of the child with his mother. The fifth (pages 154–55, in chapter eight, which opens with the prison records for Molina and Arregui and then continues with the dialogue between Molina and the warden) focuses on the function of patriarchal dominance in the workings of repression, mentioning for the first time the so-called Freudian left or heterodoxy—Wilhelm Reich, Herbert Marcuse, Norman O. Brown—and the Australian political scientist and ideologist of gay liberation Dennis Altman. The sixth (pages 168–71, in chapter nine, the first chapter of the second part of the novel, in which Molina tells the first half of the Jacques Tourneur film I Walked with a Zombie) discusses the fortunes of the Freudian concept of sublimation in the work of these heterodox Freudians and opens the discussion of a new topic: the possible function of sexual liberation in broader social change. The seventh (pages 199–200, at the end of chapter ten, in which Molina continues the retelling of I Walked with a Zombie) begins with the assertion that the stigma against homosexuals is stronger than that on alcoholics, compulsive gamblers, ex-cons, and former mental patients (derived from J. L. Simmons's work on deviance), continues with Freud's disapproval of this stigma (in his well-known "Letter to an American Mother"), and proposes that if the original "polymorphous perverse" were released, that strong changes in society, sexual roles, and human liberation in general would follow. The eighth and final note (pages 209–11, in chapter eleven, which begins with another interview between Molina and the warden, continues with the conclusion of *I Walked with a Zombie*, and finishes with the first time that Molina and Arregui have sex) argues once more for the liberation of the "polymorphous perverse" (again mentioning Marcuse's and Brown's interpretations of Freud), recalls Fenichel's idea that the only gender roles that are available are those that are based on imitations of our mothers and fathers, and ends with an extensive discussion of the ideas of the Danish woman doctor Anneli Taube on the link between sexual liberation and revolution.

The eight notes, then, provide a fairly broad survey of twentieth-century ideas on the dialectics of sexual oppression and liberation; Pamela Bacarisse calls them "a homogeneous collection, orientated towards the theories proposed by the politico-sexual liberation movements of the sixties, and at least some of the sexual idealists of that epoch" (Bacarisse 1988, 114). A total of twenty-six authorities are quoted or paraphrased (from Freud and Lenin to Dr. Taube), from a total of thirty-one texts (five Freud texts are cited, as well as two of Marcuse's). This extensive treatise on sexual repression and liberation is noteworthy for the seeming diversity of its sources and for its strong final thesis: that sexual liberation in general and gay liberation in particular are essential parts of the widely desired social change (we are in the seventies, after all) and that there are strong links—Lenin, Marcuse, Taube—between ideas of sexual liberation and the Marxist tradition.[4]

Such an abundance of authorities, quotations, summaries, and paraphrases suggests considerable research. However, a careful examination of the quotations and paraphrases from the twenty-six authors reveals that with only three exceptions all of them are cited in the two sources that Puig relied on the most: *Homosexuality* (1967), by the British psychologist D. J. West, and *Homosexual Oppression and Liberation* (1971), by the Australian political scientist and activist Dennis Altman. The first exception is a passing reference to C. S. Lewis's memoir *Surprised by Joy*, which includes a discussion of homosexual practices among boys in British boarding schools (a situation parallel to that of the prisoners in the novel, and one often studied in relation to other segregated male situations such as military bases and prisons in the literature on the subject). The second is a passing reference to Freud's authorship of *The Interpretation of Dreams,* a work not cited directly by West or Altman (although the ideas of Freud's that are discussed here do appear in West, but with notes referring to others of Freud's works). The final exception is the discussion of the ideas of Dr. Taube, for reasons revealed years ago by Lucille Kerr in her book on Puig, *Suspended Fictions:* that said Danish doctor is our author in drag.

In general terms notes 1 to 4 are based on Puig's readings of West and notes 5 to 8 on Altman, although there are some exceptions to this pattern. In any case the summaries of the sociological and psychological studies of homosexuality, particularly the empirical ones, derive from West, whereas the discussions of the work of the heterodox Freudians (Reich, Marcuse, Brown), of ideas on sexual revolution and counterculture (Millett, Roszak), and even the reference to Lenin's ideas on sexual liberation, derive from Altman. The odd thing about the almost total reliance on this particular pair of sources is that West's book is sharply criticized by Altman for its reliance on the normative language of 1960s social science: West uses descriptive terms that imply a strong moral sanction, such as *normal, perverse,* and *deviant,* without apparent irony. Altman comments: "however able a psychologist West may be, he is a poor logician, and a man too apt to confuse social prejudice with natural laws" (Altman 1971, 48), and later: "his use of words like 'natural,' 'perversion,' etc. powerfully reinforce conventional morality. . . . Like too many psychologists, West is strongly conformist, even where his own expert knowledge tells him that social norms are not necessarily sensible"(Altman 1971, 49).

By using West almost exclusively in the first half of the notes (concerned mostly with theories of the origin of homosexuality), leaving Altman as the main source for the second half of his treatise, Puig privileges the latter's ideas on gay liberation and its ties to social transformation over West's more conventional or conformist ideas on the origin and nature of homosexuality (as an exotic Other). What interests Puig in the last instance is not what the homosexual is but what he or she could become. As Altman writes:

> It seems to me that the connection between sexual liberation and total liberation should be made somewhat differently. Liberation is a process

that individuals strive toward, and part of this striving involves a recognition of the way in which oppression is implanted in the very structures of our society. To overcome the stigma society places on homosexuality, for example, does mean radical alterations in the way in which we order the socialization process. More than this, as individuals come to a greater acceptance of their erotic/sexual being, they tend spontaneously to reject the "performance principle" that underlies the dominant ethos of property, competition, and aggression. Thus, between individual and social liberation there is a dialectic relationship, and as Marcuse puts it in his *Essay on Liberation,* "radical change in consciousness is the beginning, the first step in changing social existence: emergence of the new Subject." (Altman 1971, 92).

There is a startling unevenness in the importance of the authors cited in the notes (or rather, quoted from prior quotations, since these almost always derive from West and Altman). One feels a bit embarrassed to encounter the quotation from Theodore Roszak on the woman who is hidden within every man waiting to be liberated; his book *The Making of the Counter-Culture,* published in 1969, is very much of its time and barely intelligible today. So it is a bit comforting to think that Puig did not necessarily read Roszak (but encountered Roszak in Altman), although it is in fact very likely that he did read him, because it was impossible to live in the United States and to follow the pseudointellectual discussions of the time without reading Roszak or, even worse, Charles Reich's embarrassing *The Greening of America,* which was excerpted in *The New Yorker* in the early seventies and widely commented on as if there were ideas to be found in it. Altman's book is very informed by discussions of the period—about the relations between gay liberationist ideas and those of the women's movement, the New Left, or the Black Panthers—but for the most part Puig avoided quoting from the most lightweight material that found its way into Altman's early book (his more recent work is quite different in tenor, I should clarify); instead, Altman is mostly used for his useful digest of the ideas of Reich, Marcuse, and Brown and Altman's provocative use of the heterodox Freudian tradition for discussing gay liberation.

In numerous instances, when comparing the quotations or summaries in Puig's footnotes with the texts cited in West and Altman, I have found small but significant changes of title, confusing of opinions, even the conflation of two or more authorities into one. For instance, the first note claims to summarize the ideas of Dr. Foss, from his article "La influencia de andrógenos urinarios en la sexualidad de la mujer," in the following words:

las grandes cantidades de hormonas masculinas administradas a mujeres producen sí un notable cambio en dirección a la masculinidad, pero sólo en lo que concierne el aspecto físico: voz más profunda, barba, disminución de senos, crecimiento del clítoris, etc. En cuanto al apetito sexual, aumenta, pero continúa siendo normalmente femenino, es decir que el objeto de su deseo sigue siendo el hombre, claro está si no se trata de una mujer ya con costumbres lesbianas. (Puig 1976, 66)

This is a fairly full translation of the following passage in West:

The effect of large doses of androgens on women is well known as a result of naturally occurring adrenal tumours, which secrete excessive amounts of androgens, and because big doses of androgens have been given as treatment for certain cancers. The woman's appearance undergoes a striking change in the direction of masculinity. The voice deepens, a beard grows, breasts regress, clitoris enlarges, features coarsen, and feminine fat disappears. Sexual desire usually increases, but remains normal feminine desire, unless of course lesbian inclinations were already present. (West 1967, 158)

Apart from the slight condensing of the original material in Puig's translation (and of the addition of the idea that "normal" feminine desire is directed toward men, not in West), what is most interesting in this passage is that West's notes refer not only to G. L. Foss's article "The Influence of Androgens on Sexuality in Women" but also to two other sources: R. B. Greenblatt's "Hormonal Factors in Libido" and W. H. Masters and D. T. Magallon's "Androgen Administration in the Post-Menopausal Woman." Puig, that is, simplifies the critical apparatus, referring to only one of the three articles. In the same note, when he refers to a Dr. Swyer, author of "Homosexualidad, los aspectos endocrinológicos," he paraphrases material from page 159 of West, which is based on the work of C. A. Wright, author of "Endocrine Aspects of Homosexuality." I will not try your patience with an excessive number of examples of this sort of error or simplification, but they confirm the hypothesis that the bibliographical research on the topic was minimal, apart from the two books mentioned.

The case of Dr. Taube is interesting in part because the author disguises himself as a woman (as he is said to do in the letters that are preserved in the Princeton library), but the Danish doctor is also a sort of double of Dennis Altman. Like him, she sees the gay liberation movement as parallel to, and in solidarity with, movements of women's liberation and Black power, and part of a broader united front. Both use the language of the New Left of the sixties and seventies. The author himself calls attention on page 210 to the great similarities between the ideas of Taube and Altman. Dr. Taube says that the homosexual child is a future revolutionary: "el rechazo que un niño muy sensible puede experimentar con respecto a un padre opresor—símbolo de la actitud masculina autoritaria y violenta—, es de naturaleza consciente" [the rejection that a very sensitive child can feel with regard to an oppressive father—the symbol of an authoritarian and violent masculine attitude—is of a conscious nature] (Puig 1976, 209). It is worth noting that *taube* in German means "dove" or "pigeon" ("pichón" in Argentine Spanish), a possible reference to the Argentine psychiatrist Enrique Pichon Rivière but also to the use of *pichón* as a term of endearment; the German form of the surname is reminiscent of "taboo," thus recalling Freud's *Totem und Tabu*. The doctor is Danish, I suppose, because of the celebrated early sex change operation performed on Christine Jorgensen, recalled at the moment that our author changes sex. (José Amícola mentions that when the novel was translated into Danish, Puig attempted—but too late to affect the published form of the translation—to change the doctor's name and nationality, so as not to give away the game [Amícola 1992, 238 n. 8].)

The ideas of Taube/Altman on sexual revolution and the polymorphous perverse make possible the entanglement of Molina and Arregui and their change of roles in the course of the novel: the reading of the "bottom" of the page alters the "top." In this game of "top" and "bottom" there is an interesting inversion of roles: if the active figure (male, top, "lector cómplice") normally subjects the passive one (female, bottom, "lector hembra"), then Puig uses the footnotes, and invents the authority of Dr. Taube, to destabilize this schema.[5]

Another example of the use of the sources, now with respect to the topic of sexual revolution, is when Puig writes, "Marcuse señala que la función social del homosexual es análoga a la del filósofo crítico, ya que su sola presencia resulta un señalador constante de la parte reprimida de la sociedad" [Marcuse signals that the social function of the homosexual is analogous to that of the critical philosopher, since his or her very present is a constant indicator of the repressed part of society] (Puig 1976, 199). This is derived from Altman, who in turn is summarizing the arguments of Paul A. Robinson, author of *The Freudian Left,* on Reich, Roheim, and Marcuse: "Robinson interprets some of [Marcuse's] writings as suggesting that 'in a certain sense, then, the social function of the homosexual was analogous to that of the critical philosopher'" (Altman 1971, 65, quoted in Robinson 208). Here there can be no doubt that Marcuse is thinking of the famous phrase of Karl Marx: "Philosophers have only interpreted the world in various ways, but the real task is to change it." In the diverse intonations of the same idea there is continuity but also rupture: it is obvious that Marx would not have affirmed that the homosexual is the "critical philosopher," the conscious rebel, the hero of history.

That is perhaps why there is one series of notes and not two (one on sexuality, the other on Marxist theory and urban guerrilla practice). The critical philosopher in the cell turns out not to be Valentín Arregui but the seemingly frivolous Luis Alberto Molina. He needs the voice of the other, and his ears (and other appendages), to make himself heard. The voice from below, the voice of the reader or spectator who chooses the subaltern or "bottom" role—a space occupied here by Taube, Marcuse, Freud, even Lenin, and certainly Puig—is closer to the vital center of this story, in which the private is public and the personal is political. A careful look at the manuscript material reveals that the earliest document is probably a list of quotations from Freud, Fenichel, Marcuse, and numerous others, culled from Puig's readings of West, Altman, and others. These were typed, and later numbered, in Puig's handwriting with a series of letter codes: a, b, c, and so forth through the entire alphabet, then starting again with a', b', c', etc. (That these quotations were collected prior to their being organized into the present notes is proven by the fact that they are assembled in the notes in orders very different from their ordering in the collection of quotations: note 5, for instance [in chapter 8] contains quotations in the following order: k - ı - b - e - j - d - h - ñ - o - t - u.) There is then a series of handwritten pages where Puig struggles with the ordering of the material and with determining what chapters it should be paired with. A crucial document is a schematic outline of the first eleven chapters, a scrap of paper on the other side of which Puig noted some page numbers from Altman and jotted down that his "next novel" would be called—or about—Man and Beauty. The outline reads:

1.	Pantera A	
2.	Pantera B (y Jane)	
3.	Leni A (y mozo)	Homo I {teorías 3 que termina con consenso de causas psic.
4.	Leni B, dolores SHE	Vulgo y start psic.
5.	Seef [?] Cottage	
6.	50's guerrilla, dolores HE Madre She, He's film	Edipo Narcisismo ¿Anal?
7.	"Mi carta"–Dolores HE, He's film	Represión I
8.	Director	
9.	Comida, Mejoría, Zombies A, carta dictada, lava	Rep. II
10.	Salud HE, Zombies B Desplante He por mimos	Rep. III
11.	Director–Vuelve She triste	Corolario ME alone!!! + Nombre INVENTADO . . . . PARA DEDUCCIÓN . . . Rechazo Imagen Represor

This outline is substantially that of the novel that was later published, although only of the first eleven of the sixteen chapters. The HE and SHE are Arregui and Molina, and the films that are narrated are indicated in shorthand. The importance of the outline resides in the crucial structural role played from early in the project by the footnotes, summarized in the right column after the arrows. The summary of the content of the notes is

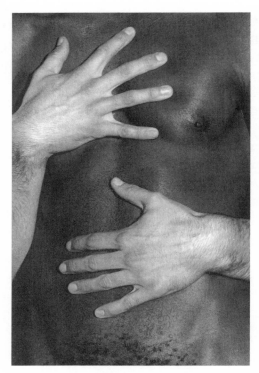

Black and white. HIV/AIDS prevention postcard
used in interventions in gay commercial venues.
Brazilian Interdisciplinary AIDS Association (ABIA).

perhaps clearer than the summary of the main action: "Director–Vuelve
SHE triste" is a somewhat inadequate summary of a chapter that includes
the first time that Molina and Arregui make love. It is also of particular
interest that the last five chapters, which include preparations for Molina's
release, the Mexican cabaretera film, Molina's release and death, and Arregui's spider woman fantasy after being tortured, are absent: what interested Puig at the moment he scrawled this outline was the pairing of the
footnotes to the main action, and the footnotes end in chapter 11. The note
on the eighth footnote is particularly revealing, as he calls it a "Corollary"
to the three notes on repression, and adds: "ME alone!!!" The reader of the
novel is left to deduce that Dr. Taube is Puig (Nombre INVENTADO PARA
DEDUCCION, with *DEDUCCION* heavily underscored).[6]

226 ▪ ▪ ▪ Daniel Balderston

Altman's title *Homosexual Oppression and Liberation* is echoed in Taube's *Sexuality and Revolution* and in the general structure of the last four notes, which move through three versions of Repression (Rep. I, II, and III, in the manuscript) to the final note on Liberation (although this theme is present earlier in the quotations and paraphrases from Marcuse, Brown, Roszak, Millett, and Altman).

The presumed next step in the process of composition is the typescript of the first seven notes, some with heavy handwritten corrections, including arrows to rearrange the paragraphs. The eighth note, the one about Dr. Taube's theories of the relations between sexual liberation and revolution, is, tellingly, handwritten rather than typed, as Puig was not working directly from his typed collection of numbered quotations but from ideas of his own. The handwritten manuscript is extraordinarily rough compared to the relatively neat typescripts of the rest of the notes, showing intense rewriting of this section. Roberto Echavarren, in a perceptive article on *El beso* published in 1978, just two years after the publication of the novel, asks near the end, in the title of the final section (which is concerned with the footnotes), whether the novel could be considered didactic. He explains:

Tal vez [las notas] irriten a ciertos lectores, tal vez resulten en parte superfluas a otros. El propósito fundamental de las notas es enriquecer la visión de la homosexualidad abriendo un campo de posibilidades que rebasa las características concretas del personaje Molina. (Echavarren 1978, 74)

[Perhaps the notes will irritate certain readers, perhaps they will seem superfluous to others. The notes' fundamental purpose is to enrich the vision of homosexuality opening up a field of possibilities that surpasses the concrete characteristics of Molina the character.]

And he later adds: "Quizá la mayor ventaja de las notas es la distancia que establecen entre una homosexualidad 'posible' y el 'modelo reducido' de la homosexualidad de Molina" [Perhaps the greatest strength of the notes is the distance they establish between a "possible" homosexuality and the "reductive model" of Molina's homosexuality] (Echavarren 1978, 75). José Amícola argues in similar terms that "las notas tienen la cualidad de establecer una convivencia con el lector mediante un efecto de ruptura de la ilusión que, a la manera brechtiana, permite considerar el problema desde la perspectiva de una equidistante lectura racional" [the notes establish a sort of complicity with the reader through an effect of the breaking of the illusion, which, in the Brechtian manner, allows the reader to consider the problem from the perspective of an objective and distanced rational reading] (Amícola 1992, 95), whereas Elías Miguel Muñoz calls the notes a "texto científico" [a scientific text] (Muñoz 1987, 71). Juan Pablo Dabove has written in his book on *El beso, La forma del Destino:*

> los personajes viven un conflicto de naturaleza afectiva, política, sexual. Por lo mismo, desconocen las variables fundamentales que en él se articulan, las repeticiones, las comunidades históricas. El saber eminentemente libresco que las notas exhiben cumpliría la función de distanciar al lector de la trama, de mostrar a la luz de las diversas disciplinas constituidas aquello que los protagonistas no ven, ampliar y relativizar los términos del debate o el amor que entre ellos se suscita. (Dabove 1994, 14 n)

> [the characters embody a conflict of an affective, political, and sexual nature. For that very reason they do not know the fundamental variables that are articulated in that conflict, the repetitions, the historic communities. The supremely bookish knowledge that the notes exhibit would thus fulfill the function of distancing the reader from the plot, of showing through the discourses of the various disciplines that are invoked that which the characters cannot see, to expand and relativize the terms of the debate or the love that grows between them.]

The problem with these readings, three of which make use of the Brechtian notion of distancing, is that the perspective from below that is opened up by the notes, and that supplements the discourse of Molina, can only be described as "objective" or "rational" if one reads these notes as if they were notes to an article or critical book. Roxana Páez allows for a richer reading of the notes when she says that they

> reintroducen fantasmáticamente lo que Puig reprime, el narrador, que deviene Puig mismo con una postura que no deja resquicios librados al lector. Enriquecen la narración/relación, porque la apostrofan o la con-

tradicen. Y por momentos, de tan brechtianas, las interrupciones se vuelven cómicas. (Páez 1995, 77)

[reintroduce in a phantasmatic way what Puig represses, the narrator, who becomes Puig himself in a posture that leaves no opening for interpretation by the reader. They enrich the narration/telling, but they apostrophize or contradict it. And at times, due to the Brechtian character, the interruptions become comic.]

Julia Romero's comments on the destabilization effects of Dr. Taube's ideas of the polymorphous perverse are also pertinent:

La nota de Anneli Taube, incluida en el mismo capítulo donde los personajes llegan a la consumación sexual, deja ver la ironía: el perverso polimorfo no es Molina, sino el viril Valentín. Recordemos que Molina discrimina (se siente "una mu-jer," y es por eso que quiere a un "hombre de verdad," no a los homosexuales amigos suyos) y el sujeto de la enunciación lo critica. (Romero 1996, 455 n. 12)

[The note by Anneli Taube, included in the same chapter in which the characters achieve sexual union, leaves room for irony: the polymorphous perverse is not Molina but the virile Valentín. Let's remember that Molina discriminates (he feels himself a "wo-man," and for that reason seeks a "real man," not his homosexual friends) and the subject of the enunciation criticizes him.]

She then quotes in extenso from Dr. Taube on the bourgeois models that afflict both heterosexuality and homosexuality, that is, above all, the models of "hombre fuerte" and "mujer débil," thus suggesting the same subversion of the upper text by the lower that I suggested earlier.

Notes in a fictional text, as Shari Benstock has observed in a fine article in *PMLA* in 1983, have a somewhat different, and often more subversive, dimension:

Footnotes in fictional texts do not necessarily follow the rules that govern annotation in critical texts: they may or may not provide citation, explication, elaboration, or definition for an aspect of the text; they may or may not follow "standard form"; they may or may not be subordinate to the text to which they are appended. Most significant, they belong to a fictional universe, stem from a creative act rather than a critical one, and direct themselves toward the fiction and never toward an external construct, even when they cite "real" works in the world outside the particular fiction. The referential and marginal features of these notes serve a specifically hermeneutic function; to the extent that notations in fictional texts negotiate the distance between writer and reader, they do so in terms that differ radically from those of scholarly discourse. (Benstock 1983, 204–5)

Although Benstock focuses her attention on notes in Henry Fielding, Laurence Sterne, James Joyce, and Vladimir Nabokov, and never refers to Puig (or to Jorge Luis Borges), her ideas are a useful corrective to Echavarren, Amícola, and Dabove, all of whom assume a scientific stance in these footnotes, some of which refer to empirical scientific research or to the pseudoscience of psychoanalysis yet do not speak from a scientific viewpoint. The treatise on sexuality and revolution that is Puig's footnotes to *El beso* is closer to the mock-philosophical tradition that we know from Jonathan Swift, Sterne, and Borges than to the "equidistante lectura racional" invoked by Amícola, and the clincher is Puig's disappearing act at the end into the female body and voice of Anneli Taube. As Benstock writes at the end of her article:

Because footnotes in fiction cannot serve the ends they serve in the scholarly tradition, they parody the notational convention and draw attention to the faulted authority present in all such structures, most especially those employed by scholars. Language always embodies both authority and the threat to authority; it is always a dialogue between self and other; it is always turned back on itself. The very fact of writing both extends and undercuts the claims of language. Thus footnotes in any text, whether scholarly or fictional, illustrate the rhetorical double bind that keeps all language at the margin of discourse. (220)

The sex change that Manuel Puig performs on himself at the end of the treatise on sexuality, whether we choose to read the treatise as a whole as mock-philosophical or not, is at least a signal to the fact that authority can be put into question or "turned back on itself" in the "bottom" text, as well as in the "top" one.

Notes

1. The focus of this essay is deliberately narrow, on the footnotes to the novel and the theories of homosexuality that inform them; it may seem at times that the multiple "masculinities" with which other essays in this volume are concerned are referred to only obliquely. I would argue, however, that Puig's 1976 novel is an early and decisive intervention in debates about masculinity in Latin America, certainly one of the most widely read texts to be concerned with these questions. In addition, Molina and Arregui's debates in the novel are centrally concerned with what it is to be a man, and it is certainly not the case that Arregui's performance of masculinity is the only one available here.

2. See, e.g., Bacarisse: "The reader should not ignore the footnotes, for if he does, a major key to at least some kind of understanding of the novel will have been passed over" (1988, 113).

3. A Spanish version of this essay appeared in Daniel Balderston, *El deseo, enorme cicatriz luminosa* (Caracas: Ediciones eXcultura, 1999).

4. "Their quasi-scientific nature gives them an impersonal, even objective air, but they are not, of course, either impersonal or objective. Like the sixties movements, they constitute an explicit plea for freedom from repression, a repression that was seen then as the pervasion of society by a ruthless masculinity" (Bacarisse 1988, 114).

5. In a 1984 talk (published in part in the British journal *Index on Censorship* in 1985), "The Loss of a Readership," and in a subsequent 1990 talk "El error gay," Puig develops his ideas about sexual liberation, polymorphous perversity, and the fluidity of sexual categories. See Romero 1999, 305–15, which includes a transcription from the manuscripts of these important texts, showing Puig's careful revision of his expression of these ideas.

6. Juan José Sebreli, in a long 1997 essay on the secret history of homosexuality in Buenos Aires, argues that Puig based *El beso* on the outcry by the ERP (one of the urban guerrilla groups in the early 1970s in Argentina), which "denunció con horror que sus militantes eran recluidos en las mismas celdas que los homosexuales" [denounced with horror that their militants were imprisoned in the same cells as homosexuals] (Sebreli 1997, 337). Sebreli also mentions that Puig took part in the first meetings in 1971 of the Frente de Liberación Homosexual in Buenos Aires, although he claims that Puig "advirtió que no participaría en el movimiento a causa de su carrera literaria" [announced that he would not participate in the movement because of his literary career] (Sebreli 1997, 332).

References

Altman, Dennis. 1971. *Homosexual Oppression and Liberation.* New York: Outerbridge and Dienstfrey.

Amícola, José. 1992. *Manuel Puig y la tela que atrapa al lector: Estudio sobre El beso de la mujer araña en su relación con los procesos receptivos y con una continuidad literaria contestaria.* Buenos Aires: Grupo Editor Latinoamericano.

Bacarisse, Pamela. *The Necessary Dream: A Study of the Novels of Manuel Puig.* Cardiff: University of Wales Press, 1988.

Balderston, Daniel. *El deseo, enorme cicatriz luminosa.* Caracas: Ediciones eXcultura, 1999.

Benstock, Shari. 1983. "At the Margin of Discourse: Footnotes in the Fictional Text." *PMLA* 98, no. 2:204–25.

Dabove, Juan Pablo. 1994. *La forma del destino: Sobre "El beso de la mujer araña" de Manuel Puig.* Rosario: Beatriz Viterbo Editora.

Echavarren, Roberto. 1978. "*El beso de la mujer araña* y las metáforas del sujeto." *Revista Iberoamericana* 102–3:65–75.

Kerr, Lucille. 1987. *Suspended Fictions: Reading Novels by Manuel Puig.* Urbana: University of Illinois Press.

Muñoz, Elías Miguel. 1987. *El discurso utópico de la sexualidad en Manuel Puig.* Madrid: Editorial Pliegos.

Páez, Roxana. 1995. *Manuel Puig: Del pop a la extrañeza.* Buenos Aires: Editorial Almagesto.

Puig, Manuel. *El beso de la mujer araña.* 1st ed. Barcelona: Seix Barral, 1976.

Romero, Julia. 1996. "De monólogo al estallido de la voz." In *Materiales iniciales para La traición de Rita Hayworth,* ed. José Amícola, 451–67. La Plata: Centro de Estudios de Teoría y Crítica Literaria.

———. 1999. "Manuel Puig: Del delito de la escritura al error gay." *Revista Iberoamericana* 65, no. 187:305–25.

Sebreli, Juan José. 1997. "Historia secreta de los homosexuales en Buenos Aires." *Escritos sobre escritos, ciudades bajo ciudades,* 275–370. Buenos Aires: Editorial Sudamericana.

West, D[onald]. J. 1967. *Homosexuality.* Chicago: Aldine.

PETER M. BEATTIE

Measures of Manhood: Honor,

Enlisted Army Service, and

Slavery's Decline in Brazil, 1850—90

■ ■ ■ ■

He who would travel abroad and, as a result, see foreign army troops will notice the enormous difference that exists between their [enlisted soldiers] and our own. . . . What Brazilian considered decent would dare walk down the street arm in arm with a simple private? Let's be frank: no one! We cannot attribute this type of repugnance to anything but the individual quality of a soldier, and the barbarous methods employed to fill the ranks of our army. The recruiters hunt down all the dregs of society and bring in their recruitment sweeps thieves, vagabonds and vagrants . . . and with these elements of infamous dissolution our battalions are formed and our cavalry squadrons! . . . He who is unfit to be admitted to the national guard is fit to serve as an army regular.—O Alvorado, Jaguarão, Rio Grande do Sul

As this writer rued, most Brazilians in the late 1800s equated regular army enlisted service with "dishonor." Privates and noncommissioned officers (NCOs) formed part of an untouchable stratum of Brazil's free poor, whose very presence embodied a kind of dangerous social pollution to the "honorable." Brazilian soldiers were not unique in this sense. In Russia at this time public city park signs barred both dogs and army enlisted men from entering; peasants performed mock funeral rites for young men tapped for army service, and the doleful inductees went on a socially sanctioned drinking binge.[1] Although this essay will focus on Brazil, the Russian comparison shows that the low status of common soldiers was not unique to Latin America, and it suggests that their disrepute was linked to surrounding coercive labor systems such as slavery, serfdom, and debt peonage, whose decline coincided with the rise of nationalist militarism on a global scale.[2] Although many coercive labor practices were abolished in the 1800s, the cultural values they begot were slower to change. No "decent" Brazilian would socialize with privates, much less walk with them in public. Instead, "honorable" poor freemen sought out posts in the national guard to exempt themselves from army service. Not all Brazilians viewed soldiers in such a negative light, but the majority, rich and poor, evinced contempt or pity for regular troops and enlisted service.

The rules, practices, and assumptions surrounding military impressment (coercive recruitment, not to be confused with conscription) offer privileged insights into how individuals and authorities contested ideals of honorable manhood as the institution of slavery receded.[3] This essay explores the disputes over "manhood" that army enlisted recruitment and service throws into relief by analyzing broadly recognized traits that conferred an honorable reputation on poor free males that protected them from military impressment. Not all Brazilians identified with the ideals of honorable manhood formulated in law and custom. Competing ideas of manhood were at work among groups and within individuals, but some patterns arose in disputes over measures of manhood. Rich and poor Brazilians of both genders gauged manhood against four major tropes or stereotypes of subordinate social categories: slaves, convicts, women, and children.[4] The analysis that follows will show how these tropes became vital touchstones to appraise the quality of a poor male's honor. Although this essay stresses cultural perceptions, it links them to the free poor's economic security and liberty. The inquiry necessarily begins with a brief digression to establish historical context surrounding the decline of slavery and the status of enlisted military service.

Slavery and Soldiering in Brazil from 1850 to 1888

Nowhere in the Americas had slave ownership been so historic, ubiquitous, and democratic (in that a broad sector of the population, including many nonwhites, owned slaves) than in Brazil. Because Brazil's bonded population had never sustained itself through natural reproduction, its decline began in 1850, when the state enforced laws prohibiting the international slave trade. Relatively few studies have plumbed how the decline of bondage affected gender roles, much less ideals of manhood, among the free poor.[5] This slow but dramatic transformation of labor and social relations destabilized cherished benchmarks of status that authorities, the free poor, elites, and slaves themselves had used to measure status and privilege. Without bondage freedom alone began to lose cachet as a marker of social standing.

The distinction between the manhood of free poor males and the childlike stereotypes of women and bondsmen worked in concert with ideas of racial hierarchy.[6] The Portuguese brought not only African slaves to the New World but also ideals of honor that venerated "purity of blood." In the New World purity of blood placed those of light skin tone and European features and birth at the top of a racial and ethnic scale of honor in which African-born slaves occupied the lowest rungs and free people of mixed racial heritage dominated the middle strata. By providing opportunities through patronage to free nonwhites, a white minority negotiated an uneasy rule over a nonwhite majority. Brazil's army hierarchy mirrored larger society. It had a mostly "white" officer corps whereas its lower ranks included blacks, whites, and Indians, but most troops were of mixed race. Nonwhites were overrepresented in the ranks, but whiteness itself did not protect men from impressment. In Brazil and other Latin American militaries necessity and the low status of soldiering deterred authorities from using a color bar to prevent men of color from serving, nor did they segregate men of different races in the ranks.

A Brazilian bondsman had few privileges, but he was not legally subject to impressment because that would violate his owner's property rights.[7] Poor freemen depended on patronage and reputation to protect them from impressment. The law defined who was "recruitable." Most men who practiced a skilled trade were legally exonerated from impressment, as were those who could certify their marriage, verify a national guard post, pay for pecuniary exemption, or rely on a prominent patron to intercede on their behalf.[8] To protect their free male dependents and workers, many influential landowners and politicians obtained an officer's rank in the national guard in order to name clients to guard posts that shielded them from peacetime impressment. In times of war, however, guardsmen could be designated for regular service. Whereas peacetime impressment targeted the patronless poor, wartime mobilizations tapped into the ranks of the honorable poor. A guard post also qualified men to vote, which allowed political bosses to mobilize their troops for elections. This local electoral organization was so common that it was dubbed *coronelismo* (colonelism) because of the guard rank held by many political bosses.

Slavery's decline in Brazil and elsewhere was intertwined with war mobilization. The rise of conscripted and insurgent independence forces in nations such as the United States, Cuba, Haiti, Colombia, and elsewhere undermined the discipline of the slave regime and ran counter to the logic of social and racial hierarchies that slavery helped to shape.[9] In rhetoric, modern militarist nationalism called for social leveling by drafting able-bodied male citizens of all classes and races. Political theorists of the day made impressionistic comparison of Greek, Roman, and modern North Atlantic nations and argued that republics emerged when the importance of infantrymen in warfare was paramount: it was "the man on foot who made democracies." These new ideals and the real needs for tribute labor in the form of universal male conscription brought to the fore language that repudiated aspects of traditional hierarchies of race, patriarchy, station, and age.

For Brazil it was the Paraguayan War (1864–70), not the mobilizations for the brief struggle for independence in the 1820s, that brought to a head tensions surrounding recruitment. The Paraguayan War pitted tiny Paraguay against the Triple Alliance of Brazil, Argentina, and Uruguay. Brazil would mobilize to a distant front for a lengthy campaign at least four times the troops deployed in any previous war. It is vital to note that the campaign's logistics, dimensions, and length made it a modern war, more akin to the total war campaigns of the 1900s than those that preceded it. The war strained the Brazilian army's capacities and public coffers. What most Brazilians had assumed would be a brief campaign turned into an unpopular five-year ordeal largely because of mobilization problems. Some Brazilians quickly answered Emperor Pedro II's call for volunteers to drive out Paraguayan troops who had invaded national territory, but this initial burst of patriotic fervor soon waned. Already in 1865 Brazil's Parliament offered new enlistment bounties and promises of land grants to volunteers, but these initiatives failed to attract enough men. The state began to call up national guardsmen for wartime service, but only a minority of them reported for duty voluntarily.[10] Desperate, authorities organized press gangs to arrest designated guardsmen and to dragoon other able-bodied freemen. These dragnets captured many men who would have normally been protected from peacetime impressment.

Meanwhile, Brazil's emperor informed a delegation of French abolitionists that as soon as the war was over, new legislation to hasten abolition would be a priority. Brazil's Liberal Parliament anticipated this promise when it passed legislation in 1866 to fill depleted regiments by purchasing slaves to serve as soldiers. Slaves purchased or donated by patriotic masters received a conditional letter of manumission as long as they served on the front. Out of approximately 110,000 men mobilized, some 4,000 to 7,000 manumitted slaves served as soldiers.[11] Alongside slaves, the state freed able-bodied convicts from prisons to fight in return for an imperial pardon. A motley crew of volunteers, ex-slaves, convicts, national guardsmen, career officers, and a handful of nobles from across Brazil served side by side at the front. For the respectable poor forced to serve alongside convicts and ex-slaves, wartime recruitment blurred important distinctions that tainted their claims to honor. Instead of exalting the virility of men who served the nation, the army's recruitment methods bolstered an association of soldiering with the status of criminals and slaves.

A crisis broke out on the front when the Brazilian army's commander, the duke of Caxias, who was also a Conservative senator, threatened to resign his post. He accused the Liberal Parliament of lacking patriotism and of meddling with his officers. Fearful that Caxias's resignation would demoralize the war effort, the emperor disbanded his Liberal Council of Ministers and called for new elections that brought the Conservative Party to power. Conservatives used the threat of impressment to intimidate Liberal Party supporters at the ballot box. This election led to a period of bitter partisan rivalry, and it inspired the founding of the Republican Party in 1870. Wartime abuses and impressment's links to free poor labor discipline and high politics made it an object of caustic contention during a wave of postbellum legislative reform.

In the 1870s reforms accelerated slavery's demise and challenged impressment's legitimacy as a tribute labor system. In 1871 a Conservative Parliament passed the Free Womb Law, which stated that any child born henceforth would be free once he or she reached the age of majority. Subsequently, the 1874 Recruitment Law set out to implement a system of limited conscription and to abolish the manhunts that had created protests and violence during the Paraguayan War. Unlike the Free Womb Law the Recruitment Law met with widespread resistance, both passive and active. Most Brazilians refused to cooperate with the registration process that the law required, and in many localities crowds stormed draft boards, intimidated officials, and shredded enrollment lists. Although the state would repeatedly attempt to implement conscription, it would only succeed in doing so during the unsettling years of World War I.

Impressment survived slavery's abolition in 1888, but Brazil's monarchy soon yielded to an army coup in 1889 that proclaimed a republic. Army officers, in part disgruntled because of the imperial state's lack of resolve in reforming recruitment, took the reigns of power for themselves. This brief account hardly captures the complexity of trends and events that shaped the battles to end slavery and reform recruitment, but it affords the background needed to examine resistance to conscription and measures of manhood. As slavery declined, vulnerability to recruitment became a more consequential mark of distinction for the status-conscious free poor.[12]

Impressment and the Status of Common Soldiers

That many contemporaries often compared the status of soldiers to that of slaves, women, convicts, and children shows how racial, gender, class, and age hierarchies were mutually constitutive. Impressment compelled poor freemen to conform to honorable stereotypes of manly comportment. Disputes over impressment reveal a number of traits, privileges, and codes by which poor free "men" identified themselves. *Man* was a title of status often denied to slaves. As Bert Barickman has observed of postmortem inventories in Bahia, adult male slaves were classed by general age categories such as *moço* (a youth), *ainda rapaz* (still a boy), *idoso* (aged), *de boa idade* (of a good age), and *já velho* (already old). Appraisers could have used terms such as *já homem* (already a man) or *homem feito* (a full-grown man) to convey similar information about age and productive capacity, but they consistently chose not to do so. Only in the 1870s did these records in Bahia begin to record specific ages *as appraisers had in other parts of Brazil.* Still, outside of abolitionist literature, slaves were not commonly referred to as "men."[13]

The servile nature of enlisted army service in the late 1800s was incompatible with prevailing ideals of manly privilege. Impressment itself resembled slaving methods. The phrase *recrutas à pau e corda* (club and rope recruits) described the crude means by which agents subdued and restrained inductees in operations referred to as *caçada humana* (human-hunts). Like *capitães da mata* (bounty hunters who tracked down runaway slaves) recruitment agents stalked their prey in cities and countryside. Local police pressed troublemakers and designated armed escorts to transfer inductees to recruit depositories. Police escorts often grouped recruits and deserters with convicts destined for jails in provincial capitals. This undifferentiated treatment further confused soldiering with criminality and slavery in the public mind.

Other practices also made aspects of soldiering appear similar to slavery. Before dawn, bugles awoke soldiers for morning roll calls, a rite similar to the morning assembly of slaves on large plantations and at mines.[14] Dietary statutes in Salvador, Bahia, asserted equities among slaves employed in the public granary, mendicant convicts, and soldiers: all three were allotted the same daily ration of manioc flour.[15]

Other markers distinguished soldiers from less desirable stations. Officers and politicians aimed to distinguish between soldiers and slaves by flogging privates with *pranchadas* (sword-flat blows) rather than with the whips used to punish slaves or the *chibatas* (nautical cords) used to flog sailors. In Parliament senators distinguished between honorable and dishonorable instruments of castigation and, in this seemingly trivial way, differentiated army privates from the lower castes of slaves and sailors. For the free poor, however, being subject to flogging before their peers smacked of the humiliation of bonded status. After all, an increasing distaste for cruelty forced the dismantling of *pelourinhos* (slave whipping posts) from most of Brazil's public squares in the 1820s, when the police began to castigate slaves inside prison walls. Thus, Parliament abrogated flogging soldiers in 1874 (but not for sailors) in an effort to make conscription acceptable to the honorable free poor. Prominent social conventions held that "men" should resist aggressions by peers against themselves and their dependents. If they submitted to beatings by a superior, subordinates could still prove their manhood by not exhibiting fear. The right to wear shoes and bear arms were markers of freedom forbidden to slaves. Boots and arms were badges of free status, but for most these markers did not remove soldiering far enough from stereotypes of slave status. Indeed, when press gangs approached, some freemen of color removed their shoes and masqueraded as slaves; others cross-dressed or feigned physical handicaps. Thus, some freemen briefly disavowed their status to preserve it. Individual males creatively developed their own ways of interpreting and acting out ideals of manhood according to their circumstances, class, culture, age, race, and region.

To better grasp the status of soldiering in relation to ideals of manhood, an example of everyday police work clarifies the hazards poor men faced when migrating even short distances. In 1874 the police delegate of the hardscrabble farming town of Botucatá, São Paulo, jailed João Nepomoceno de Almeida Nobre as an army recruit. But before going to the trouble and expense of sending João to a distant recruit depository via an armed escort, the delegate inquired about the recruit's reputation and exemption status with the police delegate of his prisoner's hometown, Porto Feliz, São Paulo. Porto Feliz's delegate replied that he did not know João, but after making inquiries (which normally involved talking with the prisoner's family and neighbors), he came up with five reasons why João should not be pressed. First, João was the son of an honest widow, whom he supported and protected, and, second, he provided the same "manly" security for a sister whose husband had abandoned her. Third, he was a carpenter who practiced his trade; indeed, he had migrated to Botucatá and other nearby towns in search of work to sustain his family. Fourth, João had a brother who died some years earlier in the Paraguayan War. Finally, João was "well-mannered." On the basis of this letter the Botucatá delegate freed João, confirming the value of an honorable reputation with one's neighbors and kin to a free poor man's livelihood and liberty.

It is difficult to know from documentation whether the Porto Feliz police delegate shaped the information to secure João's release or if his family and friends knew what conditions would favor his liberation. It is likely, however, that the free poor were cognizant of the measures of status that would prevent a man from being pressed because it was essential to family security. João's brother had probably been dragooned for service in the Paraguayan War. If João had been unable to prove his exemption status, he would have faced a minimum six-year service contract (often extended by years because of a lack of timely discharges) with low wages and a posting in a garrison far from his home. For a humble family military impressment could signify not only humiliation and dishonor but disaster for the household economy. The Botucatá delegate mentioned that he had been informed that João was disorderly and that he had kidnapped and seduced (raptado) a young woman of Porto Feliz whom he later abandoned.[16] In the eyes of a police delegate such disreputable acts against family honor clearly merited impressment. In this manner police across the nation acted to protect family honor, public morality, and order. Free poor men and women, like João, struggled to protect themselves from slanderous gossip in an age when authorities depended on oral memory, not bureaucracy, to assess most individuals' records, as it were. Public perceptions often mattered more than the "truth" of statements in a society of honor; hence men sometimes fought over seemingly trivial slights to protect themselves and their families. If unchecked, rumor or insult could be ruinous for family honor and security.

Local authorities willingly tread on the right of unfamiliar poor freemen to come and go as they pleased on the basis of rumor alone to protect local "families" from dangerous male and female "loners" like João. The documents do not mention João's race, but racial traits influenced interpretations of honor and respectability. Black and mixed-race men who migrated were at greater risk than their white counterparts because those suspected of being runaway slaves were sometimes held by police until a family member or patron could vouch for their status. The right to geographic mobility is a marker of manly competence in many patriarchal societies. Poor Brazilian freemen treasured the right to come and go as they pleased because it was a liberty denied to slaves, convicts, sailors, and soldiers and by custom to most women and children.[17]

Even in São Paulo, where army recruitment levels were low compared to most other provinces, police relied on impressment rather than the courts to punish men, like João, suspected of wrongdoing. Major prisons were filled with men convicted of homicide, leaving little room to punish lesser offenders. Thus, military impressment was a much more common punishment for those who committed crimes against property, family honor, or who were "criminally idle." Hence, the barracks were often compared to jails. In 1874 the war minister defended the need for conscription by conceding, "It is said with reason, that manhunts (impressment sweeps) . . . have reduced the army to a penitentiary that should be proscribed as soon as possible."[18]

Because João reputedly fulfilled the role expected of a poor patriarch, he did not deserve such summary punishment. He provided for and "protected" his widowed mother and his sister, whose husband had failed in his patriarchal duty. He was obliged to leave his hometown to find work to support his female kin. Conventional ideals of manhood favored those who headed households and provided for and "protected" the honorable reputations of their dependents. An important part of protection was to shield female kin and dependents from the sexual aggressions of other males. To help protect a household head's honor, Brazilian law protected the home's inviolability by limiting the power of authorities to enter them in the daytime. It further prohibited nighttime searches except when natural disasters threatened, cries of help came from within, or crimes were in progress within a household. In part, the law prevented the violation of the home to protect "women of family" from real or putative sexual aggressions by strangers or authorities. The law was not always respected, but Brazilians expressed heated offense if authorities or strangers violated this principle. Complaints against impressment abuses normally included accusations that agents disrespected the inviolability of the family home.[19]

Necessity pushed João and many other poor freemen to migrate to provide for themselves and their families. This made it hard for poor freemen to live up to elite standards of patriarchal protection, and it illuminates an important intersection between class and manhood. The code of honor reinforced class distinctions by casting doubts on the poor patriarch's ability to protect his dependents.[20] Police often suspected loners like

João of abandoning patriarchal obligations. Rumors or perhaps the delegate's supposition about João's honor cost him worrisome days in jail.

Brazilian law had traditionally exempted married men who "protected" their wives from impressment. Responsible poor freemen were expected to marry, to exhibit their virility by fathering children, and then to protect and to provide for their progeny. Officials often punished with military impressment men who seduced young women with false marriage promises, who abandoned their wives, and who failed to support and protect widowed mothers, decrepit fathers, or younger orphaned siblings with military impressment. In this sense even though João was single, he was protected by codes that exempted men who provided protection to more vulnerable members of their families. The 1874 Recruitment Law conceded all these customary exemptions except for one: marriage. The fear that married men might be drafted and parted from their wives fueled resistance to conscription. Instead of protecting families by pressing wayward males, conscription threatened to remove "natural" patriarchal protectors from their homes, leaving their wives unprotected.

Officials dragooned men to make an example of a portion of less tractable poor freemen and to caution those who would seek to escape family obligations. The police delegate of Juiz de Fora, Minas Gerais, sent a letter along with the prisoner Bernardo Amâncio de Souza to army headquarters in Rio de Janeiro in 1874. It described Bernardo as *"recrutável"* (recruitable) and revealed what made him so: "he resides in this borough where he is not known, living in a state of emancipation, provoking disorders according to his neighbors, and it is also known that he is a married man from São João del Rey, thirty leagues away." The War Ministry responded that Bernardo "will be [transferred to and] enlisted in one of Rio Grande do Sul's garrisons if he cannot prove his exemption and passes the army's health inspection."[21]

For police Bernardo was "recruitable" because he had abandoned his wife and maintained a dissolute life in a town where he was a stranger. Documents do not reveal Bernardo's final fate or the truth of the accusations leveled against him, but they do indicate the risks poor freemen ran when they migrated, especially if they caused disturbances, abandoned a wife, or had no employer or patron to protect them. The delegate hints that "neighbors," presumably the household heads of "honorable" poor families, requested police intervention to deal with Bernardo. Once again, this example indicates the importance of maintaining the respect of one's neighbors. An honest reputation could help to protect poor free males from impersonal police action, the vengeance of powerful social superiors, or even the ire of malicious peers. A man pressed in the mountainous coffee-growing town of Valença, Rio de Janeiro, in 1859 confirmed the notion that authorities only pressed disorderly, immoral, and violent men. He held that his impressment was unjust because he had always lived "meekly and peacefully" in his town. One officer recalled that many soldiers in the early 1900s were "disorderly drunken criminals" sent to serve from a prison cell.[22]

Marriage itself was a title of honor and privilege that many poor men and women proudly flaunted. Untitled Brazilians usually identified themselves first as *casados* (married men) when interacting with authorities.[23] Marriage was an honor denied to most slaves, and it was an important marker of privilege for the free poor. Slaves were assumed to be immoral and depraved in part because they normally lived outside of a nuclear family household.

Family honor, considered the foundation of "good" public order in Brazilian law and custom, was strongly associated with the idea of the home in Romance languages. The very verb *casar* (to marry) derives from *casa*. In Brazil the expression *quem se casa quer casa* (one who marries wants their own house) reiterates the ideal that a married couple live in their own home. Thus, it is no accident that Gilberto Freyre titled his 1933 classic analysis of patriarchy *Casa Grande e Senzala* (The big house and the slave's quarters, later translated as *The Masters and the Slaves*).[24] He made a direct comparison between the master's house and the slaves' quarters. On large plantations and mines most slaves lived not as family units but in large barracks-like common dwellings that often segregated slaves by gender. Brazilian masters permitted few slaves to marry or to establish their own private households on provision grounds.[25]

The primacy of the independent household or hearth (*fogo*) as a measure of status is confirmed by electoral law. The right to vote required an adult male to head an independent household, unless he held a medical or law degree or bore an officer's rank in the military. Lawmakers deemed

244 • • • Peter M. Beattie

this a cardinal criterion for the freedom of conscience required of a citizen to vote. The law assumed that a household dependent lacked this font of manly liberty. Thus, the rule was one male head of household, one vote, rather than one man, one vote.[26]

As Gilberto Freyre and, subsequently, anthropologist Roberto DaMatta and many other scholars have shown in works on the urban geography of honor, the family home is commonly contrasted with the street. Whereas the home is identified with order, safety, honor, private authority, legitimacy, and marriage, the street is more often associated with disorder, danger, illegitimacy, vagrancy, prostitution, and susceptibility to impersonal public authority. Clearly ambiguities and contradictions existed in these conceptions. Individuals filtered diverging perceptions of house, street, and manhood through lenses of class, race, gender, ethnicity, region, occupation, and circumstances. For those who lived under the thumb of a patriarch, the street could represent liberty and safety from abuses. Even so, the conceptual and linguistic realms of house and street remained part of a common language that individuals (rich, poor, and slave) shared, even as they disputed their interpretations. The term used for privates and NCOs, *praça,* also meant public square. Thus, army enlisted men were linguistically located in the dangerous world of the street. The term used to distinguish a private's rank *(soldado)* in colonial times was also a synonym for an unmarried man and a euphemism for penal exiles expelled from Portugal. This usage confirmed the traditional exemption from military impressment that "well-mannered" married men enjoyed and the use of penal exiles to fill the ranks of colonial armies.[27]

Like the *senzala,* the prison, and the bordello the barracks rested on the opposite end of the spectrum of values associated with the family home. Authorities sought to congregate and to supervise a portion of society's dangerous male "loners" in the barracks. In some ways barracks were the male counterpart of the bordello. Officials tried to use both spaces to separate dangerous "loners" from respectable family homes. The barracks, like the *senzala,* prisons, and even urban tenements, often crowded mostly single men into promiscuous common lodgings. Thus, barracks became associated with slavery, and the moral and sexual degradation was ascribed to convicts and servants. A Pernambucan police chief made the association of the barracks with sexual danger explicit when he defended the impressment of a number of men because they caused disturbances and were "known to practice the repugnant vice of sodomy."[28]

Rank, Distance, Deference, and Homophobia?

Within more developed army compounds the use of social space and custom explicitly sought to reinforce the hierarchy of rank. Separate latrines, cantinas, and stockade cells existed for officers, NCOS, and privates. Rules forbid privates to enter spaces reserved for superiors without permission to avert what officers called "social pollutions." In one court martial case a second lieutenant was accused of irregular conduct. Witnesses, mostly NCOS under the lieutenant's command, discredited their officer's integrity by noting that he had participated in a popular dance with common soldiers under his command and sang indecent songs with civilians aloud in the streets of Boa Vista, Goiás.[29] Such familiarity was assumed to breed contempt and weaken the soldiers' and civilians' respect for the authority of officers. The court judged public fraternization with the "rabble" unseemly in an officer whose social origins were assumed to be more elevated than that of his troops. As in caste societies, army hierarchies affirm that familiarity can breed contempt and weaken respect for privilege.[30] Like slaves and humble peons, army subordinates were admonished to show deference by not looking into the eyes of superiors and ceding the right of way. The out-ranked manifested submission by saluting, and for many these practices gave army service the look of servility analogous to the deference of slavery.

The association of words describing slavery, exile, and sodomy elucidate strong links among the barracks, immorality, and sexual submissiveness. The urban slang for a male prostitute, *bagaxa*, derived from *bagaço*, or the dregs that remained after sugar cane, olives, or fruit were pressed. This term was in use in Italy, Spain, and southern France since at least the early modern period, and its meaning was similar to the Portuguese term *bagaxa* to describe a "cheap whore."[31] *Bagaceira* means the place where *bagaço* accumulates, a lax moral environment, or a collection of useless things. The association of slavery, sodomy, and the *bagaceira* was confirmed by bigoted Brazilian medical assertions that blamed Africans and Indians for "contaminating" the Portuguese with this same-sex "perversion." These associations marked the close links among sex, domination, and hierarchy. In depicting the sexual awakening of the sons of sugar planters, Gilberto Freyre noted that they anticipated their experience of physical love by way of sadistic and bestial practices. He added that the first victims were plants, domestic animals, and their young black childhood companions.[32] Regardless of the comment's veracity, it is shot through with assumptions about domination in relation to class, race, sexuality, and masculinity. Planters' sons rehearsed a kind of manhood by sexually dominating subordinates, be they human, vegetable, or animal. By playing the active role, privileged youths manifested their virility, and the lion's share of any shame for the act rested with the submissive male.

In a similar way the term for a penal exile *degredado* (degraded one) implies ties among concepts of criminality, perversion, and soldiering. In colonial times the term for private, *soldado,* was also a euphemism for a penal exile because many ended up serving in colonial armed forces. Thus, Portuguese officials subjected exiles to a coerced transatlantic migration that resembled that suffered by many more African slaves. Before and after independence Brazilian authorities used impressment to relocate men strategically through a type of internal exile. Exile status bore a relationship to "perversion," as moralists often described sodomy as a "degrading" sin, one often associated with prisons and other institutions that segregated men from women.[33] Because impressment often resembled a sentence of exile and the barracks segregated mostly unmarried men into common abodes, many believed that barracks, along with prisons, *senzalas,* monasteries, and boarding schools, prompted sodomy.

From the evidence I have examined, one could not easily describe the fears of institutions that segregated men from the company of women or the men who participated in a same-sex subculture of desire as "homophobia." Although some Brazilian sexologists in the 1900s employed the term *homosexual,* it was not part of informal or legal parlance. Men who behaved in an effeminate manner or who were suspected of playing the passive role in same-sex intercourse bore the brunt of social stigma because in doing so they ceded their claims to manly status. "Passive sodomites" often did become targets of violent sexual advances from those who sought to assert their virility. Oftentimes, these men sought out protectors among fellow soldiers who would defend them from the violence and sexual advances of other men. In this sense their relationship resembled stereotypes about the proper relationship between a man and wife, and in military prisons officers noted that soldier convicts "married" one another. By rationalizing this behavior as a result of a lack of accessible women, authorities did not recognize what some would call a third sex, but at the same time others noted that some men preferred sex with their own gender. Those who observed this factor tended to view this "unnatural" desire as part of a social pathology that had twisted an individual's sexuality. The few men who were convicted of "sodomy" by the army were not expelled; that would have been a reward. Rather, they were required to serve out new contracts or to remain in the ranks longer. If one sees this as "homophobia," then it certainly was one that sought to contain this vice in the barracks rather than suppressing it outright. Perhaps attempts to reform "inverts" would have to await the popularization of psychology during World War I.[34] The move to implement conscription in the 1900s would have to rework the image of the barracks as a site of sexual danger and immorality.

Many clearly equated the barracks with sexual dangers that could menace a soldier's claims to manhood. Most Brazilians in the late 1800s identified men not by their sexual preference but by the role they performed in same-sex copulation. Those who played the active role were seen as manly, whereas those penetrated were considered sexually passive, as women and children were assumed to be. Many fights between *praças* were punctuated by slights that impugned a foe's manhood by labeling him a passive sodomite or, in slang, as "serving as a woman" for another man's lascivious pleasure. As one soldier rudely propositioned by a comrade retorted, "I am not a boy nor a woman to serve such ends." Being a sexual aggressor marked manly privilege, and men who failed to demonstrate virility by protecting themselves and their dependents from the aggressions of other males could find their reputations as "men" shattered.

Most physicians, politicians, labor leaders, and laypersons believed that men were "natural" sexual aggressors whose organism required sexual release, without which, a "mummification" of passion occurred, imperiling their physical health and psyches. By contrast, women and children were "naturally" sexually passive and required manly "protection" from the sexual predations. This was an ideal most explicitly espoused by more privileged men; but most poor free men and women also viewed marriage as a touchstone of "honorable" status, and they shared a language of gender stereotypes. For many, prostitution was a necessary evil because it served as an escape valve to protect honest women from the aggressions of unmarried males. It was assumed that if soldiers were unable to satisfy their lust with prostitutes, they would turn their lust on other men or, perhaps even worse, on "honest" women of family.

These sexualized assumptions about gender permeated the imagery and rhetoric of national honor, often symbolized as an honorable female who had to be defended from foreign interlopers.[35] Thus, nationalists tapped into the loyalty men of honor "naturally" feel for their family. As a Brazilian army song of the 1860s warned, "A bad people armed for war comes to conquer us and rape our wives . . . to deflower our daughters." Conversely, this "wife stealing" logic could serve as a stimulus. Another army song touted, "All brave soldiers returning from the cursed [Paraguayan] war brought in their packs a beautiful mestizo backland woman (cabocla)."[36] These metaphors implied that men of defeated nations were cuckolds unable to defend their collective honor and that the spoils of victory included sexual conquests. With the rise of nationalism this rhetoric became more pronounced because it depicted the heterosexual nuclear family as the primary building block of social order and metaphor for the nation. National honor is thus charged with deep-seated preoccupations over sexual dominance. Since ancient times, patriarchs utilized this sexualized imagery to justify and to promote war mobilizations. The threat invaders posed to women of families inspired a common identification with the virile defense of collective honor. These metaphors could only come to fuller closure in Brazil with conscription's implementation because impressment filled the ranks with men associated with dishonor.

There were men in the wake of slavery's demise who escaped some of these constricting ideas of honorable manhood. Some became admired outlaws who defied many conventions. In most bandit legends, however, outlaws began their Robin Hood–like careers only after their family was wronged by authorities; thus, their criminal vocation could be seen as an attempt to vindicate injustice. As Linda Lewin shows, Antônio Silvino, celebrated as a noble bandit in popular culture, began his career in 1897 when his father was killed by an enemy who could count on the political protection of incumbent state officials. Thus, the acts of most popular bandit legends took on the cast of a blood feud undertaken to defend respect for family honor rather than brigandage for its own sake. Antônio Silvino depended on ties to powerful, although not politically incumbent, landowners who served as his patrons. Thus, as Lewin argues, the image of legendary bandits as rugged, independent alternative icons of "manhood" is somewhat exaggerated, as they often formed part of a broader patronage network and served to enforce the will of landowners rather than directly challenge them.[37] Legendary bandits were thus the exceptions who proved the rule in that they defied public authority to defend family after their manhood had been vilely assaulted.[38]

Conclusions

Vulnerability to impressment implied a lack of manhood for most poor freemen in Brazil in the late 1800s. The decline of slavery, urbanization, state building, and the controversy over conscription destabilized ideals of manhood, race, class, family, and nation that had held sway during the age of impressment. The conscription controversy touched on these notions in a profound way that perhaps no other issue save slavery's abolition did. As slavery faded, vulnerability to impressment became a more important mark of distinction for the respectable free poor.

By way of contrast, in the United States, Confederate and Union Civil War foot soldiers were publicly venerated in popular memory and lore as paragons of republican manhood. The Union army had grudgingly allowed black volunteers the manly honor of wearing the uniform, and even then, it was careful to segregate them from white soldiers. Only later in Brazil and other nations like Russia would a willingness to pay this tribute come to be considered a more broadly accepted measure of an able-bodied poor male citizen's honor. This ensued when large-scale conscripted armies spread to nations across the world during the great war mobilizations and decolonizations of the 1900s, widening the circle and reshaping measures of honorable manhood.

In an age when government-funded social assistance was minimal, military impressment was the most assertive way that the Brazilian state attempted to police family honor and to pressure poor patriarchs to uphold their commitments to their families and local communities. This threat encouraged men to work for prominent citizens who could vouch for them and facilitated the formation of a more dependent free wage-labor force as slavery ebbed. The state also sought to compel men to fulfill patriarchal duties to prevent the social problems linked to unprotected single mothers. Officials feared that these women would be forced into prostitution or mendicancy and that their children would likely turn to crime to survive.

Wartime impressment during the Paraguayan War, followed by attempts to implement a limited conscription lottery from 1875 forward, threatened to undermine common measures of manhood for poor freemen at a time when slavery began to dwindle. By probing how manhood was measured against the statuses of slaves, convicts, women, and children, resistance to conscription becomes more intelligible. Changes in attitudes toward convicts, women, and childhood in the 1900s also reshaped conceptions of manhood. When the government implemented conscription in 1916, it accelerated the formation of inchoate but new social pacts among poor women, men, and children that were being negotiated and contested among individuals, families, and the state.

Notes

1. See, e.g., Mary Douglas, *Purity and Danger: An Analysis of Concepts of Pollution and Taboo* (London: Routledge, 1966); John Bushnell, *Mutiny Amid Repression: Russian Soldiers in the Revolution of 1905–1906* (Bloomington: Indiana University Press, 1985), 6.

2. On *praça* status see, e.g., Antônio Edmilson Martins Rodrigues et al., *A guarda nacional no Rio de Janeiro, 1831–1918* (Rio: Pontífica Universidade do Rio de Janeiro, 1981), 14–15; Joan E. Meznar, "The Ranks of the Poor: Military Service and Social Differentiation in Northeast Brazil," *HAHR* 72, no. 3 (Aug. 1992): 337–40; Hendrik Kraay, "Soldiers, Officers, and Society: The Army in Bahia, Brazil 1808–1889" (Ph.D. diss., University of Texas, 1995), chap. 7.

3. See, e.g., Sandra Lauderdale Graham's "Honor among Slaves," in *The Faces of Honor: Sex, Shame, and Violence in Colonial Latin America*, ed. Lyman L. Johnson and Sonya Lisett-Rivera (Albuquerque: University of New Mexico Press, 1998), 18–44.

4. This essay builds on ideas of honor I examined in "The House, the Street, and the Barracks: Reform and Honorable Masculine Social Space in Brazil, 1864–1945," *HAHR* 76, no. 3 (Aug. 1996): 439–73. Some of the insights herein can be found in

Peter M. Beattie, *The Tribute of Blood: Army, Honor, Race, and Nation in Brazil, 1864–1945* (Durham, N.C.: Duke University Press, 2001); Meznar, "Ranks of the Poor," 335–51; Kraay, "Soldiers," chap. 7.

5. Joan Scott, "Gender as a Category of Analysis," *American Historical Review* 95, no. 1 (Dec. 1986): 259–306. For works that examine gender and race in the wake of slavery see, e.g., George Reid Andrews, *Blacks and Whites in São Paulo, Brazil, 1888–1988* (Madison: University of Wisconsin Press, 1991); Sandra Lauderdale Graham, *House and Street: The Domestic World of Servants and Masters in Nineteenth-Century Rio de Janeiro* (New York: Cambridge University Press, 1988); Martha de Abreu Esteves, *Meninas Perdidas: Os populares e o cotidiano do amor no Rio de Janeiro da Belle Epoque* (Rio: Paz e Terra, 1989).

6. Sidney Chalhoub, *Trabalho, lar, e botequim: O cotidiana dos trabalhadores no Rio de Janeiro da belle epoque* (São Paulo: Ed. Brasilense, 1986); Hebe Maria Mattos de Castro, *Das cores do silêncio: Os significados de liberdade no sudeste escravista* (Rio: Arquivo Nacional, 1995).

7. Hendrik Kraay, "Slavery, Citizenship, and Military Service in Brazil's Mobilization for the Paraguayan War," *Abolition and Slavery* 18, no. 3 (Dec. 1997): 228–56; Hendrik Kraay, "The Shelter of the Uniform: The Brazilian Army and Runaway Slaves, 1800–1888" *Journal of Social History* 29, no. 3 (Mar. 1996): 637–57.

8. *Collecção das leis do Império do Brasil* (Rio: Typ. Nacional, 1831), 3:215–16.

9. Ada Ferrer, *Insurgent Cuba: Race, Nation, and Revolution, 1868–1898* (Chapel Hill: University of North Carolina Press, 1999); Carolyn Fick, "Black Peasants and Soldiers in the St. Domingue Revolution: Initial Reactions to Freedom in the South Province," in *History from Below: Studies in Popular Protest and Popular Ideology in Honour of George Rudé,* ed. Frederick Krantz (Montreal: Concordia University, 1985). See readings in *A Question of Manhood: A Reader in U.S. Black Men's History and Masculinity,* ed. Darlene Clark Hine and Earnestine Jenkins, (Bloomington: University of Indiana Press, 1999); Ira Berlin et al., *Slaves No More: Three Essays on Emancipation in the Civil War* (New York: Cambridge University Press, 1992); Kenneth S. Greenberg, *Honor and Slavery* (Princeton, N.J.: Princeton University Press, 1996). Kraay, "Slavery," 249–50; Ricardo Salles, *Guerra do Paraguai: Escravidão e cidadania na formação do exército* (Rio: Paz e Terra, 1991).

10. On guardsmen see Luiza Rios Ricci Volpato, *Cativos do sertão: Vida cotidiana e escravidão em Cuiabá em 1850–1888* (São Paulo: Marco Zero, 1993), 64–65; Márcio Lucena Filho, "Pernambuco e a Guerra do Paraguai: O recrutamento e os limites da ordem" (Dissertação de Mestrado, Universidade Federal de Pernambuco, 2000); Beattie, *Tribute of Blood,* chap. 2.

11. Wartime mobilization is beset by the numbers game. Júlio José Chiavenato makes widely cited but unsubstantiated claims that mobilization led to a "40 percent decline in Brazil's black population" (Júlio José Chiavenato, *O negro no Brazil: Da senzala à Guerra*

do Paraguai, 14th ed. [São Paulo: Brasiliense, 1982], 11, 199); Hendrik Kraay argues that army statistics were accurate (see Kraay, "Slavery," 228–56). Jorge Prata de Souza, *Escravidão ou morte: Os escravos brasileiros na Guerra do Paraguai* (Rio: ADESA, 1996). Vitor Izecksohn argues that official army numbers were somewhat low. See Vitor Izecksohn, "War, Reform, and State-Building in Brazil and in the United States: Slavery, Emancipation, and Decision-Making Processes in the Paraguayan and Civil Wars, 1861–1870" (Ph.D. diss., University of New Hampshire, 2001).

12. Manolo Florentino and José Roberto Góes, *A paz das senzalas: Famílias escrava e tráfico Atlântico, Rio de Janeiro, c. 1790–1850* (Rio: Civilização Brasileira, 1997). On honor and color see Greenberg's *Honor and Slavery*.

13. Bert Barrickman, conversation with author, Barraca do Jô, Copacabana Beach, Rio de Janeiro, July 28, 2000. For records elsewhere see Stanley Stein, *Vassouras, a Brazilian Coffee County, 1850–1900: The Roles of Planter and Slave in a Plantation Society* (Princeton, N.J.: Princeton University Press, 1985); Florentino and Góes, *A paz das senzalas*.

14. Matt D. Childs, "A Case of 'Great Unstableness': A British Slaveholder and Brazilian Abolition," *Historian* 60, no. 4 (summer 1998): 717–40; Stein, *Vassouras*, 161–69.

15. B. J. Barickman, *A Bahian Counterpoint: Sugar, Tobacco, Cassava, and Slavery in the Reconcôncavo, 1780–1860* (Stanford, Calif.: Stanford University Press, 1998), 46.

16. Emilio de Cerqueira Lima to the Police Chief, Jan. 18, 1874, Porto Feliz, Secretária da Polícia, Arquivo do Estado de São Paulo, *ordem* 2560, ma. 1. Delegate Antonio Eugenio do Amaral to the Police Chief, Jan. 24, 1874, Botucatá, *ordem* 2560, ma. 1.

17. On geographic mobility and manhood in comparative perspective see, e.g., David D. Gilmore, *Manhood in the Making: Cultural Concepts of Masculinity* (New Haven, Conn.: Yale University Press, 1990); de Castro's *Das cores do silêncio*, 31–40; Walter Fraga Filho, *Mendigos, moleques, e vadios na Bahia do século XIX* (Salvador: Ed. Hucitec, 1995), 165–67.

18. Army and police *praças* involved in crime became an increasing embarrassment. See *O Diário do Rio de Janeiro*, June 8, 1874, 1; Thomas Holloway, "A Healthy Terror: Police Repression of *Capoeiras* in Nineteenth-Century Rio de Janeiro," *HAHR* 69, no. 4 (1989): 637–76.

19. *Collecção das leis do Império do Brasil* (Rio: Imp. Nacional, 1831), 3:215–16.

20. George Reid Andrews argues that many ex-slaves who headed households sought to remove their wives and daughters from fieldwork to protect them from advances by overseers. Andrews, "Black and White Workers: São Paulo, Brazil, 1888–1928," *HAHR* 68, no. 3 (Aug. 1988): 85–118.

21. Governor of Minas Gerais to the War Ministry, Juiz de Fora, July 28, 1874, Arquivo Nacional, *maço* IG¹214, *folha* 151.

22. Petition from Francisco de Souza de Barros to the Governor of Rio de Janeiro,

Dec. 29, 1959, Valença, Arquivo Público do Estado de Rio de Janeiro, *fundo* PP, *col.* 8, *maço* 7; Nélson de Melo, *depoimento,* Centro de Pesquisa e Documentação/Fundação Getúlio Vargas, História Oral, Rio de Janeiro, 1983, 4–5.

23. Many freemen and women lived together based on a marriage promise either because of a lack of funds to pay for the rite or because of the lack of clergy in rural areas. Both local leaders and everyday Brazilians often referred to couples who resided as man and wife based on a marriage promise were considered *casados* (married). A man who abandoned such a marriage promise, however, could be censured with impressment. See Graham, *House and Street,* 71–80; Dain Borges, *The Family in Bahia, 1870–1945* (Stanford, Calif.: Stanford University Press, 1992).

24. Gilberto Freyre, *Casa grande e senzala: Introdução à história da sociedade patriarchal no Brasil,* 39th ed. (Rio: Editora Record, 2000).

25. As Bert Barickman shows, the privilege of provision grounds and the permission to establish an independent household was usually granted to trusted slaves. They were more likely to be allowed to take a consensual spouse. See Bert Barickman, "A Little Piece of Ground They Call *Roça:* Slave Provision Grounds in Nineteenth Century Bahia," *HAHR* 74, no. 4 (1993): 649–88. Despite the nature of living arrangements, recent research has revealed the existence and resilience of slave families countering stereotypes that denigrated slaves as living outside the moralizing family unit. See, e.g., Florentino and Goes, *A paz das senzalas.*

26. Bert Barrickman emphasizes this point in his analysis of parish census returns in "Citizenship, Kinship, Slavery, and Household in the 1835 Parish Censuses from Bahia: Santiago do Iguape" (paper presented to the Social Science History Conference, New Orleans, Nov. 1997).

27. Timothy J. Coates, "Exiles and Orphans: Forced and State-Sponsored Colonizers in the Portuguese Empire, 1550–1720" (Ph.D. diss., University of Minnesota, 1993), 113–15; M. N. Pearson, "The Crowd in Portuguese India," in *Coastal Western India,* ed. M. N. Pearson (New Delhi: Concept Publishing, 1981), 42.

28. Police Chief Antonio Francisco Correia d'Araujo to Governor Henrique Pereira de Lucena, Recife, Nov. 10, 1874, Arquivo Público do Estado de Pernambuco, li. PC-140, fo. 237; also ibid., Dec. 29, 1874, fo. 441.

29. Alferes Antonio Brederodes, São Luis, Maranhão, 1896, Arquivo Nacional, processo 210, caixa 13.203.

30. Celso Castro, *O Espírito militar: Um estudo de antropologia social no Academia Militardas das Agulhas Negras* (Rio: Jorge Zahar, 1990); James Scott, *Domination and the Arts of Resistance: Hidden Transcripts* (New Haven, Conn.: Yale University Press, 1990).

31. I thank Professor Thomas V. Cohen for bringing to my attention the longevity of the term *bagasse.* I found his work helpful in reflecting on honor in Brazil. See Thomas V. Cohen, "The Lay Liturgy of Affront in Sixteenth-Century Italy," *Journal of Social History* 25, no. 4 (summer 1992): 857–77.

32. Freyre, *Casa grande,* 209; José Ricardo Pires de Almeida, *Homosexualismo (a libertinagem no Rio de Janeiro)* (Rio: Laemmert, 1906), 75–76, 85.

33. The terms *degredar* (to banish) and *degradar* (to debase) are not one and the same, but my *Novo Michaels Dicionário Ilustrado* notes under its third definition that *degradar* is used as an equivalent of *degredar.*

34. James N. Green, *Beyond Carnival: Male Homosexuality in Twentieth-Century Brazil* (Chicago: University of Chicago Press, 1999), chap. 3.

35. José Murilho de Carvalho, *A Formação das Almas: O Imaginário da República no Brasil* (São Paulo: Companhia das Letras, 1990), chap. 4; Beattie, *Tribute of Blood,* chap. 2.

36. Peixoto, *Cancioneiro militar* (São Paulo: Escola do Lyceu da Coração Sagrada de Jesus, 1923), 38, 74–75.

37. Linda Lewin, "The Oligarchic Limitations of Social Banditry in Brazil: The Case of the 'Good' Thief Antônio Silvino," in *Bandidos: The Varieties of Latin American Banditry,* ed. Richard W. Slatta (New York: Greenwood Press, 1987), 67–96.

38. Although their claims to honor were much more tenuous and less celebrated in song, some urban toughs became serviceable villains in the informal security forces of powerful men. One senator denied that it was easy to punish *capoeiras* with impressment because "in this city there exists a class of individuals, against which the authorities fight and who possess a thousand means of escape, I refer to *capoeiras.*" Another retorted, "The good [capoeira] artist is sure to find someone who will give him money to exempt himself [from military service]." But these claims contradict the protests of Rio's police who avowed that there was little he could do to punish recidivist *capoeiras* who were army veterans, national guardsmen, arsenal employees, or active duty *praças.* Undoubtedly, some *capoeiras* were protected from impressment, but their security hinged on the intercession of prominent men. See *O Diário do Rio de Janeiro,* Sept. 2, 1874, 1–2; Thomas Holloway, "Healthy Terror," 648, 668; Carlos Eugênio Líbano Soares, *A negregada instituição: Os caipoeiras no Rio de Janeiro* (Rio: Biblioteca Carioca, 1994).

MIGUEL DÍAZ BARRIGA

Vergüenza and Changing

Chicano/a Narratives

■ ■ ■ ■

Un hombre con vergüenza *tiene* firmeza. *(A man with* vergüenza *is firm.) Although he is helpful, he is not a meddler. He is a private person,* un poco aparte. *He is an aloof man who has come to be recognized as having stature in the community. . . . Another part of* firmeza *is a man's willingness to challenge authority. . . . He knows when to stand his ground. This is another manifestation of his being a private person: one who consults himself and feels no need to find out what people in general think before making up his mind. In fact, the role of the male is so imposing that* vergüenza *is really a male characteristic, and a woman derives her* vergüenza *from her father and later her husband. If she acts* sin vergüenza, *it always implies that the man responsible for her had not performed his responsibilities effectively.—Facundo Valdez, "Vergüenza"*

Facundo Valdez, a Chicano writer from New Mexico, describes the role *vergüenza* (shame) plays both in the formation of a Chicano political identity and the maintenance of traditional gender relations. On the one hand, a man with *vergüenza* is capable of challenging authority and standing his ground. On the other hand, *vergüenza* encodes traditional gender relations by defining Chicanas as being dependent on males. In this essay I explore how *vergüenza* is linked to the construction of a male political identity through an analysis of Ernesto Galarza's (1971) well-known autobiography, *Barrio Boy*. I then show how two equally well-known Chicana writers, Sandra Cisneros and Gloria Anzaldúa, have displaced *vergüenza* because it reinforces patriarchy and limits one's ability to resist racism. My principal concern here is to outline the connections between the displacement of *vergüenza*, the critique of patriarchy, resistance against racism, and the construction of borderland identities.

In relating changing conceptions of *vergüenza* to the construction of borderland identities my study takes its cue from Renato Rosaldo's (1989) analysis of changing Chicana and Chicano narratives. In *Culture and Truth: The Remaking of Social Analysis* Rosaldo describes changing narratives in terms of both the infusion of feminist perspectives into Chicana and Chicano studies and the development of new representations of culture as borderland regions. Arguing against traditional views of culture as homogeneous and static, Rosaldo explores how Chicana and Chicano writers have described themselves and their characters as "complex sites of cultural production [rather] than as representatives of a self-contained, homogeneous culture" (Rosaldo 1989, 217). According to Rosaldo, changing narratives involve a movement of representations of "Chicano identity from bounded cultural purity through the mockery of patriarchs to encounters at the border zones of everyday life" (Rosaldo 1989, 149).[1] For anthropologists these changing narratives suggest a reorientation of social analysis that more fully explores social creativity and power dynamics in the context of migration and globalization: "In the present postcolonial world, the notion of an authentic culture as an autonomous internally coherent universe no longer seems tenable, except perhaps as a 'useful fiction.' In retrospect, it appears that only a concerted disciplinary effort could maintain the tenuous fiction of a self-contained cultural whole. Rapidly increasing global interdependence has made it more and more clear that neither 'we' nor 'they' are as neatly bounded and homogenous as once seemed to be the case" (Rosaldo 1989, 217). The notion of cultural borderlands involves viewing culture both as a physical (and visceral) movement across national and cultural boundaries and as a series of creative intersections along the lines of ethnicity, class, and gender. As such, cultural borderlands produce social actors who are engaged in redefining identities and challenging and shaping relations of power. These redefinitions and engagements can include, as in the case of *vergüenza*, a subtle reworking of everyday emotions.

Because *vergüenza* informs uniform notions of proper behavior and gender relations, its transformation has involved both critiquing notions of cultural homogeneity and challenging patriarchy. Chicana writers, such as Cisneros and Anzaldúa, have criticized *vergüenza* because of its ideological function in justifying male dominance. As Alvina Quintana (1990) notes, both the Chicano movement and mainstream feminism have silenced Chicana voices. Chicana authors such as Cisneros and Anzaldúa have transformed both traditional Chicano ideology and feminism to create new conceptions of Chicana culture. The result is a "fertile soil [where] Chicana writers are concentrating their efforts, planting the seeds for Chicana re-vision and self-definition" (Quintana 1990, 258–59). For Chicanas this has meant greater attention to diversity within our own culture and reinterpretations (often differing) of key symbols such as Aztlán, La Llorona, and La Malinche.[2] Chicana writers have also focused on how homogenous notions of Chicano and Chicana identity, including notions of *vergüenza*, have limited our abilities to challenge racism.

Each of the authors studied in this essay has inhabited cultural borders. As a boy Ernesto Galarza migrated from Mexico to Sacramento, where he took on a variety of jobs, including farm labor, before attending college at Stanford and later Columbia. Galarza is highly regarded in Chicana and Chicano studies both for his history of political activism around farmworkers' rights and his publications, which include bilingual children's stories. Galarza's (1971) autobiography is a richly detailed history of his migration to the U.S. and the development of his political will to gain an education and become an activist for his community. Sandra Cisneros grew up in a racially mixed neighborhood in inner-city Chicago. In addition to her writing she has been involved in educational programs for high school dropouts and worked as a poetry teacher in various schools. Cisneros's (1984) first novel, *The House on Mango Street*, tells the story of a young woman's experiences in the inner city and the formation (as in the case of Galarza) of her political consciousness. Gloria Anzaldúa is a Chicana-Tejana who grew up in south Texas near the Mexican border. She has written two books on Chicana feminism and has become a major voice in expressing borderland conceptions of Chicana and Chicano culture.

Anzaldúa's (1987) *La Frontera/Borderlands: The New Mestiza* is a "bio-mythography" that combines autobiography with discussion of Chicana and Chicano history and analysis of Mesoamerican archetypes.

The Meanings of Vergüenza

Chicana and Chicano perspectives on *vergüenza* have challenged standard anthropological wisdom, which emphasizes how shame acts as an external regulator, based on fear of group sanctions, whereas guilt relies on an internalized set of norms. According to the classical formulation, "true shame cultures rely on external sanctions for good behavior, not, as true guilt cultures do, on an internalized conviction of sin" (Benedict 1946, 223).[3] In contrast, Facundo Valdez (1979) and Ernesto Galarza (1971) have noted that in Chicana and Chicano culture *vergüenza* is based on both what other people think and an internalized set of beliefs about what constitutes proper behavior and norms.[4] On the one hand, *vergüenza* involves a sense of living up to the standards of a community and is therefore founded on a fear of rejection or scorn. On the other hand, *vergüenza* encodes a sense of social responsibility and well-being. As Galarza points out, *vergüenza* is not necessarily "based on the fear of being caught" but involves a sense of "personal dignity; conscience; doing right; modesty; responsible behavior; trustworthiness" (Galarza 1971, 275).

In the context of village culture, as Valdez (1979) suggests, the meanings of *vergüenza* include being trusted and respected by members of a community. A man *con mucha vergüenza* (with shame) "is a helpful person to other people. Someone whom they can call on in an emergency." Valdez continues, "Along with moderation and his private nature, a man with *vergüenza* does not violate confidences. He has respect not only for older people, but for people in general, even youngsters, so that in turn he gets respect from them" (Valdez 1979, 100–101). In addition to the values of *confianza* (trust) and *respeto* (respect), a man *con mucha vergüenza* also knows when to defend his community and his rights. This does not mean that a man *con vergüenza* is a politician: "He is a crisis leader, but he is not a politician. If a crisis situation arises, he is likely to be put into responsibility because everybody has trust and confidence in him. He will retire from public position when the crisis has passed" (Valdez 1979, 100–101).

Vergüenza therefore encompasses not only one's internal sense of proper behavior and of being a part of a community but also one's ability to resolve crises within the community.

The values associated with *vergüenza* also involve the ability to feel ashamed when one's sense of right and the norms of a community are broken or violated. On the one hand, the values associated with *vergüenza* encode having a sense of modesty, integrity, respect, and trustworthiness / mutual trust. On the other hand, they involve the ability, when these values are not realized, to feel shame, expressed as embarrassment, shyness, timidity, or disgrace. An obvious example of this meaning of *vergüenza* is parents feeling ashamed of a child's misbehavior. These expressions of *vergüenza*, however, go beyond feeling ashamed of specific acts but rather encompass one's social, economic, and political sense of belonging and engagement in a community. For example, according to Valdez (1979), a man *con mucha vergüenza* usually has the means to support himself economically. In general, poverty can cause an individual to feel *vergüenza* because it reflects his or her standing in the community and can prevent him or her from fulfilling social responsibilities.[5] A good example of this sense of *vergüenza* is found in Barger and Reza's (1994) account of Alfredo, a Mexican migrant farmworker who lives in south Texas but travels with his family to Michigan and Ohio to harvest cucumbers and tomatoes. In their description Barger and Reza emphasize both Alfredo's internal sense of dignity and his feelings of shame at being unable to provide for his children's future: "Alfredo is a quiet man with a warm smile and gentle manner. He has a deep concern about his children's future and believes education will improve their situation in life. He worries that they have been behind in school, but the children's earnings have been necessary for the family's survival. He has also been ashamed when he could not provide them with new clothes at school" (Barger and Reza 1994, 2).

This sense of *vergüenza*, expressed both as a gentle dignity and ability to feel ashamed, is one of the factors that leads Alfredo to join a labor movement. According to the authors, after years of struggling for and gaining basic rights and better work conditions, Alfredo has gained a greater sense of belonging, a deeper respect for others, and economic security. Barger and Reza (1994) are, of course, focusing on the importance of union organizing. Their recounting of Alfredo's experiences is telling, however, because it shows how feeling ashamed is enmeshed in wider webs of power. And, as we will see in Cisneros's work, feeling ashamed of not being able to provide one's children with decent clothing for school can have different outcomes and meanings.

For those not familiar with Mexican and Chicano and Chicana culture these meanings of *vergüenza* can seem confusing given that having a sense of *vergüenza* (as opposed to being someone *sinvergüenza*, without shame) and the ability to feel ashamed are related. Because the values associated with *vergüenza* are relational—shaped by one's internal sense of dignity and acting responsibly within a community—they encompass expressions of feeling ashamed. This relational aspect of the concept points to the complexities of reconfiguring its meanings in cultural borderlands, where distinct moral and ethical dimensions of correct behavior and belonging to a community come into contact. In the case of gender relations these articulations are complex because traditional meanings of *vergüenza* are an aspect of male domination, yet these meanings are also an aspect of cultural identity and belonging.

Valdez (1979), I should note, emphasizes that the meanings of respect, firmness, and trustworthiness are gendered because *vergüenza* for women in village culture is conditioned by their being controlled and protected by men (Valdez 1979, 102). According to Valdez, traditional understandings of *vergüenza* can push women into a more reserved pattern of behavior because women's roles are mainly defined in terms of domestic respon- sibilities that limit the roles they can take in public. Valdez's understand- ing, I think, underestimates the ways that the values of *vergüenza, firmeza,* and *respeto* can inform women's participation in wider community issues. Nonetheless, I should emphasize that the role of shame in maintaining gender inequality is well known. Research on various cultures has shown that values associated with shame reinforce traditional notions of mas- culinity and femininity.[6] The problem with this research is that it has not focused on the ways that social actors have transformed and challenged the values associated with shame, including redefining gender relations. As Stanley Brandes (1987) points out, little is known about changing conceptions because researchers have focused on village culture without exploring how the meaning of shame is transformed "when cities grow or villages die, or when migrants move here or there, with or without their families" (Brandes 1987, 133).

Valdez (1979) hints at this project by arguing that *vergüenza* in Hispano villages of New Mexico no longer functions as a coherent moral code because of increasing contact with non-Hispanic society:

> So long as villages are relatively autonomous and so long as most of the individual's life is carried on within the village, *vergüenza* guides the individual to proper behavior and helps hold the village together. But when Hispanic villagers have to cope with urban and especially non-Hispanic society, in the county, state, or the region, then *vergüenza* impedes adjustment. *El hombre con vergüenza* is the ideal citizen of his village; he is not a skillful actor on a wider stage. (Valdez 1979, 106)

Valdez (1979) begins to rethink the usefulness of the values associated with *vergüenza* in the context of emerging interactions in cultural borderlands (rural/urban, Hispanic/non-Hispanic). Chicano writers, such as Galarza, have taken this project further by redefining shame in the context of migration and linking its transformation to new understandings of culture and politics. Cisneros and Anzaldúa, in contrast, have displaced these meanings by vindicating (and at times writing from the perspective of being) *sinvergüenza*.

Vergüenza *and the Displacement of Patriarchy*

Throughout his life Ernesto Galarza dedicated himself to working with and writing about agricultural workers. Although he never held an academic post, he wrote several books on farm labor organizing, as well as novels about the lives of migrant workers. Given his history of activism, one might expect that his autobiography would more overtly focus on politics. Instead, Galarza's (1971) autobiography tells the story of his early boyhood and his family's migration from Jalcocotán, Mexico, to Sacramento, California. At the level of "structures of feelings," however, Galarza's autobiography is about how he learned to challenge authority by internalizing a sense of *vergüenza*. I employ Raymond Williams's (1977) notion of structures of feeling because it emphasizes how emotions shape, reflect, and transform social relations. As such, structures of feeling inter-weave thought and feeling, "not feeling against thought, but thought as felt and feeling as thought: practical consciousness of a present kind, in a living and inter-relating community" (Williams 1977, 132). In Galarza's (1971) autobiography *vergüenza* reflects and transforms patriarchy and class relations while shaping, both as thoughts and feelings, perceptions of his community, migration, and inequality.

In *Barrio Boy* a young Ernesto Galarza's transition from the somewhat carefree days of childhood into adolescence is marked by learning *ver-güenza*. Galarza (1971) describes how his brother, José, and mother, Doña Henriqueta, taught him the rules of *respeto* and *vergüenza:*

> In addition to all these rules [of *respeto*] there were the proverbs and folk sayings my mother and José used frequently in their conversation. Something strange, something funny, something sad was put into a familiar phrase that not only explained matters but also gave you a safe rule to go by. . . . As to *vergüenza*, I learned by a hundred examples what it was to have it or not have it. Doña Henriqueta wrapped all hypocrites and deceivers in one of her sayings: "They are born naked, which they can't help; and they die without *vergüenza*, which they can." (148)

Learning *vergüenza* is also linked to Galarza's future ability to become a proper *jefe de familia* (head of family):

> My standing in the family, but especially with my mother depended on my keeping these rules [of *respeto*]. I was not punished for breaking them. She simply reminded me that it gave her acute *vergüenza* to see me act thus, and that I would never grow up to be a correct *jefe de familia* if I did not know how to be a correct boy. I knew what *vergüenza* was from feeling it time and again; and the notion of growing up to keep a tight rein over a family of my own was somehow satisfying. (237)

Throughout Galarza's (1971) autobiography, the themes of adhering to the rules of *respeto*, becoming a *jefe de familia*, and having a sense of *vergüenza* are intertwined.

Although Galarza (1971) links *vergüenza* to becoming a reigning *jefe de familia*, he is critical of traditional masculine ideology. Galarza even defines *jefe de familia* ironically: "the head of the family, called *el jefe* for short; by whichever name now rapidly becoming extinct" (271). On several occasions Galarza mocks traditional Mexican patriarchs by telling humorous stories about the singing of *corridos* (49), becoming a soldier (116), and watching men act *macho* at a dance (242). Galarza's mocking, however, has a larger target.[7] His criticisms are also directed at a group of individuals who constantly reappear in a repressive role, *autoridades* (authorities). In contrast to his mocking of *jefes de familia* and *autoridades,* Galarza affirms his mother's and aunt's resistance to patriarchal authority. Galarza emphasizes his mother's ability to stand up to her brother-in-law, Don Catarino, the *jefe* of the extended family in Jalcocotán: "Doña Henriqueta knew about people in deep trouble for she was one of them. But unlike most of them, she believed in rebelling against it, in resisting those who caused it. As the oldest of the four migrants from Miramar, Doña Henriqueta stood between us and Don Catarino when he was in one of his cantankerous moods. She drew a line between respect, which we were expected to show, and fear, which we were not" (18).

Recognizing this distinction between *respeto* and fear is one of the valuable lessons that Galarza learns from Doña Henriqueta. This everyday resistance against patriarchal authority is the first of four confrontations around which Galarza structures his autobiography. In the second, which also takes place in Mexico, Doña Henriqueta directly confronts a *patrón* who attempts to kill José instead of paying him. After learning of the incident, Doña Henriqueta bravely leads José and Ernesto to the offices of the *patrón:* "We stood during the brief encounter. My mother looked the *patrón* level in the eye and said: 'The wages—that is all—the wages.' I was afraid. The *patrón's* face was red with anger and perhaps fear. He called a clerk who counted out fifteen pesos to José" (170). By standing her ground in this brief but dangerous encounter, Doña Henriqueta displays *firmeza* (firmness). Indeed, this conflict shows that while recognizing its role in maintaining gender equality readings of *vergüenza,* such as Valdez's (1979), must provide a more nuanced view of how women in "village" culture engage its values.

Although they are capable of challenging authority in Mexico, Doña Henriqueta and José have a more difficult time confronting North American officials. In a powerful scene Galarza (1971) writes about a long-awaited reunion with members of his extended family who had just migrated from Mexico. After traveling to greet the migrants at Angel Island, the Galarzas return to Sacramento empty-handed because their relatives had been deported:

> The trip back to Sacramento was like returning from a funeral. My uncles exchanged puzzled questions, bitter and despairing, anger and grief in their faces, staring out the window to avoid looking at each other. They paid little attention to my comments, caught up in their own distress. The man in uniform had merely shown us some papers but he had not told us why. He had not even said what would have to be done to bring our family back and take them home with us. I saw him vividly in my mind, ugly and menacing, and silently called him all the names I could think of, like *gringo pendejo* [damn gringo]. But my secret revenge did not make me feel better as I tried to guess what Gustavo meant when he had said on the launch: "*Es una injusticia* [It is unjust]." Our hopes had been denied and our joy had been turned to sadness by people we were powerless even to question. (215–16)

Although Galarza (1971) does not dwell on this point, the more disturbing realization here is that his family has lost the ability to stand firm before authority.

In the last part of the autobiography Galarza begins to occupy a bicultural zone that allows him to mediate between his English- and Spanish-speaking worlds. He regularly becomes involved in challenging *autoridades*: "When troubles made it necessary for the *barrio* [neighborhood] people to deal with the Americans uptown, the *Autoridades*, I went with them to the police court, the industrial accident office, the county hospital, the draft board, the county clerk. We got lost together in the rigmarole of functionaries who sat, like *patrones*, behind desks and who demand licenses, certificates, documents, affidavits, signatures, and witnesses" (256). Taking on the characteristics of *vergüenza*, Galarza displays the qualities of *confianza* (trustworthiness/mutual trust) that make him a person with stature in his community.

The fourth and final confrontation with *autoridades* occurs while Galarza is still in high school. At the farm where Galarza worked during the summer as a laborer, several children died because of the lack of potable water. The migrant workers chose Galarza to contact *autoridades* in Sacramento. It is during this incident that Galarza, without realizing it, makes his first organizing speech. For the reader familiar with his life history, this event marks the beginning of Galarza's lifetime concern and activism over the plight of farmworkers.

It is important to note that for Galarza (1971) *vergüenza* and *respeto* are not simply a set of rules and norms but feelings. Galarza's sense of *vergüenza* is an example of structures of feeling because it engages lived experience and involves an appreciation of "impulse, restraint, and tone" (Williams 1977, 132). Concerning cultural emergence, Galarza's occupation of a bicultural border zone and his juxtaposition of North American *autoridades* with Mexican *patrones* give him a "critical idiom" on social injustice (Rosaldo 1989, 160). As Valdez (1979) would say, Galarza has learned *firmeza*, the ability to "stand his own ground." Galarza, however, links his learning of *vergüenza* to the education he received from Doña Henriqueta. Indeed Doña Henriqueta's ability to challenge authority (in Mexico) makes her a powerful figure. However, even though Galarza mocks traditional conceptions of masculinity, he embeds his own political identity in *vergüenza*. In contrast, Cisneros and Anzaldúa focus on how *vergüenza* is an aspect of male domination.

Vergüenza *and the Creation of an Imagined/Real Community*

In Sandra Cisneros's (1984) novel, *The House on Mango Street,* the themes of the oppressiveness of shame and the construction of a new political identity, symbolized by the protagonist's search for a home, are intertwined. The novel begins with the young protagonist, Esperanza, being made to feel shame about her home and identity. Her shame derives from her family's poverty and from the limitations imposed on women by male domination in the household. Shame is first inflicted onto Esperanza by outsiders and Anglos. In two key passages at the beginning of the novel, nuns make Esperanza feel ashamed of her house (9, 43). In another incident a white neighbor girl causes shame by remarking that her family is moving because the neighborhood is turning bad; Esperanza's family had just moved in (15). Esperanza refuses to go see the rich houses where her father works because it gives her shame: "I want a house on a hill like the ones with the gardens where Papa works. We go on Sundays, Papa's day off. I used to go. I don't any more. You don't like to go out with us, Papa says. Getting too old? . . . I don't tell them I am ashamed—all of us staring out the window like the hungry. I am tired of looking at what we can't have" (81). Finally, Esperanza's mother points out the limitations of shame: "Shame is a bad thing, you know. It keeps you down. You want to know why I quit school. Because I didn't have nice clothes. No clothes, but I had brains" (83–84). Even though Esperanza's mother is a creative person, her poverty and the limitations of *vergüenza* prevented her from continuing her education. Cisneros presents this as a sad irony because *vergüenza* and poverty work only to push a young woman out of school.

Later in the novel Esperanza relates shame not only to poverty but also to male domination and the maintenance of traditional gender relations. The oppressiveness of shame and its links with patriarchy are made apparent in the lives of two women, Esperanza's friend Sally and Aunt Guadalupe. In Sally's case the full force of male domination is made apparent. Sally is treated like an "animal" by her father because she threatens the family's sense of shame: "But Sally doesn't tell about the time he hit her with his hands just like a dog, she said, like if I was an animal. He thinks I'm going to run away like his sister who made the family ashamed" (85). Here Sally's father enacts the traditional notion of *vergüenza* (as described by Valdez [1979]), in which it is men's "responsibility" to control wives and daughters. In the case of her Aunt Guadalupe, Esperanza expresses surprise when learning her aunt has died: "We didn't know. She had been dying such a long time we forgot. Maybe she was ashamed. Maybe she was embarrassed it took so many years. The kids who wanted to be kids instead of washing dishes and ironing their papa's shirts, and the husband who wanted a wife again" (57). Because she is dying, the notion that Guadalupe would feel ashamed because she cannot function as a housewife is, to say the least, disturbing.

Esperanza, in contrast, refuses to allow her creative potentials to be limited by male domination and shame. As Rosaldo (1989) notes, Esperanza uses her "social grace" and cunning to effectively counteract the threats of poverty and patriarchy. Rosaldo links Esperanza's ability to "move on" with her construction of a "borderland" identity. "Esperanza inhabits a border zone crisscrossed by a plurality of languages and cultures. Multiple subjectivities intersect in her own person, where they coexist, not in a zone of free play but each with its own gravity and density" (Rosaldo 1989, 163). These multiple subjectivities are partially the result of the intersecting oppressions that Esperanza faces—class, race, and gender—as well as the physical space she inhabits, a racially mixed, inner-city neighborhood. The emotional subtext, which Rosaldo does not explore, is that to thrive in the borderlands, Esperanza must not only construct her own multiplex identity but also transform the meaning of shame. Cultural emergence—the construction of cultural borderlands—is therefore articulated through the reconfiguration of shame.

The themes of overcoming patriarchy and transforming shame are fused during a visit by three magical figures who appear at the end of the novel, *las comadres* (the godmothers). "They came with the wind that blows in August, thin as a spider web and barely noticed. Three who did not seem to be related to anything but the moon: one with laughter like tin and one with eyes of a cat and one with hands like porcelain. The aunts, the three sisters, *las comadres*, they said" (Cisneros 1984, 96). Throughout the novel *las comadres* are the only relatives to whom Esperanza refers in Spanish. Esperanza calls her parents Mama and Papa (which has a bilingual sensibility but is not italicized in the text), and she refers to the rest of her relatives in English as aunts, uncles, cousins, and so forth. This reference to *las comadres* in Spanish, and the mystical nature of their visit, marks Esperanza's sense of belonging to her community. This sense of identity, however, also involves creating an imagined/real women's community, as symbolized by *las comadres,* while transforming the meaning of *vergüenza.*

To fully understand the significance of *las comadres'* visit allow me to introduce José Limón's (1994) discussion of the loss of values such as *vergüenza* among Chicanos and Chicanas. In *Dancing with the Devil: Society and Cultural Poetics in Mexican-American South Texas* Limón explores how social dynamics such as the emergence of consumer culture and the displacement of communities through migration have led to a sense of historical and social lack of depth. Limón highlights this point by characterizing how *Mexicano* and *Mexicana* elders characterize his generation (post–World War Two):

> All of their lives are marked by divorce and shifting relationships. And, if ties to the nuclear family are often tenuous, they spend even less time with members of their extended family, save seeing relatives at a dance by accident rather than design. Only weddings and funerals bring them together and sometimes not even then. While all of them have been co-parents in baptismal rites *(compadrazgo)*, there is no consistent follow through on these obligations. They rarely see their co-parents *(compadres)* or their godchildren, and there is little, if any, of the traditional gifting for the latter on their birthday. Most telling, when they do see their co-parents—the child's parents—they do not address each other with the honorific *compadre* and *comadre* that traditionally take the place of first names. But above all, notions of self-worth and social responsibility to others are also now in tenuous state. There is precious little socialization of their children with ideas of *respeto, vergüenza,* etc., and the elders among them constantly noted and lamented the absence of this aspect of culture. (113)

The lack of values that Limón's (1994) elders lament are in part reflected in Esperanza's community, where relatives are mainly seen at family events and characters struggle with notions of self-worth. Clearly, Esperanza's links to her Mexican past are tenuous, although they exist in powerful moments, such as when Esperanza listens to her father's Mexican music. Cisneros's (1984) novel, however, also provides a powerful reflection on and perhaps answer to the laments of Limón's elders. For one, values such as *vergüenza* and *respeto* are not simply lost but questioned and transformed by Cisneros's characters. For another, the elder's nostalgia for "lost" values such as *vergüenza* does not take into account patriarchy. The appearance, then, of *las comadres* at a funeral speaks to a world where relatives and friends only come together, as Limón's elders would note, for weddings and funerals. However, their visit also provides for the possibility of a world where *vergüenza* generates a sense of belonging and the honorific *comadre* does not simply mark respect for traditional culture but signifies the creation of an imagined/real community: one that displaces patriarchy.

During this mythical moment, in which a sense of community is reconstituted, *las comadres* grant Esperanza a wish. When Esperanza wishes to leave Mango Street, a sense of shame reconnects her to her community:

> When you leave you must remember to come back for the others. A circle, understand? You will always be Esperanza. You will always be Mango Street. You can't erase what you know: You can't forget who you are.
>
> Then I didn't know what to say. It was as if she could read my mind, as if she knew what I had wished for, and I felt ashamed for having made such a selfish wish.
>
> You must remember to come back. For the ones who cannot leave as easily as you. You will remember? She asked as if she was telling me. Yes, yes, I said a little confused. (Cisneros 1984, 98)

This process of leaving and coming back is mediated both by the force of shame, this time in a woman's context, and the ability to write, which becomes a source of personal empowerment. At the end of the novel Esperanza associates writing with overcoming patriarchy and her search for a home. Writing becomes the vehicle for creating a new political space and creating a circle back to the community: "Friends and neighbors will say, What happened to that Esperanza? Where did she go with all those books and paper? Why did she march so far away? They will not know I have gone away to come back. For the ones I left behind. For the ones who cannot out" (Cisneros 1984, 101–2).

In contrast to Galarza (1971), Cisneros (1984) problematizes the impact of *vergüenza* on women by linking it closely to male dominance. In terms of their political identities, the reconfiguration of *vergüenza* plays a central role in the ability to stand firm before authority (Galarza) and to link writing to empowerment (Cisneros). For both authors, albeit in different circumstances, reinterpreting *vergüenza* is an aspect of creating a sense of identity within cultural borderlands. In both cases the protagonists are entrusted to return to and represent their communities (for Galarza migrant workers and for Esperanza an inner-city neighborhood whose meaning is reconstituted by *las comadres*). Esperanza's reconfiguration of *vergüenza* therefore involves a displacement of feeling ashamed about her poverty and community to *firmeza* about her identity and background. For

Cisneros the presence of *las comadres* in generating an imagined/real sense of community and reconstituting *vergüenza,* the dream of a house independent of men, and the use of writing as creative resistance all inform a larger Chicana feminist project.

Vergüenza *and the New Mestiza*

In the essay "La Prieta," in the volume *This Bridge Called My Back: Writings By Radical Women of Color,* Anzaldúa (1983) describes how poverty and racism have caused her to feel shame. It is worth quoting a section from the essay, entitled *"Vergüenza,"* keeping in mind that Anzaldúa is not writing about the isolated villages of New Mexico but the borderlands of south Texas:

> . . . eating at school out of sacks, hiding our "lonches" *papas con chorizo* behind cupped hands and bowed heads, gobbling them up before the other kids could see. Guilt lay folded in the tortilla. The Anglo kids laughing—calling us "tortilleros," the Mexican kids taking up the word and using it as a club with which to hit each other. My brothers, sister and I started bringing white bread sandwiches to school. After a while we stopped taking our lunch altogether. (201)

Like Cisneros's (1984) Esperanza, Anzaldúa's (1983) sense of shame is cast in terms of racism and a sense of regret, which is initially inflicted by Anglos, for being both culturally different and poor. With the publication of *La Frontera/Borderlands,* Anzaldúa (1987) returns to the theme of *vergüenza* but this time to displace it with a new *mestiza* form of social consciousness.

In her biomythography Anzaldúa (1987) constructs a new physical, historical, and archetypal identity that is based on inhabiting cultural borderlands. The book begins with a description of the Mexico/U.S. border and then examines ethnic, sexual, gender, and psychological borders. In all cases borders are not natural but imposed and artificial: "Borders are set up to define the places that are safe and unsafe, to distinguish *us* from *them.* A border is a dividing line, a narrow strip along a steep edge. A borderland is a vague and undetermined place created by the emotional residue of an unnatural boundary" (3). By the end of her biomythography

Anzaldúa has redefined the meaning of borders. A key part of this re-definition involves reconfiguring the values associated with *vergüenza;* "I will not be shamed again. Nor will I shame myself" (87).

Similar to Cisneros's (1984) Esperanza, Anzaldúa's (1987) initial criticism of *respeto* and *vergüenza* are based on the fact that they are an aspect of male domination:

> Culture forms our beliefs. We perceive the version of reality that it communicates. Dominant paradigms, predefined concepts that exist as unquestionable, unchallengeable, are transmitted to us through culture. Culture is made by those in power—men. . . . *Respeto* carries with it a set of rules so that social categories and hierarchies will be kept in order: respect is reserved for *la abuela, papá, el patrón,* those with power in the community. Women at the bottom of the ladder are one rung above the deviants. (16–18)

In contrast to Galarza (1971), whose demonstrations of *respeto* for his elders are touching, Anzaldúa (1987) links *respeto* to an attitude of humility among women as well as to a lack of tolerance for deviance in Chicana and Chicano culture as a whole. For gays this lack of tolerance is devastating: "The Chicano, *mexicano,* and some Indian cultures have no tolerance for deviants. . . . The queer are the mirror reflecting the heterosexual tribe's fear: being different, being other and therefore lesser, therefore sub-human, in-human, non-human" (18). The heterosexism encoded in traditional understandings of *vergüenza* and *respeto* therefore require not only reinterpretation but displacement.

For Anzaldúa (1987) *vergüenza* prevents us from realizing our own creative potential. It causes us to take on a variety of pathological defense mechanisms (45). The personal project of overcoming shame in order to express intersecting identities is part of a larger goal of gaining "equal power." Anzaldúa writes about the possibilities of establishing alliances with Chicanos:

> Though we "understand" the root causes of male hatred and fear, and the subsequent wounding of women, we do not excuse, we do not condone, and we will no longer put up with it. From the men of our race, we demand the admission/acknowledgement/disclosure/testimony

that they wound us, violate us, are afraid of us and of our power. We need them to say they will begin to eliminate their hurtful put-down ways. But more than the words, we demand acts. We say to them: We will develop equal power with you and those who have shamed us. (83–84)

The last sentence indicates the intensity through which oppression is mediated by shame. The reference to "others" also indicates how oppression by Anglos can be inflicted by causing shame. Anzaldúa (1987) therefore locates *vergüenza* in a complex web of oppressions that silence borderland voices.

As is true for Cisneros's (1984) Esperanza, Anzaldúa (1987) views writing as a source of empowerment because it shatters the silence surrounding the Chicana experience and acts as a form of creative resistance. "When I write it feels like I'm carving bone. It feels like I'm creating my own face, my own heart—a Nahuatl concept. My soul makes itself through the creative act. It is constantly remaking and giving birth to itself through my body. It is this learning to live with *la Coatlicue* that transforms living in the Borderlands from a nightmare into a numinous experience. It is always a path/state to something else" (73). The reference to *Coatlicue*, an Aztec deity, is part of Anzaldúa's (1987) larger project of realigning Chicana and Chicano identity with Mesoamerican archetypes. A key part of this project is to reaffirm the indigenous roots of *La Virgen de Guadalupe* (Our Lady of Guadalupe) by linking her meanings to *Coatlicue* and *Tonantzín*. I should note here that *La Virgen de Guadalupe* is the most important symbol of Mexican nationalism, culture, and identity. Her appearance marked the beginning of a new nation and race. After the 1519–21 conquest of Mexico by Cortés, indigenous peoples were forced to practice Catholicism and leave aside their traditional religions. This history is beyond the scope of this essay. However, I would like to highlight that *La Virgen de Guadalupe*'s appearance to Juan Diego, a poor Indian peasant, on December 12, 1531, has come to symbolize identity, truth, and hope within Mexican and Mexican American culture. She has also been represented as an ideal of passive womanhood—a suffering, pure, and patient female. As Anzaldúa notes, however, *La Virgen de Guadalupe* appeared at the same site where the Aztecs worshipped the goddess *Tonantzín*. By emphasizing

Men wearing Virgin of Guadalupe scarves dance at the Basilica in Mexico City, December 12, 1992. Photograph by Matthew C. Gutmann.

this relation between *Tonantzín* and *La Virgen de Guadalupe* Anzaldúa shows how traditional understandings of *La Virgen* have deemphasized Her active and sexual meanings along with Her indigenous roots.

Anzaldúa (1987) argues that the reconfiguration of the meanings of key symbols such as *La Virgen de Guadalupe* breaks down sexual and ethnic barriers, thus making possible border crossings and the emergence of the new *mestiza:* "The new *mestiza* copes by developing a tolerance for contradictions, a tolerance for ambiguity. She learns to be an Indian in Mexican culture, to be a Mexican from an Anglo point of view. She learns to juggle cultures. . . . Not only does she sustain contradictions, she turns the ambivalence into something else" (79). The expression of this new *mestiza* identity thus places Chicanas at the center of an increasingly diverse and creative interaction of cultures, a borderland region. Transcending the effects of shame is a central part of Anzaldúa's larger project of establishing a borderlands identity: "I will no longer be made to feel ashamed of existing. I will have my voice: Indian, Spanish, white. I will have my serpent's tongue—my woman's voice, my sexual voice, my poet's voice. I will overcome the tradition of silence" (59).

According to Anzaldúa (1987), the oppressive effects of *vergüenza* and patriarchy occur at the level of everyday life and are displaced, in part, by the formation of a new *mestiza* consciousness that rejects feelings of shame. Similar to Cisneros's (1984) Esperanza, Anzaldúa (1987) displaces *vergüenza* in the construction of a multiplex identity. For Esperanza, *vergüenza* takes on positive meanings—firmness and trustworthiness—only after a sense of an imagined/real community is reconstituted (that is, by the visit of *las comadres*). Anzaldúa's writings offer new possibilities for reinterpreting *vergüenza* because she maps its meanings onto a variety of cultural traditions, including Aztec social thought, and a political practice based on breaking the silence around the Chicana lesbian experience. In this context the potential for reconfiguring *vergüenza* and being *sinvergüenza* (shameless), and the reconstitution of a new sense of a community through the deployment of a *mestiza* consciousness, remains to be explored.

Conclusions

Within Chicana and Chicano literature the meanings of *vergüenza* are not fixed but rather in a constant state of flux and open to a variety of interpretations.[8] Indeed, a number of lines of literary analysis can be drawn from this exploration of changing narratives. For one, the complex nostalgia for patriarchal village life that is expressed by Américo Paredes (1958) can be interpreted as a longing for traditional values of *vergüenza* and *respeto*.[9] For another, the mediations between having a sense of *vergüenza* and being *sinvergüenza* are often linked to border crossings. For example, the *chilanga tejana*[10] poet Liliana Valenzuela (1991), in a poem titled "Sinvergüenza," writes about the lack of *vergüenza* she feels in the United States.

> . . . En este país
> me es más facil hablar de cosas
> prohibidas
> like tu culo, el mío, and other cochinadas
> cosas que no se mencionan
> because they can activate a spell
> and freeze you on your tracks. (65–66)

[. . . In this country
it is easier for me to speak about
prohibited things
like your ass, mine, and other nastiness
things that are not mentioned
because they can activate a spell
and freeze you on your tracks . . .]

This lack of *vergüenza* signifies the loss of a moral code in which *co-chinadas* (nasty things) are permitted and a sense of decency is absent. In the end the poet leaves unresolved how she intends to mediate between the two cultures and her ambivalence toward feeling a lack of *vergüenza*. This type of meditation on having a sense of *vergüenza* and being *sin-vergüenza* is also expressed by characters in Cisneros's (1991) essays. Several characters in her collection of short stories *Woman Hollering Creek and Other Stories* (1991) express a variety of understandings of shame. One young Chicana character, in the story "One Holy Night," wears the title *sinvergüenza* (without shame) with a degree of irony and pride (32). Another young Chicana character, in "Little Miracles Kept Promises," feels ashamed of *La Virgen de Guadalupe* because of the way she is portrayed as suffering and passive (128). Only when the protagonist realizes that the true name of *La Virgen* is *Tonantzín* does she no longer feel ashamed of *La Virgen*. In this instance, rather than reinforcing the quiet suffering associated with traditional representations, shame becomes an emotional force in creating a more feminist understanding of *La Virgen*.

Both Cisneros (1984) and Anzaldúa (1987) have noted the negative aspects of shame for men in the context of border crossings. Shame can prevent Chicanos from reacting to injustice and limit their ability to maneuver in borderland zones. For example in the chapter "Geraldo No Last Name" Cisneros (1984) describes undocumented male migrants as always looking ashamed (63). As in the case of Esperanza's mother, who feels shame about her poverty, there is a painful irony here given the living conditions and hardships undocumented migrants face. Anzaldúa (1987), at the beginning of *La Frontera/Borderlands*, also writes about shame and fear of being captured by *la migra* (the border patrol):

In the fields, *la migra*. My aunt saying, "*No corran*, don't run. They'll think you're *del otro lado*." In the confusion, Pedro ran, terrified of being caught. He couldn't speak English, couldn't tell them he was fifth generation American. *Sin papeles*—he did not carry his birth certificate to work in the fields. *La migra* took him away while we watched. *Se lo llevaron*. He tried to smile when he looked back at us, to raise his fist. But I saw the shame pushing his head down, I saw the terrible weight of shame hunch his shoulders. (4)

In both cases *vergüenza* only confuses and humiliates men as they attempt to support themselves and their families while living in constant fear of the border patrol. Cisneros (1984) and Anzaldúa (1987) thus show how traditional understandings of *vergüenza* have outlived their usefulness in the context of racism and border crossings. Indeed, their writings on *vergüenza* should be understood as a call for Chicano writers to expand the projects started by Galarza (1971) and Valdez (1979) in reinterpreting and displacing its meaning for men.

The study of changing Chicana and Chicano narratives also calls into question traditional anthropological understandings that draw a rigid dichotomy between shame and guilt cultures. For Chicana and Chicano writers the values associated with *vergüenza* are based both on a fear of group sanctions and internalized convictions. In other words, the values of *firmeza* (firmness), *confianza* (trustworthiness/mutual trust), and *respeto* (respect) are relational because they both involve belonging and/or contributing to a community and maintaining an internalized sense of right and wrong. The study of changing Chicana and Chicano narratives also offers insights into understanding, as Brandes (1987) states, the cultural transformations surrounding the meaning of shame. For Chicana and Chicano authors these transformations are not only linked to social processes, such as migration, but also to the emergence of new understandings of culture, politics, and everyday emotions. Indeed, these changing narratives point to the possibilities of exploring the structures of feeling, the intersections of thought and emotion, that shape borderland experiences. And, because *vergüenza* encodes a wide set of values based on *confianza*, gender identities, and *firmeza*, its meanings are sure to undergo further transformations as Chicanas and Chicanos continue to write about and challenge the relations of power through which these values are articulated. For anthropology, then, the task that remains is to follow the lead of these changing narratives by exploring how Chicanos and Chicanas in their everyday lives have reinterpreted and displaced the meanings of *vergüenza*.

Notes

I would like to thank Alejandro Lugo, Matthew Gutmann, Peter Schmidt, Renato Rosaldo, Jonathan Inda, and Laurie Fitzmaurice for their comments on this essay. Earlier drafts were presented at the American Studies Association meeting in Boston, November 4–7, 1993, on the panel, "Imaginary Homelands and Contingent Traditions: The Cultural Politics of Representational Practices," and at the American Anthropological Association meeting in San Francisco, November 20–24, 1996, on the panel, "Mexican and Chicano Family, Marriage, and Gender in a Changing World."

1. The notion of cultural borderlands has gained wide circulation in ethnic studies. See, e.g., hooks (1990) and Kondo (1991).

2. Aztlán, the mythical homeland of the Aztecs, was an important symbol of the Chicano and Chicana civil rights movement. For a good discussion of changing conceptions of Aztlán see Daniel Cooper Alarcón (1992). La Llorona (the weeper), an ethereal mother who is searching for her lost children, is a central element of Mexican and Mexican American folklore. From an anthropological perspective José Limón (1985) offers an interesting interpretation of La Llorona. La Malinche served as a translator for Cortés, the Spanish conqueror. In Mexican and Mexican American culture she is often seen as having betrayed her people, although a number of writers have developed a fuller understanding of La Malinche's actions (see Alarcón 1983). Also see Chabram-Dernersesian (1992) for a discussion about the production of Chicana identities.

3. Benedict (1946) continues: "Shame is a reaction to other people's criticism. A man is shamed either by being openly ridiculed and rejected or by fantasying to himself that he has been made ridiculous. In either case it is a potent sanction" (223). Recently, anthropologists studying Japanese culture have challenged this view by pointing out that the external/internal distinction is overdrawn because shame also relies on an internalized set of norms (Creighton 1990, 282).

4. Chicana and Chicano understandings of shame also challenge the notion that shame and honor are inextricably linked. In Valdez's (1979) discussion of *vergüenza* little mention is made of the concept of honor. This same finding has been reported about other cultures. Brandes (1987), for example, argues that among his Spanish informants, notions of shame play a key role in everyday life, but the concept of honor is rarely mentioned (123).

5. Creighton (1990) makes a similar point about shame in Japanese culture, where notions of belonging to the group include not falling behind others either economically or socially (295).

6. Several essays in David Gilmore's (1987) edited volume *Honor and Shame and the Unity of the Mediterranean* make this point. Also, see Melhuus (1990). I should also note that this link between shame and gender inequality is not as pronounced in some cultures, such as Japanese (Asano-Tamanoi 1987) and Ilongot (Rosaldo 1983).

7. *Corridos*, a form of Mexican balladry, cover a range of themes including cultural resistance to class and race domination.

8. These changing narratives point to a new dimension—the level of everyday emotions—in which representations of Chicana and Chicano identity "respond to real and perceived pressures that are constantly in flux" (Alarcón 1992, 62).

9. Paredes's (1958) pastoral description of Mexican villages, where patriarchs ruled through trust and respect, focuses on south Texas before the 1848 U.S. invasion.

10. Valenzuela (1991) has lived both in Mexico City and Texas. *Chilanga* is a somewhat derogatory reference to the residents of Mexico City, who are seen as thinking they are superior to residents of rural areas. Residents of Mexico City sometimes use the word to refer to themselves in a slightly ironic and undercutting way.

References

Alarcón, Daniel Cooper. 1992. "The Aztec Palimpsest: Towards a New Understanding of Aztlán." *Aztlán* 19, no. 2:33–68.

Alarcón, Norma. 1983. "Chicana's Feminist Literature: A Re-vision through Malintzin/ or Malintzin: Putting Flesh Back on the Object." In *This Bridge Called My Back: Writings by Radical Women of Color*, ed. Cherríe Moraga and Gloria Anzaldúa, 182– 90. New York: Kitchen Table/Women of Color.

Anzaldúa, Gloria. 1983. "La Prieta." In *This Bridge Called My Back: Writings by Radical Women of Color*, ed. Cherríe Moraga and Gloria Anzaldúa, 198–209. New York: Kitchen Table/Women of Color.

———. 1987. *La Frontera/Borderlands: The New Mestiza*. San Francisco: Spinsters/Aunt Lute.

Asano-Tamanoi, Mariko. 1987. "Shame, Family, and State in Catalonia and Japan." In *Honor and Shame and the Unity of the Mediterranean*, ed. David D. Gilmore, 104–20. Washington, D.C.: American Anthropological Association.

Barger, W. K., and E. Reza. 1994. *The Farm Labor Movement in the Midwest: Social Change and Adaptation among Migrant Farmworkers*. Austin: University of Texas Press.

Benedict, Ruth. 1946. *The Chrysanthemum and the Sword: Patterns of Japanese Culture*. Boston: Houghton Mifflin.

Brandes, Stanley. 1987. "Reflections on Honor and Shame in the Mediterranean." In

Honor and Shame and the Unity of the Mediterranean, ed. David D. Gilmore, 121–34. Washington, D.C.: American Anthropological Association.

Chabram-Dernersesian, Angie. 1992. "I throw punches for my race, but I don't want to be a man: Writing us—Chica-nos (girl, us)/Chicanas—into the movement script." In *Cultural Studies*, ed. Lawrence Grossberg, Cary Nelson, and Paula A. Treichler, 81–95. New York: Routledge.

Cisneros, Sandra. 1984. *The House on Mango Street.* Houston, Tex.: Arte Publico.

——. 1991. *Woman Hollering Creek and Other Stories.* New York: Random House.

Creighton, Millie R. 1990. "Revisiting Shame and Guilt Cultures: A Forty Year Pilgrimage." *Ethos* 18, no. 3:279–307.

Galarza, Ernesto. 1971. *Barrio Boy.* Notre Dame, Ind.: University of Notre Dame Press.

Gilmore, David D., ed. 1987. *Honor and Shame and the Unity of the Mediterranean.* Washington, D.C.: American Anthropological Association.

hooks, bell. 1990. *Yearning, Race, Gender, and Cultural Politics.* Boston: South End.

Kondo, Dorine. 1991. "M. Butterfly." *Cultural Critique* 16, no. 5:5–29.

Limón, José. 1985. "La Llorona, the Third Legend of Greater Mexico: Cultural Symbols, Women, and the Political Unconscious." In *Renato Rosaldo Lecture Series Monographs.* Vol. 2, ed. J. R. García, 58–92. Tucson: University of Arizona Press.

——. 1994. *Dancing with the Devil: Society and Cultural Poetics in Mexican-American South Texas.* Madison: University of Wisconsin Press.

Melhuus, Marit. 1990. "A Shame to Honour—A Shame to Suffer." *Ethnos* 1, no. 2:5–25.

Paredes, Américo. 1958. *With His Pistol in His Hand.* Austin: University of Texas Press.

Quintana, Alvina. 1990. "Politics, Representation, and the Emergence of a Chicana Aesthetic." *Cultural Studies* 4, no. 3:257–63.

Rosaldo, Michelle. 1983. "The Shame of Headhunters and the Autonomy of Self." *Ethos* 11, no. 3:135–51.

Rosaldo, Renato. 1989. *Culture and Truth: The Remaking of Social Analysis.* Boston: Beacon.

Valdez, Facundo. 1979. "Vergüenza." In *The Colorado College Studies: The Survival of Spanish American Villages*, ed. Paul Kutsche, 99–106. Colorado Springs: Colorado College Research Committee.

Valenzuela, Liliana. 1991. "Sinvergüenza." *Americas Review* 19, no. 1:65–66.

Williams, Raymond. 1977. *Marxism and Literature.* Oxford, U.K.: Oxford University Press.

X. ANDRADE

Pancho Jaime and the
Political Uses of
Masculinity in Ecuador

∎ ∎ ∎

This essay explores the uses of dominant notions of masculinity for constructing representations of political power in Ecuador. This is a case study
of the work and audience of Pancho Jaime (1946–89), the prominent and
controversial political journalist in Ecuador during the 1980s. Jaime's
mastery of selective elements of popular culture made him legendary
in Guayaquil, the country's largest city and a place renowned in popular imagination for its *machismo* and flamboyant politicians. Between
1984 and his death at the hands of unknown political enemies in 1989,
Jaime illegally produced magazines sold through underground distribution networks. These magazines totaled nearly one thousand pages and
included hundreds of caricatures. Jaime's writing style followed local patterns of speech and embellished sexual stereotypes, insults, gossip, and
rumors about public figures. Although his articles were generally well
documented, one of his main strategies was to reveal the corruption of
politicians by making connections between their conduct in public office
and their supposedly "deviant" sexuality. Seizing on particular events involving public figures from key institutions in Ecuador, such as Congress

and the Catholic Church, Jaime critically assessed local and national politics through long tirades of heavily charged, obscene language. He presented these texts alongside outrageous images of his targets in a variety of heterosexual and homosexual positions. Portraying enemies as grotesque characters motivated by shameful, "perverted" instincts, Jaime criticized the establishment by creating a carnivalesque representation of political life in Ecuador.

In this essay I use *machismo*—a term both shared and contested locally—to describe a political form of public masculinity. Jaime's work aids in elucidating the local meanings of politics, the masculine language in which these meanings are expressed in everyday life, people's perceptions about the masculinity embodied by elites and authorities, and the extent to which people take for granted that corruption and vulgarity are inherent in the exercise of power. My approach emphasizes issues of production, circulation, and consumption of political meanings and as such could be described as an effort to understand a political economy of images and representations of power. The concept of "economy" helps to put informants' conflicting views into a larger, more systematic framework for understanding the ways in which people's ideas about power relations, and the sentiments they hold about elites and their own social position, relate, although not directly, to a social structure (see Poole 1997, 8–13). In addition, the concept of "political economy" (of images and representations of power) aids in analyzing the perception held by some informants' that both the public imagery of politicians and the political caricatures advanced in Jaime's magazines were commodities that circulated within unequal systems of political marketing.

Keeping a focus on larger fields of production, as well as on how local audiences read these materials, I explore how obscene images and vulgar discourses are used to forge a link between *machismo* and politics. My ethnographic fieldwork took place between 1998 and 1999 in Guayaquil. I conducted participant observation among different male social formations to gather information on the local meanings of masculinity, conducted over sixty interviews with readers of Jaime's works, and carried out informal surveys about the extent of his popularity. In addition, I assembled focus groups with selected female readers and conducted detailed interviews with some of Jaime's closest collaborators.

Exploring some of the reactions generated by Jaime's writings among informants of different social backgrounds, this essay shows the importance acquired by dominant notions of masculinity in confronting and/or affirming mainstream representations of political power. Jaime's work, although unique in Ecuador, was hardly idiosyncratic. On the contrary, his writings belong to a politics of masculinity that can be broadly identified with *populismo* in Guayaquil. For this reason it is important to read his materials as part of the traditions of political rhetoric, print media, and local expressive culture.[1]

Comentarios

Victor Francisco Jaime Orellana, widely known as Pancho Jaime, or PJ, was born in Guayaquil in 1946 and assassinated there in September 1989.[2] Conducting fieldwork almost a decade after his death, I interviewed many people who remembered him more as a *rockero* (rocker) than as a political journalist. Others saw PJ either as a puppet in the hands of populist leaders or as the last truly honest, independent fighter for popular causes. Equally important, many saw PJ as *un verdadero macho* (a true macho man), an honor conferred on him for the ballsy, personal flair with which he denounced political corruption. At the same time, Jaime was widely considered an example of a "style" believed to be common among working-class sectors, one characterized by vulgar, violent language, and a disproportionate emphasis on sexual references.

PJ grew up in Los Angeles, where his family had moved in the early fifties as part of the first massive wave of Ecuadorian immigrants to the United States. Jaime, an observant Seventh Day Adventist, was proud of having been a Vietnam veteran and a participant in the California hippie movement, details in his colorful life history that differentiated him from most of his readers and provided him with a certain status in Ecuador. PJ presented himself to his Guayaquil readers as a cross between a hippie and a working-class intellectual, appearing in caricature in his own magazines wearing jeans, T-shirt, baseball cap, flip-flops, round glasses, and a ponytail. At the same time, PJ built a bridge between himself and his working-class readers by underscoring his personal experience with poverty and oppression.

While in Los Angeles, Jaime worked an endless series of odd jobs, such as dishwashing, selling newspapers, and cleaning restaurants and service stations. Nevertheless, he earned a technical degree at a community college. In the 1970s he got involved as the music editor of *L.A. Touch,* an adult magazine devoted to pornography and the hippie lifestyle. According to PJ, shortly after the beginning of his career as a journalist, his luck changed dramatically. He claimed to have found a large sum of money that he used to return to Guayaquil, where he lived for the remainder of his life.

Promoting rock music was Jaime's top mission on his return, and, in so doing, he acquired local celebrity. His knowledge of North American pop culture and his hippie experience became the symbolic capital that he exploited in the course of various enterprises. His first publications were devoted entirely to music and emerging bands. By the time Jaime started criticizing the music industry for its discriminatory practices toward local bands, he had already toured with his own group, Texaco Gulf, and opened the city's first rock discotheque and "head shop." PJ's notoriety spread further through his stint at a radio station, where he worked as a DJ under the professional name *La Mamá del Rock.*

Although the tone of Jaime's allegations against the music industry became increasingly virulent in the final issues of his early magazines, his jump to a more clearly political form of journalism was the direct result of a violent incident with local police. During November 1984 PJ was tortured and incarcerated. His torturers, government officers, made him eat both his hair and his paper, and then they broadcast a photograph of his bloody, disfigured face on national television. This episode occurred during León Febres Cordero's ultraconservative presidency, a time when Jaime had begun printing a tabloid, *Censura* (here translated as *Censured* rather than *Censorship* in reference to PJ's constant subjection to state terrorism). In the years that followed this episode Jaime was tortured on several occasions by local authorities, was kidnapped by government agents, and was even once illegally incarcerated for several months. When legal charges were pressed against him, he was accused of "spreading false rumors" or of "making attempts against national security."[3]

In defiance of his torturers' threats, to which he made frequent reference in his magazines, PJ spent the rest of his life speaking out. Throughout Febres Cordero's regime (1984–88) and the first year of the presidency of social-democrat Rodrigo Borja (1988–92), PJ published approximately thirteen issues of *Censura*, followed by twenty issues of *Comentarios de Pancho Jaime*.

Although the format of the publications gradually changed from that of a tabloid newspaper to a magazine, the main feature added over time was the use of crude caricatures instead of photographs. Advertising, always marginal, gradually disappeared altogether, although Jaime did occasionally publish propaganda from friends and from populist and leftist figures. The magazines were printed on cheap paper, colored ink reserved only for the cover. They consisted on average of forty pages, which included approximately thirty articles and an editorial page about current political developments. Generally speaking, each page had at least one illustration, most often a single cartoon. Sometimes articles were accompanied by reproductions of original documents, such as letters or certificates, offered as proof of the veracity of the contents. The small typesetting and crowded layouts created the impression of each page being packed with information. The saturation of space resulted in part from economic constraints, a limitation that Jaime frequently lamented in his writings. More important, the narrative structure itself created a space-consuming effect. For instance, entire pages were filled by only two or three paragraphs. Each paragraph was composed of several sentences, not necessarily about related topics but somehow intertwined to form a continuous, single account. Jaime possessed a fair level of orthographic expertise, but his grammar and punctuation departed from the standard.

Estimating the numbers of readers is difficult. First of all, it is hard to determine the actual print runs. No laws in Ecuador require even registered publications to disclose the number of copies sold, and PJ's magazines were never officially approved for open distribution. The estimates of the ex-collaborators I interviewed fluctuated between eight thousand and eighteen thousand copies, both impressive numbers in the case of Ecuador. Second, the circulation of the magazines increased as they were photocopied, borrowed, and/or transmitted via networks of gossip in public offices, educational centers, and neighborhoods all over the city.[4] Although Jaime targeted local bureaucrats and politicians, and mostly male working-class audiences, the widespread consumption of his magazines suggests that there was a far more diverse readership that included male and female, upper- and middle-class readers.

PJ's works were sold primarily in downtown Guayaquil, the financial and administrative center, as well as an important meeting place for all social classes. Members of a local association of disabled persons, who in the last few decades have dominated the selling of lottery tickets and newspapers, were eventually recruited to distribute the magazines at the height of their popularity, around 1987. Vendors advertised the publications on the sly by whispering to potential and/or well-known clients as they passed by in the streets.

Public Masculinity

Mirroring similar developments in the newspaper industry in the United States in the late nineteenth century (Soper 1999), political caricature in Guayaquil originally appeared as a key element of *periódicos satíricos,* a genre of critical publications that were generally articulated to the political agendas of *Liberales* in Ecuador and Latin America at large during the turn of the century. Indeed, the period of major proliferation of this type of literature in Ecuador coincides with the advent of the Liberal Revolution of 1895. In the Ecuadorian case early references to homosexuality in political caricature, although exceptional, were made specifically in relation to Peruvians, nicknamed "chickens," as part of a long tradition of ideological confrontation between the two countries around issues of territorial sovereignty (Hidalgo 2001). However, the most familiar style of caricature for Guayaquilean readers during the first half of the twentieth century was *costumbrista,* a dominant visual legacy that owes its origins to early photography and painting of racial and ethnic "native types" with no explicit references to sexuality (Biblioteca Municipal de Santiago de Guayaquil 2001; Muratorio 1994; Poole 1997). Even though there are some formal similarities with the cartoon tradition in newspapers during the following decades (for example, black-and-white ink drawings of renowned political figures as part of day-to-day commentaries), the style of sexualized humor that Pancho Jaime inaugurated during the 1980s was a completely different story.

Departing from the tradition of political publications in Ecuador (see Gómez Iturralde 1998, 3:467–73), PJ wrote exclusively in the first person, at times as if in conversation with political figures, at other times as though addressing personal written correspondence to them. In both cases he shifted abruptly from wider, national topics to details of the perceived sexual inclinations of those to whom he directed himself. PJ also inserted stereotypes about masculinity into his descriptions of characters to spice up his political commentary.[5] For example, in the following excerpt PJ criticized how President Borja handled a political appointment, among other issues:

> Dr. Rodrigo Borja, Mr. President, Dear Gentleman, low-life dick-face, wake up you fucker, you stick the people into deeper shit every time, there is not one thing that you do well, you kept the Secretary of Agriculture in office for too long, you tried to cover up the "rice affair" in different ways while the easiest way would have been to incarcerate a couple of assholes, and to make it even worse, you appoint a fool as the current Secretary of Agriculture, he is the cousin of a fugitive delinquent who stole many millions during the past government, this fucker, the first thing that he did as Secretary was to cover up the "rice affair."
>
> Dr. Rodrigo Borja I don't know how I can wake you up, because pussy is pussy, and, as the people say: a pair of panties can be replaced by another pair of panties, so change, look for another ass since the one you've got now is making you scared. How is it possible that you can say that that political alliance is patriotic, when all of the guys in that party are a bunch of faggots, and everyone in the Secretary of Housing distributes housing as they wish, while the people who made requests years ago continue waiting around like fools? (*Comentarios* 18, 4)[6]

This sense of personal indignation lay at the base of Jaime's textual constructions. Offensive remarks, to a large extent with sexual content, occupied different positions in the texts, from inscriptions in illustrations, to whole titles, to the main argument and/or conclusion of an article. Jaime used insults to confront elements of power head-on, whether they were individual authorities or entire institutions at either the local or national levels. Through the recurrent use of insults to highlight his own volatility as a Guayaquilean macho and the negative features of his political enemies, PJ personalized every debate while referencing a repertoire of stereotypes about sexuality. In the excerpt directed at President Borja PJ appealed to *estar calzoneado,* a local concept generally used to describe faithful love for one woman. Such love is conceptualized as the obsessive thinking about just one "panty," and is associated with smelling or dreaming about the same "pussy" all the time (*panty* and *pussy* are terms used in local slang to refer to a woman). It is implied that a man who maintains a monogamous relationship cannot think straight. The suggested cure for such cases is sentimental detachment and/or promiscuity, which is what Jaime referred to in advocating a change of panties. The cartoon accompanying this article portrayed PJ trying to wake up President Borja, who lay passively in bed, dreaming of the scent of a pair of panties. In showing the president in this way, Jaime was also playing on regional stereotypes. At issue is that manliness is a quality of coastal men. Coastal people see men from the highlands, like Dr. Borja, as less masculine and somewhat effeminate and therefore incapable of fulfilling the role of a multiple penetrant.[7]

Although the bold, antiestablishment stance in passages such as this one made Jaime infamous, it was hardly an idiosyncratic creation on his part. On the contrary, Jaime's comments built on established styles of political rhetoric, in particular a style based on obscenity and vulgarity. PJ's particularity was to reveal secrets, to print defamatory or sexualized insults, and to inscribe them on grotesque caricatures from the political body. Exploring political pornography in different social and historical contexts, scholars have noted the political ends to which vulgarity can be put (Cohen 1995; Hunt 1993). As pointed out by Mbembe (1992) and his critics (e.g., Coronil 1992), vulgarity can function as a discursive technology associated with either the State in its exercise of power and/or with subaltern sectors in their daily confrontations with the State. Trouillot (1992) notes that vulgarity is subject dependent and culturally defined. This point is relevant in thinking about both the highly local flavor of Jaime's magazines and the varied opinions that his readers had of his style. In some cases how readers interpreted Jaime's vulgarity depended on how closely they allied themselves with his political views. Jaime's detractors repeatedly claimed that he used obscenity as a mere marketing ploy to

288 ▪ ▪ ▪ X. Andrade

"Wake up, you cunt!" Pancho Jaime is addressing President Borja. Originally published in *Comentarios* 18, no. 2.

attract "ignorant" readers. Jaime's enthusiasts, on the other hand, conceded that obscene, scatological, and pornographic references could be a suitable strategy for denouncing corruption. They frequently expressed their admiration for Jaime in relation to their contempt for what they perceived as submissiveness on the part of the rest of the Ecuadorian press.

Although Jaime's irreverence was generally considered unique, the kind of sexist discourses that appeared in his magazines were familiar to many of his readers. These discourses surface repeatedly in public, everyday life and in politics in Guayaquil. Studies on Latin America (see Fonseca 2001; Gutmann 1996; Lancaster 1992) show how gossiping, games, and insults using sexual innuendo characterize everyday male interaction among working-class sectors, although they are exclusive neither to men nor to this social class or region. In Guayaquil my own ethnographic observations of a particular working-class barrio, as well as of a network of middle- and upper-class contacts, showed how homosociality in that city is constituted by a well-defined set of practices, including cross-naming (the deployment of nicknames with female connotations), the impromptu performance of humorous routines involving the inversion of heterosexual positions, and, finally, a grandiloquent manner in referring to body parts laden with sexual meanings. The importance of sexual references in local society was explained to me by a lawyer-cum-local intellectual as *machismo dialéctico* (dialectical machismo). He coined this term to refer to both vulgarity and the omnipresence of *macho* bravado in everyday life. By *dialectical* he meant the "fake" or constructed nature of male, public displays:

> Pancho insulted with grace, a very *criolla* [local] grace indeed, because in Paris that style does not make anyone laugh, and in Madrid it makes everybody cry. In Ecuador it makes us laugh because this [Guayaquil] is a violent city. When you drive around, here comes another driver who screams at you: "*Hijueputa*" (son of a bitch). It's a city where, when you bump into a friend of yours, he will welcome you with: "How is it going *chucha tu madre*" [mother's cunt], and then he will burst out laughing. It's a city where, when you go to Court they will tell you, "You are a *chucha*" (cunt) as a lawyer. They won't say, when you win a case, that you are intelligent or very intelligent. This is a false machismo, this is a dialectical machismo. (Reader 50)[8]

Leaving aside the author's opaque analysis and use of the term *dialectical,* this quote shows not only that forms of machismo are central to some men's public performance but also that Guayaquileans are very aware of their presence and power. In addition people perceive the ambiguity of the term *macho* (see Gutmann 1996, 223), even if only from a patriarchal perspective.

Pancho Jaime drew from the performative elements of this local culture to create the textual and visual narratives of his magazines. The images reenacted the ways in which certain dominant forms of maleness are publicly performed. Many were created by the illustrator as he sat and watched Jaime model the kinds of poses and gestures he wanted. Furthermore, some articles were transcripts of actual improvised speeches that PJ delivered to the secretary of *Comentarios,* who was in charge of typing and proofreading them. The end products of these sessions were not so much editorials or articles in the typical sense as they were Jaime's efforts to script his own performances. When interviewed, the secretary referred to these sessions almost as if they were the result of some sort of "spirit possession." According to her, Jaime appeared as if he were standing right down on the street corners where "dialectical machismo" takes place. Whoever these spirits were, it was clear that they "spoke" to PJ in street tongues.

To understand the significance of Jaime's work, one must also contextualize his magazines in relation to populism and politics at large. Since the 1930s Ecuadorian populism has tended to revolve around a Manichean style of discourse in which social struggle, the goodness of the poor, and the wickedness of the rich are defined within a moralistic narrative. The beginnings of this trajectory in Guayaquil can be traced back at least as far as the 1950s, when the first populist party was founded. The manipulation of basic oppositions, such as the oligarchy versus the people, rich versus poor, and the highlands versus the coast characterized the discourse used by early populist figures (see Guerrero Burgos 1994). These dualities, which contemporary leaders continue to mobilize, helped form the basis of Pancho Jaime's orientation.

Populismo, already a slippery sociological term, is hard to define in the Ecuadorian context, where the term has been confined to analyzing the traditional populist parties or historical leaders. In my perspective populist style characterizes a larger political field, including at least two distinctive fronts that hold electoral power in Guayaquil, the social-Christian and the populist. These fronts correspond to two opposing segments of the Guayaquilean bourgeoisie. The social-Christians are oriented around the traditional export oligarchy led by the above-mentioned former president, and Guayaquil's mayor for the last decade, Febres Cordero. The populist party corresponds to an emergent elite linked to commercial capital and contraband and is represented by the former president Abdalá Bucaram (1996–97), himself the main subject of studies on Ecuadorian populism in recent years based on his antioligarchic stance, ambiguous ideology, and *populachero* style. In spite of these two leaders' mutual animosities, ideological discrepancies, and different social origins, important commonalities emerge when examining the imagery surrounding them. They share a regionally based rhetoric, an authoritarian style of rule, and a *macho* public image, elements that serve to create a political style recognized by local people as particularly Guayaquilean and not necessarily confined to that city's working classes.

So conceived, one of the most problematic aspects of populism in Guayaquil is the extent to which leaders convert hegemonic notions of masculinity into either a powerful, albeit imaginary, weapon for popular redemption against the oligarchy and/or to affirm the power of the elites.

The most visible aspects of this political style in recent history emerged during several electoral campaigns shortly after the return to democracy in 1979. An illustration of this trend is, without doubt, the election and brief administration of President Abdalá Bucaram (1996–97), a notorious Guayaquilean "macho" icon. During his campaigns in the 1980s and 1990s, Bucaram proclaimed his sympathy for Hitler as a means of highlighting his own tough-as-nails personality. He accused his opponents of having "watery sperm" and emphasized the "size of [his] own balls." During his brief tenure as president Bucaram also danced in the palace with his honorary guest, Lorena Bobbitt, an Ecuadorian who attained brief notoriety in the United States when she cut off her *gringo*, rapist husband's penis. Although some feminist activists and academics in the United States embraced Bobbitt's act as an example of radicalism (see Deem 1996), in Guayaquil Bucaram managed to frame his boogie with Bobbitt as both the act of a gentleman and a nationalist statement.

Today references to maleness continue to play an important role in regional political rivalries. For example, since the very beginning of the Ecuadorian republic there has been a venomous regional conflict between coastal Guayaquil and the inland capital city of Quito (see Quintero 1991). Among other ways, this conflict takes the form of opposing sexual meanings that are attached alternately to the coast and to the highlands. An example emerged with force at the time of my fieldwork as a deep financial crisis began in Ecuador at the outset of 1999. The situation eventually triggered massive mobilizations in Guayaquil against what was perceived as the overly centralized government in Quito, embodied by the figure of the Quito-based president, Jamil Mahuad (1998–2000). Although Mahuad tried to manage the crisis with erudite calm, some sectors of the Guayaquilean elite-controlled press accused him of "lacking the balls" to deal with it. The press contrasted Mahuad with the "fearsome" Febres Cordero, at the time mayor of Guayaquil, who is always portrayed as the ultimate patriarch of the traditional, local oligarchy. Mahuad, a Harvard-educated technocrat, did not respond with the open, verbal aggression for which Febres Cordero is well known. Instead, Mahuad took advantage of the recent release of the Hollywood blockbuster *Titanic* to describe a sinking country in need of a rational, modern "captain" to overcome the crisis. Calling to mind Bederman's (1995) discussion about the effeminate character associated with the new, "civilized" man at the turn of the century in the United States, informants immediately reinterpreted this metaphor as a desperate recourse to a "prosthetic maleness."

Audiences

I used Pancho Jaime's magazines as cultural materials to stimulate people from different social classes to reflect on issues of local identity, inequality, and power. At one level informants identified these materials as typical of a Guayaquilean "culture," thereby acknowledging the existence of meanings shared by a whole community. Some readers regarded the magazines in more specific terms, namely as characteristic of the "popular" or "populist" culture associated with the Guayaquilean working class. When it came to evaluating the contents of Jaime's works, however, and his textual and visual language, there was a broad spectrum of opinion. Describing the magazines as "trash" or as "documents," people's reactions ranged from fear, disgust, and condemnation to laughter, praise, and admiration. The process of reading these materials was also diverse, from secretive, embarrassed, individual readings to collective, out-loud gatherings. There were also those who never actually read the originals but were systematically updated about their contents via networks of gossip.

The different forms of circulation and consumption of these materials bear witness to the ways the connection between masculinity and politics is constructed throughout society. Jaime's works are a privileged source for understanding this process. For reasons of space, I will present here only a few examples of readerships and reactions. This sample, although limited, provides a window on what informants themselves perceive as the distinctly "cultural" dimensions of a broader political field. In many ways PJ tailored his political rhetoric to meet the expectations of his target audiences. The fact that he so consistently relied on Guayaquilean idioms and slang indicates that he oriented his magazines toward a working-class local or coastal audience and only secondarily considered readers at a national level. A merely textual analysis of the sexist content of PJ's work might lead one to conclude that he was not concerned with attracting female readers. Fieldwork, however, revealed that Jaime's audience was actually composed of a large number of women, in addition to men, from all social classes. Jaime's reliance on exaggerated ideas about masculinity and offensive remarks toward women were not obstacles to consolidating female readership. On the contrary, the creation of a "grotesque effect" (Russo 1995), through reference to bodily images and fluids, appealed to both women and men.

With respect to the deprived sectors of Guayaquilean society, Jaime's political denouncements made him for many the ultimate working-class hero. He was viewed as a loyal representative of their politics and style and as a receptacle of popular feelings directed toward the establishment:

> Panchito was in touch with the essence of *el pueblo's* sentiments. He had good feelings for the poor people, his beloved people. He witnessed the injustice of the *aniñado* (girlish) politicians, the *niños bien* (well-off girls and boys) as we call them because of their endless *sinvergüencería* (shamelessness). And he devoted himself in soul and life to discredit them, (to show them as) they really were, having fun with the people's money that they swore to respect. . . . Pancho Jaime was a correct man because he printed the magazine out of his own sacrifice and his tenacious desire for the people to find out the *sinvergüencería* of certain men who are in politics not precisely for just causes. (Reader 27)

The centrality of values such as *vergüenza* to the construction of masculinity in certain social contexts is well documented (see Díaz Barriga 2001). Attacking a political elite that was seen both as effeminate and shameless fostered a sense of commonality with popular sectors. In the words of a street seller of *Comentarios*:

> I sold (PJ's) product because I was sympathetic towards his personality and work. I didn't sell it to make money. For me, his work was monumental, a huge work, a fantastic work to guide and to enlighten the Guayaquilean people, to direct and to manifest their expressions. I really liked reading it because he didn't restrain himself. He had a lexicon that was understandable, that corresponded to our people's culture. . . . He had both an *aggressive* and a *passive* lexicon. It was *aggressive* because of its direct, spontaneous expression, direct and graphic. *Passive* because it was also relaxing reading, meant to educate and teach. (Informant 47; my emphasis)

The informant asserted that the twofold character of Jaime's work ex-plained also the attraction the materials held for "more educated people," the middle- and upper-class audiences. In what follows I explore some responses from female readers that both complicate sexual politics and illustrate the varying uses to which the magazines were put. Often *Comentarios* served purely recreational ends. Many women (and men) from the elites skimmed through the magazine in search of gossip that ridiculed hated members of opposing segments of their exclusive circles. Jaime was positioned by opposing elite factions as a repository of exclusive informa-tion that well-situated citizens could wield in hurting one another. One informant from this milieu, a woman from a prominent law firm, recalled parties at which women enthusiastically chatted about the most recent issue of *Comentarios*. She also told me that immediately after Jaime's assassination powerful men jokingly fought among themselves to take credit for his death.

Middle-class female readership is particularly interesting because women from this strata underscored the political and/or humorous con-tent of the magazines, while downplaying Jaime's sexist agenda. For exam-ple, a feminist activist used PJ-inspired aesthetics while fostering her own agenda through community workshops for women. The local branch of her social-democratic political movement printed pamphlets depicting politi-cal enemies in ways similar to Jaime's cartoons. When asked what was the appeal in PJ's writings, a professional architect put things into perspective:

> The ways in which he described people (in positions of power) and the things they did. For example, that they had a party at someone's house, and that everybody got drunk and then they got naked. He added who had fucked whom during these orgies. And the drawings were also that way. The funny way in which he described those orgies, it was as if he were directing a satire. For us [the reader and her female college friends] it was a satire about what can go on right in the middle of an orgy. State problems were solved, politics negotiated and deals accom-plished. That is what caught our attention. On the one hand, he created doubt in us, he made us question the formality [of politics]. On the other hand, [politics] were shown to be like domestic stuff that is solved among friends, between acquaintances. (Reader 19)

"Angry because I called them thieves." This image depicts members of the local city council. Originally published in *Comentarios* 10, no. 24.

Another interesting example came to my attention one day after I had finished an interview at the office of a woman who held Jaime's work in high regard. She was not bothered by the images, nor did she think they were sexist: "I have no problem with dirty, loud talking or with seeing all those *vergotas* [big penises]. They made me laugh and made me learn something about real political life" (Reader 5). Once I had finished recording this session, the informant invited her colleagues into the office one by one. Before I knew it, I was leading an improvised focus group with six well-educated, middle-class professional women in their late thirties or forties. At first a few seemed shy, if not reluctant, to talk about PJ in this setting during office hours. Nevertheless, over the course of a couple of hours the session gathered an increasingly joyful tone. What did these women immediately recall about the magazines? They remembered specific images, such as the one with the caption *Nueva Pieza,* in which Elsa Bucaram, a former mayor of Guayaquil and the sister of the former Ecuadorian president, carried an enormous penis. She was depicted as if exhilarated, because she had supposedly just acquired "a new piece," meaning a new piece of meat, a new male lover with a much larger penis than her former partner's. The readers also recalled the cartoon of a presumed homosexual congressman and president of one of the most important soccer clubs sticking a recently inaugurated stadium into his ass. Did obscene images and foul language shock these readers? Although some were clearly uncomfortable with the visual vocabulary, they admitted that they could not help reading the magazines to catch up on the latest de-

NUEVA PIEZA

"New piece." The image depicts Elsa Bucaram, a former mayor of Guayaquil. Originally published in *Comentarios* 19, no. 8.

nouncements and the intimate lives of politicians. Most important, the women disagreed about the tone of the publications, but they concurred about the need to speak out and to denounce the corruption of bureaucrats, the press, and the ruling elites.

The festive, impromptu workshop reached its peak when a new reincarnation of Pancho Jaime was called on. She turned out to be a workmate referred to by her colleagues as "our own Pancho Jaime." Although she did not draw caricatures, she assembled collages from newspaper photos, inking in conversations in the dialogue bubbles common to comic strips and *Comentarios*. Her colleagues encouraged her to show me a series of collages she had made of their former boss, also a woman, but from *las encopetadas,* as the female upper-class elite is known. Members of this class were always appointed as heads of this office because of their political connections. These materials had been distributed among the employees on different occasions, but the author decided to show me one series released at Christmastime. The texts attached to each of the images suggested that the boss was a closet lesbian who longed for a tryst with any of her female colleagues to whom the collage was addressed. In the cartoon the boss comments on the sexy color of the potential lover's lipstick, the size of her breasts, the height of her skirt, and so forth. Although the participants in the joke were not certain about their boss's sexual orientation, the fact that she was widely rumored to be a lesbian became the means for attacking her lack of knowledge and skill in directing the institution.

Jaime's project did not limit the appeal of his magazines to an audience oriented toward a narrow conception of populism. The volatile tone of his magazines, in addition to his use of insults as a rhetorical strategy, must be identified as an aggressive discursive style that has historically captivated broader local audiences. In Jaime's work we see how different discursive fields, including local politics and the media, contributed to the construction of a larger public culture. The uniqueness of Jaime's work lies in the singular creativity with which he forged a grotesque visual and textual language for documenting its local foundations.

Public Secrecy

Part of Jaime's popularity stemmed from the viciously humorous way he linked political enemies' private sexual practices, whether real or imagined, with their competence in public office or institutions. He bestowed politicians with some of the stereotypical attributes associated with subordinated masculinities, such as different forms of sexual "perversion," including homosexuality, bisexuality, effeminacy, and transvestism. As in the case of the "secret literature" studied by Cohen in India (1995), many images depicted sex between men. This "circulation of homosocial penetration" (414), to use Cohen's words, was embellished with images of public figures as *cachudos* (cuckolds). They were described as compulsive masturbators and sexually impotent. Their genitals were depicted as tiny and flaccid in contrast with their lovers' gigantic, hairy penises. Their anuses were shown open, facing the reader, ready to be penetrated or expulse excrement. Their corruption was marked by their bodies' feminine curvatures. Finally, the gender of their given names or nicknames was changed to the feminine to indicate the essence of the identity hidden away inside their bodies, out of the eye of public scrutiny but very much known in their own social circles.

To these features PJ attached yet another set of negative values to erase what was left of his targets' public faces. They were exposed as incompetent as bureaucrats, corrupt as authorities, clumsy as politicians, immature and hypocritical as persons, and mentally retarded by nature. Jaime then equated these elements with the inability to manage positions of power. As for female enemies, Jaime usually presented them as either the objects of compulsory heterosexuality or as whores. Occasionally, Jaime mentioned lesbianism. As such, his attitudes reflected the wider social concern with specifically male homosexuality as opposed to other practices that are still quite invisible in Ecuador.

The *machista* lexicon that contributed to PJ's enormous popularity can be interpreted in relation to the audiences' everyday practices of imagining political power. As noted above, the ways in which the magazines traveled around Guayaquil, the uses to which they were put in different circles, the broadcasting of a *machista* masculinity by the elites and assorted public figures, and the existence of audiences across lines of class, gender, and even political affiliation point to the fact that masculinity occupies a prominent place in the public images of Guayaquilean society at large. In accomplishing his aims, however, he reproduced an authoritarian language, reinforced dominant notions of sexuality with their accompanying gender-based forms of discrimination, and fostered a political style historically capitalized on by elites (see de la Torre 2000).

The familiarity of Jaime's vocabulary is based on the secrecy underneath heterosexual hegemony. PJ exposed the inherent ambiguities of heterosexuality. His readers recognized that he was moving along a very thin line, "balanceándose peligrosamente entre la verdad inmencionable y la calumnia irrepetible" (Reader 22). Jaime's "dangerous balancing act" built on a destructive narrative structured by the revelation of "unmentionable truths and the repetition of unrepeatable calumnies." Frequently I came across characterizations of PJ's writings as the work of a "negative," destructive force recklessly bent on pursuing a sometimes heroic yet suicidal and, by definition, impossible task (that is, the desecration of the public personae of revered figures of authority).

PJ's task exemplifies what Taussig (1999) refers to as "defacement," meaning the revelation of "public secrets" or knowledge that is widely known "but cannot be articulated" (5). Although *defacement* is a term that has no literal translation in Spanish, I repeatedly came across similar concepts when reviewing ethnographic data. Informants used terms such as *unmasking, disfigurement, mutilation, despoilment, vandalism, destruction,* and *damage* to describe either the effects of PJ's writings or his depictions of those in power. These forms of creative negativity express the essence of Pancho Jaime and are central to Guayaquileans' memories about him.

Defacement, however, should not be confused with exposing any kind of "truth" that may exist behind secrets. It is rather the very act of publicly stating that such secrets exist that works to make evident the inner core of power, thereby destabilizing it. Jaime's work involved the production, circulation, and consumption of nonknowledge, that is information generally held as unspeakable "truths." In his work he attacked the silence required to keep the political/gender system in place. In Guayaquil one view that is widely held, yet rarely articulated, is that homosexuality is pervasive among the elites. What I regarded as a homophobic stereotype was a "fact" for many of my informants. Nevertheless, it is not important to establish any kind of correspondence between this belief and "truth." In spite of Jaime's claims for the veracity of his journalistic enterprise, his art of exaggeration and transgression demanded adding to the facts, embellishing them with poignant elements drawn from the *machista* lexicon to accomplish his communicative goals. The "over-the-top" character of his material was on par with his audience's *morbo* (morbidity) for the gossip, vulgarity, and obscene language that could "do justice" to the imagery of power.

PJ's information regarding the wild festivities about which he wrote came from both documented denouncements and from rumors and gossip. Jaime took clever advantage of his unique position as the main repository of harmful information launched between opposing factions of the Guayaquilean elite. Using his self-conferred poetic license to embellish on this information freely, he orchestrated a circus by placing into the spotlight of his magazines the freakish bodies of those in power. The repeating images of oligarchs, well-known journalists, and priests dressed as women and/or engaged in orgies made readers of Jaime's magazines feel like morbid spectators of an endless parade of debauchery. Male politicians in Ecuador, struggling to keep up "big man" profiles, encountered crude images of themselves in print for everyone to see. The drawings were all the more scandalous given that PJ emphasized not only the "twisted" nature of politicians' sexuality but also their taste for the scatological. In doing so, he construed national and local politics as a spectacle performed by "perverted" political subjects:

There are not only 3 social classes, the oligarchy, the middle class and the low life people, which we are, but also the supposedly privileged class, the oligarchy, the children of perfumed armpits, is itself subdivided into three classes composed of the families of Plaza Luque, Valdez, Amador Icaza, Vernaza, Baquerizo Gómez, Febres Cordero, Noboa, and other sons-of-bitches, who are the members of the National Lottery and who believe they are the owners of Guayaquil and steal pieces of land using false documents. These assholes think they are hot shit, and to avoid mixing with the rest of the oligarchs they created the CLUB DE LA UNION, to conduct healthy gatherings, educational ones, not the flaming fagottry that they do on a daily basis, especially in the sauna, where it is likely that all of them walk around naked butt-fucking each other, with the participation of faggots, queens, whores, nymphomaniacs, transvestites and other kinds of faggots, they make the "FAMOUS NAPOLITAN BAGEL" ("la famosa rosca napolitana") which is nothing more than each one butt-fucking the other to form a train, and to give themselves more flair they call themselves "THE KNIGHTS OF THE ROUND TABLE." (*Comentarios* 7, 6; PJ's emphasis)

In placing himself outside of the world he depicted, PJ made a profound comment. His portrayal of himself as a comic or antihero asserted his working-class status as a regular citizen who had to confront severe limits placed on his power to comment on politics. PJ reminded his readers of this constantly when he directed the illustrator to depict his abuse at the hands of authorities or as if speaking from inside a coffin. These prophetic images rang true one day when he was gunned down in his own neighborhood. The ribald circus that Jaime officiated throughout the 1980s came to an end in the fearful silence that surrounded his death. The continued and irrepressible flow of gossip and rumors about the "corrupt" sexuality of power, however, are proof of the ongoing importance of the kind of secrecy that Jaime so creatively publicized.

Notes

I would like to acknowledge Matthew Gutmann, Deborah Poole, Carlos de la Torre, and Carlos Calderón Chico for helping me to rethink preliminary findings. Shanti Pillai, Gabriela Pólit, and Javier Auyero provided insightful readings. Shanti also edited this article. Funding for fieldwork was generously provided by a predoctoral grant from the Wenner-Gren Foundation for Anthropological Research.

1. This essay forms part of my doctoral dissertation, in which I explore these various fields of cultural production in detail. Here they are mentioned to highlight Jaime's reliance on these traditions and to provide a more accurate context for my own interpretation.

2. Biographical information provided in this section is based on Jaime's own writings.

3. On at least one occasion official rationales for Jaime's arrest and torture alleged that he was a drug trafficker, an easy excuse given Jaime's hippie fame and highly visible role as a rock producer. Censorship and harassment against mainstream journalists were a matter of public concern, as in the case of writers affiliated with the *Hoy*, a newspaper published in Quito that voiced opposition to Cordero's regime. Jaime's arrests, however, received only marginal attention from the national press. For an extensive account of PJ's systematic repression see his only book, *Otra obra de León: Pancho Jaime tiene razón pero va preso* (Jaime 1986).

4. The magazines were also sold in the capital, Quito, and a few other cities. In addition, they circulated among Ecuadorian immigrants in cities such as New York, Los Angeles, and Toronto.

5. *Comentarios* was, to a large extent, a one-man enterprise. Only at first, however, did PJ author every single article. As time went on, he began to include submissions from a pool of occasional writers, including other journalists, leftist activists, and people close to the populist party known as the Partido Roldosista Ecuatoriano (PRE).

6. Translations of PJ's writings are mine. The punctuation is an attempt to mirror that used in the originals.

7. This stereotype is based on racial prejudices that are the product of the ideology of *mestizaje. Serranos* (highlanders) are seen as physiognomically closer to aboriginal Andean people, who, in turn, are seen as less masculine (see Larrea 1999).

8. Because of the continuing controversy over these materials informants must remain unnamed. Here I distinguish between "informants" and "readers." Informants are people who were willing to talk to me about PJ's place within the Guayaquilean popular imagination. Readers are actual members of networks of readership.

References

Bederman, Gail. 1995. *Manliness and Civilization: A Cultural History of Gender and Race in the United States, 1880–1917*. Chicago: University of Chicago Press.
Biblioteca Municipal de Santiago de Guayaquil. 2001. *Estampas de Guayaquil*. Guayaquil: Biblioteca Municipal.

Cohen, Lawrence. 1995. "Holy in Banaras and the Mahaland of Modernity." *Gay and Lesbian Quarterly* 2:399–424.

Comentarios de Pancho Jaime. Issues 1 to 20. Guayaquil: Pancho Jaime y Asociados.

Coronil, Fernando. 1992. "Can Postcoloniality Be Decolonized? Imperial Banality and Postcolonial Power." *Public Culture* 5, no. 1:89–108.

de la Torre, Carlos. 2000. *Populist Seduction in Latin America: The Ecuadorian Experience.* Athens: Ohio University Press.

Deem, Melissa D. 1996. "From Bobbit to SCUM: Re-memberment, Scatological Rhetorics, and Feminist Strategies in the Contemporary United States." *Public Culture* 8, no. 3:511–37.

Díaz Barriga, Miguel. 2001. "*Vergüenza* and Changing Chicano and Chicana Narratives." *Men and Masculinities* 3, no. 3:278–98.

Fonseca, Claudia. 2001. "Philanderers, Cuckolds, and Wily Women: A Reexamination of Gender Relations in a Brazilian Working-Class Neighborhood." *Men and Masculinities* 3, no. 3:261–77.

Gómez Iturralde, José Antonio. 1998. *Los periódicos Guayaquileños en la historia, 1821–1997.* 3 vols. Guayaquil: Archivo Histórico del Banco Central del Ecuador.

Guerrero Burgos, Rafael. 1994. *Regionalismo y democracia social en los orígenes del "C.F.P."* Quito: CAAP.

Gutmann, Matthew C. 1996. *The Meanings of Macho: Being a Man in Mexico City.* Berkeley: University of California Press.

Hidalgo, Angel Emilio. 2001. "La Caricatura en Guayaquil: Arte y Sarcasmo (1883–1900). Guayaquil: Museo Antropológico y de Arte Contemporáneo." Unpublished manuscript.

Hunt, Lynn. 1993. "Pornography and the French Revolution." In *The Invention of Pornography: Obscenity and the Origins of Modernity, 1500–1800,* ed. Lynn Hunt, 301–39. New York: Zone Books.

Jaime, Pancho. 1986. *Otra obra de León: Pancho Jaime tiene razón pero va preso, gobernación del Guayas.* Guayaquil: Publicitaria Pancho Jaime.

Larrea, Fernando. 1999. "'Cómo un indio va a mandarnos!' Frontera étnica y masculinidades." *Iconos* 8:87–102.

Lancaster, Roger N. 1992. *Life Is Hard: Machismo, Danger, and the Intimacy of Power in Nicaragua.* Berkeley: University of California Press.

Mbembe, Achille. 1992. "The Banality of Power and the Aesthetics of Vulgarity in the Postcolony." *Public Culture* 4, no. 2:1–30.

Muratorio, Blanca. 1994. "Nación, Identidad y Etnicidad: Imágenes de los Indios Ecuatorianos y sus Imagineros a Fines del Siglo XIX." In *Imágenes e Imagineros: Representaciones de los indígenas ecuatorianos, siglos XIX y XX,* ed. Blanca Muratorio, 109–96. Quito: FLACSO.

Poole, Deborah. 1997. *Vision, Race, and Modernity. A Visual Economy of the Andean Image World*. Princeton, N.J.: Princeton University Press.

Quintero, Rafael, ed. 1991. *La cuestión regional y el poder*. Quito: Corporación Editora Nacional.

Russo, Mary J. 1995. *The Female Grotesque: Risk, Excess, and Modernity*. New York: Routledge.

Soper, Kerry. 1999. "Seriously Funny: A History of Satirical Newspaper Comic Strips in Twentieth Century United States." Ph.D. diss., Emory University.

Taussig, Michael. 1999. *Defacement: Public Secrecy and the Labor of the Negative*. Stanford, Calif.: Stanford University Press.

Trouillot, Michel-Rolph. 1992. "The Vulgarity of Power." *Public Culture* 5, no. 1:75–81.

Sexuality

and Paternity

■ ■ ■

RICHARD PARKER

Changing Sexualities:

Masculinity and Male

Homosexuality in Brazil

■ ■ ■

Over the course of the past decade significant new attention has been given to the study of masculinity throughout Latin America. The reasons for this are multiple, of course, including the growing impact of feminism (with its problematization of gender systems more generally), the gradual emergence of gay and lesbian movements throughout the region, the impact of HIV and AIDS, questions related to women's and men's reproductive health, and so on. The end result, however, has been an increase in attention to the social construction of masculinity in Latin American societies not as a single unified experience but as a complex field of meanings and exchanges built up in diverse ways throughout the region: the study of Latin American masculinities and male sexual identities, very much in the plural, rather than as a single gender category (see, e.g., Parker and Cáceres 1999; Valdés and Olavarría 1998; Viveros 2001). Equally important, within this broader conception of the importance of diversity in relation to both gender and sexuality, a rapidly growing literature has begun to focus on issues of social change—to explore the complex transformations that appear to be taking place in the construction of masculinities and male sexualities throughout the region (see, e.g., Gutmann 1996, 2001; Lancaster 1988, 1992, 1995; Parker 1991, 1999; Parker and Cáceres 1999).

This chapter seeks to contribute to this broader collective effort by drawing on work that colleagues and I have been carrying out in Brazil over the course of nearly two decades now (see, e.g., Parker 1985, 1989, 1991, 1994, 1999; Parker and Terto Jr. 1998). It focuses, in particular, on the changing shape of male homosexualities during the 1980s and the 1990s, with particular attention to the ways in which a changing political economy of sexuality and the profound impact of HIV and AIDS have contributed to a range of transformations in the social construction of (homo)sexual identities, cultures, and communities. It suggests that such transformations are present not only in the visible expressions of emerging gay communities but even in the most intimate expressions of sexual practice, which has been restructured and reinvented perhaps above all in response to the perceived threats posed by the HIV/AIDS epidemic in heavily affected communities (see Parker and Terto Jr. 1998).

With these goals in mind the text is divided into three major sections. The first of these focuses on the changing social organization of male homosexuality in Brazil and in particular on the emergence of urban gay communities and cultures in the late twentieth century (as an important part of broader reorganization of the political economy of gender and sexuality in Brazilian life). The second section reviews briefly some of the ways in which both gay rights groups and AIDS-service organizations have sought to develop HIV/AIDS prevention activities within the context of these changing communities and cultures and the ways in which such activities have contributed to the increasing visibility of homosexuality itself, as well as to the construction of a growing range of institutions and community support structures. Finally, drawing on research carried out in Rio de Janeiro from the late 1980s through the mid-1990s, the third section explores the ways in which such activities have fed into a range of changes in the subjective experience of sexual identity and erotic practice among sexually active homosexual and bisexual men. Taken together, these discussions aim to contribute to a growing understanding of the processes of social and sexual change taking place not only in Brazil but throughout the Latin American region.

The Changing Social Organization of Male Homosexualities

As I have argued at length elsewhere (Parker 1991, 1999), in seeking to develop some understanding of the experience of male homosexuality in Brazil, it is fundamental to realize that the very notion of homosexuality, as a distinct sexual category, is actually a relatively recent development—in Brazil, as well as in other parts of Latin America. Although a whole set of new (and rapidly changing) ideas related to homosexual behavior, as well as to gay identity, have begun to emerge in Brazilian culture in recent years, these ideas have in large part been the product of a complex and ongoing cultural dialectic in which the traditions of Brazilian society have necessarily had to confront and interact with a wider set of cultural symbols and sexual meanings in an increasingly globalized world system. Making sense of the increasingly diverse and complex range of meanings that organize same-sex relations in contemporary Brazilian life thus requires at least some understanding of the very different economy of sexuality in traditional culture—an economy organized less around the symbolic value of sexual desires or sexual identities than of sexual roles (see Daniel and Parker 1991, 1993; Parker 1989, 1991, 1994, 1999).

As I have tried to point out, this "traditional" system of sexual meanings is hardly a free-floating cultural domain. On the contrary, it is anchored in a wider set of meanings and practices that throughout the Latin world have come to be known rather generically as "machismo" (see, e.g., Brandes 1980; Gutmann 1996, 1998; Lancaster 1992, 1995; Parker 1991). And in Brazil—as in many parts of the circum-Caribbean region, I suspect—it can be further rooted in the complex social and cultural system that gradually built up around a highly concrete mode of production—the rural plantation economy (dependent, initially, on the use of slave labor but later adapted to capitalist wage labor after the abolition of slavery) that dominated Brazilian life for nearly four centuries and that has only very recently given way (even if only partially) to the rapid urbanization and industrialization that have characterized the past fifty years (see Freyre 1956, 1963; Parker 1991, 1999). In spite of the important changes that have recently taken place in the organization of Brazilian society, particularly in the most developed urban areas, the heritage of this traditional system continues to exert profound influence over the flow of daily life,

constituting a kind of cultural grammar that continues to organize important aspects of experience even in settings that would otherwise seem far
removed from the past (see Parker 1991).

Within this traditional cultural system understandings about the nature
of sexual interactions can hardly be separated from the social construction
of gender; indeed, the body itself, particularly in its sexual performances,
becomes the raw material for the construction and reconstruction of gender, just as the relations of power that traditionally circumscribe and organize the universe of gender become the basic structures organizing the
sexual field. Within this model of sexual life cultural emphasis seems to be
placed not merely on sexual practices in and of themselves but on the relationship between sexual practices and gender roles—in particular, on a distinction between perceived masculine *atividade* (activity) and feminine
passividade (passivity) as central to the organization of sexual reality. It is in
terms of this symbolic distinction between *atividade* and *passividade* that
notions of *macho* (male) and *fêmea* (female), of *masculinidade* (masculinity)
and *feminilidade* (femininity), have traditionally been organized in Brazil.
In everyday life, of course, these notions are constructed rather informally
in the discourses of popular culture. They are less a product of self-
conscious reflection than of the implicit values encoded in the gendered
language that is commonly used to speak about the body and its practices,
about the combination of gendered bodies, and about the classificatory
categories that flow from such combinations: a distinction between sexual
atividade and *passividade* that is translated into relations of power and
domination between *machos* and *fêmeas*, between *homens* (men) and *mulheres* (women).

What is particularly important to understand, however, is not simply
the structure of this hierarchy but the fact that, within the traditional
context of popular culture, it has been used to organize and to conceptualize sexual relations both between members of the opposite sex and between members of the same sex. The symbolic structure of male/female
interactions seems to function in many ways as a kind of model for the
organization of same-sex interactions in Brazilian culture. Within the
terms of this model, what is centrally important is perhaps less the shared
biological sex of the participants than the social/sexual roles that they play
out—their *atividade* or *passividade* as sexual partners and social persons.

The *homem* who enters into a sexual relationship with another male, then, does not necessarily sacrifice his culturally constituted *masculinidade*—at least so long as he performs the culturally perceived active, masculine role during sexual intercourse and conducts himself as a male within society. The male who adopts a passive, female posture, however, whether in sexual intercourse or social interaction, almost inevitably undercuts his own *masculinidade*. By upsetting the culturally prescribed fit between biological sex and social gender, he sacrifices his appropriate categorization as *homem* and comes to be known as a *viado* (originally from the term, *veado*, which literally means "deer," but more commonly spelled with the accentuated "i" replacing the "e") or a *bicha* (literally, worm or intestinal parasite, but also, instructively, the feminine form of *bicho* or animal, and thus a female animal) thanks to his inappropriate femininity. On the basis of his/her perceived passivity and internalized femininity, then, the *bicha* or *viado* is seen as a kind of walking failure on both social and biological counts—as a being who is unable to realize his natural potential because of inappropriate social behavior yet equally unable to cross the culturally constituted boundaries of gender because of the unavoidable constraints of anatomy. Not surprisingly, he is thus subject to the most severe symbolic, and often physical, violence found anywhere in Brazilian society and is a constant object of ridicule and shame, a circumstance that serves to stigmatize and marginalize deviant gender performances and at the same time reinforce normative patterns of masculinity and femininity (for more extended discussions of this system see Parker 1991, 1999).

What is perhaps most difficult to understand in this cultural construction, however, is the degree to which the role of the *viado* or *bicha* is simultaneously stigmatized *and* institutionalized in traditional popular culture. On the one hand, the *bicha* is subjected to constant ridicule and discrimination. And all too frequently such stigma breaks out in outright violence, socially sanctioned and approved. Yet, at the same time, in spite of the very real and powerful stigma, discrimination, and even violence associated with the *bicha* and the *viado*, there is also a socially constructed space for the *bicha* in popular culture, often in quite unexpected places. Any number of studies have pointed to the importance of effeminate *bichas* in the structure of Afro-Brazilian religious cults, for example (see, e.g., Birman 1985; Fry 1982, 1985; Landes 1946; Wafer 1991). Much like female prostitutes, *bichas* or *baitolas* can be found in virtually any small town or city in the interior of the country or on the frontier and are often highly valued, much like the female prostitute, for (sexual) services rendered to the local male population. And in the working-class communities and *favelas* or shantytowns in all major cities similar figures can be found, specializing in a range of otherwise feminine professions (such as hair stylists or makeup artists), and surprisingly integrated in community life. Precisely because the *bicha* violates the traditional expectations of *masculinidade* in popular culture, then, s/he is at one and the same time rejected yet necessary—subjected to violent discrimination, and often to outright physical violence, particularly in the impersonal world of the street, yet also accepted as a friend and neighbor, integrated into a network of personal relationships, in the traditional culture and highly personalized social relations of what in Brazil, as in other parts of Latin America, are described as the *classes populares* (the popular classes, that is, the poor, in what is still an overwhelmingly poor country).

Ultimately, then, this traditional system of meanings and practices, in Brazil as in other parts of the Latin/o world, takes shape as a quite specific economy of the body, organizing the sex/gender system in particular ways and opening up a determined range of possibilities for the experience of sexual life. It defines what a *homem* is and what he is not, what he can do and what he cannot, what he should desire and what he should not. It determines how both opposite-sex and same-sex relations can be organized and the range of practices and identities that can be produced around such relations within the flow of daily life and the structures of popular culture. Bringing meaning and power together in highly specific ways, it provides what is still today (even in social settings that are far removed from the context in which this system originally emerged) perhaps the most deeply rooted, and deeply felt, framework for the organization of sexual relations between men.

Emerging Cultures and Spaces of Desire

In Brazil, as in the Anglo-European world, however, this traditional emphasis on popular notions such as *atividade* and *passividade* in the conception of same-sex relations should not be read to suggest that nothing in the way of a gay world existed prior to the 1980s or 1990s. On the contrary, a complex (and only partially secretive) sexual subculture organized around male same-sex desires and practices has clearly been present in urban Brazil since at least the early twentieth century and has continued to become more diverse and complex, particularly in rapidly modernizing cities such as Rio de Janeiro and São Paulo, over the course of the past fifty years (see Green 1999; Trevisan 2000). In recent decades this urban subculture has rapidly become increasingly visible and multidimensional, at least in part breaking down into any number of diverse (although overlapping) subcultures, each with its own particularities and specificities—multiple social worlds that might best be thought of as diverse cultures of desire, organized around varying forms of same-sex practice, and, simultaneously, as cultures of resistance that provide at least partial protection from the violence, stigma, and oppression encountered in the outside world.

Although this emerging gay world crosses constantly with both the traditional world of active/passive gendered relations, it is nonetheless also distinct from it. Again, it is rooted in a specific social and economic system, linked to the processes of urbanization and industrialization that have transformed Brazil into a predominantly urban society in a period of fewer than fifty years, and that have created the relatively new (at least in Brazil) social space of a rapidly expanding industrial working class, together with the relative anonymity and impersonality of urban existence. Its history thus contrasts sharply with that of the active/passive gender hierarchy inherited from the plantation past. Yet in daily life it intersects constantly with this more traditional system—just as the constant flow of rural migrants entering the city merges with the industrial proletariat in the living conditions of the *favelas* and the *subúrbios* (poor, suburban areas on the outskirts of all major Brazilian cities) or in the vicissitudes of the informal labor market (see Parker 1998, 1999).

Within this immense, often impersonal, and remarkably complex urban system it has generally been through their shared sexual desires and practices, and the complex sexual geography present within the relative anonymity of city life, that diverse types of men who have sex with men have nonetheless been able to find one another and to establish a shared social world. The symbolic center of this urban subculture has thus been less psychological than spatial—the cafés or bars, the plazas and streets where individuals seeking such sexual contacts were known to meet. Protected, at least up to a point, by the increased anonymity of urban life, a loosely organized, flexible, and constantly shifting homoerotic subculture (or set of subcultures) began to take shape in the streets of Brazil's larger cities at the same time that a notion of *homosexualidade* (homosexuality) as a distinct mode of sexual being was beginning to form in the salons and studies of the well-to-do and well-educated.

Since at least the mid-twentieth century, then, and increasingly over the course of the 1960s, 1970s, and 1980s, yet another model for the conceptualization and organization of same-sex desires and practices had clearly emerged. At first glance this new model, organized around homoerotic desire and practice, seems to contrast rather sharply with the traditional, gender-based model of active/passive same-sex interactions available in popular culture. It seems to have focused largely on the eroticization of otherwise public space while at the same time carving out at least partially protected safe havens in an otherwise hostile world. Within this model virtually any public space might become a focus for homoerotic interaction. Public toilets, parks, plazas, public baths, and the like were invested with erotic meaning, mixing pleasure and danger in an almost constant game of *caça* (hunting) or *pegação* (cruising).

Gradually, over time, however, more private commercial settings began to emerge as well, offering protected alternatives to the potential dangers of homoerotic contacts in public settings. In part this took place through the almost determined invasion of what would otherwise be perceived as nonhomosexual spaces, such as (heterosex) pornographic movie theaters in the center of most major cities. Increasingly, however, particularly during the 1960s and 1970s, such spaces were carved out through the opening of establishments specifically focusing on a gay clientele, such as bars and nightclubs catering to homosexual patrons. Public baths that had long been known, at least secretively, as the focus for same-sex interactions suddenly had to compete with newer, better-equipped saunas that had opened exclusively for a gay clientele.

Like the world of homoerotic pleasures in public space, these enclosed private or commercial spaces also took shape primarily against a backdrop of sexual desire—concretely represented in the *quartos-escuros* (dark rooms) of popular nightclubs and successful saunas. Together with the furtive *pegação* in city streets or the shadowy embraces of the parks and plazas, this growing range of commercial establishments opened yet another set of possibilities for the organization of same-sex interactions—a growing, alternative sexual subculture, or set of overlapping subcultures, closely linked to the rapidly changing realities of urban life, in which sexual desire could open up the transgressive possibilities of pleasure, at least in theory, at almost any moment, and could become, at least for some, almost a distinct style of life.

By the late 1970s, and increasingly in the 1980s and 1990s, the emergence of a self-identified urban gay subculture and, somewhat more tentatively, a gay liberation movement together with a gay-friendly AIDS activist movement, began to become increasingly significant forces in contemporary Brazilian society. Although this subculture continued to be organized, in important ways, around homoerotic practices independent of any kind of sharply bounded homosexual identity, in many of the very same physical and social spaces (ranging from public cruising grounds to bars or discos, saunas, and even the offices or meeting places for gay groups or AIDS-service organizations), it also came to intersect with the increasingly conscious and articulate use of homosexual or gay identity as an equally important organizing principle. Indeed, this emerging gay subculture gradually became a point of convergence where the elite appropriation of modern medical/scientific classifications related to homosexuality and heterosexuality and the popular reality of a relatively open-ended erotic field of same-sex practices could be brought together and, at least up to a certain point, integrated. Throughout the 1980s and on into the 1990s these various currents continued to flow together and mix, increasingly merging, in some cities at least, in the growing sense of a *comunidade gay* (gay community) with its own traditions and institutions (see Green 1999; MacRae 1990, 1992; Trevisan 2000).

With the emergence of AIDS in the early to mid-1980s, and the ongoing association between HIV/AIDS and the experience of gay and bisexual men in Brazil, the relatively gradual social and political mobilization that had been taking place within the emerging gay community over the course of more than a decade would increasingly begin to go hand in hand with intensive AIDS advocacy (see Bessa 1997; MacRae 1990; Parker 1994;

Parker and Terto Jr. 1998; Terto Jr. 1996, 1999, 2000). In Brazil, as in other parts of the developing world (and, for that matter, even in the developed countries), AIDS would provide an important basis, as well as a significant source of funding, for increasingly visible gay organizing and mobilization. From the mid-1980s through the mid-1990s, AIDS-related work and gay political advocacy would build on the substratum of the different cultural models described above, ironically reinforcing the distinctive difference of same-sex relations as constituted through traditional sexual culture, as well as the growing sense of homosexual or gay identity as a key foundation for gay community, and thus contributing in important ways to the progressive formation of what is now probably the largest and most visible gay subculture to be found anywhere outside of the fully industrialized West.

In short, what seems to have emerged over the course of the past decade in large urban centers such as Rio or São Paulo—and only to a slightly lesser extent in smaller cities such as Belo Horizonte, Porto Alegre, Recife, Salvador, or Fortaleza—is a relatively complex sexual subculture (or set of overlapping and intersecting subcultures) that nonetheless provides an alternative model for the organization of sexual reality that contrasts sharply with the more traditional patterns of popular culture, as well as with the rationalized sexuality of scientific discourse. Although emergent gay communities and subcultures have decentered and relativized preexisting gender systems and power hierarchies in a number of important ways, however, they have of course also produced and reproduced other forms of power, discrimination, and social exclusion. In particular, reflecting the wider process not only of social transformation but of social exclusion in modern Brazilian society, gay communities and subcultures throughout the country continue to be permeated by the same divisions of both class and race that are found in Brazilian society more broadly, just as they are characterized by a range of other forms of exclusion (related to age, aesthetics, and so on) all too typically associated with the constitution of gay communities in contemporary capitalist/consumer societies.

Yet in spite of the divisions that (in Brazil as elsewhere in the capitalist world) might lead us to question whether the notion of community is really the best way to designate such emerging social and sexual configurations, there can be little doubt concerning the construction of a whole new range of social/sexual spaces in contemporary Brazilian society. And if these new social configurations are, at one level, the product of a set of largely impersonal social, political, and economic transformations taking place not only in Brazil but far more broadly in the contemporary global system, they are also very much a product of human agency—of often quite conscious action aimed at making, unmaking, and remaking the world, and the possibilities that it offers, and at creating options that may not have existed previously. Although this remade world may at times reproduce many of the characteristics typical of other systems of sexual meaning and social inequality, it would seem to organize them and link them to the formation of identities and experiences in rather different ways. And it clearly offers those individuals whose lives it touches a very different set of possibilities and choices in the constitution of their own sexual and social lives (Parker 1999).

Responding to AIDS

Precisely because the HIV/AIDS epidemic was originally perceived, in Brazil as in so many other societies, as somehow inextricably linked to stigmatized homosexual practices and communities, the early history of the epidemic in Brazil during the 1980s and the early 1990s was characterized by widespread denial and neglect on the part of most government officials. In countries such as Australia, Great Britain, or the United States the preexistence of a range of gay commercial institutions and gay rights political organizations contributed to an early community-based response to the epidemic. The general absence of such preexisting structures in Brazil (and the other countries of Latin America), however, meant that such a response was slower to take shape and have an impact. Yet in Brazil, as much as in these other societies, it was almost entirely as a result of the efforts of gay political groups and AIDS-service organizations, as they emerged over the course of the mid to late 1980s and the early 1990s, that the mobilization of gay communities and homosexually and bisexually active men in major urban centers throughout the country began to take place (see Klein 1998, 1999; Parker 1999; Parker and Terto Jr. 1998; Terto Jr. 1996, 1999, 2000).

317 ▪ ▪ ▪ Changing Sexualities

Although the history of such initiatives is difficult to reconstruct (given that the available documentation exists largely in the gray literature of project reports, newspaper accounts, oral histories, and the like), it is clear that for nearly two decades now AIDS-related work aimed at responding to the epidemic and its impact in relation to homosexually and bisexually active men has been centrally important to the reconfiguration of homosexuality (and, by extension, heterosexuality) in Brazilian life. A number of very important early activities, such as the maintenance of an AIDS hot line and free condom distribution services, were developed during the mid to late 1980s by a range of gay rights organizations, such as Atobá in Rio de Janeiro and the Grupo Gay de Bahia (GGB) in Salvador (see Daniel and Parker 1993). For the most part, however, these early initiatives were both poorly funded and relatively unsystematic (because of their lack of resources).

By the early 1990s, however, a number of larger, more ambitious projects began to emerge in different parts of the country. Perhaps the most ambitious, and certainly the largest-scale, project was what came to be known as the "Homosexualities Project" developed for men who have sex with men in Rio de Janeiro and São Paulo from mid-1993 until the end of 1997 (see Parker et al. 1995; Parker and Terto Jr. 1998). This project was developed in collaboration by ABIA (the Brazilian Interdisciplinary AIDS Association), the Pela VIDDA Groups in Rio de Janeiro and São Paulo, and the Institute of Social Medicine at the State University of Rio de Janeiro, with support provided by a range of donors, including the USAID-funded AIDSCAP Project, the Brazilian Ministry of Health, and the Ford Foundation. The project was based on a number of key points of departure: (1) that high-risk sexual practices continued to be common on the part of many homosexually and bisexually active men in spite of relatively widespread knowledge and information about HIV/AIDS; (2) that the continued practice of high-risk behaviors on the part of men who have sex with men is often closely associated with social isolation and psychological conflicts caused by widely disseminated prejudice and discrimination in relation to homosexuality and bisexuality; and (3) that only by responding to this wider context of sexual oppression, and by situating AIDS prevention positively as a key element in the construction of a culture of "safer sex as community practice" (Watney, 1990), responsive to and respectful of the

SILÊNCIO = MORTE

"Silence = Death." HIV/AIDS advocacy poster.
Brazilian Interdisciplinary AIDS Association (ABIA).

universe of sexual or erotic meanings described above, can we effectively respond to the epidemic. Ultimately, then, it sought to bring together some of the key insights that had emerged from AIDS-prevention work among gay communities in the Anglo-European world, with the long tradition of liberation pedagogy in Latin America, inspired, above all by Paulo Freire's notion of education as a dialogical and dialectical process of individual as well as collective transformation (see Freire 1970; Parker 1996; see also Paiva 2000).

Taking these assumptions as a point of departure, the Homosexualities Project sought to develop a range of activities and strategies aimed at demystifying the relationship between homosexuality and HIV/AIDS and at creating a supportive social environment for risk-reducing behavioral change on the part of the emerging gay community. It aimed to address the stigma and discrimination related to homosexuality in Brazilian society, seeking to demystify homosexual behavior and develop a more realistic assessment, on the part of the population as a whole, of the relationship between AIDS and homosexuality. Intervention methods included a range of outreach activities aimed at reaching men who have sex with men in the diverse sites in which work was carried out, as well as the development of a range of cultural activities such as theater workshops, video and theater production, and related artistic events (Almeida 1996; Klein 1999; Parker 1996; Parker and Terto Jr. 1998). To monitor the impact of the intervention activities, cross-sectional surveys of homosexual and bisexual behavior were carried out in both 1993 and 1995, and results were compared with data collected in 1990, in seeking to assess the impact of HIV/AIDS-prevention activities within the emerging gay communities in both Rio and São Paulo (see Parker and Terto Jr. 1998; for a brief summary of these results see below).

Because of its size and scope, as well as its relatively high visibility, the Homosexualities Project provided an important model for the development of HIV/AIDS-prevention programs for sexually active homosexual and bisexual men in cities around the country. Throughout Brazil a growing range of programs and interventions has sought in recent years to address the needs of men who have sex with men, as well as men involved in sex work or in prison. AIDS-service organizations and gay groups such as GAPA-Minas Gerais in Belo Horizone, GAPA-Ceará and Asa Branca in Fortaleza, Nuances in Porto Alegre, Grupo Dignidade in Curitiba, as well as Atobá and the Grupo Arco-Íris in Rio de Janeiro, and GGB in Salvador, have all initiated prevention programs, in large part funded by the National AIDS Programme of Brazilian Ministry of Health (see Klein 1998, 1999; Parker and Terto Jr. 1998). In a number of cases special programs have been developed for behaviorally bisexual men, sex workers, and men in prisons (see Parker and Terto Jr. 1998).

Such programs have both drawn on the emerging gay communities and homoerotic subcultures of major urban centers in Brazil during the 1990s and played an important, and fairly direct, role in influencing and shaping their development. In particular, the prevention interventions developed by gay and AIDS-service organizations have played an important role in transforming what might be described as the aesthetic of homosexuality in Brazilian society. Whereas both the mass media and popular opinion typically produced stereotyped images of effeminized queens or unruly transvestites as its most frequent way of imaging (and imagining) homosexuality, the "targeted educational materials" of AIDS-prevention programs quickly countered such images with the eroticization of same-sex interactions. Highly masculine bodies seductively photographed, hard penises dressed in condoms, relatively explicit scenes of homosexual sex, and so on all became part of the expanding sexual imaginary in Brazil during the 1990s, and all were placed on display for public view (rather than wrapped in plastic and sold in the back of the newsstand, as in the case of most homoerotic pornography).

To this changing imaginary was added the equally important reconfiguration of the social (and socioeconomic) spaces of homosocial and homoerotic interaction. Although the commercial gay scene had expanded rapidly in the 1980s and continued to do so over the course of the 1990s, it nonetheless suffered from a variety of barriers similar to those typical of Brazilian society more generally—in particular, barriers related to class and, closely associated, race. Given the importance of socioeconomic class differences in Brazilian society, and the continued gap of inequality between a relatively small yet highly privileged elite and a far larger and for the most part excluded population living in poverty (the *classes populares*), many AIDS-related activities played an especially important role in opening up alternative and accessible spaces for homosocial exchange and community building. Whereas the commercial world of bars, saunas, discos, and the like excludes by its very nature large segments of the poorer population, the workshops and support groups developed by gay rights and AIDS-service organizations have come to provide one of the most important alternatives for the development of alternative homosocial networks organized around leisure, as well as around activism. A new range of alternatives began to open up for individuals whose economic circumstances or skin color often meant exclusion from the most highly prized commercial spaces (see Klein 1999; Parker 1999; Parker and Terto Jr. 1998; Terto Jr. 2000).

Indeed, even at the most basic economic level, if the commercial gay

"It doesn't matter with whom." HIV/AIDS prevention
poster promoting condom use. Brazilian Interdisciplinary
AIDS Association (ABIA).

world had for the first time begun to open up a kind of gay economy
complete with employment opportunities (beyond those found in commercial sex work) based in large part on their sexual preferences for sexually active homosexual and bisexual men, over the course of the 1990s
the project-driven world of community-based AIDS prevention and control
work would provide yet another alternative with a somewhat different
dynamic and profile—as well as a social visibility and legitimacy that few
individuals employed in the nightlife of the commercial sector could hope
to obtain in Brazilian society more generally. If, by the beginning of the
1990s, the mainstream Brazilian media seemed to have discovered

homosexuality and homoerotic subcultures, and *go-go boys* or *drag queens* had become relatively common commodities on the talk-show circuit or in the pages of major magazines or newspapers, with the advent of AIDS and the growing response to the epidemic on the part of gay groups and AIDS-service organizations, an entirely new species of public figure began to emerge, with so-called AIDS experts taking their place alongside the exotic species drawn from the world of gay nightlife, occupying important spaces in the media, in government AIDS-prevention commissions, and even in public offices of various types (see Klein 1999; Parker 1999; Terto Jr. 2000).

The importance of this development can hardly be overemphasized, as it has marked a major shift from what might be described as a kind of exhibition of the exotic (which may well be important in its own right, but which nonetheless shrouded homosexuality not only in the aura of difference but also in an almost implicit sense of underlying stigma), to what has increasingly taken shape as a legitimate social role defined in terms of its respected expertise and valued for its broader contribution to the well-being of Brazilian society. If AIDS clearly impacted the emerging gay communities taking shape across Brazil throughout the late 1980s and the 1990s, inflicting terrible levels of individual and collective suffering and robbing these communities of many of their political leaders and their most talented resources, the growing (and increasingly visible) response to the epidemic on the part of these communities contributed not only to the elaboration of new community support structures but also to the increasing visibility (and growing respect and legitimacy) of these communities in the eyes of Brazilian society more generally. Although deeply rooted homophobia and heterosexism continue to characterize Brazilian society at every level, the growing visibility of homosexuality and of gay communities throughout the country has nonetheless become a fact of life at the turn of the century, and the struggles for sexual diversity, sexual rights, and sexual citizenship that characterize contemporary Brazilian life, together with the changing understandings of masculinity that seem to be taking place even within mainstream Brazilian society, would surely look very different if not for the intensive work carried out in the face of AIDS over the course of the past decade.

Given the major changes that have taken place in the social construction of male homosexualities in Brazil during the closing decades of the twentieth century, together with the intensive AIDS-prevention work developed by community-based organizations that have clearly contributed to changing perceptions of homosexuality, it is also worth examining, even if only briefly, the changes that may be taking place at an individual level in response to these changing circumstances. Surely, few phenomena are more capable than HIV/AIDS of demonstrating both the deeply rooted character of gender systems and sexual meanings *as well as* the quite remarkable plasticity of gender and sexuality. Just one example of this can be found in the results from a series of cross-sectional surveys that a team of researchers carried out in Rio de Janeiro in 1990, 1993, and 1995 in order to examine changes in sexual identities and practice that seem to have been adopted during this period in response to the epidemic.

Based on these studies, it is clear that one of the most important transformations that has taken place in recent decades is the changing nature of sexual classification on the part of men who have sex with men—the categorization of sexual identity and self-identification. From 1990 to 1995, for example, there was a constant and consistent decrease in the number of men who define themselves as "bisexual": in our sample of 1990, 12.1 percent defined themselves as "bisexual," a figure that fell to 10 percent in 1993 and then to a mere 8.7 percent in 1995. The number of men defining themselves as "homosexual" remained more or less steady: 50.1 percent in 1990, 48.3 percent in 1993, then rising to 56.7 percent in 1995. The number of men who define themselves as "gay," however, rose considerably, growing from only 4.8 percent in 1990 to 9.7 percent in 1993 and then to 16.7 percent in 1995.

Ultimately, these changes in the nature of sexual self-identification may prove especially important, both in relation to HIV prevention (given that much of the research literature on HIV/AIDS both in Brazil and the rest of the world suggests that there is a strong correlation between homosexual and/or gay identity, on the one hand, and the development of a sense of gay community, on the other, as central elements in HIV/AIDS prevention [Parker 1994]), as well as in the development of gay communities. The

Table 1. Knowledge Concerning HIV Transmission
and Prevention—1990, 1993, 1995*

	1990	1993	1995
HIV is transmitted via semen	94.2	98.0	99.0
HIV is transmitted via the blood	97.8	99.3	99.0
Using a condom prevents HIV infection	88.7	94.0	90.6
Apparently healthy people can transmit HIV	92.4	93.7	96.3

*Percentage of respondents answering "certainly" or "I think so."

Source: Brazilian Interdisciplinary AIDS Association (ABIA) and Institute of Social Medicine/State University of Rio de Janeiro (IMS/UERJ).

development of support structures in the gay community, in turn, has been seen as central to the community response to the epidemic, in what would seem to be a kind of feedback circle (Parker 1994; Parker et al. 1995). Although it is too early to determine the extent to which community organization to deal with HIV and AIDS, together with the kind of prevention programs that have been described above, has contributed to the changes that have been taking place in the classification of sexual identity, or the potential impact they may have borne on forming a base for the community to respond more positively to the epidemic, it nevertheless seems clear that these questions will be of utmost importance in the future.

The data from 1990, 1993, and 1995 show clearly that major changes have taken place not only in relation to sexual identification but also with regard to AIDS-related knowledge and, perhaps most important, what might be described as a sense of sexual agency. The results of all three cross-section surveys reveal very high levels of knowledge about AIDS among the men interviewed. If we look at the indicators of basic knowledge on HIV as a sort of "ABC of AIDS," then practically 90 to 100 percent of the men interviewed were clearly "AIDS-literate," that is, capable of providing correct answers about the ways that HIV is transmitted. And these percentages rose to almost 100 percent in 1995 (see Table 1).

Increasing levels of knowledge and information also seem to have been accompanied by several major changes in attitudes relating to the risk of infection. In 1990, for example, 81.9 percent of the sample had reported the potentially dangerous supposition that reducing the number of partners (without necessarily altering risk behavior) would bring down the risk. This dropped to only 75.3 percent in 1993 and then to 70.4 percent in 1995. Just as important, a feeling of responsibility and individual capacity to act constructively toward reducing the risk of transmission seems to have grown significantly. In particular, we see impressive changes in the capacity of those surveyed to control their own state of health and ability to negotiate safer sexual practices. In 1990, for example, 50.9 percent of the men interviewed agreed that "luck or destiny is responsible for the state of my health," whereas 16.1 percent agreed completely or partly that "nothing can be done to avoid HIV infection," and fully 60.2 percent disagreed. By 1993 these convictions had undergone a significant transformation, with only 21 percent of the men interviewed on that occasion agreeing that luck or destiny controlled their health and a total of 76 percent stating their disagreement, whereas only 9 percent agreed that nothing could be done to avoid infection, with 89.3 percent disagreeing with that view. In 1995 these changes had either expanded or solidified: only 10.3 percent of the men interviewed on that occasion agreed that luck or destiny controlled their health, whereas 87.3 percent showed disagreement; only 8.4 percent agreed that nothing could be done to avoid infection, whereas 91.3 percent disagreed.

These changes in attitude and convictions as to the capacity to control infection seem to be confirmed by the perception of one's individual capacity to negotiate safer sex. In 1990, 61 percent of the men interviewed agreed that "they would not practice anal sex without a condom," while 19.7 percent disagreed. In 1993 the percentage of those in agreement rose to 75.7 percent, and those in disagreement dropped to 14 percent. In 1995 the percentage of those in agreement had grown to 80 percent, whereas those who did not agree had plummeted to 11 percent. Similarly, in 1990, 51.5 percent were in complete or partial agreement that "in the heat of passion it is hard to practice safe sex," whereas 40.1 percent disagreed. In 1993 the percentage of those in agreement had dropped to 36.4 percent, whereas the percentage of those who disagreed had risen to 56.3 percent. In 1995 the figure for those in agreement fell to 18 percent, but the percentage of those who disagreed rose to 74.3 percent.

Another equally important item points directly toward the question of self-sufficiency with regard to sexual negotiation, with 28 percent agreeing entirely or in part in 1990 that "they could do nothing if their partners refused to practice safe sex," whereas only 59.5 percent disagreed. In 1993 the percentage of those interviewed believed they could do nothing to negotiate safe sex with an intransigent partner had dropped to 21.3 percent, with the number of those in disagreement swelling to 74.7 percent. In 1995 the percentage of those who believed they could not negotiate safe sex had dropped even more, to 14.6 percent, whereas the number of those who disagreed had soared to 83.3 percent.

In short, during the period documented by our three stages of data collecting, significant changes seem to have occurred with regard to the extent to which the men interviewed felt capable of facing the questions relating to HIV transmission. This appears most clearly in their ever-greater rejection of the type of fatalism that seemed so general in 1990, their conviction of their ability to negotiate safer sexual practices with their partners, and even in the heat of passion to reject high-risk sex.

From the point of view of HIV prevention the final measure of efficacy is certainly the way that these representations translate into practices that actually increase, or conversely reduce, the risk of infection. Indeed, the main concern that emerged from the survey carried out initially between 1989 and 1990—and the concern that to a great extent motivated HIV/AIDS prevention in men who have sex with other men during the following years—was the apparent contradiction between information, attitudes, and self-declared behavioral change, on the one hand, and the continued incidence of risk practices, on the other. By far the most important result of the long-term study of homosexual and bisexual practices among men in Rio de Janeiro is the documentation of the extent to which these changes in convictions and attitudes related to HIV transmission and safer sex seem also to have been confirmed by the declared changes in sexual practices. In 1993, for example, 20.3 percent of the men interviewed stated they had adopted "some" changes in their sexual behavior, whereas 63.3 percent claimed to have made "many" changes. In 1995, 35 percent reported some changes, against 43.7 percent who reported many changes. In 1993, 61 percent said that they had reduced the number of sexual partners, 55 percent claimed to have sought a steady relationship, 46.7 percent reported avoiding penetration, and 83.3 percent claimed to use condoms as an answer to HIV/AIDS. In 1995, 48 percent declared less partners, 42.7 percent claimed to seek steady relationships, 25.3 percent reported avoiding penetration, and 84 percent claimed to use condoms.

These changes in what might be described as the "strategies" that seemed to have been adopted in order to reduce sexual risk are also confirmed by self-reported changes in actual behavior. In 1990, 65.6 percent of the men sampled reported having practiced receptive anal sex at least once during the month prior to the interview, and 47.3 percent reported having done so without the use of a condom. By 1993 the number reporting receptive anal sex remained steady at 66.0 percent, but those reporting receptive anal sex without a condom had dropped quite significantly to only 21.0 percent. By 1995 the number reporting receptive anal sex was 76.7 percent of the sample, but those reporting receptive anal sex without a condom had remained steady at 22.0 percent. Receptive anal sex with a condom, in contrast, had increased from 35.4 percent in 1990 to 59.3 percent in 1993 and 68.7 percent in 1995. These important changes in rates of unprotected receptive anal sex were also evident in rates of unprotected insertive anal sex. In 1990, for example, 74.4 percent of respondents reported insertive anal sex during the six months prior to their interview, but only 34.0 percent reported having used a condom. In 1993, 72.0 percent reported insertive anal sex, but the percentage reporting having used condoms increased to 64.0 percent. In 1995, 76.3 percent reported insertive anal sex, but the percentage reporting having used condoms was 73.0 percent (see Parker and Terto Jr. 1998).

These substantial reductions in the rates of unprotected anal sex obviously do not mean that the risk of HIV infection no longer exists or that the battle against AIDS has in a way been won. They do, however, offer important proof that significant changes in sexual practices effectively took place among homosexual and bisexual men in Rio de Janeiro for the purpose of lowering the risk of vulnerability to infection. With the higher levels not only of knowledge and information in respect to infection but also, and more important, of what might be described as awareness or responsibility, there is growing conviction that it is possible to assume responsibility for one's own life in order to respond to the epidemic and reduce the risk of infection. It is possible to feel hope for increasing success in bringing down the risk of HIV infection in the future.

Conclusion

Whether at the level of the social organization of sexual subcultures, the formation of institutions and communities, or the recreation of sexual meaning and practices in response to HIV and AIDS, it is clear that important transformations have taken place in recent decades in relation to male homosexuality in Brazil, as in many other parts of Latin America (Parker and Cáceres 1999). It is perhaps less clear to what extent these changes can be interpreted as a function of broader changes taking place in the organization of masculinity (or masculinities) or as a dynamic force for change that is itself helping to shape the changes taking place in relation to masculinity more broadly. Although it is likely that both interpretations have important insights to offer, my own suspicion is that emerging gay cultures and communities have had an especially important role in pushing the envelope for change in relation to masculinity and male sexuality more generally.

Acting as a kind of vanguard, pushing at the limits of the acceptable and the tolerated, and running the constant risk of discrimination and violence, homosexual and bisexual men of all different types have been central players in redefining the possibilities and the limits of the transformation of masculinities and male sexualities and contemporary Brazilian life. In so doing, they have simultaneously transformed the very nature of their own experience—their sexual identities and practices, their bodies and pleasures. To predict how such changes will continue to evolve and change as we enter the new millennium would of course be little more than an exercise in futurology. Even if we are unable to predict the exact dimensions or directions of such change, however, we have some reason for optimism from the whirlwind of transformations that seem to characterize the current moment—a world in which the possibilities for sexual diversity seem to be expanding in important ways, in which it is increasingly possible to shape and reshape one's own sexual subjectivity. Whether in Brazil, in Latin America, or anywhere else, sexualities are changing—and the world will never be the same again.

References

Almeida, Vagner, ed. 1996. *Cabaret Prevenção*. Rio de Janeiro: ABIA.

Bessa, Marcelo Secron. 1997. *Histórias positivas: A literatura (des)construindo a AIDS*. Rio de Janeiro: Record.

Birman, Patrícia. 1985. "Identidade social e homossexualismo no Candomblé." *Religião e Sociedade* 12, no. 1:2–21.

Brandes, Stanley. 1980. *Metaphors of Masculinity: Sex and Status in Andalusian Folklore*. Philadelphia: University of Pennsylvania Press.

Daniel, Herbert, and Richard Parker. 1991. *AIDS: A Terceira Epidemia*. São Paulo: Iglu Editora.

———. 1993. *Sexuality, Politics, and AIDS in Brazil*. London: Falmer Press.

Freire, Paulo. 1970. *Pedagogy of the Oppressed*. New York: Continuum.

Freyre, Gilberto. 1956. *The Masters and the Slaves: A Study in the Development of Brazilian Civilization*. New York: Alfred A. Knopf.

———. 1963. *The Mansions and the Shanties*. New York: Alfred A. Knopf.

Fry, Peter. 1982. *Para Inglês Ver: Identidade e Política na Cultura Brasileira*. Rio de Janeiro: Zahar.

———. 1985. "Male Homosexuality and Spirit Possession in Brazil." *Journal of Homosexuality* 11, nos. 3/4:137–53.

Green, James N. 1999. *Beyond Carnival: Male Homosexuality in Twentieth-Century Brazil*. Chicago: University of Chicago Press.

Gutmann, Matthew C. 1996. *The Meanings of Macho: Being a Man in Mexico City*. Berkeley: University of California Press.

———. 1998. "El machismo." In *Maculinidades e equidad de género en América Latina*, ed. Teresa Valdés and José Olavarría, 238–57. Santiago, Chile: FLACSO/UNFPA.

———. 2001. "The Vicissitudes of Men and Masculinities in Latin America." *Men and Masculinities* 3, no. 3:235–36.

Klein, Charles. 1998. "Gender, Sexuality, and AIDS Prevention in Brazil." *NACLA Report on the Americas* 31, no. 4:27–32.

———. 1999. " 'The Ghetto Is Over, Darling': Emerging Gay Communities and Gender and Sexual Politics in Contemporary Brazil." *Culture, Health, and Sexuality* 1, no. 3:239–60.

Lancaster, Roger N. 1988. "Subject Honor and Object Shame: The Construction of Male Homosexuality and Stigma in Nicaragua." *Ethnology* 27, no. 2:111–25.

———. 1992. *Life Is Hard: Machismo, Danger, and the Intimacy of Power in Nicaragua*. Berkeley: University of California Press.

———. 1995. " 'That We Should All Turn Queer?': Homosexual Stigma in the Making of Manhood and the Breaking of a Revolution in Nicaragua." In *Conceiving Sexuality:*

Approaches to Sex Research in a Postmodern World, ed. Richard G. Parker and John H. Gagnon, 135–56. New York: Routledge.

Landes, Ruth. 1946. *The City of Women*. New York: Macmillan.

MacRae, Edward. 1990. *A construção da igualdade: Identidade sexual e política no Brasil da "abertura."* Campinas: Editora da Unicamp.

——. 1992. "Homosexual Identities in Transitional Brazilian Politics." In *The Making of Social Movements in Latin America*, ed. Sonia Alvarez and Arturo Escobar, 185–203. Boulder, Colo.: Westview.

Paiva, Vera. 2000. "Gendered Scripts and the Sexual Scene: Promoting Sexual Subjects among Brazilian Teenagers." In *Framing the Sexual Subject: The Politics of Gender, Sexuality, and Power*, ed. Richard Parker, Regina Maria Barbosa, and Peter Aggleton, 216–39. Berkeley: University of California Press.

Parker, Richard G. 1985. "Masculinity, Femininity, and Homosexuality: On the Anthropological Interpretation of Sexual Meanings in Brazil." *Journal of Homosexuality* 11, nos. 3/4:155–63.

——. 1989. "Youth, Identity, and Homosexuality: The Changing Shape of Sexual Life in Brazil." *Journal of Homosexuality* 17, nos. 3/4:267–87.

——. 1991. *Bodies, Pleasures, and Passions: Sexual Culture in Contemporary Brazil*. Boston: Beacon Press.

——. 1994. *A construção da solidariedade: AIDS, sexualidade e política no Brasil*. Rio de Janeiro: Relume-Dumará Editores.

——. 1996. "Behaviour in Latin American Men: Implications for HIV/AIDS interventions." *International Journal of STD and AIDS* 7 (suppl. 2):62–65.

——. 1998. "Hacia una economía política del cuerpo: Construcción de la masculinidad y la homosexualidad masculina en Brasil." In *Maculinidades e equidad de género en América Latina*, ed. Teresa Valdés and José Olavarría, 106–27. Santiago, Chile: FLACSO/UNFPA.

——. 1999. *Beneath the Equator: Cultures of Desire, Male Homosexuality, and Emerging Gay Communities in Brazil*. New York: Routledge.

Parker, Richard, and Carlos Cáceres. 1999. "Alternative Sexualities and Changing Sexual Cultures among Latin American Men." *Culture, Health, and Sexuality* 1, no. 3:201–6.

Parker, Richard, et al. 1995. "AIDS Prevention and Gay Community Mobilization in Brazil." *Development* 2:49–53.

Parker, Richard, and Veriano Terto Jr., eds. 1998. *Entre homens: Homossexualidade e AIDS no Brasil*. Rio de Janeiro: ABIA.

Terto, Veriano, Jr. 1996. "Homossexuais soropositivos e soropositivos homossexuais: Questões da homossexualidade masculina em tempos de AIDS." In *Sexualidades Brasileiras*, ed. Richard Parker and Regina Maria Barbosa, 90–104. Rio de Janeiro: Relume-Dumará Editores.

———. 1999. "Seropositivity, Homosexuality, and Identity Politics in Brazil." *Culture, Health, and Sexuality* 1, no. 4:329–46.

———. 2000. "Male Homosexuality and Seropositivity: The Construction of Social Identities in Brazil." In *Framing the Sexual Subject: The Politics of Gender, Sexuality, and Power,* ed. Richard Parker, Regina Maria Barbosa, and Peter Aggleton, 60–78. Berkeley: University of California Press.

Trevisan, João Silvério. 2000. *Devassos no Paraíso,* 2d ed. Rio de Janeiro: Record.

Valdés, Teresa, and José Olavarría, eds. 1998. *Maculinidades e equidad de género en América Latina.* Santiago, Chile: FLACSO/UNFPA.

Viveros Vigoya, Mara. 2001. "Contemporary Latin American Perspectives on Masculinity." *Men and Masculinities* 3, no. 3:237–60.

Wafer, James. 1991. *The Taste of Blood: Spirit Possession in Brazilian Candomblé.* Philadelphia: University of Pennsylvania Press.

Watney, Simon. 1990. "Safer Sex as Community Practice." In *AIDS: Individual, Cultural, and Policy Dimensions,* ed. Peter Aggleton, Peter Davies, and Graham Hart, 19–34. London: Falmer.

JOSÉ OLAVARRÍA

Men at Home? Child Rearing
and Housekeeping among
Chilean Working-Class Fathers

■ ■ ■

I like doing housecleaning. This has nothing to do with being a man or a woman, I still have to do my share. . . . What woman wouldn't like her man to help?—Alex, age twenty-one

This essay examines changes in fathering among working-class men who live with their children in Santiago, Chile.[1] Despite the fact that hegemonic masculinity and patriarchal fatherhood in the nuclear family are reference points for urban fathers, in gathering their life histories and conducting in-depth interviews I have observed that the growing autonomy of women, the demands of modernity, economic adjustment policies, and the requirements of the nuclear family itself have had an impact that has changed the subjective meanings of domesticity, introducing new practices (at least according to the men themselves) and creating a series of new dilemmas that they have been forced to confront.[2]

In Chile, as elsewhere, the workplace and the home were separated—particularly in urban areas—only as a result of the industrial revolution, which detached the site of production from where people lived. This situation "gradually gave rise to the public/private distinction, leading to a separation in the spheres of action of women and men, of power and affection" (Jelin 1994, 76). Simultaneously, in response to the requirements imposed by the economy and those of reproducing the labor force, in conjunction with family policing policies that sought to impose discipline on the family life of low-income urban sectors (Donzelot 1979), a particular type of family gained strength: a nuclear family in which the father/patriarch played the role of head of the household and provider and in which the mother took charge of domestic matters and child rearing in the home. This type of family was idealized as the normative model—particularly in the twentieth century—assumed to be "normal" and "natural." Its existence gained ideological dominance through the theory of gender-determined roles, despite discrepancies with lived experience. In this sense the distinction between the domestic and public spheres, achieved through an abrupt division in social reality based on gender differences—placing men in charge of public duties and women in charge of private and domestic matters as if this were a universal constant of social organization—is a historical artifact, as has been militantly demonstrated by the women's movement, by feminism, and, in recent years, by some men who aim to transform gender relations in order to achieve greater equity with and autonomy for women.

Objective transformations in the conditions of everyday life in recent decades, particularly because of economic adjustment policies and the values of modernity, are generating profound changes in behavior, replete with new demands, deficiencies, and possibilities. The latter are not necessarily consciously perceived by men in their own lives or by other members of their nuclear families, as has been demonstrated by research involving men not only in Chile (Olavarría 2001a, 2001b) but in other Latin American contexts as well (Fuller 2000; Gutmann 2000; Viveros 2000). Many men assume that these new realities do not, and will not, affect them, although they are feeling the effects of these transformations in their daily existence.

Awareness among men that the separation between home and workplace does not reflect their own experiences or that of their partners has begun to gain force in recent years, although at times the disruption of the dual world—the public and the private—has gone unnoticed by men. The main trigger in this recognition has been the massive incorporation of women into the world of gainful employment, a situation that has become the norm among working-class families. Once a woman joins the workforce, it is unlikely that she will leave it and return to domestic work as her single and/or main activity, except, for instance, temporarily after the birth of a child. Men are beginning to notice that women are not "returning to their homes," although many are unwilling to accept this reality, and despite the fact that the actors are often the same, they are confronted by a new reality in which the patriarchal nuclear family is subject to changes not only in the power resources available to men and women but also in the relationships and meanings articulated between them.

The explanation that fathers have for these two processes—women moving into the public sphere, specifically toward "the market space," to use de Barbieri's term (1996), and men moving to the private sphere, child rearing, and domestic chores—is closely linked to power resources and to the position of authority assigned to fathers in the patriarchal nuclear family. Men interpret these changes from this standpoint. In general, even if they are not consciously aware that the basis of patriarchal fatherhood is going through a crisis, it is increasingly difficult for men, particularly working-class men, to achieve these positions of authority. Objectively, fatherhood takes place in a context of growing insecurity linked to recent demographic processes that highlight a family order in Chilean society (that of the patriarchal nuclear family) that is increasingly unstable, as evidenced by a drop in the number of marriages, an increase in marriage annulments,[3] and a rising number of children born out of wedlock in situations in which many men, initially at least, do not legally acknowledge paternity.

Paradoxically, gainful employment among women has turned into one of the pillars supporting this type of family, while concurrently creating new realities that undermine its permanence. If women do not work, the family's quality of life deteriorates, at least in relative terms. When women are providers, their role gives rise to tensions for many fathers, especially because remunerated employment provides women a certain autonomy that they previously lacked. Earning their own money and being able to decide how to spend it and going out and establishing relationships with other people, including other men, affect the authority of the patriarch. The father cannot exercise effective control over what "his" woman does when she is not at home. And men are not indifferent to these changes.

Men describe their partner's financial collaboration as "assistance" and "the leftovers," certainly not the main contribution, which is what the men are supposed to provide. Within the home, although men may help women with housework, most continue to see this as women's responsibility. In general, the explanations and justifications that men use in these situations do not alter the position afforded them by dominant notions of fatherhood, although the underpinnings of their position are actually eroding and their discourse is therefore contradictory.

Nevertheless, despite changed behavior among many working-class men in Santiago and their own reinterpretation of their domestic activities, the patterns of hegemonic masculinity continue to be strongly rooted in the discourse separating the home from the workplace. As thirty-nine-year-old Alexis explains, "I have never liked having my wife work; I want to have a job myself and have her take care of the children until they grow up. I work and I provide for all their needs. I fulfill all my duties, [and] I pay the bills. Maybe this is a very chauvinistic system, but I feel self-sufficient because I was raised this way. I was raised to look out for my family."

The Sense of the Domestic

Particularly among younger men, helping in the home can be a spontaneous affair, although this occurs less frequently among older men as well. By their own accounts young fathers are apparently more willing to help women "do anything," an attitude that they do not feel reflects poorly on their manhood. On the contrary, they actually feel satisfied doing it. As thirty-five-year-old Víctor explains, "I don't find anything unpleasant;

when I'm home I do the ironing every day; if dishes need to be washed, I do so; if my little girl needs her diaper changed, I change it."

But this predisposition is limited by the time men actually find or claim to be available for such activities. Men work long hours, often on weekends, holidays, and overtime, to increase their income, which effectively prevents fathers from becoming more involved in domestic activities.[4] They help out mainly on weekends. Even so, men feel that women are grateful they do any household chores. Although some men dislike doing so, they help out when they see that their partner is tired or that she is running out of time to complete "her duties." Twenty-seven-year-old El Sardina clarifies, "I think she likes me to help. On weekends I help her make the beds or when I get home early and she is still busy with chores; but I don't like this very much because she is picky." For some, helping women is a problem of conscience.

Permanently taking charge of household chores is for most men impossible to imagine. This is particularly true for older men, who more uniformly believe that domestic chores are the responsibility of women. Forty-eight-year-old Antonio states:

> I'm not going to tell you that I enjoy doing it; I wouldn't do it willingly. I would feel obliged by circumstances, and maybe I would not stay [at home]; I would be out looking for any kind of job. I would feel bad because I've already become accustomed to work; I've been working for a very long time. Maybe I would feel all right not working for one or two weeks, but then I would feel that something is missing, like a vacuum. Perhaps it is a little bit chauvinist. Yes [it is], because, for instance, I wouldn't like being dependent on my children or on my wife.

Moreover, it is one thing for a father to want to help with household chores and another for him to be told to do them. He can help his partner, as a way of showing affection, companionship, and/or love, but this help is born out of his own will and is, at most, a "moral" duty. It is not imposed by a third party. This sentiment is expressed by twenty-nine-year-old Moncho: "I used to like doing housework, painting, sweeping the yard, because I believe I am a clean person. What I dislike the most is to be ordered around. Because, I don't know, in the life I lead on the street, or when I was in jail, I was the one who gave the orders." When a woman orders a man around—if she dares do so—a man becomes offended and his reaction can range from indifference to, at the very least, verbal violence. Fathers do not like women to give them orders: men are the ones in charge, even in a field in which women hold the upper hand.

Getting Involved in Reproductive Duties

According to the men interviewed in our study in Santiago, their engagement and participation in child rearing and household chores are determined mostly by the demands and expectations of their partners, their own interest in helping their partner and being closer to their children, the needs that arise when their partners join the labor force, and the insecurity of their own jobs. These factors reinforce each other and give some weight to the ways men describe their involvement in these tasks. But we must not forget that the share of child rearing and household chores undertaken by men is considerably smaller than that of women. Thus, when men say that they help in this regard, we need to keep in mind precisely what they are talking about, how much time they actually devote to these duties, and the fact that they would be unlikely to exchange their share in the division of labor with women (Sharim and Silva 1998).

The attitude adopted by women when they start living with their partners defines to a great extent the involvement of men in household reproductive activities. Life as a couple is determined by the type of relationship that a woman hopes to establish; it depends on her ability and the power resources available to her to negotiate and to involve her partner in child rearing and household chores. According to men's testimonies, they have been involved in reproductive activities if, from the outset, women made it clear that they wished to maintain some independence and equality in the relationship: that the women would continue working at a paying job or that they intended to join the labor market in the future, even with small children. Forty-six-year-old Pedro explains this dynamic in his relationship: "She has always worked. When I met her she was working, and even now, she is working two days a week. [Since] it breaks her heart to leave the baby . . . I have to take on that responsibility so that the child will not be alone, because it makes me sad for the child to be alone. It is a way to help her, but it causes me problems." The strength of the affective link at the beginning of the relationship is also important and gives women power resources that allow them to negotiate their partner's potential involvement. This is particularly the case for young men whose partners have clear demands about the type of relationship they wish to establish.

Some fathers who had not been involved in domestic chores in previous relationships may alter their practices with subsequent partners, either by doing what they failed to do before or by ceasing to do what irritated their earlier partners. As thirty-five-year-old Daniel reveals, "Occasionally I'll tidy up the house, fix electrical things or anything else that's broken. I like doing all kinds of things around the house. I didn't do this with my previous wife because it bored me, plus the fact that I was tired when I came home." But women who do not involve their partner from the moment they start living together may also change later in the relationship and begin demanding more independence. According to the men interviewed, some women change during their time together as a couple; they become more consciously aware of their situation and "dare" to point out this fact. Forty-eight-year-old Antonio describes this process:

> I have noticed a really positive change in recent times, compared to several years ago. My wife pointed out things that I had no idea I was doing wrong, or what was wrong. Before that, she didn't dare bring it up; she was more submissive, a lot more. Recently, she has started saying, "No way!" and explaining why. . . . At first, I get mad, but afterwards I think about things and I say, "She's right," and may even tell her so. Sometimes I apologize and say, "You're right, I like the way you're doing things. I like what you've changed; it's helped you." I say something like that and that way I encourage her.

When men hear these "new" demands, some acknowledge them, accept them, and begin, by their own accounts, to change.

Men's involvement in domestic tasks, initially considered women's work, is also triggered by women's participation in the labor force. A paying job places limits on women's possibilities to perform domestic work and makes evident the need for the father to help at home. Realizing the demands faced by his partner, thirty-five-year-old Nano clarifies: "I help my wife with everything because she gets tired and women work more than men. She has a lot more duties in terms of household chores, cooking, ironing, washing, all that. . . . I don't like ironing because I sweat a lot and I get very tired. Occasionally, when she has a lot of work and is stressed, I help her do the ironing." "Helping" women is a necessity about which men cannot be indifferent, even though they may refrain from becoming involved.

When they have to replace women, men may finally acknowledge all that is involved in women's work. The domestic order that they thought was natural becomes altered and involves a cost: they assume duties at home for which they were not previously responsible. Forty-three-year-old Pez explains: "That was when I realized that women really do a huge job at home, that they have to be on call twenty-four hours a day. Because, what happens, a man works eight or ten hours, comes home and sits down to be catered to. But I realized what it is to be there, for instance, when one of the girls couldn't sleep or got sick during the night." Coming to an agreement with their partner to handle chores that she previously assumed by herself, particularly if there are small children at home and schedules to keep, can force men to share in child-rearing duties.

Unemployment—a common situation among working-class men— makes them face a twofold dynamic: on the one hand, they are forced to confront the importance of women's work in the home, even if they may have verbally acknowledged it repeatedly in the past, and, on the other hand, they have to assume some of these duties. The generally insecure and unstable nature of working-class men's work makes unemployment a "normal" experience (Olavarría, Benavente, and Mellado 1998). Being left without a job produces multiple effects on these fathers. Becoming unemployed means being left very quickly without money. Their savings are minimal, and they have no other resources except for their own ability to work and that of their female partners, older children, and other family members. Unemployment compels many of them to temporarily assume household chores. During this time they have no choice but to do these chores, especially if their wives work or are looking for work.

Taking charge of household chores can depress some men, even if wives are careful not to reproach them for their joblessness and are supportive while they are unemployed. Men, especially at the beginning, may feel worthless; they have no ready cash for their own expenses and have to ask their wives for money. And they cannot talk about this with anyone because they would be viewed as "loafers." Later on, however, they are obliged to acknowledge their unemployment and somehow adapt until they find a new job. In the meantime they assume the chores of rearing, feeding, and keeping the children clean, caring for them, teaching them, and responding to their needs. This situation brings home, often with a destructive force, the fact that they are crossing the threshold of the forbidden because they have lost part of the power that ensures their authority and self-esteem; they are now dependent on women and they are crossing into the feminine world. Although unemployment is, for some, an opportunity to feel the love, fondness, and solidarity of their female partners, for others, on the contrary, the experience is characterized by women's contempt and rejection.

Raising and Spending Time with Children

The space for rearing and spending time with children—generational reproduction—is one of the areas of fatherhood where the effects of modernity have had the greatest impact on the intimate lives of couples and people in general. The often contradictory demands imposed by modernity, of seeking individual independence on the one hand and more intimacy in relationships on the other, have had a special effect on the lives of couples and on the expectations and feelings of fathers. Women are increasingly demanding more independence and equality from men, and both women and children are demanding more intimacy and intensity from their emotional relationships. Similarly, fathers search for enhanced physical and emotional closeness with their children; for many men this means a willingness to respond to the demands made by their families, although they acknowledge that they do not always achieve this goal and that this is a source of conflict. This situation generates many tensions in the feelings and practices of these men, tensions that are expressed in the ways they bring up and socialize their children. Encouraged to speak about raising their children, men present a favorable self-image, which reflects the fact that they have assimilated a more egalitarian view of their relationships with their partners and more emotional intimacy with their children. But we should not be deceived: it is necessary to distinguish between what

Man carrying his son in Mexico City. Photograph
by Matthew C. Gutmann.

the men interviewed report they have done and their actual practices. We
know too little of the latter except, occasionally, as byproducts of what men
have done.

Men in Santiago learn what is expected of a father through their own
experiences and what they have been taught by their own fathers and
mothers. Fathers have been many-sided characters: they are loved, cherished, and respected, but at the same time they are feared, distant, and
sometimes hated. Their behavior has been frequently ambiguous and
confusing; they are conscientious in some instances and unprincipled in
others (Fuller 1997; Olavarría 2000a; Olavarría, Benavente, and Mellado
1998).

In general, the contradictory perceptions of men regarding their fathers with respect to child rearing and socialization make them feel unprepared to be fathers when their first child is born. As the saying goes, "When the child arrives, the father is born." Yet they make negligible efforts to find out about fatherhood before the fact in order to identify approaches that might differ from the contradictory ways in which they were fathered. This approach leads, in principle, to the reproduction with their own children of the type of fathering they experienced. Fatherhood is confronted spontaneously; it is something that catches many of them by surprise. Thirty-five-year-old Nano maintains, "I wasn't ready to be a father. I wanted to be one, but I wasn't ready." Apart from having a clear idea of what their obligations are in terms of the responsibilities of being a father, for example, acknowledging the child and providing for him or her, child rearing is not an issue, even though it may be long awaited. But with current changes in the objective situations that these fathers experience, things have not been easy for them.

Demands on fathers to participate more actively in the rearing and socialization of their children have existed for some decades. These demands, nonetheless, have intensified in recent years across all social sectors. Now, according to their accounts, young fathers generally help mothers with child rearing, particularly during the first months and years. This assistance continues over time, with some men continuing to help their partner do household chores, even occasionally cooking, washing the clothes, and other "household things" to ensure that the woman gets a break, especially during the weekends. As twenty-five-year-old Yayo specifies: "Occasionally I may change a diaper. I check to see that my child is combed, that she has washed her face; the two of us do it. As soon as I get home from work I start playing with her. It's the first thing I do. I play with her. I like to make her laugh. I like to teach her." Nevertheless, there are some boundaries that men will not cross.

Experiences and Lessons during a Child's Life Cycle

In child rearing the moments of greatest physical contact are during the first months of the child's life. This is repeatedly mentioned by younger fathers, although some of the older ones have also had this experience. They feel the need to watch, to touch, to caress their children and to make them feel the father's love and affection. Some men take their child for a walk at night, put the child to sleep, feed him or her, change her or his diapers, and wash the baby. Twenty-five-year-old Yayo's experiences are similar: "I used to look at her [my baby], pick her up. I spent my time watching her. I was concerned for her comfort and cleanliness, her welfare, as I am to this day." This happens especially with the first child— frequently, the ones that follow do not enjoy this privilege, as some men lose their enthusiasm after the first child and, although they say that they also love the others, do not make as great an effort as they did with their first child because that is what the mother is there for; and in their minds she is the one ultimately responsible for the children.

Fathers feel demands for further involvement when their partner works during the first months or years of their child's life. Younger fathers tend to help more with child rearing and socialization, although among this group of men such work is still deemed principally the duty of mothers. It is their "role." When children are older, fathers try to establish spaces and times to spend with them, which is not always possible, according to their accounts. They watch television together, dance, talk, go out shopping together, go for strolls, and listen to music. A few take them to their daycare centers or to school. They may talk about school and homework with older children.

Although going out for walks or to the park may occur only occasionally, they are activities that both fathers and children remember for a long time. As thirty-four-year-old Alexis recounts, "Last week we went to the Metropolitan Park on an outing organized by the company and we had a great time. We had a barbecue; the kids got on all the rides; we rode the train; it was great!" When children become teenagers, however, tension arises in their lives and those of their parents. Teenagers challenge parental authority, disobey, and start becoming independent. Nonetheless, according to the testimonies of these fathers, their children often still demand emotional contact with them. The intensity that these fathers believe characterizes their relationship with the children, especially with the boys, starts to weaken; they feel that a distance begins to set in, and disagreements and conflicts emerge.

Fathers, in general, acknowledge that they should give more freedom to their teenage children, especially boys, because regardless of what the parents say, the youths will find ways to become more independent. Teenagers no longer accept parental authority and demands without question. As thirty-nine-year-old Herman relates regarding his son, "My relationship with Víctor, now that he is older, has changed a bit, because he is more of a man, he is starting to make his own decisions and he no longer likes certain things." When children set up their own homes, parents generally continue to keep an eye on their lives. They keep up the relationships through regular visits held both in their own homes and in those of the children. There they talk, reminisce over stories and anecdotes, and eat and drink together. Yet the worries do not end.

Dilemmas: Married Life and Fatherhood

The experiences that men currently face as fathers in Santiago challenge what they have learned about fatherhood, which often does not coincide with their actual lives. In their relationships with the mothers of their children, many men are forced to question the subjective meanings of fatherhood. Masculine identities have been reproduced in men's own nuclear families by reference to a hegemonic masculinity that encourages a patriarchal type of fathering. But they feel that this pattern of fatherhood is losing hold and does not allow them to address the new demands that confront them. Similarly, they believe that they lack adequate responses to their partners and children, who continually ask for more independence, demand respect for their own decisions, and seek closer affective relationships with their fathers. Furthermore, particularly among younger men, ambitions create questions about their role as fathers, questions for which they lack clear answers.

The fusion between the dictates of patriarchal fatherhood to be the provider, authority, and protector, and those of modern fatherhood, which calls for democratic, intimate, affectionate, and close fathering, creates new demands for fathers manifested in an emerging pattern that is proving thoroughly untenable. It is impossible to be a good father, one who complies with the demands imposed by this mixture, because these requirements are just too demanding for a single person. Thus, in exercising their roles as fathers, men seek answers and find themselves in the midst of a series of choices and dilemmas that are linked to those subjective meanings and practices that they must somehow resolve, either by active intervention or by letting things be, giving new meanings to fatherhood or reaffirming what they learned from their original models of how to be good fathers.

The birth of a child, especially the first one, frequently causes a conflict for these men. Until the child is born, the father experiences pregnancy through the mother, but once the child is born, the father often feels his world has been invaded, and he may view the child as a competitor for the devotion and affection of the mother, who also needs to be cared for. Thirty-three-year-old Negro explains: "That's where one's freedom ends and that of the other individual begins to emerge. One ceases to function for one's own benefit and starts functioning for the benefit of another."

Working and being with children is a contradictory experience because it is mediated by the ability to provide, to be the family's source of livelihood. The possibility of supporting one's family financially, however, is not always available to men, and in some cases it can become an obstacle that prevents them from achieving their desire to establish bonds of affection, of deeper and more intense family ties. Twenty-one-year-old Marcelo feels this pressure: "She [Marcelo's wife] would definitely like me to spend more time at home, to spend more time with the child." This is one of the main dilemmas reported by men, that they resolve through work the activity they see as their primary responsibility; even though they may help in the house, child rearing is the duty of women.

Generally fathers feel that they spend very little time with their children, that "now" they are less dedicated, insinuating that "before" they used to be more so. "Now" this has changed even though they would like to spend more time with their children. Their duties, however, prevent them from closer contact although, at the same time, they are aware that if they had more time, they would be bored, that they would not know what to do with it. As forty-eight-year-old Emilio said, "Unfortunately, my job is very enslaving, so I have very little time. At this moment, I have time [to go home], but I don't do it because I fear going home. I am not really afraid of going home, but what am I going to do once I'm there? Be bored? I'd rather stay out with my friends."

Demands for more affective closeness and intimacy in their relationship with their children is perceived by fathers as a requirement that they cannot easily satisfy; this demand becomes stronger as children grow up, especially in adolescence, and it is expressed both in the way these fathers listen and are listened to by their children. For fathers seeking to be closer to their children, being a parent implies moving within two spheres that are sometimes contradictory and difficult to resolve: trying at the same time to be the one in charge and a friend. Where is the boundary? On the one hand, they feel obliged to show their children the difference between right and wrong, values and norms, and simultaneously to set limits on them. On the other hand, these same fathers also often seek friendship, affective closeness, and a degree of intimacy with their children.

According to their testimonies, fathers in Santiago need to teach children rules and moral values, self-respect and self-esteem. They must take care of them, protect them, occupy and preoccupy themselves with their children. But preparing their progeny for life also involves introducing them to the laws of the street and its contradictory practices of respect for others and the use of power. Fathers find that they need to guide and accompany their children so that they will be honest, worthy, and upstanding adults while simultaneously teaching them to defend themselves from the dangers of life and to enjoy what life has to offer. The trick is to do so with respect and understanding, without overpowering or overprotecting them. Jano, a thirty-five-year-old father, states his philosophy:

> A father should allow children to be what they want to be and support them in the process. The important thing is not for the father to ask his children to be better than he is or for them to have things that he didn't have, but to let them be and always be there for them. But a child is also a being who is there to be shaped, taught values, and trained to be proud of herself or himself.

Some fathers fluctuate between allowing their children more freedom and autonomy and the urge to place limits and regulate their children. The choice lies between supporting what the children want and guiding the children based on the fathers' own experiences.

Many fathers reported that they feel uncomfortable when they have to acknowledge that their children, especially girls, are sexual beings, and, in general, they refrain from talking about sex with their own girls and boys. At most, they make an offhand comment, to acknowledge their son's experience with women, or point out the necessary precautions to avoid getting a young woman pregnant. Conversations with daughters about men and sexuality are deemed unsuitable; no one knows what may happen, and fathers are often afraid to initiate this type of conversation. In short, they pay no attention to the issue or they transfer the question to their spouse; mothers are expected to speak to daughters. Fathers will take care of the sons, of course, when they get a little older. . . .

Men, like women, believe that the demands requiring them to be the providers and to participate in child rearing and spend time with children leave them practically no room for a more intimate life with their spouses. Forty-eight-year-old Antonio explains this dilemma: "We have devoted ourselves solely to the family, and therefore we have lost some room for our own relationship. We are always putting the children first and I sometimes tell her 'I'm fed up,' tired of being a father. I would like to be only a husband." The need to have space and time for themselves is another requirement that they face, but they view this more as a wish than as an actual possibility.

Some men also feel that their partners need more room for themselves. Thirty-two-year-old Marco, for example, is relatively open about this point: "She has her own space. She sometimes tells me that she is going to get together with her classmates, with the same ones she used to go to parties with. I take her there and then I bring her back." It is not always easy, however, for men to accept that their partners do things in which they do not participate or somehow cannot oversee. What will she do while she is not at home and not at work? The uncertainty caused by the possibility of another man "conquering" her is something that many men cannot tolerate; scenes caused by jealousy are usually based on this fear. But there also are men, like Marco, who believe that their partners, like themselves, are entitled to their own space and thus acknowledge greater autonomy for women.

Final Remarks

We are experiencing a process of deep transformations in the configuration of families and of fatherhood. This transformation is evidenced by the testimonies of working-class fathers in Santiago, Chile, and by statistics over the past twenty years that show a decrease in marriages and births and an increase in marriage annulments, in children born out of wedlock, and in households headed by females (Olavarría 2000b). These developments are giving rise to changes in the perceptions that men have about the sexual division of labor and also about their relationships with their partners and children.

The patriarchal nuclear family and its relevant father figure are being subjected to severe tests in Santiago. This ideal of fatherhood is being increasingly challenged, both in the subjective sense and in the practice of fatherhood itself. It produces tensions, frustration, conflicts, and pain among many men because it generates dynamics in the relationships between genders and generations that presuppose a redistribution of men's prerogatives and abilities. The challenges also originate in the search for relationships that are closer and more intimate, invoking a greater affective and loving intensity with their family.

Some men hold on to the view of fatherhood that they learned from their own fathers, a view that is no longer possible to maintain. But the changes observed among men do not challenge patriarchal fatherhood as such; no alternative models have yet won wide support. Nevertheless, there are new practices among some men that point to relationships of greater intimacy and equality with their partners and children, which in turn will allow men to understand their families and encourage the independence and interests of other members of these families.

Notes

1. Material used in this paper is based on in-depth interviews with seventy working-class fathers in Santiago, Chile, based on the following studies: "Construcción social de la masculinidad en Chile: Crisis del modelo tradicional. Un estudio exploratorio," financed by the Ford Foundation; "Construcción social de la identidad masculina en varones adultos jóvenes de sectores populares," financed by CONICYT; "Ser padre: La vivencia de los padres de Santiago. Estereotipos, subjetividades y prácticas de la paternidad," financed by FONDECYT grant no. 1980280.

2. This essay specifically refers to "los sectores populares," roughly translated here as the working class, which include those populations classified in Chile as "poor" and "extremely poor." The former are unable to satisfy their basic needs, and the latter cannot even satisfy their need for food. Patriarchy is understood here as the system of domination that allows men to control women's capacities (including their reproduc-

tive, erotic, and labor skills, among others), a patriarch as one who exercises this power, and the patriarchal nuclear family as one in which all members are subordinate to a patriarchal father.

3. There exists no divorce law in Chile.

4. The average workday in Santiago for males lasts 11 hours, plus 2.7 hours for commuting, with an average work week of 55 hours (Sharim and Silva 1998).

References

de Barbieri, M. Teresita. 1996. "Los ámbitos de acción de las mujeres." In *Encrucijadas del saber: Los estudios de género en las ciencias sociales,* ed. Narda Henríquez, 107–32. Lima, Perú: Pontificia Universidad Católica del Perú.

Donzelot, Jacques. 1979. *La policía de las familias.* Valencia, Spain: Editorial Pre-textos.

Fuller, Norma. 1997. *Identidades masculinas: Varones de clase media en el Peru.* Lima, Perú: Pontificia Universidad Católica del Perú.

———. 2000. "Significados y prácticas de la paternidad entre varones urbanos del Perú: Lima, Cuzco e Iquitos." In *Paternidades en América Latina,* ed. Norma Fuller, 35–89. Lima, Perú: Pontificia Universidad Católica del Perú.

Gutmann, Matthew C. 2000. *Ser hombre de verdad en la ciudad de México: Ni macho ni mandilón.* Mexico City: El Colegio de México.

Jelin, Elizabeth. 1994. "Las familias en América Latina." In *Familias siglo XXI,* ed. ISIS, 75–106. Santiago, Chile: Edición de las Mujeres No. 20.

Olavarría, José. 2000a. "Ser padre en Santiago, Chile." In *Paternidades en América Latina,* ed. Norma Fuller, 129–73. Lima, Perú: Pontificia Universidad Católica del Perú.

———. 2000b. "De la identidad a la política: Masculinidades y políticas públicas. Auge y ocaso de la familia nuclear patriarcal en el siglo XX." In *Masculinidad/es: Identidad, sexualidad y familia,* ed. José Olavarría and Rodrigo Parrini, 11–28. Santiago, Chile: FLACSO-Chile, Red de Masculinidad and Universidad Academia de Humanismo Cristiano.

———. 2001a. *Y todos querían ser (buenos) padres: Varones de Santiago de Chile en conflicto.* Santiago, Chile: FLACSO-Chile.

———. 2001b. *¿Hombres a la deriva? Poder, trabajo y sexo.* Santiago, Chile: FLACSO-Chile.

Olavarría, José, Cristina Benavente, and Patricio Mellado. 1998. *Masculinidades Populares: Varones adultos jóvenes de Santiago.* Santiago, Chile: FLACSO-Chile.

Sharim, Dariela, and Uca Silva. 1998. "Familia y reparto de responsabilidades." Santiago, Chile: SERNAM, Documento No. 58.

Viveros, Mara. 2000. "Paternidades y masculinidades en el contexto colombiano contemporáneo." In *Paternidades en América Latina,* ed. Norma Fuller, 91–127. Lima, Perú: Pontificia Universidad Católica del Perú.

HÉCTOR CARRILLO

Neither *Machos* nor *Maricones*:

Masculinity and Emerging Male

Homosexual Identities in Mexico

. . . .

In Mexico, as in other parts of Latin America, popular discourses about male homosexuality have traditionally emphasized effeminacy and a "loss of manhood." These associations are changing as more men who are sexually attracted to men disclose their homosexuality yet retain masculine identities. The emergence of their male identities as homosexuals is the central topic of this chapter.

My analysis is not limited to men who identify as *homosexuales* or *gays*.[1] Discussion of masculine male homosexuality in urban Mexico is becoming relevant to understanding the identities of all Mexican men—precisely owing to the increased visibility of masculine homosexual men who contribute to a broader social questioning of previously accepted male identities and the dominance of machismo. Because of this visibility, the notion that everyone who calls himself a man is by definition sexually attracted to women is strongly challenged. This challenge forces all men to reflect on where they fit within the landscape of possible male identities.

Men who could in other times easily distance themselves from the world of homosexuality because of their apparent masculinity are now realizing that being masculine is no longer a sufficient precondition for a man if he wishes to reassure the rest of Mexican society of his being *normal,* the term chosen by many Mexicans to refer to people who are sexually attracted exclusively to the opposite sex. Furthermore, the visibility of masculine homosexuals challenges the essentialist and widely accepted connection in Mexico between *machismo, hombría* (manhood), and masculinity. The existence of these masculine homosexual men also adds validity to new ideas about masculinity being adopted by those Mexicans, men and women, who oppose what they consider obsolete *machista* values.[2]

In this regard the identities of masculine homosexuals send two strong messages to Mexican society. One is that a man can continue to be a man despite not being sexually attracted to women. The second is slightly more abstract. It involves the notion that because homosexual and heterosexual men can be quite similar in their demeanor and behavior, except for the object of their sexual attraction, a man need not be *macho* to prove to the world that he is not a *maricón*—an effeminized man who has lost his manhood. In other words, and perhaps ironically, masculine homosexuality in Mexico is helping to lift the burden of expectations about machismo off the shoulders of all men.

To further understand this phenomenon, *hombría* and, by extension, *masculinity* ought to be defined in terms of what they traditionally were not. Prior to the adoption of an understanding of categories of sexual identity and sexual orientation, Mexican society dichotomized men almost exclusively into two broad categories that were defined by demeanor. Masculine men were *hombres* or *machos.* Their counterparts were the effeminate men, the *maricones,* who were perceived as having forfeited their manhood altogether (Carrier 1972, 1995; Paz 1985; Taylor 1978, 1986). The existence of the latter confirmed the "normality" of the former. The *hombres*—those who were seen as legitimately manly and who were allowed to assert their dominance via the abuses of machismo—needed the *maricones* as a point of reference that defined where manhood ended. The identity of the *maricón* marked the point at which "a man stops being a man." *Maricones* defined the socially undesirable end of the spectrum of male identities; the abusive *macho* defined the other end.

The identities of masculine men who today declare themselves to be *homosexuales* or *gays* shifts the location of the boundary marked by the *maricones* and expands the range of possible male identities. Because the masculine *homosexuales* often prove to be as "manly," or even as *macho*, as the rest of masculine men, their identities lend validity to a new and growing sense that manhood in Mexico has to be measured by more than masculinity, machismo, or a man's sexual attraction to women. It is in this sense that openly homosexual, masculine men force a redefinition of what being a man in Mexico means.

On the other hand, despite the changes and shifts that I have described, many people in Mexico still rely on signs of effeminacy to decide who is a homosexual man and still often measure male homosexuality against an essentialist notion of manhood and not against heterosexuality. As the examples that I analyze below indicate, the separation between contemporary understandings of masculine homosexuality and previously existing associations of homosexuality with effeminacy is not always clear cut. In fact, I have found that in interpreting the roles and identities of male actors in everyday interactions—sexual and nonsexual—men in Mexico often find themselves using criteria that equate sexual orientation with sexual attraction and simultaneously think of sexual orientation in terms of masculine or feminine demeanor. I have discussed the origins of this phenomenon elsewhere, as part of a larger investigation into what I call—borrowing a term developed by García Canclini (1995)—"cultural hybridity" in the evolution of ideas and practices about sexuality in Mexico's recent history (Carrillo 1999, 2002).

In this chapter I analyze how indications of a complicated shift in boundaries and identities emerge in current perceptions of homosexuality shared by Mexicans, as well as in recent depictions of homosexual Mexican men in the mass media in that country. I also discuss the interplay between contemporary ideas about homosexuality and the entrenched need among many men who call themselves *homosexual* or *gay* to conform to widespread social expectations regarding manhood and masculinity. For my analysis I rely on data from an ethnographic study of sexuality in Guadalajara that I conducted between 1993 and 1995.[3] I also discuss representations of male homosexuality in a 1999 Mexican *telenovela*, the Mexican version of a soap opera, *La vida en el espejo* (Life in the mirror). This telenovela, which was broadcast nationally and was very popular among the urban middle class, included a prominent character who over the course of the series acquires a Mexican gay identity: from realizing he is sexually attracted to men, to disclosing his sexual orientation to his family, to developing a fully open relationship with another gay man.

Who Is a Man? Who Is a Homosexual?

Masculinity was an important feature of the identities of many of the men in my study who thought of themselves as *homosexuales* or *gay*. Being masculine was extremely valued by these men because it allowed them to retain a status as regular men—to prevent others from questioning their manhood and avoid being stigmatized for their difference. They regarded this status as crucial for their careers and their family relations and for maintaining membership in social networks where they believed they could not fit should they appear to be effeminate.

The need to maintain a reputation as regular men was interpreted in two different ways. For some it meant that they had to be selective about where and to whom they disclosed their sexual attraction to men. These men used masculinity to hide their homosexuality as needed. They often maintained two separate worlds, one where they passed as *hombres normales* (normal men) and another where they were open about their sexual orientation. They often justified such separation because they feared the potential consequences of disclosure, such as discrimination at work or rejection by relatives and friends. Within the circles of their life where they could be open about their sexual attraction to men, these men tended to play an important didactic role. They taught others what male homosexuality was all about, modeling behaviors for those who were in the process of acquiring a homosexual identity and enlightening heterosexuals who could, in turn, help change attitudes about homosexuality in their own social and family circles.

Some of these men chose to disclose their sexual orientation only within social networks consisting of *homosexuales* and sympathetic heterosexuals. They were careful to ensure that news about their sexual orientation did not invade the worlds where they fully passed as *hombres normales*, and those who knew about their sexual attraction to men generally respected their desire for controlled disclosure. These men often assumed that as they aged and did not marry a woman, everyone around them would eventually realize that they were different and would silently tolerate this fact without necessarily acknowledging it openly. Their being masculine facilitated the ability of everyone involved to maintain the pretense of "normality" even when it was clear that the man in question was *homosexual*. In other words, using what I and others have labeled "sexual silence," these men often achieved a veiled form of disclosure that provided them with unspoken tolerance (Carrillo 1995, 2002; Díaz 1998).

For other men masculinity allowed them to disclose their sexual orientation fully to their immediate or extended families, to coworkers and supervisors, to classmates, or to friends, including those who had known them previously as "regular" men. These men used their masculinity to establish that they were men and that one of their male characteristics was that they were homosexual. Two interesting cases are those of Julio and Enrique. Julio had not disclosed his homosexuality to his family but had decided that he could not tolerate antihomosexual attitudes at work. "When I started working I told my boss that a friend of mine had been fired from his job for being *homosexual* and that I did not want that to happen to me. She said to me, 'There is no problem here, your life is your life, work is work.' She made me feel good."[4]

By the age of twenty-three Enrique had managed to live what was close to full disclosure. Over a period of five years his family had learned about his sexual orientation, he had disclosed his sexual orientation to his boss and other people in his job, and a great majority of his friends knew about his homosexuality. His parents rejected him at first but slowly learned to accept him, and Enrique had managed to bring his male lover into the life of the family, where he was introduced as a close friend to relatives and family friends with whom Enrique's homosexuality had not been openly acknowledged. Although he had not fully disclosed his homosexuality everywhere, Enrique did not feel threatened by the idea that someone in his life might find out about his sexual orientation or reveal it to others.

For many of the masculine men who identified as *homosexual* or *gay*, the demeanor of men who were openly effeminate or who had adopted identities as women were very threatening. They saw them as a barrier to the eventual acceptance of homosexuality in Mexican society and as a burden that prevented homosexual men from moving beyond the stereotype of the *maricón*. As Eugenio, a forty-eight-year-old man put it, "To a great degree they are responsible for the stigma against *homosexuales*, because with their public displays they make the rest of society believe that all *homosexuales* are like that, which is definitely not true. I believe they are responsible for much of society's rejection of *homosexuales*."

Eugenio identified as *homosexual*, which to him meant that "I am *varón* [male], but my sexual preference is for other males, because I feel completely male. I don't believe I am effeminate, either in my looks or in my demeanor. Nothing." Interestingly, the long-term love relationships to which Eugenio referred in his interview had taken place with masculine men who did not identify as homosexuals. Within these relationships Eugenio had typically played the role of a *homosexual* who is having sex with a *normal* (meaning here a man who is masculine and who has a primary sexual attraction to women, despite his also being attracted to men). His partners had tended to be married to women or to have a steady woman partner and treated the relationship with Eugenio as something that happened on the side. It is also worth noting that these men sought to have sex with Eugenio, a masculine man, and not with an effeminate man who fit the more traditional image of the *maricón*.

Masculinity allowed some of the openly homosexual or gay men not only to maintain a status as regular men but also to enact behaviors that could be seen as typically *macho*. One interesting example is that of Antonio, a young man whose case I have described more extensively elsewhere (Carrillo 1999). Antonio was very masculine and was frank about being *gay* in all spheres of his life, including his workplace. He reported seducing heterosexual men in his office and asserting himself as a dominant sexual partner with them. He described incidents where he had taken the penetrating role in sexual interactions with these heterosexual co-workers, refusing to be penetrated by them when they had requested reciprocity. It is noteworthy that the heterosexual men being seduced were not expected to take "the role of the man" and that they were being seduced by a homosexual who could be regarded, to use a stereotype, as "more of a man than they."

The impact of close contact with masculine and openly masculine homosexuals on the heterosexual men around them was varied. Some heterosexual men established direct interactions, at times even sexual, with *homosexuales* who did not fit the category of *maricones* and who were generally masculine. These homosexual men were often open with the heterosexuals about their sexual attraction to men and sometimes about being sexually attracted to them in particular. When there was sexual involvement, as in the cases described by Eugenio and Antonio, these heterosexual men probably realized that they were having sex with a man and not with "a man who has lost his manhood," as the traditional definition of *maricones* suggests. They were in a position in which they could hardly claim that their sexual partners were women, or even quasi women, because they knew that their partners were masculine and they thought of themselves as *homosexual* or *gay*.

This situation is different from that found by Prieur (1998) in her study of working-class men in an economically marginal zone in Mexico City's metropolitan area. Prieur's main focus was on the *jotas*, extremely effeminate men who made every effort to pass as women. Prieur also interviewed some of the *jotas'* masculine partners, whom she labeled *mayates*. She found that the *mayates* often managed to justify their actions by convincing themselves that they were having sex with a woman or by minimizing the contact with any part of their partners that reminded them that these women were indeed men, in particular the genitals.

In the case of the men who identified as *normal* or *heterosexual* and who engaged in sex with masculine men, such as the ones in my study, they were usually fully aware that they were having sex with men. Despite this awareness, however, they sought special rationales to justify their actions. They seemed to conceive of such relationships as ones between masculine men where one is *homosexual* and the other is not. As Gerardo, a self-identified *heterosexual* put it: "To me the homosexual is the one who receives, the one who seeks the relationship, the penetration. The other, well he is the heterosexual, even when he is penetrating a man, because he can have sexual relations with a woman or with a man." Here the separation between the homosexual and the heterosexual man is measured not by masculinity—or lack thereof—but by the ability to penetrate. The man who identifies as *normal* or *heterosexual* can still make a claim that he is more of a man than the other.

Clearly, this last argument would work only for those men who, while engaged in sex with another man, consciously decide not to take any roles that could be interpreted as being those of a woman. This would certainly be difficult for the partners that Antonio seduced and penetrated. I would speculate, however, that these men might still find some way to convince themselves that their role is that of the man who is having sex with a homosexual.

Nonsexual Homosociality

When heterosexual men were involved in nonsexual friendships with homosexual men, they felt forced to be careful about drawing a line that too narrowly defined the boundaries of their interactions. It was important to them to let it be known that they were not threatened by the homosexual person's lifestyle but that they had no interest in becoming involved in ways that could suggest they themselves were homosexual or had an interest in having sex with a man.

Gerardo, for instance, talked about having had good friends who were homosexual and feeling that they were extremely loyal and easygoing. He emphasized that there was mutual respect among all concerned. He added, nonetheless, that he felt some repugnance when he thought about homosexual sex, about the fact that men would seek to obtain pleasure from each other. When I asked for clarification, he said, "As people, in their everyday lives I respect them. But within their environment and in terms of their relations, I don't." Describing his friendships with homosexual men he mentioned, "Many people say, 'If you want a good friend, have a homosexual friend.' I don't know. Perhaps it's because they are more attuned to feelings, more so than women. I don't know exactly how to express myself, but it's like you have more trust. A homosexual does not disappoint you as easily as a woman." The friendship was not unconditional, however. In order to participate, Gerardo felt a strong need to set strict boundaries, "as friends, and that's it, drawing a line."

Francisco, a twenty-two-year-old man, expressed a similar need when discussing his identification as a *heterosexual,* claiming that "I even had experiences that led me to identify more deeply as a heterosexual." Francisco was referring to interactions with a male friend who was expressing strong interest in him. He had realized that his friend was different because of "some features and attitudes that were a bit effeminate." Mauricio had accepted an invitation to move in with him and to sleep next to him. One time, his friend attempted to touch him as they slept. "That's when I told him that I felt respect for him but that I did not share that [interest in men]." Francisco told me that for a reason unknown to him he tended to attract homosexual men and added that this caused him "no conflict."

In Francisco's case his contacts with homosexual men had created a distinction in the kinds of interactions that he had with different types of male friends. With his heterosexual friends he could engage in what he called *mayor acercamiento corporal* (greater corporal closeness), referring to expressions of affection that involved touching. Such expressions included kissing each other on the forehead, making jokes about wanting to caress them and then enacting the caresses, and even slapping them on their buttocks. With his openly homosexual friends such interactions were absent. He could express full respect for them and for their lifestyle, but he also thought that he should be careful not to do anything that could trigger their sexual or emotional interest. This is an interesting consequence of the disclosure of homosexuality.

Traditionally in Mexico, men have used playfulness as an avenue for seduction because homoerotic interactions have created a space for the initiation of sex between men. But once friends are known to be homosexual, men's participation in the kind of homoerotic games and affectionate interactions that are common between male friends can easily become restricted because, as in Francisco's case, heterosexual men may become wary and make efforts to ensure that no action is interpreted as an invitation for sex.

The most general effect that the visibility of masculine homosexual men have had on heterosexual men in Mexico has to do with the recognition that masculinity does not guarantee that a man will be sexually attracted to women. When speaking of classifications of sexual orientation, a majority of men and women in my study referred to a man who is sexually attracted to men with the words *homosexual* or *gay*. In their explanations of what this meant they typically placed an emphasis on sexual attraction based on the assumption that both partners in a same-sex sexual encounter are homosexual, regardless of their demeanor or the roles that they take (insertive or receptive, dominant or responsive) during sexual interactions.

Much like Gerardo a few people had adopted interpretations of homosexuality that reflected knowledge of the object-choice categories but that were also influenced by an understanding of the roles and identities defined by older, demeanor-based classifications. Additionally, a similar superimposition of classifications was evident in participants' comments about the origins of homosexuality, which often resorted to clues like signs of effeminacy in a boy as indicators that the child would grow up to be a homosexual. In this interpretation people struggled to accept that a masculine boy who never showed any signs of effeminacy could also "naturally" turn out to adopt a homosexual identity as an adult. They accepted the notion that as an adult a homosexual man could be completely masculine, but, in the absence of effeminacy, they considered that the main cause of homosexuality in such a man was probably initiation into sex with other men by a homosexual, especially if this occurred during childhood.

These examples illustrate that, in their adoption of contemporary notions of male homosexuality, many Mexicans are seeking to make sense of who are homosexuals and how they are different from the *maricones* and *hombres normales* and *heterosexuales*. Indeed, this felt need to categorize men under different labels is beginning to force men who identify as *normal* or *heterosexual* to reflect on where they themselves fit in the spectrum of male identities. Perhaps the most explicit example in my study of this development was offered by Francisco, the young man who had shared a home with a homosexual friend. Francisco said that as part of his training in psychology, and owing to the experiences he had with this friend, he began to ask himself whether he was attracted to men. He had gone as far as to force himself to fantasize about having sex with a man to test whether there were any traces in him of same-sex attraction. He said he never found any such traces. In the context of his fantasizing he could visualize a handsome naked man. He could see his features and imagine himself caressing him and kissing him. He could also picture the man's anus as offering a potential site for penetration. However, once he tried to envision the coitus, he could no longer see the man but instead would think about women. He took this as proof that he was not even remotely attracted sexually to men.

In a different case, Eduardo defined his identity as that of a "person who is fundamentally heterosexual but who has some homosexual tendency every so often." Eduardo had been involved in a few sexual interactions with men throughout his sexual life. On those occasions he had been somewhat submissive and had had a strong interest in being penetrated. The fact that these partners were men did not represent a threat to his sense of manhood, but he had felt uncomfortable when he realized that he was "losing control of the situation," which meant that his male sexual partner was being dominant.

Eduardo's assessment was that his sexual attraction was overall very strongly oriented toward women. The fact that he had only pursued sex with men on a few occasions and under specific circumstances—being drunk or very aroused—indicated to him that he was not *gay*. He had also decided that he did not regard himself as bisexual because his sexual attraction toward both sexes was not equal.

In a final example, Rafael, who was married to a woman and, like Antonio, was extremely masculine, had been involved in a four-year love relationship with another man, whom he described as equally masculine. I met Rafael in a gay disco, where he was socializing with a group of gay friends. He was fully aware that being a masculine man who is exclusively gay was an option, yet he chose to continue identifying as a "normal" man. What he wished to emphasize during our conversation was the relationship that he had had with another "normal" man. The two men had enacted this relationship in the context of friendship between the two married couples, and Rafael had never told his wife about the full nature of his friendship with their common friend. One could say that his handling of this situation was "very *macho*," which seemed to be an important feature of his primary identification. Yet he was not shy about being seen in a gay environment because he knew that his identity was ultimately similar to those of certain self-identified *gays* who lived double lives. In addition, he was clear in his interpretation that all this made sense and fit well in a Mexican context. In other words, the identities of masculine homosexuals had not pushed the boundaries so far that he could not continue to think of himself as just a regular man who happened to also be physically and emotionally attracted to men.

In the world of masculine men, there is in Mexico an increasing understanding that some masculine men are *normales* or *heterosexuales*, that some are *homosexuales* or *gays*, that some are *bisexuales*, and that they are all "men." There is also an awareness that some masculine men pretend to be *normales* for social reasons even when their main interest is in other men. This awareness is not new. As I mentioned before, a previous classification of men into *hombres* or *machos* on one hand, and *maricones* on the other, positioned some *hombres* as sexually attracted to men. Those men were the sexual partners of the *maricones*. The shift in interpretations is not, as a result, some new and widespread acknowledgment that some masculine men are attracted to men but rather the acknowledgment that those men are in fact different from the men who are exclusively interested in women.

Another central shift in interpretation is the awareness that masculine men who openly state an attraction to other masculine men do not automatically acquire an identity as *maricones,* at least not in terms of effeminacy. This shift is having a profound effect on social understandings of manhood and is forcing many Mexicans to resist arriving at the automatic conclusion that a man must be exclusively attracted sexually to women for the simple reason that he is masculine.

In the section that follows I present an example of how the relationship between masculinity and homosexuality is becoming visible at a social level that is broader than that illustrated by the examples that I presented here. My focus is on certain depictions of masculine homosexuals in the Mexican mass media.

La Vida en el Espejo

In 1999 Televisión Azteca, a national television network in Mexico, aired the *telenovela La Vida en el Espejo*.[5] This telenovela focused on contemporary Mexican men, their identities, and their issues, including homosexuality. The last topic played a prominent role because in the course of the program Mauricio, the eldest son in the family on which the telenovela centered, realized that he was attracted to men. Mauricio was depicted as a young, twenty-three-year-old masculine man—as smart, secure, and entrepreneurial a son as any upper-class Mexican couple could presumably wish to have. At the time of his realization of same-sex attraction he had a girlfriend, Irene, with whom he was involved in the type of relationship that typically leads to marriage.

The topic of Mauricio's sexual orientation was introduced in the following way: At first he showed no desire to have sex with Irene, who insisted that they have premarital sex. Mauricio responded to her by saying that he was conservative and he believed in waiting until marriage before having sex. She then began to imply that he was impotent, which was in itself an affront to his manhood. While this was happening, Jim, a visiting professor in Mauricio's university who had become Mauricio's friend, disclosed his homosexuality to Mauricio. A Mexican expatriate who taught at Stanford University, Jim had learned to accept his homosexuality while living in California. Referring to why he did not return to live in Mexico, Jim explained to Mauricio, "I have thought about returning several times, but I would not have the same peace, the same freedom."

> "Freedom? Why not?" asks Mauricio.
> "Well . . . here there is still a lot of discrimination against homosexuals," Jim responds.
> "What do you mean?" asks Mauricio in disbelief.
> "Homosexuals here still can't express themselves as openly as in other countries."
> "And you . . . ?" Mauricio begins.
> "Come on!" replies Jim. "Don't tell me you haven't figured it out. Well, I don't know, you are too, aren't you?"

At this point in the dialogue Mauricio reacted violently and was completely closed to Jim's suggestion, which was the first indication in the telenovela of Mauricio's latent homosexuality. Nonetheless, at the same time as he was rejecting such innuendo by Jim, Mauricio began to show signs of an internal struggle. He began noticing the bodies of young men during swim practice—men who looked at him with that special glance commonly recognized among Mexican men to be a sign of interest. Enough hints were given to suggest that Mauricio might not be that interested in women after all. However, at the same time that all this was happening, Mauricio resolved to ask his girlfriend to marry him, a decision that was presented as a desperate act designed to convince himself that he was not attracted to men. The proposal also provided a critique of what many masculine men in Mexico are assumed to do in order to cover up their same-sex attraction.

The charade did not last long. When Mauricio learned that Jim had decided to leave Mexico and return to Stanford, he ran out after him and encountered him as he was leaving for the airport. In a moment of high drama and intense passion, Mauricio embraced Jim and asked him to stay. This was the point at which the telenovela's audience, along with Mauricio, became fully aware of his dormant sexual attraction to men.

Jim stayed and ended up playing a didactic role by teaching Mauricio, and the telenovela's audience as well, what being a masculine gay man in a contemporary world is all about. In a conversation between the two, Mauricio complained about his new self-awareness. "I don't like what I am. I don't understand it. Not yet. . . . You grow up thinking that you'll live your whole life a certain way, then suddenly something happens and you've turned into something that you used to criticize."

In response, Jim offered Mauricio a lesson about what he should expect will happen as he acquires an identity as gay. This lesson culminates with a statement about masculinity and the implications of being *gay*—in a Mexican sense—for a man's ability to stand up and demand his rights:

> The irony is that you have to be a real man to declare yourself a homosexual. But you'll see that when you do it your fears slowly dissipate and eventually everything is in the right place. You will be in the place where you belong and those who really love you will also be there, in that precise place. . . . And, besides, there is a huge difference between being homosexual and being gay. Homosexuals, there are a lot of them. Some are even married and with children. But being gay means having a [different] attitude about life.

This last statement is consistent with the distinction made by men in my study who identified themselves as gay when they distinguished between being gay and being homosexual. In characterizing what being gay is, they commonly emphasized the fact that they would not marry women or have children—signs of leading a double life. At the same time, however, they did not view their own double lives as necessarily contradicting their sense of being *gay* and not *homosexual*.

In the telenovela, as a result of his interactions with Jim and his conscious decision to adopt a gay lifestyle, Mauricio decided to leave the family home, rent an apartment, and disclose his new identity to his father. In a particularly long scene taking more than twenty minutes of the one-hour episode, Mauricio and his father engaged in a painful dialogue that eventually led to Mauricio's disclosure. In their conversation Mauricio slowly hinted that there was something difficult that he had to say. With deep concern his father inquired what his son wants to tell him, thereby demonstrating his interest in helping Mauricio. Mauricio finally revealed that he was *homosexual*. His father responded by yelling, "No, I do not have sons who are *maricones*. I do not have sons who are abnormal."

His father's first impulse was to invoke the image of the effeminate *maricón*. For the rest of the scene Mauricio tried to explain to his father that his decision was based not on any desire to be less of a man but on his realization that he was exclusively attracted to men in sexual ways. In formulating his explanation, however, the writers used several stereotypes about the kinds of boyhood activities that homosexuals are assumed to detest, at the same time making it clear that Mauricio was not an effeminate boy. "Look, I never wanted to wear dance slippers and to be taken to ballet [class], Dad, but I hated having to go to boxing matches and to the soccer stadium with my pals." Mauricio's monologue also included statements about his continuing to be normal despite his homosexuality, his need to take off the mask that he was wearing, and his realization that he had fallen in love with Jim. By the end of this episode the audience witnessed this masculine young man declare his love for another equally masculine man.

Following a number of twists and turns in the story, everyone in Mauricio's immediate family ended up accepting him as a gay man. In the telenovela's final scene the father made a toast to his family, reunited to celebrate his birthday. As he acknowledged his children, he expressed gratitude for their bringing three wonderful *parejas* (partners) to the family. The camera panned around the long table and Jim was sitting next to Mauricio with his arm wrapped around his back. The solution to Mauricio's homosexuality, in the eyes of the writers of this telenovela, was that a son's homosexuality should be accepted as a lifestyle option and that the son should follow the path expected of any child: To find a life partner with whom one may form a couple and to bring this partner into the extended family life so strongly valued in Mexico. Implicit in this message is another that says to gay men that they can be accepted if they at least conform to family expectations, including expectations about their masculinity.

The treatment of contemporary male homosexuality in this telenovela reflects both how many changes have occurred in Mexico regarding attitudes about masculine male homosexuality and the limitations that still exist in representations of homosexuality in media such as television, which reaches such a large national audience.[6] Those who watched this telenovela were exposed to a view of contemporary homosexuality that had never been presented with such detail on Mexican television. Never before on a popular Mexican television show had viewers been privy to this kind of questioning of negative attitudes and discrimination against homosexuals or comparable messages about the validity of a masculine gay lifestyle. In addition, very strong messages about the validity of romance and attraction between two men were sent to the audience, with a particular emphasis on the role that family, and especially parents and siblings, have in making the lives of gay men better.

Despite these positive representations, the writers were very restrained about portraying any images that suggested actual sexual acts between men, the existence of an organized gay community in Mexico City—where the telenovela is set—or many expressions of gay culture. Absent also was any sense of diversity within gay identities or suggestions that acceptance should be extended to men who display public behavior that others might perceive as effeminate. Mauricio and Jim were presented throughout the entire telenovela as a couple living in a completely heterosexual world, devoid of any gay friends, and never attending gay bars or clubs. When they went out dancing or for drinks, they were always shown in hip heterosexual clubs, where they could demonstrate a bare minimum of affection toward each other. The most daring scenes regarding affection between them showed them standing on the street about to subversively kiss each other on the lips, disappearing behind a wall to embrace, or walking away from the camera while holding hands. These were the telenovela's attempts to show that they indeed loved each other without making any reference to the nature of their sexual acts and roles.

Both characters were, as a result, explicitly desexualized, and many in the audience were no doubt left wondering who did what to whom sexually. The message seemed to be that, in the context of this interaction between two masculine gay men, complete equality prevailed and that no questions about roles needed to be raised. Nothing remotely questioning their masculinity or manhood was presented. These men did everything to avoid showing the rest of the world that they indeed had sexual lives and that such lives involve acts such as anal penetration or oral sex where, in the eyes of society, one or both of the partners could be regarded as taking a more "feminine" role. Instead of sex, the telenovela emphasized love and stability, masculinity and equality, and participation in family life.

Conclusion

In this essay I have begun to present a picture of a social phenomenon that is not yet fully understood. My analysis raises certain questions about the roles of masculinity and open male homosexuality in the context of larger transformations of male identities in Mexico. The increasing social visibility of masculine men who declare themselves to be exclusively *homosexual* or *gay* is likely to continue challenging Mexicans' association of male homosexuality with effeminacy. In reacting to this visibility heterosexuals will probably create new boundaries between them and homosexuals, effectively delimiting the social space granted by society to homosexuals for the enactment of their sexual identities.

As some of my examples here have illustrated, research about masculinity in places such as Mexico would greatly benefit from asking heterosexuals about homosexuality, as well as from asking homosexuals about heterosexuality. Such a crossover approach would likely yield fascinating data—data that could help fully elucidate how the range of male identities is being redefined as new ideas about masculinity, normality, heterosexuality, and homosexuality in Mexico take shape.

Notes

1. Throughout the chapter I italicize all Spanish words. In the case of the word *gay*, it is the Spanish version of the English word. *Gay*, along with the words *homosexual* and *lesbiana*, have been adopted by many in Mexico to refer to homosexual men and women.

2. For an account of the types of cultural changes that are leading to new ideas about men and masculinity in Mexico see Gutmann 1996.

3. This study consisted of participant observation in a variety of settings and social networks; sixty-four semistructured, individual interviews with men and women, ages eighteen to fifty-three, of different sexual orientations, and of lower-middle-class to upper-middle-class status; and three discussion groups conducted in a local public clinic. The study investigated local constructions of sexual identities, prevalent forms of sexual socialization, individuals' perceptions about sex and sexual communication, and the influence of locally accepted ideas and values about sexuality on individual decisions about HIV prevention and safe sex.

4. All interviews were conducted in Spanish. The excerpts presented here were translated by me into English. As much as possible, I was careful to maintain the original tone and intention of the statements.

5. The *telenovela* is the Mexican version of the soap opera. This genre is extremely popular in Mexico and Latin America and differs from its U.S. counterpart in two ways. First, the telenovelas are shorter, lasting anywhere from six to twelve months. Second, the more popular telenovelas are shown during prime time as opposed to exclusively in the late morning or early afternoon, as is customary in the United States.

6. This telenovela had average national ratings of thirteen points, which represents a considerable segment of the Mexican television audience. These ratings were about half of what the most popular telenovelas had around the same time.

References

Carrier, Joseph M. 1972. "Urban Mexican Male Encounters: An Analysis of Participants and Coping Strategies." Ph.D. diss. University of California, Irvine.

———.1995. *De Los Otros: Intimacy and Homosexuality among Mexican Men*. New York: Columbia University Press.

Carrillo, Héctor. 1995. "Lifting the Veil of Silence: Sexuality, Social Influence, and the Practice of AIDS Prevention in Modern Mexico." Ph.D. diss., University of California, Berkeley.

———. 1999. "Cultural Change, Hybridity, and Male Homosexuality in Mexico." *Culture, Health, and Sexuality* 1, no. 3:223–38.

———. 2002. *The Night Is Young: Sexuality in Mexico in the Time of AIDS*. Chicago: University of Chicago Press.

Díaz, Rafael M. 1998. *Latino Gay Men and HIV*. New York: Routledge.

García Canclini, Néstor. 1995. *Hybrid Cultures: Strategies for Entering and Leaving Modernity*. Minneapolis: University of Minnesota Press.

Gutmann, Matthew C. 1996. *The Meanings of Macho: Being a Man in Mexico City*. Berkeley: University of California Press.

Paz, Octavio. 1985. Reprint. *The Labyrinth of Solitude: Life and Thought in Mexico*. Trans. Lysander Kemp. New York: Penguin. Original edition, New York: Grove Press, 1961.

Prieur, Annick. 1998. *Mema's House, Mexico City: On Transvestites, Queens, and Machos.* Chicago: University of Chicago Press.

Taylor, Clark L. 1978. "El Ambiente: Male Homosexual Social Life in Mexico City." Ph.D. diss., University of California, Berkeley.

———. 1986. "Mexican Male Interaction in Public Context." In *The Many Faces of Homosexuality,* ed. Evelyn Blackwood, 117–36. New York: Harrington Park Press.

DONNA J. GUY

Rape and the Politics of Masculine Silence in Argentina

■ ■ ■ ■

If historians had to rely solely on police statistics to measure the incidence of sexual crimes in late-nineteenth- and early-twentieth-century Argentina, they would come to the conclusion that the capital city of Buenos Aires was an extremely safe place for young boys, girls, and women. The number of arrests made yearly for the several categories of sexual violence was small. In 1882, for example, there were 2 cases of rape, out of 1,273 arrests for major crimes, and the following year there was 1 case of sodomy out of 1,105 arrests.[1] During some years no one would be arrested in one or more categories. A 1906 census of all Argentine jails revealed that in Buenos Aires city twelve men were imprisoned for rape, yet thirty-five men were imprisoned for the same crime in the province of Buenos Aires. Only one man in the national capital had been imprisoned for deflowering (seduction of a virgin) and two for sodomizing a child.[2] At the same time thousands of people were arrested yearly for misdemeanor crimes, principally disorderly and often violent behavior.

Continued European immigration prompted the growth of the city, as well as an increase in the number of reported crimes, yet the number of sex offenses remained almost nonexistent. Between 1902 and 1911 no cases of bigamy, corruption of minors, deflowering, rape, or attempted rape were taken to court.[3] Between 1919 and 1923 police did not bother to mention any of these categories in their statistics, yet they mentioned that there had been 62 infanticides and 521 cases of abortion. Although women were being arrested for sex-related cases, the police were cooperating in silencing rape by refusing to report its existence.[4]

Why were women committing crimes against unborn children when there were no honor crimes to cover up? This was precisely the period when the Buenos Aires Defenders of Minors were complaining that placing minor girls into foster care usually resulted in their rape by foster fathers or brothers.[5] Clearly the codes and laws designed to punish rape did not protect women from sexual dangers. Instead they forced women into silence along with the men.

The scarcely reported rape crimes contrasted the vigorous apprehension of males accused of other infractions. As Julia Kirk Blackwelder and Lyman Johnson (1982) demonstrated in their study of male crime in Buenos Aires between 1885 and 1914, the number of arrests for public drunkenness declined from a high of 46,679 in 1887 to a low of 12,558 in 1903, whereas arrests for violent disturbances increased from a low of 12,779 in 1894 to a high of 35,295, and crimes against property soared. These authors were unconcerned with sexual crimes, and based on the frequency of arrests, such crimes would have constituted an insignificant concern.[6]

Does the infrequency of reported rape cases indicate an absence of such crimes or a general unwillingness to report such incidents? Do those few crimes reported and taken to trial represent typical incidents of rape, or are they indicative of other factors? Perhaps even more important, what was the purpose and intent of antirape laws in Argentina, and why were there no anti-incest laws?

I argue that laws in Buenos Aires were designed *not* to protect women from sexual aggression. Indeed, they were enacted to keep sexual crimes from being reported, discussed, and adjudicated, and they promoted a world of masculine silences where patriarchal men ensured that their sexual secrets would not be made public. These laws prevented married women from reporting crimes without their husbands' permission and punished men for admitting their criminality in public. Therefore masculine silences also imposed female silences.

In this sense the silences modify Michel Foucault's ideas that there has been an increasingly vocal discourse about sexuality. At the same time physicians and moral reformers talked more about sexuality, legal structures, rooted in some post-Absolutist nation-states, particularly those with a dominant Catholic population (including Argentina), began to separate morality from civil society. This meant that civil authorities preferred to ignore sexual acts defined as criminal by religious laws. Instead these activities became matters of conscience to be dealt with only by religious authorities. What began as an absolutist state effort to separate itself from religious authority shaped the modern nation-state's efforts to impose fewer legal restrictions on male sexual activity and lessened penalties for women who had unwanted pregnancies. New penal codes decriminalized many sex acts and specifically protected men and patriarchy as long as public silence was maintained. Thus the statistics mentioned above are indications of how successful the politics of silence in Buenos Aires had become by the late nineteenth century, a reality that continued after 1900, and continues to this day.[7]

Honor Concepts

Rape and silence, concepts rooted in masculine ideals, are historical and thus subject to change over time. In Argentina laws designed to keep sexual crimes from being denounced were late-nineteenth-century phenomena, but they were based on modernized colonial visions of honor. Most studies of masculine honor refer to the publications of Julian Pitt-Rivers. His classic works on the concept of honor in Mediterranean societies ascribed the role of maintaining family honor to the male head of the nuclear family, whereas the cause of shame, and hence the removal of honor, was attributed to the inappropriate sexual behavior of female family members. As he put it in his essay "The Moral Foundations of the Family": "These concepts display the moral division of labour, but they are aspects of honour manifested by either sex rather than opposed concepts of honour, for they are united in the family honour of which they are the external facets. As such they imply each other in the sense that female honour un-defended can be taken not to exist while in its absence male honour cannot be transmitted."[8] Thus for Pitt-Rivers the locus of sexual honor resided within the nuclear family, and its burden was placed on the female body.

At the same time that men were supposed to guard the honor of their family, they had other privileges that potentially contradicted this impor-tant responsibility. Men had the right to pursue the conquest of all women, even if this meant dishonoring both the women and their male protectors. Honor for men could mean shame and dishonor for women. Honor, however, could be challenged if the wrong women were accosted sexually. Pitt-Rivers noted that even the famous mythical character of Don Juan maintained his honor despite deceiving many women. He accomplished this because he engaged neither in adultery nor had sex with any woman who had been claimed by another.[9] What maintained Don Juan's honor, however, shamed the women deceived by him, as well as the honor of their male guardians. Thus, this renowned anthropologist believed that each act of emotion and sexuality carried within itself a complex pattern of political, ethical, social, religious, and economic implications for the family, many of which were often contradictory and antagonistic.[10] But not all men were as careful as Don Juan, and their actions are also part of the historical record. These actions include vengeance against families or individuals through the rape of their women.[11]

Therefore, as useful as Pitt-Rivers's anthropological perspective has been to studying how honor systems affect social attitudes toward rape in Latin America, honor concepts are often considered enduring, ahistori-cal principles unaffected by change. Equally important, Pitt-Rivers never contemplated the actions of men who dishonored their own family and themselves through incest or pederasty. But all modern societies either made these distinctions through laws or refused to acknowledge them in civil law.

From the independence period onward, some Latin American coun-tries criminalized incest, whereas others did not; few criminalized sod-omy, but most retained laws against pederasty (called sodomy, it occurred when an older man had sex with a minor); a few passed laws to redefine rape, and others made efforts to introduce concepts of forensic medical proof, rather than family statements, to prove the incidence of rape and

"We're already thinking about revenge." Poster produced by Tulipan, an Argentine manufacturer of condoms, after Argentina lost to Brazil in the World Cup. Photograph by Donna Guy.

thereby remove the crime from the honor arena. Some continued to frame rape cases in an explicit honor context. Many, like Argentina, criminalized the sexual violation of boys as well as girls.

Brazil serves as an interesting contrast to its neighbor to the south. The last country in South America to end slavery, Brazil had a large Afro-Brazilian population and a legacy of rural plantations. Within the cities governments struggled to promote new European visions of society, ones that redefined honor concepts that had had little relevance during slavery. One consequence was a system of family honor that led to hundreds of deflowering cases adjudicated in Rio de Janeiro courts every year. According to Sueann Caulfield, "the defense of sexual honor [became] a central component of their mission to 'civilize' the recently proclaimed Republic [1889–1930]."[12] By 1940, however, the passage of new Brazilian codes led to the "disappearance" of these honor crimes because the negotiation of sexual honor was no longer considered a measurement of modernity. The crimes were still being committed, but, as in Argentina it became much harder to report them. Why did Brazil persist in encouraging the prosecution of rape and deflowering as honor crimes whereas Argentina ended this custom so quickly? The answers are as complex as the questions and are rooted in a combination of local conditions and international influences.

Historicizing Rape and Honor in Argentina

It might seem strange to analyze turn-of-the-century Argentine rape cases by quoting a specialist in contemporary Mediterranean anthropology, but Julian Pitt-Rivers has been cited by a number of Latin American historians in studies of rape and sexual deception and deflowering of virgins ranging from colonial Argentina to early-twentieth-century Mexico. They have generally used him to explain not only the patterns of honor expressed in sexual crimes but also how men, often from the lower classes, defended their honor in a courtroom. This recourse was often shunned by upper-class men because they could sort out their private affairs without discussing them in public.[13]

The recent works of several Latin American historians provide the framework for this paper. Specialists in colonial Latin American history, and eighteenth- and nineteenth-century Europe make it possible to historicize rape and the decriminalization of certain sex crimes that led to masculine silences. Ann Twinam's extensive research on honor in colonial Latin America provides a promising background for late-nineteenth-century historical research in Argentina because she looks at honor as a social process negotiated in *public*, not in private by male patriarchs. Thus her work suggests that the notion of silence and keeping family secrets from being uncovered dates back to the colonial period, although it changed over time, and *the interpretation of honor was not absolute* but varied from region to region. Nevertheless, Twinam perceived of honor as an asset that could only be identified and negotiated in the public sphere.

Studying illegitimacy and the renegotiation of class and race, Twinam pointed out cogently in *Public Lives, Private Secrets* that "honor was located in the public sphere, where an individual's reputation was malleable and ultimately defined by other peers."[14] There was no difference between public and private honor, and only the public world could negotiate these notions. Laws such as the right to seek specific public statements that in effect rewrote family histories (documents called *gracias al sacar*) made it possible to legitimate parents, whiten one's heritage, and improve one's public honor.

Although Twinam included Buenos Aires in her study of colonial cities, Susan Socolow specifically studied rape in eighteenth-century colonial Buenos Aires. She noted that women were most often attacked by men whom they knew, not by strangers. Furthermore their rape served as a form of revenge against the woman's family, and it was the family, rather than the woman, who took the successful case to court. "When married women were the victims of violent sexual crimes, the legal complaints were always initiated by their husbands."[15] If women were unable to get a male family member to defend them, they couldn't take their case to court. Unmarried women could accuse a man in court, but they had to defend their own honesty at the same time. This reality provided the foundation of patriarchally forced silences implemented by Buenos Aires police after 1850.

After the colonial period the link between rape and honor persisted in Argentina, but gradually discussions regarding honor occurred less frequently in rape cases, unlike in the eighteenth century. The Argentine courts remained the last resort for honor crimes, but the terms of the negotiations changed during the course of the nineteenth century.[16] Argentina created new norms for sexuality and sex crimes as part of nineteenth-century nationalism and nation building in Argentina, ones that gradually chose silence over the negotiation of honor.

Rape and Argentine Law

During the nineteenth century Argentina struggled to create a modern nation-state and only began to produce codes of laws in the latter half of the century. The criminal code was not in force until 1886, although the civil codes had been implemented since 1871. The influence of the judicial system on the prospects of securing a legal judgment against a rapist has rarely been analyzed in Latin American rape cases.[17]

The Argentine penal system developed in the late nineteenth century as part of a general effort to codify new laws suitable for a modern nation-state. Between 1810 and 1865 various Spanish penal codes were used to define criminal law. Several years after the 1853 Constitution was ratified, specialists were appointed to draw up commercial, civil, penal, mining, and other codes. Like other Latin American countries, Argentina relied on code law, often drawn from Napoleonic, Spanish, Bavarian, and other models. It also drew on existing Argentine customs.

Under code law no action was considered criminal unless it was cited in the law. Hence jurists were quite specific about what they wanted to criminalize and what remained beyond the law, but they also recognized that there were deeds that occurred in private, ones that became crimes only when they were revealed. These *crimes were not supposed to be uncovered by public authorities*, thereby frustrating the negotiation of honor. Indeed, no crimes of rape could be lodged against a person on the basis of discoveries made by the police or any public official unless someone had been murdered as part of the event. Instead they had to be denounced by a private citizen, and once the court procedures began, they could not be canceled.[18]

Furthermore, in Argentina aspects of rape could be dealt with by other types of law, particularly the 1869 Civil Code, in force after 1871. A few examples will demonstrate how this feature could affect perceptions of male behavior. The civil code declared that incestuous marriages were not recognized by law. An incestuous relationship was not a criminal act, but neither was it legitimated by marriage.[19] Although incest was condemned by the Catholic Church, as well as by popular sentiment, it was not criminalized. Yet violent rape of a relative, in the 1886 penal code, particularly if the victim was under fourteen, could lead to a longer jail sentence.[20] This same act, in a civil court, resulted in the loss of patriarchal privileges *(patria potestad)* over the child. Even in the criminal court, jail terms effectively removed custodial privileges. Furthermore, under the same laws all children born of incestuous relationships were automatically barred from inheritance rights by the civil code.[21] So incest was not a crime, but once it became public, it was penalized in other ways.

The Argentine Penal Code was designed by Carlos Tejedor in the 1860s, but it was not adopted immediately by the national government. Instead it was adapted and passed by various provinces. This meant that different traditions regarding honor crimes were inscribed in law. Finally in December 1886 a modified version of the Tejedor Code was adopted by the national government. For the first time since 1810 there was a unified body of criminal law.[22]

Significantly, all forms of rape were incorporated into a section entitled *Delitos contra la honestidad* (Crimes against honor). These crimes included adultery, rape, crimes of seduction, corruption, *ultraje al pudor* (acts that offend modesty) and *rapto* (a form of rape that involved kidnapping). Rather than breaking down categories of sex crimes, these terms tended to look at the event from the point of view of degree of violence, the sexual purity of the victim, age, and gender. If the victim was married or under the age of twelve, the punishment was six to ten years in the penitentiary. If a minor girl or boy died, hard labor for ten to fifteen years was the price. If the victim was an honorable woman (that is, not married but chaste and above twelve), the convicted was sentenced to the penitentiary for three to six years. However, if the victim was a prostitute, the sentence was only one to six months in jail. The same punishments were specifically applied to sodomy of minors.[23]

Although women of all ages could lodge charges of sexual violence, mothers could not lodge formal protests of rape of their children unless the father did not reside in the household. If children were orphans, only then could a public official, such as the *Defensor de Menores* (Defender of minors), go to court for the victim. Most cases that had any chance of conviction without a confession involved child victims under age fourteen, which eventually became the designated age instead of colonial use of age twelve. Then other factors determined what the crime would be called. For example, cases of *violación* by law only had to demonstrate violence, but judges demanded evidence of both complete penetration and violence for convictions. By the nineteenth century this information was obtained through the examination of forensic physicians rather than midwives.

Prior to 1886 it had been possible to get a conviction with only a limited amount of forensic proof, but after that date conviction was unlikely without a confession or clear evidence of penetration and violence.[24] The punishments, as mentioned before, depended on who was raped rather than the act itself. Under these circumstances who could or would want to go to court? Some of these criteria were changed in 1921, and this marks yet another way to historicize rape. Nevertheless, for purposes of explaining why most late-nineteenth- and early-twentieth-century cases never went to court, it becomes clear that prostitutes had little or no chance of convicting a rapist. Married women could not charge a husband with rape because of a colonial concept that stated that there was a sexual marital debt that women owed their husbands, and no conditions were placed on how it was paid off as long as vaginal sex occurred.[25] The bodies of young girls and boys had to provide evidence of complete penetration, an act difficult to accomplish in very young children. And mothers alone could not lodge complaints against husbands or male family members who raped their daughters.

Rape and Nationalism

The relationships connecting sex crimes, silence, and nationalism are complicated. George Mosse's pioneering *Nationalism and Sexuality: Middle-Class Morality and Sexual Norms in Modern Europe* offers clues about how the relationship between rape and masculine honor was historicized in the nineteenth century. He argued that religion, sexuality, and the development of new forms of morality were significant lenses through which to view this process. Catholics thought about sexuality differently from Protestants, and these differences were often essentialized:

> The eighteenth-century Protestant revival affected these two countries [Germany and England] directly, leaving a unique impact on the tenor of life that other regions did not share; of course, the substance of bourgeois morals and sexuality . . . spread throughout Europe. The *difference in tone* between Protestant and Catholic nations was well reflected in the love-hate relationship of so many Germans and Englishmen with the so-called Catholic South. When German writers like Thomas Mann equated the South with sin and immorality, or English popular literature swarmed with "dagos" and "Portuguese" villains, the North-South contrast was merely one more device to shore up respectability.[26]

Although Mosse emphasized "difference in tone," I would argue that it was a difference in the increased legal separation between civil society and morality. The Catholic Church had its list of venal and mortal sins, and few dared flaunt these sins in public. Before the nineteenth century the Inquisition in Spain and the criminal and civil courts in the colonies regulated the investigation of such crimes. The punishments were draconian, and some for sodomy and bestiality included death. By the eighteenth century, however, fewer sexual sins came to the courts' attention. Instead, the confessional rather than the courtroom increasingly became the place to admit sins and be forgiven.

Even anticlerical groups did not challenge most definitions of morality, but the emerging nation-state in many Catholic countries was more interested in the regulation of heterosexual marriage than immorality. Thus the so-called difference found in Catholic France and in the Catholic-dominated German states meant experimenting with the decriminalization of male sex crimes, particularly consensual sodomy, and attenuating the punishment of men for rape and incest and for women accused of infanticide. Even though there were substantial Protestant populations in these countries, the rise of Napoleon and his European conquests disseminated Napoleonic codes that decriminalized homosexuality and reduced the severity of punishment for many other sex crimes all over Europe, and eventually Latin American nations also adopted the codes.

Isabel Hull has shown how eighteenth-century Bavarian jurists, as well as monarchs such as Frederick the Great, began to justify decriminalizing a number of sex-crime laws.[27] The end result was an absolutist separation of morality and law and a decriminalization of most consensual sexual acts except incest (included over the objections of its principal architect) in the Bavarian penal code enacted in 1813 under the guidance of Anselm Feuerbach. This code represented a major change that mirrored both absolutist desires and Napoleonic reforms. It was eventually replaced, but rather than British common law that maintained sex crimes, the Bavarian code became an ideological backdrop for the Argentine penal code, although the rape clauses came from Spanish law.[28]

Argentina followed the path of Catholic Europe by decriminalizing certain sex acts by the eighteenth century. Cristian Berco has examined how sodomy among consenting males in Argentina became an invisible crime. He noted that only one case of sodomy has thus far been found in late-eighteenth-century Río de la Plata, and that involved a child. In Paraguay Jerry Cooney and Thomas Whigham have identified a series of eighteenth-century cases dealing with bestiality in rural areas, as opposed to cases of male-to-male sex, which were few.[29] The decriminalization of sodomy began before the creation of the new nation after 1810, and the adoption of French-influenced Spanish codes prior to the passage of the first national penal code presaged the further decriminalization of other sex acts among adults. Thus nationalism in Argentina reinforced earlier colonial attitudes.

Not only did nationalism construct a political entity, but it also ordered the society within. As Mosse put it:

> Nationalism and respectability assigned everyone his place in life, man and woman, normal and abnormal, native and foreigner; any confusion between these categories threatened chaos and loss of control. . . . Alongside the idealization of masculinity as the foundation of the nation and society, woman . . . was at the same time idealized as the guardian of morality, and of public and private order. . . . Woman was not confined to the family, yet the roles assigned to her were conceived of as passive rather than active. She was to be a guardian, protector, and mother.[30]

To be respectable in late-nineteenth-century Argentina meant that both men and women, in public, accepted the public norms of that society. The private possibilities, however, were quite different, and occasionally they became public. In Argentina the legal system and the police privatized many types of family and sexual violence in a way that made it difficult to report sex crimes. For example, usually only immigrant women working as maids were charged with infanticide, mostly for killing their children in a "public place"—the homes of their employers. Nevertheless, the consequences were much milder than during colonial times and were attenuated by many factors.[31] At the same time, Argentine women of all classes rarely had their honor challenged in court in infanticide cases.

Case Studies of Rape in Buenos Aires

How did new national laws attenuate the crime of rape, and how did it become detached from honor crimes? The only way to answer these questions is to delve into the few rape cases that ended up in criminal courts. In the past few years I have uncovered in Buenos Aires and other Argentine cities a few court cases that offer some rare glimpses into the world of personal sexual violence. The cases I reviewed do not constitute all those taken to trial. Indeed, one group of Buenos Aires criminal records was only available for the letters *A* through *E*. In regional archives I also sampled some of the few files that were made available. What struck me was neither the quantity nor the quality of the documents but rather the high incidence of rape cases involving incest or sodomy of young boys. The selection presented offers a glimpse into the complex world of rape and honor. We begin with an incest case.

In February 1888 Manuel Donato, a forty-two-year-old Spanish postmaster, was brought before the Criminal Court of Buenos Aires. Asked whether he knew that his daughter had given birth three years earlier, and whether he had buried the child in the backyard, he responded resolutely that he knew nothing about it, nor did he know a midwife by the name of Adelaida. The court record, as in so many of these cases, identified the man with the use of the honorific *don,* despite the fact that he was an immigrant worker. Despite the heinous acts he was accused of, for the courts of Buenos Aires all who entered, including Manuel, had honor, no matter what the crime.[32] Manuel was eventually accused of rape and abortion.

That same day his daughter Manuela was interrogated. The twenty-one-year-old single woman claimed that three and one-half years earlier her father had raped her when he found her alone in the house and then threatened to kill her if she told anyone about it. He then forced her to submit four more times. When she found out she was pregnant, he told her he would take her to Adelaida Méndez, a midwife who eventually inserted a surgical probe several times until Manuela aborted a seven-month baby, born alive according to Manuela. At that moment her father, who had been assisting the midwife, took the crying infant and buried it. Both Manuel and Adelaida denied any knowledge of the abortion, although Manuel subsequently admitted that he had known about the birth, that his recently departed wife had attended her daughter, and that the fetus was only about three months old, too young to have survived.

This story became public because Manuela had recently heard her sister screaming while her father attempted to rape her. Manuela's screams prevented the consummation of the act, but she was so angry she wrote a garbled letter to the chief of police denouncing her father and had her brother mail the letter. Pedro, a seventeen-year-old, confirmed the story. Subsequently the father again denied the story but admitted having broken his son's arm with a stick after Pedro had lost some money.[33]

Both Manuela and Adelaida were kept in prison awaiting the final sentencing. Manuela's twelve-year-old sister, María, corroborated the story of how her father had tried to rape her. The police doctor confirmed that the skeleton exhumed was that of a seven-month-old fetus, further confirming what Manuela had claimed. Nevertheless, in less than a week Adelaida was released from the women's jail, and in August the judge also released the father. Their silences made it impossible for Manuel's children to protect themselves against their father. All minors, they had to submit to his authority because of the lack of corroboration both by Manuel and Adelaida, both of whom would have incriminated themselves by their evidence. Part of the justification for dismissing the case was related to the fact that the crime of infanticide and abortion had taken place before the 1886 law was enacted, but the reality was that without public admission of his crime, Manuel's silence weighed in more heavily than his children's accusations.

In another rape case Francisca Leduc was not raped by a relative, but she had few chances of getting the rapist convicted because of her age and where the crime occurred. On May 11, 1890, Juana Mayor, a thirty-four-year-old German woman went to the police to lodge a complaint against Juan Bautista Figari, Juan Mülders, and Julieta Tany de Mülders, accusing them all in a conspiracy to rape sixteen-year-old Francisca Leduc. Francisca, a French girl, had arrived in Buenos Aires to join her sister, Josefa. Their parents were living in the province of Buenos Aires, but city life seemed to compel these young girls to stay in Buenos Aires city. Josefa tried to help her sister and had enlisted the aid of Juana, but Francisca had no luck with jobs because she spoke little Spanish. After being unsuccessful as a governess, Francisca put an ad in the French newspaper *Courrier de la Plata,* looking for a job as a servant.

On May 4 a man came to the door saying he needed a servant for his wife and niece. Juana wanted to send the girl the following day, but while she was out of the house, the man returned with a young woman and talked to Juana's son. He then accompanied Francisca to her new place of employment. One week later Francisca returned and told Juana that she arrived at the house and was given a variety of assignments, including washing clothing and going to the market. On the ninth of May, however, Madame Julieta, the wife, told her to remove some dirty water from the room closest to the street. As soon as she entered Madame Julieta insisted Francisca have sexual relations with Juan Bautista Figari. When she refused and said she was not a prostitute, Madame Julieta removed Francisca's clothes, and while Julieta held her pinned down by the arms, Figari raped her. The following evening the man who first came to the house left her near Juana's house and told her not to say anything.

According to a man present in the house the day before, the house was a bordello, and a man had approached Julieta and offered to pay fifty pesos to be with Francisca, but the young servant had refused. On May 12 Julieta and Juan Mülders were arrested. The following day Juan Figari told his story. He claimed Julieta said she had a license to operate a bordello. He had frequented the establishment several times and had seen Francisca working in the kitchen. In contrast to Francisca's story, Juan claimed that she sat down on a sofa with him and allowed him to kiss and caress her. Then he took her to a room and tried to entice her to have sex by arousing her passion, but when he finally had sex with her, she started to exclaim several times, "Mon Dieu! Mon Dieu!" Afterward Julieta let go of the girl (he admitted there was duress), and Francisca seemed willing to hug him. Then she went to the kitchen, and Julieta charged Juan 50 pesos. Juan Figari admitted that Francisca was *una mujer buena* (a decent woman), that is, a virgin. After this was all over, Juan had dinner there and returned to his home while Julieta tried to force Francisca to get drunk on wine.

To figure out what happened, the judge in the case went to the house where the incident occurred to see if it was a house of prostitution. He decided it was an unlicensed bordello because it had pornographic pictures (at least according to him). The police doctor examined Francisca and declared that she had been deflowered. On September 24 the accused, Juan Batista Figari, asked the judge to order another hearing to prove his contention that Francisca had hugged and kissed him. Less than a week later Figari was released from jail, and the money he had to put down for deposit (to pay for his incarceration) was returned to him. In contrast, the

Mülders were fined $2000 and had their property seized by the courts and auctioned off.[34]

Francisca was over the age of fourteen and thus was considered adult enough to know right from wrong. She also got work in the wrong type of business, and even though she claimed ignorance of what went on, the judge sided with Figari, who admitted having sex with her but argued that anyone working in a bordello should be considered a prostitute, even a virgin. Although the penal code provided for the rape of a prostitute, Figari left the jail as a free man, even though he admitted his guilt!

In contrast, the next case demonstrated how dangerous it was for a man to admit a sex crime not involving a prostitute. In July 1909 Buenos Aires police began to investigate Pedro Berruti. They had heard from others that the fifty-year-old Italian immigrant practiced "all kinds of obscenities with his two daughters María, 13 and Enriqueta, age 10." When the police began to talk to Enriqueta, the father began to swear and commented, "since I am the head of the household, I have the right to do what ever I want to." When Enriqueta was finally able to talk to the police, she claimed that the father had tried to rape her the night before, and he would probably do it again. Furthermore, he had been raping her for some time.[35]

Pedro made the mistake of openly admitting having forced sexual relations with his daughter María because "his fellow countrymen (from Italy) believed that it was commonplace to have relations with their daughter in order to avoid getting venereal diseases from prostitutes." As for his daughter Enriqueta, he argued that she had submitted without threats of violence and with her own consent.[36] During the course of the trial, María offered a poignant description of her father's actions, and Enriqueta contradicted her father's version by claiming that her father threatened her with a pistol as he raped her.[37]

Pedro presumed he was safe because there were no laws against incest. Instead he was incorrectly accused of the crime of *violación* (rape with violence) instead of *estupro* (deflowering). The father was sentenced to jail, mostly because he so arrogantly defended incest, a crime totally against Catholic beliefs, and he threatened violence; but that was not the end of the story. The girls were considered immoral for having given in to their father. María was rewarded for her testimony by being incarcerated in the Women's Jail. Enriqueta and her brother, Santiago, were sent off to the Sociedad de Beneficencia, a state-supported charity for women and children, as orphans because the father lost patriarchal custody over the minors.

The interaction of family honor and criminal law is a complicated issue in many areas of the world. This particular case dealt with a family whose private dilemmas had been made public by rumors spread by some anonymous person and by an unmarried daughter's desire to be freed of the sexual advances of her father. Pedro did not try to defend his honor but rather claimed that his paternal rights empowered him to do whatever he wanted. Although this might have been true behind closed doors, once his deeds became public, these rights and his honor were taken away as part of his punishment. As for the daughters, they were both spared from their father but were treated harshly by the courts.

Pedro thought it was honorable to have sex with his children, but the dishonor of a male relative could put great strains on the family. The next case involved rape by the brother-in-law of the victim who was charged with the crime of deflowering. The case began when his mother-in-law, Exequiela Santana, accused Salustiano Baach of raping her youngest daughter, Leonor, who was fourteen at the time. Exequiela was a cook with several children. The youngest remained at home while her mother went out to work. According to Leonor, Salustiano had been urging her to have sexual relations with him ever since he married her sister. Finally on July 28, 1906, he forcibly disrobed her and raped her three times. Although he had threatened her if she told anyone, she confided in her mother, who lodged the charges. Baach claimed he never touched her; but neighbors had heard the noise, and several had peeked through the keyhole and viewed what was happening. Furthermore, the medical report revealed that she had been recently deflowered. Thus Salustiano was sent to the penitentiary awaiting final sentence, and his money and material goods were embargoed by the courts, a common procedure.[38]

After realizing that her older daughter and grandchildren were left without any material support while Salustiano was in jail, Exequiela relented. She realized that there was no way to restore the honor of her youngest daughter and that as long as her son-in-law remained in jail, she would have to support her older daughter and grandchildren. Thus in

August 1906 Exequiela wrote the judge to let Salustiano out of jail and return his material possessions. The judge initially ignored this letter and sentenced Salustiano to prison, but after receiving a second letter written by the mother-in-law on April 25, 1907, the judge seemed to relent. He reversed his decision on a technicality.[39]

Incest clearly was considered unacceptable if it became public. But what about sex with a minor who is not a relative? We can look at another case, this time involving the rape of a young boy. In 1909 Enrique Carena was accused of having sodomized a four-year-old neighbor in a nearby garage. In this case the man admitted to the crime, but that did not resolve the issue completely. First of all, because the boy was so young, it had been difficult to proceed with the rape. Thus there was no evidence of complete penetration. On the basis of the confession, rather than the strength of forensic evidence, on August 4, 1910, Enrique was sentenced to jail for one year for attempted sodomy.[40]

Enrique never defended his honor. In fact he demonstrated embarrassment at his actions, for when publicly revealed, same-sex relations were never deemed appropriate, even if they were pursued in public and, among adults, bore no criminal stigma. Sex with a child, however, was completely unacceptable. This time the private action of a male had been revealed publicly. Of all the sodomy cases I saw, this was one of the few convictions, and I am convinced that here, too, there would have been no conviction if Enrique had not admitted his guilt.

What do these cases have in common? First of all, they represent a universe of crime that distorted the concept of family, as well as demonstrate how violence affected childhood and gender relations. Most of the men had transgressed both religious and public moral beliefs, but they were invulnerable to criminal punishment if they kept quiet. The only reason they ended up in court was because either the victims or the perpetrator told what happened, or outsiders observed the events, or it became news in the public domain. In many senses the nature of the crime was not intrinsic to what happened but rather how it was announced publicly.

The victims of these attacks won nothing by taking their cases to court, and the scarce number of cases implied that the victims, too, generally kept silent because of the consequences of speaking out. In the case of daughters they, too, could be sent to prison for having participated in the rape. If their fathers won, they had to return to a violent household and accept the reality that they could be blamed for publicly accusing their father, the retribution for which was determined by the father or relative, not the court. Young boys who were raped could be confronted by jokes accusing them of having been feminized. Francisca Leduc lost her virginity, her job, and saw her rapist freed without serving time. Exequiela Santana ended up supporting her older daughter after turning in her son-in-law and had to beg for his release. Only men who left clear evidence of their dishonor were convicted by the courts.

In many ways the leakage of these cases into the public domain emphasized the limited tolerance Argentine society had for any man who boasted of incest or sodomy. Although the rape of a presumed prostitute could be understood, the acknowledgment of child rape was clearly beyond the limits that patriarchal judges could tolerate. This meant that such public cases were not necessarily typical but rather the ones that leaked through the perimeters marked by silence. The politics of silence could protect men so long as they did not transgress these limits. In the last analysis antirape laws served to define the private from the public and the limits of tolerance men had for the misdeeds of other men. They demonstrated how the modern nation-state in Argentina constructed a complex code of patriarchy based on *both public and private rules*. Under these circumstances only remnants of the colonial honor system persisted. Modernization of patriarchy meant that honor was no longer fought principally over the public disciplining of female bodies.

Notes

This research was conducted with a Social and Behavioral Sciences Summer Research Grant from the University of Arizona. The author would like to thank Cristian Berco, Julia Clancy Smith, Sarah Deutsch, Dora Barrancos, Susan Socolow, and Matthew Gutmann for their comments on earlier drafts. I would also like to thank Ana María Presta for the translation.

1. Buenos Aires Police, *Memorias*, 1882, 255; 1883, 115.

2. República Argentina, Ministerio de Justicia é Instrucción Pública, *Resultados generales de primer censo carcelario de la República Argentina, 1906* (Buenos Aires: Talleres Gráficos de la Penitenciaria, 1906), 34. There were even fewer arrests for these crimes in the other provinces.

3. Buenos Aires Municipality, "Delitos por especies géneros y años perpetrados en el decenio, 1902–1911," *Anuario estadístico de la ciudad de Buenos Aires*, 1911, 381.

4. Buenos Aires Municipality, "Delitos cometidos contra las personas. Años 1919 a 1923," *Anuario estadístico de la ciudad de Buenos Aires*, 1923, 257.

5. Archivo General de la Nación Argentina [hereafter referred to as AGN], Fondo Ministerio de Justicia e Instrucción Pública, División Expedientes Generales, Letra D, 1908, Legajo 110, Letter of Defensores Figueroa, de Elizalde and Cabal, Feb. 25, 1908.

6. Julia Kirk Blackwelder and Lyman L. Johnson, "Changing Criminal Patterns in Buenos Aires, 1890–1914," *Journal of Latin American Studies* 14, no. 2 (1982): 359–79.

7. Michel Foucault, *The History of Sexuality*, 3 vols. (New York: Pantheon, 1978). For an analysis of the sexuality discourse in Argentina see Donna J. Guy, *Sex and Danger in Buenos Aires: Prostitution, Family, and Nation in Argentina* (Lincoln: University of Nebraska Press, 1991); and Jorge Salessi, *Médicos maleantes y maricas: Higiene, criminología y homosexualidad en la construcción de la nación argentina (Buenos Aires, 1871–1914)* (Rosario: B. Viterbo Editora, 1995).

8. Julian Pitt-Rivers, "The Moral Foundations of the Family," in *The Fate of Shechem or The Politics of Sex: Essays in the Anthropology of the Mediterranean* (Cambridge, U.K.: Cambridge University Press, 1977), 78.

9. Julian Pitt-Rivers, "The Anthropology of Honour," in *The Fate of Shechem or The Politics of Sex: Essays in the Anthropology of the Mediterranean* (Cambridge, U.K.: Cambridge University Press, 1977), 11.

10. Pitt-Rivers, "Moral Foundations," 93.

11. I thank Julia Clancy-Smith for her observations about clan-based vendettas in the Middle East.

12. Sueann Caulfield, *In Defense of Honor: Sexual Morality, Modernity, and Nation in Early-Twentieth-Century Brazil* (Durham, N.C.: Duke University Press, 2000), 3.

13. Sonya Lipsett-Rivera, "The Intersection of Rape and Marriage in Late Colonial and Early National Mexico. *Colonial Latin America History Review* 6, no. 4 (fall 1997): 559–90. Sueann Caulfield and Martha de Abreu Esteves, "Fifty Years of Virginity in Rio de Janeiro: Sexual Politics and Gender Roles in Juridical and Popular Discourse, 1890–1940," *Luso Brazilian Review* 30, no. 1 (summer 1993): 47–74. See also the essays in Lyman L. Johnson and Sonya Lipsett-Rivera, eds., *The Faces of Honor: Sex, Shame, and Violence in Colonial Latin America* (Albuquerque: University of New Mexico Press, 1998). Rebecca Earle relies on the historiography of revolutionary societies. Rebecca Earle, "Rape and the Anxious Republic: Revolutionary Colombia, 1810–1830," in *Hidden Histories of Gender and the State in Latin America*, ed. Elizabeth Dore and Maxine Molyneux, (Durham, N.C.: Duke University Press, 2000), 127–46.

14. Ann Twinam, *Public Lives, Private Secrets: Gender, Honor, Sexuality, and Illegitimacy in Colonial Spanish America* (Stanford, Calif.: Stanford University Press, 1999), 33.

15. Susan Socolow, "Women and Crime in Buenos Aires, 1757–1797," in *The Prob-*

lem of Order in Changing Societies: Essays on Crime and Policing in Argentina and Uruguay, 1750–1940, ed. Lyman L. Johnson (Albuquerque: University of New Mexico Press, 1990), 7. See also Osvaldo Berreneche, "'Esos torpes dezeos': Delitos y desviaciones sexuales en Buenos Aires, 1760–1810," *Estudios de historia colonial* (La Plata) (1993): 29–45.

16. See Jeffrey Merrill Shumway, "Between Revolution, Power, and Liberty: Continuity and Change in Family, Gender, and Society in Buenos Aires, Argentina, 1776-1870" (Ph.D. diss., University of Arizona, 1999).

17. Even Pitt-Rivers cautioned readers that the role of the legal system, among other factors, often affected the implementation of honor systems in important ways: "The conflict between honour and legality is a fundamental one which persists to this day. For to go to law for redress is to confess publicly that you have been wronged and the demonstration of your vulnerability places your honour in jeopardy. . . . Moreover, it gives your offender the chance to humiliate you further" (Pitt-Rivers, "Anthropology of Honour," 9). This comment was directed more toward the accused male than to the female victim.

18. Mario A. Oderigo, *Código Penal anotado*, 3d ed. (Buenos Aires: Ediciones Depalma, 1965), Título XI, Del Ejercicio de las Acciones, Artículo 71, p. 92. These complaints were called *instancias privadas*. I would like to thank Osvaldo Barreneche for lending me this book.

19. República Argentina, *Código civil de la República Argentina* (Buenos Aires: Pedro Igon y Cía, 1892), Sección Segunda, Título Primero, Capítulo Primero, Artículo 159, p. 32.

20. Ibid., Título II, Art. 122, pp. 165–66.

21. Donna J. Guy, "Parents Before the Tribunals: The Legal Construction of Patriarchy in Argentina," in *Hidden Histories of Gender and the State in Latin America*, ed. Elizabeth Dore and Maxine Molyneux (Durham, N.C.: Duke University Press, 2000), 172–93.

22. "Código Penal," *Enciclopedia Jurídica OMEBA*, tomo 3 (Buenos Aires: Editorial Bibliográfica Argentina, 29 vols.), 193–94.

23. Argentine Republic, *Código Penal de la República Argentina* (Buenos Aires: Imprenta de Sud-América, 1887), Libro II, Título 4, Capítulo 2, Artículo 128, pp. 159–60. See the commentary made by Rodolfo Rivarola, *Exposición crítica del código penal de la República Argentina*, 3 vols. (Buenos Aires: Lajouane, 1890), 2:133–265.

24. A case tried before 1886 went all the way to the Supreme Court for a successful pardon on the argument that partial penetration could not be considered the sole grounds for conviction under the new national law. AGN, Fondo Ministerio de Justicia e Instrucción Pública, Leg. 105, 1886, Agustín Trucco, solicitando gracia.

25. Asunción Lavrin, "Sexuality in Colonial Mexico: A Church Dilemma," in *Sexuality and Marriage in Colonial Latin America*, ed. Asunción Lavrin (Lincoln: University of Nebraska Press, 1989), 70–72. Other forms of heterosexuality, particularly anal intercourse, maintained their Catholic definition of *contra natura*, or unnatural acts, and could be grounds for legal separations in both religious and secular laws.

26. George Mosse, *Nationalism and Sexuality: Middle-Class Morality and Sexual Norms in Modern Europe* (Madison: University of Wisconsin Press, 1985), 20 (my emphasis).

27. Isabel V. Hull, *Sexuality, State, and Civil Society in Germany, 1700–1815* (Ithaca, N.Y.: Cornell University Press, 1996), 127.

28. *Enciclopedia Jurídica OMEBA*, 3:193–94, specifically cites Feuerbach and the 1813 Bavarian penal code as an influence on Carlos Tejedor and the Argentine penal code.

29. Cristian Berco, "Silencing Sodomy: The Re-Imagination of Argentina, the Virreinato, and Criminality" (unpublished paper); Jerry Cooney and Thomas Whigham, personal correspondence.

30. Mosse, *Nationalism and Sexuality*, 16–17.

31. For the attenuation of infanticide laws in Argentina see Kristin Ruggiero, "Honor, Maternity, and the Disciplining of Women: Infanticide in Late Nineteenth-Century Buenos Aires," *Hispanic American Historical Review* 72, no. 3 (Aug. 1992): 353-73.

32. AGN, Tribunales Criminales, Legajo 23, 1888, Letra D., Donato, Miguel por violación en la persona de su hija y Adelaida Mendes por aborto violento en la misma, 2.

33. Ibid., 2–13.

34. AGN, Tribunales Criminales, Letra F., 1890, Figari, Juan Bautista, Mülders Juan y Julieta Tany de Mülders por violación a la menor Francisca Leduc el primero y complicidad los subsiguientes, 1–66.

35. AGN, Tribunales Criminales, Letra B., Leg. 112, 1907–1908. Pedro Berutti, por violación de sus hijas, July 17, 1909, 1–3.

36. Ibid., 5

37. Ibid., July 18, 1909, 7–8.

38. AGN, Tribunales Civiles, Letra B, Legajo 110, 1906, 1–34. Baach, Salustiano, acusado de estupro en la persona de la menor Leonor Gregoria Gonzalez.

39. Ibid., 37–53. The technicality was that Exequiela had failed to report Gregoria's birth in the Registro Civil, thereby making it difficult to prove that Gregoria was under the age of fourteen.

40. AGN, Tribunales Criminales, Letra C, Legajo 177, 18–39, Enrique Carena por sodomía, 1909.

■ ■ ■ ■

X. Andrade is a Ph.D. candidate in Anthropology at the New School for Social Research and a visiting professor at FLACSO-Quito. His doctoral dissertation explores issues of masculinity, visual representation, and political culture in Ecuador. Other research interests include drug trafficking, a subject about which he has published extensively, most recently in the *Journal of Drug Issues*. Andrade is currently documenting the public worship of Tamil male cinema icons in South India and coediting a book on masculinities in Ecuador.

Daniel Balderston is Professor in the Department of Spanish and Portuguese at the University of Iowa. His recent publications include the books *El deseo, enorme cicatriz luminosa* (Caracas: Ediciones eXcultura, 1999) and *Borges, realidades y simulacros* (Buenos Aires: Editorial Biblos, 2000), as well as the edited journal issue *Erotismo y escritura* (*Revista Iberoamericana* [1999]) and the edited book *Sexualidad y nacion* (Pittsburgh: Instituto Internacional de Literatura Iberoamericana, 2000). He is also one of the three general editors of the *Encyclopedia of Contemporary Latin American and Caribbean Cultures,* 3 vols. (New York: Routledge, 2000).

Peter Beattie is Associate Professor of History at Michigan State University and the author of *The Tribute of Blood: Army, Honor, Race, and Nation in*

Brazil, 1864–1945 (Durham, N.C.: Duke University Press, 2001). He is currently researching prisons, penology, and social control during slavery and emancipation in Pernambuco, Brazil, from 1830 to 1945. Beattie is also conducting a comparative study of the adoption of military conscription in nations of the Southern Cone and is editing a reader of nonelite biographies, *The Human Tradition in Modern Brazil*, for SR Books.

Stanley Brandes holds a doctorate from the University of California, Berkeley, where he is Professor of Anthropology. For more than thirty years he conducted fieldwork in Spain, Mexico, and the United States. His principal areas of investigation include folklore, visual anthropology, popular religion, and the cultural dimensions of food and drink, particularly alcohol. He is the author of five books and more than a hundred articles, book chapters, and brief reviews and communications. Among his most well-known works are *Metaphors of Masculinity: Sex and Status in Andalusian Folklore* (Philadelphia: University of Pennsylvania Press, 1980); *Forty: The Age and the Symbol* (Knoxville: University of Tennessee Press, 1985); and *Power and Persuasion: Fiestas and Social Control in Rural Mexico* (Philadelphia: University of Pennsylvania Press, 1988). His *Staying Sober in Mexico City* was published by the University of Texas Press in 2002.

Héctor Carillo is a researcher at the Center for AIDS Prevention Studies, University of California, San Francisco, and at the Center for Community Research, Institute on Sexuality, Inequality, and Health at San Francisco State University. Carrillo currently studies sexuality and HIV risk among Latino gay men in the United States. His ethnography on sexuality and HIV prevention in Guadalajara, Mexico, which focuses on the formation of sexual identities, has recently been published as *The Night Is Young: Sexuality in Mexico in the Time of AIDS* (Chicago: University of Chicago Press, 2002).

Miguel Díaz Barriga received his Ph.D. from Stanford University in 1991 and is Associate Professor of Anthropology at Swarthmore College. He has conducted research on urban social movements in Mexico City and with Mexican migrants in Pennsylvania. His publications include articles on gender relations and grassroots organizing in *American Ethnologist*,

Mexican Studies/Estudios Mexicanos, and several edited volumes. He is currently editing a volume on regional issues in Latin American anthropology for Blackwell and completing a research project entitled "La Virgen de Guadalupe in Pennsylvania."

Agustín Escobar Latapí has written extensively on Mexican urban labor markets, Mexico-U.S. migration, and social policy. He focuses particularly on the consequences of economic and regional restructuring on work, social mobility, gender at work, migration, and poverty. Among his many books are *Hombres, trabajo y hogar,* coauthored with Santiago Bastos (Costa Rica: FLACSO, 1999); *La dinámica de la emigración mexicana,* coauthored with Frank Bean and Sidney Weintraub (Mexico City: CIESAS/Porrúa, 1999); and *Social Responses to Mexico's Economic Crisis of the 1980s,* edited with Mercedes González de la Rocha (San Diego: University of California San Diego, 1991). Currently, he is regional director at the Centro de Investigaciones y Estudios Superiores en Antropología Social in Guadalajara.

Francisco Ferrándiz received his Ph.D. from the University of California at Berkeley. He is currently an Associate Professor of Anthropology at the University of Deusto (Bilbao, Spain). He has taught at the University of California Berkeley and at the Universidad Autónoma del Estado de Morelos (UAEM) in Cuernavaca, Morelos, México. He has held visiting appointments at the Universidad Central de Venezuela (UCV) in Caracas; at The Virginia Foundation for the Humanities at the University of Virginia (UVA), Charlottesville; at the University of Utrecht (The Netherlands); and at the Centro de Investigaciones y Estudios Superiores en Antropología Social (CIESAS) (México, D.F.). He has carried out research on informal economy, popular religion, healing, memory, embodiment, social trauma, and everyday violence—as expressed in the spirit possession cult of María Lionza—in the shantytowns of Caracas and Catia la Mar, Venezuela.

Claudia Fonseca (Doctorat d'État, Université de Nanterre) is Professor of Anthropology at the Universidade Federal do Rio Grande do Sul. Her research interests include family organization and gender relations in Brazilian working-class populations, with special emphasis on human rights issues and international adoption. Dr. Fonseca's recent publications include *Caminhos da Adoção* (São Paulo, Brazil: Cortez, 1995) and *Família, Fofoca e Honra: Etnografia de Relações de Gênero e Violência Em Grupos Populares* (Porto Alegre: Editora da UFRGS, 2000).

Norma Fuller is Professor of Anthropology and Chair of the Social Sciences Department at the Pontificia Universidad Católica del Perú (UCP). She received her Ph.D. in anthropology from the University of Florida in 1996. Among her publications, Dr. Fuller has written *Identidades masculinas: Varones de clase media en el Perú* (Lima, Peru: Pontificia Universidad Católica del Perú, 1997) and *Dilemas de la femineidad: Mujeres de clase media en el Perú* (Lima, Peru: Pontificia Universidad Católica del Perú, 1993), and edited *Paternidades en América Latina* (Lima, Peru: Pontificia Universidad Católica del Perú, 2000). Her research interests include gender, the anthropology of subjectivity, theory, and methods in Peru.

Matthew C. Gutmann is the Stanley J. Bernstein Assistant Professor of the Social Sciences–International Affairs at Brown University, where he teaches classes in cultural anthropology, Latin American studies, ethnic studies, and medical anthropology. He is also Visiting Professor at the Centro de Investigaciones y Estudios Superiores en Antropología Social—Istmo in Oaxaca. His publications include *The Meanings of Macho: Being a Man in Mexico City* (Berkeley: University of California Press, 1996); Spanish version, *Ser hombre de verdad en la ciudad de México: Ni macho ni mandilón* (Mexico City: El Colegio de México, 2000); *Mainstreaming Men into Gender and Development: Debates, Reflections, and Experiences*, written with Sylvia Chant (Oxford: Oxfam, 2000); *The Romance of Democracy: Compliant Defiance in Contemporary Mexico* (Berkeley: University of California Press, 2002); and *Perspectives on Las Américas: A Reader in Culture, History, and Representation*, edited with Félix V. Matos-Rodríguez, Lynn Stephen, and Patricia Zavella (Malden, Mass.: Blackwell, 2003). His present research in Oaxaca, Mexico, is concerned with negotiating men's reproductive health and sexuality.

Donna Guy is Professor of History at Ohio State University. Her publications include *Sex and Danger in Buenos Aires: Prostitution, Family, and Nation in Argentina* (Lincoln: University of Nebraska Press, 1991);

Argentine Sugar Politics: Tucumán and the Generation of Eighty (Tempe, Ariz.: Center for Latin American Studies, Arizona State University, 1980); *White Slavery and Mothers Alive and Dead: The Troubled Meeting of Sex, Gender, Public Health, and Progress in Latin America* (Lincoln: University of Nebraska Press, 2000); *Sex and Sexuality in Latin America*, edited with Daniel Balderston (New York: New York University Press, 1997); *Contested Ground: Comparative Frontiers on the Northern and Southern Edges of the Spanish Empire*, edited with Thomas E. Sheridan (Tucson: University of Arizona Press, 1998); *Feminisms and Internationalism*, edited with Mrinalini Sinha and Angela Woollacott (Oxford: Blackwell, 1999). Currently she is working on a book about street children in Argentina.

Florencia Mallon is Professor of History at the University of Wisconsin-Madison. She is the author of *The Defense of Community in Peru's Central Highlands: Peasant Struggle and Capitalist Transition, 1860–1940* (Princeton, N.J.: Princeton University Press, 1983); and *Peasant and Nation: The Making of Postcolonial Mexico and Peru* (Berkeley: University of California Press, 1995); as well as numerous articles on agrarian, political, and social history. Since 1996 she has been researching the twentieth-century relationship between the Mapuche indigenous people of southern Chile and the Chilean state. She is the editor and translator of Rosa Isolde Reuque Paillalef, *When a Flower Is Reborn: The Life and Times of a Mapuche Feminist* (Durham, N.C.: Duke University Press, 2002), and she is completing her next book, *The Mapuche Indigenous Community of Nicolás Ailío and the Chilean State, 1906–2000.*

José Olavarría is Profesor Investigador and Coordinador de Estudios sobre Hombres del Area de Estudios de Género at FLACSO-Chile in Santiago. He is the author, coauthor, editor, and coeditor of several books and articles on gender and men. Recent research includes "Qué significa ser padre para los hombres de los sectores populares hoy día en Chile"; and "Ser padre: La vivencia de los padres de Santiago: Estereotipos, subjetividades y prácticas de la paternidad." He is currently working on a project titled "Varones adolescentes: ¿Responsabilidades y derechos?: Cuestiones en torno a la sexualidad, salud reproductiva y paternidad."

Richard Parker is Professor and Chair of the Department of Sociomedical Sciences in the Mailman School of Public Health at Columbia University and in the Institute of Social Medicine at the State University of Rio de Janeiro. He has carried out long-term field research in Brazil and has published extensively on issues related to gender, sexuality, and the politics of health. In addition to his work as a researcher, he has been actively involved in a range of advocacy and program activities, and he currently serves as president of the Brazilian Interdisciplinary AIDS Association (ABIA), an HIV/AIDS-service and advocacy organization based in Rio de Janeiro. He is also a member of the board of directors for the Commission on Citizenship and Reproduction (CCR), a reproductive and sexual rights coalition based in São Paulo.

Mara Viveros Vigoya is Associate Professor of Anthropology at the Universidad Nacional de Colombia. Viveros is the author of *De quebradores y cumplidores: Sobre hombres, masculinidades y relaciones de género en Colombia* (Bogotá: Universidad National de Colombia, 2002), and coeditor of *Cuerpo, diferencias y desigualdades: Mujeres, hombres y cambio social* (Universidad Nacional de Colombia, 1998). Her recent articles include "Stérilisation masculine et rapports de genre: Une étude de cas en Colombie," in *Femmes et hommes dans le champ de la santé*, ed. Pierre Aïach, Dominique Cèbe, Geneviève Cresson, and Claudine Philippe (Lille: Editions ENSP, in press); and "Dionysian Blacks: Sexuality, Body, and Racial Order in Colombia," *Latin American Perspectives* 123, no. 2 (March 2002).

INDEX

■ ■ ■

A.A. *See* Alcoholics Anonymous (A.A.)

ABIA. *See* Brazilian Interdisciplinary AIDS Association (ABIA)

Abolition: military impressment and, 237, 238

Abortion: men and, 15, 45, 46

Absent fathers, 39, 149

Acevedo, Oscar Fernando, 34

Acquired immunodeficiency syndrome. *See* AIDS (acquired immunodeficiency syndrome)

Active/passive dichotomy: in discussions of Latin American sexualities, 7–12, 16–18, 48; in homosexuality and masculinity discourse, 48, 173, 247–49, 310–11, 361

Adolescent fatherhood, 40–41

Adultery: women and, 70–71, 73–76, 80 n.11, 169–70. *See also* Cuckolds; Vila São João

Aesthetic beauty, 140

Afro-Brazilian religious cults, 311. *See also* Spiritists: masculine identity and

Age: classification of male slaves by, 238–39; effect on men's migration and urbanization, 92–95; effect on men's priorities, 108; elderly parents and, 104; homosociality and, 33; household chore help and men's, 150–51, 337 (*see also* Division of labor, household; Domestic sphere), impact on male attitudes toward women, 85, 87–88, 151; intergenerational assistance and, 32, 91, 101–6, 110; marriage and, 96–101, 109–10, 145–47; perception of masculine body and, 138–42; politics and, 142–43; work and, 143–45, 149–50

"Age, Gender, Family, and Work in Urban Mexico, 111–12 n.1

Agrarian Reform Law (Chile), 195–96

Agricultural cooperatives, 195–96

AIDS (acquired immunodeficiency syndrome): emergence of, 315–16; individual responses to prevention of, 326–28; knowledge about transmission of, 325–26; programs and responses to, 7, 41, 49, 50, 69, 226, 317–23

AIDSCAP Project, 318

Ailío, Eduardina, 215 n.43
Ailío, Heriberto: agrarian reform and, 195, 196; capture of, 207–8; community/family ties of, 198–99; post-coup, 215 nn.41, 43; on providing economically for family, 197
Ailío, Hugo, 208
Ailío, Robustiano, 196, 198, 199, 215 n.43
Aires de Familia (Monsiváis), 1
Alcohol/alcoholics: affirmation of heterosexuality and, 173–74; alternative masculinities among, 166–71; *esposa* versus *compañera* among former, 165–66; homosexual desire expressed by, 172–73; impact on families, 161–62, 164, 168; impact on marriage, 162–63, 168–69; impact on women, 162–64; life-cycle rituals and community fiestas and, 154–55; male friendships and, 155, 157–61, 166, 172; masculine identity and, 19–20, 153–54; mortality and morbidity from, 155–56; unmarried, 171–72; women's use of, 154, 155, 156–57
Alcoholics Anonymous (A.A.), 19–20, 156, 161, 165, 174
Allende, Andrés Pascal, 180
Altman, Dennis, 219, 220–21, 227
O Alvorado (Jaguarão), 233
Amâncio de Souza, Bernardo, 243–44
Amícola, José, 217, 223, 227–28
Andrade, X., 7, 10, 44
Andrews, George Reid, 252 n.20
"Androgen Administration in the Post-Menopausal Woman" (Masters and Magallon), 222
Antiautobiography, 118, 130 n.7
Anzaldúa, Gloria: background of, 258–59; *La Frontera/Borderlands: The New Mestiza*, 258–59, 271, 276–77; new conceptions of Chicana culture, 258; "La Prieta," 271; on vergüenza, 257
Archetti, Eduardo P., 43–44
Argentina: rape and masculine silence in, 10–11, 370–91
Argentine Penal Code, 377–78
Army songs: masculinity represented in, 249
Asa Branca, 320
Asentamiento Arnoldo Ríos, 195–200, 207
Atobá, 318, 320
Attractiveness: male bodies and, 140–41
Autoridades: vergüenza and, 264, 265–66
Aztlán, 278 n.2

Baach, Salustiano, 386–87
Bacán (suave and generous man), 43
Bacarisse, Pamela, 219
Bagaceira (lax moral environment), 246–47
Bagasse (cheap whore), 254 n.31
Bagaxa (male prostitute), 9, 246
Balderston, Daniel, 7, 15–16
Barbudo (romantic revolutionary), 14, 180–81, 210. *See also* Revolutionary masculinity
Barger, W. K., 260
Barickman, Bert, 238–39, 254 nn.25, 26
Barracks: negative associations with, 245–46, 248
Barrenechea, Ana María, 217
Barrientos, Manuel ("El Indio," alias), 186–94, 208–10, 213 n.10
Barrio Boy (Galarza), 257, 262–66
Bastidas, Julián, 191, 192–93
Bastos, Santiago, 33–34
Beattie, Peter, 5, 11
Beauty: male bodies and, 140–41
Bederman, Gail, 292–93

Beltrán, Luciano Ernesto, 208, 215 n.43

Beltrán, Orlando, 208

Benedict, Ruth, 278 n.3

Benstock, Shari, 229–30

Berco, Cristian, 380

Berruti, Enquieta, 385, 386

Berruti, María, 385–86

Berruti, Pedro, 385–86

Berruti, Santiago, 386

El beso de la mujer araña (The kiss of the spider woman, Puig), 16; authors cited in footnotes in, 219–24; order and content of footnotes in, 216–19, 225; on physical origins of homosexuality, 218; role changes in, 223–24; scholars on, 227–30; Taube character in, 223, 226, 229, 230

Bestiality, 380

Beyond Patriarchy (Kaufman), 47

Bicha (female animal), 311–12

Birth control, 13, 45–46, 47

Birth order: versus gender, 94–95

Bisexuality, 48–49, 356

Black men: masculinity and, 36. *See also* Slavery

Blackwelder, Julia Kirk, 371

Blood feuds, 122, 123, 250

Blood ties: versus conjugal relationships, 72–73

Bly, Robert, 5, 51

Bobbitt, Lorena, 292

Bodies: age and perception of masculine, 138–42; beauty and, 140–41; dichotomized cultural values and practices and, 9–11; gender and, 310; importance of athletic, 152 n.2; life stage and, 140; sex and, 139; strength and, 139–40

Borderlands, cultural, 257–58, 271–72, 276–77, 278 n.1

Borja, Rodrigo, 287, 288, 289

Brandes, Stanley, 15, 39; on changing concepts of shame, 261–62, 277, 278 n.4; on male remorse, 19–20

Brazil: army service and slavery in, 5, 233–55; cuckolds and gender relations in, 10, 61–83; cultural identity versus gender identity in, 35–36; deflowering cases in, 11; male socialization in, 30, 31, 42–43; masculinity and homosexuality in, 9, 15, 49–50, 307–32; paternity in, 38, 40–41

Brazilian Interdisciplinary AIDS Association (ABIA): illustrations by, 41, 49, 69, 226, 319, 322; projects of, 318

Brazilian Ministry of Health, 318, 320

Brown, Norman O., 218

Brusco, Elizabeth, 9

Bucaram, Abdalá, 291, 292

Buenos Aires Defense of Minors, 371

Butecos (bars), 42

Caça (hunting), 314

Cáceres, Carlos, 48–49

Canelón, 123, 125

Capitãoes da mata (bounty hunters), 239

Capoeiras, 255 n.38

El caracazo (rebellion against austerity measures), 130 n.5

Cárdenas, José [alias], 183–86, 193, 197–98, 202, 211, 213 n.7

Cardoso, Luiz, 40–41

Careers: marriage and, 99–100, 101, 103–4. *See also* Work

Carena, Enrique, 387

Caricatures: political, 285, 286, 289, 296, 297

Carnal transactions, 127

Carrillo, Héctor, 7, 48

Casa Grande e Senzala (The Masters and the Slaves, Freyre), 244

Catholic Church: "Christians" and, 112 n.8; on *contra natura*, 391 n.25; impact on pronatality, 15; on incest, 377, 385; morality versus civil society and, 372; relationship to masculinity, 24 n.7; on sexuality, 379–80

Caucasian beauty, 141

Caulfield, Sueann, 374

Censura, 284, 285

Chiavenato, Júlio José, 252 n.11

Chicano identity: cultural borderlands and, 257–58, 271–72, 276–77; *mestiza*, 271–75; narratives about, 257, 277. *See also* Anzaldúa, Gloria; Cisneros, Sandra; Galarza, Ernesto

Chifrudo (cuckold), 80 n.1

Chilanga (derogatory term for Mexico City residents), 275, 279 n.10

Childbirth: female employment after, 101

Childhood: impact on men's attitudes, 88, 119–20, 342–43; sex crimes and, 387, 388. *See also* Rape

Child rearing (generational reproduction): fatherhood duties in, 341–43; women and, 41, 73. *See also* Intergenerational assistance

Chile: child rearing and working class fathers in, 14, 33, 333–50; MIR and masculinity in, 14, 179–215

Chimarrão (erva mate), 80 n.9

Christians. *See* Catholic Church; Protestants

Cisneros, Sandra: *House on Mango Street*, 258, 266–71; new conceptions of Chicana culture, 258; on *vergüenza*, 257; *Woman Hollering Creek and Other Stories*, 276

Civil Code (1869, Argentina), 377

Class. *See* Social class

Clatterbaugh, Kenneth, 28

Coatlicue, 273

Coen, Tanya, 23 n.5

Cohen, Lawrence, 298

Cohen, Thomas V., 254 n.31

Colección Archivos, 217

Colombia: black males and bodies in, 36–37; cultural pacification of men in, 9; fatherhood in, 38; *lealtad* and homosexuality taunts in, 4–5; male sterilization in, 45–46; obstacles to parental roles in, 34; prostitution and violence in, 48

Las comadres (godmothers), 268–69

Comentarios de Pancho Jaime: content and focus of, 284–86, 302 n.5. *See also* Pancho Jaime (Victor Francis Jaime Orellana)

Comer (to eat): as slang term, 80 n.8

Comisión Política (Political Commission) (MIR), 180

Communication: in marriage, 97–98

Communist Party (Bolivia), 184

Communist Party (Chile), 182, 191

Compadrito (elegant seducer), 43

Compañera: versus *esposa*, among former alcoholics, 165–66

CONACYT (Science Council, Mexico), 111 n.1

Concentration camps: at Cuatro Alamos, 209; at Tejas Verdes, 209; at Tres Alamos, 209

Condoms: use of, 318, 321, 326, 328, 374

Confianza (confidence), 277

Conjugal relationships: blood ties versus, 72–73; cheating in, 70; formal expectations in, 65; study methods for, 63–64; types of, 89–90. *See also* Marriage

Connell, R. W., 23 n.1, 28, 53 n.2, 81 n.13

Conscription: impact on families, 243. *See also* Impressment, military

Conservative Party (Brazil), 237
Contraception, 13, 45–46, 47
Contreras, Manuel, 215 n.40
Cooney, Jerry, 380
CORA (agrarian reform agency), 196, 197
Corno manso (tame or willing cuckold), 69
Cornudo (cuckold), 80 n.1
Coroa (older man), 70
Corridos (Mexican ballads), 279 n.7
Corruption: concept of masculinity and, 282
Cortázar, Julio, 217
Cortés, Hernán, 53 n.4
Costumbrista (caricature style), 286
Coup, of September 1973 (Chile), 202
Creighton, Millie R., 279 n.5
Crisis of masculinity, 28, 29, 53 n.2
Cross-class mobility, 96
Cross-naming, 289
Cruz, Luciano, 180, 184, 203, 204
Cuaderno de Bitácora, 217
Cuates (twins), 158. *See also* Homosociality
Cuckolds, 61–63, 80 n.1, 169–70, 249, 298. *See also* Vila São João
Culebras (blood feuds), 122, 123
Cultural hybridity, 353
Culture and Truth: The Remaking of Social Analysis (Rosaldo), 257

Dabove, Juan Pablo, 228
DaMatta, Roberto, 245
Dancing with the Devil: Society and Cultural Poetics in Mexican-American South Texas (Limón), 268–69
Davis, Natalie, 77
Death: impact of parental, 90–92
De Barbieri, M. Teresita, 51, 335
Decriminalization: of sexual crimes, 380–81
Defacement, 299–300

Defensor de menores (Defender of minors), 378
Deflowering cases *(defloramento/defloramiento)*, 11, 374–75, 386–87
Degendering, definition of, 152 n.2
Degredado (degraded one): soldiers and terminology associated with, 246–47, 255 n.33
De Keijzer, Benno, 38–39, 46, 47
Delinquents, 121–22. *See also Malandros*
De Suremain, Marie Dominique, 34
Desviaciones obreristas (workerist deviations), 189
Díaz, María, 107
Díaz Barriga, Miguel, 6–7, 22
Dichotomous dualities. *See* Active/passive dichotomy
Dime capitán: Reflexiones sobre la masculinidad (What it means to be a man: Reflections on Puerto Rican masculinity, Ramírez), 30
Dirección de Inteligencia Nacional (DINA) (Chile), 207, 209, 215 n.40
Displacements, 34, 53 n.3
Division of labor, household: among recovering alcoholics, 168; changes in, 336–38; employment patterns impact on, 13; intergenerational assistance and, 101, 102, 110. *See also* Domestic sphere
Divorce, legalization of, 78
Doctrina Betancourt, 131 n.12
Domestic sphere: men and, 137, 138, 336–38, 341–43; women and, 100–101, 138, 145–48. *See also* Division of labor, household; Marriage
Dominance, male: active/passive dichotomy and, 7–12, 16–18, 48, 173, 247–49, 310–11; alcoholics' remorse about,

Dominance, male (*cont.*)
19–20, 164–65, 167; global changes impact on, 78, 84–85; in homosexual relationships, 361; illegitimate births and roots of, 35; male image and, 34, 147; La Malinche as founding myth of, 35; public sphere and, 13–14; veiled justifications for, 86; vergüenza and, 267, 270, 272–75. *See also* Marriage; Rape

Domingo Cañas, José, 209

Donato, Manuel, 382–83

The Doors, 17

Drouilly, Jacqueline, 209

Duke of Caxias, 237

Eber, Christine, 154

Echavarren, Roberto, 227

Ecuador: political uses of masculinity in, 10, 44, 281–303

Education: delayed marriage and, 103; middle class and, 104, 144; of peasant children, 93–94; state-sponsored versus private, 95; women and, 13, 145

Educational mobility, 96

Egalitarian negotiations, 32

Elderly parents: impact of, 104, 111

Elites: Pancho Jaime attacks on, 294–97

Employment patterns: in banks, 107–8, 112–13 n.13; gender and, 84–85, 88–90, 105, 107, 150; masculinities and, 13–14, 68; of women, 84–85, 88, 99, 100–101, 104–5, 335–36. *See also* Informal employment

Las encopetadas (Chilean female upper class), 297

"Endocrine Aspects of Homosexuality" (Wright), 222–23

Enlistment bounties, 237

Enríquez, Edgardo, 180

Enríquez, Miguel, 180, 207

ERP, 231 n.6

"El Error Gay" (Puig), 231 n.5

Escobar Latapí, Agustín, 14, 32–33, 88

Europe: influence on concepts of Latin manliness, 18. *See also* El beso de la mujer araña (The kiss of the spider woman, Puig)

Exile: masculinity and, 210–11, 247

Family relationships: discourse on responsible, 181–82; friendship equated with, 166; versus households, 91; impressment impact on, 242; masculine socialization and, 47, 87–88; nuclear family as idealized, 334, 335; revolutionary masculinity and, 182, 197–98. *See also* Marriage

Fatherhood: adolescent, 40–41; child rearing duties and, 341–45; clichés related to, 14–15; different practices of, 40; hegemonic masculinity and, 334–36; historical changes in concept of, 38–39, 42; idealization of, 151; married life and, 345–48; masculine identity construction and, 37–38, 53 n.6, 148–49; over child's life cycle, 343–45; reproductive duties and, 338–41; status and, 73; of teenage children, 344–45, 347–48. *See also* Domestic sphere; Paternity

Fathers: abandonment of families by, 91; absent or fugitive, 39; changes in concept of, 39; intermediate category of, 14; men's attitudes toward, 87, 193–94; migration and urbanization and, 92–93; obstacles to idea of ideal, 34; substitutes for, 198–99; traditional image of, 38, 39

Fausto-Sterling, Anne, 8

Febres Cordero, León, 283, 291, 292

Femininity: in homosexuality/homo-
sexuals, 48, 310–11, 353, 355–58, 360,
365; masculine identity construc-
tion and, 6, 36, 141; repudiation of,
137
Feminist theoretical frameworks, 5, 21,
27, 31, 52
Ferrándiz, Francisco, 15, 20–21, 45
FER. *See* Revolutionary Student Front
(FER)
Fertility, 15, 46, 102
Figari, Juan Bautista, 383–85
Figueroa, Juan Guillermo, 45, 46
Finkler, Kaja, 163–64
Firmeza (firmness), 264, 266, 277
Fonseca, Claudia, 7, 10
Football songs: masculinity represented
in, 43, 44
Ford Foundation, 111 n.1, 318
La forma del Destino (Dabove), 228
Foss, G. L., 222
Foucault, Michel, 372
Free poor males: distinction between
bondsmen and, 235; enfranchisement
and, 244–45; exemptions from im-
pressment, 235–36, 240–41, 243; flog-
ging of, 239–40; honor and, 237, 238;
marriage and, 242, 243, 244–45, 254
n.23; migration and male role, 242–43;
patronage and, 236–37, 240–41, 251,
255 n.38; Recruitment Law and, 238,
243; stereotypes of slave status and,
240. *See also* Soldiers
Free Womb Law, 238
Frei, Eduardo, 195
Freire, Paulo, 319
Freitas, Julio de, 116
Frente de Liberación Homosexual, 231
n.6
Freud, Sigmund, 220, 223

The Freudian Left (Robinson), 224
Freyre, Gilberto, 244, 245
Friendship: alcohol use and, 155, 157–61,
166; equated with family, 166; equated
with Moral Support group, 172. *See also*
Homosociality
La Frontera/Borderlands: The New Mestiza
(Anzaldúa), 258–59, 271, 276–77
Fuga (elopement), 66–67
Fugitive fathers, 39
Fuller, Norma, 6, 30; on middle class mas-
culinity, 34–35; on paternity, 37; on
public sphere, 13–14
Fundo Chesque, 203
Fundo Nehuentúe, 207, 208
Fundo Rucalán, 194–95

Galarza, Ernesto, 257, 277; background of,
258; *Barrio Boy* autobiography of, 262–
66; on vergüenza, 259
Galarza, Henriqueta, 263, 264
Galarza, José, 263
GAPA-Ceará, 320
GAPA-Minas Gerais, 320
García, Carlos Iván, 48
García Canclini, Néstor, 353
Garrido, Omar, 187
Gastaldo, Edison Luis, 43
Gaúcho identity, 36, 53 n.5
Gay: versus homosexual, 364, 367 n.1
Gay communities, 7, 318, 320, 364, 366
Gay liberation movement, 220–21, 315
Gender: alcohol and male, 174; versus
birth order, 94–95; bodies and, 310;
definition of, 136; differences in sex-
ualities, 10–11; differences in virginity,
10–11; in employment patterns, 84–85,
88–90, 105, 107, 150; identity, 6, 33,
35–36, 50, 136; income differentials
and, 85, 89; inequalities and, 52, 88–

Gender (*cont.*)
89, 112–13 n.13; masculinity as configuration of, 53 n.2; mediumship and,
127, 128–29; national honor and, 249;
overlap with ethnic-racial identities, 6,
35–37; patterns of, 174; relations and
humor, 63, 64–66; scholarship on
masculinity and, 28–29; segregation in
workplace, 107; spiritists and, 127–30;
vergüenza and, 261–62
Gender studies, 20, 27–28
"Geraldo No Last Name" (Cisneros), 276
Gilmore, David, 64–65, 279 n.6
Global changes: impact on chicano identity, 257; impact on male domination,
78, 84–85, 334–35; impact on women,
12–18, 34–35, 108; sexualities and, 12–
18, 32
Goldchluk, Graciela, 217
Gomensoro, Armando, 46, 47
Gómez, Fredy, 45
Gossip: about cuckolds and sexuality, 66,
67, 71–73, 77; military impressment
and, 241, 244; politicians and elites
and, 300
Grandchildren, 32, 91, 110
Greenblatt, R. B., 222
The Greening of America (Reich), 221
Grupo Alfa, 100
Grupo Arco-Íris, 320
Grupo Dignidade, 320
Grupo Gay de Bahia (GGB), 318, 320
Grupo Monterrey, 92
Guampudos, 61–62, 80 n.1. *See also*
Cuckolds; Vila São João
Guard posts: military impressment and,
236–37
Guatemala, 33–34
Guevara, Che, 183, 184, 204, 211
Gutiérrez, Nelson, 180, 210

Gutmann, Matthew: on alcohol and male
friendship, 155; on degendering, 152
n.3; on fatherhood, 40; on gender patterns, 174; on traditional role changes,
31–32; on variation in men's roles, 85;
on women in relation to masculinities,
65
Guy, Donna, 10–11, 12
Guzmán, Virginia, 44

Heads of households, 33–34
Hegemonic masculinity, 23 n.1; fatherhood and, 334–36; impact on men's
health, 47; *populismo* and, 291–92,
298; prototype of, 115–18; public
sphere and, 44–45; revolutionary, 181–
83; social stigma of cuckoldry and, 73–
76; study of, 3–4, 33, 51–52; working
wives and, 100–101
Henao, Hernán, 31, 38
Henríquez, Miguel, 184
Heterosexuality, 360; alcoholics affirmation of, 173–74; association with masculinity, 48, 360; homosexuality/
homosexuals effect on, 356–57, 359;
vergüenza and, 272
Higgins, Michael, 23 n.5
HIV. *See* AIDS (acquired immunodeficiency syndrome)
*Hombres de Hierro: Los ritos de iniciación
masculina del Nuevo Hombre* (Bly), 5, 51
Hombría (manhood), 137–38, 151, 352. *See
also* Manhood
Home: concept of, 242, 244–45, 334
Homeownership, 108, 113 n.15, 126–27
Homoerotic pornography, 321
Homophobia, 4–5, 16, 247–48
Homosexuality (West), 219, 220
Homosexual/homosexuals: ac-
tive/passive dichotomy and, 48, 173,

406 ••• Index

247–49, 310–11; in Afro-Brazilian religious cults, 311; alcoholics and, 172–73; changes in sexual practices of, 327–28; characteristics of, 358; classification of, 360–61; class/race issues and, 316, 321; commercial settings for, 314–15, 321–22; as constructed category, 48; definitions of, 354–58; derogatory terms for, 4–5, 8–9; disclosure of, 354–55, 359, 365; effect on male heterosexuals, 356–57, 359; effeminacy and, 48, 310–11, 353, 355–58, 360, 365; versus "gay," 364, 367 n.1; as *hombres normales,* 352, 354–55, 357, 361; integration into communities, 311–12; machismo and, 352; in masculinity studies, 48–50; meanings of, 8–9, 309, 352–53; media portrayal of, 322–23, 362–67; nonsexual homosociality and, 358–62; origins of, 218; in political caricatures, 286; programs and responses to AIDS, 317–23; public sphere and, 312–17; Puig footnotes on, 217–23; revolutionary masculinity and, 194, 213 n.14; self-identification as, 8, 9, 48, 324–25, 352–53, 355–56, 360–61; sexual roles and, 15, 356; social changes and, 231 n.6, 307–12, 321; stereotypes of, 364; taxonomy of, 48–49, 311, 324–29; theories of origins of, 218; urban subcultures of, 312–17. *See also* AIDS (acquired immunodeficiency syndrome); *El beso de la mujer araña* (The kiss of the spider woman, Puig)

"Homosexuality Project," 318–20

Homosexual Oppression and Liberation (Altman), 219, 227

Homosociality: alcohol use and, 155, 157–61; generational differences in, 33; Moral Support group and, 172; nonsex-

ual, 358–62; public figures and, 298–302; revolutionaries and, 187, 199–200; spaces of, 42–45, 147; spiritists and, 129; study of, 5; work as site of, 44, 143

Honor and Shame and the Unity of the Mediterranean (Gilmore), 279 n.6

Honor/shame: Chicanas on linkage of, 278 n.4; concept of home and, 244–45; cultural borderlands and, 257–58, 271–72, 276–77, 278 n.1; free poor males and, 237, 238; gender relations and, 64–66; versus legality, 390 n.17; literature on, 63, 64–66, 279 nn.5, 6; *malandros* and, 119–20; of male relatives and women, 65, 74; military impressment and, 237; nationalism and, 249; outlaws and, 249–50; rape and concepts of, 372–76, 386; scholarly use of, 80 n.3; skin color and, 235; soldiers and, 249; vergüenza and, 261, 267, 270, 271, 276–77 (*see also* Vergüenza); women in literature of, 65, 74

"Hormonal Factors in Libido" (Greenblatt), 222

Household studies, 33–35, 85

House on Mango Street (Cisneros), 258, 266–71

Huasi, Julio, 215 n.38

Huaso (boorish), 181

Huentelaf, Felix, 203

Huentelaf, Moisés, 192, 203–6

Hull, Isabel, 380

Human rights abuses, 130 n.4, 131 n.13

Humor: gender relations and, 63, 64–66; intergenerational transmission of values by, 77

Identity: alcohol and masculine, 19–20, 153–54; bodies and, 9–10; construction

Identity (*cont.*)
of masculine, 29–31, 32, 35, 36, 37–38, 42, 46–47, 53 n.6, 148–49; cultural, 206–7; ethnic-racial, 35–37; femininity and masculine, 6, 36, 141; gaúcho, 36, 53 n.5; gender, 6, 33, 35–36, 50, 136; social context and male, 31–33; spiritists and masculine, 125–30, 131 nn.10, 16; work and masculine, 138, 143, 150. *See also* Chicano identity; Homosexuality/homosexuals: self-identification as; Vergüenza

Illegitimate births, 35

Impressment, military: abolition and, 237, 238; versus courts and legal punishment, 242, 243–44; exemptions from, 235–36, 240–41, 243; as form of exile, 247; gossip and, 241, 244; honor/shame and, 237; impact on families, 241; inviolability of family home and, 242; marriage, effect on, 242, 243, 244–45, 254 n.23; patriarchal role and, 242, 243, 251; patronage and, 236–37, 240–41, 251, 255 n.38; Recruitment Law and, 238, 243; similarity to slaving methods, 239; slaves and, 235–36, 237; status and, 238–46

Imprisonment/punishment, 124, 239–40

Incest, 373, 377, 382–83, 385–86

India, 298

Infanticide, 381, 382

"The Influence of Androgens on Sexuality in Women" (Foss), 222

Informal employment, 112 n.11; among spiritists, 126; as chief source of family income, 113 n.15; impact on gender equality, 89; impact on occupational performance, 105; shantytown dwellers and, 119, 123–24

Ingham, John M., 155

In-laws: gossip about sexuality of female, 71–73, 77

Institute of Social Medicine, 318

Interethnic relations: masculinity and, 146

Intergenerational assistance, 32, 91, 101–6, 110

The Interpretation of Dreams (Freud), 220

Iron John (Bly), 51

I Walked with a Zombie (film), 218, 219

Jaguarão, 233

Jardim, Denise Fagundes, 42–43

Jefes de familia, 264

Johnson, Lyman, 371

Jorgensen, Christine, 223

Jotas (effeminate homosexuals), 357

Kaufman, Michael, 47

Kerr, Lucille, 217, 220

Kimmel, Michael, 28

Kinship networks, 196–97

Kiss of the Spider Woman (Puig). See *El Beso de la mujer araña* (The kiss of the spider woman, Puig)

Klubock, Thomas, 181

Labor unions, 107, 108

Lacho (popular working-class lovers), 181

Lamas, Marta, 51

Lancaster, Roger, 127

Land ownership, 112 n.5

Latin American Studies Association, 12

Latinos, in United States, 22

Laws: Agrarian Reform Law (Chile), 195–96; decriminalization of sodomy, 380, 381; Free Womb Law, 238; Recruitment Law, 238, 243

Leal, Ondina Fachel, 35–36

Lealtad (loyalty), 4–5
Leduc, Francisca, 383–85
Leduc, Josefa, 383
Legendary bandits, 249–50
Leñero, Luis, 46
Lesbianism, 275, 297–98, 299, 367 n.1
Leverenz, David, 45
Lewin, Linda, 249–50
Lewis, C. S., 219
Liberal Party (Brazil), 237
Life transitions: age and, 87–88; employ-
    ment inequality as, 88–90; inter-
    generational assistance as, 101–6;
    migration and urbanization as, 92–95,
    135, 242–43; parental death as, 90–92.
    See also Employment patterns: of
    women; Marriage
Limón, José, 268–69
Lindisfarne, Nancy, 81 n.13
"Little Miracles Kept Promises"
    (Cisneros), 276
La Llorona, 278 n.2
Lomnitz, Larissa Adler, 157–58
"The Loss of a Readership" (Puig), 231 n.5

Machismo: *dialéctico*,290; historical roots
    of, 309–10; homosexuality and, 352;
    Latin American scholars on, 30–
    31;/*marianismo* model, 80 n.3; neo-
    machismo, 46–47; public masculinity
    and, 282, 290; sexuality studies and,
    18; stereotypes of, 15, 18, 32, 64–68,
    79, 288, 302 n.7
Macho: stereotype of, 30, 37, 66–68
Magallon, D. T., 222
Mahuad, Jaime, 292
Mäkelä, Klaus, 157
The Making of the Counter-Culture
    (Roszak), 221
Malandragem (roguishness), 68

Malandros (street-smart hustlers): case
    study of, 115–32; family life of, 118–20,
    123; honor/shame and, 119–20; im-
    prisonment and, 124–25; police repres-
    sion of, 130 n.4, 131 n.13; socialization
    and image of, 43; spiritists and, 125–30;
    stereotypes of, 130 n.256; women as,
    68–70
Male-female dimorphism, 8
La Malinche, 35, 53 n.4, 278 n.2
Mallon, Florencia, 14, 23, 52
Manhood, 3; conventional ideals of, 240,
    242; *hombría* as concept of, 137–38, 151,
    352; images of, 34, 147; republican, 250;
    slavery and, 235–36, 238–39, 240;
    versus social class, 242–43; soldiers'
    status and, 240–41
Manliness, 3
Mann, Thomas, 379
Manque, Alejandro, 195, 203–4
Maoist organizations, 187
Mapuche peasants: cooperatives and MCR,
    194–203; MCR images of, 203–7
Marcuse, Herbert, 218, 224
María Lionza cult, 125–30, 130 n.1
Maricas (queers), 4–5
Maricones (homosexuals), 8–9, 352, 353,
    362
Marinao, María, 184
Marqués, Josep-Vincent, 42
Marriage: age and, 96–101, 109–10, 145–
    47; alcohol/alcoholics impact on, 162–
    63, 168–69; careers and, 99–100, 101,
    103–4; class differences in, 146, 165–
    66; communication in, 97–98; con-
    tracts, 97, 98–101, 109–10, 145–46;
    education and delayed, 103; horizon-
    tality, 99; impact of fatherhood on,
    345–48; impressment and, 242, 243,
    244–45, 254 n.23; older men on, 96,

Marriage (*cont.*)

98; revolutionary male attitude toward, 193–94; slavery and, 244; status enhancement due to, 63, 150, 249; women's attitudes at beginning of, 338–39; younger men on, 96–97, 98, 146

Marx, Karl, 224

Masculinity: active/passive dichotomy in, 48, 173, 247–49, 310–11, 361; beauty and, 141; concepts of, 3; crisis of, 28, 29, 53 n.2; definitions of, 3, 37, 136–38, 138, 352; domestic, 137, 138, 336–38, 341–43; double system of, 34; employment patterns and, 13–14, 68; exile and, 210–11, 247; heterosexuality and, 48, 360; nationalism and, 249; natural, 137; politics of, 18–21; public, 137, 138, 282, 286; as risk factor in health, 47; social class and, 6, 34–35, 43, 68, 117, 146, 151; in songs, 43, 44, 249, 279 n.7; topics for future study of, 50–52; transgressive, 181–82; variant, 79, 81 n.13, 85, 167–71; wounded, 21, 117. *See also* Hegemonic masculinity; Heterosexuality; Machismo; *Malandros* (streetsmart hustlers); Revolutionary masculinity; Vergüenza

Masculinity studies: ethnic-racial identities and, 35–37; fatherhood in, 37–42; homosexuality in, 48–50; public sphere in, 42–45; reproductive health and sexuality in, 45–48; social classes and, 33–35; social context and, 31–33; unexplored themes in, 50–52. *See also* Identity: construction of masculine

Masculinity tracks, 21, 127, 128–29

Masters, W. H., 222

Masturbation, 170

Mayate concept: definition of, 8–9, 23–24 n.5, 357

Mayor, Juana, 383, 384

Mbembe, Achille, 288

MCR. *See* Revolutionary Peasant Movement (MCR)

Mediums: masculinity tracks and, 21, 127, 128–29

Men and Masculinities (journal), 21

Méndez, Adelaida, 382

Merino, Marcia, 209

Mestizos: definition of, 112 n.2; masculinity and, 6; stereotypes and, 302 n.7; women's work and income impact on, 85

Mexico: alcohol and masculine identity in, 19–20, 153–76; gender and life transitions in urban, 14, 32–33, 38–40, 84–114; homosexual male identity in, 8, 9, 48, 351–69; illustrations, 13, 17, 93, 157, 274, 342; impact of 1982 economic crisis on, 31–32

Middle class: definition of, 136; as descendants of migrations, 135; education and, 104, 144; ethnic-racial identities and, 36–37; masculine characteristics defined by, 145; taxonomy of sexuality in, 48–49; women, 34–35, 43; work and, 143

Migration: impact of, 92–95, 135, 242–43

Miguel, Leopoldo de, 186, 192

Military Intelligence (Chile), 209

Military service: impact on men, 122–23. *See also* Impressment, military; Soldiers

Milonguitas (young unmarried lower-middle class women), 43

Mineworkers, 181

MIR. *See* Movement of the Revolutionary Left (MIR)

O mito da masculinidade (The myth of masculinity, Nolasco), 29–30, 38

Momio (ultraconservative), 213 n.16

Monsiváis, Carlos, 1

Montecino, Sonia, 35

Mora, Ricardo, 195

"Moral agreement," marriage and, 97, 110

"The Moral Foundations of the Family" (Pitt-Rivers), 372–73

Morality: definitions of, 372, 379–80, 391 n.25; family and Leftist, 182, 197–98

Moral Support program. *See* Alcohol/alcoholics

Morris, Karen, 45, 46

Morrison, Jim, 17

Mosse, George, 379, 381

Mothers: abandonment of families by, 91; discourse of traditional father and, 38; Freudian theories of homosexuality and, 218; life histories of, 130 n.8; men's attitudes toward, 68–69, 87, 94–95, 185; role in experiences of sons, 32, 86, 93, 119, 125; as single-head of household, 91, 92

Movement of the Revolutionary Left (MIR), 14, 179; homosexuals expelled from, 194, 213 n.14; peasants and, 194–207; post-September 1973 coup, 207–11; working-class students and, 183–94

Mülders, Juan, 383

Mülders, Julieta Tany de, 383, 384

Muñoz, Elías Miguel, 228

Mutual help networks, 142

National AIDS Programme, 320

Nationalism: impact on social leveling, 236; impact on social order, 381; masculinity, honor, and, 249; rape and, 374, 379–81

Nationalism and Sexuality: Middle-Class Morality and Sexual Norms in Modern Europe (Mosse), 379

National Worker's Party (PT) (Brazil), 78

Natural masculinity, 137

Neomachismo, 46–47

Nepomoceno de Almeida Nobre, João, 240–41, 242

Nicolás Ailío, community of, 195

Nolasco, Sócrates, 29–30, 31

North America: influence on concepts of Latin manliness, 16, 18, 79

Nuances, 320

Nuclear family: as idealized family, 334, 335

Object-choice categories, 360

Occupational mobility, 96

Oil economy: impact of, 131 n.11

Olavarría, José, 14, 33

"One Holy Night" (Cisneros), 276

Opportunity inequality: in employment, 88–89

Orellana, Victor Francis Jaime. *See* Pancho Jaime (Victor Francis Jaime Orellana)

Padres de cheque, 14

Páez, Roxana, 217, 228–29

Palma, Milagros, 35

Pancho Jaime (Victor Francis Jaime Orellana), 281; background of, 283–85, 302 n.3; circulation of publications of, 285–86, 302 n.4; critics of use of vulgarity by, 288–89; effects of writing of, 299–300; first-person style of, 287; illustrations, 289, 296, 297; on public secrecy, 298–302; readership of, 293–98; sexist discourses of, 289–90; significance of work of, 291; use of insults by, 287–88; use of regional stereotypes by, 288; vocabulary of, 299

Paraguayan War, 236–37, 251

Parental death: impact on men, 90–92

Parker, Richard, 7, 8, 12, 15, 49–50

Partido Roldosista Ecuatoriano (PRE), 302
n.5

Passive migration, 93

Passivity: assumed, 9; cultural origins of,
11; homosexuality and, 48, 173, 247–
49, 310–11

Paternity: adulthood and, 148, 151; biological versus social, 38–39; legal acknowledgment of, 335; status and, 40–
41, 73; virility and, 37–38. *See also*
Fatherhood

Patriarchy: definition of, 349 n.2; patriarchal privilege and children, 377;
rape and, 371–72; vergüenza and displacement of, 262–66, 270, 275,
277

Patronage: impressment and, 236–37,
240–41, 251, 255 n.38

Paz, Octavio, 35

Pederasty, 373

Pedro II, 237

Pegação (cruising), 314, 315

Pela VIDDA Groups, 318

Penal codes, 372, 376–79

Periódicos satíricos, 286

Peru: gender identity in, 6, 34–35, 37–42,
44, 48–49, 134–52

Philippine Codes, 80 n.11

Pichon Rivière, Enrique, 223

Pinto, Jorge, 181

Piranha (promiscuous woman), 68–69

Pitt-Rivers, Julian, 64, 372–73, 375, 390
n.17

Poetry, revolutionary, 205–6

Political economy, 282

Political pornography, 44, 288. *See also*
Pancho Jaime (Victor Francis Jaime
Orellana)

Politics: public sphere and, 18–21, 142–
43, 292–93

Popular sector: alcohol use and, 155–56;
definition of, 349 n.2; household studies of, 33–34; masculinity versus beauty
in, 141; taxonomy of sexuality in, 48–
49; work and achievement in, 144, 145.
See also Fatherhood

Popular Unity, 196

Populismo: hegemonic masculinity and,
291–92, 298

Pornography: homoerotic, 321; political,
44, 288

Portocarrero, Patricia, 44

"The Power of Women, The Weakness of
Men" (Gilmore), 64–65

Praça (public square/privates and NCOs),
245, 252 n.18

PRE. *See* Partido Roldosista Ecuatoriano
(PRE)

Priests, discourse of traditional father
and, 38

Prieur, Annick, 9, 357

Production Center Jorge Fernández, 200

Pronatality, 15

Prostitution, 9, 48, 246, 379

Protestants, 112 n.8, 158–59, 379, 380

PROVEA, 131 n.13

PT. *See* National Worker's Party (PT)

Public Lives, Private Secrets (Twinam), 375–
76

Public masculinity, 137, 138, 282, 286

Public shaming rituals (*vito/charivari*), 64

Public sphere: definition of, 137; home
versus street as, 245, 334; homosex-
uality/homosexuals and, 312–17;
homosociality in, 42–45, 147; male
dominance and, 13–14; politics and,
18–21, 142–43, 292–93; soldiers and
derogatory terminology for, 245–47,

248, 255 n.33; women in, 145, 150. *See also* Employment patterns: of women; Homosociality; Work

Puerto Rico, 30–31

Puig, Manuel, 16, 231 n.5. See also *El beso de la mujer araña* (The kiss of the spider woman, Puig)

Quidel, Gertrudis, 208

Quijón, Luis Ernesto, 202

Quintana, Alvina, 258

Ramírez, Rafael L., 12, 29–31

Rank, 246

Rape, 10–11; age and, 391 n.39; arrests for, 370, 378; case studies of, 381–88; charges of, 378; confessions of, 385–86; convictions for, 377, 378, 390 n.24; as deflowering case, 386–87; father-daughter, 382–83, 385–86; honor concepts and, 372–76, 386; laws and, 376–79, 380; of married women, 371–72, 379; master-servant rape, 383–85; nationalism and, 374, 379–81; patriarchy and, 371–72; proof of, 379; of prostitutes, 379; punishment for, 378; as revenge, 376; silence about, 371–72; statutory, 11; terminology for crimes of, 378; of young boys, 387, 388

Rayuela (Cortázar), 217

Reaction formation, 166

Recruitment: for military service, 236–37, 239

Recruitment Law, 238, 243

Reich, Charles, 221

Reich, Wilhelm, 218

Reproductive health, 45–47. *See also* AIDS (acquired immunodeficiency syndrome)

Republican manhood, 250

Republican Party (Brazil), 237–38

Respect/reputation model, 80 n.3

Respeto, 264, 269, 272

"The Resurrection of Moisés Huentelaf," 205–6

Revolutionary masculinity, 14; attitudes toward homosexuality, 194, 213 n.14; definition of, 181–83, 191; family relationships in, 182, 197–98; hegemonic masculinity in, 181–83; images of, 14, 180–81; marriage attitudes in, 193–94; peasants, 1970–1973 and, 194–207; post-1973 coup and, 207–11; working-class students, 1967–1971 and, 183–94. *See also* Movement of the Revolutionary Left (MIR)

Revolutionary Peasant Movement (MCR), 179; coastal region, 194–203; images of Mapuche in, 203–7

Revolutionary Student Front (FER) (Chile), 184, 213 n.8

Reza, E., 260

Ricardão, 62

Rich men: feminization of, 6, 36, 141

Ríos, Arnoldo, 203, 213 n.17

Ritual spheres, 44

Roberts, Bryan, 88

Robinson, Paul A., 224

Romantic revolutionaries, 14, 180–81, 210. *See also* Revolutionary masculinity

Romanucci-Ross, Lola, 156

Romero, Julia, 217, 229

Romero, Mariana, 45, 46

Romo Mena, Osvaldo, 209, 211

Rosaldo, Renato, 257, 267

Rosemblatt, Karin, 182

Rosovsky, Haydée, 170

Roszak, Theodore, 221

El roto macanudo (hobo/mineworkers), 181

Salcedo, Hernando, 45, 46

Salinas, Marcelo, 209

Sanctions: against unchaste women, 74–75

Santa (good mother and faithful wife), 68–69

Santana, Exequiela, 386–87, 388, 391 n.39

Santana, Gregoria, 391 n.39

Santana, Leonor, 386

Science Council (CONACYT) (Mexico), 111 n.1

Sebreli, Juan José, 231 n.6

Seeger, Anthony, 77

Serrano, José Fernando, 48

Sexist discourses, 289–90

Sexual bragging, 170

Sexual contracts: marriage and, 97

Sexualities: active/passive dichotomy in, 7–12, 16–18, 48, 173, 247–49, 310–11, 361; in caricatures, 285, 286, 289, 296, 297; gender differences in, 10–11; global changes and, 12–18, 32. *See also* Identity: construction of masculine

Sexual revolution: Puig on, 224–30

Sexual silence, 355, 388

Shantytown dwellers, 117. See also *Malandros* (street-smart hustlers)

Sharecroppers, 196

Silvino, Antônio, 249–50

Simmons, J. L., 218

Sinvergüenza, 275

"Sinvergüenza" (Valenzuela), 275–76

Skin color: beauty and, 141; honor and, 235

Slavery: black population decrease and mobilization, 252 n.11; decline in Brazil, 236; independent households and, 244, 254 n.26; letters of manumission and army service, 237; manhood and, 235–36, 238–39, 240; marriage and, 244; soldiers and terminology associated with, 246–47

Social class: case studies and, 85; children and, 89; feminization of dominant, 6, 36, 141; gendered resentment and, 190, 191, 200–202; household studies and, 33–35; versus manhood, 242–43; masculinity and inferior, 6, 34–35, 43, 68, 117, 146, 151

Social context: male identities and, 31–33

Social mobility, 95–96, 99, 105

Social stigma: of cuckoldry and hegemonic masculinity, 73–76; *malandros* and, 116

Socolow, Susan, 376

Sodomy: decriminalization of, 380, 381; as pederasty, 373; soldiers and terminology associated with, 246–47, 248

Soldiers: conditions of service of, 241; *degredado* and terminology associated with, 246–47, 255 n.33; flogging of, 239–40; homophobia and, 247–48; low status of, 234; manhood status and, 240–41; mobility of, 241; national honor and, 249; public sphere and terminology associated with, 245–47, 248, 255 n.33; rank and, 246; similarities to slaves, 239. *See also* Free poor males; Impressment, military

Songs: masculinity represented in, 43, 44, 249, 279 n.7

Spanish rule: influence of, 152 n.1

Speech patterns, male, 172, 181, 214 n.31

Spiritists: masculine identity and, 125–30, 131 nn.10, 16

Statutory rape, 11

Stephen, Lynn, 12

Sterilization, male, 45–46

Street children, 130–31 n.9

Streicker, Joel, 36

Structures of feelings, 262–63

Substance abuse: masculine identity and, 121, 122. *See also* Alcohol/alcoholics: masculine identity and

Sugar daddies, 67–68, 80 n.6

Surprised by Joy (Lewis), 219

Suspended Fictions (Kerr), 220

Symbols: reconfiguration of meanings of, 273–74

Taibo, Paco Ignacio, II, 211

Tango texts: masculinity represented in, 43–44

Tejedor, Carlos, 377–78

Tejedor Code, 378

Telenovel: definition of, 368 n.5

Terradas, Ignasi, 130 n.7

Textile workers' union, 107

Third Congress (MIR), 180

This Bridge Called My Back: Writings By Radical Women of Color, 271

Tinsman, Heidi, 181, 213 n.14

Tolbert, Katherine, 45, 46

Tonantzín, 273–74, 276

Torture, 208, 283, 302 n.3

Totem und Tabu (Freud), 223

Tourneur, Jacques, 218

Transformative vs. archaic consciousness, 79

Triple Alliance, 236

Twinam, Ann, 375–76

Two-career families, 103–4

Unemployment: impact on men, 340–41

United States: influence on concepts of Latin manliness, 16, 18, 79; Latinos in, 22. See also *El beso de la mujer araña* (The kiss of the spider woman, Puig)

Upper class: feminization of, 6, 36, 141; gendered resentment against, 190, 191, 200–202; morality as social control and, 182

Urbanization: impact of, 92–95, 135, 313–14

Uruguay, 47

Vaillant, George, 166

Valdés, Teresa, 12, 33

Valdez, Facundo: definition of vergüenza of, 256, 259; on displacement of patriarchy, 262–66, 277; shame versus honor in work of, 278 n.4

Valentía, 139

Valenzuela, Liliana, 275–76, 279 n.10

Valenzuela, Patricia, 215 n.43

Van Schowen, Bautista, 180

Vega, Margarita, 156–57

Venezuela: *malandros* and masculinity in, 20–21, 45, 115–33

Vergüenza: definitions of, 256, 259–62, 276–77; displacement of patriarchy and, 262–66, 270, 275, 277; gendered meanings of, 261–62; heterosexuality and, 272; male dominance and, 267, 270, 272–75; new *mestiza* and, 271–75; non-Hispanic society impact on, 262; oppressions and, 273; in Pancho Jaime attacks on political elite, 294–95; real/imagined communities and, 266–71; values associated with, 259–60, 263–64; in village culture, 259–61; women's roles defined by, 261–62. *See also* Honor/shame

"Vergüenza" (Valdez), 256

Viado, 311

La Vida en el Espejo (TV show), 353–54, 362–67

Vidal, Hernán, 179, 180

Videla Moya, Lumi, 209

Vila: definition of, 80 n.7

Vila São João: cuckolds and wily wives in, 68–71; honor/shame in, 65–66; on men as sexmongers, 66–68; social

Vila São João (*cont.*)
stigma and adultery in, 73–76; virginity
and male wiliness in, 66–67; women's
use of cuckoldry, 71–73
Violence: masculine socialization and, 47,
48; use of alcohol and, 155–56. *See also*
Rape
La Virgen de Guadalupe, 273–74, 276
Virginity: female, 66–67, 384; gender differences in, 10–11
Virility: active/passive issues in, 247–49;
definition of, 137; versus *hombría*, 137–
38; paternity and, 37–38; procreation
associated with, 15; sexual organs and,
139; women from subordinate classes
and, 68, 146, 151
Vitalidad (vitality), 139
Viveros, Mara, 4–5, 6, 12, 36–37, 45
Voting criteria, patriarchal role, 244–45

Wage inequality: in employment, 88–89
Warrior-victim, 14
West, D. J., 218, 219, 220
Whigham, Thomas, 380
Whiteness, 135, 141
Williams, Raymond, 262–63
Woman Hollering Creek and Other Stories
(Cisneros), 276
Women: adultery and, 70–71, 73–76, 80
n.11, 169–70; alcoholism of husbands
and, 162–64; alcohol use by, 154, 155,
156–57; arrests for sex-related cases,
371; attitudes at beginning of marriage,
338–39; beating of husbands by, 169;
child rearing and, 41, 73; cultural pacification of men by, 9, 21; division of labor
in household and, 13, 101, 102, 110, 168,
336–38; domestic sphere and, 100–
101, 138, 145–48; education and, 13,
145; effect of male military impress-

ment on, 242, 243, 244; effect of parenting on marriage and, 345–48; global
changes and impact of, 12–18, 34–35,
108; gossip about cuckoldry and, 71–73;
grandchildren and, 32, 91, 110; in
honor/shame literature, 65, 74; infanticide and, 381, 382; intergenerational
assistance and, 101–6; lesbianism and,
275, 297–98, 299, 367 n.1; as *malan-
dras*, 68–70; male attitudes toward, 32–
33, 85, 87–88, 106–8, 110–11, 151; middle class, 34–35, 43; Pancho Jaime publications and, 286, 293–94, 295–97;
public sphere and, 145, 150; rape of
married, 371–72, 379; reproductive
control of, 24 n.5; significance in negotiation of masculinities, 3, 65; slang for,
288; stereotypical qualities associated
with, 23, 79; in studies of men and
masculinities, 6, 19–20; from subordinate classes and sex, 68, 146, 151; as
symbols in MIR propaganda, 204–5;
transformation of middle class by, 34–
35; utilitarian attitudes toward men,
67–68; views on men, 52; in work sites
and homosociality, 44. *See also* Employment Patterns: of women; Marriage
"Women on Top" (Davis), 77
Work: average hours worked, 350 n.4; impact on family relationships, 85, 88;
male perceptions of achievement at,
105–6, 143–45, 149–50, 197, 346; masculine identity and, 138, 143, 150; public
sphere and, 143–45; as site of homosociality, 44, 143
Working-class male: image of, 181, 289,
294
Wounded masculinity, 21, 117. See also
Malandros (street-smart hustlers)
Wright, C. A., 222–23

We are grateful to Richard Parker and the Associação Brasileira Inter-disciplinar de AIDS for permission to reprint the photograph by Em-manuelle Barbaras.

The chapter "Drink, Abstinence, and Male Identity in Mexico City" includes reprinted portions of *Staying Sober in Mexico City*, by Stanley Brandes (Austin: University of Texas Press, 2002), with kind permission from University of Texas Press.

We are grateful to Sage Publications, Inc., for permission to reprint the following:

– "Philanderers, Cuckolds, and Wily Women," by Claudia Fonseca. *Men and Masculinities* 3, no. 3 (July 2001): 261–77; copyright 2001 by Sage Publications, Inc. Reprinted by permission of Sage Publications, Inc.

– "*Vergüenza* and Changing Chicano and Chicana Narratives," by Miguel Díaz Barriga. *Men and Masculinities* 3, no. 3 (July 2001): 278–98; copyright 2001 by Sage Publications, Inc. Reprinted by permission of Sage Publications, Inc.

– "Pancho Jaime and the Political Uses of Masculinity in Ecuador," by Xavier Andrade. *Men and Masculinities* 3, no. 3 (July 2001): 299–315; copyright 2001 by Sage Publications, Inc. Reprinted by permission of Sage Publications, Inc.

– "Contemporary Latin American Perspectives on Masculinity," by Mara Viveros. *Men and Masculinities* 3, no. 3 (July 2001): 237–60; copyright 2001 by Sage Publications, Inc. Reprinted by permission of Sage Publications, Inc.

– "The Social Constitution of Gender Identity among Peruvian Males," by Norma Fuller. *Men and Masculinities* 3, no. 3 (July 2001): 316–31; copyright 2001 by Sage Publications, Inc. Reprinted by permission of Sage Publications, Inc.

Library of Congress Cataloging-in-Publication Data
Changing men and masculinities in Latin America /
[edited by] Matthew C. Gutmann.
p. cm.   Includes bibliographical references and index.
ISBN 0-8223-3034-2 (cloth : alk. paper)
ISBN 0-8223-3022-9 (pbk. : alk. paper)
1. Men—Latin America—Identity. 2. Masculinity—
Latin America. 3. Men—Latin America—Sexual behavior.
I. Gutmann, Matthew C.
HQ1090.7.L29 C43 2003   305.31′098—dc21   2002010206

Books by Gish Jen

Fiction

Typical American. Houghton Mifflin, 1991.
Mona in the Promised Land. Knopf, 1996.
The Love Wife. Knopf, 2004.
World and Town. Knopf, 2010.

Short Fiction

Who's Irish? Knopf, 1999.

Nonfiction

Tiger Writing: Art, Culture, and the Interdependent Self. Harvard University Press, 2013.
The Girl at the Baggage Claim: Explaining the East-West Culture Gap. Knopf, 2017.

Contents

Preface   ix

Introduction   xi

Chronology   xxiii

The Intimate Outsider: Gish Jen   3
  Marilyn Berlin Snell / 1991

Writing about the Things That Are Dangerous:
A Conversation with Gish Jen   10
  Martha Satz / 1991

Interview with Gish Jen   20
  Yuko Matsukawa / 1991

Gish Jen: Interview   30
  Rachel Lee / 1993

Gish Jen: "So, Aren't You Going to Ask If I'm Jewish?"   42
  Ron Hogan / 1996

Gish Jen: An Interview on the American Experience   47
  Lilli Leggio / 2002

An Interview with Gish Jen   52
  Sarah Anne Johnson / 2002

Interview with Gish Jen   60
  Bill Moyers / 2003

A Conversation with Gish Jen about *The Love Wife*   78
   BookBrowse / 2004

Gish Jen Talks about How She Became a Writer   82
   Rob Neufeld / 2007

A Conversation with Gish Jen   89
   Suzanne Koven / 2013

Interview with Gish Jen: Tiger Writer Whose Novels
Reflect the Ways in Which We View Ourselves and Our Culture   109
   Jennifer Haupt / 2013

Interview with Gish Jen   112
   Paul Peppis / 2014

An Interview with Gish Jen   122
   Katie Young Foster / 2014

"Give Me My Daily Wickedness": Celebrated Novelist Gish Jen
Talks with *Chapter 16* about Truth-Telling and the Project of Fiction   125
   Sarah Norris / 2014

An Interview with Gish Jen   128
   Ryan Kim / 2016

Gish Jen: The Self in the World   132
   Jason Gots / 2017

A Conversation with Gish Jen   147
   Biling Chen / 2017

Index   159

Preface

Gish Jen, with her sensitivity to the language, her unique depiction of characters, and her subtle representation of various subject matters, including racial relations, has given an authentic voice to Chinese Americans, whose images have often suffered from stereotyping under the pens of earlier authors. Jen's witty, humorous, and ironic narrative voice effectively explains East-West cultural differences and helps mainstream readers adjust their perceptions of Asians and Asian Americans, as Jen asserts in her latest interview: "My emphasis is not on bridging it. People in the West don't even understand what the gap is. It's 2017 and to me it's unbelievable that there is still so little understanding. They see the copycat phenomena. Everywhere they go, they see things like 'What? That's weird,' and immediately they feel they must reject it. I want to explain these things in a different way that, I hope, will make things clearer than they have been. I am trying to de-familiarize East and West. Heaven help me!" (Chen). Jen is a contemporary writer concerned about cultural understanding, gaps, and clashes; about an individual's independence and interdependence in a multicultural society; and about a writer's obligation to help people understand cultures unfamiliar to them. She says, "I have more of a sense of wanting to open things up for other people. A writer makes a cultural space. And that cultural space can be very helpful" (Foster).

A decade ago when I read *Who's Irish?*, Jen's short story collection, I was immediately fascinated by its humorous language, and adopted it for my course on introduction to fiction. I should admit it was the first time that an Asian American writer became so appealing and impressive to me. In December 2014, during a family vacation in San Francisco, we visited the City Lights Bookstore one evening. Stacked up on a table was Gish Jen's *Tiger Writing*. I picked up a copy and told my son that it was a Christmas gift for him, even though I knew he would never want to be a tiger writer at the *age of erli* (a Chinese phrase to signify the age of independence at thirty). On our way back to the hotel I told my son and wife that I had been collecting interviews with Gish Jen and would soon start a book project on Jen as soon as I wrapped up the project *Conversations with Sterling Plumpp*.

I chose to work on this project simply because, as an immigrant, I had been impressed by Jen's humorous language and her desire to present culture in a way different from other Chinese American writers. Having gotten tied up with editing and teaching, I invited Biling Chen, an associate professor of English at the University of Central Arkansas, to coedit the Gish Jen project, for I had known her since our fellowships at the Asian Studies Development Program at the East-West Center in Hawaii in 2007. Her specialty in Asian American literature and her essay on Gish Jen published in the *Journal of Ethnic American Literature* demonstrated her qualifications as a coeditor for this volume. Biling wrote an introduction, worked on copyright permissions, and conducted an interview with Gish that covers all of Jen's fiction and nonfiction writings, including *The Girl at the Baggage Claim: Explaining the East-West Culture Gap*, while I wrote the book proposal, produced the chronology and index, worked on copyright permissions, and copyedited the interviews.

I am grateful beyond measure to the University Press of Mississippi for publishing this book and my editor, Katie Keene, for her patience with this project and for her charming words that Gish Jen had been a longstanding name on the press's wish list. We would like to jointly extend our gratitude to all interviewers and original publishers for granting their permissions, without which our project would have been still an embryo. We would also like to sincerely thank a number of people who have generously helped us with this project: Angela Ball for finding an interview we were unable to get, Ben Huang for listening to an interview to check on a transcription, Julia J. Heydon for communicating with us about a permission, and, of course, Gish Jen, for her significant contribution to American literature and her permissions.

To borrow Gish's words from *Tiger Writing*, "And now off with these words—*send!*" we hope this book will do some good and make some significance to the study and reading of Gish Jen's works.

JZ

Introduction

When Gish Jen (b. 1955) started writing fiction in the 1980s, mainstream American readers and the publishing industry were largely unaware of the cultural nationalism and ethnic nationalism that had been simmering within the Asian American community ever since the civil rights movement. In the imagination of the American majority, the sense of Asian Americans as exotic remained a given stereotype. Thus, writers of Asian origins, for all their efforts to assert their American identity while coming to terms with their ancestral values, could not shed their image of perpetual foreigners, and their works, fiction or nonfiction, were constantly received as a voyeuristic window to Asian ways of living rather than as a representation of Asian American hybridity in the contemporary United States. Due to this warped lens, books by such fine authors as Maxine Hong Kingston (b. 1940) and Amy Tan (b. 1952) suffered, one way or another, crude reading as well as the label of exoticism. It was in such a milieu, Jen tells Katie Young Foster decades later, that she made it her primary goal to create "artifice" rather than "artifact," writing "real fiction" that would not become an autobiography or a memoir in disguise.

Gish Jen, in fulfilling her project of de-exoticising Asian Americans in general and Chinese Americans in particular, moves her characters out of Chinatown, highlighting their acculturation into American society while avoiding the appropriation of myths, legends, and folklore from the old world. More importantly, the author employs humor and wit—skills and traits rarely associated with Asian American ethnicity—to tackle racial discrimination, ethnic stereotyping, and identity politics. From her first novel, *Typical American* (1991), to her latest *World and Town* (2010), tensions between the Confucian ideology and the Emersonian ethos are frequently peppered with a comic flavor. The unique angle and tone the novelist adopts to depict her characters and address social issues have won her critical acclaims. Besides a few awards and fellowships, John Updike in a 1999 special issue of the British publication *The Times Magazine* considers Gish Jen his literary successor; Elaine Showalter in her essay "The Female

Frontier" on May 8, 2009, for the British newspaper *The Guardian* puts Jen in the same league with Toni Morrison, Joyce Carol Oates, and Marilynne Robinson; Junot Diaz at the Key West Literary Seminar on January 9, 2016, credits Jen's *Typical American* as his guidebook and "ally" when he was writing *The Brief Wondrous Life of Oscar Wao* (2007). All of these recognitions bespeak Jen's influence on what's being written and read in an ethnically diverse contemporary literary scene.

Throughout her more than thirty years of writing, the author has been endlessly evolving. In recent years, apart from fiction writing, she has actively assumed such roles as public intellectual and cultural critic. An intellectual autobiography based on the Massey Lectures she delivered at Harvard University in 2012 was published in the following year, titled *Tiger Writing: Art, Culture, and the Interdependent Self.* The ease with which she explicates the aesthetics, ethics, and selfhood in the East and the West demonstrates that the now well-established writer has sustained and even thrived on the pulls of her multicultural heritage and affinity, be they by birth or by choice, be they Chinese, Jewish, Irish, or mainstream American. In the same vein, her newest book, *The Girl at the Baggage Claim: Explaining the East-West Cultural Gap* (2017), investigates causes of the West's misunderstanding of the East, accentuating the two worlds' contrasting ways of teaching and learning, modes of self-formation and self-perception, and attitudes toward creativity and plagiarism.

The conversations in this collection are arranged in chronological order, allowing the reader to gain a sense of how Gish Jen's thematic and technical choices developed over the course of her career, as well as her various thoughts regarding assimilation, multiculturalism, and the status of minority women writers. Invariably, Jen's interviewers would ask about her background as a daughter of first-generation Chinese immigrants; Bill Moyer, in fact, makes it the focus of his conversation with her. Students of literature who feel liberated by Roland Barthes's notion of "the death of the author" could relearn the validity of the authorial intention by bearing in mind Barthes's critic Camille Paglia's argument that there IS an author behind a book. Although Jen herself is not keen on galvanizing her readers to search for her shadow in the characters she creates, her revelations of her Chinese upbringing; of growing up under a Jewish cultural influence in Scarsdale, New York; of attending the MFA program at the University of Iowa after dropping out of the Stanford Business School; of her marriage to an Irish American; of her penchant for veering away from the I-centered tradition in the Western novel; and of her aversion to experimentation for its own sake, all provide us with extra keys to unlock the complexity of her narrative voices.

Jen's conversations with Yuko Matsukawa and Rachel Lee illuminate how she came to understand the plurality of Chinese American ethnicity, and how the ideology of the American Dream could help ameliorate the old-world feudalism embedded in immigrant communities. The novelist, drawing upon her parents' Shanghai upper-class origins and American graduate education, creates Ralph Chang and Helen Chang in *Typical American*. The couple shares with their real-life counterparts a snobbish attitude toward the predominantly working-class Chinese immigrants from Guangdong Province. But unlike Jen's father, the fictional patriarch fails to receive tenure, which forces him to abandon an academic career (a highly esteemed profession in Chinese culture) and switch to a restaurant business (which, due to its association with the merchant class, represents the lowest status in traditional Chinese society), selling such typical American food as pancakes and fried chicken. "Typical American," Jen tells Matsukawa, originally is a derogatory term her family used to express their disapproval of certain "vices" that mainstream Americans see as merits, including self-advertisement, unrestrained social ambition, and greed. Ironically, the Changs, by putting aside their class pride and adopting all of these qualities, not only rise from their downfall but also achieve great financial success. The narrator's claim in the beginning of the novel—"This is an American story"—becomes a reality in the end of the novel, demonstrating the young author's determination to equalize the Americanness of Chinese Americans with that of any other Americans.

De-exoticizing Chinese Americanness is, nevertheless, not the sole purpose of *Typical American*. More importantly, Jen tells Martha Satz, the novel aims to make her readers "think about what our myths and realities are." The Changs, having assimilated middle-class American values, realize the dangers of unbounded personal and social freedoms—an aspect of American culture that immigrants, because of their comparative cognitive framework, recognize readily, but that most mainstream Americans are unwilling to acknowledge. In her conversation with Marilyn Berlin Snell, Jen agrees with the interviewer on the American "tragedy of optimism," advocating the value of such immigrants' perspectives as the Changs': "Immigrants see America through different eyes: They see the potential, but they also see the shortcomings. They are the intimate outsider." The fledgling novelist's critique of American society's disregard of immigrants' voices still rings true today:

Unfortunately, many assimilated Americans aren't conscious of the risks of freedom. They don't have the Old World point of reference. Their forefathers have already shed the concept of social, cultural, ethical limits and the descendants do not like to be reminded of them. That is why Americans have so much trouble with an idea like regulating the amount of gas they use; the firearms they purchase; or their energy consumption. They don't like the idea that there are limits in this world.

While capitalist America believes in exceptionalism and expansionism, racist America denies its people of color equal access to social power. Not every individual's prosperity entails a positive social sanction that will enable her to transcend her ethnic origin and choose her own cultural, religious, and any other alliances without having the validity of her choices questioned. "So, aren't you going to ask if I'm Jewish?" Jen jokingly asks her interviewer Ron Hogan after the publication of her second novel, *Mona in the Promised Land* (1997), in which Ralph and Helen's teenage daughter, influenced by the "typical American" ideology that in America, one can be whoever one wants to be, decides to find her true self by converting from Catholicism (her parents' religion) to Judaism (her best friend's). Given the fixed assumption of the general reader that only insiders are able to portray accurately and vividly the lives of their ethnic group, many had thought Gish Jen was Jewish, and had been amazed that she was not. Jen tells Hogan that she, living in the time when public embrace of ethnic roots was becoming a trend, wanted to show how lives in America were much more complex than the cultural and ethnic identity they inherited at birth. Undoubtedly, socialization and schooling contribute as much as home culture to an individual's development of selfhood.

Although Jen did not go so far as to convert to Judaism, she credited the Scarsdale Jewish community for bringing out her comic voice and for opening her eyes to the value of fiction writing, while acknowledging that her parents, having grown up in China, had a higher regard for scholarship. Examined more deeply, "Aren't you going to ask if I am Jewish?" has a serious dimension to it. That is, to what extent does one's race become a liability and reduce the legitimacy of one's voluntary identity-switching? With Jen's unmistakable Asian face in front of him, would her conversationalist believe she was Jewish if she so proclaimed? By extension, would the majority of people in the United States accept that a Chinese American, such as Mona Chang in Jen's novel, could know more about as well as identify with Jewish culture more than with Chinese tradition? Why is it not weird and laughable when

Mona's Jewish boyfriend experiments with a Japanese identity? Through *Mona in the Promised Land*, Jen challenges the reader to take a closer look at the issue of interracial power in the light of self-invention: "Nobody asks an Irish American if he knows Gaelic, or if she celebrates Saint Patrick's Day, and if you don't, you are not seen as a fallen Irish. But for Chinese, it's different—how is it that people who don't even know us very well feel free to tell us about our identity and how we're living up to it?" (Hogan).

Mainstream America's impulse to push Asian Americans back to their own cultural enclave is, ironically, a byproduct of the civil rights movement—a movement that encouraged minorities to take pride in their ethnic heritage as a way to counter society's biases against them. Seen from another angle, white Americans' foray into other cultures suggests their uneasy awareness that the mainstream culture they embody is inadequate to represent the whole reality of the United States. A parody of such awkward conditions can be found in Pammie and Sven's Galatea-Pygmalion marriage in "House, House, Home"—the final story in Jen's third book, *Who's Irish?* (1999). Through the couple's arguments about the purposes of art, the novelist subtly exposes the disparities between socially imposed isolation and self-inflicted alienation, while poking fun at the trends of roots-finding, of bourgeoisie-bashing, and of restless experimentation popular among the liberals in the 1960s and '70s. On her male protagonist's superficial radicalism, Jen comments: "In Sven's mind being an artist is a self-glorifying thing. From his purely Western point of view, art is a tool of self-expression, like an individual, in and of itself" (Chen). The former college art lecturer, lacking the will to finish his dissertation and the talent to become an artist, tries to force his new-found interest in traditional Chinese painting on his Chinese American wife, a young architect in favor of applied art. If the couple's unbalanced power relation serves as a microcosm of racial inequality in American society, her ultimate refusal to be his tool of vicarious self-expression signifies that ethnic conflicts cannot be solved by a perfunctory celebration of multiculturalism. Jen thinks "everyone should be multicultural," but not "in the way that everybody's holiday is celebrated or everyone carries a flag waving their nationality." Rather, "everyone should be foundationally multicultural and able to use this in a way most productive for themselves as well as for their society" (Chen). Indeed, it is one thing to appreciate an ethnic minority's ancestral culture and absorb it to expand one's humanity; it is, however, quite another thing to appropriate it to conceal one's sense of inadequacy and aggrandize one's progressive image. Although in their struggle to find meaning in life both Sven and Pammie suffer an existential sense of alienation, his comes mainly from the stranger within himself whereas hers is largely pressured from without, including from him.

Jen explicates nuances of these alienations to Lilli Leggio when asked if she has ever met anyone who does not at times feel a little out of place in the contemporary United States:

> My observation has been that many people, male or female, feel themselves not quite at home in their town or office or whatever. We are a country, it seems, of misfits. I often try to emphasize this when I speak with Asian Americans and people who consider themselves people of color—that feelings of alienation are pretty general. But it's also true that for some groups it's an internal phenomenon and for other groups there's an external factor—and that makes a huge difference. The world intrudes more upon you.

Because of her race, Gish Jen, though well-adjusted in American society, does receive more of the world's intrusion into her being. For example, strangers on the street often assume that her Caucasian-looking baby daughter's German au pair is the biological mother and that Jen is the little girl's nanny.

Notwithstanding, the novelist sublimates her vexation into a contemplation on the fluid nature of the contemporary family in her fourth book, *The Love Wife* (2004). Conversing with *BookBrowse*, Jen remarks: "In my novel, of course, the racial breakdown of the family is completely different. And the Wong family is not my family. But the questions raised by my real life experience—questions about what a 'real' family is, about what's 'natural,' and about what choice we have in these matters—do inform the book." Under her pen, Jen's personal frustrations become Blondie's anxieties, including her status as the only white member in the Wong family; her inability to communicate in Chinese with the two daughters she and her Chinese American husband adopted from China; and her fear of losing her family's love to the Chinese nanny hired by her mother-in-law on account of their shared racial and cultural roots. Unlike Jen's previous two novels where characters' different perspectives of the same issues are articulated by an implicit omniscient narrator, *The Love Wife* allows all major characters to tell their own stories that could shed a different light on one another's narratives. This new approach is the result of the author feeling more self-assured in her mid-career: "I have finally become confident that my voice will never leave me, and I seem to want to absent myself, that I might inhabit others. In truth, I am not wholly absent from this book, and back when I was 'finding my voice', I never lost sight of other points of view. But I strike a different balance in *The Love Wife* than I did in my early career." Indeed, the intricate plot and cacophonous soliloquies correspond to the characters' inner struggles as well as their tensions with one another; identities by descent battle heart-wrenchingly with identifications by consent. A good exercise for her best novel yet, *World and Town*.

Perhaps because identity issues have been a major obsession in our times, Jen has to emphasize periodically to her interviewers that the roles of art and religion in the human life have also been portrayed in her fiction. These two subject matters are delineated with a richer depth and a larger scope in *World and Town*. The author, troubled by the post-9/11 American xenophobia and intolerance of non-Christians, especially Muslims, imagines a corrective, depicting how a group of retirees, while dealing with their own physical, financial, and existential crises related to aging, help a traumatized Cambodian refugee family adjust to the New England life. World religions and living philosophies collide here. Christian fundamentalism clashes with Confucian secularism in the friendship between Sophy Chung and Hattie Kong. The Cambodian teenager, unable to find nurturance from her Buddhist mother and alcoholic father, seeks a sense of belonging in an Evangelical church, but the retired biology teacher wants to save her from the narrow faith that her own Caucasian maternal grandparents used to impose on her. The widow, meanwhile, strives to reach a Daoist state of magnanimity through practicing Chinese landscape painting, so that she could handle the request of her *fengshui*-obsessed Hong Kong relatives to relocate the bones of her deceased parents. The conflicts between sense and sensibility, between science and spirituality, and between autonomy and intimacy are further aggravated by Hattie's reencounter with her old flame Carter Hatch, an agnostic who believes in worldly glory and self-fulfillment as vehemently as a born-again Christian does in God. The ultimate product is quite satisfying and has consistently received positive reviews, although to *Boston Globe*'s Richard Eder *World and Town*, for all its many merits, is still over-storied. This comment, I think, indirectly propels Jen to examine the tension she has felt between the way she wants to write and the way she is supposed to write—an aesthetic as well as ethical issue she explores in her next book, *Tiger Writing*.

Preparing the Massey lectures gives the author a good opportunity to reflect on her tendency to "over-story" her novel and on her reluctance to center her narrative on a single protagonist according to the rule of Western modern fiction. She finds from cross-cultural psychology two terms to articulate her hybridity—interdependent self and independent self—and attributes her "digressive" narrative style to her interdependent self, mostly cultivated by her Chinese upbringing. In the process of writing, her interdependent self constantly interacts with her American independent self, desiring to have an equal say. The author comments on her own work to Jennifer Haupt:

> I see that my books are often hybrid works, and tend to have, for example, an ensemble feel. The protagonist is a little bigger than the other characters but not much, and his or her status may be questioned by the work overall. For example, in my last book, *World and Town*, there are five sections. Three are given to one character, so she's the protagonist. But by having these two other interrupting sections, with related but fairly separate narratives—narratives that do not represent different views of the same events, but focus on different sets of events—there's the sense that this could be a totally different book if one of the other "protagonists" was given more space. What's more, there is a suggestion that these two other possibilities are just two of a number of possible narratives. The main protagonist's story has an independent arc, that's to say, but its context is quite interdependent.

Those who are familiar with cultures where the self is mostly defined by his or her relationships with others rather than by the individual's uniqueness need not search hard to find that such Eastern classics as *A Thousand and One Nights* and *The Dream of Red Chamber* are written in a meandering narrative style and with a large ensemble cast. In this type of works the male and female protagonists' stories invariably dominate the opening and the concluding chapters, but other characters could respectively take on the central role of various chapters in between. Their stories, though self-sustaining, are in essence related to those of the protagonists, revealing an aesthetic anchored in a worldview that evaluates individuals in context (as opposed to in isolation). Although Jen has never compared her narrative style to those of the above-mentioned two books, her "apology for *World and Town*" invites her readers to read outside the box—to expand their vision of the novel by adopting a different artistic lens: "With globalization in full swing, it's a good time to take stock of our ideas about art and what ideas about art are in other cultures" (Burns).

To Jen, art, especially fiction, carries a tremendous social responsibility. Experimenting solely for the sake of formal inventiveness does not appeal to her. Authors she admires are those who succeed in challenging their readers to reappraise the norms of their society and culture, including Jane Austen,

Philip Roth, Alice Munro, Jhumpa Lahiri. But Jen is also keenly aware that what is eye-opening in one era can become blinding in another, because even serious literature cannot completely avoid feeding on as well as feeding back to readers certain esteemed values of their society, even if these values themselves are overdue for reassessment. As demonstrated in the conversations about her *Tiger Writing*, the author wonders if individualism in the West today has ceased to be liberating but has become a prison, in which the practitioners of this ideology navel-gaze at their jealously guarded independent self, oblivious of the humanity of others. The unique and autonomous I, a concept invented by the Enlightenment philosophers and evangelized in Emerson's Transcendentalism, has morphed into a hyperindividualism that guides not only the conduct of the majority of contemporary Americans but also the artistry of most novelists. Jen remarks in her talk with Suzanne Koven in *The Rumpus*: "The novel is always on the side of the individual, the individual, the individual, the individual, freedom, freedom, freedom. . . . It's never about maturity and balance." In so critiquing the cultural and literary biases of the West, Jen thinks the current mainstream American culture and fiction writing can benefit from a more interdependent worldview and way of living.

The overwhelmingly positive response to her *Tiger Writing* encouraged Jen to continue examining the cultural gap between East and West, the result of which is *The Girl at the Baggage Claim*. East and West here mainly refer to East Asian societies and the United States. The author, speaking mostly to people in the West who do not know much about the East, hopes that "in addition to literary people, lawyers and business people will find this book very relevant to what they are doing" (Chen). The story of the Asian girl in the title—the story about her admission into Milton Academy by having her sister, who spoke better English, do a Skype interview for her with the school—is used as "a jump-off point" to discuss issues ranging from selfhood and education to intellectual properties and brand names.

Jen's conversation with Jason Gots illuminates how the operations of human relationships, ethics, and laws differ in societies where the flexi-self/interdependent self dominates, and in those where the big pit self/independent self prevails. By Western standards, the aforementioned girl's behavior is unethical and deserves expulsion, but most East Asians would be rather lenient about her cheating, because siblings are each other's flesh and blood—the boundary between self and other in this case is beside the point. The East's flexible attitude toward personhood can also be found in its approach to education. As opposed to the West's emphasis on self-discovery and disposition, the East believes in training and discipline. In

China, Jen tells Gots, if a child is not good at math or music, adults, instead of attributing it to the kid's aptitude, would insist that he should spend more time and work harder on the subject. Most Westerners would feel such a demand a violation of the child's natural being:

> I think very foundationally this avocado pit self is an introjective divinity. In other words, we feel God lies within, whereas in many places in the world, God, whatever it is, lies without. So, because we feel God lies within, everything God says within is what we pay attention to, but that's simply an idea. It's an idea with roots. It's not an objective truth, right? It is just an idea that's been very, very powerful. It's relatively new; it's very, very, very powerful, and the dominance of the West rests on this idea.

The practice of this God-within-oneself ideology has certainly led to the West's supremacy in technological and economic developments, but Jen thinks it is unjust to use the West's model of success as the universal standard by which to define creativity, morality, and legality. In arts and sciences, the West tends to privilege geniuses/innovators over masters (those who work within a tradition or refine a product based on a prototype); hence, the former's legal right to long-term financial gains from their intellectual properties is deemed logical and fair while the latter's efforts and accomplishments are seen as second best and worth relatively less. The same rationale applies to businesses. Having a distinctive and unique brand is thought in the West essential to success. "And yet if you look at Asia, there are spectacularly successful businesses based on this incremental model. They did not invent the smartphone, but they refine it just like Jiro with sushi. The result is something that is pretty cool, and I'll say, very successful" (Gots).

Jen's enthusiasm to "correct" the West's misperception of the East and her sense of humor sparkle all over the conversations collected in this book. Issues that get on her nerve could make her sound a little exasperated, bespeaking the strength of her conviction. For instance, when Ryan Kim asks her thoughts about Michael Derrick Hudson, a white male writer who builds his literary career by adopting an Asian pen name, Jen states: "It's just somebody being a jerk." "I will devote exactly one nanosecond of my time worrying about that kind of con-artist." In such a multicultural society as the United States, readers' evaluations of literary works have become inevitably, though not always justifiably, intertwined with their knowledge (or assumption) of the author's race, ethnicity, or gender. The authors themselves and the publishing industry have particular stakes in who and what get published, read, and promoted. Considering this topic worth exploring,

I try to elicit from Jen more comments on whether an author's true gender and racial identities should play a role in our judgment of his work; she gives a short response for literary critics to ponder over: "I think they matter when the value of the work is tied up with its authenticity." Obviously, Jen is quite protective of and always ready to de-stereotype socially and culturally misrepresented people. Queried by *The Rumpus* about the significance of the title of her first nonfiction book, *Tiger Writing*, she explains that it is partly to take issue with the parenting method Amy Chua portrays in her *Battle Hymn of the Tiger Mother*, since she feels that the latter's memoir, though a self-parody, would reinforce the image of Asians as dogged workers without critical thinking. That said, in her conversation with Gots, we find Jen accentuating the merits of Chinese parenting and schooling (i.e., the benefits of the Tiger Mother's way). Seemingly contradictory, these views indicate the complexity of all cultures and of Jen as a cultural critic.

The author, though not afraid of contradictions, is aware of the danger of generalization, as she repeatedly emphasizes in my conversation with her, "I hate to generalize." Yet, without generalizing a culture first, one can hardly begin to address its various shades and shapes. By taking the risk of sounding dualistic, Jen is in essence creating a temporary structure for her readers to understand the two fundamentally divergent mindsets, while at the same time reminding us that culture, like identity, is not set in stone but constantly changing. The West could learn from the East to rediscover the interconnectedness of things and people, and contemporary Chinese culture could put into practice the Western ideas of individual rights and freedom. Ultimately, Jen makes it clear that, in the applications and evaluations of values, historical and cultural contexts should be taken into consideration. It is safe to say that, in the years to come, Gish Jen will continue to promote intercultural communication so that the multiplicity of contemporary America and of the worlds beyond can be viewed with undistorted lenses.

BC

Works Cited

Burns, Carole. "Interview with Gish Jen, Author of *Tiger Writing.*" *Washington Post*, March 19, 2013. Web.

Eder, Richard. "This American Life: Aging, Lonely Chinese Immigrant Struggles with Shadows of Past. "*Boston Globe*, October 10, 2010. Web.

Chronology

1955   Born Lillian Jen on August 12 in Long Island, New York, to immigrant parents, Norman Chao-pe and Agnes Jen, from China.

1973   Graduates from Scarsdale High School in New York.

1977   Graduates from Harvard University with a BA in English and works for Doubleday Publishing.

1979–80   Attends Business School at Stanford University.

1980   Teaches in a coal mining college in China.

1981   Publishes "Bellying-Up" in the *Iowa Review*.

1982   Publishes "The Small Concerns of Sparrows" in *Fiction International*.

1983   Graduates from the University of Iowa with an MFA in fiction; receives the *Transatlantic Review* award from Henfield Foundation.

1984   Publishes "The White Umbrella" in the *Yale Review*, reprinted in *Home to Stay: Asian American Women's Fiction*, edited by Sylvia Watanabe and Carol Bruchac (New York: Greenfield Review Press, 1990), and in *My Mother's Daughter: Stories by Women*, edited by Irene Zahava (Freedom, CA: Crossing Press, 1991).

1985   Publishes "Eating Crazy" in the *Yale Review*.

1986   Receives a Radcliffe College Bunting Institute Fellowship; serves as a lecturer in fiction writing at Tufts University; publishes "In the American Society" in the *Southern Review*, reprinted in *New Worlds of Literature: Writings from America's Many Cultures*, edited by Jerome Beaty and J. Paul Hunter (New York: Norton, 1989), *The New Generation: Fiction for Our Time from America's Writing Programs*, edited by Alan Kaufman (New York: Anchor P, 1987), and *Imagining America: Stories from the Promise Land*, edited by Wesley Brown and Amy Ling (New York: Persea Books, 1991).

1987   Resident at MacDowell Colony; publishes "The Water Faucet Vision" in *Nimrod*; receives the Katherine Anne Porter Contest Prize.

1988   "The Water Faucet Vision" is included in *The Best American Short Stories 1988*, edited by Mark Helprin; receives a National Endowment for the Arts Fellowship, a Massachusetts Artists Foundation Fellowship, and the Urban Arts Project Prize (Boston MBTA).

1990   Publishes "What Means Switch" in the *Atlantic Monthly* and "Grover at the Wheel" in the *New Yorker*.

1990–91 Visiting writer at the University of Massachusetts.

1991   Publishes *Typical American* with Houghton Mifflin; Finalist for the National Book Critics' Circle Award; publishes "Challenging the Asian Illusion" and "Our Luck: Chips, But No Breaks" in the *New York Times Magazine*.

1992   Receives a Guggenheim Foundation Fellowship.

1993   Publishes in *Nimrod Awards XIV: Making Language*.

1994   Publishes "Birthmates" in *Ploughshares*.

1995   "Birthmates" is included in *The Best American Short Stories 1995*.

1996   Publishes *Mona in the Promised Land* with Knopf; *Mona in the Promised Land* is named to the *New York Times* notable books of the year and *Los Angeles Times* best ten books of 1996; publishes "An Ethnic Trump" in the *New York Times Magazine*.

1997   Publishes "Who's to Judge? Identity Politics v. Inner Lives" in *New Republic*.

1998   Publishes "Who's Irish?" in the *New Yorker*, "Lulu in Exile" in the *New York Times Magazine*, "Just Wait" in *Ploughshares*, and "Chin" in the collection *Shorts* (Granta Books).

1999   Publishes *Who's Irish? Stories* with Knopf; receives a Lannan Literary Award for Fiction; "Birthmates" is included in *The Best American Short Stories of the Century*, edited by John Updike.

2000   Publishes "Inventing Life Steals Time; Living Life Begs It Back," "Coming into the Country," and "For Wen Ho Lee, a Tarnished Freedom" in the *New York Times Magazine*.

2001   Receives a Radcliffe Institute for Advanced Study Fellowship.

2003   Receives a Fulbright Fellowship to China and a Mildred and Harold Strauss Living Award from the American Academy of Arts and Letters; publishes "Racial Profiling" in *Time* (Asia Edition), August 18, vol. 162, no. 7.

2004   Publishes *The Love Wife* with Knopf; receives honorary PhD from Emerson College.

2005	Publishes "A Short History of the Chinese Restaurant" in *Slate*.
2006	Featured in a PBS American Masters Program on the American Novel; publishes "Amaryllis" in *Paris Review* and "Gratitude" in *Ploughshares*.
2008–10	Serves as professor of creative writing and codirector of the Creative Writing Program at Brandeis University.
2009	Elected a member of the American Academy of Arts and Sciences; publishes "Updike Remembered" in *New Republic*.
2010	Publishes *World and Town* with Knopf.
2011	*World and Town* wins the Massachusetts Book Prize in Fiction and is nominated for the 2012 International IMPAC Dublin Literary Award; publishes "Bringing Context to the Page" and "My Muse Was an Apple Computer" in the *New York Times*.
2012	Delivers the Massey Lectures at Harvard University; publishes "Asian Men Can Jump" in the *New York Times*.
2013	Publishes *Tiger Writing: Art, Culture, and the Interdependent Self* with Harvard University Press; "The Third Dumpster" is included in *The Best American Short Stories 2013*, edited by Elizabeth Strout.
2013	Named Sidney Harman Writer-in-Residence, Baruch-CUNY.
2015	Receives honorary PhD from Williams College.
2016	Visiting professor of literature at New York University–Shanghai.
2017	Publishes *The Girl at the Baggage Claim: Explaining the East-West Culture Gap* with Knopf. Receives the MOCA Legacy Award from the Museum of Chinese in America.
2018	Publishes "No More Maybe" in the *New Yorker*.

Conversations with Gish Jen

The Intimate Outsider: Gish Jen

Marilyn Berlin Snell / 1991

From *New Perspectives Quarterly*, Summer 1991, 56–60. Reprinted by permission of Marilyn Berlin Snell.

Author of the widely acclaimed novel *Typical American*, Gish Jen has thought a great deal about what it means to be American, what sacrifices assimilation demands, what is lost in the process of migration and mutation and what America has to gain by accommodating the infusion of different cultures. In the following interview with *NPQ* Senior Editor Marilyn Berlin Snell, Jen—the daughter of Chinese immigrants to the US—discusses the odyssey of the immigrant in the New World.

NPQ: In *Typical American*, which recounts the lives of three Chinese immigrants in America in the 1940s, you illustrate an ironic clash of cultures. As the Confucian ideal of hard work and filial piety, along with the Chinese belief in the value of education, comes into conflict with the immigrants' assimilation process into the American mainstream, one can't help but wonder what the term "middle-class Americana values" actually means.

Did you intend this culture clash to be so ironic? That certain fundamental Chinese cultural traits are harmonious with the American myth but out of sync with the American reality?

Gish Jen: I don't know that hard work and educational attainment are exactly congruent with the dreams of middle-class America. "Middle-class American values" are ideals, myths Americans aspire to, values they would like to believe they really cared about. But this is not the America the immigrant meets.

The average suburban dweller is not particularly anxious for his or her child to go on and get a PhD. For instance, education in the US is viewed as a road to economic achievement and, for the most part, most middle-class

American parents would greatly prefer their sons and daughters were successful businessmen rather than scholars.

This reality is very different from the situation in China, where learning for learning's sake is much more respected. It's not that the Chinese are a nobler people. In fact, the reason that scholarship is so revered in China is that there has always been a very direct link between scholarship and power. Historically, the civil service exams were operated as a path for the scholar to become, say, a governor of a province. In the US, there is almost no link between scholarship and power.

As for the "value" of work in the US, the US did at one point have a strong Protestant work ethic that was linked to work for its own sake. For the early immigrants, work was the way to spiritual salvation. But that ideal changed radically once the Push Westward began.

Of course, much of America's attraction and vitality are directly related to its rejection of Old World verities. Americans don't believe that they inherit their destiny from their fathers, for instance. They don't want to live the lives of their fathers, or grandmothers. They want the freedom to make their own lives.

Yet there are also great costs involved, costs which directly affect the most enshrined American institution: the family. Relative to anywhere else in the world, the family structure in America is very weak. The divorce rate is 50 percent; extended family networks are tenuous.

There is no guarantee that the values immigrants bring to the New World—strong extended family ties, or belief in scholarship in the case of the Chinese—will withstand the pressures of assimilation.

Any group that comes to America attempts to reestablish the Old World on new soil, which is natural. And yet they are changed by their environment. They are changed by its opportunities as well as by its changers. And people are changed differently depending on their individual predispositions. The immigrant who longs for economic achievement will be affected by certain opportunities and influences much differently than the immigrant who comes to America to take advantage of one of its universities, for instance. And the women who come to this country see the freedom it offers in different terms still. For instance, they see the opportunity for romantic love. Or they see in their new home the opportunity to study and to excel on their own for perhaps the first time in their lives.

These are typical American opportunities, but they are accompanied by responsibilities. Indeed, when one escapes the circumscribed life of the Old

World, new questions surface: Who am I? What can I make of myself? In the US, where there is so much more freedom, the immigrant sees that he or she also has a responsibility to attain at least some degree of self-knowledge. That is very different from the Old World, where one is born into a preordained life, remains in that circumscribed role, and never has to think about it very much.

NPQ: Immigrants bring that culture of limits to America. But in *Typical American* you write about the challenge posed when the culture of limits meets the land of opportunity: "In spread-out America, this loose-knit country, where one could do as one pleased, a person had need of a different understanding. Ralph needed to know what his limits were, and his impulses, what evil and what good he had in his soul and with his hands to fashion." What are the hazards of opportunity?

Jen: America is a place of great opportunity and great danger; a place with so many fewer social limits that one begins to feel a kind of vertigo and see a land without *any* limits. The danger occurs when we come to believe that there are no limits, not even personal limits. The land of dreams, of imagination and positive thinking must also be grounded in *terra firma*, whether that grounding is based on an Old World sense of limits or on some New World awareness of the responsibility demanded by freedom.

Unfortunately, many assimilated Americans aren't conscious of the risks of freedom. They don't have the Old World point of reference. Their forefathers have already shed the concept of social, cultural, ethical limits and the descendants do not like to be reminded of them. That is why Americans have so much trouble with an idea like regulating the amount of gas they use; the firearms they purchase; or their energy consumption. They don't like the idea that there are limits in this world.

NPQ: Isn't the knowledge that life is circumscribed—that there are limits—a somewhat timely lesson for an adolescent America facing family disintegration, eroding business and personal ethics, diminishing natural and economic resources? Will it be the immigrants who construct the cultural boundaries we need? Will they be the ones that infuse America with a sense of limits?

Jen: It is interesting you say "adolescent America." That is exactly how I see us—as "coming of age." Perhaps we are moving from delinquency to malaise but I believe we may be ready as a nation to begin the process of maturation, which necessarily involves coming to terms with tragedy.

I find it incredible that in American literature there is no established tradition of tragedy. Such denial keeps us from a balanced view of life, and it also separates it from the literary and philosophical traditions of most other societies in the world.

As to whether the immigrant will have any effect on the American growth process: whether we like it or not, America is being infused with other perspectives all the time. The problem is that the voices are not always heard, and if they are, they are not always respected.

Many people think immigrants are all just delighted to be in the US. Some of them are. A lot of them work very hard to get here. And yet it is amazing how critical they are of this country. Get into any cab and some Lebanese or Ethiopian or American cabby will tell you exactly what he thinks of this country. Immigrants see America through different eyes: They see the potentials, but they also see the shortcomings. They are the intimate outsiders.

However, by and large, we don't listen to them. We would listen to a Lebanese cab driver on the subject of Lebanese, but we are not going to listen to what he has to say about America. And that is a mistake.

NPQ: We don't hear that voice, that accented voice.
Jen: No! We could be in the cab with Alexis de Tocqueville and we would be saying, "Tell me about France."

Immigrants have a comparative framework which is essential in gaining any sort of perspective. They can appreciate what Americans take for granted and they can point out what Americans would prefer to deny.

NPQ: In your book, you had a masterful way of drawing America's cultural land mines: the rootlessness, greed, and misplaced values—all the dangers that exist in a society that doesn't have a strong sense of limits. At one point you write of America's rootlessness, "The way Americans in general like to move around, the Chinese love to hold still; removal is a fall and an exile." In coming to maneuver these land mines, your characters become more American but they also experience a kind of tragedy of optimism when they realize that "America is no America."
Jen: They realize that America is not the idealized version of itself, which is not necessarily bad. But they do indeed experience the "tragedy of optimism"—a phrase that captures a necessary transition in the process of individual, or societal, development and growth.

NPQ: Yet none of your characters were left unscathed by this process of assimilation. Could you imagine a less painful process, one less determined to flatten out difference and impose a kind of uniformity on "the other" as a rite of passage into the American mainstream?

Jen: "Untouched" is perhaps a more appropriate term. The family I write about almost falls apart but they come to a new point of maturity that they otherwise would never have reached.

My characters are searching out the texture of evil. They want to push the limits and test the opportunities presented by this country and their own individual characters.

But let me answer by giving a real example of how immigrants can retain a vibrant sense of themselves in the New World: There is a town near Los Angeles called Monterey Park, which could be a town in Asia. Though it is not possible to live in the US and not become part of the New World, it is possible to still remain 85 percent Chinese. People speak their native language; they live in a vibrant ethnic community; they buy and sell their goods to one another. In the case of Monterey Park, difference was definitely not flattened out.

NPQ: The example of Monterey Park is an important one. America allows the immigrant to create economic space, but what about gaining access to the mainstream? While those in Monterey Park can maintain strong cultural connections and create economic space and sell to one another, will they ever be "assimilated"? They are living in ethnic enclaves.

Jen: True. But one can have quite a lot of economic achievement in that little enclave. However, it is also true that in order to assimilate, almost by definition, one must sacrifice part of one's culture.

I believe that the challenge for the new America, the one that is being fashioned at the end of the millennium, is to find a balance between the old and the new, the immigrant and the native, the white and the nonwhite. In striking a balance, we are not going to be exactly the way we were when we came from China. We will speak a different language, our manner will be different. But all growth involves change and all change involves loss. Our children will never do what we do and thank God. Otherwise we would still be in a cave.

Am I in favor of the melting pot? Of course not. I don't like Asian American boys and girls dying their hair blonde to look like Barbie and Ken. The melting pot is an obsolete metaphor.

In a way, the immigrant—or the immigrant literature of which I am a part—is pushing the limits and expanding the notion of America's view of itself. The fact is that there are many social forces at work on the American mind that are acting as catalysts for change. What is the "typical American" these days? Somehow, we must found a new American myth that is more inclusive of diversity than any of the myths we have had so far. Our old myths are not holding. Today, we are a nation of tribes; units of unbridgeable differences. We need to create a new notion of what it means to be American, one that acknowledges our diversity.

NPQ: You rarely touch on the issue of prejudice in your book. It is addressed indirectly, but one of the few and most poignant moments is when you are talking about baseball, the great American pastime. "The one time they went to an actual game, people had called them names and told them to go back to their laundry. They in turn had sat impassive as the scoreboard. Rooting in their hearts, they said later. Anyway, they preferred to stay home and watch it on TV. 'More comfortable.' 'More convenient.' 'Can see better,' they agreed."

They never went back. They became observers rather than participants in the great American pastime. What role does prejudice play in the lives of immigrants? Is it as American as baseball? Or is it a minor irritant for the immigrant, hardly worth mentioning?

Jen: It is most certainly worth mentioning. I just prefer understatement, since so much has been made of it already. People don't have to be hit over the head with the issue of prejudice. They understand.

People often ask me why there is a surge of interest in Asian American writers. America is embracing the Asian American now partly because they are the easiest minority to embrace. As racial tensions become more and more heightened in the US—note only the police beating of the black motorist in Los Angeles or the recent riots between Hispanics and police in Washington, DC—it is nice to be able to point to a "model minority."

In general, the subtext of all these articles about how well the Asian Americans are doing is that the system is functioning fairly. If the blacks and Hispanics worked harder, they too would manage to succeed.

But touting Asian Americans as the model minority cloaks the full scope of the Asian American experience. A great many Asians are stuck in America's Chinatowns and are having a very, very difficult time getting out. When people talk about the model minority they forget that Asians, too, are stratified by class.

Also, it is an act of ignorance to blur the differences between different groups of Asians. For instance, my sense is that Japanese Americans feel rather more separate than Chinese Americans in the US. Unlike Japan, China has been a country where borders have fluctuated wildly, taking in many foreign influences over the years. China's ability to be flexible with its sense of self began with its flexible geography. Today, the Chinese are well known throughout Asia as business people able to transplant themselves to other countries.

Further, when one looks at the success of the Asian Americans, a lot of those success stories are sons and daughters of upper-class immigrants. They came to the US with a strong sense of self, even if they didn't have a lot of money. They didn't grow up with somebody telling them they were ugly, no good, or inferior. They were well educated. They grew up with an incredible sense of entitlement. They come to this country and have to work hard. But in a very basic way, they operate from the principle that America is going to give them what was owed them to begin with.

NPQ: In your book, you discuss what the nonwhite immigrant, lacking the position of class, needs to survive in America: "To be non-white in this society was indeed to need education and accomplishment—some source of dignity. A white person was by definition somebody. Other people needed, across their hearts, one steel rib."

Jen: Well, the fact is that if you are a minority, you never know when the rug is going to be pulled out from under you—whether or not you have education, dignity, or accomplishment.

I do not want to be put in the position of being a professional victim, but that is not to say that I do not have to endure a fair amount of discrimination. One has to put it in perspective. There are a lot of people in this country who are feared, even hated, because of their race and class. Out of respect for them, I feel I must distinguish between the degrees of discrimination we experience.

If we as a society were sophisticated enough to acknowledge the gradations of discrimination that exist, I would feel much more comfortable addressing the issue of racism. But I do not want to become a professional victim and I do not want to obscure from viewing those people who are truly suffering.

Writing about the Things
That Are Dangerous:
A Conversation with Gish Jen

Martha Satz / 1991

From *Southwest Review* 78.1 (1993): 132–40. Reprinted by permission of Martha Satz.

Interviewer's note: In November 1991, I interviewed Gish Jen on the occasion of the publication of her first novel, *Typical American*. The novel deals with a young Chinese man, Ralph Chang, who comes to do graduate work in engineering and pursue the American Dream as he understands it in China. In this country, he is reunited with his sister Theresa and marries her friend Helen. Much of their lives is a series of misadventures and disasters. Their idea of America and the American Dream is continually changed and ultimately transformed.

Martha Satz: I wanted to ask you about the choice of a male protagonist for your first novel, *Typical American*. Can you say why you chose to write about a male?

Gish Jen: It was partly a technical choice. When I started out to write this book, I thought that in order to fill 350 pages or whatever (which seemed to me quite intimidating at the time) you would be better off with somebody active, somebody who does things. You and I might appreciate people who simply think, but they don't always make good fiction. And it occurred to me that in this generation and culture, men had a greater latitude than women and that therefore a male protagonist might make for a broader book. Also, Ralph as a character came very easily to me, and I was interested in him.

Satz: How did he come to you?

Jen: He first arose in a story titled "In the American Society," which was the original title of this book. That story was from the point of view of Callie, the daughter.

Satz: You created the second generation first?

Jen: Yes and no. That story was about Callie, but the father figured very heavily too. Especially young novelists like myself (relatively young—I'm not as young as perhaps I look) often write books about their parents' generation. I think that's one of the big basic tasks a person is confronted with, to figure out what reality was like for her parents.

Satz: You have said you found yourself writing often with a self-consciously explicating voice. I think you do very well with this. You explain for me, or as I envision for my students, what it's like to try to find one's home in a new and different culture. That is, it seems to me that one of the issues in your novel is the nature of home. There are buildings that are torn down and transported. Is this an example of what you had in mind as issues you consciously explicate?

Jen: Well, those are the kinds of themes that are less conscious. Those are the kinds of things I notice myself when I get to the end of a draft. I say to myself, "God, there are a lot of roof problems." And then I go back and heighten those motifs by having Ralph comment, for example, "Why do we have so many problems with roofs?" I do not start with ideas about the nature of home or whatever and then try to shoehorn them into the work.

Satz: There's a little story Theresa tells about the family that transports a house, tears it down, and builds it again.

Jen: Yes, that's right. In a different place.

Satz: It had a leak and the question was, why would they move the house if it were flawed. And the answer was—well, maybe they were used to it. Wasn't that a conscious explication of a cultural theme?

Jen: The concept was not initially conscious. In later drafts, I saw how Ralph and Theresa had attempted to reconstruct their family via a marriage— something many people do, by the way, not just immigrants—and then I used the story of the housemoving to reinforce it.

Satz: Well, how would you characterize your own novel? What is your conscious perception of it?

Jen: What I came to understand after I'd worked on it awhile is that this novel is about coming to America and what that means in reality. People think you set foot in America and you become American instantly. For the characters in my book, it takes a while to become American and it's not so much becoming a citizen that makes them feel American, it's something like buying a house.

Satz: And seeing the grass grow.

Jen: I think that's much more the truth. Also, I think the truth is also that America holds out this promise that a person can do anything. Right? "Be all that you can be." And Ralph believes that for a time, but he comes to realize the limits here. I hope *Typical American* will he viewed not only as an immigrant story but as a story for all Americans, to make us think about what our myths and realities are. We are not a country that likes to think in terms of limits.

Satz: Absolutely.

Jen: I can remember how much trouble there was during the gas shortages. We believe in endless expansion and endless expression of our will. The grandiose self.

Satz: Absolutely.

Jen: By the end of the book Ralph comes to a point of reflection where he starts to ask himself questions.

Satz: Instead of do, do, do—

Jen: Exactly. It's do, do, do, do, but finally he has to stop and say—My God, what have I done?—and before I do more, don't I need to know something about who I am. Ralph is at a point much like the one we are at as a country. Our adolescence is over—I hope. We're sobered. People are starting to think about the environment, about war, about our place in the world.

Satz: And maybe this is one of the advantages of getting the perspective of the immigrant because those of us who have been here a long time can't see ourselves. That's the way your title works, doesn't it? It's an inversion. *Typical American* is a kind of put-down of America by those who are themselves being put down. The immigrant family in your book says disparagingly that something is "typical American."

Jen: Right. But then in the end, of course, the irony is that they themselves become typically American.

Satz: So they have become American—
Jen: Despite themselves.

Satz: Despite themselves and so fall under the negative judgment of their own original critique.
Jen: That's right.

Satz: I admire your book.
Jen: Thank you.

Satz: Can you talk about the role of the injection of Chinese language? You use Chinese phrases that employ concepts that can't be stated in English—listening but not hearing, for example. Do you think this is a means to induce readers to enter the Chinese culture just a little bit?
Jen: Yes, to begin to understand how fundamentally different other points of view can be. You have talked about what students have to be taught. They have to be taught for one thing that there are different realities. If you have grown up in a place where you have one reality and everyone else has the same reality, you begin to believe that is reality. You are unaware of the degree to which it is artifice. Whereas if you can see the terms in which other people think you begin to realize that your reality is not so absolute.

Satz: As a writer do you feel privileged to have these two perspectives that are in some ways consonant and in some ways dissonant?
Jen: Absolutely. I think all writers have to get to the point where they can stand outside of experience and behold it, and if you are an outsider by virtue of who you are or where you were born, half the work is done.

Satz: I've talked to Sandra Cisneros—do you know her work?
Jen: Yes. She's an exciting writer.

Satz: She told me a little bit about her experience at Iowa, which for her was quite a negative experience because she felt so much the outsider. Everyone was writing about suburban neighborhoods that looked the same, and everyone had the same voice. For a while, it silenced her because her voice and her experience were so different. What was it like for you?
Jen: The student population varies widely from year to year and in my year there were a lot of cowboys. So I did feel like an outsider, but interestingly it wasn't *so* much because I was an Asian American. I felt like an outsider

because I was from the East, and I had gone to Harvard and that was not cool the year I was there.

Satz: Was it sexist?

Jen: Yes, it was, and there I was East Coast, intellectual, female. That was really my problem much more than being an Asian American.

Satz: I want to ask you about yourself. Your situation in terms of identity and culture is very different from that of your parents' generation. How do you perceive yourself in regard to these two cultures?

Jen: There is a certain amount of cultural conflict. For instance, when my son was born, a lot of my friends said you really want to have two weeks to yourself, just you and your husband and baby. It's a very intense time and really you should get your parents to come after that. So I tried to explain this to my mother, but it was just *out of the question.* The problem has to do with different ideas about what constitutes the fundamental social unit. I mean to my friends I'm starting this new group, and I'm entitled to that. To my mother I am part of the family that already exists, and the new baby is too. Take the issue of Christmas. Dave and I are trying to lobby for having Christmas Day at our own house now, especially when our son Luke gets older. We want Santa Claus to come down our chimney. But my mom wants all the grandchildren to come to her house.

Satz: May I ask you about your *Boston Globe* piece? The grounds on which you criticize multiculturalism as an artist?

Jen: What I said in effect was that multiculturalism has made more boxes for people. It has added questions to the lists with which we approach literature and that has been an enormous contribution to our understanding. Unfortunately, the result has been that readers reading a minority writer now assume that these new concerns are the ones you must be addressing. So they say to me things like, "Oh, you must be trying to preserve their heritage in this book." Meanwhile, there's a lot about business in my book. No one asks, "Oh, there seems to be a connection between religion and business."

Satz: I wanted to ask you about your wonderful comic voice. Where do you think it comes from?

Jen: It's because I'm half-Jewish. Oy.

Satz: Oy.

Jen: It's interesting—someone interviewed me from the Yale student paper who turned out to be a Chinese American who had grown up in Scarsdale, and she commented on how articulate all the Jewish American students seemed to be, and how she was forced to start talking just to survive.

Satz: So it was living in Scarsdale, basically, you think—
Jen: Basically. Don't get me wrong, my whole family also had a great sense of humor. But the humor is not so verbal. I think a lot of the verbal humor comes from growing up in Scarsdale. You know, a nice Catholic town.

Satz: My children are adopted and they're biracial, so they're black and white and Jewish.
Jen: Which is very American.

Satz: Yes, it's very American. I also think they are in a privileged position because they can't succumb to easy answers and easy stereotypes. It's on many levels an outsider's position, which I think is advantageous.
Jen: Well, it is. From the beginning, you are forced to confront the complexity of life with all its difficulties. Other people have an easier time but they never see anything.

Satz: I wanted to ask you about something else. You seem to know so much about so many things. There is the terrible realism of your portrayal of university politics. And I don't know anything about animal slaughterhouses, but your description sounded terribly authentic to me.
Jen: I only saw one chicken get killed, but it left a big impression on me.

Satz: So what would you say about yourself? That you're an especially acute and curious observer?
Jen: I'm curious about everything and it really is true that when I was trying to decide whether to become a writer, I thought I would enjoy it partly because I would get to do everything and call it work.

Satz: It's my research. It's my job.
Jen: No corner of the world is too obscure for you to be over there sniffing around. But you also have to understand that I don't know as much as it seems I may know. I don't really know about the academic world, for example. I'm just guessing.

Satz: May I say it's a very astute guess!
Jen: Oh dear, I'm so sorry.

Satz: About your earlier comment on the link between business and religion, Ralph, your protagonist, hears all these slogans and believes them, and they basically alter his life. Do you think this is American, I mean typical American?
Jen: I do think so. Norman Vincent Peale pretty much sums up the connection. Historically we've always felt that we had this special connection with God, right?

Satz: Right.
Jen: And through Norman Vincent Peale, we have a special connection with God through which we can get rich. You know what I mean? This has always been part of American culture. Religion and self-aggrandizement go hand-in-hand.

Satz: Were you also consciously working out relations between males and females? You have Ralph and his sister and his wife in very painful relations. Is that something that concerns you about American and Asian households?
Jen: I didn't consciously address that. As soon as you have men and women of that generation, though, that's what you get. I couldn't help but bring it out. What I was thinking more about when I was writing was sibling rivalry. I thought a lot about how what happens to Ralph is shaped by his experience with Theresa and his father. I was thinking too about how much what becomes of you in America is shaped at least as much by family dynamics as by America. Helen and Ralph and Theresa all find some version of the American Dream and yet it's very different for each of them. There is no one story. There are many stories.

Satz: And that's another thing that we do. We say there is a Chinese view and basically Chinese people come—
Jen: Exactly. Meanwhile, birth order was as important as anything else in this book.

Satz: This was not an issue for you as an Asian woman; that is, you weren't in any way discouraged from writing, from achieving, from going—
Jen: I have to say that I was. This is not a story of all Asian American females because many are pushed in a big way. And probably if I had started to fail I would have been pushed too, but as it was for most of my life I did well in school without too much effort and I was not encouraged to work any harder. My mother did say to me as the mother in "What Means Switch" says to Mona, "It's no good for a girl to be too smart anyway."

Satz: Pricing yourself out of the market, so to speak.

Jen: She thought I would have trouble getting married and that I should not work at being any smarter. So that while growing up a lot more attention was paid to my brother's education than to that of me and my sister. And speaking of the next generation, here he is—

[Luke, Jen's infant son, arrives in a stroller with his father and is admired by all.]

Satz: Does Luke bring up new questions about identity for you?

Jen: I realize he is very different from me. And that as much trouble as I've had with categorization, he is going to have more. Already it's starting. People will say things like, "Oh and he's half Chinese and half American." I say, no, no, no, no, he's one hundred percent American. What do they mean he's half Chinese, half American—give me a break. Or they'll say, well he looks like you. I think what they mean is that he looks more Asian than he does Caucasian but actually he doesn't look like me at all.

Satz: I wouldn't think so. They are struggling to say something.

Jen: Exactly. But they're very stuck on this race thing. He presents a challenge to them, even at this age. People will say his eyes are *blue*. They're trying to make some new category for him—they're working on it even though—

Satz: They're working on it, and they're trying to be nice.

Jen: It's a matter of education, there's no ill will. People need education, and he will be the educator.

Satz: How much Chinese do you know?

Jen: I actually don't know that much. I don't speak very well and I don't understand that well anymore these days. I've never been very good at it. I put in the book what I know.

Satz: Is it important for you that Luke know some Chinese?

Jen: I would like him to know some. In fact I would like him to know more than I know. My mom talks to him in Chinese, and I'll send him to Chinese school, but who knows what he'll learn. And in a general kind of way I think that it's more important for him to understand what it means to be Asian American than it is for him to speak Chinese, that being Asian American often means not speaking Chinese or Japanese or whatever, the same way being German American often means not speaking German. I think it's a very American think not to speak the language of your ancestors.

Satz: But a negative thing, don't you think? Or not?

Jen: I don't think it's necessarily negative. I think it would be nice if all Chinese Americans spoke Chinese, and at the same time I also think that all change involves loss. I don't mean to minimize the loss. But if you stand against change, you stand against life.

Satz: You have said that you wanted to be wicked.

Jen: Wicked. Yes.

Satz: What does that mean for you?

Jen: It means writing about the things we're not supposed to write about. For example in "What Means Switch" I'm pretty close to the edge. People are uncomfortable when one starts writing about the Jews and the Japanese. Everyone's a little bit—

Satz: Everyone's poised, right? Where's this going to go?

Jen: It's dangerous but as a writer you have to get up the nerve to write about the things that are dangerous. And it is a minefield. I don't know. I don't think anything actually explodes in my story but—

Satz: It's poised, it's poised. That was the feeling that I had.

Jen: It makes people nervous.

Satz: Which is a good thing, it seems to me. The tension of being on the edge. Are there particular topics you think are bad?

Jen: Sex in general is of course a bad topic, for a nice girl. Racism. Power. Things you wouldn't talk about in company you're not supposed to write about either. But a writer is dedicated to truth—a writer's job is to write about these things. So the naughtier you are the better. The not-nicer you are the better a writer you are.

Satz: Do you have a new novel in the works now?

Jen: I sure hope so. But you know how it is—you really can't tell what's going on for a couple hundred pages. I hope I'm not going to have to throw it all out, but—

Satz: Do you feel courageous? You have spoken about writing in the dark, just going ahead without plot, without structure. Are you doing that now?
Jen: Yes. I'm doing it again. You would think I'd have learned better by now.

Interview with Gish Jen

Yuko Matsukawa / 1991

From *MELUS* 18.4 (1993): 111–20. Reprinted by permission of Yuko Matsukawa and *MELUS: Multi-Ethnic Literature of the United States*.

With the publication of her first book, *Typical American*, in 1991 and articles such as "Challenging the Asian Illusion" (*New York Times*, August 11, 1991), Gish Jen is fast becoming a visible and vocal part of the contemporary American literary landscape. Born in New York City in 1955, Jen, who is a second-generation Chinese American, grew up in Yonkers and Scarsdale, New York. It was during high school that she acquired the nickname "Gish" (after the actress with whom she happened to share a first name, Lillian Gish), which she later adopted as her pen name. Educated at Harvard and Stanford Business School, Gish Jen embarked upon her writing career while attending the Iowa Writers' Workshop and has been writing and publishing her stories in literary magazines now for over a decade. She also has been the recipient of numerous fellowships and grants and has won awards for her short stories, many of which have been anthologized repeatedly.

Several of Gish Jen's short stories center on the Changs, an immigrant family from China. In captivating stories such as "The White Umbrella," "The Water Faucet Vision," and "What Means Switch," we witness how the daughters of the family, Callie and Mona, ingeniously and ingenuously attempt to navigate their way through the turbulent waters of childhood and adolescence, carefully mediating the overlapping relationships between cultures, between home and the outside world, and between their parents, their friends, and themselves. Through moments of revelation and their contemplative interpretations of events, Gish Jen charts the sisters' complicated, funny, and often heartbreaking process of growing up Chinese American.

It is in the short story "In the American Society," however, that we get a glimpse of the dynamics of the Chang family. Ralph, here the successful proprietor of a pancake house who prefers his own society to the American society, and his wife, Helen, who has broader social aspirations, come into their own as characters through their interactions with family, neighbors, and employees. The life stories of Ralph, Helen, and Ralph's sister Theresa are further expanded and elaborated in Gish Jen's first novel, *Typical American*, which has garnered deservedly excellent reviews. The *New York Times Book Review* declares, "No paraphrase could capture the intelligence of Gish Jen's prose, its epigrammatic sweep and swiftness. . . . The author just keeps coming at you, line after stunning line. Even her incidental description seems new-minted—purely functional, bone clean yet lustrous." The *New York Review of Books* calls the novel "poised and unsentimental," and asserts that "Gish Jen sustains her complex pattern of duality even in her prose style, sophisticatedly choosing to tell her somber story wittily." Gish Jen starts her book with the line "It's an American story"; by guiding us through one Chinese immigrant family's experiences, she perceptively and brilliantly challenges readers to reexamine their definitions of home, family, the American Dream, and, of course, what it is to be a "typical American."

This interview took place late in November 1991 at her home in Cambridge, Massachusetts, where she lives with her husband, David O'Connor, and baby son, Luke. Sitting by the fireplace—the archetypal site for listening to and telling stories—Gish Jen animatedly answered my questions about her life and her work; our conversation was delightfully punctuated by laughter.

Interviewer: Has motherhood changed your writing schedule?
Gish Jen: I have to say that it's very slow now. I used to basically write fulltime. Now I'm a mother fulltime and try to work my writing around that. But I'm hoping to start my son on twenty-hour-a-week day care soon.

Interviewer: Do you work at home?
Jen: No, I work in an office. I really admire people who work at home; they have a lot more discipline than I do. I think everyone has something which they have to reject in order to become a writer. After I rejected legitimate professions—I thought about going to med school, to law school, and I actually went to business school—I had to reject being a housewife, which was for me the last great temptation. I'm the kind of person who, if I stay home, will clean the house, for one thing. And I love catalogs—gardening catalogs are a serious threat to my career (laugh)—which is why I have to go to another environment where I have no distractions. I don't even keep books in my office. I have three choices when I'm in there: I can sleep, I can

eat, or I can work. Generally, I just go and sit there until I'm so bored that it is less painful to write than to continue sitting.

Interviewer: Did you think that you would be a writer when you were growing up?

Jen: If you had asked me at any point along the way, the answer would have been "no." But looking back, I can see that one of the biggest experiences of my young life was when I was in fifth grade and we had a literary magazine. Everybody was supposed to contribute something to it and most people did. I was the only one, though, who contributed enough to fill up fifteen of these magazines myself. There were all these different categories and I brought things in for all of them. I also wrote my first story for that magazine, which was the longest thing included—five pages. You can imagine how in a class magazine for twenty-six kids, having five pages was a major thing. The story was about a maid who had stolen some gold. She had hidden it inside this hat but when she picked up the hat, the gold fell out! (laugh). And so she was caught.

I read a lot as a child. I was very influenced by *Little Women* back then, and I'm sure it made an impression on me that Jo became a writer. Originally, I went to school in Yonkers, New York, to a Catholic school which had almost no library. When my family moved to Scarsdale, though, I took out two books a day from the school library there. Of course, I read all these books quite indiscriminately. I read *The Island Stallion Races* but I also read *The Stranger* by Camus, which I particularly remember because I remember coming across the phrase "an execrable cry of pain" and thinking "What does this mean, 'execrable'?"—I thought it had something to do with excrement, you know (laugh).

Interviewer: What other writers did you admire?

Jen: You mean growing up? I think the next writer to have a really big influence on me was Jane Austen. *Pride and Prejudice* was one of the books that I read backwards and forwards. I really wanted to be Elizabeth Bennett. Of course today, there are people who would say "Oh, that's so Anglo"; they think I should have been more influenced by Chinese opera or something (laugh). But this is not what should have happened; this is what *did* happen. I do think that it's unfortunate that all the Austen novels end in marriage, but to me, they still show us what the power of the novel can be. I think that many people lived by those books.

They showed us how to live—they were moral books. Which is what fiction is for, it seems to me. I know this is probably not the most critically sophisticated view but I'm not so interested in experimental writing unless it speaks to the limits of human knowledge, say—unless its concern is more human than formal. And of course, included in the category of books that show us how to live are books that show us how we *do* live. Those are moral too: they contrast the human chaos with some notion of civilization, even if it's implied.

Interviewer: So, whom do you admire now?
Jen: I still tend to admire people who are very moral.

Interviewer: What do you mean by moral?
Jen: What I mean by moral is that they are concerned with values and the human condition. I'm not talking about upholding morals like the Moral Majority; I'm talking about morals in the sense of a concern with the manner in which life is lived, which is not necessarily according to the accepted rules of society: in fact, I'm most influenced by people who are naughty.

Interviewer: What's naughty?
Jen: Naughty means not "nice." You know, people who write things as they really are, without sentimentalizing everything. I'm talking about people like Alice Munro and Jamaica Kincaid, whom I admire very much.

Interviewer: You've been reviewed in many newspapers and magazines lately along with other Asian American writers—how do you feel about that?
Jen: There are a few people who keep on recurring in the same article over and over and over again. We're like "the Gang of Four" (laugh). A friend of mine said—and I think there is a lot of truth in this—that either you're categorized or else you're ignored. I guess what I understand is that in modern society people are bombarded with so much information that this categorizing is necessary. Still, it's irritating to have people rewrite and rewrite and rewrite the same article over and over and over again and have it based on race, especially since this has led to distortions in the way my book has been read. Some people told me that they thought it was a book about preserving one's heritage; I felt like saying "That wasn't what I wanted to say *at all!*" You know it's this knee-jerk reaction on their part: you're an ethnic writer, so *you must* be writing about *"people striving to preserve their heritage."* I'm not

saying that on some level there isn't some kind of tug about what to retain and what to take on but that wasn't what the book was *all* about.

Interviewer: Why the title *Typical American*?
Jen: Well, I should say to begin with that the person who came up with this title was not me, it was my agent. My working title was originally "In the American Society," which was the name of the short story from which this whole novel grew. I do understand why she didn't like the title because the story once got cited as nonfiction by accident. As for the present title, there's this irony within the book which has to do with the phrase "typical American." "Typical American" is a phrase that the Changs use to describe people who are not them, and yet by the end of the book, of course, they become "typical Americans" themselves.

Also I liked it because it was a phrase that was used not only by my family but by other immigrants and their children. For instance, at one point before the book was published, I was talking to somebody who asked me what the title of my book was, and when I said, "Typical American" and explained, she said, "We say that in my family *all the time!*" And it turned out that she was *Irish*! Her family had just come over and that's what they said all the time and I thought, "Ha! This is true."

And finally, of course, I wanted to challenge ideas of what a "typical American" looks like, to put forward the idea that the Changs are not any less American than anyone else. There are people who, when they choose to read ethnic writing, want comfortably exotic stuff that makes them feel like they're traveling in some foreign country. The Changs, though, are not a foreign country. They wonder about their identity: they ask themselves who they are, who they're becoming. And therefore, they are American.

Interviewer: So do you think you're writing against or responding to a stereotype or a tradition or other writers?
Jen: Was I talking back to people or books? It's hard for me to say. I think I wasn't so much writing against a certain person as against public demand. I was writing against the public's expectation as I understood it. I was damned if I was going to give them the exotic nonsense they thought they wanted; instead, I wanted my book to succeed on character. I followed my own interests. Even though I had written other stories unrelated to this family, I had come back to them again and again—this family, I knew, meant something to me. Of course, people will always say, "Oh it must be your

family," but in fact it's not my family I wrote about. The idea of writing about a family, though, was very appealing to me.

Interviewer: I understand that your pen name, Gish, comes from a nickname you acquired during high school. What interests me is that in your first two stories—"Bellying Up" and "The Small Concerns of Sparrows"—you use your legal name, Lillian. What precipitated the change from "Lillian" to "Gish"? From your publication chronology, it looks like you started using "Gish" with the stories about the Chang family—is there a relationship between the birth of this fictional family and the emergence of the writer Gish Jen?

Jen: I'm not aware of a connection between the two but I need to review this chronologically for myself. As I recall, those first two stories were accepted for publication before the summer between my first and second year at Iowa, the summer of 1982. At the time, being in print seemed so final and important that I used my legal name "Lillian Jen." But then later I realized, "Well no, I can be whoever I want—I *am* Gish Jen!" I think my changing my name marks the point at which I discovered writing to be liberating; I discovered that just as I could create stories, I could create this self, Gish Jen. Besides, a friend of mine said to me, "Gish, that's what you *call* yourself!" My friends thought Gish Jen was a better name because it had more impact. It sounds strong because of the spondee: "Gish Jen," like "bang bang." I always associate "Lillian" with a shyer self, a received self. My family calls me "Lillian," or rather, "Lil." My parents still go around explaining to their friends, "Yes, Gish Jen's our daughter, she has this book out but that's not her name really, she just calls herself Gish, her real name's Lillian," and so on.

Interviewer: It's a great name also because people can't tell whether you're male or female—you keep them guessing.
Jen: (laugh) That's another reason I like it.

Interviewer: I'm interested in how your short stories and *Typical American* intersect. You mentioned that though you wrote many other short stories, you kept coming back to the Changs. What is the relationship between the Chang family short stories and your novel? For instance, you incorporated the story "The Water Faucet Vision" into *Typical American.*
Jen: Yes, I put it in the book. It was really, I think, a very transparent attempt to save that story; I thought that if I could work it into my novel it would

really be much better. So I tried to work it in and I think I did manage. It was probably the only thing that I knew about my novel: that at a certain point I wanted to put the story in so I wouldn't have to throw it out. The funny thing is that it's bad enough when you have an incident like that in a story; when it also occurs in your novel, people think that this really happened to you in real life. I'm happy to say my father never threw my mother out the window. They had normal adult fights where they yelled at each other and maybe one of them *walked* out of the room.

Interviewer: How about "What Means Switch"? We encounter a Mona who seems older than the Mona in *Typical American*. Does the existence of this older Mona mean that there will be a sequel to *Typical American*?
Jen: It's a terrible thing—everybody wants you to write your last book over and over and over and do whatever you did again. But the nature of being a writer is always to want to forge on and do something else, so we're at odds.

Interviewer: Some people I know who have read your recent stories said to me, "Ask her if she's really Mona."
Jen: (laugh) People always think that, you know. And the answer is, I think, that Mona is the person I would have liked to have been. When I was in junior high school, I was quiet and kind of traumatized by everything. Or at least that's how I felt, even as I was getting thrown out of class all the time for talking (laugh). But Mona's together in a way that I was not.
Before "What Means Switch," by the way, everybody thought I was Callie. And people who only read the book often think I must be Theresa, though every now and then somebody thinks that I must be Ralph! Can you imagine?

Interviewer: Well, why did you choose a male protagonist? Since I read your short stories before *Typical American* came out, I was expecting that the novel would be written from the point of view of the daughters.
Jen: In fact, because of the way it evolved, for a long time I was thinking about writing it from the point of view of the children. But gradually it became clear to me that I had a lot of energy around the older generation and then the children's point of view became a problem because there was so much happening that they couldn't know. As for why Ralph became the protagonist, at the time it just seemed like the most natural thing and I don't really know why. Maybe because Ralph threw that shirt into the pool in the story "In the American Society": from the beginning, he was a person who did a lot of things; he acted out, if you will.

Interviewer: It's interesting to hear you say that because a lot of novels by Asian American women writers do have female protagonists.

Jen: And they seem to make it go. I don't know what happened. I'm not against women or anything (laugh). I think the truth of the matter is that having never written a novel before, I wanted to make it as easy as possible, and that I realized that in that generation men were more likely to make things happen, and to range over large parts of society. And I wanted that, to write a book that included all kinds of things—an expandable book in which I could write whatever I liked.

Interviewer: Men had more latitude perhaps but the women of Ralph's generation—Janis, Helen, and Theresa—illustrate some of the options available for women, don't they?

Jen: Yes. Even though Ralph fueled the story, I wanted the women to be developed characters, not just secondary figures. And they do make things happen too—many more things than I could have predicted. Really the book is about all of them. I have this affection for Helen, and I think Janis is a good egg. As for Theresa, she was a late addition to the formulation of the story but it's clear to me now that she could have been the one to carry the whole novel—that she could have borne the burden of my interests. She's adventuresome enough and not so bound by her gender. Though she's of that older generation, her experience could have been made almost as broad as my own.

Interviewer: What triggered your decision to become a fiction writer?

Jen: We didn't get past fifth grade, did we, when we started this before? (laugh) A couple of things. In college I was an English major, which is probably not too surprising given how much I read. And this will sound stupid, but I took a prosody course taught by Robert Fitzgerald because I really didn't get it about poetry. I felt like asking, "Why does it have to be written like that?" I couldn't see the point of all those little lines. And so I thought I'd take this nuts-and-bolts course. Which sounded easy enough until Fitzgerald said there was going to be a weekly assignment. And then it turned out that he meant an assignment in *verse*. It had never occurred to me to try to write poetry before. But because I liked this class so much, I thought, "Well, I'll give it a try," so I wrote this thing in Catullan hendecasyllables which Fitzgerald xeroxed and handed out to the class—I still don't know if he did that because he liked it or because it had a mistake in every line. But anyway, I wrote these things and later he was very encouraging. He was the one who told me I should be doing something to do with literature and should give up being premed. And in fact he helped me get a job in publishing.

So there I was, at Doubleday, and working supposedly in nonfiction. But every week this colleague of mine and I would wait for the *New Yorker* and when it came we'd read it immediately and discuss the fiction all the next morning when we were supposed to be working at our desks. It was then that I started to write some fiction too. But I thought, "What should I do?" I couldn't decide; I knew I didn't want to be in publishing but should I do something more practical or less? I decided that if I couldn't decide, I might as well try being more practical first. And so I went to business school but made sure I went somewhere where there was a good writing program, i.e., Stanford. And sure enough, what happened was that the moment I got to Stanford I knew I was in the wrong place. I mean I just knew *immediately*. I spent the whole year writing novels and taking writing courses at every opportunity. And the second year I dropped out.

Interviewer: Why fiction? Would you have become a poet?
Jen: I don't know if I could have been a poet. I don't think I have the sensitivity to be one. I remember I loved Robert Fitzgerald's class but I'm glad I'm not a poet, even today. It's hard enough being a fiction writer; being a poet is, you know (throws hands up). Maybe that's my immigrant parents still talking, I don't know. But if I had to write in a different genre, I think I'd move to drama.

Interviewer: Why?
Jen: Well, because dialogue comes easily to me and also plot and structure.

Interviewer: Which playwrights did you read—Shakespeare, perhaps or . . . ?
Jen: I do love Shakespeare.

Interviewer: Which plays?
Jen: The tragedies more than comedies. *King Lear*, especially. Dramatic form and structure definitely influenced my writing. For instance, I think it is no coincidence that my book is in five parts. Not that I was modeling it on *Lear*, but you could say that *Typical American* was informed by it.

Interviewer: How does comedy function in your book? Is it a source of inspiration as tragedy is?
Jen: I think we are talking about two different things here: comedy as in comedic form and comedy as a sort of lightheartedness. Comedic form

suggests that by the end of the play, against all odds, everything gets resolved happily, which is not the case in my novel. But I do think the *tone* is sometimes comic—maybe a better way to put it is that it's tragicomic. I've been interested in complexity of tone, even though some people have found it "problematic." It's made some people uncomfortable; they've been disturbed by the indeterminacy of it. Contrary to what they thought, though, I have always considered this complexity of tone one of my strengths. I think it has to do with the fact that I come from a culture where things can have opposite attributes at the same time, like in food, sweet and sour. The world is at once yin and yang.

Interviewer: How do you come up with subject matter?

Jen: I start with a feeling: in the short story "The White Umbrella," I started with the feeling of waiting on the doorsteps for your mother to come pick you up. Then you start accumulating around that feeling and the story evolves. It's like deciding what you like to eat. It just so happens that you eat certain things more often than other things. You don't sit down and say, "Well, I think I like garlic." Over the years you discover that you like garlic—it happens, you don't plan it.

Interviewer: Now that you have a son, would you write a children's book?

Jen: Maybe. Let me put it this way. There's only one person in the world for whom I would write and that would be my son. From what I hear, there are few books out there to help him with being biracial—he's Eurasian—so I would write for him if there were books he needed that had not been written. Also I can imagine doing some for fun.

Interviewer: What's your next project? I know you've been speaking at colleges this fall (1991) . . .

Jen: Yes, at Williams and at Yale but these things invariably take up a lot of my time; they do require preparation. Also these little articles for the *New York Times* and the *Boston Globe* have taken time. I like having things coming out in a sort of steady little flow. But I have got to get back to my own writing again, which means there'll be a long silence while I try to write something more serious.

Gish Jen: Interview

Rachel Lee / 1993

From *Words Matter: Conversations with Asian American Writers*, ed. King-Kok Cheung (University of Hawaii Press, 2000), 215–32. Reprinted by permission of University of Hawaii Press and Gish Jen.

Gish Jen won the respect of a wide audience with her first novel, *Typical American* (1991), which was shortlisted for the National Book Critics' Circle Award. In this novel, as in her published short stories, Jen broadens the definition of Asian American literature by writing beyond its "typical" themes of cultural dislocation, generational conflict, and immigrant success. For instance, her short story "The Water Faucet Vision"—reprinted in *Best American Short Stories 1988*—probes the nuances of religious awakening. Though not strictly about race, it features Asian American protagonists whose ethnicity remains integral to the author's long-term project of rendering Asian Americans a familiar part of America's literary landscape.

As part of that mission, Jen crafts unexotic, "everyday" characters such as the Changs, whose trials in Northeast suburban America provide the grist for several of the author's published works (e.g., *Typical American, Mona in the Promised Land*, "What Means Switch," "The Water Faucet Vision," "The White Umbrella," "Grover at the Wheel," and "In the American Society"). Creating Asian American protagonists who are fallible, sympathetic, and even mundane remains one avenue through which Jen pursues her political goals. Another strategy involves writing about Asian Americans even in cases where ethnic identity is not crucial to the plot.

The interview first took place by telephone on the evening of September 9, 1993; it was updated on the publication of *Mona in the Promised Land*. Early in our conversation, Jen talked about switching from a "practical" profession to a career in writing. As a matter of record, her choice to "throw everything to the wind" has resulted in numerous publications and has garnered for her several fellowships, among them a 1992 Guggenheim Foundation Fellowship and a 1988 National Endowment for the Arts Fellowship.

I also asked Jen about her relationship to Asian American literature. As a writer who grew up on the East Coast in the sixties and seventies, Jen seems particularly attuned to the location and historicity of Asian America. She remarks that, when she was younger, "there was no Asian America . . . it hadn't been invented yet." While acknowledging the overwhelmingly supportive aspects of discovering an Asian American literary community, Jen also admitted to resisting a "ghettoized" identity as ethnic writer. We talked about the tensions within the Asian American literary community, particularly the ongoing debate spearheaded by Frank Chin over whether Asian American men ought to be portrayed in a blanket, positive light in order to counter the negative stereotypes of them in popular culture. Setting herself apart from writers who would argue for artistic freedom, Jen finds the political context in which she writes crucial to what she eventually publishes. One makes ethical choices when one edits, Jen seems to say, and her personal ethics decry misogyny and racism. We also discussed her engagement with various communities, her commitment to social responsibility in writing, and her opinions on the serendipitous receptivity of current readers to her kind of satiric female voice.

Rachel Lee: I saw from your résumé that you went to business school. Was writing on the back burner then?

Gish Jen: Business school was a particularly uninspired decision; the decision was just to go to professional school, meaning that, as an undergraduate, I had tried being premed and prelaw already. That left the one thing that I really had never had any interest in, which was business. A lot of that is being the daughter of immigrants. I did write poetry as an undergrad. I distinctly remember telling my roommate, "I love this, and, if I could, I would do this for the rest of my life." But it never even occurred to me for one second to try to become a poet. I didn't know anyone who was a poet. It just wasn't something that someone like me did.

I remember that, in a graduate seminar in prosody, Robert Fitzgerald, the translator, did ask, "Have you thought about doing something with words?" I told him I was premed. He said, "You should really think about writing." I told him that I simply couldn't imagine being a writer. So then he asked me, "Have you at least thought about publishing?" And, as professors at Harvard will, he got me a job in publishing. Once I was there, though, I distinctly understood that I had landed up in the middle ground between a world I was quite interested in and a world where you actually could make a living. I was making something like $5,000 a year. For a while that was fine, but it couldn't go on forever. Meanwhile, my parents were hammering at me to do something practical. I realized that I was going to do one or the other. And I said to myself, if I can't decide which to do, let me try the more practical route first. So I applied to business school. It was a lark. Then, to my amazement, I got in—to Harvard and to Stanford. It just goes to show the power of the word.

I met my husband during orientation. I remember pointing to a line in the course catalog and asking him, "What does this mean?" I didn't even understand what the courses were about. Meanwhile, he had exempted out of everything.

I read a hundred novels. I think it's safe to say that I was the only first-year business school student who read a hundred novels while she was at business school. I passed, amazingly. But, the next year, I found that I could not get myself to go to class. Literally, the first day I overslept; the second day I overslept; the third day I overslept. By the end of the week, I realized that I was never going to go to class. So I dropped out and never went back. It was difficult to drop out, but I've never regretted it.

RL: What made you switch to writing fiction?

GJ: When I was at Doubleday, there was an editorial assistant at the next desk, and we were always talking about fiction. She actually had an MFA in poetry. Still, it was fiction we talked about, nonstop, instead of working. I had started writing some stories back then—it wasn't very serious. Then, at business school, I became more serious. Life works that way. You push the pendulum in one direction, and then you swing back. You're pushing it that way in order to see that. Going to business school was good in a way. One of the hardest things about being a writer is you flagellate yourself with the idea that you could have done something else more practical. I was lucky to know that I couldn't—that I hated business and didn't want to do that. When all my friends started thinking, "Maybe I'll go to law school now," I didn't. I'd already tried other things. I had to become a writer or die.

But to back up: I dropped out of business school, went to China, came back, and got my MFA. There's no question that I would probably not have written *Typical American* if I had not gone to China. When I went to China, I saw so much that I recognized. But you see it in a purer form. I really began to understand that certain trains of thought in my parents and also in myself were Chinese. In some ways, I didn't even know what my conflicts were until I went to China—what it means to be Chinese; what it means to be American; what it means to be Chinese American.

I was supposed to be working on my Chinese, to little avail. I spoke very well when I was there. Now I'm back, and I can't speak a word. Mostly, I was absorbing; I wasn't writing. But I began to get to a place where I understood what my concerns were.

RL: What is that problem or way of thinking that drives your writing?

GJ: Somebody said, in everything there's a dragon. What's the dragon? That's what you're asking, right? Probably in *Typical American*, in addition to this concern about how much you can do—whether the self has limits or not—is being poised between two visions; one is "You're lucky to be able to do anything," and the other is "You can do whatever you want to do." Which of these is true? Another thing driving the book was coming to terms with a kind of assimilation that had to do with economic success.

People always ask me whether I'm against assimilation or for it. I'm neither. It's simply a fact of life. It's like asking someone if they're for or against growing up. It just happens. So it's not like bad characters are assimilated, or vice versa. There are certainly different patterns of assimilation, though, better and worse patterns. A pattern of assimilation that appeals to me, for instance, abhors racism. Let's face it, you don't want to talk about all the Chinese, but, in general, China's a pretty racist place. They make no bones about it. They definitely say things about blacks, for instance, that are at least publicly unacceptable in America. If part of you assimilates and learns to say, "That's wrong," that's a great kind of assimilation. As for the kind of assimilation where you come here and learn all about American greed and take that as far as you can—I'm not so sure that's so great. I have seen a range of assimilation in my family, including some of the not so good.

I came to understand a lot about America by thinking about this book. A lot of what drives the action is the negative things about America. But I also came to understand a lot of the possibilities in America. When I wrote that opening line, "This is an American story," I was redefining an American tradition. That's one level of my book. As an Asian American, I understood that I was going to be ghettoized, and I wanted to get out.

RL: So you were writing against a tradition that would pigeonhole you as an exotic Asian American?

GJ: Absolutely. *Typical American* is extremely anti-exotic, while it is still an Asian American book. I did not struggle against the pigeonholing by choosing to write a book with all white people in it. That would have been a strategy, but that wasn't my strategy.

RL: You mentioned *assimilation*. In your *New York Times* article ["Challenging the Asian Illusion"], you talked about your family identifying with white America but realizing that wasn't quite the whole story. There was this feeling of not belonging—was that something you discovered later? From my own experience, I know I didn't wake up knowing this. It took a long time to discover that.
GJ: That you weren't white?

RL: That, as well as that there was something like Asian America.
GJ: It's strictly an American invention. When we were younger, there was no Asian America. It wasn't as if we just didn't realize it was there—it hadn't been invented yet. In terms of that understanding, for me it came late, too. Not immediately knowing that you're Asian American is much more of an East Coast phenomenon. If you are in California, it's going to occur to you a lot earlier that you're not white. In San Francisco, you belong to a community. On the East Coast, there's no community.

RL: Was it immediately something you wanted to write about, or did it only later feed into some things you were already concerned with?
GJ: I had already been writing about isolation. So, at some level, the emotional truth was already there. I just had to learn to name it. Since naming it, I've written about it more explicitly.

RL: So these feelings of isolation were disconnected from race at first?
GJ: Feelings of isolation do not stem only from race. The part of myself that feels isolated is partly racially defined and partly not.

Discovering racial isolation was painful, although it was also reassuring. You know all along that something is the matter. Maybe you would have preferred that you didn't have those feelings. If you're going to have them, though, it's nice to know that you're not just loony. There's a sense of injustice that goes with it, of course. Why should you feel that way when other people wear green pants and pink shirts and get along fine? They also have problems, I realize. America is a lonely place. I think a lot of those people also have feelings of isolation, and they don't have race to fall back on as an explanation.

RL: Is there an Asian American community of writers with which you identify?
GJ: There is no question that we see each other as kindred. I was recently reading this interview with Cynthia Kadohata in which she talks about how she feels sisterhood with me. I met her once years ago. In this interview, she says that, whenever she sees me doing well, she always thinks, "Go Gish." How nice! Just today, David Wong Louie was in town and left a message on my machine.

RL: You've had a positive experience with that Asian American writing community.
GJ: I think more positive than negative.

RL: What do you think about the tensions in the Asian American literary community, however you want to define it?
GJ: I was waiting to get attacked by Frank Chin. It hasn't happened. Maybe he hasn't read my book. I don't know what to make of that. Either I haven't heard about it, or he hasn't read my book, or he couldn't figure out what to think about it.

RL: Why did you think he would attack *Typical American*?
GJ: I thought I would be attacked because of who I was. One could say that Ralph Chang is not exactly a role model for Asian American males. And the women are a lot more sympathetic in my book than Ralph is. Now, I personally find Ralph very sympathetic, but I understand that he's not as sympathetic as Theresa. I thought that, as an Asian American male, Frank Chin would be unhappy about that. And I could imagine being attacked because I'm East Coast, a woman writer, I'm married to a *haole* [a white]. I heard that he didn't like that, which is probably not even true—I don't know anything really because I haven't had any personal contact with him. It's all just this myth. From what I can tell, Frank Chin has a lot of valuable things to say, but he expresses himself in a very unfortunate manner.

To see this kind of polarization breaks my heart. There are so few of us. The atmosphere's been so difficult for so long. While it's important that we all say what we have to say, I wish that everybody could say that in a clear manner without it turning into a bloodbath.

RL: Does that inhibit your writing at all? Do you think twice about whether you're going to make a character a certain way, or do you ignore it all?
GJ: It's not just with Frank Chin. The whole atmosphere now. . . . I support social responsibility in writing. I think I'm a rare writer in saying that. Most

writers argue for artistic freedom. But to imagine that your images have no effect on what happens in society and the way people see themselves is completely naive. I think also that you are a better writer as you start considering questions like *representation*. I don't see how writing stereotypes about blacks or Asians or anybody else could possibly make you a better writer. The whole way of writing that used to be popular—in which there is a black and a white, a good guy and a bad guy, and certain people or races get to be the bad guys—is very unfortunate and stupid. We live in a much more complicated world.

There is a way in which you have to stand back before your work is published and ask yourself what it was in your unconscious that was triggering this. If you were in your heart of hearts anti-Semitic and there it is on the page—you have to think again before you send the story out.

RL: Your published work is about Asian Americans. Is that a conscious decision? Have you written works not about Asian Americans that didn't get published?
GJ: No, they did get published. Early on I wrote a number of stories about Caucasians. Then I started writing about Asian Americans, not necessarily with their Asian Americanness being the subject. For instance, "The Water Faucet Vision" is about the religious impulse. These characters came to me. Writing is like dreaming: that I would dream about Asian Americans seems to me no surprise. Later on, when I realized I had a lot of Asian Americans in my work—that I didn't write things with all white characters—I kept on with it partly as a political thing. It didn't start as a political thing, but I did feel it was important that there be Asian American representation in literature. I didn't see that it limited my subject matter in any way. There's nothing I couldn't write about using Asian American characters, and I didn't see why I shouldn't just go on. I felt I had a social responsibility—it wasn't a big burden. I just did it.

RL: So this next work of yours [*Mona in the Promised Land*]—is it on Asian Americans?
GJ: Yes.

RL: Are you keeping some of the same characters?
GJ: I'm trying not to talk about my new work. Dorothy Parker said, "The goose that laid the golden egg died looking up its crotch. Would you lay as well? Don't watch." You can't have your whole creative process out there.

RL: Has writing *Typical American* allowed you to get the issues resolved and go on to . . . ?

GJ: Yes, new issues, but related issues. I'll probably be writing more about race than I was. *Typical American* was about bigotry—the prejudice against the Changs. But that's not really the subject of the book. Society isn't really that present, except for pieces that they take down and put in their nest, if you will. It's much more about what they take of America and what they're making of it. The new book is probably more about actual social forces with which the characters have to contend. It is an angrier book, it's a funnier book. Those two things go together a lot.

RL: You use humor, then, to diffuse anger or pain?

GJ: There is for me a type of humor sometimes in my books, in my work, where that humor is a way to organize your anger. It's a way of being angry but telling a coherent story. It's not just pure rage. Maybe it's also a way of transcending it.

RL: How has your family reacted to your work?

GJ: My mom got to the end of *Typical American* in galleys, and she said, "Ah! So well written!" And then she said, "And it's not about anybody!" My favorite quote so far. My family has been very happy about it, which I was sort of surprised about because they had been very against my becoming a writer. I cannot tell you how against it they were, even after I enrolled in the workshop. I would go home, there would be fights. Walking out in the snow with no coat on. They refused to pay for any part of my writing education. They were very against it, not necessarily for such bad reasons. They were immigrants. Here are these two people; they came to America only to see their home country collapse. That doesn't exactly give you a view of the world as a stable place. Of course they value security.

But they've accepted my decision, ever since there was an article about me in the *World Journal*. You know how it is with these Chinese news articles: they're half article, half wedding announcement. The piece began: Gish Jen, daughter of Norman and Agnes Jen, and so on. All their friends called, and, after that, it was fine for me to be a writer. They've been supportive.

RL: When you look back on your work, do you see an intention that you keep coming back to or that you work out in various ways?

GJ: I can't see it across all my work exactly. It's very hard for a writer to see these things. But probably self and family is a big tension along which I write. And that's very Asian American. In America, one of the big themes is the individual in society—for me, the society that really matters is often the family.

RL: You chose a male protagonist.

GJ: There's a way in which you can see the whole story as being about a son coming to America and seeing this as an opportunity to break away from the family.

RL: Earlier, you said that you could see how Theresa is a more sympathetic character. How did you play around with the gendered subtext of Ralph's and Theresa's interaction—the male younger son with the older sister? Are you going to be doing more with gender and sexual politics, which is an especially heated subject in the Asian American community?

GJ: I just didn't see it that way. I saw it much more in a sibling-like way. I wasn't thinking so much about sexual politics—although obviously it's there. So much of both Theresa's and Ralph's problems has to do with social roles as prescribed.

RL: Do you feel that you break the stereotypes? Ralph in the end says that there are limits to America, but, in your life, you've come to the opposite conclusion.

GJ: Ralph says that on the worst day of his life. Also, it's followed by an image of incredible freedom and possibility, Theresa and Old Chao. The image is supposed to undercut the statement so that it's not only that. That's one truth, and there's also this other truth. Possibilities despite the limits.

My own story has mostly been about miraculous things happening. I don't think that I've made them all happen—a lot of them have happened to me. I've been lucky. Times happened to change in a very fruitful way for me.

RL: Has being an Asian American writer helped you in this publishing atmosphere right now, or has it not made a difference?

GJ: It hurt me early on, and now it helps and hurts me. When I was talking about this being a lucky time, I was talking less about publishing and more about the material that presented itself to me and a way of thinking about the material. This confluence of my life's experience, things in the air, a way of thinking, all came to a boil, and I got to that place of understanding where I could write my book. That's what I'm trying to say. There are writers who are not in the right time for them. I'm a writer in a time that can help me explore my preoccupations. Had I been writing in the fifties, I might not have been able to come to a point of clarity. I live in the right time for my sensibility, for this desire to play with stereotypes, for my kind of humor. I can have a satiric edge. We live in a time where that's fine for a woman, whereas, in other times, it would not have been such a great thing.

In terms of the publishing atmosphere, I think that, early on, it was an incredible disadvantage to be Asian American. Fifteen years ago—good luck. When I was at Iowa, the distinct understanding was that I would never be published in a commercial magazine. I certainly understood that; people around me understood that.

RL: Unless you wrote about white characters?
GJ: Yes. I think it was understood that nobody wanted to read about Asian Americans, even from the literary magazines. I got letters that said point blank, "We prefer your more exotic work." That was from the *Paris Review.* I still have the letter.

RL: What did they think was your more exotic work?
GJ: Things about China—stuff like that. They were more interested in stories about China than little Asian American girls running around in New York. Things have changed a lot. I have this story, "In the American Society," that has many problems but is clearly about something that can be discerned. I say this because it's been anthologized dozens of times. Today, I can look at the editor's questions at the end of the story, and I can see that people were able to read this story and figure out what it was about. Yet, when I sent that story out, I got these letters back that literally said, "Brilliant writing, but what's it about?" *Now* this story is said to be about being "between worlds." But editors didn't use to have this theme on their laundry list of things that a story could be about. So these well-meaning editors would come to the story and be baffled by it.

The present is different. As a result of multiculturalism, the list of possible themes is greatly expanded—not expanded enough probably. But it is expanded, and there's definitely a new receptivity. There is also quite a serious backlash against multiculturalism that writers like myself have definitely felt. It's very "in" to be an "independent thinker"—never mind that you're being an independent thinker in a very fashionable way. But one of the ways in which people are "independent thinkers" is to be anti-PC, whatever that means, in the publishing world and academic world. I get this feeling that Asian American writers in general are in the cross fire.

RL: Have you had different or surprising responses to *Mona in the Promised Land* from the various ethnic communities—Jewish, Asian American, and African American?

GJ: With *Typical American*, I was expecting a reaction like the one Philip Roth received in the fifties. I thought not everyone in the Asian American community would like it because Ralph Chang was so far from the model minority. But, by the time the book came out, the Asian American community was so much more sophisticated about fiction than the Jewish community had been. I was braced for being attacked. Instead, I was given awards by Chinese civic groups in Boston and New York.

By the time *Mona in the Promised Land* came out, there were so many books published by Asian Americans that I felt much freer. There was much less pressure to write something representative. Also, I was too exhausted by trying to juggle child rearing and writing to worry about other people's reactions.

RL: Did you receive any civic awards from Jewish groups?

GJ: I was offered an award from the Brandeis Library Association, but I couldn't travel to Los Angeles at the time to accept it. For the most part, Jewish American groups have been thrilled with *Mona*. Individuals come up to me and say, "Your book made me so happy and proud to be Jewish." My German publisher said, at first, that he was sure I must be Jewish, that no one could have written this book who wasn't. He was shocked and thrilled to discover I wasn't. In a way, I've tried to contribute to the process of boundary crossing, to painting pictures that are a little less black and white—a little more complicated.

There haven't been any negative reactions from black groups either. Individuals tell me that they were glad I had taken the time to portray different kinds of blacks instead of just one type.

RL: I think of *Typical American* as a book about Asians adjusting to the United States, about national character and biculturalism; you've characterized the message of *Mona in the Promised Land* as dealing with ethnicity as an unstable quantity—I believe you referred to America as a place where "all the groups . . . have rubbed off on each other." Is there a further development along these lines that you are pursuing in your current work?

GJ: My newest book [*Who's Irish? and Other Stories*] is a collection of stories that reflects a range of interests. Some of them are about ethnicity, but others about religion and art. Ethnicity is a great and big subject—I love it. Even though ethnicity is a truly large American subject—and it's a gift to have a subject that big to address—I found that, in my shorter work, I had other subjects to address. "Who's Irish?" is the title story of my newest book. It's already appeared in the *New Yorker* [in September 1998]. "Who's Irish?" is about cultural difference and cultural tension. The second story, "Birthmates," is about the price of racism, about its personal costs to a particular man. The third is about religion, and the fourth is about China—an Asian American man's romantic ideas about China.

RL: So questions of race and ethnicity overlay these stories, which are also about larger issues of home and exile?
GJ: That's right.

RL: Are *Typical American* and *Mona in the Promised Land* part of a trilogy, the third part of which you haven't yet written?
GJ: I have always thought that the Chang family would be a trilogy. I think there will be a third book, but it won't be my next book. Having just had a second child, my time is fragmented. So I'm on the fence between the long form and sticking to short stories for now. I hope, though, that within ten years there will be another Chang family book.

Gish Jen: "So, Aren't You Going to Ask If I'm Jewish?"

Ron Hogan / 1996

From Beatrice, www.beatrice.com. Reprinted by permission of Ron Hogan.

Gish Jen speaks of ethnic identity as one of the many hats that we can wear as Americans, and the protagonist of her second novel, *Mona in the Promised Land*, tries on quite a few hats during the course in the novel. Living in Scarshill, a fictional upscale New York city, during the late 1960s and early 1970s, Mona, a second-generation Chinese American (first seen as a small child in Jen's debut novel *Typical American*), becomes fascinated with the Jewish community surrounding her and, to the shock of her parents and her friends, decides to convert. That's the impetus for comic interaction between Chinese, Jews, and blacks, often centered around the diner that Mona's father owns. Through it all, Mona seems remarkably level-headed, even when beating her head against the brick wall of other characters' small-mindedness. I met with Jen during her book tour to discuss the novel and the ways in which her own ethnic and cultural identity were shaped during that era.

Ron Hogan: This is a continuation of the story from *Typical American*, but with a number of differences.
Gish Jen: It's very different in tone and feeling. The characters from my first book do appear, but the emphasis is on the younger generation. The first book is more tragic-comic, while *Mona in the Promised Land* is more purely comic.

RH: Was it something that you had in mind as you were writing your first novel, or shortly after that?

GJ: I think there was a time when I was writing the first book that I realized the potential for two books, and that the second book would be about the second generation of this family, but I can't say that I knew this is what it was going to be. Then, about three quarters of the way through *Typical American*, I was kind of stuck, and I went down to a reading in Soho, and it happened that the person taking tickets at the door was from my high school. Something about seeing that person jogged my memories, and I went home and wrote the short story that became the first chapter of this book in about three days (which is very quick for me). I knew then that this would be my next novel, and so in some ways it was difficult for me to go back and finish *Typical American*, because I had a new voice and new concerns, and I knew that I was going to be writing a very fun, very loose, very fast book.

RH: It chronicles what was not only an exciting time for you personally, but for American culture as a whole.

GJ: I wanted it to be about the Asian American experience and intergenerational conflict, though those things are there in the book. From the beginning, I wanted it to address broader concerns about the nature of ethnicity, so I did set it quite purposefully in the late 1960s, when ethnicity was being invented, because it occurred to me when I looked back on my high school years that I had been a witness to that process of invention, on the heels of the civil rights movement, when blacks were turning blacker, and young Jews were becoming more Jewish, partly because of the Six-Day War, but also following the model of black people, reembracing their Judaism in a way that was quite astonishing to the older generation: returning to temple, learning Hebrew, things that their parents had gone to great lengths to avoid.

It encouraged me that that's the model that's being used by Asian Americans and other groups today. From our latter-day perspective, the invention of ethnicity is an interesting thing to look at, because in our time it seems so obvious that one is essentially (fill-in-the-blank) American, when twenty years ago there was no such label. It's a very recent and very American construction.

RH: Did these experiences influence you earlier on to become a writer in the first place?

GJ: That's very hard to say. Probably I became a writer by the process of elimination—I was a literary type, interested in writing in a casual way in elementary school and high school, but it wasn't until college that I really tried to write. I fell into it by accident; I was a junior, an English major, and I felt that I still didn't understand why poetry had to be written in these little lines. So I took a course in prosody with Robert Fitzgerald. He said that we'd have a weekly assignment, which I took to mean a paper, but he meant a weekly assignment in verse. I immediately fell in love with it and told my roommate that if I could do this for the rest of my life, I would. But I'm the daughter of immigrants, and I'd completely internalized all their practical ideas, so I didn't even consider for a moment becoming a poet. It was just not something anybody I knew did. But I had the feeling in me, and as I went from one career plan to another—I was premed, prelaw, in business school, thought about being an architect, a contractor, an antiques dealer—it became clear that there was one thing that I loved, and that none of these were it. But I had to try them all before I realized that I was going to have to write.

RH: Getting back to the earlier point about the construction of ethnic identity, I want to explore the connections between your identity as a writer and your identity as an Asian American.
GJ: The funny thing about it is that I was one of the earliest of this wave of Asian American writers, but I can't say that being a writer is an extension of my being an Asian American. Quite the contrary. My life as a fiction writer is directly related to my assimilation, particularly to the Jewish community in Scarsdale where I grew up, which is very much like the Scarshill in the book. That was a community that greatly esteemed fiction writing, which is how I first got interested in finding my voice and expressing myself. In my Chinese heritage, scholarship is greatly esteemed, but fiction writing is not considered scholarship. So as an "Asian American" writer, the "Asian" is linked to the "writer" part by being an "American."

RH: Yet there's a shorthand in literary criticism, particularly at more mainstream levels, where a writer can get identified early on as "(fill-in-the-blank) American."
GJ: Of course you hope that the identification doesn't end up becoming a pigeonhole. I have to say that that hasn't been my experience, though I did bristle early on at being labelled an "Asian American writer," because I think every writer likes to be seen as a universal writer. But today, I look at how many of my writer friends are greatly talented and hugely unknown, it occurs to me that we live in a culture where if you're not labelled you disappear. So as much as I hope I'm not limited by that moniker, and that people

will use it as a starting point to think about my work rather than an ending point, I now see that I'm lucky to have the label, ironic as it may seem. I'm probably pigeonholed with respect to the press, but among general readers and universities I seem to have gotten out of that small cubicle.

RH: Are you working on a third project?

GJ: I don't plan until I sit down. I'm a really intuitive writer—no plan, no end point—so I can have all the ideas in the world, but until I sit down at the keyboard, I have no idea whether I've got a live fish on the line or not. I wait for my books to write themselves; the conscious mind doesn't really know much about getting that to happen on a schedule.

RH: Who are some of the fiction writers that were held in high esteem when you were growing up?

GJ: It depends on what age you're talking about. In high school Bellow, Mailer, Philip Roth, Singer, Cynthia Ozick, Grace Paley: these writers were like gods to me. I continue to greatly esteem these writers, and to admire what Roth has called "red-face literature," a literature that is out there emotionally, not quite so restrained. So, aren't you going to ask if I'm Jewish?

RH: I don't know. I thought I might try to avoid asking some of the things you've probably been asked a dozen times already.

GJ: Oh, well, nobody's asked me yet if I'm writing a new book.

RH: I just hate reading interviews full of questions like "So how autobiographical is this novel? Did this really happen to you?" Are you Jewish?

GJ: I'm not Jewish, but I thought about it a lot as a teenager, and reexamined a lot of those thoughts while writing the book. Who I am is a person who assimilated a great deal of the Jewish culture I grew up in, as I think everybody who lives in the New York area has. The fact is that you can't grow up in New York without learning some Yiddish, without the culture leaving its mark on you. In the parts of this book that were consciously controlled, I did want to honor that. One of my friends from childhood described the novel as "a love letter to Scarsdale."

In this time of huge, public embracing of ethnic roots, I wanted to show how our lives are more complex than what we're born with. While our ethnic roots are very important to us, I think that anybody who is interested in their identity would do well to learn about the place they grew up in, and learn about its culture. We make ourselves in this country; even people who are racial and ethnic minorities transform themselves. The different groups have spent a lot of time rubbing elbows, rubbing off of each other, and while the melting pot model of assimilation was unhealthy, with its one way melting of people into generic Barbies and Kens, the idea of assimilation is still with us in ways that we don't necessarily have to be afraid of. We rub elbows with each other and learn from each other, and this is a wonderful thing. It's not like we abandon our own roots; we just know more things and allow them to change our lives.

One of the reasons that I steered the interview around to the "Are you Jewish?" question is that I want to question why it's funnier for an Asian American woman to consider switching identities like that than it would be, for example, an Irish American. There's some racist component to that formulation. Nobody asks an Irish American if he knows Gaelic, or if she celebrates Saint Patrick's Day, and if you don't, you're not seen as a fallen Irish. But for Chinese, it's different—how is it that people who don't even know us very well feel free to tell us about our identity and how we're living up to it?

RH: Why are Chinese being held up to a higher standard of cultural integrity?
GJ: And why do people consider it appropriate to even raise the issue? Asian Americans are held up to a different standard in that regard than Caucasian Americans, and there's an assumed power differential there that I want to question.

RH: At the same time, white people can experiment with Asian culture in any number of different ways and don't get asked about how unwhite they're being.
GJ: Exactly. It's not as much of a joke for a white person to try Buddhism as it is for a Chinese person to try Judaism. People have found the book hilarious, from what they've been saying to me during the tour, but there are also serious issues there that I hope they'll consider as well.

Gish Jen: An Interview on the American Experience

Lilli Leggio / 2002

From *Radcliffe News* 15.1 (December–January 2002). Reprinted by permission of Lilli Leggio.

"Nobody's having more fun with American diversity than Gish Jen," a book reviewer for the *Boston Globe* declared when Jen's most recent book *Who's Irish?* was published. The collection of short stories, like Jen's two novels—*Typical American* and *Mona in the Promised Land*—is a literary traffic study, a collection of eyewitness accounts about the intersection of American and immigrant cultures. Jen, a daughter of Chinese immigrants, is a fellow this year at the Radcliffe Institute for Advanced Study, where she's working on her next novel. Despite juggling work, historical commission meetings, other interviews, colleagues' lectures, and childcare, the over-booked author found time to sit down with the Radcliffe News.

Lilli Leggio: Is it fair to say that growing up Asian American is a primary influence on your work?
Gish Jen: I do write about other things—religion and what it means to be an artist, for example—but issues of identity are the dominant concern, especially what it means to be an American.

The roots of this do lie, of course, in my growing up the child of immigrants, which has given rise not only to my subject matter but also my tone. How could I not be alert to irony, growing up the way I did? Take, for example, the matter of my language. My parents immigrated from China, so their first language was Chinese, and probably they would have preferred to bring us up bilingual. But because my older brother had a very hard time with bilingualism, my parents decided—and this was progressive for the time—to raise me and my younger siblings speaking English. It was my parents' way of accepting that there had been a revolution in China, and that they were really stuck here. My mother told me that once they had made up their minds that America was going to be their home, they also decided they wanted their kids to speak English so well no one would be able to tell their parents were Chinese. And what was the result? One of my boyfriends in college once made everyone in the room close their eyes, listen to me talk, and tell him what they heard. And, of course, they all said, "New York Jew!"

Leggio: Dealing with new languages and new cultures creates stressful conditions for immigrants. How does this affect their expectations of their children?

Jen: Of course, there are huge expectations for the children. Often the parents have had to work tremendously hard to send a child to college, for example. How can the children then go and fritter their time away? They are the family's great hope. In some American households, the kids go home at Thanksgiving and everyone nods and says, Oh yes, I loved history of science too, and isn't medieval architecture fascinating. In immigrant households, the kids need to make the case for liberal education. What's it for? Where's it going to get him or her? How is it going to help the family? Sometimes too the parents feel they have a right to pressure the child into doing something practical—which, honestly, might not be such a bad idea, given the kid's home context. But, of course, the messages from college are about finding yourself and doing what you love—ideas the family does not imagine it can afford—with the result that the parents flip out, partly because they're worried and partly because immigration in general has made them feel helpless and stripped of their rightful parental power.

Leggio: The Harvard Immigration Project conducted a study (now archived at the Murray Research Center) which found that immigrants' children tend to equate success with education and helping their families and communities, while white American children tend to measure success more in individual terms. Does this surprise you and what do you think causes it?

Jen: I don't know about other groups, but, in the case of Asian Americans, you're talking about a home culture that is, among other things, predominantly collectivistic rather than individualistic. So, of course, people in the first or second generation especially tend to define success in nonindividualistic terms. Of course, over time, the family becomes Americanized, and its ideas about success change. This is a slow and painful process.

It's interesting that you should bring this up, because just last week I was talking to my mother about one of my brothers, who is off mountain climbing. We kids all thought he was great because he had just climbed a very difficult mountain near Everest. Not only was his the first team to summit this season, but immediately after summiting my brother had to go back up the mountain on a rescue mission. This was within twelve hours; they had to leave in the middle of the night to bring down a man who had had a stroke on the mountain. Isn't that incredible? They saved the man's life. To us kids, my brother was a hero. But my mother's view of my brother was completely different. As far as she was concerned, he should have been home, he was needed at home. He was in the Himalayas, she said, for his own glory.

Leggio: You were at Stanford working toward your MBA when you decided to focus instead on writing. How did your parents react? Do the pragmatic concerns of immigrant parents undermine the artistic aspirations of their children or do they further motivate them?
Jen: My parents were completely opposed to my dropping out of business school. They could not have been more opposed or made their opposition more plain.

Whether parental pressure helps or hinders really depends on the personality of the child involved. It's like watering flowers. Some do better without water; in fact, too much water will kill them. Others just need water. It's generally true, though, I think, that there's a kind of confidence that comes with having opposed your parents and won—a sense that you proved yourself in an important way.

Leggio: Most children want to fit in and avoid being singled out. With your children, Paloma and Luke, who are biracial, have you experienced any instances where they were made to feel like outsiders?
Jen: There were a few incidents with Luke when he was little—one at the Cambridge Common and another at the Science Museum—where little boys called him "Chinese, Chinese, Chinese." I'm just glad my child is at least Chinese American; I don't know what I would have told him if he were, say, Korean American or Japanese American.

In both instances, Luke was so young that it wasn't the words so much as the aggression that took him aback. He completely understood that it was hostile. Luckily, he's now going to a school with a lot of Asians and Asian Americans. Some are biracial, some are adopted, some have parents from Taiwan—you name it. This has been very normalizing; there hasn't been even the slightest whiff of anything uncomfortable. There are so many Asian and Asian American kids in this school that nobody even calls me to do Chinese New Year. It used to be that every year doing a little something was my job.

I don't know what my daughter's issues are going to be. Where Luke has black hair, she has light hair. Where Luke is usually identified as an Asian American, Paloma is not. In fact, people sometimes think I'm her nanny.

I am trying to bring both of them up knowing a little Chinese. I'd like to bring them to China, too, so they will understand a little of what it is. I don't want their experiences to be confined to Chinatown or a Chinese culture club.

Leggio: We've talked about people who feel like outsiders. Do you think there are people in America who don't feel like outsiders?
Jen: I think the number is smaller than you'd think. My observation has been that many people, male and female, feel themselves not quite at home in their town or office or whatever. We are a country, it seems, of misfits.

I often try to emphasize this when I speak with Asian Americans and people who consider themselves people of color—that feelings of alienation are pretty general. But it's also true that for some groups it's an internal phenomenon and for other groups there's an external factor—and that makes a huge difference. The world intrudes more on you. I was once in the Cowboy Hall of Fame in Oklahoma City, about to buy a little cup, and as I fiddled with my change, the lady behind the counter reached across and took my hand and started arranging the coins on it. Then she explained, "That's fifty cents right there. It's two of the big coins."

Leggio: What were you doing in the Cowboy Hall of Fame?
Jen: I couldn't resist! Would you go to Oklahoma City and not go to the Cowboy Hall of Fame?

Leggio: What do you think of anti-Arab sentiments resulting from the September 11 terrorist attacks?
Jen: My heart completely goes out to Arab Americans. I don't want to say that I feel their pain, but I can certainly relate to what they're going through. In the wake of the Wen Ho Lee incident, for example, there were people talking about boycotting Chinese restaurants. Not that Chinese restaurants had anything to do with Wen Ho Lee; but people will do these things. When the Japanese auto industry was the bogeyman, Chinese American people

got killed; there's a wonderful movie about this phenomenon called *Who Killed Vincent Chin?*

During the Gulf War, too, I was mistaken for an Arab American—amazing, no? And yet true. A gas station owner on Concord Avenue started screaming at me, even as I tried to scream back that I was Chinese American. So I'm very aware of the way that these things spill over, and my heart breaks when I hear about Arab Americans having their cars vandalized, and so on. I know some of them feel that having survived living here during the Gulf War, they can survive anything. Still, these times are going to be very difficult.

An Interview with Gish Jen

Sarah Anne Johnson / 2002

From *The Writer's Chronicle*, December 2002. Reprinted by permission of Sarah Anne Johnson.

Gish Jen grew up in Scarsdale, New York, and graduated from the Iowa Writers' Workshop. Her work has appeared in the *New Yorker*, the *Atlantic Monthly*, and the *Best American Short Stories of the Century*. The author of two novels, *Typical American* and *Mona in the Promised Land*, as well as a collection of stories, *Who's Irish?*, she lives in Massachusetts with her husband and two children and is currently teaching at Harvard.

Sarah Anne Johnson: How did you get started writing?

Gish Jen: When I was in college I took a class with Robert Fitzgerald, the translator, in prosody. Today, it seems to me that every English major should have to take this class. Fitzgerald said at the beginning of the semester that there was going to be a weekly exercise; being an English major, I thought that he meant a paper. It turned out that he meant a weekly exercise in verse. I thought, I'd try the class and if I didn't like it, I'd drop it. But I wrote my first poem in Catullan hendecasyllabics, and immediately I loved it. I remember saying to a friend that if I could do this every day for the rest of my life, I would.

But I am the child of immigrants; it never occurred to me that I could try to be a poet. I didn't know any poets. Also, my parents had come from China where they'd seen a lot of upheaval. First their country was invaded by the Japanese, then there was a World War. They ended up in America quite by accident. I had internalized all of their desire for security.

I was a premed student when Fitzgerald pulled me aside at the end of a class and asked me why I was premed. I can't imagine what I said, given that there was no reasonable explanation, and I had just received a C in chemistry. He said that I should think about being a writer, and that if I wasn't

going to be a writer, I should go into publishing. Sure enough, when I graduated, he did get me my first job, which was in publishing, at Doubleday. He
called up Pike Johnson, the managing editor at the time, and that was that.

Once I was in publishing, I did, at Doubleday's expense, take a course in
writing at the New School. And later I went to business school for a year at
Stanford because I knew they had a good writing program. You may gather
from this how confused I was at the time. I immediately realized when I got
to Stanford that I had no interest in business, that I was only interested in
writing. I spent the entire year taking writing classes. I also read over a hundred novels. Who knows how I managed to pass business school; anyway,
I didn't go back for my second year. Instead, I went to China, and when I
came back I went to the Iowa Writers' Workshop.

Johnson: How do your novel and story ideas come to you?
Jen: They come in many different ways. Often, I identify what I like to think
of as a nerve in myself—a nerve that I've developed as a result of my contact
with the world—and I try to follow that nerve. The work is not autobiographical, exactly. The things that happen have not happened to me, but
the nerve, or the nature of the conflict, is often something with which I am
familiar. I write this way partly because I was very conflicted for a long time
about being engaged in an activity that seemed to me so selfish. I found this
to be a way of producing work that was both personally compelling and
relevant to other people.

Johnson: How do you know when an idea is worth pursuing?
Jen: My friend Martha Collins used to say that she'd write about the forbidden. When you can hear the bells going off, you're on the right track.

Johnson: What is your process like for working on a novel?
Jen: I write my novels much in the same way that I write my short stories,
which is to say intuitively. With both, I write off into the darkness and don't
know where I'm going until I get to my end. I know a lot of people don't
write novels that way. When I was writing my first novel, it seemed that
about once a month I'd go to a reading, and there would be some famous
writer up there who would say that with a novel, it's a good idea to have
some sort of a plan. I'd think, Oh my God, I don't have a plan! In fact, it's a
very nerve-wracking way to write. I swore after I finished *Typical American*
that I'd never do it again, but then I wrote *Mona in the Promised Land* in the
same way, and now I'm writing a third novel in the same way.

That said, there is a fair amount of analytical thinking that goes on. I write off into the darkness, but then I spend time reading over what I've written and trying to understand it. I try to understand why I wrote it, and where it might be going, and whether in fact I'm writing more than one story, and whether that's okay.

Johnson: What writers have influenced your work and whom do you admire now?

Jen: I admire more writers than I can name. Certainly Grace Paley has been an enormous influence on me, I think because I struggled so much with the question of what writing has to do with the world. Her humor, her humanity, her interest in society were very big influences on me. Her honesty and directness. But there have been a lot of other people, too. I've read a lot of Alice Munro. I've looked to Jamaica Kincaid for inspiration. She's very, very "bad." Whenever I hesitate to be bad, I think of Jamaica and I go ahead.

Johnson: There is a lot of humor in your work, even in the face of tragedy. Where does your comic outlook come from?

Jen: I have to say that I think that it's genetic. I say that because my father has a tremendous sense of humor, and I see now that my children do, too. My daughter started with the humor really early. Even when she was eighteen months she would stick her bum right in my face when I was trying to change her diaper and say, "Ta da!," and start laughing.

Johnson: You were at the Iowa Writers' Workshop before multiculturalism became a trend in American literature. Were you concerned at that time about how your work would be received?

Jen: It was commonly understood at the time that people like me, i.e., Chinese American people, would never be published in mainstream publications. People now say that it was obvious that multiculturalism was right around the corner. But it wasn't, and that was okay. Most people were not going to be in the *New Yorker*. It wasn't what we were doing. It's not like I carried it around like this big wound. At the same time, multiculturalism was a gift.

Johnson: What were your early attempts at publication like? When did you start to break through?

Jen: I was very lucky from very early on. My first publication was a piece I'd written for the Raymond Carver Write Alike contest in Barry Hannah's class my first year at Iowa. He had this contest and we were all supposed to write something in the manner of Raymond Carver. All the women in the class were sure that a woman would never win, so we signed our stories Raymond Carver. I still remember the shock I felt when Barry held up these pages and asked, "Now who wrote this?" There were a full three seconds before I realized that I was going to have to raise my hand. That story became my first published piece. The *Iowa Review* took it.

Johnson: You are such a quintessentially American writer in that you turn what it means to be American on its head and redefine it altogether. You first did this in *Typical American*, where you depict the Chang family pursuing the American dream and struggling with homesickness, assimilation, racism, and greed. When you're writing, are you aware of making these points, or do they rise out of character?

Jen: They rise out of character, and I bring it up a little bit. That would be the analytical part. I try to stay ahead of the critics, and see what I wrote myself. That said, no novel can be written by sitting down and saying, "Now I'm going to turn ideas about the American dream on their head." You better have a lot of cappuccino before you start that one. I write about these nerves, and some of these nerves have to do with how American I am. The whole question of whether an Asian American is an American or a foreigner has been with me my whole life, even after *Who's Irish?* came out.

Johnson: Does it make you angry?

Jen: I have to say that I mostly think it's ridiculous. It's so ridiculous that it's hard to be angry. It'd be like being angry at a child. The level of ignorance can be so unbelievable, but I see it as a kind of amiable irritant. When *Who's Irish?* came out, the first line of one of my reviews referred to the collection as a series of stories about America as seen by foreigners. I thought, this is 1999! What can you do but laugh? If I didn't feel the weight of the culture and educated people behind me, I'm sure I'd be furious, but that's not the case.

When I wrote *Typical American*, I was aware that to call a book about Chinese Americans *Typical American* was provocative, and that felt good. I don't know if that's anger, or what that is. It's a desire to set something straight at some level, sure, and there's a measure of defiance in it. The world is full of nonsense; if you can use it more than it uses you, for a writer, it's a gift.

Johnson: *Typical American* is told in the third-person personal point of view. How did you decide on this point of view?

Jen: I think that because people were so convinced that I must be writing immigrant autobiography, I instinctively shied away from first person.

Johnson: Do you find it more or less difficult to inhabit characters of the opposite sex? Are there inherent challenges in this?
Jen: I don't find it difficult.

Johnson: Ralph's assimilation begins with his renaming from Yifeng Chang to the American Ralph Chang by a secretary at the Foreign Student Affairs Office. While this is a common experience for many immigrants, it's ironic that upon entrance into America where people hope to find a new freedom, they must first give away an essential part of themselves—their name!
Jen: There are many ironies in this book, and that certainly is one of them. I have to say that, Ralph finds, ironically, a kind of freedom in his new name. For many people the new name might not be freeing, but in Ralph's case it is. One of the many things that, in hindsight, I was trying to do, was to complicate the immigrant story. There isn't one story, there are millions of stories. Some people come and find restriction here, and some people come and find liberty. Sometimes that liberty is what we think it is, and sometimes it's a totally different kind of liberty. For Ralph, it's liberty from his family. "Goodbye, Dad!" That was probably 90 percent of it for him.

Johnson: You describe that point in the immigration experience at which Ralph is no longer Chinese and not yet an American. Ralph "refused to be made an American citizen. He thumbed his nose at the relief act meant to help him, as though to claim his home was China was to make China indeed his home. And wasn't it still? Even if his place in it was fading like a picture hung too long in a barbershop—even if he didn't know where his family was anymore?" There seems to be resistance to claim a home in either China or America.
Jen: That's pretty common, don't you think? We often imagine that everybody comes here and is dying to become American. I actually think that most people are not dying to become American, even the ones who are not unhappy to be partaking of the American feast, and that's not everyone either. We don't read that much about the people who go home, and that's a lot of people. As for the ones who stay here, a lot of them are quite ambivalent for a long time, if not forever.

Johnson: In *Typical American*, the Changs eventually adopt the culture and values that they originally despised. Do you think this is an inevitable result of assimilation?

Jen: One irony of *Typical American* is that "Typical American" is something they call other people, but by the end of the novel, they are the kind of people that others might call "Typical American." It's not like they've whole hog adopted every facet of American culture. They've simply availed themselves of the freedom here in a way that makes them think hard about who they are now; they spend much more time thinking about their identities than they would have if they'd stayed in China.

Johnson: *Typical American* begins, "It's an American story: . . ." And yet, many critics labeled you as an Asian American writer, which seems to me reductive. In fact, your work seeks to redefine what it means to be American. Was *Mona in the Promised Land* written in any way as a response to those early classifications?
Jen: I suppose I wanted to complicate people's ideas about ethnicity in general and how better to do that than to write about the invention of ethnicity?

I do struggle with the Asian American thing. I don't mind it being used as a description of me, but I do mind it being used as a definition of me. Frank McCourt is an Irish American writer who writes about Irish things. And yet sometimes he's "Irish American writer Frank McCourt," and sometimes he's simply "writer Frank McCourt," or more often "best-selling writer Frank McCourt." The term "Irish American" is somehow detachable from "writer" in a way that "Asian American" is not. That said, I'm happy to report that in many places now I am seen as someone who writes about the American dream.

Johnson: In this novel you expand your territory from the Chinese immigrant experience in *Typical American*, to explore a larger canvas of characters with a variety of backgrounds including WASP, Jewish, African American, and Chinese immigrants. How do you discover and define your territory as a writer?
Jen: I write about whatever I'm interested in. I didn't for a minute wonder if I had the right to write about other groups, but I did think I needed to do my homework if I was going to. I knew that if I got one thing wrong, I would get called on it. But that's as it should be. I think anyone writing about anything should get it all right.

Johnson: As *Mona in the Promised Land* progresses, each character becomes less fixed in her or his cultural identity. Mona even converts to Judaism and her friends call her Changowitz. What interests you about the fluidity of ethnic or cultural identity?

Jen: It is a kind of reclaiming of a reality that threatens to be lost. There is a way in which someone like me is always in danger of being frozen into an ethnic mold. I think the fact that people find the book so funny is proof that it is a challenge to ideas that are held right now in our culture. Is an Irish American turning Jewish funny? But for a Chinese American to turn Jewish, now that's funny!

Johnson: You also capture a range of voices and inflections from New York Jewish to African American to Chinese American with apparent ease. Are there any pitfalls to watch for in rendering these voices?
Jen: You try to listen to the way that people really talk. If you do, it's not that complicated. I have no advice to the young writer, other than to pay attention.

Johnson: The title story of *Who's Irish?* is narrated in pidgin English by a Chinese grandmother. Did you have any concerns about writing a story in this voice?
Jen: People have suggested that the way to gain freedom as a writer is to use a pseudonym, but for the ethnic writer, freedom actually comes with having a name and creating your own context. If I had written that story twenty years ago and sent it to the *New Yorker*, I guarantee that I would've gotten a little slip back saying "please try again when your English is better." I don't think they would've assumed the voice was artifice. Today they get the story and it says Gish Jen on it, and they know I speak English.

I've seen this again and again. If I didn't have a name of some sort, I wouldn't have been able to publish a book called *Who's Irish?* with no subtitle. As it was, nobody at my publishing house said, we have to subtitle this "stories about Asian Americans."

One of my greatest satisfactions as a writer has been earning myself a context different than the one supplied to me by our culture.

Johnson: You depict this grandmother's racism with clarity, humor, and sensitivity. For example, "Even the black people doing better these days, some of them live so fancy, you'd be surprised. Why the Shea family have so much trouble? They are white people, they speak English. When I come to this country, I have no money and do not speak English. But my husband and I own our restaurant before he die. Free and clear, no mortgage. Of course, I understand I am just lucky, come from a country where the food is popular all over the world. I understand it is not the Shea family's fault they come from a country where everything is boiled." This seems a fine line to walk for any writer, yet you do it beautifully and without offense.

Jen: This is related to that desire to write about things that are hard. I don't know why it is that I seem to be able to keep my balance through difficult terrain. I don't know exactly why it is either that I'm attracted to this terrain. But there it is. I am attracted to it, and I haven't totally screwed up yet.

Johnson: In this short story collection, you continue to explore the friction of assimilation through a variety of characters of Irish and Chinese backgrounds. In the title story, you explore the difficulties between generations, as well as cultures, and in the end, the two grandmothers who share the same generation and immigrant experience wind up together in spite of their different backgrounds, rather than the grandmother winding up with her daughter. Comment?

Jen: I think it is one of the great gifts of America, that a lot of the old attitudes are remade. That happens in *Mona in the Promised Land*, too. The mother begins being very anti-Japanese, but once a Japanese woman actually drives up on her lawn, a lot of the prejudice falls away. She doesn't have the heart to actually start yelling at the lady in person. Immigrants bring their ethnic grudges with them, but a lot of that stuff tends to lose its force.

Johnson: You have two more stories about the Changs narrated this time by Callie. Can readers expect to encounter the Changs again in future works?

Jen: Never say never, but I'm not writing about them now. I've completely forgotten about them, I don't know why.

Johnson: What are you working on now?

Jen: A new novel, not about the Chang family.

Interview with Gish Jen

Bill Moyers / 2003

From "Becoming American: Personal Journeys," *PBS Television*, March 25, 2003.
Printed by permission of Bill Moyers and Public Square Media, Inc.

Bill Moyers: You once said that writing depends on an amiable irritant. What exactly is an amiable irritant?

Gish Jen: Yeah, well, that's not my phrase. That phrase is from Philip Roth. I think he developed it under circumstances that are similar to mine in the sense that he had identities assigned to him by society which he found very irritating. I know that these irritants help me overcome other anti-writing feelings such as general sloth, embarrassment, whatever, a desire to make a living.

But yeah, for me growing up Asian American, having been a child of immigrant parents—all of that difficulty did serve as a kind of amiable irritant, the grain of sand that hopefully produces the pearl.

Moyers: So, you think your writing would have been different had you not been the daughter of immigrant parents?

Jen: Absolutely. I'm not even sure that I would have been a writer.

Moyers: Why?

Jen: Oh, I don't know. In many ways I'm very social. Maybe too social to be a writer. I think I am a person who on one hand can find deep satisfaction in holing up with my computer day after day after day. But in another way I could have done something very different, if I hadn't had so much stuff to deal with. I kind of had to become a writer. Sometimes I imagine that someday I'll be done with my stuff and then I won't write anymore. But that day has not come.

Moyers: Stuff. What kind of stuff?

Jen: Well, early on, of course, it was the whole business of trying to make sense of two very different worlds that I was living in. The immigrant world and the mainstream world and all that that meant.

It really just wasn't a matter of: you ate with chopsticks and they ate with forks but the whole difference in the way that people thought. I came from a world where—in every sentence—in everything they did there was this idea that there were obstacles everywhere that one could not simply go out and do what one wanted. That one had to be canny and one had to be smart because the world opposed you.

And then I would go out into the mainstream world where it was assumed that you got what you wanted. Wasn't that what the world was for? To provide for us?

Moyers: Did you feel between two worlds?
Jen: Absolutely. And of course, I grew up in a time before we had that phrase "between two worlds." So I didn't even have that. I simply had this feeling that, "My goodness, I know people who think so differently about the world, in the most fundamental ways." Well, what am I gonna do with that?

I don't think I asked myself that explicitly but I did have this feeling that you could step through a door and step into a completely different reality at any moment. And I think that that dissonance led me to become a writer.

Moyers: You were born in America of immigrant parents?
Jen: Yes.

Moyers: Where were they from?
Jen: My parents are from China. My mother was from Shanghai, from the city. And my father was from outside the city.

Moyers: Talk about how they got here.
Jen: Well, they both came in the 1940s. My mother came for education. At that time, it was called "gilding the lily." It was something the upper-class families did. They sent their girls abroad for a little graduate school. Not that they were ever gonna have to earn a living or anything. But it was sort of a nice thing to do.

And my father came as part of the war effort. He was a hydraulics engineer. And back at the end of the Second World War there was talk of opening a second front against the Japanese in Shanghai. And so they needed some harbor engineers to come over and help coordinate that.

And so my father was sent, overland of course because the Pacific was too dangerous to cross. He was sent over the Hump, as they say, over the Himalayas into India and all the way across Europe, all the way across the Atlantic. By the time he got there the war was over. (laughter)

Moyers: Typical Army papers, right?
Jen: Exactly. Exactly.

Moyers: But [things didn't] go that way.
Jen: Exactly. And then by the time he got here he said, "Well, maybe I'll stay and go to graduate school." And so he did. Neither one of my parents ever planned to stay. For them it was a little adventure. But of course, that was before the Communists took over.

Moyers: And they couldn't go back?
Jen: Yeah, it was one of things that was very complicated about the time and what not many people realize is that a lot of the Chinese technical students were held here illegally against their will. They actually wanted to go back. My father and his fellow students wanted to go back. A lot of them did. Of course, their families are there. You can imagine if you were in China and something happened here. Of course you want to go home.
But the US government was afraid that they would help the Communists. And so they kind of cut a deal with the Guo Ming Dang [the KMT] to keep the students here. Or at least that's what my parents always told me.

Moyers: When did your father come actually?
Jen: It would have been about 1945.

Moyers: Well, at that time I wouldn't think many Americans thought Chinese knew very much about the world, right?
Jen: Yes.

Moyers: I mean, Chinese Americans were a very small number at that time. And there was a great deal of indifference if not outright hostility that grew out of the past.
Jen: Oh, absolutely. And of course, this business of keeping the technical students here because they were so valuable. Well, three years earlier it was perceived that they probably don't even know very much math.

My father worked—was out in the field with some engineer. He's actually a very highly trained person. They would give him algebra books and he would give them back and say, "Well, I can do that." And they would give him a trigonometry book and he would hand it back and say, "I can do that too." They really didn't quite believe it.

Moyers: What was the story of the bridge?

Jen: There was a very funny story where my father was out in field and there was this bridge. I guess it's a truss bridge and it needed repair and they were having trouble getting this piece in. So, my father said, "Well, if you park a truck on the end of the bridge it basically take the stress out of the piece, then you'll be able to fix it."

But of course, this was in the days when no one thought that Chinese could do engineering. They just kind of said, go back to your trig book, right?

So they struggled for another three or four hours and my father said again, "If you park a truck at the end of the bridge you'll be able to fix this." I'm not sure if they really understood what he was saying.

And so they went on and after about eight hours someone finally said, "What's with parking a truck on the end of the bridge?" And sure enough they fixed it just fine.

Something very interesting about my dad. I think a lot of people would have told that story with great bitterness. Look at that, they looked down on me. All those assumptions all day, all that prejudice. My father always thought it was the biggest joke in the world.

Moyers: How did he feel when he was told he could not go back to China, go home?

Jen: Well, that was not so funny. I think there were all those students who were offered citizenship under a refugee act. And my father said, "I am not a refugee." I mean, they were very insulted, and they did not think it was funny.

My father refused to become a US citizen with the result that for many years he was in this country with no status. He was not a citizen of any country.

Moyers: He was not even between two worlds; he was—

Jen: No, he was in no world. Yeah.

Moyers: You grew up in Yonkers, a suburb north of New York City. What was it like for you there?

Jen: Well, I have to say that a lot went on in that suburb that was not so easy, and it was not funny. We were the only Chinese family in that area, and it was kind of a rough neighborhood. So, definitely people threw rocks at us. My brother was beaten up so frequently that my mother finally sent him to judo school so that he could learn to defend himself. I mean, it was not pretty.

Moyers: This is a working-class neighborhood?
Jen: A working-class neighborhood.

Moyers: You were clearly the outsider.
Jen: Sometimes, when I'm talking to my son, and I'm trying to explain to him what my childhood was like and I say to him, "You gotta understand, when someone threw a snow ball we never knew whether or not there would be a rock in it." To him, it was of course, why would anybody throw a snowball at you with a rock in it?

Moyers: You were very young, right?
Jen: Yeah, I was probably five or six.

Moyers: What does this do to your psyche, the way you see the world?
Jen: That's a good question. I mean, I have to say that, it did make us pretty defensive. And it did have a tendency to make us wary, more apt to depend on family than on outsiders.

And don't get me wrong, a lot of people were very kind to us. Of course my parents are proud people. It was a little hard to accept the kindness also. I mean, they had been aristocrats and then all of a sudden people are like, "Oh, we'll take your daughter to ballet?" On one hand they had to accept. On the other hand it was not easy for them.

Moyers: Then you moved to an upscale community, Scarsdale? Did things change for you?
Jen: Yes, it's a very, very, very, very different kind of community. For one thing, Scarsdale is predominantly Jewish. I think probably it was really maybe 40 percent Jewish. But there were enough Jews so that it was felt to be quite a Jewish community.

And so they were acquainted with what it meant to be a minority. So, this was a place where a minority was sort of the majority. And of course, as a community it was completely committed to being open and embracing and so on.

It was still awkward there too in many ways, but always in well-intentioned ways. People would sort of say, "We'd love to hear more about your traditions." Maybe I didn't really want to talk about my traditions. But in any case it was never mean. Nobody ever threw anything at us.

Moyers: Talk about the differences in the culture inside the Chinese home and the American home and how these came to play out in how you were raised?
Jen: Well, we could talk for an entire hour just about that. But, certainly there were some things about the Chinese family that I was happy to escape, I will say. There was a view that the girl's education was not as important as the boy's. I know it's true of a lot of immigrant families. It's very pronounced in a Chinese family.

Certainly there were a lot of views about what a nice Chinese girl did and that did not include becoming an author, I hardly need to point out. There was a way that, if I had not grown up in Scarsdale, New York, in a culture where writing was this great thing, I don't know that I ever would have thought to pick up a pen. So, in that way, I'm deeply grateful to the mainstream culture.

On the other hand certainly in my home culture, this kind of familiarity, it might not always be a complete picture of peace. But certainly, you have a feeling of contact with other people. The kind of animus and isolation that I see in a lot of mainstream family experiences. You don't experience that in a Chinese family. Everybody is close.

Moyers: Once your parents had to stay here, did they say, "Well, we know our children are going to be American and we're going to raise them as American"? Or did they still want to raise you within the traditional Chinese ethos?
Jen: Yeah, well, for my parents, it took them a while to realize that they were really, truly stuck here. These Communists were not going away; they really had taken power.

But once they finally accepted that, they decided on a move which was considered quite progressive at the time—to bring us up English speaking and to bring us up as Americans. And my mother said that she hoped that our English would be good enough that somebody listening in the next room would think that our parents were American.

And they succeeded. When I was in college, one of my boyfriends said, "Okay, if you close your eyes and listen to Gish, what do you hear?" And they all said, "New York Jew." (laughter)

Moyers: So, your parents succeeded then?
Jen: They did. All too well, maybe.

Moyers: Did they speak Chinese in the home?
Jen: Yeah, they did. But mostly around Christmas time as it was always for things that they were trying to keep secret from us. I have to say today of course I greatly regret this. I have taken beginning Chinese a hundred times and I'm still working on my Chinese.

Moyers: You'd like to know Chinese now?
Jen: Of course.

Moyers: You don't need it now.
Jen: Well, now I need it more than ever.

Moyers: Why?
Jen: Well, I think I do because I am forty-seven—I'm gonna be forty-eight later this year—I'm at that age where you suddenly realize that your parents are not gonna live forever and all your heritage [is going to die]. If you don't know what happened in your family, if you don't speak the language it's gonna die.

I mean, you suddenly realize like, "Oh, my God." You can't depend on your parents to translate things for you forever. Now it seems greatly life enriching. And I guess, (unintelligible) growing up, you just want to define yourself, you want to make yourself.

Bill Moyers: You want to be like everybody else.
Gish Jen: Well, partly that; partly you want to be yourself. You don't want to just be your parents' daughter. You want to be yourself. I don't know that becoming a writer is exactly like being everybody else either.

In the beginning, you want acceptance. And then later on you want self-realization. Maybe that is a way of being like everybody else here in America.

Moyers: Well, that's very American, isn't it?
Jen: It is.

Moyers: The business of inventing ourselves?
Jen: Yeah, it is. But one hopes that one will somehow bring some inner essence out and make it manifest.

And of course, one's hope has nothing to do with one's parents whatsoever. And also I have to say, in a context where so much of the world is telling you, "You're Chinese, you're Chinese, you're Chinese," there is a way in which you want to say, "Actually that is one part of what I am. But it is not all of what I am. It does not define me." So, there is a way in which you try to push it away from you a little bit because it threatens to color everything.

Moyers: Has this informed your writing? Is this one of the reasons you write?

Jen: Well, sure. Part of my writing has been an effort to claim my Americanness in a way that does not deny my Chinese heritage. People ask me, "Oh, those Chinese shoes? You must know where to get them."

There's something baffling about Chinese politics. I think pretty much every Asian American has had the experience of being in some meeting and everything is going along fine and something comes up with Asia and everybody turns to look at them.

And I will point out that it's not just the things having to do with China; it's things having to do with Japan or Indonesia or whatever. They still look at you as if you must have some insider knowledge.

But early on, my project, like everybody, was define myself as an American, to define myself irrespective of my parents, irrespective of these messages I was getting from society, to really be my own person.

In some ways I viewed it as probably dangerous to know Chinese, the same way that for women it could be a mixed thing to know how to type because if you can type, you will type. If I had spoken Chinese, there's so much pressure for me to play this ambassador role. It's difficult to resist.

Now, everybody knows that I wrote the book after turning Jewish and staying Jewish. (laughter) No one would dare ask me whether I spoke Chinese. But the whole idea is that my authority as a writer, it clearly does not stem from my knowledge of the old country. It clearly stems from something else.

Now, it's kind of safe for me to go back. To really think, to get the old stories, to really bring up my language and my identity is born now. It's not going to change.

Moyers: What were your parents' expectations of you? They must have been huge?

Jen: Well, yes and no. Whatever their expectations were they were mostly worried that I would not get married. I think that their perception early on was that I was far too outspoken and headstrong for a nice Chinese girl and that was gonna be trouble.

Moyers: Was education important in their scheme for you?
Jen: I have to say that as the years went on, it became more important. But early on they totally did not care. I was a girl, and that was not what was important.

Quite the contrary, I was often told that I was too smart. Again, too smart to be marriageable. It was fine if I was gonna be smart as long as nobody knew. I definitely got the mixed message about education.

As a result, I have to say, there have been good things about it. Oh, I don't know. Today, when I look at these kids and how hard they work, I definitely never felt that I had to perform up to some level and I had to spend all of my time trying to get to that level or whatever. I had a great time and I paid no attention whatsoever to my school work. It did not seem to matter at all as far as I can tell.

And in a funny kind of way it might have fed my creativity that I had all this time. I was kind of on my own. Nobody really was paying too much attention to what I was doing.

Moyers: Did they applaud when you decided to become a writer?
Jen: Oh, no. That was a disaster.

Moyers: Why?
Jen: Well, by that time of course, they had begun to think that well, if nothing else I was going to have to have enough skills to support myself. I went to Stanford Business School for a year and dropped out to become a writer. I remember my parents were both very distressed about this.

My father said to me, "You have to have a meal ticket." And interestingly he said to me—and this shows some evolution on his part too of course—he said, "If you don't have a meal ticket, your husband will treat you badly." It was interesting. And so, you can sort of see their thoughts and how it had come quite a long way.

Moyers: And writing was not a meal ticket.
Jen: No, it's definitely not a meal ticket.

Moyers: Did you call home and say, "I'm gonna decide who I am. I'm gonna write a novel"?

Jen: Oh, yes. And now that I'm a parent I completely understand where they're coming from. People often ask me, "Well, would you want your child to become a writer?" And of course I would never prevent them from becoming writers, but I would start saving now. (laughter)

Moyers: So, you went to Stanford Business School?

Jen: I did.

Moyers: Intending to get into business?

Jen: I don't know. It's one of these things where I always say that I became a writer by process of elimination. I had already been pre-med and pre-law so that only left business school, one thing I had never been interested in at all.

And one thing about being able to write, you get into everything because you can write. But the minute I got there I was like, "What am I doing here?" I think I read 100 novels, and I spent the entire year taking writing classes. I never went to any of my business classes at all.

Moyers: What did your parents say when you told them this?

Jen: Well, I didn't tell them that I wasn't going to class but by the time second year rolled around and it was just clear to me that I was—I think I overslept the first day of class and then I overslept the second day. I overslept the third day. And by the end of the week it was clear to me that I was never going to class and I should just drop out.

And of course my parents would be very upset—very, very upset. My mother didn't talk to me for almost a year. My sibs also. Everybody was like, "Will you please stop this. Do you realize you're ruining Christmas? Just stop it?"

But it really wasn't me. For whatever reason I've never been able to do anything I didn't want to do. And I really didn't want to do it.

Moyers: And why did you decide on writing? You had to make a commitment at some point. Why did you say this is the way?

Jen: There did come a point where I was able to get myself into whatever other schools and it always seemed that I could do other things. But I don't know. One morning I woke up and I guess I realized that I was gonna be on my deathbed someday. Someday, I'd be lying there and my parents would be long dead. And I realized that if I had not even tried to become a writer that I would be full of regret.

I mean, it sounds sort of morbid but it is true. And I think at that moment I realized like, "Oh, my God. My life is my own." And I just realized that yeah, I would never forgive myself. And at that point, I just had to try.

Moyers: You were glib about it but you did pass beyond the point when I asked you about your parents' response. I mean, this must have been somehow difficult for them to know that you were gonna become a writer. Because as I understand it, in the Chinese home there are expectations for the child. And they do expect you to fulfill those expectations. And for you to announce that you were taking this—not reckless but uncertain path, that you were going out to do something that was foreign to them. This must have been a blow.

Jen: Yeah, it was scary to them. And of course, looking back, when I see how much instability they had lived themselves—the loss of the country, their home, I mean everything. When we were younger we had no money, we drank powdered milk, you know, that sort of thing.

Bit by bit they had built up the family, they had gotten us into good schools. Their daughter had gone to Harvard and then she had gotten into Stanford Business School and I was gonna throw it all away and go onto who knew what. Yeah, they were very upset.

Moyers: And for them to cut you off. As you said, your mother didn't speak to you for a year?

Jen: Yeah, for many, many, many, many months—many months. I think they couldn't understand it. And it was also such an assertion of the self. It's so I . . .

Moyers: So American. I think it's so American.

Jen: Yeah. I mean, besides the fact that I wasn't going to business school, I was doing something which is so individualistic, that was very counter to their whole culture.

Moyers: Did they cut you off financially?

Jen: Yes. Yes, that was also very difficult for me. It was a very difficult period. I myself wondered what I was doing. Like I say, I had this feeling like I had to do it. I had this feeling like I had no choice. You know what I mean? I kept on seeing myself lying there dead—almost dead. And I just felt that I just couldn't live any other way.

Moyers: When did they change their mind?

Jen: Well, slowly, slowly. First they realized—well, I think the first big step, in their accepting what I had done was when I married my husband who I have to say is the epitome of everything that they approved of. He had gone to Harvard. He had gone to Stanford Business School. He had a good job. So, when we got married I think a lot of their anxiety was greatly reduced.

Moyers: Was he an American of Chinese descent?

Jen: No, he's of Irish descent.

Moyers: So, you were marrying an Irishman?

Jen: Well, you've got to understand the circumstances. I think I alluded to how unmarriageable they thought I was. My father had said to me, "We'd be happy if you married a dog." (laughter)

Moyers: No comment.

Jen: No comment. But they were just relieved that some nice guy was going to marry me. And really and truly my husband is a very, very nice man.

Moyers: I'm sure of that.

Jen: —except that he had, you know, blue eyes and a beard.

Moyers: Here you were, you were becoming a writer and you were marrying an Irishman.

Jen: Yeah, like I said they were just relieved. (laughter) They were relieved I was getting married at all.

Moyers: When you married "outside the Chinese American community," how did they react?

Jen: I think they could see it coming. I mean, I think that they could see that I didn't have a lot of Asian Americans around me.

Today if you go to Harvard, there are tons of them, tons. But back when I went to school, we were still a very, very small minority. And the numbers were just against us. Plus, I think that my parents recognized, early on, that I was so far from the Chinese American ideal. (laughs)

I think they understood that early on, that I was never gonna be the sort of wife who made the soup just right and went and got slippers. And they could just see that. I don't think by the time I got married that this was any great shock.

Moyers: Even though it was an Irishman?
Jen: Even it was an Irishman. At least he had degrees.

Moyers: And so much irony in that, because in the past, it was the Irish who—
Jen: Oh, I know. No kidding.

Moyers: —took all the Chinese out in California—
Jen: That's right, that's right.

Moyers: But that's the American story you're writing here. You're living it here. You're not writing it. You're living it here.
Jen: That's right. But you know what? My parents, because they immigrated so late, had really no awareness of that history, I mean, the dimmest awareness. And they did not identify with those Chinese, either. As far as they're concerned, those are the California Chinese. They were railroad workers; we were educated, so on and so forth. They didn't see themselves as related to them at all.

Moyers: What did they think when *Typical American*, your first book, was such a success?
Jen: Well, they were happy enough. It was fine. But there was a moment where suddenly it became more than fine.

It actually became great. I had been in the *New Yorker* and I'd been in *Time Magazine*, you name it, I had been there. None of this really meant very much to them. I mean, they would still look at the notices. They would say that's fine. But then I was in the *World Journal*, which is the Chinese newspaper. And they ran this piece on the front page of the paper.

(laughs) And it was like a wedding announcement. It was, "Gish Jen, daughter of Norman and Agnes Jen. . . ." And of course, all of their friends called. People called from Canada. And just like that, it was alright.

Moyers: Like a wedding announcement?
Jen: Yes. (laughs)

Moyers: One of the reasons I was eager to talk to you is because in your work, you keep wrestling with this question of what it means to become an American, to be an American. And I'm wondering if you come to any conclusions about what it means to be an American today.

Jen: Well, I don't know if you can actually say that there's one definition. But it is striking to me that Americans ask themselves certain kinds of questions.

And it does seem to me that by the time you ask yourself, "Well, what does it mean to be Iranian American, Chinese American, Jewish American, Irish American," you are American 'cause it's not a question that people ask in other parts of the world.

Moyers: A reviewer said of your work, "If the American immigrant experience is most often construed as a process of merging and gradual assimilation like traffic on the freeway, then Gish Jen's version resembles a busy intersection with everybody laying on the horn." Is that an accurate description?

Jen: Probably. Probably. I've always been interested, in my books, not only just in capturing the Chinese American experience, but the whole American experience. And all the many groups kind of jostling and intermingling and banging against each other and coming together both.

Moyers: Like bumper cars?

Jen: It is like bumper cars. I've always tried to capture that quality, rather than simply write about one group in isolation.

Moyers: What's interesting about your work is it's not just for Chinese Americans. I mean, the rest of us learn something about us in it, about what it means to become an American.

Jen: Yeah, I hope so. I hope so. I am writing very much with this idea that the American experience includes the Chinese American experience. And the Chinese American experience is very much part of that experience. But that it's a larger phenomenon.

Moyers: Do you think that you can write true to one's ethnic past and true to the American experience too? They are the same, aren't they, in effect? They merge at some point?

Jen: I do think so. I don't think that you need to erase all the particulars of the Chinese American experience in order to capture the essential American experience. There's this idea that if you want to make it American, that you have to erase the particularities. But I don't think that's true at all. I think you can write right through them and still come out with something which is recognizably American.

Moyers: Talk to me about what it's like raising two children when their mother is American of Chinese descent and their father is American of Irish descent. What's it like for them? What's it like for you?

Jen: Well, for us it's perfectly normal. It's just our family. Do you know what I mean? It's not like we have another idea of another family that would be more normal. To us, this is normal. And in quite a wonderful way.

It is true that there's been kind of a tendency, I think, from society, to just make us more Asians, or more Asian American than we are Irish American, which has been sort of interesting. But we've tried to resist that, as best we have been able.

And we've tried to make something which is not about just kind of two things coming together. Biracial kids are called half/half, but—

Moyers: Half Chinese, half American?

Jen: Yeah, it always sounds like mismatched socks or something. (laughter) You know what I mean? We try to make something which is not half/half, which is something whole and new and integrated.

Moyers: Tell me about your two children. Now, do they look like their Irish father or their Chinese mother?

Jen (in male voice): Interestingly, they look like each other. They look like both me and my husband. But I don't think they look more like my husband than they look like me, or vice versa. Their facial features are very alike—so alike that if you looked at their black and white baby photos you could not tell them apart. Interestingly though, their hair color is very different. My son has straight black hair and therefore is often kind of typed as Asian American, whereas my daughter has very light brown hair and therefore is often typed as Caucasian.

Moyers: Do you talk to your son about this?

Jen: Yeah, I talked to him a little bit about it. He's not that interested. He's in a school where there are lots of Asian Americans, lots of biracial kids, multiracial kids. To him, it's no big deal one way or the other. He's never experienced a moment of discrimination that he can remember. It's a relatively minor part of his childhood.

What's been very interesting to us is the way my daughter was treated, which is quite differently than the way my son is treated. I mean, there is a sense that maybe she's not quite my daughter.

I noticed this from strangers. I do wonder about the effects of this gaze on her. People will ask me, "Is she yours?" For a while, we had a German au pair, six-foot-two, blond. And everybody assumed that she was the mother and I was the nanny. It's made me think a lot about what we consider natural, how much we depend on things matching in some way, kind of the visual cues are so important to us somehow in our idea of what a natural grouping is. And I do think that as a society, we need to get beyond that.

Moyers: Who do you think we are now? Where do you think we are in this whole question of becoming American? More immigrants have come here in the last ten years than in the last one hundred years. Where do you think we are with inventing this new identity?

Jen: Well, I think sometimes it's going well, and sometimes it's not going so well. Obviously, since 9/11, things have not been going so well.

I think before that, we'd experienced a rate of (unintelligible) change which is really very remarkable. From the time of civil rights until 1990, it was unbelievable, truly. Just as a writer, I know that. Like I say, this is such a small window onto what was happening. But I went from a writer where I was writing stories today would be seen as being between worlds but early on, were seen as totally baffling, as maybe not about anything.

I had this story called "In the American Society" which today every college freshman can tell you, "This is about being between worlds." But when that story first came out, editors wrote to me. It was like, "Well, wonderful writing. But what's it about?" They couldn't see.

'Cause there's a laundry list of things that a story might be about, man and nature, coming of age. If it's not any of them, it must not be about anything.

So we went from this old kind of thinking to this new kind of thinking where, "Oh well of course." You just called this book *Typical American*. It's about Chinese Americans. Can we really do that?

I still remember my agent. "Well, what is this story about? It's about coming to America." Today it's, "Oh, it's an immigrant novel?" Yeah well, in 1990, people were all like, "What are you gonna call this?" I've seen a fantastic amount of change, kind of (unintelligible) change that has very much married the social change. It's been incredibly fast.

First blacks said, "I'm black and I'm proud." Then, "I'm Jewish and I'm proud." Now everybody's proud.

Now we have the opposite problem. There are so many groups on campus, they all have their own dorms. That's its own problem. But that all happened in what, thirty years or something? But I have to say that I think now since 9/11, I do wonder—

Moyers: A lot of people still face terrible discrimination and economic difficulties.
Jen: Yes. I have to say both. But compared to many other societies where they don't ever see that kind of change to begin with, there was something there that was fast and American and full of possibility. But even that kind of leading edge of change—

Moyers: How do you think this will all play out in your children's lives? You've got Irish and Chinese in there.
Jen: I think my children will be fine. I'm hoping. I mean luckily my children are not from the Middle East. [My children] are not gonna be the first target of a lot of the backlash.

But I have to say that as a country, I think that so much of the progress we were able to make was based on a sense that we were secure. We could be open. We're like the Tong Dynasty, we were the top of our gig. We could afford to start to be open. I think now people are worried and afraid. I hear it's already very much more difficult for immigrants to get visas. I don't know what will happen. But I have to say it doesn't feel very hopeful.

Moyers: What are you going to do in China next month?
Jen: Oh, well, it's a personal thing. I am going to China for six months on a Fulbright. I'll be teaching. I am bringing my two children. My husband is gonna come visit. Unfortunately, he can't stay the whole time. But I'm going for many reasons. Partly, of course, I want to bring my children. Partly I want to go while my parents can still go. My father's eighty-four. There won't be too many more trips. And partly, I guess I do realize that I'm at the age where I have to know all the family stories, that I can't rely on my parents to be the repository. I'm not always gonna be able to ask them. So I am going in some ways, to really make that link with China as strong as I can, just so that it's not lost. Like I say, I don't think it defines me. But that's our heritage. I don't want my children not to know where my parents came from. I want them to know.

Moyers: So, it's a roots trip?
Jen: Yeah, it's a roots trip. (laughs) Finally, who can believe it?

Moyers: And yet, all of your experience has been in this country as an American?

Jen: I've been to China a couple times to visit. I mean, I was there to teach in '91 and I've always been interested, but I've been more interested in sort of the journey from the old world to the new world than I have in just the old world per se.

I've always been interested in the becoming, in the transition. Well, this is a little bit different. This is all different.

Moyers: Helen Zia says in her book and told me when I interviewed her, "The issue for us isn't any more becoming an American. We've shown that we are American in every way of our—we like hot dogs. We like baseball. We like fast cars. The issue still for us is being accepted as an American." Do you agree with that?

Jen: I think there were times when it's still an issue. I think two things. One thing as what I have come to realize is that this business of not being accepted as an American does not only affect Asian Americans. It affects so many people. You sort of wonder who really feels unequivocally American, honestly. It seems that many, many people are subject to this feeling of slight estrangement. That's the first thing.

And the second thing I would say is that in my experience, if you claim America, no one will dispute your claim. No one's gonna hand it to you but if you say, "Well, this is mine," no one is gonna stop you, either. And that's been very empowering for me.

Moyers: Thank you very much.

Jen: You're very welcome.

A Conversation with Gish Jen about *The Love Wife*

BookBrowse / 2004

From *BookBrowse*, www.bookbrowse.com, 2004. Reprinted by permission of Gish Jen.

Interviewer: *The Love Wife* is your third novel. How might this book surprise readers of your previous novels, *Typical American* and *Mona in the Promised Land*? What surprised you?

Gish Jen: *The Love Wife* is not about the Chang family, for one thing. Also this book is, I hate to say more middle-aged, but that's probably the truth. I've lived through more, and it shows.

At the same time, what really surprised me about *The Love Wife* was, paradoxically, how young I felt writing it. In my nonwriting life, I felt tired and stressed and a shadow of my younger self in almost every respect. In my writing life, though, all of that seemed to fall away: This novel wrote itself and wrote itself as if it did not realize its author got no sleep and no exercise and could barely remember what year it was. I could not have been more amazed and grateful.

Interviewer: The novel is told in the different voices of the Wong family. Why did you decide to write the novel in this form?

GJ: The novel came to me this way—as if told by the various Wongs at a very long family therapy session, only without the therapist, and with license, it seems, to soliloquize. I don't exactly know why this happened. In life I rarely witness stories unfolding in the way they conventionally do in fiction. I mostly hear what's happened to so-and-so over coffee, or on a walk. A recounted story has perhaps come to seem more "real" to me than a recreated story, rich with dynamics I recognize, and full of the information I would seek from a friend.

Other times I think that something about the complexities of our time makes me want to hear every voice I can hear. Having grown up with immigrant parents, I have always heard many voices, and understood many points of view—so many that for most of my writing career I have been concerned with trying to make out what in that chorus might be my own voice. More recently, though, I've finally become confident that my voice will never leave me, and I seem to want to absent myself, that I might inhabit others. In truth, I am not wholly absent from this book, and back when I was "finding my voice," I never lost sight of other points of view. But I strike a different balance in *The Love Wife* than I did in my earlier works.

Interviewer: Was there a particular image or idea that inspired you as you began writing this novel?

GJ: I have two biracial children, the older of whom has straight black hair like mine, and is usually "read" as Asian American, the younger of whom has fine light hair, and is usually "read" as Caucasian. From the time she was born, people have looked at my daughter and asked if she was mine, which has been, for me, both a pain and a gift. Philip Roth has written about writers needing "amiable irritants" to fuel them; I have had no shortage in this regard, and at the time I began this book, my supply was particularly abundant. This was thanks to the beautiful, blond, six-foot-two-inch basketball-playing German au pair we had then—not that she was herself in any way distressing (aside from being a dead ringer for Julia Roberts, that is). However, she was—to our mutual dismay—often taken for my daughter's mother, and I, sometimes, for my daughter's nanny. This was food for thought.

In my novel, of course, the racial breakdown of the family is completely different. And the Wong family is not my family. But the questions raised by my real life experience—questions about what a "real" family is, about what's "natural," and about what choice we have in these matters—do inform the book.

Interviewer: Carnegie Wong (Chinese American) and Janie "Blondie" Wong (WASP American) adopt their first daughter when she is abandoned at a local church. Nearly seven years later, they adopt a second daughter, from China. And eventually they are surprised with the birth of their biological son. A neighbor of the Wongs calls them "the new American family." Do you agree with this assessment, and how did that affect your writing?

GJ: I thought of Tiger Woods a lot as I wrote *The Love Wife*; he seemed a cousin of the Wongs, and like them, the tip of a very large iceberg. For we are seeing more and more families that fall outside of the Dick and Jane mold these days—mixed-race families, blended families, adopted families, and so on—as is very much in keeping with the idea of America. How very natural it is, after all, that an invented nation based on shared ideals rather than on blood and inheritance should be full of families brought together on a similar principle—by choice rather than by circumstance and biology. And yet, for all of its naturalness, how challenging this new phase of the American experiment, too.

Interviewer: When Lan arrives from China to help the Wongs with child care, alliances begin to form within the family. (Who is most like whom? Who belongs to whom?) Do you think this is a typical response to a new nanny? Is it a matter of "culture clash"? Do you think it might have more to do with the ages of the Wong daughters (preteen and teen)?

GJ: I think that, just as toddlers of a certain age simply must climb every stairway possible, preteens and teens are driven to seek out whatever it is they need developmentally. If a nanny is of use to their project, she will be enlisted. And of course, different nannies will respond differently to this. Lan, far from home, uncertain of her relationship to the family and to America, needs the children and their love; family is important to her. At the same time, what she means by "family" is not always what the Wongs mean; so yes, there is culture clash.

Interviewer: Can you tell us about your choice to have Mama Wong suffer from Alzheimer's? The condition seems to precipitate a change of identity, or at least a shift in family roles.

GJ: I am, like many people, horrified by the cruelty of Alzheimer's, of which my mother-in-law died some years ago. I wrote about it partly because I needed to write about it and partly because it brings to the surface a great fear shared by Carnegie and Blondie—a fear, not so much of loss of life, as loss of identity. Carnegie, for example, has spent most of his life rebelling against Mama Wong and her Chinese ideas. But the more she forgets, the more he strives, belatedly, to remember, record, recover, revive. The irony and vanity of this is not lost on him, and yet he cannot help himself. The anxiety precipitated by Mama Wong's Alzheimer's becomes a preoccupation with ethnic identity, and this, in turn, has repercussions in the novel as in the world today.

Interviewer: Though the Wongs are grappling, like any family, with serious matters, their lives are full of comedy. (For instance, they have a goat—a goat!—in their suburban backyard.) How do you manage, as a writer, to make your characters' lives so funny even as awful things happen to them?
GJ: I do not manage to make them funny—they simply turn funny, usually at the most inappropriate times.

Gish Jen Talks about How She Became a Writer

Rob Neufeld / 2007

From *Ashville Citizen-Times*, March 25, 2007. Reprinted by permission of Robert Neufeld.

Q: When you started writing *Mona in the Promised Land*, were you thinking that you were going to write a comedy of errors right from the start?

A: That book came out of a story. I was three-quarters of the way through *Typical American*. I took a little break and I wrote this story, and then I put it aside. The story came so easily, and sometimes when things come so very, very easily that way, it's a sign of some sort. I did think when I wrote it, "Ah! There's my next book." I did realize it as a book, but I wrote it as a story. When I wrote the story, the whole business about Mona's conversion to Judaism was not in it. Mona was a girl having adventures in her new town. The interest in and invention of ethnicity were not there yet.

Q: Is comedy a kind of a muse for you? Do you feel your way toward situations where there will be a lot of comedy?

A: You know, not necessarily. I see comedy as something that I do so easily, that I often try to pull back from it. I finished *Mona*, for instance, and I thought, this book is too funny. I'm often working to get the deeper register. In edits, I'll often rein back the broader humor. I guess that's to say that I'm not looking for humor. Humor's just there.

Q: Do you have certain hopes for bridging cultural chasms?

A: Finally, I guess I do. I would not say I wrote for that purpose—but certainly the thought that my work would make people think, and that that might help them understand cultural difference—these are things that I would love to see.

Q: When did you know you were a writer? I imagine most writers write because they can't do anything else.

A: Actually, that's very true. People come to me and ask me should they become a writer. And I ask them if they feel that they could do something else. Because if you feel that you could do something else, you're just not going to have the stick-to-it-ness that you're going to need to be a writer. I had this moment of revelation when I was in my late twenties. This is a little morbid. The daughter of immigrants, I had never been to a funeral. I went to my first funeral and I thought, "Oh my God, we're all going to die." I had this vision of myself on my deathbed, and I realized if I had never tried to become a writer, I'd be lying there thinking, "Why didn't I try to become a writer?" I think sometimes it's that knowledge that keeps me going. There are other things that theoretically I could do, but I don't think that I could have lived with myself if I had done them instead.

Q: How did you recognize—aside from the urge—that you had the skills?

A: I really didn't. I think, in retrospect, I had a lot of encouragement. There were signs, I guess, but I was somehow oblivious to them. When I finally let on, it was more because I felt that I had to do it than that I had any idea that I might succeed at it. I'm still just stunned, I have to say. *Typical American* is about to be featured in this PBS series on the American novel. It's funny because suddenly everyone is talking about that book, my first novel. I remember sitting down to write the first line of that book, and I can't even tell you how unlikely it seemed to me that anyone would ever publish that book, much less that it would go on the way it has. [When] I wrote that book, I had just gotten to the Bunting Institute, which is now the Radcliffe Institute at Harvard. It was my fifth day there. The first day, we'd gone around a circle, and people had asked what we were, and I said I was a would-be writer. It never occurred to me to try to write a novel. And then day five, being at this amazing place full of ambitious women, I said, "Oh, maybe I'll write a novel." I sat down and wrote *Typical American*.

Q: In *The Love Wife* and in short stories, you leave the Chang family. But the Chang family and all the people associated with it are so fully developed, how do you free yourself from the Chang family? Will they continue to come back?

A: You know, everyone was looking for that third Chang family book. I don't know why (laughs). I'm just in the throes of finishing up a new book, and it's not the Chang family and it's not the Wong family either!

Q: Do you have a particular attraction to Judaism?

A: Growing up in the New York area, it's not even an attraction. You grow up in the New York area as I did, you're going to have a lot of Jewish friends. There are parts of Judaism that I have to say became mine. I'm not Jewish. In fact, I grew up Catholic. I think especially of the (Jewish) interest in society. The people around me, growing up in Scarsdale, were very socially engaged. I really respect that. Also, a tolerance for other faiths. It always impressed me that B'nai B'rith so went out of their way to support not only Jews, but other religious groups. That kind of thing—I think that all those values that I hold today—toleration, social activism—came to me via Judaism, and that way I will always have a special place in my heart for Judaism.

Q: Are you ever going to write more about the Cultural Revolution?

A: It's there in the background. But I'm primarily interested in America. I did not live through the Cultural Revolution. There are so many people who did, and I'm not sure that I am the right filter for that experience. My preoccupation is really with identity, globalization, diaspora things, things that maybe I know better.

Q: You said you had various people who encouraged you in your writing. Who was your first encourager?

A: The great encourager of my life was Robert Fitzgerald at Harvard.

Q: The translator.

A: The translator—and a very erudite and wonderful man. I took his class in prosody when I was a junior because I was an English major, and I didn't understand why poetry had to be written in those little lines. I thought when he said in his class there'd be a weekly exercise, I thought he meant a paper, and it turns out he meant a weekly exercise in verse. I said, "Oh my gosh. I don't think I can do that," but I thought, first week, if I don't like it, I can always drop, let me just try. And I wrote that first poem, and I loved it. I loved writing right away. And I loved his class. I don't think I ever imagined that it was something I should do with myself. Because Robert Fitzgerald took me aside—I had written a paper on prose rhythms in Henry James, and he was going over my paper with me, and he was nodding, nodding, nodding. He was the first person to sort of say, "Now, why are you premed?"—a question not very easily answered because I had just gotten a C in chemistry. He's the first to say, "Have you thought about being a poet?" I said, "No, I have not thought about being a poet!" He said to me that he really thought

I should do something with words. He was very adamant about that. When I said I didn't think I could be a poet, he did give me a job in publishing as my first job out of college.

Q: He did?

A: Yeah, he called up the managing editor of the house that he was at then, which was Doubleday, and he said, "I have this student." Sometimes when I think of him, I'm overwhelmed with gratitude because I do feel that I have owed my whole writing life to him, and the interest that he took in me and my future.

Q: So where is the poetry of Gish Jen?

A: It's funny, but I think from the very beginning I was very narrative. I still love to read poetry, but I think my drive is narrative, even toward the novel more than the short story.

Q: There are a lot of different rhythms as you go through the book. For instance, in *Mona*, when it opens up into that 1970s scene in the Gugelstein house. Wow! What a window! Toward the end, when the novel is headed toward marriages, and people were going in and out like Marx Brothers characters, I thought, this is fun! But also there are a lot of different rhythms, partly because of the narrator's voice, and partly because of the characters and their manners of speech. Are you a student of manners of speech?

A: I'm not a student of them, but I notice and I hear. I guess that's what Fitzgerald was trying to tell me, that I had an ear, and, for whatever reason, I notice that I have a lot of these voices in me when I start to write them on the page, they just came out. I can't say how I picked them up, but clearly I did. You can hear a lot of Jewish New York voice in *Mona*, for instance. I was not aware of picking that up, but there it all is.

Q: I think that's an important ability for a writer. I'm not sure they teach that in writing classes as they teach it in acting classes. What do you think about that?

A: It's interesting. You're right. I don't know that they teach it in writing classes. But it's true that the teachers have an ear and encourage students to listen as well as to write. The funny thing about writing is that people imagine it's a very productive activity, that you're making, but I think the actual experience of it is a lot like listening. You feel that you are simply hearing and recording, and it doesn't feel that you are writing. You feel that you are receiving. I think that many writers would describe the process that way, and that in teaching writing, we would emphasize the listening aspect of it.

Q: You teach writing, right?
A: I've actually taught very little, although I've just taken a new job at Brandeis, I'm happy to say. I don't start until 2008, and I'm looking forward to it.

Q: And what is your job there?
A: I'll be professor of English, teaching writing.

Q: Great. Congratulations! Do you have an example of a writing assignment that you would give?
A: I don't have an example. I've been pretty spoiled. The teaching that I've done has been with teachers, and quite advanced, and I didn't need assignments.

Q: Okay, let's get to a few fun things now. I have some quick questions. This is the lightning round. Are you ready?
A: Okay.

Q: Do you have a family heirloom in your possession?
A: Because my family were immigrants, I don't have a lot, but I do have one piece of a tile, which came from my family's summer garden in China. In this garden, they actually had a glass-bottomed pavilion where they could look through the bottom at the fish. That pavilion is long gone. Some of the tiles from that pavilion, the shards were still on the ground. I have a shard.

Q: How did you get that?
A: I was in the garden with a cousin, and we saw the shards, and I just picked one up.

Q: Do you have a favorite comedian?
A: I do not have a favorite comedian. There are certainly many favorite comedians. I thought Richard Pryor was brilliant. I think that Steve Martin is brilliant. It's not like I follow comedy.

Q: Do you have a favorite philosopher?
A: I do not have a favorite philosopher. I mull over a lot of things that people have said.

Q: What kind of a quote, talisman, or decoration do you have at your work desk?
A: I've had different things at different times. One quote that I've had for quite a while now—you know Sister Wendy Beckett, she said, "Use everything."

Q: What is one of the funniest or oddest reviews that you have received? Do you read reviews of your work?
A: You can say I look at them. To be honest, I don't really read them exactly.

Q: Because sometimes they get them totally wrong, and sometimes they have an insight that you didn't think of.
A: Yeah, I remember reading a review in which someone said, "There's nothing here that Margaret Cho hasn't done better"—Margaret Cho being much funnier than me. I'm trying to trim my humor down. I don't see myself as being like her. Yeah, that was kind of weird. The reviews come in in big stacks, and very typically, I thumb through. It's kind of like writing class. I see that the same criticism had come through eight times; I would definitely pay a little attention and understand where people are coming from.

Q: Is there a Chinese word for which there is not a very good translation into English?
A: Oh my God, there are many Chinese words. The word that leaps to mind is *guanxi* (gwan-shee). Everybody says it's "connection," but it's a much bigger word than that, and it's so fundamental to the Chinese mindset. You can translate it as "relationship." "Connections" is not a very good word, I think. *Guanxi* is a much warmer word. Relationship is too analytical. And I don't think any of the words that we have get at how fundamental it is to your way of being in China. It's so much more of a basic psychic thing than relationship.

Q: Let's go the other way. Is there an English or American word that doesn't translate very well into Chinese?
A: I'm sure that there are a lot. (laughs) Individualism. It means a very different thing over there.

Q: A major theme in your work is about one finding one's identity, and what identity is even based on, and if one has to make a new identity, how one even looks for that, how one even has a sense of that. Do you have a response to that?

A: I'm not sure that I can answer a question such as "How does one make one's identity?"

Q: Is it even important to be considering that, or just be it?
A: I think probably it's some combination of those two things. I think that it's helpful sometimes for people to realize how many messages they have from their culture about their identity. It may help them negotiate this problem, which we all have, we want to know who we are. It's maybe helpful to realize that there are a lot of Old World voices that say, you are who you were born, or you are your station, or you are your blood, or you are your parents. Then it's helpful to realize the idea that you have some inner essence, that it's your job on Earth to discover and to realize that that's a very New World idea. I don't think that I can solve the problem for anybody, but I think it's helpful for people to have some perspective on the process itself, and the conflicting voices that they have about it. A book like *Mona* I think provides some perspective, particularly on ethnic identity and how "natural" it is. We live in a time when not to have an ethnic identity is not to be person, and there are many ideas in the world about what that means, ideas that we can consume critically or uncritically. As a writer, I would (assume) that we consume them critically.

Q: There are some strikingly weird sections of *Mona*. There are the ways in which some of the characters try on different identities. It happens a few times, and it's disturbing: Seth in his sexual play when he acts out the thug; of course, the whole thing with Sherman; and then, not as disturbing, but still striking because it's the third instance of it, when Mona plays her sister.
A: Right. Well, they're young. I do think people do try on identities. I think that they find that they stick or they don't stick. The things that they are moved to try on probably say a lot about them. You may gather from that book that I see identity as a very fluid thing, something that is very much invented. Parts of it that we think are natural are often invented or adopted. I think there's a lot of performance involved.

A Conversation with Gish Jen

Suzanne Koven / 2013

From *The Rumpus*, April 17, 2013. Reprinted by permission of *The Rumpus* and
Suzanne Koven.

This new column, "The Big Idea," features interviews with people whose
lights stay on—writers, artists, scientists, activists, and others who take a
long and broad view of an issue, problem, or concept, and pursue it over
many years. The series begins with the third installment (numbers one and
two are the *Rumpus* interviews with Neal Barnard and Andrew Solomon): a
conversation with Gish Jen. Jen has been thinking for nearly her whole life
about the cultural and aesthetic differences between China, from which her
parents emigrated, and America, in which she was born and raised. She's
written a book about these differences, and I recently sat down with her to
talk about it.

It's not so easy to get Gish Jen to talk about herself. I spent a good half
hour in the kitchen of the Cambridge, Massachusetts, home Jen shares with
her husband, David O'Connor, and their two children, drinking coffee and
answering her questions about my work and my family, before I finally managed to steer the conversation to Jen's new book: *Tiger Writing: Art, Culture,
and the Interdependent Self.* I should not have been surprised.

Tiger Writing, Jen's first nonfiction book—she's the author of four novels:
Typical American, Mona in the Promised Land, The Love Wife, and *World
and Town,* plus a short story collection, *Who's Irish?*—is a meditation on
Jen's deep ambivalence about the self. On the one hand, she was raised by
parents who emigrated to the US from China as adults, and who brought
with them a culture which valued community over the individual. On the
other hand, Jen—now fifty-seven—found in Western literature, and especially in the reading and then writing of novels, great joy in the individual
story, the singular voice.

Jen has spent many years trying to reconcile, or at least articulate, this duality—and in 2012 she got the chance to do so. Harvard University invited her to give three autobiographical lectures, which formed the basis for *Tiger Writing*. In these lectures, Jen explored her "independent" and "interdependent" selves—terms she borrows from cross-cultural psychology. She explains: "The first—the 'independent,' individualistic self [more prevalent in the US and Western Europe]—stresses uniqueness . . . and tends to see things in isolation. The second—the 'interdependent,' collectivist self [more prevalent in Asia]—stresses commonality . . . and tends to see things in context." Though she is very aware of the danger of perpetuating stereotypes, particularly of the self-effacing "robotic" or "sheep-like" Asian, Jen still finds value in thinking about these two categories as lenses through which differences in family relationships, culture, art, and literature can be better understood. *Tiger Writing* is, as Jen calls it, a "magpie," jumping from memoir to Chinese landscape painting, to experimental psychology, to the modern novel. It's also peppered—as are Jen's novels and her conversational speech—with Yiddish.

There was so much I wanted to ask Gish Jen about her life and writing, her thoughts about "tiger mothers," and contemporary fiction—if only I could get her interdependent self to stop being so interested in what I had to say.

The Rumpus: Enough about me. I want you to talk about your book!
Gish Jen: But the truth of the matter is, I like to listen. I'm much more interested in listening than in speaking, for sure. So please don't feel like you're going on. I could sit here all morning hearing about your parents. I probably should have been a therapist. No, I don't want to be a therapist. But the empathic piece is definitely an important part of fiction. It's human to hear stories and to know how people live and to imagine how that is for them. It's very interdependent! I naturally hear what you have to say and focus on that, and I'm not thinking "Oh my God, when is she going to listen to *me*?" I'm not thinking that at all. I'm totally interested in what you're saying.

Rumpus: Your parents constantly reminded you, when you were a child, about "consideration for others," not yourself. Yet the impulse to write narrative, an individual personal narrative, even if it's not about you, seems to be, as you're framing it, kind of "independent"—self-focused.
Jen: Yeah. I mean, obviously I have both sides. I've described myself as shuttling back and forth, but it's not really shuttling. It's more like a very wide-angle lens.

Rumpus: Or two sides of one coin?

Jen: They're not even that separated. It's more like a dual processing. I'm a little bit concerned that talking so much about interdependence makes it sound like there's no "I" at all in interdependence. I am clearly very hybrid, which is not the same thing as having two sides. It's about being a third thing, which is a hybrid. But there's a way in which I understand being interdependent, which I wouldn't if I didn't grow up the way I did. At the same time, I certainly understand what it is to be independent, too.

Rumpus: Is it analogous at all to being biracial?

Jen: That's another term where it makes you sound like you're split down the middle, like one side has a blue eye and one side has a brown eye . . .

Rumpus: But you're really a "third thing"?

Jen: Yes, you're a third thing. I mean, we all are "third things." I guess in this book, it comes up as more of a duality because I'm trying to introduce an idea with which many people are unfamiliar. The reality is much more gray. I'm trying to give people an idea of what black looks like and what white looks like before I introduce them to gray.

Rumpus: I want to ask you about what you write your husband calls the "CYA" ("cover your ass") portions of the book, where you acknowledge that you risk perpetuating stereotypes, but that these stereotypes may contain a truth worth exploring.

Jen: The word "truth" makes me a little bit uncomfortable. I think, a "basis." One of the reasons I tried to be so careful in this book is that when people are looking at something they don't understand they quickly label it as something that's from their own framework. And in the case of interdependence, the label is "sheep" or "robot." You hear that all the time [about Asians]: "They're sheep. They're robots. They're not human." And I think that's where you have to be careful not to say, "Well, it's true . . ." That's the stereotype. You're looking at something, you see the phenomenon, but you make it into something that isn't really about the phenomenon at all. It's really all about you.

Rumpus: So it's a phenomenon worth exploring, even if it's not an absolute duality, or even if the things that have been said about it thus far aren't accurate?

Jen: Yes. I think something that's hard for the particularly independent to understand, even though it's all around them. I talk over my novels with my hairdresser, who is Brazilian American. She's interested. She asks "What's this one about?" But *this* book! When I told her I was writing about interdependence she just lit up. She's from Brazil, and I could see that it's a reality she lives with every day, but that somehow she feels is unrecognized. Even with people she interacts with regularly, she feels they don't understand this thing about her.

Rumpus: What part of the independent/interdependent spectrum is she on?
Jen: In some ways she's from the independent side. She runs her own business, she's unmarried and has no children. She's certainly not anything like a sheep or a robot. But she has a piece of her—because she grew up in Brazil, she was one of nine children—which is very at odds with the mainstream. Now you can't say this isn't "American" because she's American. And it's not confined to immigrants from Latin American countries. A friend of mine told me she went to a basketball game in the Southwest. And there was a team that was predominantly Native American playing against a team that was predominantly non-Native American. On the non-Native American team, everyone had their own water bottle. And on the Native American team they were sharing a water bottle. You can't say one is less American than the next. But you can say that there is another self which is a different self—primarily a Protestant self, though it's more complicated than that . . . it came to America via Protestantism.

Rumpus: But in the book you talk about "the East and the West" being less accurate than "the East and the Rest"—implying that you wouldn't place Brazilians and Native Americans with Asians.
Jen: Yes, the Brazilians and Native Americans *are* with the Asians. In this book I'm trying to explain interdependence to a largely independent audience, but, in fact, it's a phenomenon with which the rest of the world is quite familiar. Even within Western Europe, Ireland is much more interdependent than England. The English always say the Irish are very "clannish."

Rumpus: Which used to be said of the Jews.
Jen: Right. And countries which are predominantly Catholic are more interdependent, as opposed to countries that are predominantly Protestant. There's a continuum, of course. If you want to know who's at the far end of the continuum, that would be Europeans and Americans, especially

those that come from Anglo-Saxon Protestant backgrounds. You know the Durkheim study? The independents are the ones who tend to commit suicide. I'm not against this way of being in the world. Individuals have brought us many treasures. You can't just say that's a bad way of being in the world—it's not. But it's not everyone's way of being in the world.

Rumpus: You know, in a funny way, we are enacting your book right now. I'm thinking, Yeah, but I want to ask her about herself. And you're contextualizing. So I'm being very independent-minded, and you're being very interdependent-minded. And I can't help thinking about the part of your book where you describe your father's "autobiography" in which he wrote more about his house and his community than about himself. But I'm going to pin you down and ask you about your early life. Your parents were from Shanghai . . .
Jen: My mother was from Shanghai and my father was from a town west of Shanghai.

Rumpus: And they came over in the 1940s?
Jen: Yes.

Rumpus: You were born in New York.
Jen: Yes.

Rumpus: For eleven years you lived in Yonkers.
Jen: Something like that.

Rumpus: And then you moved to Scarsdale. You describe yourself at that point as being "narratively naïve." It was your exposure to the well-funded library in this very affluent town that really allowed you to tap into your independent self. And you describe yourself as the black sheep of the family. What I wonder about is: when you were reading all those books in that library—obviously decades before you ever heard the terms "independent" or "interdependent"—did you have the sense that you were changing? Or did you have the sense that there was an aspect of yourself that was finally blooming?
Jen: That's a very good question. And it's the sort of question that one answers in an interview and then one thinks that night, Hmm . . . that wasn't actually the truth. Do you know what I mean? It's a little hard to cough up an answer.

I think that I was somewhat temperamentally different from my siblings. I don't know that I would have identified that as an "independent self." If you look at how my father grew up . . . he remembers his brother breaking a plate, and his mother had the urge to reprimand him for that, but the reaction of his grandmother was, "No, give him a whole set of plates and let him throw them against the wall." Because a Jen boy should not be inhibited. My father had a lot of that in him, the sense that for him—and this is very much a class thing—he should be free, within the confines of that society. And I think that I grew up with some of that. I grew up with a sense that somehow I was sort of on a different program, from very early on. That program was not the "independent self program." I don't know what program it was, exactly.

Rumpus: It sounds like it had something to do with gender. Do you think it wasn't so much that by going to that library you were being independent rather than interdependent, as that you were taking more the prerogatives of a male than of a female?

Jen: It's so interesting that you say that, because I think another part of what happened was that our family—the family I grew up in—like my father's family in China, and to some degree my mother's family, too, was very, very sexist. So you're right. There was a way in which all the attention was focused on my older brother. The next two were myself and my sister and then two younger boys. There was so much focus on that eldest son. And really, my sister and I were just kind of ignored—which was kind of a gift. In the Chinese system, I think it was really hard for my brother to have that much pressure on him. But there was a way in which, too, I probably felt that I was being neglected—you know what I mean? And that the library was some kind of world which was mine, but which I was somehow denied. And I think that this somehow dovetailed with the reading, and had something to do with why I was in that library. Also, I just loved to read! My parents kept very little in the way of records about us, but I found a bunch of report cards recently and it said in a very early report card: "She loves to write. She's very imaginative." Maybe these two things came together in the reading.

Rumpus: Self-empowerment and independence?

Jen: Yes. Some kind of self-empowerment because there was so much emphasis on my brother's education and not on mine, so there was a way in which I was getting my own education. "I'm going to get my own education since no one is going to take an interest in what I'm doing." But I don't think that I was particularly looking for this independent self. That kind of snuck in the back door. That was kind of a surprise to me. Somehow it worked for someone like me.

Rumpus: Before I get into the narrative and aesthetic aspects of independence/interdependence I want to ask a few questions about parenting.
Jen: You're a psychiatrist, right?

Rumpus: No, an internist. Probably should have been a psychiatrist.
Jen: Yeah.

Rumpus: First off, you married a non-Asian.
Jen: Yes.

Rumpus: And you have a couple of kids.
Jen: Yes.

Rumpus: And they're grown or almost grown?
Jen: One fourteen, and one twenty-one.

Rumpus: You talk a lot in the book about high-elaborative versus low-elaborative parenting—meaning parents who talk a lot to their kids versus parents who don't, the latter being more typically Asian. My husband and I never called it "elaborative parenting" but we always rolled our eyes at parents who talked and negotiated endlessly with their toddlers, like in a crowded bakery—"You want this one? Or are you sure you don't want that one?" I mean, just buy the kid a fucking cupcake! Was there any tension at all in your and your husband's parenting because you were bringing this heritage of low-elaborative parenting to your marriage and family? Did you instinctively feel, at all, like "the high-elaborative thing doesn't work for me, doesn't make sense to me?"
Jen: I would actually say that I am more elaborative than my husband.

Rumpus: Fascinating!
Jen: Well, I did grow up in Scarsdale, you know? I think I took the middle ground. Obviously I spoke much more to my children than I was spoken to, and probably in a very different way. I mean, my daughter will say: "Everything you say is an essay!"

Rumpus: The kid's got a point.
Jen: That's sort of interesting. I don't know if that's a reflection of how I learned to elaborate. I wonder whether it's a reflection of the fact that I learned to elaborate so late, so that I don't elaborate the way a two-year-old elaborates. I elaborate the way a much older person elaborates.

Rumpus: And you're a writer.

Jen: Right. You could also say that I'm a writer and that I will structure.

Rumpus: Okay, so now I have to ask about Amy Chua [author of the controversial *Battle Hymn of the Tiger Mother*]. One thing you write about her is that you were sympathetic to some of what she said but felt she didn't adequately address the sense of vulnerability that is at the root of strict Asian parenting. And I was a little confused about that because, of course, there are other vulnerable and persecuted immigrant populations or are more elaborative. For example, stereotypical Jewish parenting is very elaborative.

Jen: I don't really want to talk about her.

Rumpus: But how about that style of parenting? Where does it come from?

Jen: I think that—and, again, I hate to generalize—but in the case of China, you had a combination of incredible insecurity and a little ladder that could get you out. So you're right, the Jews were insecure, everyone is insecure. But what the Chinese had was like this big steamship, with a very little ladder leading up from the ocean. And the ladder is very, very narrow. But there is a way up. And you can imagine that there are thousands of people in the ocean and you have this one little ladder, and that ladder is . . . exams. And that's true to this day.

Rumpus: You mean, to get into universities?

Jen: The *gaokao* [college entrance exam] in China is everything. There's a lot of politics around the college entrance exams, who gets to take what exam. The exam is not the same nationwide. It's much more difficult in the provinces than in Shanghai. And one of the sources of great discontent in China is that migrant kids have to take the *gaokao* in their home town. So if they're growing up in Shanghai, they're not going to the same schools in any case, but they're also not being schooled for the *gaokao* in their home town. And the result is, basically, that the parents are taking incredible risks by staying in the city and having their kids educated in "the wrong way." And, of course, that's meant to discourage them from staying in the city. It's just one more way they make it very unpleasant for these migrant workers.

But my point is that the ability to succeed in that exam is the difference in your whole life, if you succeed in that exam, as opposed to if you don't succeed at it. Huge. So you have this system that's been in place—I think it started in the Han Dynasty and didn't get going in full swing until the Song Dynasty—but you're still talking about something that's been there for thousands of years now. And you have a population that has learned that this is what you have to do. I don't know what's on the *gaokao* today, but the nature of the exam for thousands of years was about memorization and the classics. My point is that there was always this little ladder. And there is a way in which the kind of training in Amy Chua's book was actually very well-suited for producing people who would go up that ladder. And I think we still see that culturally today. People aren't any less human; they're just from much more desperate circumstances.

Rumpus: I'm sure you're familiar with the essay by Wesley Yang called "Paper Tigers." It was in *New York Magazine* and then *Best American Essays 2012.* He makes the argument that the same ethic that gets Asian kids into Stuyvesant [a very selective public exam school in NYC, now 72 percent Asian] and Harvard prevents them from attaining a leadership position, like being CEOs, because it doesn't encourage initiative and creativity. Did that seem to you too facile?

Jen: Yeah. I mean, look at me: I didn't climb the ladder, and I didn't want to be in the corner office. Now we really are getting into stereotyping.

In my book I cite another study that is in "Inheriting the City" where the writer is looking at the population of Asian Americans in New York City and finds that they are the most creative group, bar none, in America. If we were talking about people in Shanghai, I would say that there is a lot in that system that stifles creativity. And you can see in some of the ideas that someone like Amy Chua may import to the United States vestiges of those ideas. But the truth of the matter is that once they get to New York, that model no longer applies. For students who are in the most creative group in America to somehow be presumed to be narrow is just completely *meshugga*.

Rumpus: So you think he narrows the argument to make it sexy, but that it's really too narrow?

Jen: I think it's too narrow. Anyone who is on the old Chinese program is not going to get into Harvard. Harvard's not an exam school. I don't know what the average kid at Stuyvesant High School is like, but this idea that the Asian Americans—and remember: you have to distinguish between them and their counterparts in China—the whole idea that they're like that right through high school and then they all get into Harvard, is really erroneous. Berkeley is now something like 50 percent Asian American and this has not skewed the culture at Berkeley toward math and science. You would think:

Okay, these kids all go to Stuyvesant and you didn't let them into Harvard but they went to Berkeley and what do you get? You get a campus full of robots who are only interested in doing engineering. But that's not what they get. No. They get a campus that looks a lot like a liberal arts campus on the East Coast, only everybody is not white.

Rumpus: Right. In medical schools and residencies now you have, if not a majority, a very large number of Asians and South Asians—and they're not robotic young doctors.
Jen: Totally! It's really very annoying, right? I'm sure every single one of them feels the way I feel. I will confess that I have very high-achieving children. If you ask them what we did in our household, I think they would say that the only thing they ever hear their mother say is: "Have fun!" I really mean it. All I ever say is: "Have fun!" Everybody assumes that my daughter has a "tiger mother" at home. It's very unfair! She feels it and I feel it. The most Asian American thing about her is that she feels this stereotyping. People go on because she's good at math—it's not from my side. It's from her Irish American father! It's not me! Are you kidding?!

Rumpus: Really? I had you pegged for a math genius . . . Okay, I want to go on to art and literature. You write that it's hard to translate Proust into classical Chinese.
Jen: Yes.

Rumpus: Is it hard to translate Proust?
Jen: Into vernacular Chinese? I don't know the answer to that. Actually they have translated Proust and it has done extremely well in China. I think it was a bestseller. I think this was just within the last half year.

Rumpus: And your books have been translated . . .
Jen: Some of them. Not *Mona* [*in the Promised Land*]. That's very difficult and it has not been translated.

Rumpus: Is it difficult because of the American vernacular? My sense of why you raise the point about Proust being difficult to translate into Chinese in *Tiger Writing* is that there is something about the interiority of that particular narrative that's hard to capture in Chinese. Now we're getting into the idea of the narrative structure of the Western novel versus the interdependent self. Again, making dualities where perhaps there shouldn't be dualities. I want to understand one of the essential arguments of your book, which has to do with Eastern versus Western narrative structure.

Jen: When you ask me whether there is something about contemporary Chinese language, the answer is: I would really have to think about that. My gut says probably not. There clearly is something about classical Chinese.

Rumpus: So it's not the language? It's something else?

Jen: In some ways, as you can see with Mo Yan [2012 Nobel Laureate] and others, the fundamental difference has to do with how much space you think should be taken up with "I." And that can be important in myriad ways. I would have to think about the language piece. Chinese language tends to be quick, economical. To know what people are saying, you always need to know what the context is. The verb tenses are not marked. The way you know past tense or present tense is by context. So there is a way in which it assumes that you understand what the context is. That's true. But I wouldn't want to make too much of that.

I think more important are the millions of everyday realities that give you an idea about where you stand, how much power you have relative to the society around you, how much room you can take up. And of course there are millions of things in China that tell you you cannot take up that much room, starting with the fact that you have a very small place in which to live. If you've ever gone to a student dorm in China, it's not unusual to see six people sharing a small room. There's only so much "self" that you can have. And you see it even in people who are in the West [but grew up in interdependent cultures]. I am very struck that Salman Rushdie's memoir, *Joseph Anton*, about his years under the *fatwa*—he had a lot of trouble writing that in the first person. He tried it. He hated it. He just couldn't keep going.

Rumpus: Because of his sense of personal vulnerability? Because he had been in danger?

Jen: No. I think he was just uncomfortable.

Rumpus: He's not an "I" guy?

Jen: Yes. He had to go to the third person. To me that makes perfect sense, that somehow he was very uncomfortable with "I . . . I . . . I . . . I . . . ," not being brought up to be public in that way.

Rumpus: You say in *Tiger Writing* that one of the reasons the book became, as you call it, "a magpie" is, if I am understanding this right, is you were asked to give an autobiographical lecture.

Jen: An intellectual autobiography. That was suggested to me, and I took that seriously because the truth of the matter is that in any given field, the expert in that field is at Harvard and they don't need to hear my opinions about social psychology, etc. It's not really what I'm there for.

Rumpus: Yet the book is heavily contextualized, and I daresay there's less "I" in there than there might have been if somebody else had been asked to be "autobiographical."
Jen: That's absolutely right. I give a lot of context. From reading it, you probably become aware that without the context I couldn't tell my story. There's so much about my story which is not about me, which can only be understood if you understand the context.

Rumpus: I want to dig into this idea about Eastern and Western sensibilities in art and narrative. You mention the Japanese essayist Shonagon and you also mention several times Chinese landscape paintings.
Jen: Yes.

Rumpus: Correct me if I'm misinterpreting, but I almost felt, at times, that you were somehow saying that these were exceptions that prove the rule—that the interdependent mindset is not the most compatible with making art. Am I wrong?
Jen: What I am trying to say is that there's nothing about interdependence that would keep somebody from making art. In other words, if you look at that Fan Kuan painting [*Travelers Among Mountains and Streams*], and you look at how big that mountain is and how small the people are, obviously this is not the product of a Western mindset, where you get the portrait of the person with the little landscape in the background.

Rumpus: Like the *Mona Lisa*.
Jen: Yes. It's a very different orientation. And yet that Fan Kuan painting and many, many others . . . it's not just that painting . . . I mean I think these things are indisputably great, and indisputably art. But they're not art as we understand it. It's certainly not art as we are defining it in the West right now. What I really think is that the way we are looking at art in some circles is too narrow. If you use that interdependent lens, suddenly all these things that are "not real art" are real art. There's nothing wrong with the art. The problem is with the lens.

Rumpus: In your novels, the relationship of interdependence and independence is so entangled. On the one hand, novel-writing itself has such an independent thrust to it; on the other hand, you mention that your novels are often very landscape-oriented, and they usually have Chinese and Chinese American subjects. You mention the irony that you use this independent art form to engage your interdependent self. Do you feel that your kind of novel writing is not as appreciated as it should be within the current literary climate? Or not as understood as it might be in the current literary climate?

Jen: I think that there is a bias in the current literary climate, which is not only very Western but very male. Are we headed down some wrong road in the way we're reading the novel now? Are we somehow using a lens where women lose their definition? You have to ask yourself about the lens!

Many of our greatest works don't shine, do not come into focus with this lens we're currently using. An example is *War and Peace.* I was just looking at the review of the translation by Richard Pevear and Larissa Volokhonsky that James Wood did in the *New Yorker.* He picked out this unconventional thing that Tolstoy did and that unconventional thing that Tolstoy did . . . all these things that were really quite striking to him. And every single one of them was a sign of interdependence. It's so interesting. No one disagrees that this is a great work. But if you look at the book with a lens that's a little broader, none of those things are striking at all. They're only striking if you come at it with this very particular lens. So my question is, when we start using a lens that says all these books by Asians have "odd features" and all these books by women have "odd features" . . .

Rumpus: They don't need to be "exceptions" if you broaden the lens.

Jen: You got it. It's not only about contemporary fiction by women. It's also about *War and Peace.* It's about *Middlemarch.* Maybe it's time to take a step back and think again a little bit.

When I hear all the arguments about women's fiction, about what the "problem" is . . . and I hear that it's because it's so "domestic" . . . It's a lot more than that they're so domestic. Although that's related to it because, if you remember the whole thing about the interdependent way of narration, it very much foregrounds the everyday. Everydayness is very important. *War and Peace* ends on a very domestic note, which many would feel to be very anticlimactic. "Why did he end *there*?" people say. "That's not the best part of the book. I wouldn't go so far as to say it's a weakness, because it's

Tolstoy, but it's not the best part of the book." I think that what they're really saying is that here is a person who's blended independence and interdependence in a wonderful way. I think many people get to that end and they think, "Well, okay, that's the 'Peace.'" Something is awry.

Rumpus: You write about having come of age artistically and personally after the civil rights movement and before the diversity movement. You talk about growing up in that "narrative hole." I wonder if you look at younger writers writing between cultures, people like Junot Díaz and Edwidge Danticat and Aleksandar Hemon . . .
Jen: Or Jhumpa Lahiri.

Rumpus: . . . Yes, writers who are coming from more interdependent cultures—obviously everybody's fiction is different, but do you see a new generation coming up now that's incorporating more interdependence in their fiction? Is that part of what we call "the immigrant experience in fiction"— or not so much?
Jen: I hesitate to say something where I didn't look at that particularly, but I will say that it is noticeable to me that so many of the figures we think of as distinguishing themselves today are distinguishing themselves in the short story.

Rumpus: Do you think short stories are more interdependent than novels? Or more interdependent-ish?
Jen: I don't know about "interdependent-ish." I'm thinking even of people who have distinguished themselves with novels, but still gravitate to the short story. For whatever reason they shy away a little bit from the novel. Maybe it's because they're aware that there's this yardstick and they're aware that it doesn't come naturally to them, it's not like an open door to them, it doesn't feel like an open door.

Rumpus: You're talking about the classic, independent, Western novel?
Jen: All that self in it—Oh my God! If you think about figures like Grace Paley—a wonderful, wonderful, wonderful voice—who always felt that she couldn't write a novel. What is that about? Why did she feel that it was so alien to her? Is there something the matter with the way we define the novel that she should feel it was so alien to her?

Rumpus: And Alice Munro?
Jen: And Alice Munro. And Maxine Hong Kingston. She gave me that beautiful blurb [for *Tiger Writing*]: "Oh, and the wonderful faith—that the

novel can be learned!" But there's this feeling that somehow the novel is another land, and not a land for her.

Rumpus: And yet it has been a "land" for you.
Jen: It has, yes. I have a very independent side as well. I don't think anyone has ever said, about one of my books, "Oh, that's not a novel." So I guess there's a way in which I'm not arguing exactly on my own behalf.

But I am noticing that so many people feel that there's a barrier there. And I'm wondering, well, what is that about? Why should they feel that way? I do think it is has to do with this idea about where you should be writing from, how big a self you should be projecting onto the page. The bigger the self, the better we like it. The story that gets extolled, always, is of people who define themselves, who aren't defined by society. The novel's always on the side of the individual, the individual, the individual, the individual . . . freedom, freedom, freedom, freedom . . . It's never about maturity, and balance.

Rumpus: I happened to meet a young writer whose first short story collection has been very well-received, and of course everybody assumes that she's going to write a novel now. But she doesn't want to. She wants to write more short stories.
Jen: Good for her!

Rumpus: It's funny that this is somehow considered subversive.
Jen: Not only do some people feel that the novel is a foreign land and that the door to it is not open, but also there is this knee-jerk privileging of the novel. So what is that about? When we say that, aren't we saying that in our culture our yardstick is: "How individualistic is it? And all the people who are not individualistic enough to write a novel, well, they're not artists!" That's sort of what the assumption is. I really wonder about that.

And I especially wonder about it because along with the assumption that there's a hierarchy at the top of which is the novel with all its individualism and all its assertions of freedom—that's the top—and short stories are quite a bit down, right?—don't we also assume that the people who write novels are also somehow more human than the other ones?

I think that Kazuo Ishiguro makes this point in *Never Let Me Go*. I love that book. One of the ways in which the authorities gauge whether the clones are human or not is whether or not they can produce art. I think Kazuo is right on there, in that we associate the ability to make art with being human. And so when we are saying that this group or this gender cannot make real art, I think there is a way in which we are also saying they are less human. And that I really reject. I really, really reject it.

So that's why I'm thinking. Well, it's not just a matter of "When we use this lens, does it mean that you can't get into the *New Yorker*?" You know what I mean? It's a lot more than that. It's not just that when you use this lens you're not going to get X prize. But more importantly, I think that when we use this lens we end up with a view of the world that's pretty problematic.

Rumpus: I hadn't thought about it that way, that somehow the short story is the province of "girls and foreigners" and that the novel is for . . .
Jen: The fact is, we never talk about the Great American Short Story Writer. We never talk about it that way. "Greatness" does not lie in the short story. There's something there which does not comport well with either our own multicultural society or with our new globalizing world. Something is a little off.

Rumpus: Do you think the preeminence of the novel form has not only to do with the "I" factor, the independent factor, but also with an American obsession with size? Is the novel the Big Gulp of literature? Bigger is better? *The Corrections* is bigger and therefore better than *Interpreter of Maladies*?
Jen: Right. I absolutely agree that there's an association with size—up to a point. It's partly about size, but more than size, it's about "I." So the more it is focused on the self, on consciousness, on uniqueness—the "better" it is. I think that's a useful lens, but the other lens is good, too.

Rumpus: In *Tiger Writing* you refer to the Emersonian versus the Confucian world views. Can you define those, regarding literature?
Jen: Don't get me wrong—I'm not in favor of a Confucian novel!

Rumpus: What would that look like?
Jen: That would all be about the order of the universe and how to be moral. That's too extreme, even for me. I don't see how the novel could possibly accommodate that way of thinking and not be awfully dull.

Fundamentally, Confucius was about the proper order of things, proper relationships: "What is the relationship between a man and his wife?" In his way of thinking, one is always above and one is always below. Things are never side-by-side. So the man is above and the woman is below. Now, the man also has an obligation toward the wife. I mean, it's not as if the wife simply serves the husband. There's a lot of emphasis on benevolence, on humanity. So it's not only about servitude. But nonetheless, something is dominant and something is dominated. It's very much about the ordering of society. It's also about how to get along in society.

And Emerson, of course, is about the truth within. And I think there's a way in which that can be taken too far. If you've ever been a teacher, there's always a student who's very aware of the truth within but has a lot of trouble with the truth "without." We all know the student who wants to write and doesn't want to read, who thinks writing is about self-expression, but not about giving form to that self-expression.

Rumpus: Or understanding given forms? Literary traditions and conventions?
Jen: Right. One of the big questions is: "What is your relationship to tradition?" Confucius was the original fundamentalist. He believed in allegiance to the past and being guided by the past—this is obviously not the Emersonian program! These things lie at either end of some continuum. I think we should be in between.

Rumpus: I guess the question in my mind is: have we become too individualistic in our way of thinking about the novel, and also in our habits of being? Is that more problem than gift?
Jen: The degree of individualism that we have in America is actually a distortion of reality. You know the fundamental attribution error test? In the sixties, they developed a test where they had various subjects write an essay pro- or anti-Castro. Because people were randomly assigned their positions, nobody knew who really held what position. And the essays were given to various groups of people to read and then, after reading them, they were told the real situation—which is that people had been randomly assigned. And people from most cultures readily accepted the reality of the situation. They said, "Oh, I see. You wrote you were pro-Castro but you weren't really pro-Castro." But Americans had a lot of trouble accepting that. They could not believe that somebody could write something that they didn't really believe. What the Americans resisted was, objectively, the truth. They resisted that something external to the self could have enough power over the person to make them say something that they didn't mean. They rejected it, yet, objectively it was true.

The tendency in this country is to ascribe much more to the individual than is objectively the case. We saw this in the 2012 presidential election with this whole "I built that" attitude. We have countering things in this country. We have Obama and "we're all in this together"—that's a very interdependent message.

Rumpus: Of course the irony of "I built that" is that it's a received message that's being internalized.
Jen: Absolutely. I think that's one of the things many people would say about this "inner authentic self." There's a jealous guarding of "the sacred spark," but it's based on ads they've been seeing on TV since they were two. It's really unclear whether there's a lot of authenticity in there or not. But that's an idea against which Americans tend to be very defended. We have all these cultural messages everywhere, messages that say "you're special, your specialness is very important, and if you don't feel so special you need to find out what's so special about you."

Rumpus: You need to go into therapy to find your true authentic special self.
Jen: Right, as opposed to finding a way that works better for you, whatever that means—which would be a much more Asian view. I see the novel as maybe not so sacred itself, but actually as being part of this cultural apparatus of reinforcing the self. In that way, I think we all want to feel the novel is a realm of real freedom. But, actually, I think that the novel is a way that the self is reinforced, and if we hold a certain vision of the novel in inflexible ways, we're not supporting freedom at all, but showing slavish devotion to a different god.

Rumpus: *Tiger Writing* is your first nonfiction book after four novels and one short story collection. Was it refreshing to write a nonfiction book? Did it open up different narrative possibilities for you?
Jen: Yes, absolutely! Of course I got dragged into it kicking and screaming. I had to say yes, but after I did I said, "Oh my God, what have I done?" Every novel is an adventure because you don't actually know where you're going—it's a discovery—and I was surprised by the degree to which nonfiction also was a discovery. It was not as different from fiction as I had imagined.

Rumpus: In what sense?
Jen: It was an adventure to find out the many things I knew—that was fun. You've said, "Well, it's not that much about you," and I think that I was horrified about the idea I had to write about myself, but somehow I managed to get out of writing so much about myself. I've said before that I think fiction

is a form of shyness. Maybe that's a way of saying that it's a way of expressing myself the way that a chef expresses him or herself through food.

Rumpus: Even if you're writing about yourself and even if it's nonfiction, there's still the buffer of time, the page. The experience of me reading about you is not the same as the experience of me sitting talking with you. It's a different kind of intimacy.

Jen: It's given form. And I enjoyed giving it form. You can see in my books that I have a lot of formal restlessness, and here you see the restlessness again. I can only wonder what's next. I don't know!

Rumpus: One final question: you mention at the end of your introduction to *Tiger Writing* that you hope the book will be useful—

Jen: A very interdependent statement!

Rumpus: Yes. In what way do you hope it will be useful?

Jen: I do not believe in didactic fiction or didactic nonfiction, either. I just don't. I don't think it's alive. That part of me is very firmly independent.

But I do see writing—my own writing and the writing of others—as culture-making. I have a big interest in seeing the culture open up and lighten up, which goes back to something we were saying earlier: that there's a way in which culture always has a tendency to settle down and become hard, static, and unresponsive to humans—and I have a very big interest in helping it float a little bit. Float and be fluid and responsive to humans.

And so there is a way in which this book, as with my other books, I hope will be useful to people and to the culture. I hope that it will steady the part of the culture that's reflective and thoughtful. And I hope that it will be liberating, finally. I want it to be useful and culture-making, but how so? The answer is, finally, liberating! That's the independent part. So there we go straight from the independent to the interdependent. I don't want to say, "I made it, and that's enough for the world—and they should all be happy, because I made it and I'm an artist and I make art and they should all just be glad!" It's not that.

But, finally that, yeah, it would have an effect on the culture, that the people who are in an independent frame of mind might begin to perceive the rest of the world, have some kind of understanding of the reality that most of the world is living in. Although the world is changing, but, still, to understand what interdependent relationships are, and what that might have to do with you—that would be a wonderful thing.

Also, for the many, many people who, I think, will recognize themselves in this book and will recognize this tension—whether it's my Brazilian hairdresser or some young writer who is confronted with exactly the problem I confronted—it would give me great pleasure to feel that this person picked this book up and said: "Oh, I see. I see what the problem is and it has a name." I would just be thrilled to feel that they could go through their day with a little spring in their step. The highlight so far of the reception of this book was Maxine Hong Kingston's reaction. She wrote to me and she said: "This book is about *me*." I cried. I cried. I cried.

Rumpus: And it's about you.

Jen: And it's about me, too. But I think that she felt some struggle of hers had been described, had been explained. And I was beyond thrilled.

Interview with Gish Jen: Tiger Writer Whose Novels Reflect the Ways in Which We View Ourselves and Our Culture

Jennifer Haupt / 2013

From *Psychology Today*, www.psychologytoday.com, posted December 1, 2013.
Reprinted by permission of Jennifer Haupt.

Author Gish Jen, the daughter of Chinese immigrant parents, has always felt a bit between two worlds. Writing fiction was her way of understanding and bridging the culture gaps she perceived between the East and West. In 2012, Harvard University invited Jen to give the Massey lectures in the History of American Civilization. This series of lectures became the basis for Jen's powerful book, *Tiger Writing: Art, Culture, and the Interdependent Self*. Here's more from the author.

Jennifer Haupt: How do you describe the difference between the independent and interdependent self?

Gish Jen: It's a matter of whether you see the self as fundamentally in relationship to other selves or not—whether you see the boundary between self and the world as relatively permeable, which makes you "interdependent" (collectivist) in outlook, or relatively impermeable, which makes you "independent" (individualistic). Of course, there are shades of gray with this, as with everything. Still, these are two different ways of conceiving the self, with profound aesthetic implications, as I discuss in my book *Tiger Writing*.

JH: When it comes to writing a novel, is there a choice an author can and should make with regard to the voice of the book?

GJ: Many of the ideas we have about fiction in the West today are of quite an independent cast. There is, for example, a kind of novel that focuses on one decision or one moment on which a life hinges. There is a focus on character, and a belief that character is fate. And many novels, too, are quite linear, as if the writer believes that life is like dominos—that one thing leads to another in a cause-and-effect way, and that life is progressive rather than, say, cyclical.

These are ideas that work for many, and that may well reflect your true understanding of life. But you may in fact belong on a different place on the inter-independence spectrum, and may want your work to reflect that, even though that's not the norm in the West. And that can make a book richer, more complex, and more honest.

JH: Did you see your novels as interdependent when you were writing them? And was that a problem?
GJ: *Tiger Writing* came after my novels, so I didn't have the intellectual framework for articulating the tension I felt between how I was writing and how I was supposed to write. But now I see that my books are often hybrid works and tend to have, for example, an ensemble feel. The protagonist is a little bigger than the other characters but not much, and his or her status may be questioned by the work overall. For example, in my last book, *World and Town*, there are five sections. Three are given to one character, so she's the protagonist. But by having these two other, interrupting sections, with related but fairly separate narratives—narratives that do not represent different views of the same events, but that focus on different sets of events—there's the sense that this could be a totally different book if one of the other "protagonists" was given more space. What's more, there is a suggestion that these two other possibilities are just two of a number of possible narratives. The main protagonist's story has an independent arc, but its context is quite interdependent.

JH: You told Bill Moyers that growing up Asian American with immigrant parents serves as a kind of amiable irritant, the grain of sand that hopefully produces the pearl. How does your cultural identity shape you as a writer, and what questions does this bring up that you're trying to solve in your novels?
GJ: That phrase "amiable irritant" comes from Philip Roth. As for the influence of my background, the fact is that whatever I do in life, I'm almost always aware that there's another way to do it. I find that not just in my

writing, but even with, say, raising a child. And what's right, what's wrong—who can say? I explore these things in my writing, though I solve, sadly, nothing.

JH: Did *Tiger Writing* help you in a different way than the fiction in making sense of all this?

GJ: Yes. It gave me a vocabulary with which to look at my predicament as a writer in particular—a predicament often shared, by the way, not just by people with dual cultures, but to varying degrees by many women. I hate to generalize because there are always so many exceptions to any rule. And yet the fact remains that many women tend toward the interdependent end of things—that we tend to see ourselves in relationship to others to a far greater degree than men.

And if it's not too interdependent thing to say, I'm happy to have written *Tiger Writing* not only for myself but for others. So many people have come up to me and told me how liberating it was for them to read. Many nonwriters have said this, but of course many, many writers, too. Somebody told them it wasn't okay to have more than one protagonist or that they needed to write in a more linear way, and even if they accepted that advice and felt they profited from it, they never understood why exactly they were told that. Now, they at least understand where these ideas come from—that they are related to Kant and the Enlightenment, and America's current hyperindividualism.

JH: Does this hyperindividualism affect our literature, and vice versa?

GJ: Yes. Many writers, if they actually thought about what our society's extreme reinforcement of individualization is actually doing to us as a society, might be opposed to it, and certainly not want their books to contribute to the problem. And yet often their work is part of a cultural feedback loop of which they are unaware, and that is exactly what they are doing. It used to be that we expressed our individualism through writing novels and that was liberating. But now, I think, that same individualism has become codified, and a kind of prison.

JH: What's the one true thing that you wanted to express in *Tiger Writing*?

GJ: We are made by culture, but we make culture, too.

Interview with Gish Jen

Paul Peppis / 2014

From *UO TODAY*, May 15, 2014. Reprinted by permission of Gish Jen and Paul Peppis.

Paul Peppis: Welcome to *UO TODAY*. I'm Paul Peppis, interim director of the Oregon Humanities Center. Our guest today is fiction writer Gish Jen. Her works include four novels, *Typical American, Mona in the Promised Land, The Love Wife*, and *World and Town*. She's also the author of *Who's Irish?*, a collection of short fiction. Jen's most recent book, *Tiger Writing: Art, Culture, and the Interdependent Self*, is a nonfiction work based on the Massey lectures she gave at Harvard in 2012. Jen gave a reading at the University of Oregon on April 21, 2014, as part of the series *Asian American Voices: A Collins Literary Forum*, which was presented by the English Department. Thanks so much for coming on the show today.
Gish Jen: It's my pleasure.

Peppis: Would you mind reading something from your work?
Jen: I'd be happy to.

Peppis: Thank you.
Jen: This is a section from *World and Town*, and this is an ice fisherman from Vermont talking. (Reads from *World and Town*)

Peppis: Thank you so much; that was wonderful. Did you interview ice fishermen when you were preparing to write that?
Jen: Yeah. Well, it just so happened that I actually might have. I actually do have a house in Vermont, and we are on a lake and so there are ice fishermen right out our door. You know, a writer sees those people and she thinks material.

Peppis: Well, one of the most distinctive qualities of your fiction is your ability to create the distinct voices of these different characters. Why is that such an important part of your fiction? Why is giving this very distinctive voice to these very different people so important for you?

Jen: Well, it's just who I am, I have to say. I did a lot of research for this book *World and Town.* There's a lot in it about ethnicity, and there's also a lot about religion. So, that meant that I went to many, many churches, and I had a friend who was at the Divinity School at Harvard and who was showing me around. It was interesting because she was watching me work. After we had made three or four trips she said to me, "I always thought that a writer writes, but now I see that a writer listens." I don't know that all writers work that way, but for me, it is very much just part and parcel of what I do. Obviously in the end when people talk about voices, it's all my sensibility. It's certainly what I see, it's what I make of it, it's still my vision, but part of my vision is to capture the many ways in which people talk, which is actually the way they see things, right? It's what they say because it's what they know, and it's what they know because it's what they take in.

Peppis: Hmm, is that a kind of anthropological approach to writing fiction?

Jen: Well, I guess it is a little bit anthropological. I mean I think that in the end it is my filter, so I'm not like anthropologists just out there to see what's there. They're not trying to make a work of art out of it. I am out there looking at things, but finally I want to make something, so there's a way in which everything is itself, but also it is part of a larger thematic or metaphorical structure. So, in my work nothing is only itself. So, an anthropologist is happy just to get it straight; I must get it straight and I must. If an ice fisherman reads my book I don't want him to say, "Oh, wow, you know, we don't get smell right." (laughter) It's important to get those details right. But, in addition, it has to have, I would say, actually not just one other use but two or three or four or five other uses right before we can call it fiction.

Peppis: So I'm going to ask you some questions that you've been asked before. You're the child of Chinese immigrants. First, say a little bit about what led your parents to come to the United States in the forties.

Jen: Well, my parents came with different reasons. My mother came . . . in truth, she had an arranged marriage she did not like and sort of in the process of disengaging herself from that. She was sent for a year abroad. It's called gilding the lily. It's just the way we might take a graduate year in France or something. So she came. She never intended to get caught here. I mean she was exactly the way we might take a year at Oxford or something. She was simply abroad, broadening herself when the revolution happened. My father came as part of the war effort. During the Second World War, this talk about opening a second front against the Japanese at the Shanghai Harbor meant that they needed people to coordinate that effort, and my father was a hydraulics engineer, so he was sent all the way. He couldn't cross the Pacific, too dangerous. He was sent all the way across China over the Hump, which is the Himalayas. That was a very, very dangerous plane ride actually, very dangerous. And across India, across Europe, across the Atlantic. By the time he got here, the war was over. But he stayed to do some graduate work. But again, it was never his intention to stay in the United States. In truth, he was part of a cohort that was kept here against their will. What happened was that once it became clear that the communists were a real force to contend with, the US government and the Nationalist government got together and they knew that a lot of the Chinese scientific talent was here. They agreed that that talent should not be allowed to go back to the mainland. My father had colleagues who tried to go back. I mean their families were in China, right? They were taken off the boats in Hawaii, so they were kept there against their will. This is a story which is told in *Typical American*, and it's true. So my parents were unwilling immigrants. That meant people like my father refused to become a citizen. He was offered citizenship under a refugee act, but he said we're not refugees. Just like if you went to China, you thought you would work on your Mandarin. You went there and they said, Oops, you can't go home, but we'll make you a Chinese citizen and your reaction is "forget it," right? But the result is that we were in quite a difficult situation for most of my youth because my father was not a legal citizen. (laughter)

Peppis: So how did you guys wind up in Yonkers. I grew up in Irvington, so I know Yonkers well. So how did you wind up in Yonkers?
Jen: Well, my parents were in kind of a classic immigrant progression out of the cities. At first they were in Queens, then they moved northward to Yonkers. Eventually they moved to Scarsdale which is where my second novel, *Mona in the Promised Land*, is set, and from there they went on. Today they are in Chappaqua. Well, my mother is in Chappaqua.

Peppis: Oh, interesting. My best friend grew up in Chappaqua.
Jen: Straight north, right exactly. Now they are in the same town with the Clintons after they've arrived.

Peppis: So, for your growing up, you were living in Yonkers until fifth grade, something like that?
Jen: Yes.

Peppis: And then you moved to Scarsdale?
Jen: Exactly.

Peppis: So Yonkers was working class and more white ethnic. You moved to Scarsdale, upper-middle class, large Jewish population. What was the shift like for a Chinese immigrant family before the era of multiculturalism? What was that moving from Yonkers to Scarsdale?
Jen: Well, I would say both places were very difficult in their own way. Because we were the only Chinese American family that people had seen really in either town. In Yonkers they just never had seen one who looked like us before, and I was working class. Because I was working class, I have to say it was rough. I mean we definitely had rocks thrown at us. When I look at my own children, when snowballs are thrown at them they never have to worry there is a rock inside the snowball. When I was growing up, snowballs thrown at Jews often had a rock in it. There's a lot of trouble. My brother was always in fights. It was difficult. Scarsdale was a very different place. Again, we were the only Chinese Americans in town or the only Chinese American kids in the schools, so we were the object of a lot of curiosity, but it was very different and it was friendly. Because it was predominantly Jewish, the Jews were people we had seen a lot and they knew what it was to be an outsider, so it was a wonderful thing to have a minority as the majority in town. I can't say it was a bed of roses, but it was certainly much more welcoming and really cool, quite wonderful. There's a way in which my second novel, *Mona in the Promised Land*, is kind of a love letter to Scarsdale. I'm very grateful. I am also grateful because one feature of that particular community is that they revered writers. So there is a way in which I do feel that growing up in Scarsdale is a lot of why I became a writer.

Peppis: So, tell that part of the story. How did being in Scarsdale make you?
Jen: Well, one thing of course is this tremendous emphasis on voice. I mean voice, storytelling, all those things. I did recently write this book *Tiger Writing: Art, Culture, and the Interdependent Self*, in which I talk about the fact that being from having roots in Asian culture. I had roots in a culture which is fundamentally nonnarrative and it's very, very fundamentally

nonautobiographical. So it is a culture where you do not have baby pictures of you when you're six months old, seven months old, eight months old, where people are not looking at you to try to understand what's unique and special about you so that they can bring that forward in the world. And quite the contrary, I came from a world where what was important was what your role was, that you understood your role and that you played it well. Now all of a sudden I'm in Scarsdale, New York, which had quite an independent culture and where being able to self-narrate is very important. I do think that starting with the playground with everybody, of course, could tell a story that had beginning, middle, and end. I mean that sounds like something which is so obvious today, but honestly for people from an interdependent background, that's not a given. So, the fact is that I was steeped in it. You know, steeped in this beginning, middle, and end. Steeped in it. Steeped in a kind of narrative that focused on an individual. I understood that was the way stories were told in the West. I think that was tremendously helpful, and also helpful with the fact that Scarsdale is a rich town with wonderful libraries. I had come from Yonkers, I got to a Catholic school, and that meant there was a donation library. They had books on lawn care, and it is a kind of old room with sagging shelves, dark, not having many books. When you got to Scarsdale—I still remember the Greenacres Elementary School Library—I just couldn't believe it and I did read every book in the library. It was a fantastic thing for me. So, I don't know, had I not moved to a town with a library like that, had I not been immersed in this storytelling culture and a culture where literature was so esteemed . . . So I had fantastic, fantastic English teachers. If I had not had those teachers, I don't know . . .

Peppis: A couple of weeks ago I interviewed Samantha Chang, and she's recently more sympathetic to the argument that writers are not made but they are born, and it's interesting that you're making a somewhat different argument here.

Jen: Well, I think the truth of the matter is nature nurtures, right? It is also true that on my mother's side I actually come from a literary background.

Peppis: Interesting.

Jen: So if you look back, my grandfather was quite a literary guy. And there's a writer, Mao Dun, a very famous early twentieth-century Chinese writer. He was the one who found Mao Dun. He was a teacher. Mao Dun came to his school, and he was the one who went to Mao Dun's mother and said "you must let him write" and got him the first job in publishing in Shanghai. So, there is a way in which I did actually have literature. My mother's earliest memories are sitting on my grandfather's lap reciting poetry. It's complicated, but you can have that kind of thing in your background. You know, without the environmental support I just don't think anything else. There're seeds, the seeds of mine, but you need water if you want to see anything grow.

Peppis: You're best known for your works of fiction, you've written four novels and a book of short stories. Why is fiction your preferred genre? Why is that?

Jen: Well, I would have to say that after *Tiger Writing* I'm not sure that it is my preferred genre. It's hard to say why, but I think that I really don't know why do we have the desire to make these things up? But for me, I think that if you think about how new the world was to us as an immigrant family because we have no preconceptions whatsoever, everything is new, so it is as if you have just gone to some country that you didn't even know existed. It's fascinating to have the desire to write down what you see, to think about what it is, to try to line that up with the reality at home. I think that it is kind of amazing that all immigrants don't become fiction writers. In my view, you walk outside and there's so much and the voices, right? Because the voices that I hear at home are not these voices. So, I guess that's an answer for you exactly.

Peppis: That's a fascinating answer. So you've mentioned *Tiger Writing* a couple of times that it's a work of nonfiction, the first major work of nonfiction that you have done. It results from an invitation you received to give the Massey Lectures at Harvard. Why did you accept that invitation? What was it that made you say yes?

Jen: Well, first of all, I first said no, as I was still working on *World and Town*. I would be happy to talk when my novel is done, but it's not something that you can say no to. You know, it's a tremendous honor. I think from the beginning of the Massey Lectures, it is kind of the big lecture series associated with the American Studies Program at Harvard. I think from the beginning of the program until now it's just been a handful of writers. Let's see, Eudora Welty, E. L. Doctorow, Toni Morrison, Maxine Hong Kingston, and they all said yes. I wouldn't say no, right? So of course I said yes, and that was definitely the scariest thing I have ever done.

Peppis: So, you had something to say though. I mean you had a story to tell. You had a nonfiction narrative to present?

Jen: Well, I didn't know that at first. I first said I would do it and then I just thought, Oh no. I think the one thing that was clear to me was that people said we can write about anything, but who is going to write about Emily Dickinson with Helen Vendler sitting right there, right? So, I didn't know right away, but it is true that once I thought, well, what is it that I could usefully contribute, this thing popped out and it was rather a big thing.

Peppis: Yeah, and it's very well, I mean, you get the feeling reading it that it had been percolating for a long time.

Jen: Well, it had been one of these things when I look back at part of my master's thesis in 1983 from the Iowa Writers' Workshop. There was a scholarly component, and I wrote about individualism, so obviously this has been on my mind for a long time. You know cultural things in general are very difficult to write about, and it just so happened that as I was sitting down to these Massey Lectures, remembering this thing that I'd written in 1983. It so happened that some very significant, cultural, psychological studies were coming out, and these studies were brand-new. So, it was just a very lucky thing that these studies were coming out just as I was sitting down to look at the subject again.

Peppis: I have to ask you about the title *Tiger Writing*. Explain the title, first of all.

Jen: Well, I'm not sure that I can explain it exactly. I will say that it is partly a reaction to Amy Chua. There is a way in which I think I wanted to take back "tiger." I think that is a way of taking back really China. What it means to be Chinese. I wanted to complicate it in the way that I understand what it means to be Chinese, which is not a single thing if you think you would know what it means. I think it was also just a handy way of signaling that this is an East-West book, but of course over the course of the book, *Tiger Writing* means East, but it kind of morphs into something else, right?

Peppis: You tell a story, though, in there about the tiger. Do you remember the story?

Jen: You mean the story about the use of writing in order to tame a tiger? Yes, that's a very Chinese story. It's about somebody who writes something in order to kill this tiger that's afflicting this village, and that's a very Chinese idea. It's very instrumental for writing, which is very much at odds with the idea of writing as an ending in itself, which is a very Western idea, and also writing as a means of self-discovery, but of course writing is also a fantastic means of self-discovery, and so in my mind, *Tiger Writing* is both this instrumental thing and this very noninstrumental thing.

Peppis: Very interesting. So you begin the book with an essay about your father in the autobiography he wrote at eighty-six. What surprised you about his autobiography?

Jen: My father did write this autobiography and of course I was very excited about it as it took the form of a series of emails, but what was so surprising about it was that it didn't look anything like the narrative that I had learned from my schoolmates in Scarsdale. It should have started "I am born" like David Copperfield, and it did not start that way at all. My father did not mention himself until the eighth email and finally he mentioned himself and there he is. He mentioned himself in parenthesis and his birth in parenthesis in conjunction with another event so that when I first looked at this I just thought, What is this about? What kind of autobiography is this? Since writing this book, many, many, many people who'd come up to me were exactly in the same situation and they were all excited. A parent or grandparent just sat down to write something, and like my father's it makes apparently no sense at all. It does not begin with themselves, and moreover it seems not to be about them at all. It's very much focused in great detail on the context. Like the piece of my father, his house, everything about his house as if he cares about his house. We wonder, Where are you? That was my first view into a different self. Where they tell, what they narrate, what they see is completely different than what we see in the West.

Peppis: And that's the interdependent self that you talk about.
Jen: That is the interdependent self.

Peppis: So, do you still feel that you call yourself a changeling in the book, that there is this doubleness to your character, that you talk about strategical shift between an interdependent self and an independent self? Do you still feel that's the case?
Jen: Yes, of course. Yeah, absolutely. I do think that I have both selves and I will say that in having two selves I'm not unusual actually. Many people—I think a growing number of people—have both selves. I think when we think about these selves there has been a tendency to only think about the conflict between them, and of course there are times when the demands of the two selves are in conflict, for instance, becoming a fiction writer, you know, and the fact that I am here giving this interview when really the interdependent

part of me should be home taking care of my mother, right? So, obviously there are times when these selves are in conflict, but it is also true that they are a kind of passport. I mean you can enter so many more worlds. There's a tremendous agency in having both selves and in being able to deploy, I guess, one or the other depending on what it is or what is most helpful.

Peppis: So, are you working on anything new?
Jen: I am working on something new.

Peppis: Can you tell us anything?
Jen: No. (laughter)

Peppis: Okay, I have a different question. This one you will be able to tell me. Have you read anything recently that you'd like to tell us about that you'd like to recommend?
Jen: Well, actually it just so happened on the way here. I came in on the flight from San Francisco. I connected in San Francisco to here, and I sat there in the lounge with a galley of a new book and it did make me miss my connection so it really was very good. This is a book called *The Liar's Wife* by Mary Gordon. It's gonna be out in August. It's four novellas about Europe and America. I liked many, many things about it. One of the things I liked about it was the fact that she's so good with cultural details. She never stereotypes, but she gets all the details right, and she has a wonderful appreciation for cultural difference, but of course as in my work she makes every detail correct, and it also speaks in a fictive way. Moreover, she's just wonderful with the big questions and I did find that the big questions that she has on the table are very much questions that I am grappling with at this stage in life, and I thought it was fascinating.

Peppis: What are these questions? Can you tell me that?
Jen: Well, what really matters? This is an age in the time of novella. It's really about this woman confronted with her ex-husband who was just an incredible liar, and in her whole life she has sought clarity and truth, but there's a way in which he has lived . . . and so the very question of whether it was a good thing to have cared about the truth is on the table, I mean that's kind of a very radical idea, but I think it's something that is only when you realize that actually death is no longer something which is only gonna happen in some of those stories. You know, all of a sudden everything is on the table, and everything is up for examination—the place of beauty in your life, the

place of truth in your life—and that's a big one, right? And more and more I just found this to be a very, very gutsy and wonderful book with also some very wonderful moments in it.

Peppis: Well, we're just about out of time. I want to thank you so much for taking time out of your very busy schedule to speak with us today and tell us about your writing and your writing life.
Jen: My pleasure.

Peppis: I've been speaking with the fiction writer Gish Jen. Her most recent book is a nonfiction work titled *Tiger Writing: Art, Culture, and the Interdependent Self*. I'm Paul Peppis, thanks so much for watching.

An Interview with Gish Jen

Katie Young Foster / 2014

From *Nashville Review* 14 (Fall 2014). Reprinted by permission of Katie Young Foster.

Gish Jen is the author of four novels, a short story collection, and a volume of lectures. Jen's work has appeared in many notable venues, including the *New Yorker*, the *Atlantic Monthly*, and *The Best American Short Stories*. Jen has received many accolades and awards, including the Lannan Literary Award for Fiction, a Guggenheim fellowship, and a fellowship from the Radcliffe Institute for Advanced Study. Her latest book, *Tiger Writing: Art, Culture, and the Interdependent Self*, is based on the Massey lectures Jen delivered at Harvard University in 2012. She currently resides in Cambridge.

Interviewer: Can you talk about your progression as a writer? How have your goals or interests changed?
Gish Jen: That's a really hard question to answer because I've been writing for such a long time. As a young writer I was very focused on the *making*. I wanted to get things down, to give them form and coherence. Helen Vendler wrote a wonderful book called *The Given and the Made*. She talks about a writer's "given," but also what the writer makes of the given. People can be given amazing material, but the question is—what did they make with that material? Now, maybe, I have more of a sense of wanting to open things up for other people. A writer makes a cultural space. And that cultural space can be very helpful.

Interviewer: Many of the characters in your stories are first- or second-generation Americans. Can you speak to the way generational trauma or triumph affects the interconnectivity of your characters?
Jen: I can't say that those words ever crossed my mind, because I don't think about my stories in that way. Trauma wasn't a big word then—it was 1986, pre-multiculturalism. I was more focused on the question, What makes something

literature? I had the goal of writing a "real" novel. Almost every day someone would say, "Aren't you really writing immigrant autobiography?"; "Aren't you really making something that is not artifice but artifact?" I was very much focused on what makes something artifice and artifact, not just the facts of the matter—like generational trauma—or any of those things. For me, it's about all the ways in which materials form in a highly meaningful way.

Interviewer: As I understand it, when writing *Typical American*, you had not fully articulated the "dual processing" of the independent and interdependent selves at play in your fiction. Now that you've defined them (in *Tiger Writing*), do you find yourself paying more attention to the constructed self you draw influence from while writing? How do you navigate the boundary between these selves?

Jen: I think that I'm much more aware of it in my day-to-day life. I'm much more apt to say, "This is my interdependent part." It is very easy to know when I feel interdependent because I think that self is quieter. It is a listening self. And I see now that the listening self is part of my interdependent inheritance. Of course there's another part of me, when I'm in front of the microphone, when I'm withholding myself and it's not a time to be listening. It's a time to be speaking. In this way, I've developed quite a strong independent self. I can feel myself shifting roles—as a mother, author, and friend. I have to say that the interdependent feel in my work seems to happen unconsciously, that 90 percent of my writer self is independent.

Interviewer: You spoke earlier about your revision process. You said you compose up to fifty drafts of a novel. I was wondering—how do you know when to stop writing? When are you ready to say, "This is the draft that is the one"?

Jen: You know, I keep on going until I can't think of one more thing to write. Or until my editor says—"All right! It's time!" My editor has described having to go to various cities to wrest a manuscript away from its author. So I know that if I don't give it up, my editor will be here to claim it. However, I have faith by the time my editor would want to do such a thing, that the novel really is done.

Interviewer: What are you currently reading?

Jen: Mostly nonfiction. Right now in my bag I have Orhan Pamuk's *Istanbul: Memories and the City*. I'm about halfway through. It's wonderful. There are lots of pictures, so that's always fun.

Interviewer: What is next for you in terms of writing projects? Any upcoming publications we should watch for?
Jen: I'm working on a nonfiction book.

"Give Me My Daily Wickedness": Celebrated Novelist Gish Jen Talks with *Chapter 16* about Truth-Telling and the Project of Fiction

Sarah Norris / 2014

From *Chapter 16*, November 6, 2014. Reprinted by permission of Sarah Norris.

A prolific writer known for exploring multiculturalism with keen intelligence, grace, and humor, Gish Jen is the author of four novels, a short-story volume, and, most recently, a nonfiction book created from the talks she gave at Harvard University in 2012 as part of the William E. Massey Sr. Lectures in the History of American Civilization. Jen's acclaimed work has been widely published in magazines and anthologies, including *The Best American Short Stories of the Century*, and hailed as "hopeful and smart" (the *New York Times*), "sharply funny and wisely compassionate" (*Booklist*), and "bursting with wit, yearning and truth" (Junot Diaz). In advance of her upcoming appearance at Vanderbilt, Jen answered questions from *Chapter 16* via email:

Chapter 16: This passage in your first novel, *Typical American*, describes one of the Chinese immigrants: "He was not what he made up his mind to be. A man was the sum of his limits: freedom only made him see how much so. America was no America." In interviews and essays, you've talked about your experiences as the daughter of Chinese immigrants, including ways in which you have invented yourself. How have the limitations and expectations you were born with served you as a writer?

Jen: I do have to point out first that that line in *Typical American* is followed by an image of freedom and possibility that militates against it. I did mean it to be read in context, that's to say, though please not to feel bad: you are hardly the first to quote it solo. Looking back, I can see that I assumed more interdependence of audience than I might have.

As for the role to which life seemed to have assigned me, that was what Philip Roth might have called an "amiable irritant." Not being what I would have chosen, it galvanized me, not only to consider what I would have chosen, but to choose that, to make my life into something else. What's more, it gave me a perspective on things—especially on America—that turned out to be revealing and even liberating for some. It seems to me today that I was born to limits that begged to be shown laughable.

Chapter 16: You've said that in hindsight you recognize your teenaged act of self-naming (from Lillian Jen to Gish Jen (after the silent film star Lillian Gish), as the first sign that you would be a writer. How was that act a portent for your career?

Jen: It was the first sign that I was not afraid to go out on a limb.

Chapter 16: Following four novels and a story collection, your 2013 nonfiction book, *Tiger Writing*, marks a departure for you. Can you speak to the differences between producing imaginary and factual (or, rather, research-based) narratives?

Jen: I have done a great deal of research for my fiction as well as for *Tiger Writing*, so it wasn't much of a change to be digging around in preparation for the work itself. And, to my surprise, the writing itself wasn't as different as I expected, either. Of course, as *Tiger Writing* began as a series of lectures to be delivered at Harvard University, I had some special challenges. The work had to be a kind of triptych—three lectures that could on the one hand stand on their own and yet on the other would build on each other, so that the members of the audience could attend one, two, or all three lectures, as they liked. Also, the lectures had to be both accessible to the layperson and of interest to professors. And they had to work as a book, as the lectures in this series (the Massey Lectures) have traditionally always been subsequently published.

All of this made for much contemplation of an entirely new kind for me. However, even with these constraints, the lectures finally proved as great a discovery as fiction. Perhaps exactly because I had so much to occupy my conscious mind, my unconscious mind produced thought after thought I could not have anticipated, so that the whole process became a kind of unfolding. I don't know that I had quite the sensation of playing that I do when I write fiction, but I was not on a death march, either. It was interesting and fun.

Chapter 16: In *Tiger Writing* you argue that for the majority of Chinese people "things—even literature—should be useful." How do you reconcile that notion with writing and reading fiction?

Jen: As I am not myself Chinese, but Chinese American, I do not necessarily feel that they need to be reconciled. I think that to pique and delight is enough, though I am perhaps more than usually aware that even that can have a use of sorts. If I think of the deliciously wicked wit of a book like, say, Randall Jarrell's *Pictures from an Institution*, for example, it is actually wonderfully sustaining. Probably it makes your neurotransmitters fire at a usually high rate, and probably, too, it reinforces our best selves—the part of us that knows the truth and relishes truth-telling. I don't think that's much in line with what the Chinese would traditionally consider "useful," but I believe it a good thing for the world. Am I more than usually impatient with narcissistic navel-gazing in fiction? Yes. But as for any voices I may hear, even after all these years, that question the heart of the fictive project, the deepest part of me does answer, Get lost! Give me my daily wickedness, and deliver me from piousness, Amen.

An Interview with Gish Jen

Ryan Kim / 2016

From *Breakwater Review* 15 (2016). Printed with permission from *Breakwater Review*.

Gish Jen is a second-generation Chinese American writer whose books have won numerous awards. *World and Town*, her most recent novel, won the 2011 Massachusetts Book Prize in fiction. In this book, Jen fills the pages with humor, compassion, and deep insight, following the struggles of a Chinese American widow and her friendship with a family of Cambodian immigrants. Her latest book, *Tiger Writing: Art, Culture, and the Interdependent Self*, explores the differences of the independent and interdependent self—each crafted along radically different paradigms: West and East. Several of her stories have appeared in *The Best American Short Stories* and her piece "Birthmates" was chosen as one of *The Best American Short Stories of the Century* by John Updike. *Breakwater Review* sat down with Gish Jen to talk about her work and ideas.

Breakwater Review: Something I noticed in your stories is your use of both humor and sadness. Can you talk about the relation between the two?
Gish Jen: Of course they're related. I can't say that I'm funny in order to be sad, but with humor, there's a relaxing, there's an abandon. As soon as you abandon your guard, all sorts of things will come up—including sadness.

BR: Do you ever receive a racist reaction to your work?
GJ: No. I never have. But my audience is a particular thing. When you get out into the American mainstream, it's different. If I ever had response, I would be very worried.

BR: Do you think the writer has a responsibility to inhabit a political role?
GJ: I don't think the writer has that responsibility. But there are people who think a writer *shouldn't*. And that's not me, either. When I was younger, I

was asked in an interview what the major issues were, what I wanted the candidates to discuss, and I said campaign finance reform. I was criticized by a fellow writer, an older writer I respected immensely. She said that I was being a citizen, and that was bad. But I reject that idea. If the writer wants to be involved, I don't think they have left the high track of serious literature. It is entirely possible to be both a responsible citizen and a serious artist. I don't think those things are in conflict. It does become complicated if you start using your work to advance certain positions. Whether someone is *required* to do that? I don't think you can require the artist to do anything.

Myself, I feel like if you have the microphone—and you do have to be aware that not everybody has that—it's just the decent thing to do. To use that the same way if you pass someone on the street and they are unable to get up. I don't know if it's your responsibility or not to help the person, but it's just . . . what we do.

It's more about being human, less about being a writer.

BR: In the past couple of years there's been a rise in the appearance of Asians in mass culture. I'm wondering if you think this is being handled correctly. What do you think it will take for Asians to finally be integrated into mainstream culture?

GJ: Time. I think *Fresh off the Boat* is great. But I'd say it's still a baby step. I don't know if you saw the Academy Awards, but there were really a couple of moments that were unbelievable, with Chris Rock and Sacha Baron Cohen.

I was thinking later, after watching, we know so much about the African American experience, that's why it's easy to joke about. In other words, for a comedian like Chris Rock, he could make a joke like "Back then, we weren't protesting such and such because we were busy protesting lynching," and everybody would know what he was talking about. He doesn't need to give backstory. Whereas when it comes to Asians, the people barely realize the Japanese were in internment camps. Much less anything else.

I'm not excusing what happened at the Oscars. It was wrong.

But I will say that a bigger problem would be not even getting the chance to be joked about, to not get to be in the picture. You want to be part of the American fabric. But here's the thing: they don't even know how to joke, because they don't know anything about it. You can see how foreign we are to them. In fact they don't know how to write a joke about Asians that's actually funny without being crude.

I do think, though, it will happen with time. The fact of the matter is that Asian Americans were a tiny, tiny, tiny minority until 1965. That wave is just hitting now. So the fact is that many people my age or even younger are just *clueless* about Asian Americans.

If you didn't grow up in, let's say, New York, it's quite possible that you'd never even seen an Asian American!

I mean, how many Kosovos have you met out there? Probably none! There's just not many out there in this country.

BR: In relation to your book *Tiger Writing*, which focuses on themes of individualist versus interdependent mindsets of the West and East, what do you make of the contemporary obsession with always trying to find novel or new styles in art? Is that inherently the goal of art? Is it only a fad for the moment?
GJ: It's totally a reflection of our current individualism. Actually, most places in the world, it's not such a heavy focus on constantly remaking their fields. People don't have this fantasy of their own individual genius. In most parts of the world, people feel like they are part of a tradition, and the first thing they need to do is master the tradition. And after they've done that, perhaps they can make it their own in some important way, then pass it on. Like Fan Kuan.

Clearly, someone like Fan Kuan is a very great painter. Period. But he didn't have any of these ideas like, "I'm going to reinvent painting. I myself. The Cutting Edge." I think it's a fallacy. But a fallacy that has served our country very well. We do dominate the rest of the world.

I'm not anti-individualism. It is true that it is hugely productive in some ways. But in others, less so.

BR: Some months back there were articles written about white males using Asian pseudonyms to get published in literary journals. What are your thoughts?
GJ: It's a scam, like any scam. To me there's no excuse. They know what they're doing. There's nothing redeeming about it.

It's not like they were always longing to be Asian. If you had told them tomorrow the thing to be was to be Serbian, they would be Serbian.

Do you think it's reprehensible? Yes. It's just somebody being a jerk.

Although I will say I will devote exactly one nanosecond of my time worrying about that kind of con-artist. I'm much more worried about Ted Cruz.

Have some self-respect.

BR: What do you think of writers of color who deliberately avoid the topic of their race?

GJ: Why not? It wasn't my way. My way was try to write about what I was interested in and to use Asian Americans, because it's what I know.

We are also interested in art. We also have religious preoccupations. You know what I mean? When you're writing about Asian Americans, you're still writing about all that other stuff.

Look at Saul Bellow. He buried his Jewish background. Unlike Roth, let's say.

It reifies certain things, thinking you need to erase your ethnicity to become a major American writer. And that's probably true to a certain degree, even still. But you have to decide if that's a program you're going to accept or not.

Probably at some level I will always be an ethnic writer, but that's all right. I don't care. What I imagine the contribution I might be making is more than worth the price.

BR: What advice do you have for young writers?
GJ: Find your voice. More than ever it is important to find the thing that only you can say. You might say I'm anti-individualistic, but only up to a point!

They say an artist signs every word that he or she writes. I think you should be able to pick up a work and know, in one or two sentences, who wrote it. Certainly, by the end of the first paragraph.

If somebody else can write it, why should you write it?

Gish Jen: The Self in the World

Jason Gots / 2017

From Big Think, bigthink.com, March 4, 2017. Reprinted by permission of Jason Gots and Gish Jen.

Jason Gots: Hey there, I'm Jason Gots, your host from *Think Again*, a Big Think podcast. Starting in 2008, Big Think has been an online think tank sharing big ideas from some of the most creative thinkers on the planet. The *Think Again* podcast takes us out of our comfort zone; our producers surprise me and our guests with unexpected conversation starters from Big Think's interview archives.

I'm very happy to be here with Gish Jen. She's the author of six previous books. Her work has appeared in *The Best American Short Stories* four times, including *The Best American Short Stories of the Century*, edited by John Updike. She is a member of the American Academy of Arts and Sciences, and her work was featured in a PBS American Masters' Special on the American Novel. Her new book is called *The Girl at the Baggage Claim: Explaining the East-West Culture Gap*, and I'm told that she has a very melodious Siamese cat, who may possibly make an appearance during the interview. Welcome to *Think Again*, Gish.

Gish Jen: [laugh] It's wonderful to be here.

Gots: [laugh] The Siamese cat's meowing, so maybe we'll keep it just a little as that as a special going for this interview and then let her go. I read a lot of books for this show, especially in fact I have little reading time for anything else, aside from preparing interviews. That's good because I invite people whose books are interesting. Your book has made a major impression on me. I'm kind of filtering everything now through the lens of basic premise. I think maybe we should start with you explaining a little bit of the big picture of this idea that, in general, Westerners have what you call an avocado pit self versus the flexi-self which is more typical in the Far East.

Jen: Yes, and in the rest of the world. In a general kind of way I think that we Westerners are in a bubble, and that bubble is individualism. Because we're in this bubble we have certain ways of looking at the world, which seemed completely natural to us, so natural that it really does not occur to us that maybe other people see things differently, and I do mean very differently.

The premise of this book is that, very broadly speaking, and I know I am speaking this in an incredible generalization, in the West we value the self very, very highly, and we prioritize the self and its needs in a way which is very unlike the rest of the world; that is to say that you might imagine that here in the West we have a self that looks a lot like an avocado with a very large pit, and we are very interested in developing that pit and we are interested in making sure that pit is able to express itself. In most other places in the world, I do mean most other places in the world, and very strikingly in Asia this is not at all the case.

In Asia the self dominates, and again I know this is a broad generalization, but the self that dominates is a self which prizes flexibility. In the West the ideal is to be a soloist, like if you were a musician, right? Well, in the East the ideal is to be a member of a chamber group. That's not to say that you don't have your own voice and you don't take initiative or anything like that, but it does mean that with every note you are looking at the people around you, and you are playing in concert with them, right? That's not to say that everyone is playing the same thing, but you're very attuned to what everybody else is doing. In that way of being, the world feels entirely natural to you, and really it is inconceivable, very strange to you, that some people walk around wanting to be a soloist. You know what I'm saying?

Gots: Yeah, yeah. And something that's interesting here is like it's necessary when you're talking about this kind of thing to qualify that you're making generalizations because, of course, we are talking in big general terms, but I think there's something else going on there which you talk a little bit about in the book as well, which is that not only is it uncomfortable for everybody to have their acculturated self called out as such but also I think there's a reluctance, like on the progressive left in the US at this point, to pin down the self in any general way to culture, right? We want the idea that's completely flexible and that nobody can quite put their finger on us from the outside.

Jen: That's absolutely right. Well, because we believe that the avocado pit drives everything, and we don't like the idea that actually we are very highly formed by things outside us even though that is in fact the case, but in the United States, of course, all these kinds of discussions are incredibly politically charged because any kind of discussion of the foundational difference can easily be abused. I know my own view of this. People ask me, "Are you supporting stereotypes?"

I myself am anything but stereotyping. When I look at people I know they are anything but stereotypes. I think that the problem with stereotyping really lies with the people who stereotype. In other words, I don't think it's helpful to anyone to simply not say what's true. The objective truth is that all people really have both selves in them. You have the capacity to have to be either self, and let me just say that of course if we're really talking about a spectrum, but most people are kind of in the middle there somewhere. Also, people are situational, so they really do react very much to their immediate situation. If you are in an environment that is very supportive of the pit self, the big pit self I like to call it, that is the self that you will be aware of. If we were to run a psychological test on you; at that moment, that is the self that would be evident.

Anyone who's ever uttered the words East or West is aware of just how big those categories are. If you think about the East, you just think about China. There are enormous differences just between North and South China on the score, and I do mean measurable differences. When we talk about the West we like to think of Europe and the United States, but in fact there are enormous gradations with, in a general kind of way, the levels of individualism going up as you move westward in Europe, and the level of individualism that we have here in America is higher than anywhere in Europe and probably in the history of mankind.

There have probably never been the levels of individualism that we see in some parts of this country. And again I do think it's important to realize that within our country too, there're enormous differences, and I guess maybe let's sort of say that the part of me that says "Is it supporting stereotypes or not" is not what I'm thinking. Actually, if you understand the framework, the net effect is not to make people who are different seem more other, but actually to make them seem more understandable and more legible. They're not just strange. They're operating on a different system, a system which you can't understand.

Gots: I think what's so challenging here is, like, I wonder if there's any way around the anxiety of all of this that can provoke for people, especially people in whom the avocado pit is strong. I was watching the other day an episode of *Dr. Who* called "The Flesh," in which they were making this substance that was a kind of *vino veneno* technology flesh that could be made to imitate you perfectly—essentially a clone type of thing. We have a lot of anxiety in the West, I think, around the idea of being like anyone else, and high stakes in the idea that we are unique and different, and the idea that these things are culturally relative, which clearly they are. To a great extent, that is very personal for a lot of people, because it's the whole foundation of my life and everything that I think is my purpose, my mission, and whatever, is somehow fictional because it's grounded . . .

Jen: Well, it's not fictional but constructed, right? I think the whole question is whether we are completely socially constructed. I don't actually believe that. I don't think we know one way or the other, right? This is one of the questions like "Do we have free will?" You can argue in both ways, and clearly there is always going to be a question, but you're right. I guess my feeling would be that if you understand why the East is the way it is, you will also understand why the West is the way it is. When you understand we do have a cultural mandate to be different, there is a way that you could say maybe my whole life is a fiction, but maybe you could also find it kind of liberating (laugh). You don't have to spend twenty-four hours a day trying to establish how you are unique. Chances are someone rather like you has existed before; someone like you will exist again, and that's okay. It's more than okay. It's like saying you don't want a sun in the sky, but there IS a sun in the sky. So, you can relax.

Gots: Indeed, if we ever get to the point of artificial, general intelligence or anywhere near it, we are gonna be dealing with questions of identity anyway. We are going to basically rethink what it means to be conscious. I want to ask you a little bit about this in the context of art and writing. In the West, there is Harold Bloom's idea of "the anxiety of influence," the idea that writers are essentially great artists, and essentially overthrow their models.
Jen: Their forebears.

Gots: Yeah, their forebears. You talk about in your book the amount of copying that goes on in China specifically in this entire village. I don't remember the name . . .
Jen: Dafen.

Gots: Dafen, right, where they basically produce Van Gogh masterpieces in various sizes and so on. I wonder if you can talk a little bit about how that works in the arts. Again, these are big East and West, the flexi-self versus the avocado pit self [questions].

Jen: I guess we can say there are two models, with people inheriting these models to different degrees. You are absolutely right. I am a fiction writer and I was steeped in the school that said: "Yes, you must actually kill your forebears." That's a kind of funny thing for me to think about. One of my forebears is an Asian American writer of a certain generation—Maxine Hong Kingston. I was asked about her very often early in my career. I would say something like: "Well, she is my forebear, so I would have to kill her in order to be able to write and so on." The first time I ever met Maxine, the sweetest person on earth, she said: "I read an interview with you and you said you wanted to kill me!" (laugh). That was just awful. I said: "No, no, no." But it is the model we grow up with, right? It is very, very deeply ingrained in us that we must be utterly original; we must break them all; we must basically start the whole history of fiction. Start again with us! That's our ideal. You will see even people not in arts exactly, people in other fields and businesses; their ideal is Steve Jobs the Genius. He himself had this ideal when he first got to college; he didn't want his parents to be anywhere near him. He had wanted to be seen as if he had just come out of nowhere, [as if] he had given birth to himself, right?

Gots: What's interesting though, as you say, there are collectivist (or flexi-self) tendencies in tension with avocado pit tendencies even in American culture. When I think about hip-hop or jazz, which is of course emerging out of black American experience and which can trace its roots back to Africa, those guys and girls talk about their influences all the time. There is a major tradition of saying, "I want to give respect to this person or that person who taught me what I know." And that's as distinct, I think, from rock and roll, where the emphasis is very much on "I give birth to myself."

Jen: Yeah, and I think that actual difference can be very much traceable to the roots of these different genres, also to the way, to the degree in which they are recognized as Art—capital A—in Western culture. Every type of art that is more interdependent, more of a flexi-self that reflects a view of pinnacle figure as not being a genius but a master (meaning somebody who has absorbed a tradition and then made something new, but who identifies himself as belonging to a tradition), is always seen as second best in Western culture, especially in the US. Our pinnacle figure is always the genius. That's very different than most places in the world, including Africa, including the Middle East, including South America, including most of Europe, and very much including the Far East where clearly, from their point of view, a great figure is the figure of a master. There is a kind of condescension here in the West. Whether you want to say a master figure really represents art-dominant culture and therefore can be seen as the ultimate figure or not, I do think you cannot look at other cultures and just say: "That's fine they have the flexi-self, but they will never be as great as us."

Gots: Right, right. There is the idea—I mean this is the stereotype—that somehow we produce more ground-breaking or important things than other cultures that way.

Jen: Or works that are classified as great. If something that I hope my book will dispel is that that is completely wrong. We can absolutely look at some of the painting and other artwork that come out of the East, and I think they are indisputably Great, capital G, and they are indisputably the works of masters and indisputably reflect the flexi-self, not the big pit self.

Gots: You could argue that great works in the West may well have great subtle substance to them in addition to unique surface features and there is an emphasis on reinventing forms and maybe on the visibility of difference. I am recalling the documentary, *Jiro Dreams of Sushi*, about the sushi master Jiro in Japan. He is over eighty years old. The whole thing is about how he basically does the same, exact routine every day for forty or fifty years. He is focusing on slicing the fish slightly better. There are substantial differences but there are not formal differences. His progress is not immediately visible from the outside.

Jen: It's incremental.

Gots: Yeah.

Jen: It's incremental, and the idea that you are going to refine and refine and refine. Let me just say that greatness absolutely results from that endless refinement. You will see this in business as well. Here the idea that you must have a distinctive brand, and that your brand must be unique, is a very important thing. That's seen as key to success. And yet if you look at Asia, there are spectacularly successful businesses based on this incremental model. They did not invent the smart phone, but they refine it just like Jiro with sushi. The result is something that is pretty cool, and I'll say, very successful. So, we like to think of the geniuses having this tremendously wonderful avocado pit that just comes out, even though you talk to anyone who has accomplished anything, there's a nobody for whom that has just popped out (laugh).

Gots: That's what I was gonna say. When I think of the master writers that I had the chance to talk to on the show, they arrived at some point at the idea that discipline is essential, showing up at their desk even if they don't feel that writing is essential. All of the shiny ideas dominating the PR in their business are about talent and individuality. In the day-to-day craft, most accomplished writers seem to have arrived at this point, even Western writers as well, that you just have to sit down. It's a struggle; you have to edit it and basically learn not to take your own words so seriously and completely rewrite them. Right?

Jen: Absolutely. And it's not just in writing. This would be true in any field. The question is: "Why do we have this narrative that in so many ways kind of buries the truth?" I guess it's kind of the point of my book that we have these cultural narratives that we ourselves understand to be a little out of sync with reality, but we tell those stories anyway. And that's problematic not only because these writers or young people in any field think that talent is everything; it leads them to be unprepared for the sheer doggedness that's involved in getting anywhere. So, that's one problem, but another problem is it leads us to completely miss other forms of human endeavor. What are they doing? It leads us to view them as somehow not legitimate, and that's very problematic.

Gots: Yeah, definitely. This gets very fraught in the area of education. I have a nine-year-old son, and I spend some time teaching in my career. I am very firmly grounded in this progressive model of engaging children's natural curiosity and the idea that if you make the curriculum hands-on and interesting enough that kids will learn; obviously you could be there to help them along and so on. From that perspective, it's hard to see the model of education in, say, China or Korea, where many kids, even elementary school kids, are in school for ten to twelve hours a day and sometimes go to after-school as anything but terrifying and smashing down the spirit of the child. But your book problematizes that as well, right? Or kind of suggests that?

Jen: I think that in the end educational systems exist to create adults who can function in the world they are in, so there is not one bone in my body that thinks we should take Asian educational system and bring it here. If you're looking at the system, the question to me is: Does it work for them, given the givens? I think we are often asking the wrong question. Let me just say that it's not clear to me that the education system that dominates in China right now even works for China. This is the whole other subject.

Gots: Got you. Well, ours doesn't really work for us either.

Jen: Exactly (laugh). It works for some, but not for everyone. I am not saying we should take the Asian educational system here. But we might look at what they are doing and ask whether the fact that they are doing it DOES work for some people, like what that tells us what we refuse to do here.

Gots: Right.

Jen: It's not that they don't recognize that some students are more talented than others, and that gets very interesting in their view. They think anybody can do math, but to do literature, you have to have talent.

Gots: Oh, really, interesting! (laugh)

Jen: That's kind of interesting. Their view is everybody can do math. Here we are like: this person is just not naturally disposed to math. Their view is if you are not disposed to math, you need to start earlier and work harder.

Gots: That's interesting.

Jen: You see, they have this flexible view of the self. We are not talking about whether they can become mathematicians or are going to get PhDs in pure math and move the whole field of number theory forward. We are talking about whether we can get everybody to a level where they can do the trigonometry. The Chinese view is: Of course!

Gots: That's reminding me of the difference between the ways we teach music here and the Suzuki approach. My son plays guitar and he's been taking lessons from a Suzuki teacher since he was little. And the idea there is exactly that. We expect every human child to learn his native language, so why do we assume with music that we sort of put them near a piano and let them try it three times? And if they are not feeling it, then, oh, they are not into music. But this [Suzuki] approach, I guess, fits with the flexi-self idea that assumes anyone can learn that language. Not everyone is gonna be Mozart, but . . .

Jen: Right. They may understand that everybody can learn it, and by the way, they will lead richer lives as a result of learning it. It's not pointless. This is not we are making them do this because we want to. In fact it will better equip them to lead what we might think as a fulfilling life. So, this is a good thing, and just do it, right? Do your scales. It's a very different emphasis.

Don't get me wrong. The Far East has taken this, I think, way too far. A lot of it is just that there are very limited resources. There just aren't enough schools literally for all the people, and there aren't enough art teachers. So, if you were very good at hip-hop in China, they might very well say you need to do math. You might never have one minute in the day to be able to practice your hip-hop. That is also very problematic, and I am not arguing for that at all, but I do think we need to ask ourselves: Are we right to be so focused on the avocado pit of the child? There are actually many educators who are trying to get us out of that model also, Carol Dweck, for instance, at Stanford, because the trouble with the avocado pit is we'll just start looking at "Does this person have a natural aptitude?" Instead of something which opens a person's life up, it actively closes it down, because you measure them early on and discover they are not particularly good at math and then it's kind of over. We don't expect you to do math, 'cause you are not good at math. And then later on their options in life have been narrowed, because nobody ever sort of said: "You know you are not good at math, but you are gonna do it anyway" (laugh). So in a funny kind of way we are so focused on natural aptitude that becomes a kind of trap.

Gots: Right.
Jen: So I think there is a middle ground that we need to think about things like the word training. In China, the word training is, of course, you train children. Here, it's like a dirty word. The idea of training a child has this feeling that you have gone against their natural being. It's almost like a violation to train somebody to do something.

Gots: It's exactly right. You want them to discover themselves.
Jen: Right. And that's only an ideal. If you have a young Yo-Yo Ma, please give him a cello and leave him alone (laugh).

Gots: Right.
Jen: Definitely if you have a little Mozart, just leave him alone. But for many, many people, leaving them alone is not the answer, for whom training shouldn't be such a dirty word. Our attitudes toward training may actually be doing them harm.

Gots: Yeah, it's like we don't want to accept that we are creatures of habit on one level, but we are also higher-thinking beings. But we are creatures of habit that learning certain habits that are good through training can actually be beneficial in terms of your resilience over life.

Jen: Absolutely. I think we have to understand that our ideas about these things are ideological. We don't want to think that, but that is simply the case.

Gots: Right, right.

Jen: I think very foundationally this avocado pit is an introjective divinity. In other words, we feel God lies within, whereas in many places in the world, God, whatever it is, lies without. So, because we feel God lies within, everything God says within is what we pay attention to (laugh), but that's simply an idea. It's an idea with roots. It's not an objective truth, right? It is just an idea that's been very, very powerful. It's relatively new; it's very, very, very powerful, and the dominance of the West rests on this idea.

As I talk about in this book, whether you focus on the big pit within or on the environment without leads you to actually perceive things differently. So, if you have a lion in a savannah, the big pit self is gonna see that lion, and the flexi-self is gonna see the savannah and the relationship with the lion to the savannah.

And the answer is there's truth in both of these perspectives, and I think actually one of the reasons why the Western business has been successful is because we look at things in a new way, and really nobody else looks that way. It gave us a whole avenue into a way of thinking that turned out to be very, very powerful, probably because no one else was using it. It led to analytical thinking which was the foundation of scientific method. These things were very powerful ideology, and I would feel: Wow, what an invention! That said, it's still limited. I wouldn't want us to abandon it, but I think it's time to think in a both/and kind of way rather than an either/or kind of way.

Gots: No, no. It's just things that get complicated. People like things to be simple (laugh). But the real picture actually is fairly complex. But it's oaky. There's a lot of overlapping. I could go on and on like this for three hours. But maybe we should take a look at the surprise video; otherwise, the whole premise of the show will be compromised. Let's take a look at Paul Root Wolpe, who is a bioethicist, talking about the ethics of designer brains. [Paul Root Wolpe's talk omitted. Interested readers can listen to his talk at http://bigthink.com/videos/the-ethics-of-designer-brains-2.]

Jen: Well, the first thing I'd like to say is, of course, the idea of enhancement is something that is very uncomfortable for people with the big pit self. If you think the naturally given big pit is divine, any thought of monkeying with it is extremely disconcerting. It would be interesting to see if these technologies take hold. I would not be surprised to see them much more widely adopted in societies with the flexi-self, because it's less taboo.

My second thought is that when he talks about this kind of mindless race to the top, he associates it with American. We were talking about the flexi-self and the big pit self, I would have to say that you have also to ask yourself whether the society where the two selves are created is hierarchical or not. Listening to the video, you might have the idea that, well, the flexi-self is gonna have it right. They are gonna care more about social harmony and real riches of life, unlike us crazy big pit self. (laugh) I think that would be mistaken.

Gots: Right, right, right.
Jen: I think that China is a great example of a society which is both a flexi-self and also very hierarchical, even though, yes, they place an enormous emphasis on being attuned to other people. Finally it is about getting your group to rise in the social structure, and so the ways in which they would self-enhance, ironically I would think, very much resemble the ways in which we in America might enhance. That is my initial reaction to it.

Gots: Right, because you can only care intensely about status if you see yourself embedded in the network of relationships and what other people think of you as being extremely important. Right?
Jen: Yeah, and let me just say that not all flexi-self societies are hierarchical. Obviously, Cambodia was not that hierarchical. Some might say that because their flexi-self is so influenced by Buddhism rather than Confucianism, [their society] was not so hierarchical. But you might also argue that because they were not so hierarchical, it made them very vulnerable to be invaded and so on.

Gots: Right. You can argue in that sense Buddhism is not entirely revolutionary; it tends to encourage you to make peace with your situation in the world.
Jen: That's fine as long as your neighbor is doing the same.

Gots: Exactly, exactly. We are out on a limb here when we are going to the future. I am trying to think of what the first genetic enhancements Americans would primarily go for would be. My instinct says genetic and, oh, also pharmaceutical; whatever way we could upgrade ourselves.
Jen: The first thing you probably could make yourself so we could work ourselves 24/7 and didn't have to sleep. Right? (laugh)

Gots: I guess we would, I guess we would.

Jen: I myself love to sleep and so I would be against it (laugh).

Gots: Right.

Jen: I guess people in Cambridge, Massachusetts, would. We have so much skewed view of the world, perhaps. But it seems to me many people around me resent having to sleep. They often try to get by without sleep.

Gots: Sure. I guess [it's about] what would constitute brilliance, right? I suspect if we were offered a memory pill versus a creativity pill, we would go for the creativity pill first.

Jen: Absolutely.

Gots: Again, we are speculating, but do you think that would be different in China?

Jen: (laugh) Well, I think actually today. We need to be aware of how they think and how different it is, and we might think about some of the self that they have that might be useful to us. They are ahead of us in that way, in the sense that they are aware that creativity is not their strong suit. So, if you ask them what pill they want, I think they would go for the creativity pill. They are aware this is a challenge for them. I think they would like to have a little Steve Jobs in them.

Gots: Yeah, we would never take the discipline pill. I mean, I might, but the discipline and resilience pill would just seem decidedly unsexy in the West, I think. (laugh)

Jen: Right. Although a number of people who, I think, if you could actually test their lives before and after the resilience pill, maybe they would feel differently (about taking it). But you are right that on the gut level, they wouldn't think, like: wow, there's a pill for resilience!

Gots: Yeah, I think that's right. Shall we take a look at the next video, which is Nato Thompson?

Jen: Sure.

Gots: He is the director of *Creative Time* in New York. Let me see what the video is called. It is *Game Over: Is Anti-Establishment Just Another Corporate Product?* [Nato Thompson's talk omitted. Interested readers can listen to his talk at http://bigthink.com/videos/nato-thompson-game-over-nil-is-anti -establishment-just-another-corporate-product.]

Jen: Oh, that was pretty interesting. Yeah, of course, the anti-establishment thing is about individualism. We are talking about the very dominant narrative that we have in America, which is the individual versus society, with the individual being the good guy and all the society being bad. But his point that this is a corporate product is very well taken. And in fact if we think about where this narrative came from; this narrative is very much the product of the Cold War. I don't think it began with the Cold War, but if we're to try to track how many people thought this was a very important narrative to them. We don't have such a graph, but if we did, we would see a very sharp upward turn during the Cold War.

Our idea that we stand against evil (and that's the original stand, a stand which has to do with our nature) is actually a product of the US propaganda. I think as the US became more and more embroiled with the Soviet Union, our way of differentiating ourselves was to generate these narratives. We were Jackson Pollock, and they were robots.

Gots: Right.

Jen: The government very actively promoted that. They were promoting art shows that featured people like Jackson Pollock the abstract expressionist. They were even actually supporting literary magazines where this kind of narrative was being advanced. They were literally buying up 50 percent of certain journals in order to keep them afloat. (Chuckle) And sure enough, their propaganda efforts paid off. The efforts were mostly international, but there were domestic as well.

So in order to fight with the Soviet Union, not only did we have to convince other nations in the world about this evil nation of collectivists, but they had to promote it domestically as well. By the way, I avoid in my book the word *collectivists* as best as I can, because the political overtone of the word *collectivism* is just overwhelming—collectivism is bad. So this guy, Nato, is saying corporate product and before that, it simply was US propaganda, and we are now buying this corporate product! He is absolutely right that it's enabling us to feel great and powerful as we sit there at the video game through which they are making a very handsome profit!

Gots: Right, right. And it's ironic. There's an obvious irony in enormous businesses built on the idea that you are a rugged individualist against the machine.

Jen: Exactly, exactly.

Gots: While all that, I can see the obvious truth in what you are saying, I also think back to the beginning of America. It is a foundational idea of this country that we don't want to be ruled. Especially, we want individual freedom. Of course, the founding fathers argued over what exactly that might mean, but we overthrew the tyrant, and that was that.

Jen: It is one thing to be free of a tyrant, and it's another thing to imagine that you could live without society.

Gots: Sure.

Jen: It's kind of a trend we make people like Emerson and Thoreau. There is a difference between not wanting to be taxed without representation—there's still a government there, and you might not like the rules under which you were being subjugated. But that's not to say you reject the idea of government all together. There's a big difference between that and a more anarchist view, which is, we don't want any government.

I am not saying Emerson or Thoreau thought that. I think that some of the ideas that we have now and that your expert Nato was talking about in his tape are that all guys are bad guys. It's like individual versus everyone, all the society. He was sort of saying that this was an amazing level of individualism. I would have to agree that it is one thing to stand up and say that this is not fair; your aim is to generate some new form of social order based on rules that are fair. Another thing is to say: "Wow, it's me against everyone, and me against all social order." I am thinking, first of all, "Wow, it's very sad, very, very sad." Also, it's a fantasy. We are just not evolved to live by ourselves with no other people, and not to be able to trust anyone else. It's just a really tragic thing.

Gots: I think so, and I think there's an interesting manifestation of that like this kind of internet-driven in some ways in popular culture where we have this idea of haters, which I think is coming from rap music. But I see young people wearing, not just young people—you see the message—"Ignore the Haters" as kind of me and our culture. I think this is idea that somehow whoever you are, you will be beset by haters who simply don't like your individualism. Anyone who might criticize you is in some way trying to stop your meteor star from rising, and you must steer yourself against the possibility of outside criticism which seems like a dangerous place to be. Whatever you do should be okay fundamentally.

Jen: Right. This just leaves a lot of room for education . . .

Gots: Right (laugh), or inside growth.

Jen: Or inspiration.

Gots: Well, Gish Jen, thank you so much for being on *Think Again* today to talk to me about your wonderful book, *The Girl at the Baggage Claim.*

Jen: It's been my pleasure.

A Conversation with Gish Jen

Biling Chen / 2017

Interview conducted via Skype and email, May 5, 2016, and March 25, 2017. Previously unpublished. Printed by permission of Biling Chen.

Biling Chen: Your new book, *The Girl at the Baggage Claim: Explaining the East-West Culture Gap*, just came out in March. Do you mind telling us what motivated you to write another nonfiction right after *Tiger Writing*, as well as the major differences between them?

Gish Jen: I felt I wasn't done with the subject. I have so much more to say than just about art. Knopf was shocked that I wanted to do another nonfiction. They asked me: "Where is your next novel?" I think they were humoring me by taking this book, but they are happy now. It starts with the Tiananmen tank in that iconic picture, so I think this book will never be published in China, and my real question is whether I will be allowed to be back in China (laugh). Seriously, I don't feel I am steering this boat. I am just in dialogue in a practical way with many things that are happening. I will be talking to a lot of different audiences. I am hoping that in addition to literary people, lawyers and business people will find this book very relevant to what they are doing. Just as the US government and the Chinese government have real conflicts of interest, American lawyers and businesspeople in the Far East have real things with real problems. But they don't really have the cultural layers on top of those problems, so I can't help thinking that cultural understanding is going to be very good for all of that. I am talking mostly to people from the West about what they don't get about the East.

BC: Where is the girl in the baggage claim now, and is she doing fine?

GJ: I don't know where she is now. I never met her and I don't really know much about her except for what's in the book, which really is a jump-off point. The book is not just about her; it's more about how she is in the situation that she is in. But because she is an actual girl, there were concerns about whether this would violate her privacy in some way. Knopf's legal department had to determine that in fact people can't sue me.

BC: Then why didn't you simply write her story in the form of fiction?

GJ: Because I really had something to say, which can't be said in the form of fiction. It had to be this way. And it's been fun to go off and do something different than what you have done before, and it's challenging. I definitely felt that I was in a rut. Writing this book for me is like working in another key, similar to some novelists writing movies, or classical musicians/composers writing a film score. Sometimes they bring those things back to their main work. So writing nonfiction opens up possibilities for me. But the book does have much more story-telling in it than most books of this kind. The desire to focus on a person is emblematic of what I have to say. It's a narrative, a nonfiction, but for a book of this genre, it's a bit unusual. It's kind of resistant to categorization.

BC: The subtitle reminds me of Salman Rushdie's collection of short stories, *East, West*. But there is a comma between his East and West. I noticed on your website that originally there was no comma or hyphen between your "East West," but the published version has a hyphen between East and West. What changed your mind?

GJ: Actually the copywriter wanted to see a hyphen or a slash. I don't know why I didn't like either. To me, it is intuitive. I guess a slash or a hyphen looks kind of defining the space between East and West, which makes you feel you know exactly what East and West is. I like the subtitle the way it was because it is less defined. I can't remember the exact back-and-forth with my editor, but I think that "East West" without a hyphen was just finally felt to be distracting.

BC: Also, why do you prefer "explaining" to "bridging" the culture gap?

GJ: My emphasis is not on bridging it. People in the West don't even understand what the gap is. It's 2017 and to me it's unbelievable that there is still so little understanding. They see the copycat phenomena. Everywhere they go, they see things like "What? That's weird," and immediately they feel they must reject it. I want to explain these things in a different way that, I hope, will make things clearer than they have been. I am trying to defamiliarize East and West. Heaven help me! (laugh)

BC: I found myself agreeing with you when you explain in your book that because of their flexi-selves, Chinese people tend to have a rather relaxed attitude toward intellectual property. I wonder if most Westerners today have defamiliarized themselves from the old universal notion that imitation is the sincerest form of flattery. I also wonder if we could apply this viewpoint to evaluate the poem by Michael Derrick Hudson that was anthologized in *The Best American Poetry 2015*. The Asian American community was outraged by his usage of a Chinese pen name to pass as a Chinese American author writing about his childhood as an immigrant. You call him a con-artist in your interview with Ryan Kim. Do you still maintain this view, and do you think an author's real racial and gender identities matter when we assess his or her artistry?

GJ: I think they matter when the value of a work is tied up with its authenticity.

BC: Some of your works have been translated into Chinese. Do you think translation could create a defamiliarizing effect and do you worry about "wrong" reception as a result?

GJ: My feeling will be that you just can't control them. I don't think anybody can control meaning-making. You've got to have some kind of faith in readers, even if you are aware that the meaning to the reader might be opposite to what you intended to. I remember when my first novel *Typical American* came out in Chinese in the 1990s, somebody said that it is all about how terrible America is. Of course that was not my point, but I can see why my book might be read in this way. American writers are all critical of society; it is the nature of depicted process of novel as we understand it in the States. Our fundamental idea of fiction is not to uphold the State. Being critical in America is no problem. I don't want to generalize, but I think Chinese novels are critical of Chinese society in a more indirect way because of censorship. When we are bringing an American novel into the Chinese context, it can look very different.

BC: Your story "Who's Irish?" has been translated into Chinese and is about to appear in China in a multi-volume anthology of world literature as the final piece of the whole series. Judging by the title of the volume—*The Modernity of Literature: From Empires to the Globe*—I guess the anthologized works more or less address various forms of imperialism and globalization. I wonder whether the editors, David Damrosch and Yongguo Chen, have a Chinese take on the issues of imperialism and globalization. I also wonder how they situate your story in this frame. Have you read their introduction to the volume?

GJ: Unfortunately, I haven't. I don't read Chinese. David Damrosch has done other anthologies in the US, so I have a general faith in the project. That said, because it is not in English, I can't parse it. When things are done in China, one never really knows what's going on. We don't know what the words are. These things have lives of their own; they mean things different in other context. I don't want to put my words into Damrosch's mouth, but I think this could also be his view of world literature. World literature finds their own new contexts and meaning wherever they go. I don't really know the Chinese coeditor, so I have no idea if he would give "Who's Irish?" a Chinese take. I guess what you are asking is if the anthology is a tool of the state.

BC: I hope it isn't! It's just that the title of that volume stimulated my curiosity because it is related to my research and scholarship. In any case, I notice that you've visited China frequently in the past couple of years. Is it a "getting in touch with one's cultural roots" thing?

GJ: Many people think since I visit China often, I must have a deep emotional tie to it. The reasons are more complicated. My uncle just died, and my mother was separated from her sister for forty years. Having one's family torn apart is . . . you know. Also, now that my children are grown, I can finally accept invitations to teach and to give talks in conferences. I want to bring my daughter to China. It's good for her. She just graduated from high school and will take a gap year. She wants to become a lawyer, so there will be seven years of tuition bill. A lot of people think writers don't have to worry about tuition bills, but they do. Somebody at NYU read my *Tiger Writing* and loved it. She invited me to teach a course based on that book at NYU Shanghai. I will be teaching a course on fiction writing this fall. They pay you well, which is a major reason for me to go. I am interested in culture. Culture has a way of shaping and strangling us. We can easily become its slave. I am not a revolutionary and I don't advocate getting rid of culture. I am interested in narrative difference, and in helping students/writers see how culture works, so that they can make informed decisions [in their lives and writings].

BC: I have some questions about your novels. You have explored the meaning of art and of being an artist in your fiction. Why is it that your artistic characters are painters rather than writers?

GJ: Good question. I guess it is because I can't paint. I have a strong visual sense and I love visual arts. I have a lot of architect friends. Maybe in another lifetime I would be an architect. Maybe this is another way of orienting my other potential into fiction writing. Some writers write about things they know. But a lot of writers write about things they half know. Writing is a form to work with all people. I loved writing about the Cambodians for my novel *World and Town*. I could have done researching for the next four years! I just love researching! It's like some people spending a lot of time in museums looking at different things to enlarge their world.

BC: Many artists seem to see their creative works as a way to achieve immortality, including Sven Anderson in your "House, House, Home." Do you share this view?
GJ: No, I am much more like Pammie. Maybe this is a cultural thing. In Sven's mind being an artist is a self-glorifying thing. From his purely Western point of view, art is a tool of self-expression, like an individual, in and of itself, and should not be about teaching. I am kind of in the middle. My ideal type of artist is someone like Maya Lin. Her work is clearly not about her. Although she does see herself as someone who wants to teach through her art, it is not self-aggrandizing in any way. Her art speaks in an elevated language, with a quality which is transcendent. She may be teaching, but this is not a teacher in an ordinary classroom. In her mind, her art is still about culture-making and people-making. It has some sort of purpose, not simply because it is, for example, her art is not just art for art's sake. I am with her. The point of art is to enlarge people's sensibility and freedom, to help culture evolve in a healthy way. These purposes are like vitamins, and it's nice to have them. But art is more than just a purpose. I absolutely reject the idea that arts should be a servant of the State! Why should we sing when we can speak? Why must we have beauty? Why does Maya Lin make art? Why must we have these things that are strange in this way or that way? The answer is whatever it is, I am in support of it. I am against suppression. So I am kind of in the middle, like Maya Lin.

BC: Do you think the kind of transcendence created by art is larger than religious transcendence? In your *World and Town* these two kinds of transcendence seem to be in conflict, embodied by Hattie Kong and Carter Hatcher.
GJ: No. The reason why I wrote the book in that way is because so much about the town of Riverlake is about religion. I am not against religion. But

when I was writing that book many things happening in the world made me feel these kinds of ideas could be very destructive. Carter has devoted his life to neuroscience like a religious person to his religion. I certainly don't want to equate these things, because one is based on methods and inquiries that are tied to some kind of reality, and the other is based on a belief and a text like the Torah or the Bible or the Koran. But there is a culture of science that is very much like the culture of religion. Both afford a sense of meaning, a sense that your life really matters. Also, just as religious people could feel their religion is so important that it could supersede everything else, and that it is okay to impose it on others and bring them enlightenment somehow, Carter has those kinds of ideas too. To him, there is only one way; to do anything to stray becomes kind of fallen. He sees Hattie as fallen because she quit neuroscience research. But Hattie thinks he has just caught himself in a web of meaning. It is a meaning like one meaning or any other. Meaning is a construct, but if it is constructed in the way that becomes the only way for me to be, it becomes a form of fundamentalism, either to string up others or to string up oneself. The book takes a very skeptical view of every system of thought that imagines its way is the only way.

BC: Do you try to adopt the Daoist concept, *Da Quan*, as Hattie does in her life and her painting? Is this idea of having no self, being everywhere and nowhere and rising above life part of your living philosophy and artistic endeavor?

GJ: Hmm . . . it's a hard question. I am not Hattie. None of my characters are representative of my views. It is more like I can always feel the tension between different views. I do not see myself as having gone in a very Eastern direction. I am trying to introduce these ideas to the West to some degree, partly because, as you will see in my new book, I am so tired of the way the East is misunderstood, and partly because some moments of Eastern transcendence, one kind or another, are useful and calming. Just like the Cambodian mother in *World and Town* says: "You are not Buddhist yet. But when you are fifty, you will be Buddhist." I actually think it is a good thing to have in one's repertoire some Buddhist strategies in calming acceptance. In the West, you have to defy everything, standing up to everything. But some of these things simply cannot be stood up to or fought. There is time to reach and do something else. And yet at the same time, some of these Eastern ideas just paved the way in big time trouble in Cambodia, enabling Pol Pot's extremism. However you see Buddhism on the cosmic level, some of the results have just been beyond horrifying. So I guess I see myself as a kind of mosaic. I can use either Eastern side or Western side. I think Maxine Hong Kingston is more Eastern. She clearly embraces many Eastern ideas. I am more skeptical of any isms.

BC: I don't see that in her *The Woman Warrior.*

GJ: That's true. But she is always in favor of peace. Of course, I am not in favor of war, and I wish peace were always the answer. But sadly, it is not always the answer. I can't tell you how much it pains me but it's true in my view. I guess what I am really in favor of is that everyone should be multicultural. I don't mean in the way that everybody's holiday is celebrated or everyone carries a flag waving their nationality. I mean everyone should be foundationally multicultural and able to use this in a way most productive for themselves as well as for their society. It would be good for people to have Eastern and Western worldviews in their repertoire. We should definitely not be all Western. The Western way of doing things is so dominant that many Americans feel they have to hide their interdependent self in the closet. Even if that's something in their family life, they feel it so "old world" that in order to be really American, to be independent, they have to get rid of it. They should celebrate it and hopefully encourage others to be this way.

BC: In one of your interviews you mention that the novel is a genre in which the protagonist asserts himself or herself. I personally like very much Callie Chang in "The Water Faucet Vision." Compared to Mona, she is certainly more conventional, but I feel that she has a refined soul. Is there any chance that you will complete your trilogy about the Changs and use her as the central character?

GJ: Hmm . . . I don't know why I haven't used her. The novel is a Western form and runs on conflicts. If there is no conflict, you are gonna find it a real trouble to go on. But maybe it's a good idea (laugh). Certainly when you look at books from outside over time, there are patterns with your books. Yes, I like art. I like science. I took a lot of biology classes as a premed, and it was fun to use them on the character Carter. But a lot of the writing process is serendipitous. Something that I decided to write is just like that. Something interested me at that moment. If it interested me a lot, I would just go with it. But don't get me wrong. During this whole process, I do ask myself what it is with this character or situation that's so important to me. And you can see it in my *World and Town.* It's a mid-life book. I am wondering about what life is, and these life decisions people make one way or another. You can see me asking questions that I didn't even know how to ask when I was younger. Whatever my next question is, maybe Callie will be animating me, or maybe she won't. There's no seeing really.

BC: Mona is surely a very animating character. A student of mine did have an issue with Mona's daughter's name, Io. He asked: "Isn't Io the young woman turned into a heifer by Zeus? Why would a strong woman like Mona give her daughter a victim's name?" I told him that Io manages to turn her life around by being resourceful; she eventually even becomes an Egyptian goddess of fertility. The ending of the Greek myth is quite uplifting and culturally expansive. I wonder if this is what you had in your mind when writing that ending.

GJ: First, don't worry, the Io I raise is not gonna be a victim (laugh). I can't say exactly why I like the name. I like that Io roams around the world. You can see it's neither Mona nor Callie; it's entirely different. A lot of people are critical of the ending; they think it is a kind of tying up with a bow. But I always thought it was a twist on the marriage ending, because there is a strong suggestion that Mona is marrying her mother. It is a marriage ending, but nothing is what it is supposed to be—the baby is there. Everything is wrong, but in a good way.

BC: Io helps Mona reconcile with her mother.

GJ: She does. She does. It was a tongue-in-cheek marriage ending, like "What? What? What?" And it opens up cultural spaces. So I was very surprised by "tying up with a bow" comment. I think they were reading it in a very conventional way. A straight-up kind of marriage will never be in the end of my book.

BC: Speak of cultural spaces. Do you think one's cultural identity can be completely separated from one's political identity? In your 2003 essay, "Racial Profiling," you mention that, to the Chinese you met, a very large part of their definition of Chineseness is their having no choice. Were they talking about cultural or political restrictions or both? Do you think this definition has changed?

GJ: When I am in China I spend most of my time on the east coast, like Beijing and Shanghai; this could really skew my view of what's going on in the whole country. Obviously, most people with whom I am in contact are highly educated and very aware of choice. I don't really see people related to politics. I probably would steer away from it, because I don't have any leverage on China's politics at all. I am more interested in culture. Anyway, compared to the China in the 1980s when I was there for the first time, and the China in 2003, today's China is very different. Its economic development has hugely changed people's awareness of choice. Just think of their consumer choices. Now, everybody is like: "What am I gonna wear?" Their sense of wardrobe is . . . wow! So there is a lot of choosing—but not just in clothing. There is more of a focus of their being. Now if they don't have a choice, they are aware they don't have a choice. And they are aware some people have a choice. But the difference in importance of choice to them and to Americans is still huge. Americans must choose everything all the time (laugh). This is what I also go over in my new book. Anyway, even though the Chinese are more aware of choices, I would certainly argue that there is quite a distance between their choosing and Americans'. It just doesn't occupy . . . it just doesn't have the same importance to them.

BC: Are you saying that they have not become very individualistic in the sense like Americans?
GJ: They have become much more individualistic, but there is still a huge gap between their individualism and ours. We are without equal in this way; even the Brits are shocked by how individualistic we are.

BC: Are they fine with the sort of choices they have? Do you sense that they wish they would have the kind of choices as Americans do?
GJ: Again, I really hate to generalize. What I get from some of them is that they would just like . . . well, it's not that they want Western freedom exactly so much as they would like to have a nice life without having to be subject to some of the things that could happen in China. For instance, perhaps they have a little network that got set up when they are in college. They don't want some important people in their network that get suddenly brought on corruption charges, and their lives would become a kind of mess.

BC: It seems to me this is related to their political system. Do you sense that they are longing for democracy? Do they articulate that kind of desire?
GJ: Some of them would say that. Nobody likes oppression. Nobody likes to be sent to jail. But there is a doubt about the American style of democracy, partly it is because of the way it is portrayed to them. They see it as a very unstable, very unpredictable way of running a country. It barely works for us and they cannot imagine it can work for them. I think they kind of have a point. If you look at the crowd on the New Year's Eve. They had a terrible trampling thing in Shanghai in the New Year's last year. It's a lot of people.

It's hard to imagine having a system which is fundamentally chaotic as our system is and how that can really work in China. I don't want to sound like an apologist for a government that is extremely repressive. I don't think anybody condones it—none that I know of. But there is a distinct distance between not wanting to see people locked up and thinking that they would want democracy.

BC: How about the Chinese students in America whom you know—do they also feel the American system would not work for China?

GJ: A number of young people whom I know do want to stay here; they feel they can say whatever they want in America, and they like that. But their view of American democracy is like: "This is fine for you, but it's not suitable for China." Frankly, I think they are right. I don't know what the answer is. There is a lot of reason why the American system of democracy should work here, but it just barely does. I don't think that's what they really want.

BC: What do you think they really want?

GJ: I think they want to be able to pursue whatever they are pursuing without feeling that in any minute anything could happen to them. They would like a little stability. I don't think anyone wants that one day you are doing fine, and next day something happens, and next day there is another revolution. They do not want the rug pulled out under them for political reasons. But this is very different from having inalienable rights. If you really ask them about the inalienable rights—because you are a human being, no government should take them away from you—they feel that's not their major concern. Inalienable rights sound very abstract; they are more practical. They just want to have a good life. All the Chinese I know do have this genuine wondering about what the path forward for China is, while maintaining a general skepticism about America.

Our view is informed by individualistic views of things. To me, this is a reflection of culture. So to answer your question: "What is hard to shed?" I would not say so much the political views but culture. To me, what's hard to shed is my interdependence. My answer is also not to shed it. It is not something you should shed but should add to. You should use both your right hand and left hand. I am aware that in some places where these things are in conflict. But it's not everywhere. I find one hard thing in America is it is cold here. We are too independent as a country. The American way is: "I am sure you will be just fine; you will find the key yourself." The Chinese way is: "I will accompany you. I will take you there."

BC: Yeah. I remember a study abroad trip I participated in when I was a graduate student. I assumed we would get on the plane as a group. But the professor/leader simply handed out our tickets to us and said: "I'll see you at the baggage claim when we arrive in Heathrow Airport."

GJ: (laugh) Exactly. These kinds of things are difficult to change—the expectations. There are many foundational things that can be modified, but I don't think we can get rid of them. Nor do I think we should. I was horrified when I saw a French movie, *Amour*. It's a very moving, very beautiful movie. The woman is so sick, and she cannot accept that she cannot be independent and that she needs others to care for her. I was like: "You are a human being and you are about to die. Just accept the care of others!" What message is being taught? You cannot be a human being and sick?!

BC: Her husband shares her view too. He suffocates her to death by putting a pillow over her nose, which he thinks is a mercy killing.

GJ: You saw that movie too. Were you shocked?

BC: Well, maybe because I have lived in the West for a long time, I wasn't shocked.

GJ: I was shocked. What is it with Western culture? I have this eighty-year-old friend. We had this party and I offered to drive her. And then I drove her back. I was very busy but happy to do it. She was offended because she thought I was being kind.

BC: Offended by your kindness?

GJ: Yeah. She thought I was being condescending. She thought I did that because she was an important person and her company would be so scintillating for me instead of just out of kindness. Really, what's with this culture that somebody is being kind and has to feel guilty about it?! I was like: you can think in that way, but I'll never think that way. When the day comes when I require the kindness of others, I will gratefully accept it.

BC: Somehow this reminds me of a story about Chinua Achebe. In the last decade of his life, he was paralyzed due to a car accident. When people asked him if he felt sorry about losing his independence, he said something like: "No. The fact that I have to rely on others reminds me that we all live in a community rather than just an isolated island." I found this kind of mentality very cool. He did not feel sorry for himself. He felt that having to rely on others is actually quite humbling.

GJ: That's a very interdependent view, and I really think the world would be a better place and people would be happier and more productive and creative if they embrace their interdependent self.

Index

Achebe, Chinua, 157
Amour (movie), 157
Austen, Jane, xviii, 22

Barthes, Roland, xii
Beckett, Sister Wendy, 87
Bellow, Saul, 45, 131
B'nai B'rith, 84
Brief Wondrous Life of Oscar Wao, The,
    xii

Camus, Albert, 22
Carver, Raymond, 54–55
Chang, Samantha, 116
Chin, Frank, 31, 35
Cho, Margaret, 87
Chua, Amy, xxi, 96–97, 118
Cisneros, Sandra, 13
Collins, Martha, 53
Confucius, 104–5
Corrections, The, 104

Damrosch, David, 149–50
Diaz, Junot, xii, 102, 125
Doctorow, E. L., 117
Dream of Red Chamber, The, xviii
Dweck, Carol, 140

Emerson, Ralph Waldo, 104–5, 145
Enlightenment, xix, 111

Fan, Kuan, 100, 130
Fitzgerald, Robert, 27–28, 31, 44, 52,
    84–85

Given and the Made, The, 122

Hannah, Barry, 54
Hudson, Michael Derrick, xx, 149

Interpreter of Maladies, 104
Ishiguro, Kazuo, 103
Island Stallion Races, The, 22
Istanbul: Memories and the City, 123

Jarrell, Randall, 127
Jen, Gish: alienation, 50; American
    culture, 16, 43, 57; Americanness,
    xiii, 36, 67; Arab Americans, 50–51;
    art, 151; Asian American writers, 8,
    23, 39, 44; Asian Americans, ix, 8–9,
    30, 36, 39–40, 43, 46, 48–50, 58, 71,
    74, 77, 97, 129–31; assimilation, xii,
    3–4, 7, 33–34, 44, 46, 55–56, 59, 73;
    authenticity, xxi, 106, 149; biracial
    issue, 29, 49, 74, 79, 91; character,
    110, 119, 122, 150, 152–54; China, xx,
    4, 9, 32–33, 39, 41, 47, 50–53, 56–57,
    61–62, 76–77, 86–87, 94–99, 114, 118,
    134–35, 138–43, 150, 154–56; Chinese
    Americans, ix–xvi, 9, 15, 18, 20, 33,

42, 49–51, 54–55, 58, 62, 71–75, 101, 105, 127–28, 149; Chinese language, 13, 99; Cold War, 144; comedy, 28, 81–82; comic voice, xiv, 14; connection (*guanxi*), 87; conscious mind, 45, 126; cultural difference, 41, 82, 120; cultural dislocation, 30; cultural tension, 41; cultural understanding, 147; culture, 13, 55–59, 65, 70, 80, 88, 99, 103–7, 111, 115–16, 136–37, 150–57; culture clash/gap, 3, 14, 80, 147, 155; dual cultures, 111; discrimination, 9, 74, 76; dissonance, 61; diversity, 8, 47, 102; doubleness, 119; education, 3, 9, 17, 37, 48, 65, 68, 94, 138–39; ethnic writer, 23, 31, 58, 131; ethnicity, 30, 40–41, 43, 57, 82, 113, 131; everydayness, 101; family, 4–7, 11–12, 14–16, 24–25, 33–34, 37–38, 48, 64–65, 74, 79–81, 90–95, 115–17, 150; feeling, 29, 34, 39, 50, 60–61, 65, 77; flexi-self, 133, 136–37, 139, 141–42; form, 28, 105, 107, 151–53; globalization, 84, 149–50; humor, 15, 37, 39, 54, 82, 87, 128, 147; hyperindividualism, 111; identity, 14, 17, 24, 31, 44–47, 57, 67, 75, 80, 84, 87–88, 110, 135, 149, 154; immigrant literature, 8; immigrants, 9, 11–12, 24, 31, 37, 44, 47–49, 52, 56–57, 59, 61, 65, 75–76, 79, 83, 92, 96, 113–15, 117, 149; immigration, 48, 56; independence, 39, 90–95, 101–4, 107, 109–10, 116, 123, 153, 156–57; individualism, 87, 103, 105, 111, 118, 130, 133–34, 144–45, 155; interdependence/interdependent, 89, 91–94, 99–102, 106–7, 109–11, 119, 123, 153; irony, 12, 24, 47, 56–57, 80, 101, 106, 144; isolation, 34, 65, 73, 90; Jewish American community, 15, 40, 44, 64; Jewish culture, 45;

kindness, 157; language, 7, 13, 47–48, 66–67, 99, 151; mainstream culture, 65, 129; mass culture, 129; melting pot, 7, 46; minority/model minority, 8–9, 40, 64, 71, 115, 129; morals, 23; multiculturalism, 14, 39, 54; outsiders, 6, 49–50, 64; peace, 153; pit self, 133–34, 136–37, 141–42; prejudice, 8, 37, 59; pseudonym (pen name), 20, 25, 58, 130, 149; race, 23, 34, 36–37, 41, 130–31; racism, 9, 31, 41, 58; religion, 16, 40–41, 47, 113, 151–52; self, 90, 92–94, 99, 102–6, 109, 119, 123, 128, 133–34, 143, 152–53; social responsibility, 31, 35–36; stereotypes, 31, 36, 38–39, 90–91, 134, 137; subject matter, 29, 36, 47; tone, 29, 47; tragedy, 5–6; values, 3–4, 6, 23, 84; voice, 6, 13–14, 31, 43–44, 58, 79, 85, 88–89, 113–17, 131, 133

Works: "Bellying Up," 25; "Challenging the Asian Illusion," 20, 34; *The Girl at the Baggage Claim*, xii, xix, 132–47; "Grover at the Wheel," 30; "House, House, Home," xv, 151; "In the American Society," 10, 20, 24, 26, 30, 39, 75; *The Love Wife*, xvi–xvii, 78–81, 83; *Mona in the Promised Land*, xiv–xv, 30, 36, 40–42, 53, 57, 59, 82, 114–15; "Racial Profiling," 154; "The Small Concerns of Sparrows," 25; *Tiger Writing: Art, Culture, and the Interdependent Self*, 89–108, 109–111, 112–23, 126–30, 147, 150; *Typical American*, xi–xiii, 3–5, 10–12, 20–21, 24–26, 28, 30, 32–35, 37, 40–43, 47, 52–57, 72, 75, 82–83, 114, 123, 125, 149; "The Water Faucet Vision," 20, 25, 30, 36, 153; "What Means Switch," 16, 18, 20, 26, 30; "The White Umbrella," 20, 29–30; *Who's Irish?*, ix, xv, 40–41,

47, 52, 55, 58, 89, 149–50; *World and Town*, xi, xvii–xviii, 110, 112–13, 117, 128, 151–53
Jiro, Ono, 137
Jiro Dreams of Sushi, 137
Judaism, 43, 46, 57, 84

Kadohata, Cynthia, 35
Kant, Immanuel, 111
Kincaid, Jamaica, 23, 54
King Lear, 28
Kingston, Maxine Hong, xi, 102, 108, 117, 136, 153

Lahiri, Jhumpa, 102
Lee, Wen Ho, 50
Lin, Maya, 151
Little Women, 22
Louie, David Wong, 35

Ma, Yo-Yo, 140
Mailer, Norman, 45
Mao, Dun, 116
Martin, Steve, 86
McCourt, Frank, 57
Middlemarch, 101
Mo, Yan, 99
Morrison, Toni, xii, 117
Mozart, Wolfgang Amadeus, 139–40
Munro, Alice, 23, 54, 102

Never Let Me Go, 103

Obama, Barack, 106
Ozick, Cynthia, 45

Paley, Grace, 45, 54, 102
Pamuk, Orhan, 123
"Paper Tigers," 97
Parker, Dorothy, 36
Peale, Norman Vincent, 16

Pictures from an Institution, 127
Pol Pot, 152
Pollock, Jackson, 144
Pride and Prejudice, 22
Pryor, Richard, 86

Roth, Philip, 40, 45, 60, 79, 110, 126, 131
Rushdie, Salman, 99, 148

Shanghai, 61, 93, 96–97, 114, 117, 150, 154–55
Sister Wendy Beckett, 87
Soviet Union, 144
Stranger, The, 22

Thompson, Nato, 143
Thoreau, Henry David, 145
Tolstoy, Leo, 101–2

Updike, John, 128, 132

Vendler, Helen, 118, 122

War and Peace, 101
Welty, Eudora, 117
Who Killed Vincent Chin?, 51
Woman Warrior, The, 153
Woods, Tiger, 80

Yang, Wesley, 97

Zia, Helen, 77

Lightning Source UK Ltd.
Milton Keynes UK
UKHW04f1324051018

330059UK00001B/50/P